Mngt - day to day stuff

Entrepreneur = Vision, Imagination, Ideas —

Reports you can generate are excellent

→ # samples diff texts —

→ adoption reports! —

→ monthly sales — book by book, etc ...

PRINCIPLES OF MODERN MANAGEMENT

PRINCIPLES OF MODERN MANAGEMENT

A CANADIAN PERSPECTIVE

THIRD EDITION

Allyn and Bacon

Boston   London   Sydney   Toronto

SAMUEL C. CERTO

Roy E. Crummer Graduate School of Business
Rollins College

STEVEN H. APPELBAUM

Faculty of Commerce and Administration
Concordia University

IRENE DEVINE

Faculty of Business
Ryerson Polytechnical Institute

Canadian Cataloguing in Publication Data

Certo, Samuel C.
  Principles of modern management

3rd ed.
Includes bibliographies and indexes.
ISBN 0-205-11990-5

1. Management.   2. Management—Canada.
I. Appelbaum, Steven H., 1941–   . II. Devine,
Irene, 1937–   . III. Title.

HD31.C38 1989   658   C88-095113-3

This edition authorized for sale in Canada only. Original U.S. edition published by
Allyn and Bacon, Inc., A Division of Simon & Schuster, 160 Gould Street, Needham
Heights, Massachusetts 02194.

ISBN 0-205-11990-5

Production Editor: Linda Gorman
Manufacturing Buyer: Sandra Paige
Cover graphic: *Roman Bath* by Katherine Hanley, AT&T Graphics Software Labs
Typesetting: Q Composition Inc.

Printed and bound in Canada by John Deyell Company

1 2 3 4 5 JD 93 92 91 90 89

Photo credits are listed at the back and constitute an extension of the copyright page.
Every reasonable effort has been made to find copyright holders. The publishers
would be pleased to have any errors or omissions brought to their attention.

To Mimi, Trevis, Matthew, Sarah, and Brian
Barbara, Jill, Wendy, Geoffrey, and Eric
Glenna and Karen

Note to Students from the Authors

Management success is what happens when preparation meets opportunity. Take advantage of this text and this course as a vehicle for preparing for management opportunities that you inevitably will have. Keep this text in your professional library as a *reference book,* which can be used to enhance your preparedness for opportunities throughout various stages of your future management career.

BRIEF CONTENTS

8 chapters

CONTENTS

SECTION 2
PLANNING 80

SECTION 3

ORGANIZING   188

MANAGEMENT IN ACTION: 235
Baseball Did You Say?

MANAGEMENT IN ACTION: 257
**Show You Care: EAPs Reduce Stress and
Increase Profits**

MANAGEMENT IN ACTION: 290
**Managing in a Changing Environment: Some
Ideas of John A. Brindle, President of Sun Life
Assurance Company (Canada)**

SECTION 4
INFLUENCING   314

MANAGEMENT IN ACTION: 333
**How to Win Friends and Influence
Co-managers**

SECTION 5

CONTROLLING   434

SECTION 6

TOPICS FOR
SPECIAL
EMPHASIS   526

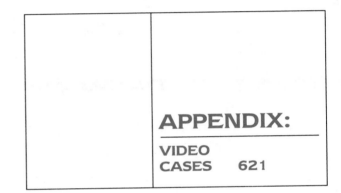

APPENDIX:

VIDEO CASES   621

It is difficult to describe the excitement and personal satisfaction we feel in writing this overview. This book reflects a distinctive tradition in management education materials that has evolved in character and scope over several years. For almost a decade, the *Principles of Modern Management* learning package—this text and its related ancillaries—has been popularly used as learning materials for management courses in colleges and universities throughout Canada.

Many credit the steadily growing popularity of this package to our conviction that appropriate management concepts must be covered and presented clearly and concisely, that learning materials must reflect an empathy for and an enhancement of the student learning process, and that instructional support materials must facilitate the design and conduct of only the highest-quality principles of management courses. Starting with the text, the following sections describe each major component of this newest management learning package and explain how this conviction has become even more pronounced in this newest edition.

The text presents appropriate management theory, enhances student learning, and facilitates the instructional process.

TEXT: THEORY OVERVIEW

As with the first two editions, the purpose of this text is straightforward: to prepare students to be managers. The overall approach employed in this book is to emphasize the wisdom of both management scholars and practising managers. Special emphasis is placed on the careful and thorough explanation of important management theory as well as the discussion of how it can be practically applied to help managers meet the everyday organizational challenges of modern organizations.

The new edition prepares students to be managers.

Deciding on the management concepts that should be included in a text of this sort and on how they should be covered is probably the most difficult task an author faces. Much insight was gleaned through careful consideration of such materials as: (1) reports and opinions of accrediting agencies—for example, the American Assembly of Collegiate Schools of Business (AACSB) and the Administrative Sciences Association of Canada (ASAC); (2) trends and issues in management research as highlighted by the work of management scholars; and (3) accounts by practising managers emphasizing the contemporary organizational problems they face and how to deal with them.

Revisions reflect ideas from AACSB and ASAC, management scholars, and practising managers.

Overall, management theory in this text is divided into six main sections: "Introduction to Management," "Planning," "Organizing," "Influencing," "Controlling," and "Topics for Special Emphasis." Naturally, updates of theory and example have been extensively made throughout each section. More specifically, Section 1, "Introduction to Management," lays the groundwork necessary for studying management. Chapter 1, "Introducing Management and Management

Theory and example updates are included.

There is a new emphasis on management careers.

Careers," has been renamed and significantly revised in this edition not only to better expose students to what management is but also to give them a better understanding of management careers in organizations. This chapter also highlights Peters and Waterman's *In Search of Excellence,* which provides insights on how to manage a successful organization. Chapter 2, "Approaches to Managing," presents several fundamental but different ways that managers can perceive their jobs. The last chapter in this section, Chapter 3, "Organizational Objectives," discusses the nature of goals that organizations can adopt and the relationship between these goals and the management process.

There is a new emphasis on environmental analysis.

Section 2, "Planning," elaborates on planning activities as a primary management function. Chapter 4, "Fundamentals of Planning," presents the basics of planning. Chapter 5, "Making Decisions," discusses the decision-making process as a component of the planning process. Chapter 6, "Types of Planning: Strategic and Tactical," has undergone significant revision. Its discussion of environmental analysis as a component of strategy formulation has been extended, and special emphasis has been given to the general, operating, and internal levels of organizational environments. Chapter 7, "Plans and Planning Tools," discusses various managerial planning tools available to help formulate plans.

There is a new emphasis on stress.

Section 3, "Organizing," discusses organizing activities as a major management function. Chapter 8 presents the fundamentals of organizing, and Chapter 9 elaborates on how to organize various worker activities appropriately. Chapter 10, "Providing Appropriate Human Resources for the Organization," discusses obtaining people who will make a desirable contribution to organizational objectives. Chapter 11 has been significantly revised; it is renamed "Organizational Change and Stress." Coverage still focuses on how managers change organizations, but it now includes additional focus on stress-related issues that can accompany such action. The discussion highlights the definition of stress and the importance of studying and managing stress.

Section 4, "Influencing," discusses how managers should deal with people. The four chapters in this section (Chapters 12–15) respectively discuss the fundamentals of influencing and communication, leadership, motivation, and managing groups.

There is new material on decision support systems.

Section 5, "Controlling," analyzes the performance of control activities as another basic management function. Chapter 16, "Principles of Controlling," presents the basics of controlling. Chapter 17, "Fundamentals of Production Management and Control," describes the basics of the production process, robotics, and a number of useful managerial tools for controlling production. Chapter 18, "Information," defines *information* and elaborates on the role it plays in the controlling process. New coverage focuses on computers and decision support systems, which managers can use to improve controlling efforts.

There is a new emphasis on ethics.

The last section of this text is "Topics for Special Emphasis." Chapter 19, "Social Responsibility: An Emphasis on Ethics," discusses the responsibilities managers have to society, as well as ethics, as a possible rationale for encouraging managers to meet these responsibilities. The focus on ethics is new to this edition. Chapter 20, "International Management," discusses the basics of international and multinational organizations. New coverage in this edition includes more comparative management focus on the study of Japanese management techniques, with special emphasis on just-in-time inventory control. Chapter 21 discusses skills people must possess in order to manage successfully in the future.

There is new emphasis on Japanese management: just-in-time (JIT) inventory control.

Current updates include future age distribution of the work force, growth of the work force, industry growth, and women in the work force. These topics lend particular relevance and timeliness to chapter revisions.

TEXT: STUDENT LEARNING AIDS

Several features of this text were designed to make the study of management more efficient, effective, and enjoyable. A list of these features and an explanation of each follow.

LEARNING OBJECTIVES   The opening pages of each chapter contain a set of learning objectives that are intended as guidelines on how to study the chapter.

CHAPTER OUTLINES   The opening pages of each chapter also contain a chapter outline that previews the textual material and helps the reader keep the information in perspective while it is being read.

INTRODUCTORY CASES WITH "FLASHES" BACK TO THE CASE   The opening of each chapter contains a case study that introduces readers to management problems related to chapter content. Detailed "Back to the Case" sections appear throughout each chapter, applying specific areas of management theory discussed in the chapter to the introductory case. Most of these cases involve real companies and highlight contemporary issues in organizations such as McDonald's, Toro, and Hospital Corporation of America.*

CONCLUDING CASES   The concluding pages of each chapter contain a real-life case that further applies chapter content to related management situations. The cases cover a wide range of subjects, including recent accounts about business, government, sports, and the like. Among the companies focused on are Crown Life Insurance, Magna International, and Northern Telecom.

There are new and updated end-of-chapter cases.

VIDEO CASE APPENDIX   A very innovative feature of this text, which is new to this edition, is the Video Case Appendix. This appendix is a collection of classroom learning activities specially designed to be used in conjunction with a series of three video tapes. The video cases and their related learning activities were carefully crafted as an integral part of this text to illustrate and extend specific text chapters. The video cases are:

New video cases focus on:
1. Management careers.
2. Strategic planning.
3. International management.

Fired: A Focus on Management Careers
Battle of the Blimps: A Focus on Strategic Planning
The Colonel Comes to Japan: A Focus on International Management

---

* All real-life materials in this text were chosen because of their special relevance to management concepts discussed in the chapter. However, because changes occur so rapidly in the real world of business and government, certain facts and figures contained in these materials may already be somewhat dated.

Extensive instructional materials are available in the Instructor's Resource Manual, and they offer detailed suggestions on how best to use these video case materials.

MARGINAL NOTES   Each chapter contains marginal notes and key words that can be helpful in the initial reading and for review.

"MANAGEMENT IN ACTION"   All chapters contain a short reading that is intended to illustrate how a management concept presented in a chapter relates to an actual company. Companies such as Alcan Aluminium, Dofasco, and Royal LePage are highlighted.

ACTION SUMMARIES   Each chapter ends with an action-oriented chapter summary. In this summary, students respond to several objective questions that are clearly linked to the learning objectives stated at the beginning of the chapter. Students can check their answers with the answer key at the end of the chapter. This key also lists the pages in the chapter that can be referred to for a fuller explanation of the answers.

INTRODUCTORY CASE WRAP-UP   Each chapter ends with several questions about its introductory case. These questions provide the opportunity to apply chapter concepts directly to the case.

DISCUSSION QUESTIONS   The concluding pages of each chapter contain a set of discussion questions that test the understanding of chapter material and can serve as vehicles for study and for class discussion.

GLOSSARY   Major management terms and their definitions are gathered at the end of the text. They appear in boldface type along with the text pages on which the discussion of each term appears.

ILLUSTRATIONS   Figures, tables, and photographs depicting various management situations are used throughout the text to help bridge the gap between management theory and authentic situations.

SUPPLEMENTARY MATERIALS

A number of ingredients have been developed to complement the use of *Principles of Modern Management*. Although the text itself was designed to offer a desirable amount of material for a high-quality course in principles of management, special supplements are available to further enrich the learning situation in which the text is used.

EXPERIENCING MODERN MANAGEMENT: A WORKBOOK, FOURTH EDITION

This is a combination study guide and sourcebook of more than sixty experiential exercises and is to be used in conjunction with the text. The fourth edition of this workbook contains several new and modified exercises that correspond to the revised text. Workbook elements that correspond to each text chapter include the following.

AN EXTENDED CHAPTER SUMMARY   Extended summaries are helpful for quick review of text material. Summaries are keyed to chapter learning objectives in the text in order to facilitate student learning.

LEARNING ASSESSMENT ACTIVITIES   For each chapter of the text, the workbook contains a series of twenty-five objective questions that test the understanding of chapter content. Correct answers and the text page numbers on which answers are explained are furnished for all questions.

EXPERIENTIAL EXERCISES, ACTIVITIES, PROJECTS, CASES   A number of diverse in-class and out-of-class learning activities that further illustrate the content of each text chapter are provided. Many exercises are available for larger and smaller classes. A suggested sequence for using the text and the workbook jointly is shown in Figure P.1.

INSTRUCTIONAL AIDS

In addition to the supplements just described, several other ingredients of the *Principles of Modern Management* learning package also have been designed to enhance the learning environment in which this text is used. These ingredients offer various optional aids to the management instructor.

INSTRUCTOR'S RESOURCE MANUAL   This unique and innovative instructor's manual contains an array of materials that instructors can use to organize their lectures and teaching materials. The separate *Lecture Enrichment Kit, Extended Lecture Outline,* and *Instructor's Manual* from the second edition have been incorporated into this new resource manual, so that all of the materials are organized in a chapter-by-chapter format.

The instructional support materials are better organized.

For each chapter in the text, the resource manual includes: (1) extended lecture outlines; (2) notes on the introductory case; (3) in-class involvement exercises with handouts; (4) transparency masters with accompanying teaching notes; (5) instructor's notes on the student workbook, *Experiencing Modern Management;* (6) notes on the concluding cases; and (7) solutions to end-of-chapter discussion questions. Detailed instructor's notes to accompany the video cases are included at the end of the manual.

Revised test bank includes:
1. Cases with questions.
2. True/false questions.
3. Multiple-choice questions.
4. Short-answer questions.
5. Matching questions.

TEST BANK   Testing instruments for the text include: (1) cases with questions; (2) true/false questions; (3) multiple choice questions; (4) short-answer questions; and (5) matching questions. The true/false and multiple-choice questions are categorized according to the learning objective they are testing and as to whether they are factual/conceptual or application questions. The matching questions focus exclusively on chapter terminology. All answers are page referenced.

Due to the importance of the testing instruments, a special Test Bank Reviewer Board, made up of management instructors, was established. This board had input into the test bank and reviewed the questions.

Test instruments reflect the insights of the Test Bank Reviewer Board.

MICROTEST—A COMPUTERIZED TEST BANK   A computerized testing program is available for the Apple, IBM PC, and Macintosh computers. This program enables instructors to choose from a bank of questions, edit them, or create their own questions.

There is an improved computerized testing program.

FIGURE P.1   Suggested sequence for using the text and student workbook jointly.

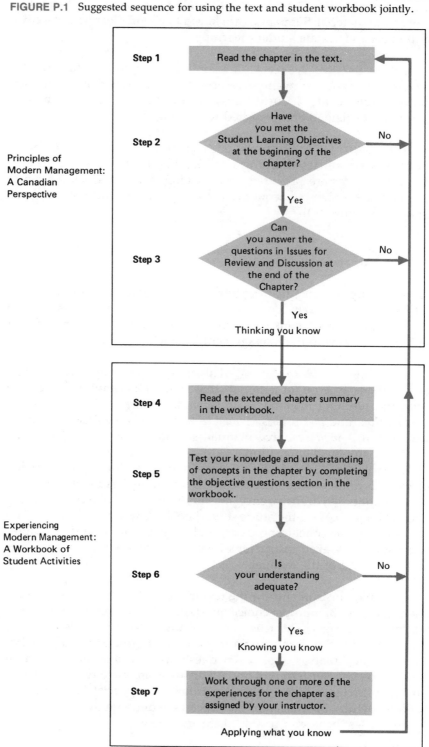

TRANSPARENCIES Sixty full-colour transparency acetates make up the transparency package, with teaching notes and strategies accompanying each acetate. Also available is the Allyn and Bacon Transparencies for Management package, which includes 100 acetates from sources other than this text.

There are over 150 transparencies available.

GOAL

Our long-term goal in publishing the *Principles of Modern Management* learning package is to make a positive contribution to society by helping to ensure the future management success of the college and university students of today. Our action plan for reaching this goal is quite simple—to constantly strive to develop the highest-quality set of management instructional materials available.

The most valuable source of ideas for improving this text and its ancillaries over the years has been colleagues and students who have used the book and the ancillaries. We apologize in advance for any frustrations we may cause you as you use our materials. We also thank you in advance for your ideas about how to eliminate these frustrations for individuals who will use the materials in the future.

ACKNOWLEDGMENTS

Positive comments generated by the *Principles of Modern Management* learning package have been very pleasing. A multitude of people have played significant roles in the design and development of this package. It is with great pleasure that we recognize these individuals and extend to them our gratitude for their insight, expertise, and warm personal support and encouragement.

As with previous editions, Professor Lee A. Graf, Illinois State University, has been a major force behind this text and its accompanying experiential workbook. Professor Graf's conceptual and organizational skills have been critical in improving this learning package to the greatest degree possible.

Several other individuals have provided this text with valuable ancillary materials, and we would like to recognize each of them for their dedication and hard work:

Robert Goldberg and Tricia McConville of Northeastern University for revising the Instructor's Resource Manual.

Philip Weatherford of Embry-Riddle Aeronautical University for revising the Test Bank.

Robert Kemper of Northern Arizona University for contributing the case studies in the Test Bank.

We would also like to thank our Test Bank Advisory board:

William Francis Herlehy, Embry-Riddle Aeronautical University
James Westwater, College of Notre Dame of Maryland
James Moreau, Rock Valley College

Every author appreciates the valuable contribution reviewers make to the development of a text project. Reviewers offer that "different viewpoint" that requires an author to constructively question his or her work. We had an excellent team of reviewers. Thoughtful comments, concern for student learning, and insights regarding instructional implications of the written word characterized the high-quality feedback we recieved. We are pleased to be able to recognize members of our review team for their valuable contributions to the development of this text:

Billie Allen, University of Southern Mississippi
Dr. Randi Ellis, North Harris Community College
Frederick Sheppard, Sylvia Keyes, and Dr. Chuck England, Bridgewater State College
Dr. Don B. Bradley, University of Central Arkansas
Robert Goldberg, Northeastern University
Valeriano Cantu, Angelo State University
Thomas Goodwin, Johnson and Wales College

Thanks are also extended to the following persons who have made valuable contributions through numerous activities:

M.C. Adams-Webber
Brock University

V. Baba
Concordia University

Ted Brown
Mt. Royal College

Harold R. Buck
Mohawk College

G.R.D. Campbell
Brandon University

R. Julian Cattaneo
University of Windsor

John A. Edds
Brock University

Ralph Flitton
Vancouver Community College

John Forde
College of New Caledonia

Anne Harper
Humber College of Applied Arts and Technology

John Holzman
Algonquin College

William C. Honey
Lakehead University

Sharon Irvine
DeVry Institute of Technology

Muhammad Jamal
Concordia University

Geoffrey Jones
Seneca College

Ralph G. Jones
Northern Alberta Institute of Technology

R.I. McLaren
University of Regina

George B. MacPherson
Malaspina College

Diane Nutik
Dawson College

Gary H. Petersen
Kwantlen College

John K. Pliniussen
College of Cape Breton

Jim Redston
Red River Community College

Roger R. Rickwood
University of Windsor

Barbara Shapiro
Concordia University

Stanley A. Shaw
Humber College

H.E. Stiver
Georgian College

G. Wright
Champlain Regional College

PERSONAL ACKNOWLEDGMENTS

I would like to recognize the personal interest and encouragement for this project shown by my colleagues in the Roy E. Crummer Graduate School of Business at Rollins College. The faculty in general has been very supportive of this project. In more specific terms, Dean Martin Schatz has been instrumental in helping me acquire the resources necessary to complete this project. Additionally, James M. Higgins, Theodore T. Herbert, and Max R. Richards, my management colleagues, have all helped me clarify the character and scope of this book. I greatly appreciate the professional orientation of my colleagues at Crummer.

The support that Allyn and Bacon has shown throughout this revision process must not go unnoticed. The attention to detail and book development skills displayed by the special projects team was absolutely critical. Clearly, this text and its ancillaries have gotten all the care and attention necessary.

Lastly, on more of a personal note, I want to thank my family for encouraging me to strive for excellence in the development of this project. In this regard, the example set by Samuel C. Certo, Sr., my father, and Annette Certo, my mother, will always be a positive influence on my life.

Samuel C. Certo

My work on the Canadian Edition was greatly inspired by Walter H. Powell and Gunther Brink who served as mentors early in my career. The managerial philosophies of colleagues V. Baba, Gary Johns, Muhammad Jamal, and William Taylor were most stimulating and treated with the greatest respect. The administrative support given by Associate Deans Ross, Wills, Rahman and Kusy allowed me to complete the manuscript a priori. I wish to thank Laurie St. John and her staff for their "virage technologique," and Vanessa Chio, a rare theoretical MBA graduating senior who assisted greatly with data retrieval and research support.

Another very special thanks is being given to Marilyn Howell for her editorial acumen and sixth sense in identifying important additions and deletions. She made a great deal of this book happen. Finally, "merci beaucoup" to Mme. Barbara Shapiro, a Professor of Management who continues to inspire my work and life. You are the "sunshine of the life" of all mutual ventures.

Steven H. Appelbaum

The impetus for my work on the Third Canadian Edition grew out of my professional relationship with Dean Steven Appelbaum. I acknowledge the privilege and honour to have him as a co-author and a friend. I thank Alison Toms and Vanessa Chio, two Concordia MBA graduates, for their assistance with library research and general research support.

Finally, but most important, I am grateful to Glenna and Karen Devine, and Paul Halpern, who willingly provided the necessary emotional support. Their patience and understanding is appreciated.

Irene Devine

PRINCIPLES OF MODERN MANAGEMENT

INTRODUCTION TO MANAGEMENT

Section 1 consists of three chapters that serve to introduce the topic of management.

Chapter 1

Chapter 1 defines management as the process of reaching organizational goals by working with and through people and other resources. Management is presented as a task important not only to society as a whole, but also to individuals who hold management positions. The management task itself is shown to involve planning, organizing, influencing, and controlling, and to be aimed solely at accomplishing organizational objectives. Chapter 1 emphasizes that managers must strive to be both effective and efficient through the judicious exercise of human, technical, and conceptual skills. The point is also made in this chapter that management principles are universal, or applicable to all types of businesses and organizations. The chapter concludes with a discussion of the different stages of a management career and suggests ways that managers can promote their careers.

Chapter 2

Chapter 2 further introduces the topic of management by discussing various approaches that managers should emphasize while managing: the classical approach, the behavioural approach, the management science approach, the contingency approach, and the system approach. The classical approach advocates that managers manage by emphasizing the "one best way" to do a job, as well as by analyzing the management task as a whole. The behavioural approach supports the idea that managers manage by emphasizing an analysis of the people within an organization. The management science approach suggests that managers manage by emphasizing the use of mathematical models and other quantitative aids. The contingency approach recommends that management action be based upon the specific situation facing a manager. And the main theme of the system approach is that managers manage by viewing and reacting to an organization as a set of interrelated parts that function as a whole to achieve objectives.

This text's approach to the principles of management emphasizes the organization as a system that managers should assess and react to from a contingency or situation viewpoint, basing their observations upon an integration of information from the behavioural, classical, and management science approaches. This integration of information will become clearer after reading the five remaining sections of the text: (1) planning; (2) organizing; (3) influencing; (4) controlling; and (5) topics for special emphasis.

Chapter 3

Chapter 3, "Organizational Objectives," concludes the introduction to the topic of management by discussing the relationship between management and organizational objectives. Organizational objectives are presented as the targets toward which a management system is directed and as being derived from organizational purpose. Since both organizational and individual objectives exist within organizations, it becomes the task of managers to encourage individuals to pursue organizational objectives even if the objectives are inconsistent with individual goals.

Chapter 3 recommends that an organization's formal objectives should reflect environmental trends that could influence the operation of the organization. It also is recommended that organizational objectives be clear, simple, precise, and operational, and that they be based upon the thoughts of managers as well as on the opinions of other organization members. Management by objectives (MBO) is presented in Chapter 3 as a tool that managers can adopt to guide an organization, mainly by using organizational objectives.

MANAGEMENT AND MANAGEMENT CAREERS

STUDENT LEARNING OBJECTIVES

From studying this chapter, I will attempt to acquire:

1. An understanding of the importance of management to society and individuals.
2. An understanding of the role of management.
3. An ability to define *management* in several different ways.
4. An ability to list and define the basic functions of management.
5. Working definitions of managerial effectiveness and managerial efficiency.
6. An understanding of basic management skills and their relative importance to managers.
7. An understanding of the universality of management.
8. Insights into what careers are and how they evolve.

CHAPTER OUTLINE

INEXPERIENCED MANAGERS AT METALCO STEEL MILL

Robert G. McTavish approached the microphones at his press conference in Dunkirk, Ontario. As president of Metalco Steel Mill, he had an important announcement to make. Perhaps unlike most press conferences, a significant proportion of the audience already knew what McTavish was going to say: A deal had been finalized whereby workers at Metalco would buy the steel mill from Oshawa Steel, its parent company. The press conference was simply part of the formality of making this deal final.

The recent financial performance of Metalco had left Oshawa Steel little choice. In the previous year, Metalco had suffered serious financial losses. In addition, since demand for the products manufactured by Metalco was declining steadily, Oshawa Steel saw little hope for a turnaround at Metalco in the near future.

Oshawa Steel had decided that it had two alternatives. The first was that it could phase out most of the operations of the Metalco plant. This action, of course, would necessitate the layoff of a significant number of Metalco's 9 500 employees. Since the entire population of Dunkirk is only 24 000, such a layoff would have a profound effect on the community's economy. In addition, this action would simply be the first step toward finally closing the plant.

Oshawa Steel's other alternative was to sell the plant to the workers. Organizing all of the employees and getting them to agree to purchase the plant was an extremely complex task, but eventually a deal was made.

Under the terms of the final agreement, the employees agree to pay $58 million for the mill and its equipment, $190 million for the current assets at the mill, and to assume $80 million worth of long-term debt that the mill has incurred. No payments of principal or interest are due until after the newly independent mill has been operating five years. The board of directors of the newly formed company will be comprised of two union representatives, two members of management, and six individuals from outside the organization.

One result of the employee decision to purchase Metalco will be that employees will play a much larger role in managing the plant in the future than they did in the past. A number of employees who have been simply line workers at Metalco until now will undoubtedly be made managers in the future.

What's Ahead

As discussed in the introductory case, the employees have purchased Metalco Steel Mill and will now have to begin taking an active role in managing this company. The information in this chapter is designed to help new managers such as these Metalco employees to understand the basics of management. Management is defined through: (1) a discussion of the importance of management both to society and to individuals; (2) a description of the management task; and (3) a discussion of the universality of management.

THE IMPORTANCE OF MANAGEMENT

Managers influence all phases of our modern organizations. Plant managers run manufacturing operations that produce our clothes, food, and automobiles. Sales managers maintain a sales force that markets goods. Personnel managers provide organizations with a competent and productive work force. The "jobs available" section in the classified advertisements of any major newspaper describes many different types of management activities and confirms this importance of management (see Figure 1.1).

Our society simply could not exist as we know it today or improve its present status without a steady stream of managers to guide its organizations. Peter Drucker makes this same point in stating that effective management is quickly becoming the main resource of developed countries and the most needed resource of developing ones.[1] In short, our country desperately needs good managers.

Society needs good managers.

In addition to being important to our society as a whole, management is vital to many individuals simply because they earn their living by being managers. Government statistics in Canada and the U.S. show that management positions have held a steady 9 to 10 percent of a sometimes quickly growing work force since 1950.[2] These managers typically come from varying backgrounds and have diversified educational specialities. Many individuals who originally trained to be accountants, teachers, financiers, or even writers eventually make their livelihood from being some type of manager. In the short term, the demand for managers may vary somewhat from year to year.[3] In the long term, however, managerial positions can yield high salaries, status, interesting work, personal growth, and intense feelings of accomplishment.

Management also has much to offer individuals.

7

FIGURE 1.1   The variety of management positions available.

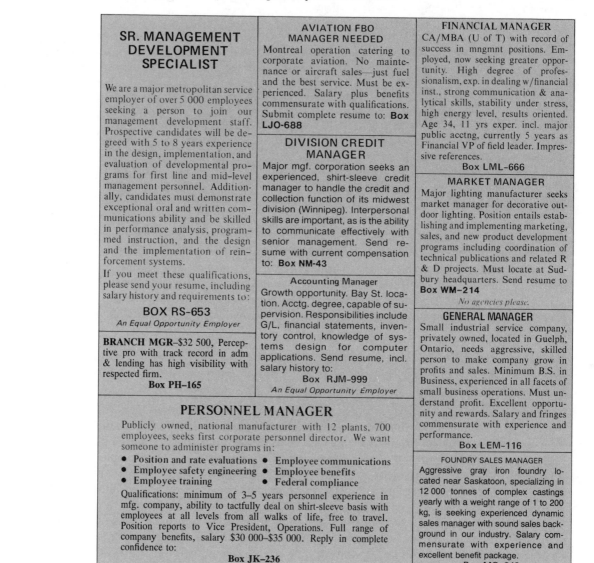

SR. MANAGEMENT DEVELOPMENT SPECIALIST

We are a major metropolitan service employer of over 5 000 employees seeking a person to join our management development staff. Prospective candidates will be degreed with 5 to 8 years experience in the design, implementation, and evaluation of developmental programs for first line and mid-level management personnel. Additionally, candidates must demonstrate exceptional oral and written communications ability and be skilled in performance analysis, programmed instruction, and the design and the implementation of reinforcement systems.

If you meet these qualifications, please send your resume, including salary history and requirements to:

BOX RS-653
An Equal Opportunity Employer

BRANCH MGR-$32 500, Perceptive pro with track record in adm & lending has high visibility with respected firm.
Box PH-165

AVIATION FBO MANAGER NEEDED

Montreal operation catering to corporate aviation. No maintenance or aircraft sales—just fuel and the best service. Must be experienced. Salary plus benefits commensurate with qualifications. Submit complete resume to: **Box LJO-688**

DIVISION CREDIT MANAGER

Major mgf. corporation seeks an experienced, shirt-sleeve credit manager to handle the credit and collection function of its midwest division (Winnipeg). Interpersonal skills are important, as is the ability to communicate effectively with senior management. Send resume with current compensation to: **Box NM-43**

Accounting Manager

Growth opportunity. Bay St. location. Acctg. degree, capable of supervision. Responsibilities include G/L, financial statements, inventory control, knowledge of systems design for computer applications. Send resume, incl. salary history to:
Box RJM-999
An Equal Opportunity Employer

FINANCIAL MANAGER

CA/MBA (U of T) with record of success in mngmnt positions. Employed, now seeking greater opportunity. High degree of professionalism, exp. in dealing w/financial inst., strong communication & analytical skills, stability under stress, high energy level, results oriented. Age 34, 11 yrs exper. incl. major public acctng, currently 5 years as Financial VP of field leader. Impressive references.
Box LML-666

MARKET MANAGER

Major lighting manufacturer seeks market manager for decorative outdoor lighting. Position entails establishing and implementing marketing, sales, and new product development programs including coordination of technical publications and related R & D projects. Must locate at Sudbury headquarters. Send resume to **Box WM-214**
No agencies please.

GENERAL MANAGER

Small industrial service company, privately owned, located in Guelph, Ontario, needs aggressive, skilled person to make company grow in profits and sales. Minimum B.S. in Business, experienced in all facets of small business operations. Must understand profit. Excellent opportunity and rewards. Salary and fringes commensurate with experience and performance.
Box LEM-116

FOUNDRY SALES MANAGER

Aggressive gray iron foundry located near Saskatoon, specializing in 12 000 tonnes of complex castings yearly with a weight range of 1 to 200 kg, is seeking experienced dynamic sales manager with sound sales background in our industry. Salary commensurate with experience and excellent benefit package.
Box MO-948

PERSONNEL MANAGER

Publicly owned, national manufacturer with 12 plants, 700 employees, seeks first corporate personnel director. We want someone to administer programs in:

- Position and rate evaluations
- Employee safety engineering
- Employee training
- Employee communications
- Employee benefits
- Federal compliance

Qualifications: minimum of 3-5 years personnel experience in mfg. company, ability to tactfully deal on shirt-sleeve basis with employees at all levels from all walks of life, free to travel. Position reports to Vice President, Operations. Full range of company benefits, salary $30 000-$35 000. Reply in complete confidence to:

Box JK-236

⧉ BACK TO THE CASE

The preceding information furnishes the employee-owners of Metalco Steel Mill with insights concerning the significance of the decision they have just made. Their role as management will not only be important to society as a whole, but also to themselves as individual managers. In general, managers make some societal contributions to creating the standard of living we all enjoy and thereby obtain some corresponding rewards for making these contributions. Given the present status of the Metalco plant in Dunkirk, the contributions that this organization will be able to afford society will probably be relatively modest in the near future. If the plant is successful, however, these contributions will undoubtedly be more significant as time passes.

THE MANAGEMENT TASK

Besides understanding the significance of being a manager and its related potential benefits, prospective managers should know what the management task entails. The sections that follow introduce the basics of the management task through discussions of the role and definition of management.

The Role of Management

Essentially, the role of managers is to guide organizations toward goal accomplishment. All organizations exist for some purpose or objective, and managers have the responsibility for combining and using organizational resources to ensure that the organizations achieve their purposes. Management moves organizations toward these purposes or goals by assigning activities that organization members perform. If these activities are designed effectively, the production of each individual worker represents a contribution to the attainment of organizational goals. Management strives to encourage individual activity that will lead to reaching organizational goals and to discourage individual activity that hinders organizational goal accomplishment. "There is no idea more important to managing than goals. Management has no meaning apart from its goals."[4] Management must keep organizational goals clearly in mind at all times.

Management entails reaching goals

Defining Management

To minimize confusion, students of management should be aware that the term *management* can be and often is used in several different ways.[5] For instance, it can simply refer to the process that managers follow to accomplish organizational goals. The term can also be used, however, to refer to a body of knowledge. In this context, management is a cumulative body of information that furnishes insights on how to manage. Management also can be the term used to pinpoint those individuals who guide and direct organizations. It is also commonly used to designate a career devoted to the task of guiding and directing organizations. An understanding of these various uses and related definitions of management should help students and practitioners eliminate miscommunication during management-related discussions.

by working with and through people and organizational resources.

As used most commonly in this text, **management** is defined as the process of reaching organizational goals by working with and through people and other organizational resources. A comparison of this definition with definitions of management offered by several different contemporary management thinkers (see Figure 1.2)[6] shows that there is some agreement that management has the following three main characteristics: (1) management is a process or series of continuing and related activities; (2) management involves and concentrates on reaching organizational goals; and (3) management reaches these goals by working with and through people and other organizational resources. A discussion of each of these characteristics follows.

FIGURE 1.2   Contemporary definitions of management.

Management —

1. Is the process by which a cooperative group directs actions of others toward common goals. (Massie and Douglas)
2. Management is the process of working with and through others to effectively achieve organizational objectives by efficiently using limited resources in a changing environment. (Kreitner)
3. Is the coordination of all resources through the processes of planning, organizing, directing, and controlling in order to attain stated objectives. (Sisk)
4. Is establishing an effective environment for people operating in formal organizational groups. (Koontz and O'Donnell)
5. Entails activities undertaken by one or more persons in order to coordinate the activities of others in the pursuit of ends which cannot be achieved by any one person. (Donnelly, Gibson, and Ivancevich)

The Management Process: Management Functions

The four basic **management functions** or activities that make up the management process are:

The four basic management functions are:

1. Planning.

1. *Planning*   Planning involves choosing tasks that must be performed to attain organizational goals, outlining how the tasks must be performed, and indicating when the tasks should be performed. Planning activity focuses on attaining goals. Managers, through their plans, outline exactly what organizations must do to be successful. They are concerned with organizational success in the near future or short term as well as success in the more distant future or long term.

2. Organizing.

2. *Organizing*   Organizing can be thought of as assigning the tasks developed during planning to various individuals and/or groups within the organization. Organizing creates a mechanism to put plans into action. People within the organization are given work assignments that contribute to goal attainment. Tasks are organized so that the output of individuals contributes to the success of departments, which contributes to the success of divisions, which in turn contributes to the overall success of organizations.

3. Influencing.

3. *Influencing*   Influencing* is another of the basic functions within the management process. This function is also commonly referred to as motivating, leading, directing, or actuating and is primarily concerned with people within organizations. Influencing can be defined as the process of guiding the activities of organization members in appropriate directions. Appropriate direction, as used in this definition, is any direction that helps the organization move toward goal attainment. The ultimate purpose of influencing is to increase productivity. Human-oriented work situations usually generate higher levels of production over the long term than work situations that people find distasteful.

4. Controlling.

4. *Controlling*   Controlling is the management function for which managers: (a) gather information that measures recent performance within the organization; (b) compare present performance to pre-established performance standards; and (c) from this comparison, determine if the organization should be modified to meet pre-established standards. Controlling is an ongoing process. Managers continually gather information, make their comparisons, and then try to find new ways of improving production through organizational modification.

* Although the term *motivating* is used to signify this people-oriented management function more commonly than *influencing* in early management literature, the term *influencing* is used consistently in this text because it is broader and allows more flexibility when discussing people-oriented issues. Later in this text, motivating is discussed as a major part of influencing.

FIGURE 1.3   Interrelations of the four functions of management to attain organizational goals.

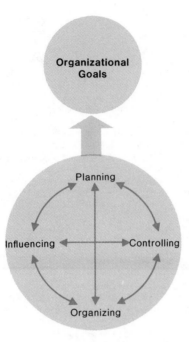

Naturally, if managers wish to be successful, they must perform all four of the management functions well.

Management Process and Goal Attainment

Although the four functions of management have been discussed individually, planning, organizing, influencing, and controlling are integrally related and cannot be separated. Figure 1.3 illustrates this interrelationship and also that managers use these activities solely for the purpose of reaching organizational goals. Basically, these functions are interrelated because the performance of one depends upon the performance of the others. To illustrate, organizing is based on well-thought-out plans developed during the planning process, while influencing systems must be tailored to reflect both these plans and the organizational design used to implement the plans. The fourth function, controlling, proposes possible modifications to existing plans, organizational structure, and/or the motivation system to develop a more successful effort.

To be effective, a manager must understand how the four management functions must be practised and not simply how they are defined and related. Thomas J. Peters and Robert H. Waterman, Jr. studied numerous organizations, such as Frito-Lay and Maytag, for several years to determine what management characteristics best described excellently run companies. Figure 1.4 contains the list and descriptions of characteristics finally developed by Peters and Waterman and published in their book, *In Search of Excellence*. This list implies that planning, organizing, influencing, and controlling within organizations should be characterized by a bias for action; a closeness to the customer; autonomy and entrepreneurship; productivity through people; a hands-on, value-driven orientation; sticking to the knitting; a simple form with a lean staff; and simultaneous loose-tight properties.

Management functions are integrally related and are used solely to attain organizational goals.

FIGURE 1.4   Characteristics of excellently run companies.

1. *A bias for action*, for getting on with it. Even though these companies may be analytical in their approach to decision making, they are not paralyzed by that fact (as so many others seem to be). In many of these companies, the standard operating procedure is "Do it, fix it, try it." Says a Digital Equipment Corporation senior executive, for example, "When we've got a big problem here, we grab ten senior guys and stick them in a room for a week. They come up with an answer *and* implement it." Moreover, the companies are experimenters supreme. Instead of allowing 250 engineers and marketers to work on a new product in isolation for fifteen months, they form bands of 5 to 25 and test ideas out on a customer, often with inexpensive prototypes, within a matter of weeks. What is striking is the host of practical devices the excellent companies employ to maintain corporate fleetness of foot and counter the stultification that almost inevitably comes with size.

2. *Close to the customer*. These companies learn from the people they serve. They provide unparalleled quality, service, and reliability—things that work and last. They succeed in differentiating— à la Frito-Lay (potato chips), Maytag (washers), or Tupperware—the most commoditylike products. IBM's marketing vice president, Francis G. (Buck) Rodgers, says, "It's a shame that, in so many companies, whenever you get good service, it's an exception." Not so at the excellent companies. Everyone gets into the act. Many of the innovative companies got their best product ideas from customers. That comes from listening, intently and regularly.

3. *Autonomy and entrepreneurship*. The innovative companies foster many leaders and many innovators throughout the organization. They are a hive of what we've come to call champions; 3M has been described as "so intent on innovation that its essential atmosphere seems not like that of a large corporation but rather a loose network of laboratories and cubbyholes populated by feverish inventors and dauntless entrepreneurs who let their imaginations fly in all directions." They don't try to hold everyone on so short a rein that he can't be creative. They encourage practical risk taking, and support good tries. They follow Fletcher Byrom's ninth commandment: "Make sure you generate a reasonable number of mistakes."

4. *Productivity through people*. The excellent companies treat the rank and file as the root source of quality and productivity gain. They do not foster we/they labor attitudes or regard capital investment as the fundamental source of efficiency improvement. As Thomas J. Watson, Jr., said of his company, "IBM's philosophy is largely contained in three simple beliefs. I want to begin with what I think is the most important: *our respect for the individual*. This is a simple concept but in IBM it occupies a major portion of management time." Texas Instruments' chairman Mark Shepherd talks about it in terms of every worker being "seen as a source of ideas, not just acting as a pair of hands"; each of his more than *nine thousand* People Involvement Program, or PIP, teams (Texas Instrument's quality circles) does contribute to the company's sparkling productivity record.

5. *Hands-on, value driven*. Thomas Watson, Jr., said that "the basic philosophy of an organization has far more to do with its achievements than do technological or economic resources, organizational structure, innovation, and timing." Watson and Hewlett-Packard's William Hewlett are legendary for walking the plant floors. McDonald's Ray Kroc regularly visits stores and assesses them on the factors the company holds dear, Q.S.C. & V. (Quality, Service, Cleanliness, and Value.)

6. *Stick to the knitting*. Robert W. Johnson, former Johnson & Johnson chairman, put it this way: "Never acquire a business you don't know how to run." Or as Edward G. Harness, past chief executive at Procter & Gamble, said, "This company has never left its base. We seek to be anything but a conglomerate." While there were a few exceptions, the odds for excellent performance seem strongly to favor those companies that stay reasonably close to businesses they know.

7. *Simple form, lean staff*. As big as most of the companies we have looked at are, none when we looked at it was formally run with a matrix organization structure, and some which had tried that form had abandoned it. The underlying structural forms and systems in the excellent companies are elegantly simple. Top-level staffs are lean; it is not uncommon to find a corporate staff of fewer than one hundred people running multi-billion-dollar enterprises.

8. *Simultaneous loose-tight properties*. The excellent companies are both centralized and decentralized. For the most part, as we have said, they have pushed autonomy down to the shop floor on product development team. On the other hand, they are fanatic centralists around the few core values they hold dear. 3M is marked by barely organized chaos surrounding its product champions. Yet one analyst argues, "The brainwashed members of an extremist political sect are no more conformist in their central beliefs." At Digital the chaos is so rampant that one executive noted, "Damn few people know who they work for." Yet Digital's fetish for reliability is more rigidly adhered to than any outsider could imagine.

The information in this section has been only a brief introduction to the four management functions. Later sections of this text are devoted primarily to developing these functions in much more detail.

Management and Organizational Resources

Management must continually be aware of the status and use of **organizational resources**. These resources, comprised of all assets available for activation during the production process, are of four basic types: (1) human resources; (2) monetary resources; (3) raw materials resources; and (4) capital resources. As Figure 1.5 depicts, organizational resources are combined, used, and actually transformed into finished products during the production process.

Human resources are the people who work for an organization. The skills they possess and their knowledge of the work system are invaluable to managers. Monetary resources are amounts of money managers use to purchase goods and services for the organization. Raw materials are ingredients acquired to be used directly in the manufacturing of products. For example, rubber is a raw material that a company like Canadian Tire would purchase with its monetary resources and use directly in the manufacturing of tires. Lastly, capital resources are the machines an organization uses during the manufacturing process. Modern machines or equipment can be a major factor in maintaining desired production levels, while worn-out or antiquated machinery can make it impossible for an organization to keep pace with competitors.

> Organizational resources include:
> 1. People.
> 2. Money.
> 3. Raw materials.
> 4. Machines.

Managerial Effectiveness

As managers use their resources, they must strive to be both effective and efficient. **Managerial effectiveness** is defined in terms of resource utilization in relation to organizational goal attainment. If organizations are using their resources to attain their goals, the managers are effective. In reality, there are degrees of managerial effectiveness. The closer organizations come to achieving their goals, the more effective the managers are said to be. Managerial effectiveness can be depicted as a continuum ranging from "ineffective" to "effective." Depending on how close organizations come to achieving their goals, managers' effectiveness may fall anywhere on the managerial effectiveness continuum.

> Managerial effectiveness is measured by how closely organizations come to achieving their goals.

Managerial Efficiency

Managerial efficiency is defined in terms of the proportion of total organizational resources that contribute to productivity during the manufacturing process. The higher this proportion, the more efficient the manager. The more resources wasted or unused during the production process, the more inefficient the manager. As

> Managerial efficiency is measured by the proportion of organizational resources used during the production process.

FIGURE 1.5 Transformation of organizational resources into finished products through the production process.

Organizational Resources		Transformation		Products
People Money Raw materials Machines	INPUTS	Designing goods/services Assembling goods/services Storing goods/services et cetera	OUTPUTS	Finished goods Finished services

FIGURE 1.6   Various combinations of managerial effectiveness and managerial efficiency.

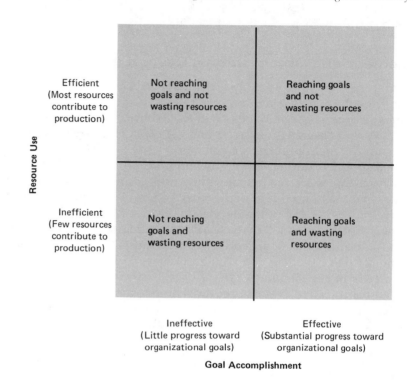

with management effectiveness, management efficiency is best described as being on a continuum ranging from inefficient to efficient. *Inefficient* assumes that a very small proportion of total resources contributes to productivity during the manufacturing process, while *efficient* assumes that a very large proportion contributes.

As Figure 1.6 shows, the concepts of managerial effectiveness and efficiency are obviously related. A manager could be relatively ineffective, with the organization making very little progress toward goal attainment, primarily because of major inefficiencies or poor utilization of resources during the production process. On the other hand, a manager could be somewhat effective despite a lack of efficiency. Perhaps demand is so high for the company's finished goods that the manager can get an extremely high price per unit sold and thus absorb inefficiency costs.

For example, some oil companies in Saudi Arabia could probably absorb many managerial inefficiencies simply because of the high price at which oil sells. Management in this situation has a chance to be somewhat effective despite its inefficiency. Thus, a manager can be effective without being efficient and vice versa. To maximize organizational success, however, a manager must be both effective and efficient.

The following Management in Action feature describes the causes leading to, and efforts undertaken by, top management at Alcan Aluminium Ltd. to maintain its effective and efficient performance in an increasingly hostile environment. It also provides a good illustration of what will be covered in the next section on "Management Skills."

ALCAN ALUMINIUM LIMITED: THE ROAD TO PROSPERITY

From its headquarters on Montreal's fashionable Sherbrooke Street West, the top management of Alcan presides over the production in some two dozen countries of the principal ingredient in hundreds of familiar products—from beverage cans to car bumpers, electric cable to pots and pans. Much of Alcan's primary aluminium supplies are made in Quebec, where the company's own hydro-electric stations provide cheaper energy than most of its competitors can command. For decades, that was enough to ensure the business success of Canada's seventh-largest industrial corporation. But in 1985, Alcan's future—and the job security of its 10 000 workers in Quebec and the 60 000 worldwide—was clouded.

Demand for Alcan's traditional products had been growing more slowly than in the past. Prices for aluminium had plummeted and competition from other producers of aluminium and rival materials was stronger than ever. The period of tremendous growth was over and the company seemed set for a slow decline in a maturing industry. Alcan's top management, consequently, ordered a change of course judged vital by the industry's experts.

According to David Culver, Alcan's chairman and CEO, the company's continued success at that time was dependent upon three factors: a clear and continuing vision of where it was going, the resources to get it there, and the flexibility to deploy those resources at the right time in the right place. As a result, Alcan abandoned what Culver calls a "mission" to encourage the use of aluminium around the world. Instead, the company is to be more selective about its markets for aluminium products, and use the profits from those areas to diversify into more promising lines of business in aluminium-related products. To him, the company must not only move in new directions, but it must also be able to do so quickly. This necessity for flexibility has led to the simplification of Alcan's management structure.

The new strategy was fleshed out by seventy senior company managers who gathered during the summer of 1986 at a secluded hotel in the Laurentians. From the week-long meeting emerged a three-sentence statement that promised that Alcan would become "the most innovative, diversified aluminium company in the world" by the 1990s: it wanted one dollar in four to come from the sale of products it didn't yet make.

Cutting costs to live and innovating to grow has since become Alcan's new modus operandi. The key to the successful implementation of its new strategy is the

"Alcan's top management . . . has ordered a change of course . . ."

flexibility required to put its goals into a concrete form. Hence the company's concentration only upon those aluminium businesses which have the potential to show long-term competitive advantages. The company has, to this end, moved out of a number of businesses over the past few years, wherever it seemed that the business had the kind of future that did not measure up to the company's profit targets or basic strategies. It also wrote down the book value of its alumina and bauxite assets by $215 million after taxes. These moves meant the company had to report a loss of $180 million in 1985, the largest in its history. But it estimated the action would cut operating costs by $150 million in 1986.

Meanwhile, Alcan has begun selling more fabricated products that are bringing in bigger profits—shipments increased by 40 percent from 1982 to 1985. Much of this increase has stemmed from the company's 1982 purchase of British Aluminium Co. and the 1984 acquisition of the U.S. aluminium assets of L.A.-based Atlantic Richfield Co. The prize in the latter acquisition was a 40 percent stake

15

in a modern U.S. sheet-rolling mill in Kentucky that Alcan hoped would increase by half its U.S. capacity to produce sheet for beverage cans. Through new subsidiaries and equity interests in other firms, Alcan has also become involved in such areas as the aerospace industry, ceramics, gallium-arsenide computer wafers, and the aluminium-air battery. In 1986 alone, fifty-seven new and improved products as diverse as pharmaceutical packaging, oil pipelines, and microwave cookery were introduced in markets in North America.

The cost-cutting and the improved mix of products, combined with a 10 percent increase in ingot prices, have started showing up on Alcan's bottom line. Profit for the first nine months of 1986 jumped to $192 million from $32 million in the corresponding period in 1985. Revenues rose to $4.5 billion from $4.3 billion. Analysts estimated the company would earn about $240 million for all of 1986, equivalent to $2.40 a share. But some former Alcan employees warn that the company's diversification efforts may be hampered by its wide-ranging staff cuts. "The company has lost a lot of valuable expertise," said one former employee, who asked not to be identified. "It might not show up now, but the impact could be felt later on."

The company is well aware that its human and material resources are equally important determinants of success. According to Culver in his 1987 report during the annual meeting of shareholders, it is a measure of Alcan's talent and effectiveness that it has achieved record sales with 4000 less employees than it had in 1983. In 1986, cashflow reached a three-year high of $725 million. With numbers like that, who can—or would—argue?

Based on "Aluminium Giant Gropes Toward Prosperity," by Craig Toomey in *The Gazette* (Montreal), November 15, 1986. Used with permission.

BACK TO THE CASE

Metalco employees now have specific information on what management is and what managers do. Employees who actually become managers will have to acquire a clear understanding of company objectives and guide the parts of the organization in which they work toward reaching these objectives. This guidance, of course, will involve working not only with other people at Metalco but also with all other department resources.

These new managers will be heavily involved in planning, organizing, influencing, and controlling. In other words, they will have to outline how jobs must be performed to reach objectives, assign these jobs to appropriate workers, encourage the workers to perform their jobs, and make any changes necessary to ensure reaching company objectives. Also, as these new managers perform these four functions, they will need to remember that the activities themselves are interrelated and must blend together appropriately.

The wise use of organizational resources by these new managers will be imperative. The new managers should strive to be both effective and efficient, and to reach company goals without wasting company resources.

Management Skills

No discussion of organizational resources would be complete without mentioning management skills, perhaps the primary determinant of how effective and efficient managers will be. The cartoon shown here makes the point that certain skills are needed to successfully manage an organization.

According to an article by Robert L. Katz, managerial success depends primarily on performance rather than personality traits.[7] Katz also states that managers' ability to perform is a result of the managerial skills they possess. If managers have necessary management skills, they will probably perform well and be relatively successful. On the other hand, if they do not have necessary management skills, they will probably perform poorly and be relatively unsuccessful.

Katz indicates that three types of primary skills are important for successful management performance: technical skills, human skills, and conceptual skills. **Technical skills** involve using specialized knowledge and expertise in executing work-related techniques and procedures. Examples of technical skills include engineering, computer programming, and accounting. Technical skills are mostly related to working with "things"—processes or physical objects. **Human skills** are those that build cooperation within the team being led. Human skills involve working with attitudes, communication, individuals and groups, and individual

Successful management performance depends on:

1. Technical skills.

2. Human skills.

"Oh, I believe in free enterprise, sir—I'm just not good at it."

Wall Street Journal, *September 17, 1987. From the* Wall Street Journal*–permission, Cartoon Features Syndicate.*

FIGURE 1.7   As a manager moves from the supervisory to the top management level, conceptual skills become more important than technical skills, but human skills remain equally important.

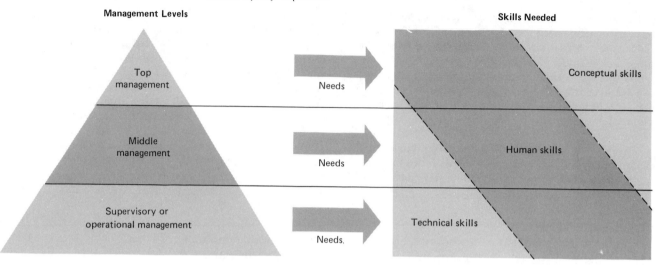

Paul Hersey/Ken Blanchard, *Management of Organizational Behavior: Utilizing Human Resources*, 5th ed., © 1988, p. 8. Reprinted by permission of Prentice-Hall, Inc., Englewood Cliffs, N.J.

3. Conceptual skills.

interests; in short, working with people. **Conceptual skills** involve the ability to see the organization as a whole. A manager with conceptual skills is better able to understand how various functions of the organization complement one another, the relationship of the organization to its environment, and how changes in one part of the organization affect the rest of the organization.

Basically, as one moves from lower management to upper management, conceptual skills become more important and technical skills become less important (see Figure 1.7). The supportive rationale is that, as managers advance in an organization, their tasks become less involved with the actual production activity or technical areas, and they become more concerned with guiding the organization as a whole. Human skills, however, are extremely important to managers at top, middle,[8] and lower or supervisory levels.[9] The common denominator of all management levels is people.

THE UNIVERSALITY OF MANAGEMENT

The four basic functions of management can be applied in all organizations.

Management principles are **universal**, or applicable to all types of organizations (business organizations, churches, sororities, athletic teams, hospitals, etc.) and organizational levels. Naturally, a manager's job is somewhat different in each of these organizations because each organization requires the use of specialized knowledge, exists in unique working and political environments, and uses different technology. However, job similarities also exist because of the common basic management activities necessary in all organizations: planning, organizing, influencing, and controlling.

Henri Fayol stated that all managers should possess certain characteristics, such as positive physical qualities, mental qualities, and special knowledge related to the specific operation.[10] B.C. Forbes, also describing managerial characteristics, emphasized the importance of certain more personal qualities in successful managers. He inferred that enthusiasm, earnestness of purpose, confidence, and faith in their worthwhileness are primary characteristics of successful managers. Forbes describes Henry Ford as follows:

> At the base and birth of every great business organization was an enthusiast, a man consumed with earnestness of purpose, with confidence in his powers, with faith in the worthwhileness of his endeavors. The original Henry Ford was the quintessence of enthusiasm. In the days of his difficulties, disappointments, and discouragements, when he was wrestling with his balky motor engine—and wrestling likewise with poverty—only his inexhaustible enthusiasm saved him from defeat.[11]

Fayol and Forbes can describe these desirable characteristics of successful managers only because of the universality concept: the basic ingredients of the successful management situation are applicable to organizations of all types.

BACK TO THE CASE

The new employee-owners of Metalco will be successful as managers only if they possess technical skills, human skills, and conceptual skills. A relatively low-level management position at Metalco would require human skills, technical skills, and conceptual skills, probably ranked respectively in terms of their order of importance to a lower-level manager. Of course, as lower-level managers take over middle- and upper-level management positions, this ranking of skill importance would change, and there would be increasing emphasis on conceptual skills.

As Metalco employees gain experience in managing, they probably will find that their cumulative management experience is valuable at whatever management position they assume, whether that position is at Metalco, in some other steel company, or even in some other business altogether. They may also discover that enthusiasm, earnestness, confidence, and faith in their worthwhileness are important personal qualities of successful managers in every organization.

MANAGEMENT CAREERS

Thus far, this chapter has focused on outlining the importance of management to our society, presenting a definition of management and the management process, and explaining the universality of management. Individuals commonly study such topics because they are interested in pursuing a management career. This section presents information that will help students preview what might characterize their own management careers and describes some of the issues they might face in attempting to manage the careers of others within an organization. The specific focus is on career definition, career and life stages and performance, and career promotion.

A Definition of Career

A **career** is an individual's perceived sequence of attitudes and behaviours associated with the performance of work-related experiences and activities over the span of the person's working life.[12] This definition implies that a career is cumulative in nature. As individuals accumulate successful experiences in one position, they generally develop abilities and attitudes that qualify them to hold more advanced positions. In general, management positions at one level tend to be stepping-stones to management positions at the next-highest level.

Careers involve attitudes and behaviour.

Career Stages, Life Stages, and Performance

There are four career stages: exploration, establishment, maintenance, and decline.

Careers are generally viewed as evolving through a series of stages. The evolutionary stages—exploration, establishment, maintenance, and decline—appear in Figure 1.8. This figure highlights the performance levels and age ranges commonly associated with each stage. The levels and ranges indicate what is likely at each stage, not what is inevitable.

Exploration Stage

In the exploration stage, individuals analyze themselves and explore available jobs.

The first stage in career evolution is the **exploration stage**, which occurs at the beginning of a career and is characterized by self-analysis and the exploration of different types of available jobs. Individuals at this stage are generally about fifteen to twenty-five years old and involved in some type of formal training, such as college or vocational education. They often pursue part-time employment to gain a richer understanding of what it might be like to have a career in a particular organization or industry. Typical jobs held during this stage might include cooking at Burger King, stocking at a Bay department store, or being an office assistant at a Sun Life Assurance office.

Establishment Stage

In the establishment stage, individuals become more productive.

The second stage in career evolution is the **establishment stage**, during which individuals who are about twenty-five to forty-five years old typically start to become more productive, or higher performers (as Figure 1.8 indicates by the upturn in the dotted line). Employment sought during this stage is guided by what was learned during the exploration stage. In addition, the jobs sought are

FIGURE 1.8   The relationships among career stages, life stages, and performance.

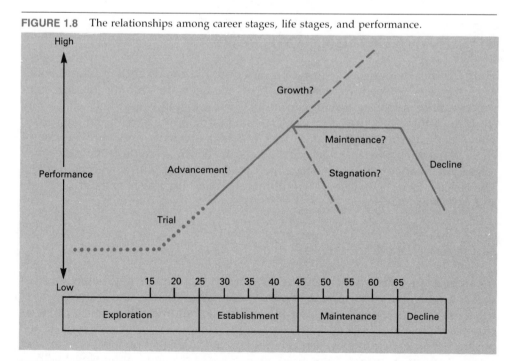

From *Careers in Organizations* by Douglas T. Hall, © 1976 Scott, Foresman and Company. Reprinted by permission.

usually full-time. Individuals at this stage commonly move to different jobs within the same company, to different companies, or even to different industries.

Maintenance Stage

The third stage in career evolution is the **maintenance stage**. In this stage, individuals who are about forty-five to sixty-five years old show either increased performance (career growth), stabilized performance (career maintenance), or decreased performance (career stagnation).

> *The maintenance stage involves growth, maintenance, or stagnation.*

From a managerial viewpoint, it is better to have growth than maintenance or stagnation. Some companies, such as IBM, attempt to eliminate career plateauing.[13] Figure 1.9 shows how Coca-Cola USA tries to avoid career maintenance and stagnation by ensuring that employees know where to go for career development guidance, know what jobs are open within the company, and know what avenues are available for self-development.[14]

Decline Stage

The last stage in career evolution is the **decline stage**, which involves people of about sixty-five years and older whose productivity naturally is declining. These individuals are either close to retirement, semi-retired, or retired. People at this stage commonly find it difficult to maintain prior performance levels because they begin to lose interest in their careers or fail to keep their job skills up-to-date. As people live longer and stay healthier, many of them become part-time workers in businesses such as Dominion supermarkets and McDonald's and in volunteer groups such as Centraide and the Canadian Heart Foundation.

> *The decline stage brings declining performance.*

FIGURE 1.9   Aspects of Coca-Cola USA that help enhance career growth of employees.

- *Newsmakers* is a monthly publication listing moves within Coca-Cola USA. This gives people information on the kinds and number of internal career moves taking place.
- Job posting and the Exempt Job Opening Listing indicate specific open positions of the lower and mid-level management levels.
- Career opportunities booklets provide a broad overview of each department, as well as specific qualifications for typical positions.
- The 30-page *Career Planning Workbook*, designed specifically for Coca-Cola USA, gives individuals an opportunity to assess their strengths, values, and alternative career directions and provides a structured means of developing a career plan. A worksheet captures all the critical information in one place.
- Career planning can also be explored through a two-day "Career Strategies Workshop." Participants examine themselves, possible career options, and strategies for attaining their goals. A special feature of the program is the opportunity to meet key human resource people representing each functional area in Coca-Cola USA as well as the larger structure of the Coca-Cola Company.
- The company helps employees develop their skills through an extensive in-house training program. The *Employee Training Catalog*, distributed annually with quarterly updates, lists courses offered by Coca-Cola USA by performance factor, such as organizing and planning. Therefore, if a particular skill area is identified during a performance evaluation or a career discussion, the appropriate course can easily be selected.
- A 100 percent reimbursement tuition aid program offers employees the opportunity to return to school to enhance their formal education.
- On- and off-the-job developmental activities are considered primary opportunities for growth. Employees may ask for feedback from their managers, act as an instructor or trainer, take on new projects, participate on a task force or project team, or join professional organizations. All of these activities allow the development of new professional skills and contribute to professional growth.

FIGURE 1.10   Manager and employee roles in enhancing employee career development.

Dimension	Professional Employee	Manager
Responsibility	Assumes responsibility for individual career development	Assumes responsibility for employee development
Information	Obtains career information through self-evaluation and data collection: What do I enjoy doing? Where do I want to go?	Provides information by holding up a mirror of reality: How manager views the employee How others view the employee How "things work around here"
Planning	Develops an individual plan to reach objectives	Helps employee assess plan
Follow-through	Invites management support through high performance on the current job by understanding the scope of the job and taking appropriate initiative	Provides coaching and relevant information on opportunities

Reprinted by permission from Paul H. Thompson, Robin Zenger Baker, and Norman Smallwood, "Improving Professional Development by Applying the Four-Stage Career Model," *Organizational Dynamics* (Autumn 1986): 59, © 1986 American Management Association, Inc. All rights reserved.

Promoting Your Own Career

Career success can be enhanced with appropriate tactics.

Practising managers[15] and management scholars generally agree that the careful formulation and implementation of appropriate tactics can enhance the success of management careers.[16] Perhaps the most important tactic is to work for managers who carry out a realistic and constructive role in the career development of their employees.[17] Figure 1.10 outlines what career development responsibility, information, planning, and follow-through might include. This figure also contains an example of a complementary career development role for a professional employee. Figure 1.11 lists several additional tactics for enhancing career success.

Success comes with demonstrations of abilities and accomplishments.

To enhance their career success, individuals must be proactive rather than reactive.[18] That is, they must take specific action to demonstrate their abilities and accomplishments. They must also have a clear idea of the next position they are seeking, the skills they must acquire to function appropriately in that position, and a plan for how they will acquire those skills. Finally, they need to think about the ultimate position they want and the sequence of positions they must hold in order to gain the skills and attitudes necessary to qualify for that position.

FIGURE 1.11   Tips for enhancing your management career.

- Remember that good performance that pleases your superiors is the basic foundation of success, but recognize that not all good performance is easily measured. Determine the real criteria by which you are evaluated and be rigorously honest in evaluating your own performance against these criteria.
- Manage your career; be active in influencing decisions, because pure effort is not necessarily rewarded.
- Strive for positions that have high visibility and exposure where you can be a hero observed by higher officials. Check to see that the organization has a formal system of keeping track of young people. Remember that high-risk line jobs tend to offer more visibility than staff positions like corporate planning or personnel, but also that visibility can sometimes be achieved by off-job community activities.

- Develop relations with a mobile senior executive who can be your sponsor. Become a complementary crucial subordinate with different skills than your superior.
- Learn your job as quickly as possible and train a replacement so you can be available to move and broaden your background in different functions.
- Nominate yourself for other positions: modesty is not necessarily a virtue. However, change jobs for more power and influence, not primarily for status or pay. The latter could be a substitute for real opportunity to make things happen.
- Before taking a position, rigorously assess your strengths and weaknesses, what you like and don't like. Don't accept a promotion if it draws on your weaknesses and entails mainly activities that you don't like.

FIGURE 1.11   Continued.

- Leave at your convenience, but on good terms without parting criticism of the organization. Do not stay under an immobile superior who is not promoted in three to five years.
- Don't be trapped by formal, narrow job descriptions. Move outside them and probe the limits of your influence.
- Accept that responsibility will always somewhat exceed authority and that organizational politics are inevitable. Establish alliances and fight necessary battles, minimizing upward ones to very important issues.
- Get out of management if you can't stand being dependent on others and having them dependent on you.

- Recognize that you will face ethical dilemmas no matter how moral you try to be. No evidence exists that unethical managers are more successful than ethical ones, but it may well be that those who move faster are less socially conscious. Therefore, from time to time you must examine your personal values and question how much you will sacrifice for the organization.
- Don't automatically accept all tales of managerial perversity that you hear. Attributing others' success to unethical behavior is often an excuse for one's own personal inadequacies. Most of all, don't commit an act which you know to be wrong in the hope that your supervisor will see it as loyalty and reward you for it. Sometimes he will, but he may also sacrifice you when the organization is criticized.

BACK TO THE CASE

Assume that Martin Plane is a plant manager for Metalco Steel. He is forty-five years old and is considered a member of Metalco's middle management.

As with many individuals, Plane began his career (exploration stage) in college by considering various areas of study and by holding a number of different types of primarily part-time positions. He delivered pizzas and worked for a lawn care company. He began college at age eighteen and graduated when he was twenty-two.

Plane then moved into the establishment stage of his career. For a few years immediately after graduation, he held full-time trial positions in the steel industry as well as in the restaurant and retailing industries. What he learned during the career exploration stage helped him choose the types of full-time trial positions to pursue. At the age of twenty-six, he accepted a trial position as an entry-level line worker at Metalco. Through this position, he discovered that he wanted to remain in the steel industry in general and at Metalco in particular. From age twenty-seven to age forty-five,

he held a number of supervisory and middle management positions.

Now Plane is moving into an extremely critical part of his career, the maintenance stage. He could probably remain in his present position and maintain his productivity for several more years. However, he wants to advance his career. Therefore he must emphasize a proactive attitude by formulating and implementing tactics aimed at enhancing his career success, such as seeking training to develop critical skills, or moving to a position that is a prerequisite for other, more advanced positions.

In the future, as Plane approaches sixty-five years of age (the decline stage), it is probable that his productivity at Metalco will decline somewhat. From a career viewpoint, he may want to go from full-time employment to semi-retirement. Perhaps he could work for Metalco or another steel company on a part-time advisory basis or even pursue part-time work in another industry. For example, he might be able to teach a management course at a nearby college.

Action Summary

Reread the learning objectives that follow. Each objective is followed by questions. Answering these questions accurately will help you to retain the most important concepts discussed in this chapter. After answering each question, check your answer with the answer key at the end of this chapter. (*Hint*: If you have doubt regarding the correct response, consult the page that follows the answer.)

Circle:

From studying this chapter, I will attempt to acquire:

1. **An understanding of the importance of management to society and individuals.**

T, F   **a.** Managers constitute less than 1 percent of the Canadian work force.

T, F   **b.** Management is important to society.

2. **An understanding of the role of management.**

a, b, c, d, e   **a.** The role of a manager is: (a) to make workers happy; (b) to satisfy only the manager's needs; (c) to make the most profit; (d) to survive in a highly competitive society; (e) to achieve organizational goals.

T, F   **b.** Apart from its goals, management has no meaning.

3. **An ability to define *management* in several different ways.**

a, b, c, d, e   **a.** Management is: (a) a process; (b) reaching organizational goals; (c) utilizing people and other resources; (d) all of the above; (e) a and b.

T, F   **b.** Management is the process of working with people and through people.

4. **An ability to list and define the basic functions of management.**

a, b, c, d, e   **a.** Which of the following is *not* a function of management: (a) influencing; (b) planning; (c) organizing; (d) directing; (e) controlling.

a, b, c, d, e   **b.** The process of gathering information and comparing this information to pre-established standards is part of: (a) planning; (b) influencing; (c) motivating; (d) controlling; (e) commanding.

5. **Working definitions of managerial effectiveness and managerial efficiency.**

T, F   **a.** If an organization is using its resources to attain its goals, the organization's managers are efficient.

T, F   **b.** If a manager is reaching goals and wasting resources, you would say that he or she is efficient but ineffective.

6. **An understanding of basic management skills and their relative importance to managers.**

a, b, c, d, e   **a.** Conceptual skills require that management view the organization as: (a) a profit centre; (b) a decision-making unit; (c) a problem-solving group; (d) a whole; (e) individual contributions.

T, F   **b.** Managers require fewer and fewer human skills as they move from lower to upper management.

7. **An understanding of the universality of management.**

T, F   **a.** The statement that management principles are universal means that they apply to all types of organizations and organizational levels.

T, F   **b.** The universality of management means that management principles are taught the same way in all schools.

8. **Insights concerning what management careers are and how they evolve.**
   a. In general, as careers evolve, individuals tend to further develop job skills but show very little or no change in attitude about various job circumstances.   T, F
   b. Individuals tend to show the first significant increase in performance during the establishment career stage.   T, F
   c. Tips for enhancing the success of your career should not be seen as too useful over the long term.   T, F

INTRODUCTORY CASE WRAP-UP

"Inexperienced Managers at Metalco Steel Mill" (p. 6) and its related back-to-the-case sections were written to help you better understand the management concepts contained in this chapter. Answer the following discussion questions about this introductory case to further enrich your understanding of the chapter content:

1. If you were an employee-owner at the Metalco plant, would you like to become a manager? Why?

2. What concerns would you have as an employee who just shared in the purchase of the Metalco plant?

3. A Metalco employee-owner has just taken a Metalco management position. List and describe five activities that you think this individual must perform as part of the new job.

Issues for Review and Discussion

1. What is the main point illustrated in the introductory case at the beginning of the chapter?
2. How important is the management function to society?
3. How important is the management function to individuals?
4. What is the basic role of managers?
5. How is *management* defined in this text? What main themes are contained in this definition?
6. List and define each of the four functions of management.
7. Outline the relationship between the four management functions.
8. List and describe five of Peters and Waterman's characteristics of excellent companies, and explain how each of these characteristics could affect planning, organizing, influencing, and controlling.
9. List and define the basic organizational resources managers have at their disposal.
10. What is the relationship between organizational resources and production?
11. Draw and explain the continuum of managerial effectiveness.
12. Draw and explain the continuum of managerial efficiency.
13. Are managerial effectiveness and managerial efficiency related concepts? If so, how?
14. According to Katz's article, what are the three primary types of skills important to management success? Define each of these types of skills.
15. Describe the relative importance of each of these three types of skills to lower-level, middle-level, and upper-level managers.
16. What is meant by "the universality of management"?
17. What is a career?
18. Discuss the significance of the maintenance career stage.
19. What tips for promoting the success of a career are most valuable to you? Explain.

Sources of Additional Information

Alpander, Guvenc G. "Training First-Line Supervisors to Criticize Constructively." *Personnel Journal* (March 1980): 216–21.

Burack, Elmer H., and Nicholas J. Mathys. *Introduction to Management: A Career Perspective.* New York: Wiley, 1983.

Burgelman, Robert A., and Leonard R. Sayles. *Inside Corporate Innovation.* New York: Free Press, 1986.

Drucker, P. *Management: Tasks, Responsibilities, Practices.* New York: Harper & Row, 1974.

Elliott, Clifford, and Jang H. Yoo. "Innovations in the Japanese Distributive System: Are the Barriers to Entry Being Lifted?" *Akron Business and Economic Review* (Spring 1980): 28–33.

Garfield, Charles A. "The Right Stuff." *Management World* 13 (July 1984): 18–20.

Hamermesh, Richard G. *Making Strategy Work: How Senior Managers Produce Results.* New York: Wiley, 1986.

Hayes, James L. "Making a Professional Manager." *Management Review* 69 (November 1980): 2–3.

Heide, Dorothy. "I Can Improve My Management Skills By:" *Personnel Journal* 63 (June 1984): 52–54.

Kamerschen, David R., Robert J. Paul, and David A. Dilts.

"Ownership and Management of the Firm — Another Look." *Business and Society* 25 (Spring 1986): 8–14.

Koontz, Harold, Cyril O'Donnell, and Heinz Weihrich. *Management,* 8th ed. New York: McGraw-Hill, 1984.

Lorsch, Jay W., and Peter F. Mathias. "When Professionals Have to Manage." *Harvard Business Review* (July/August 1987): 78–83.

Molz, Richard. "Entrepreneurial Managers in Large Organizations." *Business Horizons* 27 (September/October 1984): 54–61.

Ozawa, Terutomo. "Japan's Industrial Groups." *MSU Business Topics* (Autumn 1980): 33–41.

Ruch, Richard S., and Ronald Goodman. *Image at the Top.* New York: Free Press, 1983.

Taylor, James W., and Ronald N. Paul. "The Real Meaning of Excellence." *Business* 36 (April/May/June 1986): 27–33.

Veiga, John F. "Do Managers on the Move Get Anywhere?" *Harvard Business Review* (March/April 1981): 20–22, 26–30, 34–38.

Webber, Alan M. "Red Auerbach on Management." *Harvard Business Review* (March/April 1987): 84–91.

Notes

1. Peter F. Drucker, "Management's New Role," *Harvard Business Review* (November/December 1969): 54.
2. U.S. Bureau of the Census, *Statistical Abstract of the United States,* 93d ed. (Washington, D.C.: Government Printing Office, 1972), 230.
3. "Who Are the Unemployed?" *U.S. News & World Report.* November 16, 1970, 54.
4. Robert Albanese, *Management: Toward Accountability for Performance* (Homewood, Ill.: Richard D. Irwin, 1975), 49.
5. For a more detailed description of each of these definitions of management, see Dalton E. McFarland, *Management: Principles and Practice,* 4th ed. (New York: Macmillan, 1974), 6–10.
6. Joseph L. Massie and John Douglas, *Managing: A Contemporary Introduction* (Englewood Cliffs, N.J.: Prentice-Hall, 1973), 24. Robert Kreitner, *Management,* 2d ed. (Boston: Houghton Mifflin, 1983). Henry L. Sisk, *Management and Organization,* 2d ed. (Cincinnati: South-Western, 1974), 13. Harold Koontz and Cyril O'Donnell, *Principles of Management: An Analysis of Managerial Functions,* 5th ed. (New York: McGraw-Hill, 1972), 42. James H. Donnelly, Jr., James L. Gibson, and John M. Ivancevich, *Fundamentals of Management:*

Functions, Behavior, Models (Homewood, Ill.: Business Publications, 1975), 4.
7. Robert L. Katz, "Skills of an Effective Administrator," *Harvard Business Review* (January/February 1955): 33–41.
8. W. Earl Sasser, Jr., and Frank S. Leonard, "Let First-Level Supervisors Do Their Job," *Harvard Business Review* (March/April 1980): 113–21.
9. Peter D. Couch, "Learning to Be a Middle Manager," *Business Horizons* (February 1979): 33–41.
10. Henri Fayol, *General and Industrial Management* (London: Sir Isaac Pitman & Sons, 1949).
11. B.C. Forbes, *Forbes,* March 15, 1976, 128.
12. Douglas T. Hall, *Careers in Organizations* (Santa Monica, Calif.: Goodyear Publishing, 1976), 4.
13. John W. Slocum, Jr., William L. Cron, and Linda C. Yows, "Whose Career Is Likely to Plateau?" *Business Horizons* (March/April 1987): 31–38.
14. Lynn Slavenski, "Career Development: A Systems Approach," *Training and Development Journal* (February 1987): 56–59.
15. Joseph E. McKendrick, Jr., "What Are You Doing the Rest of Your Life?" *Management World* (September/October 1987): 2.

16. Carl Anderson, *Management: Skills, Functions, and Organization Performance*, Second Edition. (Boston: Allyn and Bacon, 1988).

17. Paul H. Thompson, Robin Zenger Baker, and Norman Smallwood, "Improving Personal Development by Applying the Four-Stage Career Model," *Organizational Dynamics* (Autumn 1986): 49–62.

18. Buck Blessing, "Career Planning: Five Fatal Assumptions," *Training and Development Journal* (September 1986): 49–51.

Action Summary Answer Key

1. a. F, p. 7
   b. T, p. 7
2. a. e, p. 9
   b. T, p. 9

3. a. d, p. 10
   b. F, p. 10
4. a. d, p. 10
   b. d, p. 10

5. a. F, p. 13
   b. F, pp. 13–14
6. a. d, p. 18
   b. F, p. 18

7. a. T, p. 18
   b. F, p. 18
8. a. F, p. 19
   b. T, p. 20
   c. F, p. 22

FRANK STRONACH: MAGNA'S STRONGMAN

In his mid-fifties, Frank Stronach, chairman of Magna International Inc., is in top condition and looks exactly like what he is: the quintessential multimillionaire who likes to stay in shape. He is also one of Canada's most successful and highest paid executives. In 1985 Stronach almost single-handedly pushed Magna, an auto parts manufacturing company, up to sales of $690.4 million, an increase of 40 percent, or $197 million, over the previous fiscal year.

Born in Austria, Stronach worked as an apprentice at a local tool-and-diemaker at the age of fourteen, and left for Canada at the age of twenty-two. Arriving in Montreal in 1954, he had nothing more than a couple of hundred dollars and a lot of determination. Unable to find work in Montreal, he drifted off to Kitchener, Ontario, where he found a job as a machinist with a small company making aerospace components. A year later, the company began losing orders and Stronach, a junior employee, was laid off. He then found a job in Toronto as a toolmaker. Six months later, he was running the place. This afforded him an opportunity to experience what it felt like to run a business. He liked it.

By 1957 Stronach was ready. He rented a small garage, bought $15 000 worth of used tools on a down payment of less than $4000 and loosed Multi-Matic Investments Ltd. upon the world. "My first job was to

Stronach, "one of Canada's most successful and highest paid executives."

make a tool that could turn out a metal bracket, a metal stamping, for American Standard. They were just around the corner." Two years later, Multi-Matic had fifteen employees and was grossing $150 000 making tools and dies for the auto industry. Business improved steadily. But then he found out that his foreman was thinking of leaving. With a slowdown in growth and more work for himself as possible consequences, Stronach decided to offer his foreman a partnership: Together they would open a new factory, with Stronach providing the capital, and the foreman would have an earn-in opportunity, based on performance, to one third of the new factory.

And so was born the doctrine of enlightened greed, a doctrine central to the operating philosophy of Frank Stronach: If someone wants to get ahead, and you want to keep that person, then you harness that ambition and you both grow. A second factory was born that way, and a third. Then Stronach decided to sweep all of his employees into his participatory vision. The company turned public because it was "the best way for management and employees to participate in the company." In 1969, Multi-Matic was sold to Magna and Stronach took shares in Magna as payment, becoming the largest shareholder in the process.

For Stronach, Magna is an engine of socio-economic policy. It is an instrument of state rather than a place where people are engaged, profitably, in turning out 4 000 different car parts, from brake pedal assemblies to the little motors that drive the windshield wipers back and forth. Some of the dreams thriving within Stronach's vision include training facilities, sports arenas, daycare centres, clinics, and factories. All·of these, he insists, can flow from his company to society at large.

A strong belief in the moral right of workers to some of the profits they help create is part of the capitalist philosophy that Stronach spreads with relentless evangelism. It is this philosophy of social responsibility that has also led him to accept countless memberships on task forces and committees for both industry and government. He has even enshrined his precepts in a charter known as the Corporate Constitution. This is the document that guarantees the thousands of workers on the shop floor their 10 percent share of the profits—3 percent as an end-of-year cash payment and the other 7 in class A shares worth one vote each, of which there are 22.6 million outstanding. This document also lays out Magna's charitable and political obligations, to a maximum of 2 percent of profits. Finally, the document also establishes management's share of profits, including the staggering 6 percent that can fall to the fewer than twenty key managers of the executive group.

In March of 1986, Magna had about 9 000 employees running eighty plants in Canada and ten in the United States. They were opening a new plant every three weeks. The company's content per vehicle manufactured in North America was almost sixty-five dollars. Stronach's goal is one hundred dollars by 1988, and as a greater

share of his business moves south of the border, so will an increasing proportion of his plants. "The jobs should go to the people buying the product," says Stronach, nailing in place another plank in his philosophy of social responsibility.

Stronach's employees seem happy enough: Magna's low turnover is enviable. The plants are small, with Magna's ideal being 100 employees per plant. Employees bright enough to come up with a new product or who demonstrate superior qualities can win their way into management and the enhanced profit-sharing that that brings. Magna's approximately 250 managers, excluding the top executives, own about 12.5 percent of the company; some 7 000 workers own the same. As for Frank Stronach, he too seems to have earned his share of Magna the employee's way.

DISCUSSION ISSUES

1. Identify the important management skills Stronach appears to possess. How might these skills aid in the continued success of the company?
2. Does Stronach understand the management process? Elaborate.
3. Which one of the four basic management functions do you think contributed the most to the success of Stronach's organization?

Based on "Frank As He'll Ever Be," by Matthew Hart in *Financial Post Moneywise Magazine*, May 1986. Used with permission.

APPROACHES TO MANAGING

STUDENT LEARNING OBJECTIVES

From studying this chapter, I will attempt to acquire:

1. An understanding of the classical approach to management.
2. An appreciation for the work of Frederick W. Taylor, Frank and Lillian Gilbreth, Henry L. Gantt, and Henri Fayol.
3. An understanding of the behavioural approach to management.
4. An understanding of the studies at the Hawthorne Works of the Western Electric Company.
5. An understanding of the management science approach to management.
6. An understanding of how the management science approach has evolved.
7. An understanding of the system approach to management.
8. An understanding of how triangular management and the contingency approach to management are related.

CHAPTER OUTLINE

Management in Action: "We're all in this together, pulling in the same direction."

MCDONALD'S RECIPE FOR SUCCESS

"Wow, we just had a customer walk out on us!" Jim Delligatti drops his Big Mac in midbite and bolts from the booth, rushing past four rows of customers who make up the noonday rush at this downtown McDonald's. Taking a command position behind the counter that stretches the width of the restaurant, Jim Delligatti, by his mere presence, spurs his twelve workers to hustle even faster.

It's not enough that Delligatti has opened forty-seven of the famous hamburger outlets over the past twenty-six years and has become a millionaire in the process. He hates to see anyone leave one of his "stores" unhappy, and his white-suited crews in their white "McNugget Mania" painter's caps know it.

"Production—twelve burgers, six Macs," barks the fresh-faced assistant manager posted behind the warming bin, where wrapped burgers can remain no more than ten minutes before being discarded. "Coming up," says a high school boy, who slaps a handful of frozen patties on the hot, stainless steel grill. Behind him, a young woman takes buns from a toaster and "dresses" them with quick squirts of mustard and ketchup from a silver dispenser. She puts the pickles on by hand, taking care to spread them out so the customer will not get everything in one gulp. At the french fry station, another young woman shakes salt onto a hot batch of golden brown potatoes and then scoops the fries into red paper containers. With today's crowd, none will remain in the warming bin over the seven-minute maximum.

The lunchtime whirl all comes together to meet one goal: to serve the customer within sixty seconds of the order's being placed.

As huge as it is, the McDonald's empire really is built around individual stores, each striving to conform to the company motto of "quality, service, cleanliness, and value." These standards are hammered into new franchisees at McDonald's Hamburger "U" training centre in Oak Brook, Illinois. The way the firm sees it, customers should get the same McDonald's quality no matter where they buy their hamburgers, anywhere in the world.

Based on "Recipe for Success in the Fast-Food Game," in *U.S. News and World Report*, November 21, 1983.

What's Ahead

A manager like McDonald's Jim Delligatti knows that there are several ways to analyze management situations and to solve organizational problems. This chapter explains five such approaches to management: (1) the classical approach; (2) the behavioural approach; (3) the management science approach; (4) the contingency approach; and (5) the system approach.

Chapter 1 focused primarily on defining management. This chapter presents various approaches to analyzing and reacting to the management situation. Each approach recommends a basically different method of analysis and a different type of management action as a result of this analysis.

Over the years, disagreement on exactly how many different approaches to management exist and what each approach entails has been common. In an attempt to organize and condense the various approaches, Donnelly, Gibson, and Ivancevich[1] combined the ideas of Koontz, O'Donnell, and Weihrich,[2] and Haynes and Massie[3] and offered these three: (1) the classical approach; (2) the behavioural approach; and (3) the management science approach. They stated that their objective was to simplify a discussion of the field of management without sacrificing significant information.

The following sections build on the work of Donnelly, Gibson, and Ivancevich and present the classical approach, the behavioural approach, and the management science approach. The contingency approach is also discussed as a fourth primary approach to analyzing the management task. The fifth approach, the system approach, is presented as a more recent trend in management thinking and is the approach emphasized in this text.

This chapter presents five approaches to management:
1. The classical approach.
2. The behavioural approach.
3. The management science approach.
4. The contingency approach.
5. The system approach.

THE CLASSICAL APPROACH

The **classical approach to management** resulted from the first significant, concentrated effort to develop a body of management thought. Management writers who participated in this effort are considered the pioneers of management study.

The classical approach to management stresses efficiency and recommends that managers continually strive to increase organizational efficiency to increase production.

The classical approach emphasizes efficiency.

For discussion purposes, the classical approach to management breaks into two distinct areas. The first area, lower-level management analysis, consists primarily of the work of Frederick W. Taylor, Frank and Lillian Gilbreth, and Henry L. Gantt. These individuals mainly studied the jobs of workers at lower levels of the organization. The second area, comprehensive analysis of management, concentrates more on studying the management function as a whole. The primary contributor to this category was Henri Fayol. See Figure 2.1.

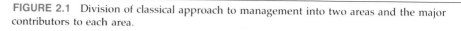

FIGURE 2.1   Division of classical approach to management into two areas and the major contributors to each area.

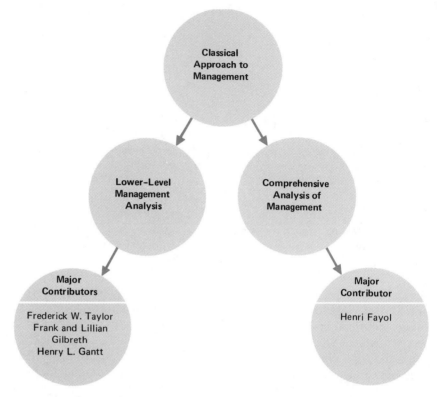

Lower-Level Management Analysis

Lower-level management analysis concentrates on the "one best way" to perform a task; that is, how can a task situation be structured to get the highest production from workers? The process of finding this "one best way" has become known as the scientific method of management or, simply, **scientific management**. Although the techniques of scientific managers could conceivably be applied to all management levels, the research, research applications, and illustrations relate mostly to lower-level managers. The work of Frederick W. Taylor, Frank and Lillian Gilbreth, and Henry L. Gantt is summarized in the sections that follow.

Frederick W. Taylor (1856–1915)

Because of the significance of his contributions, Frederick W. Taylor is commonly called the "father of scientific management." His primary goal was to increase worker efficiency by scientifically designing jobs. His basic premise was that there was "one best way" to do a job and that "way" should be discovered and put into operation.

Perhaps the best illustration of Taylor's scientific method and his management philosophy lies in a description of how he modified the job of employees whose sole responsibility was shoveling materials at the Bethlehem Steel Company.[4] During the modification process, Taylor made the assumption that any worker's job could be reduced to a science. To construct the "science of shoveling," he obtained answers—through observation and experimentation—to the following questions:

1. Will a first-class worker do more work per day with a shovelful of two, five, ten, fifteen, or twenty kilograms?
2. What kinds of shovels work best with which materials?
3. How quickly can a shovel be pushed into a pile of materials and pulled out properly loaded?
4. How much time is required to swing a shovel backward and throw the load a given horizontal distance accompanied by a given height?

As Taylor began formulating answers to these types of questions, he developed insights on how to increase the total amount of materials shoveled per day. He increased worker efficiency by matching shovel size with such factors as men, materials, and height and distance materials were to be thrown. After the third year that Taylor's shoveling efficiency plan was in operation, records at Bethlehem Steel indicated that the total number of shovelers needed was reduced from about 600 to 140, the average number of tonnes shoveled per worker per day rose from fifteen to fifty-four, the average earnings per worker per day rose from $1.15 to $1.88, and the average cost of handling a tonne dropped from $0.072 to $0.033—an obviously impressive application of scientific management to the task of shoveling.

Frederick W. Taylor

Frank Gilbreth (1868–1924), Lillian Gilbreth (1878–1972)

The Gilbreths were also significant contributors to the scientific method. By definition, therefore, they ascribed to finding and using the "one best way" to perform a job. The primary investigative tool in their research was **motion study**, which consisted of reducing each job to the most basic movements possible. This motion analysis was then used to establish job performance standards and to eliminate unnecessary or wasted movement.

During a motion analysis, the Gilbreths considered the work environment, the motion itself, and behavioural variables concerning the workers. Figure 2.2 lists the primary factors that fall into each of these groups. The analysis of each

A motion study reduces a job to its basic movements.

FIGURE 2.2   Primary variables considered in analyzing motions.

Variables of the Worker	Variables of the Surroundings, Equipment, and Tools	Variables of the Motion
1. Anatomy	1. Appliances	1. Acceleration
2. Brawn	2. Clothes	2. Automaticity
3. Contentment	3. Colours	3. Combination with other motions and sequence
4. Creed	4. Entertainment, music, reading, etc.	4. Cost
5. Earning power	5. Heating, cooling, ventilating	5. Direction
6. Experience	6. Lighting	6. Effectiveness
7. Fatigue	7. Quality of material	7. Foot-pounds of work accomplished
8. Habits	8. Reward and punishment	8. Inertia and momentum overcome
9. Health	9. Size of unit moved	9. Length
10. Mode of living	10. Special fatigue-eliminating devices	10. Necessity
11. Nutrition	11. Surroundings	11. Path
12. Size	12. Tools	12. "Play for position"
13. Skill	13. Union rules	13. Speed
14. Temperament	14. Weight of unit moved	
15. Training		

of these variables in a task situation was obviously a long, involved, and tedious process.

Frank Gilbreth's experience as an apprentice bricklayer led him to motion studies of bricklaying. He found that bricklayers could increase their output significantly by concentrating on performing some motions and eliminating

Frank and Lillian Gilbreth.

FIGURE 2.3   Partial results for one of Gilbreth's bricklaying motion studies.

Operation No.	The Wrong Way Motions Per Brick $\frac{1}{4}\frac{1}{2}\frac{3}{4}\frac{4}{4}$	The Right Way Motions Per Brick $\frac{1}{4}\frac{1}{2}\frac{3}{4}\frac{4}{4}$	Pick and Dip Method. The Exterior Four Inches (Laying to the Line).
1	Step for mortar	Omit	On the scaffold the inside edge of mortar box should be plumb with inside edge of stock platform. On floor the inside edge of mortar box should be twenty-one in. from wall. Mortar boxes never over four ft. apart.
2	Reach for mortar	$\frac{4}{4}$	Do not bend any more than absolutely necessary to reach mortar with a straight arm.
3	Work up mortar	Omit	Provide mortar of right consistency. Examine sand screen and keep in repair so that no pebbles can get through. Keep tender on scaffold to temper up and keep mortar worked up right.
4	Step for brick	Omit	If tubs are kept four ft. apart, no stepping for brick will be necessary on scaffold. On floor keep brick in a pile not nearer than one ft. nor more than four ft. six ins. from wall.
5	Reach for brick	Included in 2	Brick must be reached for at the same time that the mortar is reached for, and picked up at exactly the same time the mortar is picked up. If it is not picked up at the same time, allowance must be made for operation.
6	Pick up right brick	Omit	Train the leader of the tenders to vary the kind of brick used as much as possible to suit the conditions; that is, to bring the best brick when the men are working on the line.
7	Mortar, box to wall	$\frac{4}{4}$	Carry stock from the staging to the wall in the straightest possible line and with an even speed, without pause or hitch. It is important to move the stock with an even speed and not by quick jerks.
8	Brick, pile to wall	Included in 7	Brick must be carried from pile to wall at exactly same time as the mortar is carried to the wall, without pause or jerk.
9	Deposit mortar on wall	Included in 7	If a pause is made, this space must be filled out. If no pause is made, it is included in No. 7.
10	Spreading mortar	Omit	The mortar must be thrown so as to require no additional spreading and so that the mortar runs up on the end of the previous brick laid, or else the next two spaces must be filled out.
11	Cutting off mortar	Omit	If the mortar is thrown from the trowel properly, no spreading and no cutting is necessary.
12	Disposing of mortar	Omit	If mortar is not cut off, this space is not filled out. If mortar is cut off, keep it on trowel and carry back on trowel to box, or else butter on end of brick. Do not throw it on mortar box.

From William R. Spriegel and Clark E. Myers, *The Writings of the Gilbreths* (Easton, Pa.: Richard D. Irwin, 1953), p. 56. By permission of Hive Publishing Company.

others. Figure 2.3 shows a portion of the results of one of Gilbreth's bricklaying motion studies. For each bricklaying activity, Gilbreth indicated whether or not it should be omitted for the sake of efficiency and why. He reduced the twelve motions per brick listed under "The Wrong Way" to the two motions per brick listed under "The Right Way." Gilbreth's bricklaying motion studies resulted in reducing the number of motions necessary to lay a brick by approximately 70 percent and tripling bricklaying production.

Henry L. Gantt (1861–1919)

A third major contributor to the area of scientific management was Henry L. Gantt. He, like Taylor and the Gilbreths, was interested in increasing worker efficiency. Gantt attributed unsatisfactory or ineffective tasks and piece rates (incentive pay for each product piece an individual produces) primarily to the fact that they were set on what had been done in the past or on somebody's *opinion* of what could be done. According to Gantt, *exact scientific knowledge* of what could be done should be substituted for opinion. He considered this the role of scientific management.

> Gantt increased worker efficiency through scheduling innovation and reward innovation.

Henry L. Gantt.

Gantt's management philosophy is described by his statement that "the essential differences between the best system of today and those of the past are the manner in which tasks are 'scheduled' and the manner in which their performance is rewarded."[5] Following his own rationale, Gantt tried to improve systems or organizations through task scheduling innovation and reward innovation.

Scheduling Innovation

The Gantt chart, the primary scheduling tool that Gantt developed, is still used in many organizations today. Basically, this chart provides managers with an easily understood summary of what work was scheduled for specific time periods, how much of this work was completed, and by whom. The Gantt chart is covered in much more detail in Chapter 7.

Reward Innovation

Gantt seemed more aware of the human side of production than either Taylor or the Gilbreths. Gantt wrote that "the taskmaster (manager) of the past was practically a slave driver, whose principal function was to force workmen to do that which they had no desire to do, or interest in doing. The task setter of today under any reputable system of management is not a driver. When he asks the workmen to perform tasks, he makes it to their interest to accomplish them, and is careful not to ask what is impossible or unreasonable."[6]

While Taylor had developed a system that allowed for all workers to be paid at the same rate, Gantt developed a system wherein workers could earn a bonus in addition to the piece rate if they went beyond their daily production quota. Gantt felt strongly that worker compensation needed to correspond not only to production through the piece-rate system but also to overproduction through the bonus system.

> Gantt believed in encouraging workers to higher levels of production through bonuses.

BACK TO THE CASE

Jim Delligatti, the owner/manager of forty-seven McDonald's outlets who was discussed in the introductory case, could use a classical approach to management to stress organizational efficiency—the "one best way" to perform jobs at McDonald's—to increase productivity. As a simplified example, Delligatti might want to check whether the silver dispenser used to apply mustard and ketchup is of the appropriate size to require only one squirt or whether more than one squirt is necessary to adequately cover the hamburger bun.

Delligatti also could use motion studies to eliminate unnecessary or wasted motions by his employees. For example, are hamburgers, french fries, and drinks located for easy insertion into customer bags, or must an employee walk unnecessary steps during the sales process? Also, would certain McDonald's employees be more efficient over an entire working day if they sat, rather than stood, while working?

The classical approach to management might also guide Delligatti in scheduling more efficiently. By ensuring that an appropriate number of people with the appropriate skills are scheduled to work during peak hours and that fewer such individuals are scheduled to work during slower hours, Delligatti would maximize the return on his labour costs.

Delligatti also might want to consider offering his employees some sort of bonus if they reach certain work goals. But he should make sure that the goals that he sets are realistic, since unreasonable or impossible goals tend to make workers resentful and unproductive. For example, Delligatti might ask that certain employees reduce errors in filling orders by 50 percent during the next month. If and when these employees reached the goal, Delligatti could give them a free lunch as a bonus.

Comprehensive Analysis of Management

Comprehensive analysis of management involves studying the management function as a whole.

Whereas scientific managers approach the study of management primarily in terms of job design, managers who embrace the comprehensive view—the second area of the classical approach—are concerned with the entire range of managerial performance.

Among the well-known contributors to the comprehensive view were Chester Barnard,[7] Alvin Brown,[8] Henry S. Dennison,[9] Luther Gulick and Lyndall Urwick,[10] J.D. Mooney and A.C. Reiley,[11] and Oliver Sheldon.[12] Perhaps the most notable of all contributors, however, was Henri Fayol. His book *General and Industrial Management* presents a management philosophy that many modern managers still look to for advice and guidance.[13]

Henri Fayol (1841–1925)

Fayol suggested five elements of management

Because of his writings on the elements of management and the general principles of management, Henri Fayol is usually regarded as the pioneer of administrative theory. The elements of management he outlined—planning, organizing, command, coordination, and control—are still considered worthwhile divisions under which to study, analyze, and put into action the management process. (Note the similarities between Fayol's elements of management and the management functions outlined in Chapter 1—planning, organizing, influencing, controlling.)

The general principles of management suggested by Fayol also are still considered by most managers to be useful in contemporary management practice.

These principles follow in the order developed by Fayol and are accompanied by corresponding definitional themes:[14]

and fourteen general principles of management.

1. *Division of work*   Work should be divided among individuals and groups to ensure that effort and attention are focused on special portions of the task. Fayol presents work specialization as the best way to use the human resources of the organization.

2. *Authority*   The concepts of authority and responsibility are closely related. Authority is defined by Fayol as the right to give orders and the power to exact obedience. Responsibility involves being accountable and, therefore, is naturally associated with authority. When one assumes authority, one also assumes responsibility.

3. *Discipline*   A successful organization requires the common effort of workers. Penalties, however, should be applied judiciously to encourage this common effort.

4. *Unity of command*   Workers should receive orders from only one manager.[15]

5. *Unity of direction*   The entire organization should be moving toward a common objective, in a common direction.

6. *Subordination of individual interests to the general interests*   The interests of one person should not have priority over the interests of the organization as a whole.

7. *Remuneration*   Many variables, such as cost of living, supply of qualified personnel, general business conditions, and success of the business, should be considered in determining the rate of pay a worker will receive.

8. *Centralization*   Fayol defined centralization as lowering the importance of the subordinate role. Decentralization is increasing the same importance. The degree to which centralization or decentralization should be adopted depends on the specific organization in which the manager is working.

9. *Scalar chain*   Managers in hierarchies are actually part of a chainlike authority scale. Each manager, from the first-line supervisor to the president, possesses certain amounts of authority. The president possesses the most authority; the first-line supervisor possesses the least authority. The existence of this chain implies that lower-level managers should always keep upper-level managers informed of their work activities. The existence of and adherence to this scalar chain are necessary if organizations are to be successful.

10. *Order*   For the sake of efficiency and to keep coordination problems to a minimum, all materials and people that are related to a specific kind of work should be assigned to the same general location in the organization.

11. *Equity*   All employees should be treated as equally as possible.

12. *Stability of tenure of personnel*   Retaining productive employees should always be a high priority of management. Recruitment and selection costs, as well as increased reject rates, are usually associated with hiring new workers.

13. *Initiative*   Management should take steps to encourage worker initiative. Initiative can be defined as new or additional work activity undertaken through self-direction.

14. *Esprit de corps*   Management should encourage harmony and general good feelings among employees.

Fayol's general principles of management cover a broad range of topics, but organizational efficiency, the handling of people, and appropriate management action seem to be the three general themes stressed. With the writings of Fayol, the study of management as a broad comprehensive activity began to receive the attention it deserved.

Limitations of the Classical Approach

Although the classical approach generally improves productivity, people emphasis is inadequate.

Individual contributors to the classical approach were probably encouraged to write about their experiences largely because of the success they enjoyed. Structuring work to be more efficient and defining the manager's role more precisely yielded significant improvement in productivity, which individuals such as Taylor and Fayol were quick to document.

The human variable of the organization, however, may not be adequately emphasized in the classical approach. People today do not seem to be as influenced by bonuses as they were in the nineteenth century. It is generally agreed that critical interpersonal areas, such as conflict, communication, leadership, and motivation, were not emphasized enough in the classical approach.

THE BEHAVIOURAL APPROACH

The behavioural approach emphasizes people.

The **behavioural approach to management** emphasizes striving to increase production through an understanding of people. According to proponents of this approach, if managers understand their people and adapt their organizations to them, organizational success usually follows.

The behavioural approach is usually described as beginning with a series of studies conducted between 1924 and 1932. These studies investigated the behaviour and attitudes of workers at the Hawthorne (Chicago) Works of the Western Electric Company.[16] Accounts of these studies are usually divided into phases: the relay assembly test room experiments and the bank wiring observation room experiment.

The Relay Assembly Test Room Experiments

The relay assembly test room experiments originally had a scientific management orientation.[17] The experimenters believed that if productivity was studied long enough under different working conditions (including variations in weather conditions, temperature, rest periods, work hours, and humidity), those working conditions that maximized production would be found. The purpose of the relay assembly test room experiments was to determine the relationship between intensity of lighting and efficiency of workers as measured by worker output. Two groups of female employees were used as subjects. The light intensity for one group was varied, while the light intensity for the other group was held constant.

Production increased continuously, regardless of working conditions.

The results of the experiments surprised the researchers. No matter what condition employees were exposed to, production increased. A consistent relationship between productivity and lighting intensity seemed non-existent. An extensive interviewing campaign was begun to determine why the subjects continued to increase production. The following are the main reasons, as formulated from the interviews:

1. The subjects found working in the test room enjoyable.
2. The new supervisory relationship during the experiment allowed subjects to work freely without fear.
3. Subjects realized that they were taking part in an important and interesting study.
4. The subjects themselves seemed to become friendly as a group.

The experimenters concluded that human factors within organizations could significantly influence production. More research was needed to evaluate the potential impact of this human component in organizations.

The Bank Wiring Observation Room Experiment

The purpose of the bank wiring observation room experiment was to analyze the social relationships in a work group.[18] More specifically, the study focused on the effect of group piecework incentives on a group of men who assembled terminal banks for use in telephone exchanges. The group piecework incentive system dictated that the harder a group worked as a whole, the more pay each member of that group received.

The experimenters believed that the study would find that members of the work group would pressure one another to work harder so that each group member would receive more pay. To the surprise of the researchers, the opposite occurred. The work group pressured the faster workers to slow down their work rate. In essence, the men whose work rate would have increased individual salaries were pressured by the group rather than those men whose work rate would have decreased individual salaries. Evidently, the men were more interested in preserving the work group than in making more money.

The experiment showed that social groups in organizations can be preserved, even when monetary incentives are offered.

The researchers concluded that social groups in organizations could effectively exert enough pressure to influence individuals to disregard monetary incentives.

When taken together, the series of studies conducted at the Hawthorne plant gave management thinkers a new direction for research. Obviously, the human variable in the organization needed much more analysis since it could either increase or decrease production drastically. Managers began to realize that they needed to understand this influence in order to maximize its positive effects and minimize its negative effects. This attempt to understand people is still a major force of today's organizational research. More current behavioural findings and their implications for management are presented in much greater detail in later sections of this text.

The following Management in Action feature illustrates the behavioural approach to management at L.E. Shaw Ltd., emphasizing some of the ways in which the company has transformed its beliefs into concrete organizational policies and experiences for its employees. It also provides a comprehensive description of the employees' reactions to the company's efforts.

WE'RE ALL IN THIS TOGETHER, PULLING IN THE SAME DIRECTION

Allan Shaw is the president of a company started in 1861, when ancestor Robert Shaw began firing brick at a small plant in rural Nova Scotia. On the surface L.E. Shaw Ltd. looks like just another family firm.

But, in this case, appearances are deceiving, because Allan Shaw didn't inherit his presidency—he earned it. When his father retired from the firm in 1979, nine senior managers, including Allan Shaw, grouped together and bought the company. Only after he worked his way through various positions did the owners elect Allan to the top job.

Today there are seven owner-managers, and they are considering broadening the ownership base to include more employees. With this long-term aim in mind,

they have sent five employees to a Halifax college for an employee management participation course, two days a month for two years.

With the new ownership has come a fresh atmosphere and a variety of changes, all positive, say employees. A union president calls the improvements "nothing short of dramatic." He goes on to add: "A number of programs have been brought in that recognize people's contributions. Wages have risen significantly. There's a feeling here that we're part of something that's going somewhere."

Another worker says: "Allan Shaw said to us, 'People are our main asset,' and to prove his point we've seen increases in pay, a sickness protection plan, a quality-of-working-life program and a profit-sharing program—all brought in during the past few years. Everything has reinforced that statement."

Although the company maintains a small corporate office in downtown Halifax, the largest group of em-

"Many of the decisions made within the company are taken only after consultations with employees."

Pay:	GOOD
Atmosphere:	EXCELLENT
Benefits:	GOOD
Job satisfaction:	VERY GOOD
Promotion:	AVERAGE
Communications:	EXCELLENT
Job security:	VERY GOOD
Personal development:	EXCELLENT

L. E. Shaw is a diversified manufacturer of construction products, specializing in clay brick and concrete block. In addition, the company owns a trucking division and land developer, Clayton Developments Ltd. Manufacturing plants are located in Nova Scotia and New Brunswick, with head office in Lantz, N.S. Employees number about 400, half of whom are unionized. The company is owned by seven of its senior managers. Annual sales are approximately $35 million.

ployees works out of Lantz, N.S., approximately sixty kilometres east of the provincial capital. The site of one of the company's old clay quarries, it is now being transformed into a superlative and unusual work environment. The old clay pits have been partially filled in and flooded to create ponds, which have been transformed into a bird sanctuary. A flock of wild Canada geese is fed and nurtured here. A jogging trail has been built through the woods for fitness enthusiasts.

The central office building has been built in a pleasing colonial style, centred around the employees' lounge, a cathedral-ceilinged living room with a large fireplace, easy chairs and a lunchroom area. A hot lunch is served daily at a nominal cost.

Many of the decisions made within the company are taken only after consultations with employees. For example, there is the annual employee-benefit meeting to decide on what new benefits, if any, the company should bring in. Up to now, employees have always resisted bringing in a dental plan, feeling that other benefits, like vision-care, mattered more to them. Although not all employees agree on this course of action, the majority opinion rules.

Salaries are fairly good in the company, especially if you take into account regional disparities. As one employee explained: "It's a privilege to work for a good company in the Atlantic provinces—and we accept a little lower pay in order to work and live in the Maritimes."

The profit-sharing program is another attraction. The company puts 10 percent of pre-tax profits into the plan, and workers share the proceeds equally. In 1985, each worker received $2084, half in cash and half deferred and invested on the employee's behalf. The company does have a separate pension plan.

Employees take the plan seriously. One secretary said: "You really think twice about taking a sick day, because you know it might mean a loss in the profit share." Another worker said, "Profit sharing has communicated to everyone that 'You're all in this together and pulling in the same direction.'"

Turnover is very low, and there is a tradition of several generations of the same family working at L.E. Shaw. Since the company's reputation is so good, there is a thick pile of potential applications for the occasional job opening.

Workers are generally very positive about the company, which allows them great freedom and creativity to do their jobs. As one woman worker said: "I left my previous two jobs because I couldn't stand the pressure. Here you have incredible freedom to do your job the way you want. The pressure is still there, but you want to perform—it's not imposed from above."

The only potential problem stems from the company's popularity. Low turnover means fewer chances for promotion. Workers see possibilities for lateral moves, but not many for upward changes. "We're not big enough yet to leave much room for promotion," said one employee.

And lastly, one proud worker says: "I don't think we wave the flag enough and tell people how great we are. We're proud of this beautiful building, and of the excellent people the company has been able to attract."

"We're all in this together, pulling in the same direction," by Eva Innes in *The Financial Post*, March 29, 1986, section 2, p. 17. Reprinted by permission.

BACK TO THE CASE

Comprehensive analysis of management implies that Jim Delligatti might be able to improve his McDonald's restaurants by evaluating the entire range of his managerial performance—especially with regard to organizational efficiency, the handling of people, and appropriate management action. For example, Delligatti should check with his employees to make sure they are receiving orders from only one source—that a manager isn't instructing an employee to handle the french fry station while moments later an assistant manager tells the same employee to tend to the grill. Along the same lines, Delligatti might want to verify that all of his employees are being treated equitably—that fry cooks, for example, don't get longer work breaks than order takers.

The behavioural approach to management suggests that Delligatti should consider the people working for him and evaluate the impact of their feelings and relationships on the productivity of his restaurants. He could, for example, try to make the work more enjoyable, perhaps by allowing his employees to work at different stations (grills, beverage, french fry, cash register, etc.) each day. He might also consider creating opportunities for employees to become more friendly with one another, perhaps through company-sponsored softball teams. In essence, the behavioural approach to management stresses that Delligatti should recognize the human variable in his restaurants and strive to maximize its positive effects.

THE MANAGEMENT SCIENCE APPROACH

The management science approach involves using the scientific method and mathematical techniques.

Churchman, Ackoff, and Arnoff define the management science or operations research (OR) approach as: (1) an application of the scientific method to problems arising in the operation of a system; and (2) the solving of these problems by solving mathematical equations representing the system.[19] The **management science approach** suggests that managers can best improve their organizations by using the scientific method and mathematical techniques to solve operational problems.

The Beginning of the Management Science Approach

The management science or operations research approach can be traced back to World War II. During this era, leading scientists were asked to help solve complex operational problems that existed in the military.[20] The scientists were organized into teams that eventually became known as operations research or OR groups. As an example of a problem that these groups encountered, one OR group was asked to determine which gunsights would best stop German attacks on the British mainland.

The scientific method involves:

1. Observing.

2. Constructing.

These OR groups typically included physicists or other "hard scientists" who used the problem-solving method with which they had the most experience: the scientific method. The **scientific method** dictates that scientists:

1. Systematically *observe* the system whose behaviour must be explained to solve the problem.

2. Use these specific observations to *construct* a generalized framework (a model) that is consistent with the specific observations and from which consequences of changing the system can be predicted.

3. Use the model to *deduce* how the system will behave under conditions that have not been observed but could be observed if the changes were made.
4. Finally, *test* the model by performing an experiment on the actual system to see if the effects of changes predicted using the model actually occur when the changes are made.[21]

3. Deducing.

4. Testing.

The OR groups were very successful in using the scientific method to solve their operational problems.

Management Science Today

After World War II, the world again became interested in manufacturing and selling products. The success of the OR groups had been so obvious in the military that managers were anxious to try management science techniques in an industrial environment. After all, managers also had complicated operational problems.

By 1955, the management science approach to solving industrial problems had proven very effective. Many people found this approach valuable and saw great promise in refining and sophisticating its techniques and analytical tools. Managers and universities alike anxiously began these refinement and sophistication attempts.

By 1965, the management science approach was being used in many companies and applied to many diverse management problems, such as production scheduling, finding a location for a new plant, and product packaging.[22]

Characteristics of Management Science Applications

Four primary characteristics usually are present in situations in which management science techniques are applied.[23] First, management problems studied are so complicated that managers need help in analyzing a large number of variables. Management science techniques increase the effectiveness of these managers' decision making. Second, a management science application generally uses economic implications as guidelines for making a particular decision. Perhaps this is because management science techniques are best suited for analyzing more quantifiable factors, such as sales, expenses, and units of production. Third, the use of mathematical models to investigate the decision situation is typical in management science applications. Models are constructed to represent reality and then used to determine how the real-world situation might be improved. The fourth characteristic of a management science application is the use of a computer. The great complexity of managerial problems and the sophisticated mathematical analysis required of problem-related information are two factors that make the computer very valuable to the management science analyst.

Today, managers are using such management science tools as inventory control models, network models, and probability models as aids in the decision-making process. Future sections of this text outline some of these models in more detail and illustrate their applications to management decision making. Because management science thought is still evolving, more and more sophisticated analytical techniques can be expected.

Characteristics of management science applications include:

1. Large number of variables.

2. Use of economic implications.

3. Use of mathematical models.

4. Use of a computer.

THE CONTINGENCY APPROACH

With the contingency approach, management action depends on the situation.

In simple terms, the **contingency approach to management** emphasizes that what managers do in practice depends on, or is contingent upon, a given set of circumstances—a situation.[24] In essence, this approach emphasizes "if-then" relationships. "If" this situational variable exists, "then" this is the action a manager probably should take. As an example, if a manager has a group of inexperienced subordinates, then the contingency approach would recommend that she lead in a different fashion than if she had an experienced group.

However, the situation must be perceived accurately, and the best-suited management tactics must be chosen and implemented.

In general, the contingency approach attempts to outline the conditions or situations in which various management methods have the best chance of being successful.[25] This approach is based on the premise that although there is probably no one best way to solve a management problem in all organizations, there probably is one best way to solve any given management problem in any one organization. Perhaps the main challenges of using the contingency approach are: (1) perceiving organizational situations as they actually exist; (2) choosing management tactics best suited to those situations; and (3) competently implementing those tactics.

Although the notion of a contingency approach to management is not new,[26] the use of the term itself is relatively new. In addition, the contingency approach to management has become a very popular discussion topic for contemporary management writers. The general consensus of these writings seems to indicate that if managers are to apply management concepts, principles, and techniques successfully, they must consider the realities of the specific organizational circumstances they face.[27]

THE SYSTEM APPROACH

Understanding the system as a whole requires an understanding of the interdependence of its parts.

The **system approach to management** is based upon general system theory. Ludwig von Bertalanffy, a scientist who worked mainly in the areas of physics and biology, is recognized as the founder of general system theory.[28] The main premise of general system theory is that to understand fully the operation of an entity, it must be viewed as a system. A **system** is defined as a number of interdependent parts functioning as a whole for some purpose. For example, according to general system theory, to fully understand the operations of the human body, one must understand the workings of its interdependent parts (ears, eyes, brain, etc.). General system theory integrates the knowledge of various specialized fields so that the system as a whole can be better understood.

Types of Systems

Closed systems do not interact with the environment.

According to von Bertalanffy, there are two basic types of systems: closed systems and open systems. **Closed systems** are not influenced by and do not interact with their environments. They are mostly mechanical and have necessary predetermined motions or activities that must be performed regardless of their environment. A clock is an example of a closed system. Regardless of its environment, a clock's wheels, gears, and so forth must function in a predetermined way if the clock as a whole is to exist and serve its purpose. The second type of system, the **open system**, is constantly interacting with its environment. A plant is an example of an open system. Constant interaction with the environment influences the plant's state of existence and its future. In fact, the environment determines whether or not the plant will live.

Open systems do interact with the environment.

Systems and "Wholeness"

The concept of "wholeness" is very important in general system analysis. The system must be viewed as a whole and modified only through changes in the parts of the system. A thorough knowledge of how each part functions and the interrelationships among the parts must be present before modifications of the parts can be made for the overall benefit of the system. L. Thomas Hopkins suggested the following six guidelines regarding system "wholeness" that should be remembered during system analysis:[29]

A system is changed by changing its parts.

1. The whole should be the main focus of analysis, with the parts receiving secondary attention.
2. Integration is the key variable in wholeness analysis. Integration is defined as the interrelatedness of the many parts within the whole.
3. Possible modifications in each part should be weighed in relation to possible effects on every other part.
4. Each part has some role to perform in order that the whole can accomplish its purpose.
5. The nature of the part and its function is determined by its position in the whole.
6. All analysis starts with the existence of the whole. The parts and their interrelationships should then evolve to best suit the purpose of the whole.

Since the system approach to management is based upon general system theory, analysis of the management situation as a system is stressed. The following sections present the parts of the management system and recommend information that can be used to analyze the system.

The Management System

As with all systems, the **management system** is composed of a number of parts that function on an interdependent basis to achieve a purpose. The main parts of the management system are organizational input, organizational process, and organizational output. As discussed in Chapter 1, these parts consist of organizational resources, the production process, and finished goods, respectively. The parts represent a combination that exists to achieve organizational objectives, whatever they may be.

The management system is open and consists of input, process, and output.

The management system is an open system, one that interacts with its environment (see Figure 2.4). Environmental factors with which the management system interacts include the government, suppliers, customers, and competitors. Each of these represents a potential environmental influence that could significantly change the future of a management system.

Environmental impact on management cannot be overemphasized. As an example, the Canadian Labour Code at the federal level and commissions on working conditions at provincial levels are still encouraging management to

FIGURE 2.4   The open management system.

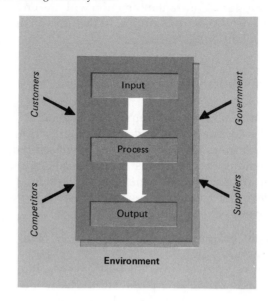

handle costly safety and health issues. However, many managers are frustrated because they feel these safeguards are not only expensive, but also unnecessary.

Information for Management System Analysis

As noted earlier, to better understand a system, general system theory allows for the use of information from many specialized disciplines. This certainly holds true for the management system. Information from any discipline can increase the understanding of management system operations and thereby enhance the success of the system. A broad, sweeping statement such as this, however, presents a problem: Where do managers go to get this information?

Triangular management uses classically based, behaviourally based, and management-science based information.

The information used to discuss the management system in the remainder of this text comes from three primary sources: (1) the classical approach to management; (2) the behavioural approach to management; and (3) the management science approach to management. Using these three sources of information to analyze the management system is referred to as **triangular management**. Figure 2.5 presents the triangular management model. The three sources of information in the triangular management model are not meant to represent all the information that can be used to analyze the management system. Rather, they are the three bodies of management-related information that probably would be most useful to managers analyzing the management system.

A synthesis of classically based information, behaviourally based information, and management-science based information is critical to the effective management of the management system. This information is integrated and presented in this text in the five remaining major sections. These five sections discuss management systems and: (1) planning (Chapters 4–7); (2) organizing (Chapters 8–11); (3) influencing (Chapters 12–15); (4) controlling (Chapters 16–18); and (5) topics for special emphasis (Chapters 19–21).[30] In addition, some information in these sections is presented from a contingency viewpoint to give added emphasis to the practical application of management principles.

FIGURE 2.5   Triangular management model.

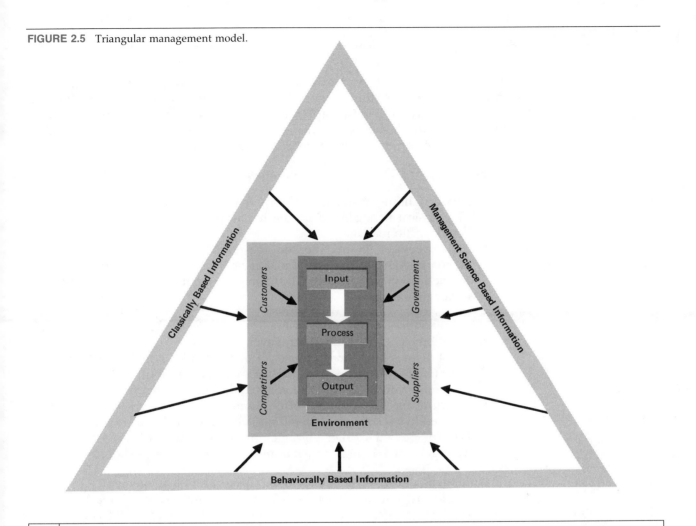

BACK TO THE CASE

Jim Delligatti could use the management science approach to solve any operational problems that arose. According to the scientific method, Delligatti would first spend some time observing what takes place in one of his restaurants. Next, he would use these observations to outline exactly how the restaurant operates as a whole. Third, he would apply this understanding of restaurant operations by predicting how various changes might help or hinder the restaurant as a whole. Before implementing possible changes, he would test them on a small scale to see if they actually affected the restaurant as desired.

If Delligatti were to accept the contingency approach to management, his actions as a manager would depend on the situation. For example, *if* some customers hadn't been served within sixty seconds because the deep-fat fryer had unexpectedly broken down, *then* Delligatti probably would not hold his employees responsible. But *if* he knew that the fryer had

broken down because of employee mistreatment or neglect, *then* his reaction to the situation would likely be very different.

Delligatti could also apply the system approach and view each of his restaurants as a system, or a number of interdependent parts that function as a whole to reach restaurant objectives. Naturally, each restaurant would be seen as an open system—a system that exists in and is influenced by its environment. Major factors within the environment of a McDonald's restaurant would include customers, suppliers, competitors, and the government. For example, if one of McDonald's fast-food competitors were to significantly lower its price for hamburgers to a point well below what McDonald's charged for a hamburger, Delligatti might be forced to consider modifying different parts of his restaurant system in order to meet or beat that price.

Action Summary

Reread the learning objectives that follow. Each objective is followed by questions. Answering these questions accurately will help you to retain the most important concepts discussed in this chapter. After answering each question, check your answer with the answer key at the end of this chapter. (*Hint*: If you have doubt regarding the correct response, consult the page that follows the answer.)

Circle:

From studying this chapter, I will attempt to acquire:

1. **An understanding of the classical approach to management.**

T, F
    a. The classical management approach established what it considered the "one best way" to manage.

a, b, c, d, e
    b. The process of finding the "one best way" to perform a task is called: (a) comprehensive analysis of management; (b) the concept of wholeness; (c) the Hawthorne studies; (d) the management science approach; (e) scientific management.

2. **An appreciation for the work of Frederick W. Taylor, Frank and Lillian Gilbreth, Henry L. Gantt, and Henri Fayol.**

a, b, c, d, e
    a. Fayol defines fourteen principles of management. Which of the following is *not* one of those principles: (a) scalar chain of authority; (b) *esprit de corps*; (c) centralization; (d) unity of command; (e) directedness of command.

a, b, c, d, e
    b. Which of the following theorists assumed that any worker's job could be reduced to a science: (a) Gilbreth; (b) Gantt; (c) Mayo; (d) Fayol; (e) Taylor.

T, F
    c. Gantt increased worker efficiency by setting standards according to top management's opinion of what maximum performance should be.

3. **An understanding of the behavioural approach to management.**

T, F
    a. The behavioural approach to management emphasizes striving to increase production through an understanding of the organization itself.

a, b, c, d, e
    b. The behavioural approach began with: (a) the Hawthorne studies; (b) the mental revolution; (c) the Industrial Revolution; (d) motion studies; (e) the Bethlehem Steel studies.

4. **An understanding of the studies at the Hawthorne Works of the Western Electric Company.**

T, F
    a. The Hawthorne studies showed a direct relationship between lighting and efficiency.

T, F
    b. The Hawthorne experimenters found that people were more concerned with preserving the work group than with maximizing their pay.

5. **An understanding of the management science approach to management.**

a, b, c, d, e
    a. Which of the following is *not* one of the philosophies of the management science approach: (a) managers can improve the organization by using scientific methods; (b) mathematical techniques can solve organizational problems; (c) models should be used to represent the system; (d) individual work is better than teamwork; (e) observation of the system must take place.

T, F
    b. In the management science theory, models are used to represent reality and then used to determine how the real-world situation might be improved.

6. **An understanding of how the management science approach has evolved.**
   a. The management science approach emerged after: (a) World War I; (b) the Civil War; (c) the Korean War; (d) World War II; (e) the 1930 depression.   a, b, c, d, e
   b. Although management science was first applied to military problems, it is now applied by companies to diverse management problems.   T, F

7. **An understanding of the system approach to management.**
   a. An organization that interacts with external forces is: (a) a closed system; (b) a model; (c) an independent entity; (d) an open system; (e) a contingency.   a, b, c, d, e
   b. Which of the following is *not* one of the guidelines proposed by Hopkins in the concept of wholeness: (a) the whole should be the main focus of analysis; (b) all analysis starts with the existence of the whole; (c) the nature of the part is determined by its position in the whole; (d) each part has some role to perform in order that the whole can accomplish its purpose; (e) modifications should be made as they occur.   a, b, c, d, e

8. **An understanding of how triangular management and the contingency approach to management are related.**
   a. The contingency approach emphasizes the viewpoint that what managers do in practice depends overall on: (a) the worker; (b) the situation; (c) the task; (d) the environment; (e) the manager's personality.   a, b, c, d, e
   b. The three sources of information in triangular management are: (a) input, process, and output; (b) management science, classically, and behaviourally based; (c) mathematics, psychology, and sociology; (d) managers, directors, and shareholders; (e) executives, administrators, and supervisors.   a, b, c, d, e

INTRODUCTORY CASE WRAP-UP

"McDonald's Recipe for Success" (p. 32) and its related back-to-the-case sections were written to help you better understand the management concepts contained in this chapter. Answer the following discussion questions about this introductory case to further enrich your understanding of the chapter content:

1. What problems do you think an individual like Delligatti faces in managing a McDonald's restaurant?
2. What action(s) do you think a manager like Delligatti would have to take to solve these problems?
3. From what you know about McDonald's restaurants, how easy would it be to hold Delligatti's job? Why?

Issues for Review and Discussion

1. List the five approaches to managing.
2. Define the classical approach to management.
3. Compare and contrast the contributions to the classical approach made by Frederick W. Taylor, Frank and Lillian Gilbreth, and Henry L. Gantt.
4. How does Henri Fayol's contribution to the classical approach differ from those of Taylor, the Gilbreths, and Gantt?
5. What is scientific management?
6. Describe motion study as used by the Gilbreths.
7. Describe Gantt's innovation in the area of worker bonuses.
8. List and define Fayol's general principles of management.
9. What is the primary limitation to the classical approach to management?
10. Define the behavioural approach to management.
11. What is the significance of the studies at the Hawthorne Works of the Western Electric Company?
12. What is the management science approach to management?

13. What are the steps in the scientific method of problem solving?
14. List and explain three characteristics of situations in which management science applications usually are made.
15. Define the contingency approach to management.

16. What is a system?
17. What is the difference between a closed system and an open system?
18. Explain the relationship between system analysis and "wholeness."
19. What are the parts of the management system?
20. What is triangular management?

Sources of Additional Information

Abernathy, William J., Kim B. Clark, and Alan M. Kantrow. "The New Industrial Competition." *Harvard Business Review* (September/October 1981): 68–81.

Boddewyn, J. "Frederick Winslow Taylor Revisited." *Academy of Management Journal* 4 (1961): 100–107.

Boone, Louis E., and Donald D. Bowen. *The Great Writings in Management and Organizational Behavior*, 2d ed. New York: Random House, 1987.

Braddick, Bill, and Denis Boyle. "Business Success in a Changing World." *Personnel Management* 13 (June 1981): 37–39, 48.

Cameron, Kim S., and David A. Whetten. *Organizational Effectiveness*. New York: Academic Press, 1983.

Carey, A. "The Hawthorne Studies: A Radical Criticism." *American Sociological Review* 32 (1967): 403–16.

Davis, R.C. *Industrial Organization and Management*, 2d ed. New York: Harper & Bros., 1940.

———. "Philosophy of Management." *Academy of Management Journal* 1 (1958): 37–40.

Feulner, Terry, and Brian H. Kleiner. "When Robots Are the Answer." *Personnel Journal* 65 (February 1986): 44.

Franklin, William H., Jr. "What Japanese Managers Know That American Managers Don't." *Administrative Management* 42 (September 1981): 36–39, 51–54, 56.

Gilbreth, F.B. *Motion Study*. New York: Van Nostrand, 1911.

Gilbreth, Lillian M. *The Psychology of Management*. New York: Sturgis and Walton, 1914.

Gilbreth, Lillian M., Orphae Mae Thomas, and Eleanor Clymer. *Management in the Home*. New York: Dodd, Mead, 1954.

Halloran, Jack. *Applied Human Relations: An Organizational Approach*, 2d ed. Englewood Cliffs, N.J.: Prentice-Hall, 1983.

Hayes, James L. *Memos for Management—The Manager's Job*. New York: Amacom, 1983.

Kakar, S. *Frederick Taylor: A Study in Personality and Innovation*. Cambridge, Mass.: MIT Press, 1970.

Kelly, John E. *Scientific Management, Job Redesign and Work Performance*. London: Academic Press, 1982.

Klein, Bruce A., and Pamela A. Posey. "Good Supervisors Are Good Supervisors—Anywhere." *Harvard Business Review* (November/December 1986): 125.

Merrill, H.F., ed. *Classics in Management*. New York: American Management Association, 1960.

Pringle, Charles D. "Managing a Closed System in an Open Systems World." *Business* 36 (October/November/December 1986): 9–16.

Riker, Richard R. "What Makes a Manager Unique?" *Journal of Systems Management* 35 (August 1984): 41.

Rogers, David. "Managing in the Public and Private Sectors: Similarities and Differences." *Management Review* 70 (May 1981): 48–49.

Thomas, Philip S. "Scanning Strategy: Formulation and Implementation," *Managerial Planning* 33 (July/August 1984): 14–20.

Yost, Edna, and Lillian M. Gilbreth. *Normal Lives for the Disabled*. New York: Macmillan, 1944.

Notes

1. James H. Donnelly, Jr., James L. Gibson, and John M. Ivancevich, *Fundamentals of Management* (Plano, Tex.: Business Publications, 1987), 6–8.
2. Harold Koontz, Cyril O'Donnell, and Heinz Weihrich, *Management*, 8th ed. (New York: McGraw-Hill, 1984), 52–69.
3. W. Warren Haynes and Joseph L. Massie, *Management*, 2d ed. (Englewood Cliffs, N.J.: Prentice-Hall, 1969), 4–13.
4. Frederick W. Taylor, *The Principles of Scientific Management* (New York: Harper & Bros., 1947), 66–71.

5. Henry L. Gantt, *Industrial Leadership* (New Haven, Conn.: Yale University Press, 1916), 57.

6. Gantt, *Industrial Leadership*, 85.

7. Chester I. Barnard, *Organization and Management* (Cambridge, Mass.: Harvard University Press, 1952).

8. Alvin Brown, *Organization of Industry* (Englewood Cliffs, N.J.: Prentice-Hall, 1947).

9. Henry S. Dennison, *Organization Engineering* (New York: McGraw-Hill, 1931).

10. Luther Gulick and Lyndal Urwick, eds., *Papers on the Science of Administration* (New York: Institute of Public Administration, 1937).

11. J.D. Mooney and A.C. Reiley, *Onward Industry!* (New York: Harper & Bros., 1931). With some modifications, this book appeared as *The Principles of Organization* (New York: Harper & Bros., 1939).

12. Oliver Sheldon, *The Philosophy of Management* (London: Sir Isaac Pitman and Sons, 1923).

13. Henri Fayol, *General and Industrial Management* (London: Sir Isaac Pitman and Sons, 1949).

14. Fayol, *General and Industrial Management*, 19–42.

15. For a provocative discussion of the principle of unity of command, see James I. Mashburn and Bobby C. Vaught, "Two Heads Are Better than One: The Case for Dual Leadership," *Management Review* (December 1980): 53–56.

16. For detailed summaries of these studies, see *Industrial Worker*, 2 vols. (Cambridge, Mass.: Harvard University Press, 1938); and F.J. Roethlisberger and W.J. Dickson, *Management and the Worker* (Cambridge, Mass.: Harvard University Press, 1939).

17. For additional information, see George C. Homans, *Fatigue of Workers: Its Relation to Industrial Production* (New York: Committee on Work in Industry, National Research Council, Reinhold Publishing, 1941).

18. Homans, *Fatigue of Workers*.

19. C. West Churchman, Russell L. Ackoff, and E. Leonard Arnoff, *Introduction to Operations Research* (New York: Wiley, 1957), 18.

20. Hamdy A. Taha, *Operations Research: An Introduction* (New York: Macmillan, 1988), 1–2.

21. James R. Emshoff, *Analysis of Behavioral Systems* (New York: Macmillan, 1971), 10.

22. C.C. Shumacher and B.E. Smith, "A Sample Survey of Industrial Operations Research Activities II," *Operations Research* 13 (1965): 1023–27.

23. Discussion concerning these factors is adapted from Donnelly, Gibson, and Ivancevich, *Fundamentals of Management*, 302–303; Efraim Turban and Jack R. Meredith, *Fundamentals of Management Science* (Plano, Tex.: Business Publications, 1981), 15–23.

24. Harold Koontz, "The Management Theory Jungle Revisited," *Academy of Management Review* 5 (1980): 175–87.

25. Don Hellriegel, John W. Slocum, and Richard W. Woodman, *Organizational Behavior* (St. Paul, Minn.: West Publishing, 1986), 22.

26. J.W. Lorsch, "Organization Design: A Situational Perspective," *Organizational Dynamics* 6 (1977): 2–4.

27. Louis W. Fry and Deborah A. Smith, "Congruence, Contingency, and Theory Building," *Academy of Management Review* (January 1987): 117–132.

28. For a more detailed development of von Bertalanffy's ideas, see "General System Theory: A New Approach to Unity of Science," *Human Biology* (December 1951): 302–61.

29. L. Thomas Hopkins, *Integration: Its Meaning and Application* (New York: Appleton-Century-Crofts, 1937), 36–49.

30. For a discussion of the value of teaching management through these management functions, see Stephen J. Carroll and Dennis A. Gillen, "Are the Classic Management Functions Useful in Describing Managerial Work?" *Academy of Management Review* (January 1987): 38–51.

Action Summary Answer Key

1. a. T, p. 34
   b. e, p. 34
2. a. e, p. 39
   b. e, p. 34
   c. F, p. 37

3. a. F, p. 40
   b. a, p. 40
4. a. F, pp. 40–41
   b. T, p. 41

5. a. d, pp. 44–45
   b. T, p. 45
6. a. d, p. 44
   b. T, p. 45

7. a. d, pp. 46–47
   b. e, p. 47
8. a. b, p. 46
   b. b, p. 48

PAUL IVANIER: MANAGEMENT AND MANUFACTURING AT IVACO

Ivaco's strong views on the subject of manufacturing excellence result from its knowledge that successful corporate growth ultimately depends on the efficiency of the manufacturing process combined with the quality of the end product.

The principles governing the management of its steel manufacturing plants are derived from the company's emphasis on continuing growth through acquisitions and internal expansion. Ivaco recognizes that although one can grow very rapidly through acquisitions, it is not possible to grow successfully through acquisitions alone; the ability to harness the intrinsic strengths of the acquired company must be there as well. This can only be done by accomplished people working to a mutually agreed upon plan — "good people" being a critical factor in its acquisition decisions. Ivaco has a distinctive and unique corporate culture relative to manufacturing management, which is based on continuous modernization and constantly broadening product lines. This often leads to a need to expand production capacities. This growth process from within reflects a strong bias within the company toward vertical integration, a move designed to capitalize on its strengths. However, worthwhile opportunities into new areas are also often pursued.

There are few rules for line managers. The principal one dictates that each enterprise be managed according to its local circumstances and on a hands-on, shirt-sleeves basis. This means decentralized decision making along with strict accountability. There are, as a result, almost as many management "trends" as there are managers at the supervisory level. The absence of a uniform trend in methods is balanced by a corporate-wide consistency of purpose — so much so that when one looks at Ivaco as a whole, the most clearly identified trend is the company's management of growth.

Ivanier: "keeping good people (is) a simple matter of creating the right kind of climate where people have the freedom to excel."

This entrepreneurial climate for manufacturing managers has four constant objectives. They're simple. They're basic. They're consistent throughout the company. They are: (1) be customer-responsive; (2) be a low-cost producer; (3) be expansion-sensitive; and (4) build on existing strengths. Each of these requires the selection and retention of good employees who can cope with decentralized autonomy by exercising responsibility and accepting accountability. For this, employees are well rewarded. Keeping good people is definitely not a problem at Ivaco, even when growth is through acquisition — most of the senior staff and employees stay on. They understand that Ivaco has confidence in, and respect for, its employees.

The making and selling of special quality steels require tremendous people-skills and a talent for precision controls. This goes for marketing as well. Technically and economically, the learning is slow and expensive. That, however, is where the better margins are and Ivaco has consistently followed a strategy of capitalizing on new and high quality operations with strong potentials for growth. Most of the managers at Ivaco are long-term, technology-oriented individuals who are used to a high degree of autonomy and accountability.

Ivaco considers the principal factor in finding and keeping good people to be a simple matter of creating the right kind of climate where people have the freedom to excel. This is consistent with the company's objective. There are probably no stronger motivators than the opportunity to meet challenges competitively and having access to the financial resources required to excel technically. By encouraging its manufacturing managers to strive constantly for improved efficiency and broader market horizons, two beneficial consequences follow. Those managers who revel in the process of winning achieve their personal goals at the same time that Ivaco's shareholders are rewarded with a larger, stronger, more efficient base for long-term growth and substantial earnings; meanwhile, the company's budgeting, financial controls, and long-term technology strategy-planning helps to watch over performance.

Ivaco's corporate head office is lean and the intellectual climate totally informal. This atmosphere is essential to achieve the type of rapid decision making that the line managers absolutely must perform. Managers cannot function creatively if the decision-making process is constantly delayed through corporate red tape.

Operations at head office are a combination of line and staff functions. The line functions provide a constant link between top divisional managers and the CEO of the corporation. This provides a continuous sounding board for line managers and allows them to reach decisions quickly. Financial controls are another important function at head office. Each business works according to a predetermined plan prepared by its management, approved by line management, and reviewed by head office. Unforeseen problems and opportunities are discussed informally as they occur and are factored into the plan at the next periodic review.

Meanwhile, tracking evolutions in technology is one area where staff and line responsibilities are shared and coordinated. While corporate headquarters must take the ultimate responsibility for the approval of capital budgets, the constant and informal exchange between managers and senior company officials provides an invaluable

forum. Out of this process emerges a consensus as to where the technology mainstream is headed. Having a solid grasp on the technology trend is vital to Ivaco's decision-making process.

This constant analysis of technological trends extends beyond steel making into the company's secondary manufacturing areas. Engineers are constantly searching for better ideas, better production machinery, and better processes. Frequently, proprietary modifications are made in order to increase efficiency. The cost of additions to fixed assets since 1980 is close to $300 million, but these additions were essential for improving efficiency and the development of new products. These are high priorities for all managers at Ivaco.

Ivaco has been upgrading its plants during the past few years, while the industry has had to cope with the double jeopardy of recession at home and a flood of subsidized imports from abroad. The past sixteen years has seen Ivaco's sales grow from $11 million in 1969 to $1.34 billion in 1985. For 1985, Ivaco reported net earnings of $35.15 million and ended the year with working capital of $395 million, shareholders' equity of $520.6 million and total assets of $1.28 billion. It now has sixty-five plants and employs approximately 12 000 people. Ivaco's concept of management has contributed to the company's success, and its achievements and emergence as a growth company during the past sixteen years are the proof.

DISCUSSION ISSUES

1. Which approaches to management has Ivaco employed to achieve its goals and why?
2. How do concepts from the behavioural approach contribute to Ivaco's management style? Explain.
3. Is Ivaco an open or a closed system? Support your answer.

Based on "Management and Manufacturing at Ivaco," by Paul Ivanier in *Business Quarterly*, Spring 1986. Used with permission of *Business Quarterly*, published by School of Business Administration, The University of Western Ontario, London.

ORGANIZATIONAL OBJECTIVES

STUDENT LEARNING OBJECTIVES

From studying this chapter, I will attempt to acquire:

1. An understanding of organizational objectives.
2. An appreciation for the importance of organizational objectives.
3. An ability to tell the difference between organizational objectives and individual objectives.
4. A knowledge of the areas in which managers should set organizational objectives.
5. An understanding of the development of organizational objectives.
6. Some facility in writing good objectives.
7. An awareness of how managers use organizational objectives and help others to attain the objectives.
8. An appreciation for the potential of a management by objectives (MBO) program.

CHAPTER OUTLINE

INTRODUCTORY CASE 3

THE DIRECTION OF FLOW GENERAL

In the early 1980s, Flow General, Inc. seemed destined for great things as a company. Its basic businesses related to the areas of cell biology and defence consulting, and business was booming. Over a three-year period (from 1979 through 1981), Flow General's earnings more than tripled, from approximately $2 million to slightly over $7 million (U.S.). The company seemed to be in excellent financial shape and poised for significant growth.

To the surprise of many outside observers as well as to company employees, however, Flow General shifted from making slightly over $7 million in 1981 to losing approximately $4 million in 1983. It was obvious that there was a problem that had to be discovered and solved as quickly as possible.

A longtime Flow General employee expressed the opinion that company losses were closely related to the fact that few people within the company seemed to clearly understand the direction in which the company was moving. According to this employee, the former president and chief executive officer at Flow General, Joseph E. Hall, "had a tendency to go off on a whim." Over recent years, the company had moved further and further away from its basic business and closer and closer to more "glamorous" research on artificial skin and interferon, a protein that has shown promise in fighting viruses and cancer.

Hall, however, disagreed with the assessment that the company lacked a clear direction during his term. In his opinion, he and other top executives had a "preconceived notion" as to where the company should go. Further, Hall felt that the company was definitely moving in this direction when he departed from Flow General.

Even if Flow General had such clear direction, there apparently was some disagreement concerning whether Hall's proposed direction was the most appropriate for the company. Chris Price, a company researcher, indicated that it was no secret that the professional scientists disagreed with the corporate objectives set during Hall's tenure. According to these scientists, Hall's objectives necessitated unrealistic timetables within which research projects had to be completed.

Current emphasis at Flow General is being placed on developing and implementing a more concrete strategy for organizational success. This strategy includes reducing investments in more "glamorous," high-risk projects and more concentration of organizational resources in the company's basic and successful products. For example, the focus on interferon-related research has been reduced to enable the biomed division to concentrate more on the mechanics of growing cell cultures.

It is hard to measure the exact extent to which past leadership at Flow General provided a clear direction for the company. Present company leadership, however, seems determined to furnish the company with a direction that all employees understand.

Based on "Flow General Tries to Settle on Future Path," by Virginia Inman in *The Wall Street Journal*, July 22, 1983.

What's Ahead

Managers like Joseph E. Hall, the former president and chief executive officer of Flow General, should recognize that organizational objectives are extremely important guidelines to be used purposefully. This chapter discusses: (1) the general nature of organizational objectives; (2) different types of organizational objectives; (3) various areas in which organizational objectives should be set; (4) how managers actually work with organizational objectives; and (5) management by objectives (MBO).

⊞ GENERAL NATURE OF ORGANIZATIONAL OBJECTIVES

Definition of Organizational Objectives

Organizational objectives are the targets toward which the open management system is directed. Organizational input, process, and output, as discussed in Chapter 2, all exist to reach organizational objectives (see Figure 3.1). If properly

Organizational objectives flow from organizational purpose.

FIGURE 3.1 Existence of open management system to reach organizational objectives.

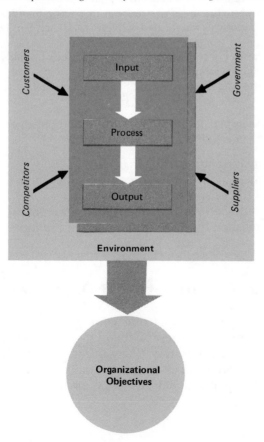

developed, organizational objectives reflect the purpose of the organization; that is, they flow naturally from organizational purpose. **Organizational purpose** is defined as what the organization exists to do, given a particular group of customers and customer needs. If an organization is accomplishing its objectives, it is simultaneously accomplishing its purpose and thereby justifying its reason for existence.

Organizations exist for various purposes and thus have various types of organizational objectives. A hospital, for example, may have the primary purpose of providing high-quality medical assistance to the community. Therefore, its primary objective focuses on furnishing this assistance. The primary purpose of a business organization, on the other hand, usually is to make a profit. The primary objective of the business organization, therefore, concentrates on making that profit. To illustrate, the primary organizational objective of the Unicorp Canada Corporation is profit-oriented and has been stated as follows:

> Unicorp Canada Corporation is an asset oriented company with diversified investments and operations in commercial real estate, energy, financial service companies, and marketable securities in the United States and Canada.
>
> Unicorp's corporate strategy is to invest in or acquire, directly and indirectly, a pool of high quality assets having the potential for long term appreciation. This is accomplished primarily by acquiring major interests in well managed public companies that own these assets.
>
> Since 1979, Unicorp's growth has been directed towards the United States, with particular emphasis on acquiring an extensive portfolio of high quality income-producing real estate.
>
> Unicorp is managed by a small, closely knit group of experienced professionals and entrepreneurs, headquartered at its corporate offices in Toronto, Ontario. Operating offices are located in New York City, San Francisco, and Calgary.
>
> Unicorp's shares are traded on The Toronto Stock Exchange and The Montreal Exchange (Symbol: UNI). Approximately 62 percent of the Class A Non-Voting Shares and Class B Voting Shares are owned by the Company's officers and directors.[1]

John F. Mee has suggested that organizational objectives for businesses can be summarized with the following comments:

1. Profit is the motivating force for managers.
2. Service to customers by the provision of desired economic values (goods and services) justifies the existence of the business.
3. Social responsibilities do exist for managers in accordance with ethical and moral codes established by the society in which the industry resides.[2]

Importance of Organizational Objectives

Organizational objectives are guidelines for:

Marshall E. Dimock stresses that "fixing your objective is like identifying the North Star—you sight your compass on it and then use it as the means of getting back on track when you tend to stray."[3] Organizational objectives give managers and all other organization members important guidelines for action in such areas as decision making, organizational efficiency, organizational consistency, and performance evaluation.

Guide for Decision Making

A significant portion of managerial responsibility involves making decisions that inevitably influence the everyday operation and existence of the organization and of organization members. Once managers have a clear understanding of organizational objectives, they know the direction in which the organization must move. It then becomes their responsibility to make decisions that move the organization toward the achievement of organizational objectives.

1. Decision making.

Guide for Organizational Efficiency

Since inefficiency results in a costly waste of human effort and resources, managers strive to increase organizational efficiency whenever possible. Efficiency is defined in terms of the total amount of human effort and resources an organization uses to move itself toward attainment of organizational goals. Therefore, before organizational efficiency can improve, managers must have a clear understanding of organizational goals. Only then are they able to use the limited resources at their disposal as efficiently as possible.

2. Increasing efficiency.

Guide for Organizational Consistency

Most organization members often need work-related directives. If organizational objectives are used as the basis for these directives, the objectives serve as a guide to consistently encourage such things as productive activity, quality decision making, and effective planning.

3. Establishing consistency.

Guide for Performance Evaluation

Periodically, the performance of all organization members is evaluated to assess individual productivity and to determine what might be done to increase productivity. Organizational goals are the guidelines or criteria that should be used as the basis for these evaluations. Those individuals who contribute most to obtaining organizational goals should be considered the most productive. Specific recommendations on increasing productivity should be comprised of suggestions about what individuals can do to help the organization move toward goal attainment.

4. Making performance evaluations useful.

▤ BACK TO THE CASE

The discussion of organizational objectives offers a manager like Joseph E. Hall, the past president of Flow General, useful insights on how a company can be put and kept on the right track. The introductory case revealed that in recent years Flow General had moved further away from its basic business and concentrated instead on researching artificial skin and interferon. This change in emphasis at Flow General apparently occurred without redefining the purpose of the organiza-tion and then formulating related objectives, or, if this was done, the new organizational purpose and objectives were not communicated or agreed upon. The communication of and agreement on such new organizational objectives within Flow General would help all managers guide the company appropriately, make better decisions, assess the level of company efficiency, be consistent, and evaluate employee performance.

TYPES OF OBJECTIVES IN ORGANIZATIONS

Objectives can be separated into two categories: organizational objectives and individual objectives. Recognizing the two categories and reacting appropriately challenges all modern managers.

Organizational Objectives

Organizational objectives are the formal targets of the organization and are set to help the organization accomplish its purpose. They concern such areas as organizational efficiency, productivity, and profit maximization.

Y.K. Shetty conducted a study to determine the nature and pattern of corporate objectives as they actually exist in organizations. Shetty analyzed 193 companies in four basic industrial groups: (1) chemical and drugs; (2) packaging materials; (3) electrical and electronics; and (4) food processing.[4] The results of Shetty's study, shown in Figure 3.2, indicate that the most common organizational objectives relate to profitability, growth, and market share. Social responsibility and employee welfare objectives are also common and probably reflect a change of managerial attitude over the last several years. The types of objectives shown in Figure 3.2 certainly do not reflect the only areas in which organizational objectives are made, but they probably indicate the most common ones.

Organizational objectives commonly focus on profitability, growth, and market share.

Individual Objectives

Individual objectives also exist within organizations. **Individual objectives** are the personal goals each organization member would like to reach as a result of his or her activity within the organization. These objectives might include high salary, personal growth and development, peer recognition, and societal recognition.

Individual objectives are one's personal goals within the organization.

FIGURE 3.2 Types of organizational objectives and organizations using each type.

Type of Objective	Number of Companies Studied Having Objective Type	Percent of Companies Studied Having Objective Type*
Profitability	73	89
Growth	67	82
Market share	54	66
Social responsibility	53	65
Employee welfare	51	62
Product quality and service	49	60
Research and development	44	54
Diversification	42	31
Efficiency	41	50
Financial stability	40	49
Resource conservation	32	39
Management development	29	35
Multinational enterprise	24	29
Consolidation	14	17
Miscellaneous other goals	15	18

*Adds to more than 100 percent because most companies have more than one goal.

A management problem arises when organizational objectives and individual objectives are not compatible.[5] For example, a professor may have an individual goal of working at a university primarily to gain peer recognition. Perhaps she pursues this recognition primarily by channeling most of her effort and energies into research. This professor's individual objective could make a significant contribution to the attainment of organizational objectives if she happened to be at a university whose organizational objectives emphasized research. On the other hand, her individual objective might contribute little or nothing to organizational goal attainment if she were employed at a teaching-oriented university. Rather than improving her general teaching ability and the quality of her courses, as the university goals would suggest, she would be secluded in the library writing research articles.

One alternative managers have in situations of this type is to structure the organization so that individuals have the opportunity to accomplish individual objectives while contributing to organizational goal attainment. For example, the teaching-oriented university could take steps to ensure that good teachers received peer recognition, perhaps by offering an "excellence in teaching" award. In this way, professors could strive for their personal peer-recognition goal while also contributing to the university's organizational objective of good teaching.

An objective or goal integration model can assist managers trying to understand and solve problems related to conflict between organizational and individual objectives. Jon Barrett's model, presented in Figure 3.3, depicts a situation in which the goals or objectives in area C are the only individual goals (area A) compatible with organizational objectives (area B). Area C represents the extent of **goal integration**.

Managers should keep two things in mind about the individual depicted in the Figure 3.3 model: (1) this individual will tend to work for goals in area C without much managerial encouragement because the attainment of these goals will result in some type of reward the individual considers valuable; and (2) this individual will usually not work for goals outside area A without some significant type of managerial encouragement because the attainment of these goals holds little promise of reward the individual considers valuable. Barrett suggests that "significant types of managerial encouragement" could be: (1) modifications to

> When organizational objectives and individual objectives are not compatible, managers should strive for goal integration.

FIGURE 3.3 Goal integration model.

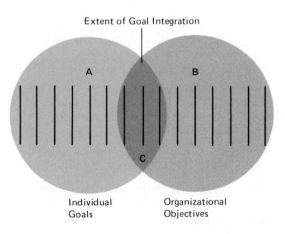

Extent of Goal Integration

A   B

C

Individual Goals   Organizational Objectives

existing pay schedules; (2) considerate treatment from superiors; and (3) additional opportunities to engage in informal social relationships with peers.

BACK TO THE CASE

Finding common ground between organizational objectives and individual objectives often is no easy task, and conflict between these two types of objectives can spell trouble for the organization. Perhaps part of the problem at Flow General was a conflict between organizational and individual objectives. For example, Joseph E. Hall, past president of Flow General, could have had individual objectives of peer recognition and

societal recognition that led him into "glamorous," high-risk projects. While the projects had merit in their own right, they may have been in conflict with Flow General's long-standing organizational objective of concentrating on its basic business. In this type of situation, it would have been to both Hall's and Flow General's advantage to seek out areas of goal integration.

AREAS FOR ORGANIZATIONAL OBJECTIVES

Peter F. Drucker, one of the most influential management writers of modern times, indicates that the very survival of a management system may be endangered if managers emphasize only a profit objective. This single-objective emphasis encourages managers to take action that will make money today with little regard for how a profit will be made tomorrow.[6]

In practice, managers should strive to develop and attain a variety of objectives in all management system areas where activity is critical to the operation and success of the system. The eight key areas in which Drucker advises managers to set management system objectives are:

In addition to profitability, there are seven other key areas in which an organization should specify goals.

1. *Market standing*   Management should set objectives indicating where it would like to be in relation to its competitors.
2. *Innovation*   Management should set objectives outlining its commitment to the development of new methods of operation.
3. *Productivity*   Management should set objectives outlining target levels of production.
4. *Physical and financial resources*   Management should set objectives with regard to use, acquisition, and maintenance of capital and monetary resources.
5. *Profitability*   Management should set objectives that specify the profit the company would like to generate.
6. *Managerial performance and development*   Management should set objectives that specify rates and levels of managerial productivity and growth.
7. *Worker performance and attitude*   Management should set objectives that specify rates of worker productivity as well as the attitudes workers possess.
8. *Public responsibility*   Management should set objectives that indicate the company's responsibilities to its customers and society and to what extent the company intends to live up to those responsibilities.

According to Drucker, since the first five goal areas relate to tangible, impersonal characteristics of organizational operation, most managers would not dispute the designation of these as key areas. Designation of the last three as key areas could arouse some managerial opposition, however, since these areas are more personal and subjective. Regardless of potential opposition, an organization should have objectives in all eight areas to maximize its probability of success.

⊞ WORKING WITH ORGANIZATIONAL OBJECTIVES

Appropriate objectives are fundamental to the success of any organization. Theodore Levitt states that some leading industries may be on the verge of facing the same financial disaster as the railroads because of objectives inappropriate for their organizations.[7] Any manager, therefore, should approach the development, use, and modification of organizational objectives with utmost seriousness. In general, an organization should have: (1) **short-term objectives** (targets to be achieved within one year or less); (2) **intermediate-term objectives** (targets to be achieved within from one to five years); and (3) **long-term objectives** (targets to be achieved within from five to seven years).

An organization should have short-term, intermediate-term, and long-term objectives.

The Mister Boffo cartoon illustrates that long-term objectives may not be useful for every individual. From a management viewpoint, however, their development and use are critical factors in maintaining long-term viability.

Reprinted by permission: Tribune Media Services.

The necessity of predetermining appropriate organizational objectives has led to the development of what is called the principle of the objective. The **principle of the objective** is that before managers initiate any action, organizational objectives should be clearly determined, understood, and stated.[8]

Establishing Organizational Objectives

The three main steps that managers must take to develop a set of working organizational objectives are: (1) determine the existence of any environmental trends that could significantly influence the operation of the organization; (2) develop a set of objectives for the organization as a whole; and (3) develop a hierarchy of organizational objectives. These three steps are interrelated and usually require input from several people at different levels and operational sections of the organization. Each step is further developed in the paragraphs that follow.

Managers take three interrelated steps in developing organizational objectives.

Analyzing Trends

The first step in setting organizational objectives is to list major trends that have existed in the organizational environment over the past five years and determine if these trends have had a noticeable impact on organizational success. Conceivably, the trends could include such factors as marketing innovations of competitors, governmental controls, and social trends, such as the move toward smaller families. Management should then decide which present trends and which new trends are likely to affect organizational success over the next five years. This decision will determine what kinds of objectives are set at various levels of the organization.

Developing Objectives for the Organization as a Whole

After analyzing environmental trends, management should develop objectives that reflect this analysis for the organization as a whole. For example, the analysis may show that a major competitor has been continually improving its products over the past five years and, as a result, is gaining an increasingly larger share of the market. In reaction to this trend, management should set a product improvement objective in an effort to keep up with competitors. This product improvement objective, then, directly results from identification of a trend within the organizational environment and also from the organizational purpose of profit.

The paragraphs that follow illustrate how management might set financial objectives, product-market mix objectives, and functional objectives for the organization as a whole.

Establishing Financial Objectives

Financial objectives are organizational targets relating to monetary issues. In some organizations, government regulations guide management's setting of financial objectives. Managers of public utility organizations, for example, have definite guidelines specifying what types of financial objectives they are allowed to set. In organizations free from governmental constraints, the setting of financial objectives is influenced mainly by return on investment and financial comparisons with competitors.

Return on investment is the amount of money an organization earns in relation to the amount of money invested to keep the organization in operation.[9] Figure 3.4 shows how to use earnings of $50 000 and an investment of $500 000 to calculate a return on investment. If the calculated return on investment is too low, managers can set an overall objective to modify the organization's rate of return.

Information on organizational competition is available through published indexes, such as Dun and Bradstreet's *Ratios for Selected Industries*. These ratios reflect industry averages for key financial areas. Comparing company figures with

---

FIGURE 3.4   Calculations for return on investment.

$$\frac{\text{Return on}}{\text{Investment}} = \frac{\text{Total dollar amount earned}}{\text{Total dollar amount invested to keep organization operating}}$$

$$\frac{\text{Return on}}{\text{Investment}} = \frac{\$50\ 000\ \text{(Earnings)}}{\$500\ 000\ \text{(Investment)}} = .10 = 10\% \text{ (Rate of return)}$$

these industrial averages should tell management in which areas new financial objectives probably should be set or ways in which existing objectives should be modified.

Establishing Product-Market Mix Objectives

Product-market mix objectives outline which products—and the relative number or mix of these products—the organization will attempt to sell. Charles Granger suggests the following five steps for formulating product-market mix objectives.[10]

1. Examination of key trends in the business environments of the product-market areas.
2. Examination of growth trends (both market and volume) and profit trends (for the industry and for the company) in the individual product-mix areas.
3. Separation of product-market areas into those that are going to pull ahead and those that are going to drag. For promising areas, these questions need to be asked: How can these areas be made to flourish? Should additional injections of capital, marketing effort, technology, management talent, or the like be used? For the less promising areas, these questions are pertinent: Why is the product lagging? How can this be corrected? If it cannot be corrected, should the product be milked for whatever can be regained, or should it be withdrawn from the market?
4. Consideration of the need or desirability of adding new products or market areas to the mix. In this regard, management should ask these questions: Is there a profit gap to be filled? Based on the criteria of profit opportunity, compatibility, and feasibility of entry, what are possible new areas of interest in order of priority? What sort of programs (acquisitions or internal development) does the company need to develop the desired level of business in these areas?
5. Derivation of an optimum yet realistic product-market mix profile based on the conclusions reached in steps 1–4. This profile embodies the product-market mix objectives, which should be consistent with the organization's financial objectives. Interaction while setting these two kinds of objectives is advisable.

Product-market mix objectives outline the relative number or mix of products an organization will attempt to sell.

Establishing Functional Objectives

Functional objectives are targets relating to key organizational functions. These key functions include marketing, accounting, production, and personnel. Functional objectives that are consistent with the financial and product-market mix objectives should be developed for these areas. People in the organization should perform their functions in a way that helps the organization to attain its other objectives.[11]

Functional objectives should be consistent with financial and product-market mix objectives.

BACK TO THE CASE

The preceding information implies that a manager like Hall should set objectives in addition to profit objectives. These other objectives should be set in such areas as market standing, innovation, productivity, physical and financial resources, managerial performance and development, worker performance and attitude, and public responsibility. Naturally, such objectives should probably be set for the short, intermediate, and long term.

Before developing such objectives, however, a manager like Hall should pinpoint any environmental trends that could influence company operations. Objectives that reflect the environmental trends could then be set for the organization as a whole. They normally would include financial, product-market mix, and functional objectives.

Developing a Hierarchy of Objectives

The third step in establishing organizational objectives involves developing a hierarchy of organizational objectives and subobjectives.

In practice, an organizational objective must be broken down into subobjectives so that individuals in different levels and sections of the organization know what they must do to help reach the overall organizational objective.[12] An organizational objective is attained only after the subobjectives have been reached.

The overall organizational objective and the subobjectives assigned to the various people or units of the organization are referred to as a **hierarchy of objectives**. Figure 3.5 presents a sample hierarchy of objectives for a medium-sized company.

Conflicting subobjectives produce suboptimization.

Suboptimization exists when subobjectives are conflicting or not directly aimed at accomplishing the overall organizational objective. Figure 3.5 shows that suboptimization could exist within this company between the first subobjective for the finance and accounting department and the second subobjective for the supervisors. Suboptimization would result if supervisors needed new equipment to maintain production and the finance and accounting department couldn't approve the loan without company borrowing surpassing 50 percent of company assets. In this situation, established subobjectives would be aimed in different directions. A manager would have to choose which subobjective would best contribute to obtaining overall objectives and should therefore take precedence.

FIGURE 3.5 Hierarchy of objectives for a medium-sized organization.

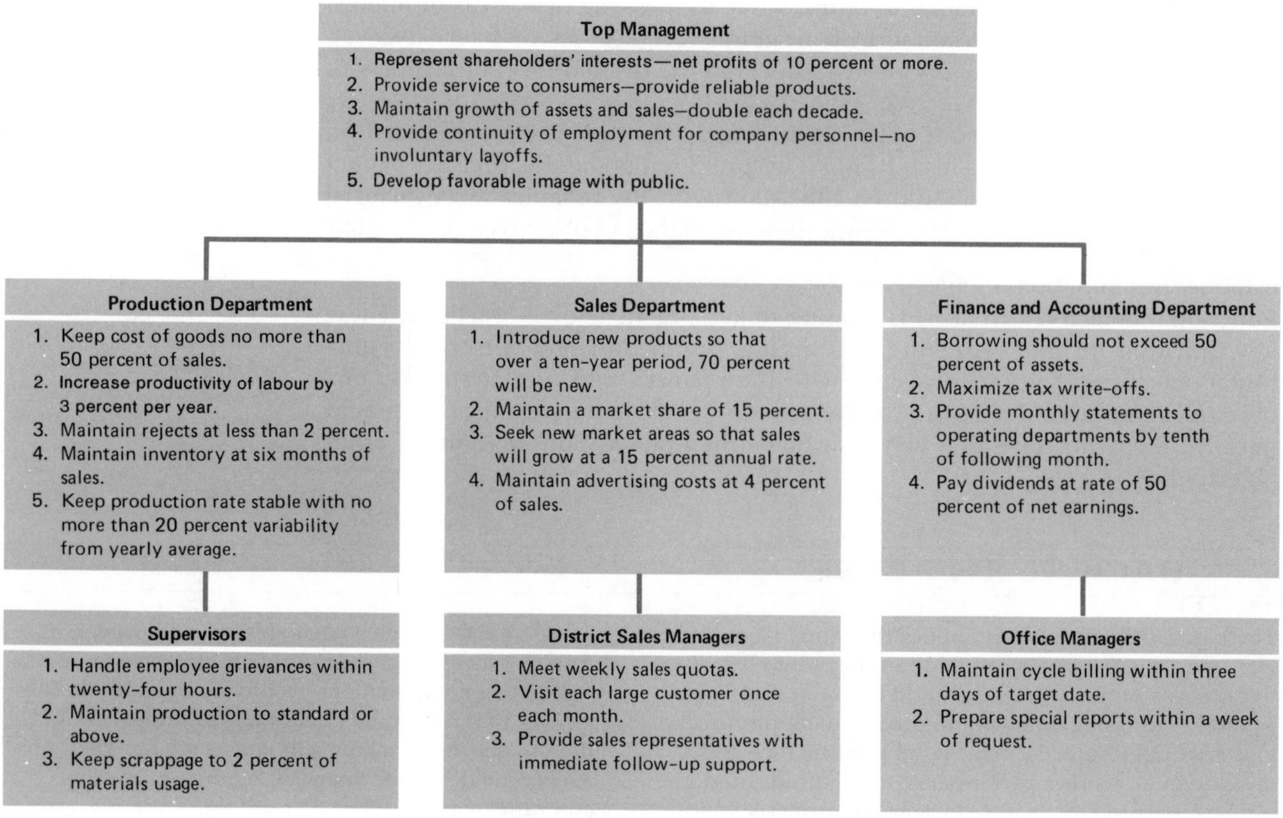
Top Management
1. Represent shareholders' interests—net profits of 10 percent or more.
2. Provide service to consumers–provide reliable products.
3. Maintain growth of assets and sales–double each decade.
4. Provide continuity of employment for company personnel–no involuntary layoffs.
5. Develop favorable image with public.
Production Department
1. Keep cost of goods no more than 50 percent of sales.
2. Increase productivity of labour by 3 percent per year.
3. Maintain rejects at less than 2 percent.
4. Maintain inventory at six months of sales.
5. Keep production rate stable with no more than 20 percent variability from yearly average.
Sales Department
1. Introduce new products so that over a ten-year period, 70 percent will be new.
2. Maintain a market share of 15 percent.
3. Seek new market areas so that sales will grow at a 15 percent annual rate.
4. Maintain advertising costs at 4 percent of sales.
Finance and Accounting Department
1. Borrowing should not exceed 50 percent of assets.
2. Maximize tax write-offs.
3. Provide monthly statements to operating departments by tenth of following month.
4. Pay dividends at rate of 50 percent of net earnings.
Supervisors
1. Handle employee grievances within twenty-four hours.
2. Maintain production to standard or above.
3. Keep scrappage to 2 percent of materials usage.
District Sales Managers
1. Meet weekly sales quotas.
2. Visit each large customer once each month.
3. Provide sales representatives with immediate follow-up support.
Office Managers
1. Maintain cycle billing within three days of target date.
2. Prepare special reports within a week of request.

From Joseph L. Massie and John Douglas, *Managing*, © 1985, p. 244. Reprinted by permission of Prentice-Hall, Inc., Englewood Cliffs, New Jersey.

Controlling suboptimization in organizations is part of a manager's job. Suboptimization can be minimized by developing a thorough understanding of how various parts of the organization relate to one another and making sure that subobjectives properly reflect these relationships.

Guidelines for Establishing Quality Objectives

As with all humanly developed commodities, the quality of goal statements can vary drastically. Managers can increase the quality of their objectives, however, by following some general guidelines:

1. *Managers should allow the people responsible for attaining the objectives to have a voice in setting them*   Often, the people responsible for attaining the objectives know their job situation better than the managers do and can help to make the objectives more realistic. Work-related problems that these people face should be thoroughly considered when trying to develop meaningful objectives.
2. *Managers should state objectives as specifically as possible*   Precise statements minimize confusion and misunderstanding and ensure that employees have explicit directions for what they should do.
3. *Managers should relate objectives to specific actions whenever necessary*   In this way, employees do not have to infer what they should do to accomplish their goals.
4. *Managers should pinpoint expected results*   Employees should know exactly how managers will determine whether or not an objective has been reached.
5. *Managers should set goals high enough that employees will have to strive to meet them, but not so high that employees give up trying to meet them*   Managers want employees to work hard, but not to be frustrated.
6. *Managers should specify when goals are expected to be achieved*   Employees must know the time frame for accomplishing their objectives. They then can be somewhat flexible and pace themselves accordingly.
7. *Managers should set objectives only in relation to other organizational objectives*   In this way, conflicting objectives or suboptimization can be kept to a minimum.
8. *Managers should state objectives clearly and simply*   The written or spoken word should not get in the way of communicating a goal to organization members.

Managers should follow these eight guidelines for making objectives effective.

Guidelines for Making Objectives Operational

Objectives must be stated in operational terms. That is, if an organization has **operational objectives**, managers should be able to tell if the objectives are being attained by comparing the actual results with goal statements.

For example, assume that a physical education instructor has set the following objectives for his students:

Operational objectives specify the activities or operations needed to attain them.

1. Each student will strive to develop a sense of balance.
2. Each student will attempt to become flexible.
3. Each student will try to become agile.
4. Each student will try to become strong.
5. Each student will work on becoming powerful.
6. Each student will strive to become durable.

FIGURE 3.6   Non-operational objectives versus operational objectives.

Nonoperational Objectives	Operational Objectives
1. Improve product quality.	1. Reduce quality rejects to 2 percent.
2. Improve communications.	2. Hold weekly staff meetings and initiate a newsletter to improve communications.
3. Improve social responsibility.	3. Hire fifty hard–core unemployed each year.
4. Issue monthly accounting reports on a more timely basis.	4. Issue monthly accounting reports so they are received three days following the close of the accounting period.

From *Management Concepts and Situations* by Howard M. Carlisle. © 1976, Science Research Associates, Inc. Adapted and reprinted by permission of the publisher.

These objectives are not operational because the activities or operations a student must perform to attain them are not specified. Additional information, however, could easily make the objectives operational. For example, the fifth physical education objective could be replaced with: Each student will strive to develop the power to do standing broad jumps the distance of his or her height plus one foot. Figure 3.6 shows four basically non-operational objectives and how each can be modified to be made operational.

BACK TO THE CASE

Once managers have set overall objectives for their organizations, their next step is to develop a company hierarchy of objectives. The development of this hierarchy entails breaking down the organization's overall objectives into subobjectives so that all organization members know what they must do to help the company reach its overall objectives. At Flow General, this hierarchy of objectives may have been confusing since, as the introductory case indicates, most employees did not seem to understand the company's overall objectives and thus probably were unclear as to their individual roles in helping the company to attain these objectives.

In establishing a hierarchy of objectives, managers must be careful not to suboptimize, or establish subob-

jectives that conflict with one another. Suboptimization also may have been a problem at Flow General, since general confusion about organizational objectives and subobjectives would have made it difficult for managers to recognize when subobjectives were in conflict.

Other guidelines for establishing quality objectives include making the objectives clear, consistent, challenging, and specific. Perhaps most important of all, organizational objectives should be operational. At Flow General, allowing workers like Chris Price to participate in establishing organizational objectives would have helped to ensure that company objectives were realistic and that organization members were committed to reaching them.

Attainment of Objectives

Attainment of organizational objectives is the obvious goal of all conscientious managers. Managers quickly discover, however, that moving the organization

FIGURE 3.7   Sample goals, means, and measures for a hotel.

Goals	Means	Measures
Increased market share	Good service	Ratio of repeat business Occupancy Informal feedback
	Employee morale and loyalty	Turnover Absenteeism Informal feedback
Financial stability	Image in financial markets	Price-earnings ratio Share price
	Profitability	Earnings per share Gross operating profit Cost trends Cash flow
	Strength of management team	Turnover Divisional profit Rate of promotion Informal feedback
Owner satisfaction	Adequate cash flow	Occupancy Sales Gross operating profit Departmental profit

Reprinted by permission from A. N. Geller, *Executive Information Needs in Hotel Companies* (New York: Peat Marwick Mitchell, 1984), p. 17. © Peat Marwick Main & Co., 1984.

toward goal attainment requires taking appropriate actions within the organization to reach the desired ends. This process is called means–ends analysis.

Basically, **means-ends analysis** entails: "(1) starting with the general goal to be achieved; (2) discovering a set of means, very generally specified, for accomplishing this goal; and (3) taking each of these means, in turn, as a new subgoal and discovering a more detailed means for achieving it."[13]

Figure 3.7 illustrates means-ends analysis for three sample goals of a hotel: increased market share, financial stability, and owner satisfaction. The goal of increased market share includes two means: good service, and employee morale and loyalty. These two means are subgoals that the hotel manager must focus on attaining in order to reach the goal of increased market share. The last column of the figure lists the measures that can be taken to operationalize the subgoals.

Effective managers are aware of the importance of not only setting organizational objectives, but clearly outlining the means by which these objectives can be attained. They know that means-ends analysis is important for guiding their own activities as well as for those of their subordinates. The better everyone within the organization understands the means by which goals are to be attained, the greater the probability that the goals actually will be reached.

The following Management in Action feature illustrates how Steinberg Inc., under the leadership of Irving Ludmer, has gone about achieving its objectives for growth. It hopes to achieve its goals through a total restructuring effort, concentrating on the new, the successful, and modern ventures.

Organizational goals are attained by taking appropriate means to reach desired ends.

STEINBERG'S "RETREAT" BRINGS COMPETITIVE EDGE

Irving Ludmer, Steinberg's president and chief operating officer since April 1984, calls the way he has been restructuring the company a "controlled retreat." The year before Ludmer took over, the giant food distributor and real estate company stumbled to a net profit of $13.3 million, or less than four-tenths of 1 percent on sales of $3.3 billion—way below average for food retailers. With Ludmer at the helm, Steinberg has far surpassed that level, recording in the year ending July 1985 a profit of $73.6 million on revenues of $3.9 billion.

But Ludmer considers talk of a turnaround premature. "I don't think we're there yet," he says. "If you look at it from the point of view of potential, which is the key, we have a long way to go before we are really good." The road back won't be easy, particularly since the whole organization is being restructured. When Ludmer took over, Steinberg was just recovering from a 1983 discount war it had triggered in Quebec that sapped $18-$20 million from the corporate treasury in less than two months. "It destroyed the bottom line."

Part of the current transformation consists of closing or selling unsuccessful stores. In the West, for instance, all twenty-seven outlets of Valdi limited-assortment units were shut. As well, the company is folding eleven Miracle Mart department stores in Quebec and Ontario; the twenty-one remaining sites will focus more on apparel and less on hardware. This division has been a drain since it was formed in 1961. Even the 212 traditional supermarkets in Quebec and Ontario, the backbone of the sixty-nine-year-old firm, are not immune. Some are being renovated, others are disappearing because they are either too small or too isolated. The executive inner sanctum has likewise been swept by internal changes and external hirings: In the last year, senior executive ranks have experienced two promotions and five hirings from outside. A third element in the turnaround has been what Ludmer calls "finding a way to put service back" into Steinberg's food stores. It was largely dropped, he says when the former regime tried to cut costs by trimming staff.

In the drive for higher margins, emphasis is shifting to items such as bulk foods, fresh fish, and a better bakery mix—all of the things the company had been eliminating over the years. Ludmer describes the old regime as "classic bureaucracy," where store managers needed approval for any disbursements in excess of five dollars. Ludmer thinks a manager who may be responsible for sales of $20 million a year should be allowed to do what he or she was hired to do—manage.

It's a fundamental change, he says. "We're turning it around from top-down (philosophy) to bottom-up, where the customer is king. That means giving each store greater autonomy, and better communications between middle-management and store management."

In the midst of restructuring, the company is rediscovering its taste for innovation and experimentation. One example is the creation of a variety of different stores. At one end of the spectrum are super-supermarkets—goliaths of 5500 square metres, twice the size of a conventional outlet. At the other is La Maisonnee, Steinberg's Quebec chain of seventy-one franchised neighbourhood stores. A more conspicuous sign of innovation is its venture into a chain of discount stores. It will be an equal partner with the fast-growing Price Co. of San Diego, which operates twenty-one warehouse stores. The new division will be called Price Club. Units will cover about 9000 square metres and carry automotive and sporting goods, appliances, and food.

But caution is still the keynote. Ludmer, his plate overflowing with challenges new and old, has little time to relax. "You can't go to sleep in any of these markets," he says. "The day we think we're good we're finished."

Based on "Steinberg's 'retreat' fattens its profit margin," by Alan D. Gray in *Financial Times of Canada*, May 12, 1986. Used with permission.

How to Use Objectives

As stated previously, organizational objectives flow naturally from organizational purpose and reflect the organization's environment. Managers must have a firm understanding of the influences that mold organizational objectives because, as these influences change, the objectives themselves must change. Objectives are not unchangeable directives. In fact, a significant managerial responsibility is to help the organization change objectives when necessary.

⊞ MANAGEMENT BY OBJECTIVES (MBO)

Some managers believe that organizational objectives are such an important and fundamental part of management that they use a management approach based exclusively on them. This management approach, called **management by objectives (MBO)**, has been popularized mainly through the writings of Peter Drucker.[14] It has three basic characteristics:

1. All individuals within an organization are assigned a specialized set of objectives that they try to reach during a normal operating period. These objectives are mutually set and agreed upon by individuals and their managers.[15]
2. Performance reviews are conducted periodically to determine how close individuals are to attaining their objectives.
3. Rewards are given to individuals on the basis of how close they come to reaching their goals.[16]

Factors Necessary for a Successful MBO Program

Certain key factors are necessary for an MBO program to be successful.[17] First, appropriate goals must be set by top managers of the organization. All individual MBO goals are based on these overall objectives. If overall objectives are inappropriate, individual MBO objectives also are inappropriate, and the related individual work activity is non-productive. Second, managers and subordinates together must develop and agree on each individual's goals. Both managers and subordinates must feel that the individual objectives are just and appropriate if each party is to use them seriously as a guide for action. Third, employee performance should be conscientiously evaluated against established objectives. This evaluation helps to determine if the objectives are fair and if appropriate means are being used to attain them. Fourth, management must follow through on the employee performance evaluations and reward employees accordingly.[18]

Management by objectives: Management and subordinates work together to develop and achieve goals.

MBO Programs: Advantages and Disadvantages

Experienced MBO managers say that there are two advantages to this management approach. First, MBO programs continually emphasize what should be done in an organization to achieve organizational goals. Second, the MBO process secures employee commitment to attaining organizational goals. Because managers and subordinates have developed objectives together, both parties are more interested in working to reach those goals.

Managers also admit that MBO programs have disadvantages.[19] One disadvantage is that, because organization members develop objectives together, they actually have less time in which to do their work. Also, elaborate written goals, careful communication of goals, and detailed performance evaluations naturally increase the volume of paperwork in an organization.

Most managers seem to think, however, that MBO's advantages outweigh its disadvantages. Overall, they find MBO programs beneficial.[20]

BACK TO THE CASE

In addition to making sure that an appropriate set of objectives has been developed for an organization like Flow General, management must also clearly outline for employees the means by which these objectives can be attained. According to the introductory case, current Flow General leadership is striving to accomplish this.

Flow General management might want to consider clarifying company objectives for employees through a management by objectives program. If so, each employee would develop with his or her manager a set of mutually agreed upon objectives. Performance reviews would give employees feedback on their progress in reaching their objectives, and rewards would be given to those employees who made the most progress.

Action Summary

Reread the learning objectives that follow. Each objective is followed by questions. Answering these questions accurately will help you to retain the most important concepts discussed in this chapter. After answering each question, check your answer with the answer key at the end of this chapter. (*Hint*: If you have doubt regarding the correct response, consult the page that follows the answer.)

Circle:

From studying this chapter, I will attempt to acquire:

1. An understanding of organizational objectives.

T, F
    a. Organizational objectives should reflect the organization's purpose.

    b. The targets toward which an open management system is directed are referred to as: (a) functional objectives; (b) organizational objectives;

a, b, c, d, e
    (c) operational objectives; (d) courses of action; (e) individual objectives.

2. An appreciation for the importance of organizational objectives.

    a. Organizational objectives serve important functions in all of the following areas except: (a) making performance evaluations useful; (b) establishing consistency; (c) increasing efficiency; (d) improving wages; (e) decision

a, b, c, d, e
    making that influences everyday operations.

    b. Implied within organizational objectives are hints on how to define the

T, F
    most productive workers in the organization.

3. An ability to tell the difference between organizational objectives and individual objectives.

    a. Which of the following is considered to be an individual objective: (a) peer recognition; (b) financial security; (c) personal growth; (d) b and c; (e) all

a, b, c, d, e
    of the above.

b. When goal integration exists: (a) there is a positive situation, desired by management; (b) managers will not see conflict between organizational and personal objectives; (c) the individual will work for goals without much managerial encouragement; (d) additional opportunities to engage in informal social relationships with peers will not be necessary encouragement for the individual; (e) all of the above. a, b, c, d, e

4. **A knowledge of the areas in which managers should set organizational objectives.**
   a. The eight key areas in which Peter F. Drucker advises managers to set objectives include all of the following except: (a) market standing; (b) productivity; (c) public responsibility; (d) inventory control; (e) manager performance and development. a, b, c, d, e
   b. Long-term objectives are defined as targets to be achieved in one to five years. T, F

5. **An understanding of the development of organizational objectives.**
   a. Which of the following factors would *not* be considered in analyzing trends: (a) marketing innovations of competitors; (b) projections for society; (c) government controls; (d) known existing and projected future events; (e) product-market mix. a, b, c, d, e
   b. Which of the following factors would *not* be considered in the "developing objectives for the organization as a whole" stage of setting organizational objectives: (a) establishing a hierarchy of objectives; (b) establishing product-market mix objectives; (c) establishing financial objectives; (d) establishing return on investment objectives; (e) establishing functional objectives. a, b, c, d, e

6. **Some facility in writing good objectives.**
   a. Which of the following is an objective stated in non-operational terms: (a) reduce customer complaints by 9 percent; (b) make great progress in new product development; (c) develop a new customer; (d) increase profit before taxes by 10 percent; (e) reduce quality rejects by 2 percent. a, b, c, d, e
   b. An example of a good operational objective is: "Each student in this class will try to learn how to manage." T, F

7. **An awareness of how managers use organizational objectives and help others to attain the objectives.**
   a. Means-ends analysis implies that the manager is results-oriented and discovers a set of means for accomplishing a goal. T, F
   b. Which of the following guidelines should managers use in changing objectives: (a) objectives should not be changed; (b) adapt objectives when the organization's environmental influences change; (c) change objectives to create suboptimization as needed; (d) adapt objectives so that they are non-operational; (e) all of the above are valid guidelines. a, b, c, d, e

8. **An appreciation for the potential of a management by objectives (MBO) program.**
   a. Both performance evaluations and employee rewards should be tied to organizational and individual objectives assigned to individuals when the firm is using MBO. T, F
   b. A method under which a manager is given specific objectives to achieve and is evaluated according to the accomplishment of these objectives is: (a) means-ends analysis; (b) operational objectives; (c) individual objectives; (d) management by objectives; (e) management by exception. a, b, c, d, e

INTRODUCTORY CASE WRAP-UP

"The Direction of Flow General" (p. 58) and its related back-to-the-case sections were written to help you better understand the management concepts contained in this chapter. Answer the following discussion questions about this introductory case to further enrich your understanding of the chapter content:

1. Should Flow General employees have clearly understood Joseph E. Hall's objectives or where the organization was going? Why?
2. What is the significance of Chris Price saying that objectives necessitated unrealistic research timetables? Explain fully.
3. Assuming that you were able to give Hall advice about how to improve himself as a manager, what would you say?

Issues for Review and Discussion

1. What are organizational objectives, and how do they relate to organizational purpose?
2. Explain why objectives are important to an organization.
3. List four areas in which organizational objectives can act as important guidelines for performance.
4. Explain the difference between organizational objectives and individual objectives.
5. What is meant by goal integration?
6. List and define eight key areas in which organizational objectives should be set.
7. How do environmental trends affect the process of establishing organizational objectives?
8. How does return on investment relate to setting financial objectives?
9. Define *product-market mix objectives*. What process should a manager go through to establish them?
10. What are functional objectives?
11. What is a hierarchy of objectives?
12. Explain the purpose of a hierarchy of objectives.
13. How does suboptimization relate to a hierarchy of objectives?
14. List eight guidelines a manager should follow to establish quality organizational objectives.
15. How does a manager make objectives operational?
16. Explain the concept of means-ends analysis.
17. Should a manager ever modify or change existing organizational objectives? If no, why? If yes, when?
18. Define *MBO* and describe its main characteristics.
19. List and describe the factors necessary for an MBO program to be successful.
20. Discuss the advantages and disadvantages of MBO.

Sources of Additional Information

Buller, Paul F., and Cecil H. Bell, Jr. "Effects of Team Building and Goal Setting on Productivity: A Field Experiment." *Academy of Management Journal* 29 (June 1986): 305–28.

Chung, Kae H. *Critical Success Factions in Management.* New York: Allyn & Bacon, 1987.

Dowst, Somerby (C.P.M.). "Classify Your Objectives." *Purchasing* 25 (April 1979): 38.

Drucker, Peter. *Managing for Results.* New York: Harper & Row, 1964.

Frisbie, Gilbert, and Vincent A. Mabert. "Crystal Ball vs. System: The Forecasting Dilemma." *Business Horizons* 24 (September/October 1981): 72–76.

Godiwalla, Yezdi M., Wayne A. Meinhart, and William A. Warde. "General Management and Corporate Strategy." *Managerial Planning* 30 (September/October 1981): 17–23.

Hughes, Charles L. *Goal Setting.* New York: American Management Association, 1965.

Kizilos, Tolly, and Roger P. Heinisch. "Special Report: How a Management Team Selects Managers." *Harvard Business Review* (September-October 1986): 6–13.

Nash, Michael. *Managing Organizational Performance.* San Francisco: Jossey-Bass, 1983.

Odiorne, George S. *Management by Objectives.* Belmont, Calif.: Pitman, 1965.

Odiorne, George S. *Management Decision by Objectives*. Englewood Cliffs, N.J.: Prentice-Hall, 1969.

Patten, Thomas H., Jr. *A Manager's Guide to Performance Appraisal*. New York: Free Press, 1982.

Scanlan, Burt K. "Maintaining Organizational Effectiveness—A Prescription for Good Health." *Personnel Journal* 59 (May 1980): 381, 422.

Smith, August W. *Management Systems: Analyses and Applications*. Chicago: Dryden Press, 1982.

Steers, Richard M. *Introduction to Organizational Behavior*. Pacific Palisades, Calif.: Goodyear Publishing, 1981.

Stewart, John, Jr. *Managing a Successful Business Turnaround*. New York: Amacom, 1984.

Stone, W. Robert, and Donald F. Heany. "Dealing with a Corporate Identity Crisis." *Long-Range Planning* 17 (February 1984): 10–18.

Wright, Norman B. "Rekindling Managerial Innovativeness." *Business Quarterly* 51 (Summer 1986): 38–40.

Notes

1. Annual Report 1983, Unicorp Canada Corporation, p. 1.

2. John F. Mee, "Management Philosophy for Professional Executives," *Business Horizons* (December 1956): 7.

3. Marshall E. Dimock, *The Executive in Action* (New York: Harper & Bros., 1945), 54. For more on objectives as the central driving force of organizations, see F.G. Harmon and G. Jacobs, "Company Personality: The Heart of the Matter," *Management Review* (October 1985): 36–40.

4. Y.K. Shetty, "New Look at Corporate Goals," *California Management Review* 22 (Winter 1979): 71–79.

5. Thomas J. Murray, "The Unseen Corporate 'War'," *Dun's Review* (June 1980): 110–14.

6. Peter F. Drucker, *The Practice of Management* (New York: Harper & Bros., 1954), 62–65, 126–29. For a worthwhile discussion about the constituencies that organizational objectives must serve, see Hal B. Pickle and Royce L. Abrahamson, *Small Business Management* (New York: Wiley, 1986), 211–12.

7. Theodore Levitt, "Marketing Myopia," *Harvard Business Review* (July/August 1960): 45.

8. Mee, "Management Philosophy for Professional Executives," 7.

9. Joseph G. Louderback and George E. Manners, Jr., "Integrating ROI and CVP," *Management Accounting* (April 1981): 33–39. For a related discussion of financial objectives, see Gordon Donaldson, "Financial Goals and Strategic Consequences," *Harvard Business Review* (May/June 1985): 56–66.

10. Adapted, by permission of the publisher, from "How to Set Company Objectives," by Charles H. Granger, *Management Review*, July 1970. © 1970 by American Management Association, Inc. All rights reserved. See also Max D. Richards, *Setting Goals and Objectives* (St. Paul, Minn.: West Publishing, 1986).

11. Granger, "How to Set Company Objectives," 7.

12. Charles H. Granger, "The Hierarchy of Objectives," *Harvard Business Review* (May/June 1964): 64–74. See also Heinz Weihrich, *Management Excellence: Productivity through MBO* (New York: McGraw-Hill, 1985), 65–84.

13. James G. March and Herbert A. Simon, *Organizations* (New York: Wiley, 1958), 191.

14. Drucker, *The Practice of Management*; also Peter Drucker, Harold Smiddy, and Ronald G. Greenwood, "Management by Objectives," *Academy of Management Review* 6 (April 1981): 225.

15. "Tailor MBO to Fit the Person," *Training* (September 1985): 58–60.

16. Robert L. Mathis and John H. Jackson, *Personnel: Human Resource Management* (St. Paul, Minn.: West Publishing, 1985), 353–55.

17. For characteristics that usually make an MBO program unsuccessful, see Dale D. McConkey, "Twenty Ways to Kill Management by Objectives," *Management Review* (October 1972): 4–13.

18. William H. Franklin, Jr., "Create an Atmosphere of Positive Expectations," *Administrative Management* (April 1980): 32–34.

19. Charles H. Ford, "Manage by Decisions, Not by Objectives," *Business Horizons* (February 1980): 7–18.

20. E.J. Seyna, "MBO: The Fad That Changed Management," *Long-Range Planning* (December 1986): 116–23.

Action Summary Answer Key

1. a. T, p. 60
   b. b, p. 59
2. a. d, p. 60
   b. T, p. 61

3. a. e, p. 62
   b. e, pp. 63–64
4. a. d, p. 64
   b. F, p. 65

5. a. e, p. 66
   b. a, pp. 66–67
6. a. b, pp. 69–70
   b. F, pp. 69–70

7. a. T, p. 71
   b. b, p. 73
8. a. T, p. 73
   b. d, p. 73

ON HURRICANES AND CONTAINING CHAOS

Executives often recognize that they must find the time to rethink their organization's primary strategies, because they know they have to develop new insights before they can do a proper job of leading. But there's always so much going on. "How do I find the time?" they complain. Definitely not by waiting for things to get back to normal—there is no normal to get back to. What these executives experience today is the way it's always going to be. For them, there is no escape from the hurricane, and the turbulence is only likely to get worse. This turbulence often includes management systems, organization charts, policies, and objectives—systems that, more often than not, do the running instead of being run.

The hurricane metaphor is used here because it is a powerful way of describing the concepts involved in bringing corporate energy to life. A hurricane is unique: It is the only weather system separate from the global weather pattern. It stands alone, is internally motivated, and can take a direction all its own regardless of what is happening around it. Its most powerful part is a wide band of rain, cloud, and violent wind; in the eye, however, the temperature is warm, the sky generally clear, and the winds are but a gentle breeze.

Successful organizations, like hurricanes, have a strong central core around which everything revolves and toward which everything is focused. At this centre are ideas about what the organization believes in and where it is going. To tap the energy of managers and individual contributors, and to organize them into a power source far greater than the sum of its parts, an organization must have a set of core values that will draw its employees in. Should management lose touch with these values, the organization's energy will dissipate and become part of the world's general weather pattern, re-

MacNeil: "Successful organizations, like hurricanes, have a strong central core around which everything revolves . . ."

acting to the environment rather than selecting a direction of its own. Just how are an organization's core values formed? They are definitely not *created* by organization leaders. What is more likely is that leaders uncover a set of beliefs that many others also share, and then shape these beliefs into a focus for energy.

There is a myth in most organizations that management is in control. Not so. Employees only let managers think they are in control. They may behave subserviently when the ineffective boss is around, but all that boss really controls is the employees' time; their hearts are reserved for things they believe in and of which they can be proud. And these days, most people seem to take more pride in what they do outside of work. Still, people generally want to contribute more than they do, want to believe in the organization they work for—want to do work that makes them proud.

Trying to motivate staff who are mired in a poor performance rut is difficult, but even in the most lethargic organization human energy is always there waiting to be tapped. (After all, no one intentionally sets out to do a poor job.) What is needed is strong leadership. If employees are convinced that their leaders care, they will begin to feel a sense of satisfaction each time a small improvement in performance moves the organization closer to its declared values. In this way, corporate energy will be created rather than dissipated.

Often, the core values that can produce that kind of employee pride and satisfaction already exist in an organization—they may be hidden, but they are there nonetheless. An easy way to discover an organization's core values is to look for sources of negative energy, for it is where dissatisfaction is highest that an organization can begin to change attitudes and, ultimately, the course of the corporation. Once a focus has been found and is directly employed at all levels of the company, changes will begin to take place—especially if leaders start to demonstrate, through personal actions, their genuine concern for it. This is nothing more than a predictable response to leadership.

Given the existence of central core values, one might ask: Where do they lead? This is a serious, yet often neglected question. Management must have a mental picture of a preferred future that will inspire people and simultaneously set them free from having to ask for interpretations of policy at every turn. This is not the same as the familiar five-year plans, goals, objectives, or much-needed analysis of strategic issues so often touted by management. Such business plans, with their cool logic and cold facts, often make employees nervous or simply turn them off. Instead, what is referred to here are "word pictures" that can bring business plans to life, such as Northern Telecom Ltd.'s "Towards the intelligent universe." This phrase comes across clearly as a declaration that the company is destined to operate on the leading edge of technology, thereby creating the positive and energetic atmosphere that can be felt throughout this successful multinational corporation.

Many organizations unable to see a preferred future are never able to move beyond where they are, regardless of how well they are suited to rapid growth in every other way. But it is also true that even for leaders of successful companies, keeping a sharp focus on the future is a full-time job, for no company can afford to rest on its laurels. Employees must, therefore, be made to understand the significance of these "mental pictures": they are no less important than a business plan or a product, for they serve as a strategic map that lets everyone know where the company is headed.

For an organization to succeed, it must create for itself an overall vision. Armed with a business plan that appeals to the mind, the organization must find for itself the vision that will grab the hearts of its employees. People do not get excited about targets that can be reached in a year—those are merely goals. A vision needs to be spiritual in nature, something people can constantly move toward and strive for but never feel pressured to reach by any particular deadline. A vision should be made up of ideals that set high standards and connect with people's emotions. Finally, a vision should be the "eye of the hurricane," the calm centre toward which management and employees can look for reassurance. For they need to know that when they are blown off course by day-to-day affairs, they can step back, focus on the vision, and reset the direction in which they want to move.

DISCUSSION ISSUES

1. What are organizational objectives and how do they relate to organizational purpose? How are they differentiated in the case?
2. According to the author, why is a "vision" of such importance to an organization and its management? Be precise.
3. Should a manager ever modify or change existing organizational objectives? Why? How does this relate to the organization's purpose? Explain.

Based on "Containing Chaos," by Art McNeil in *Canadian Business*, January 1987. Material originally published in *"I" of the Hurricane: Creating Corporate Energy*, by Art McNeil. © 1987 by Stoddart Publishing Co. Ltd. Used with permission.

2

PLANNING

Section 1 introduced the topic of management and ended with a discussion of organizational objectives. According to generally accepted management theory, once managers have developed organizational objectives, they are ready to start planning. Planning is one of the four major management functions that must be performed for organizations to have long-term success.

Chapter 4
Chapter 4, "Fundamentals of Planning," defines planning as the process of determining how the organization will get where it wants to go. Thus, the fundamental purpose of planning is accomplishing organizational objectives. Steps of the planning process are outlined and presented as an organizational subsystem. Chapter 4 also discusses the relationship between planning and the chief executive of an organization, as well as the qualifications and duties of planners and how planners are evaluated. Chapter 4 concludes with several suggestions on how to maximize the effectiveness of the planning process.

Chapter 5
The planning process inevitably involves making decisions. Chapter 5, "Making Decisions," defines a decision as a choice made between two or more alternatives. Various types of decisions and a format for determining who is responsible for making those decisions are discussed. Also covered in this chapter are the six elements of the decision situation: (1) the state of nature; (2) the decision makers; (3) goals to be served; (4) relevant alternatives; (5) ordering of alternatives; and (6) a choice of alternatives. Combinations of these elements are shown to make up the five steps of the decision-making process. Decision-making conditions—complete certainty, complete uncertainty, and risk—also are discussed in Chapter 5. In addition, the analytical tools that can help managers make decisions that minimize risk—probability theory and decision trees—are explained and illustrated.

Chapter 6
Chapter 6 discusses the two types of planning that managers should use within organizations: strategic and tactical. Strategic planning, strategy, and strategy management are defined. Strategy formulation is explored through a discussion of environmental analysis as well as various tools available to help managers in actually developing strategy. These tools include critical question analysis, SWOT analysis, and business portfolio analysis. Environmental analysis emphasizes the general, operating, and internal levels of the organizational environment. Chapter 6 concludes with a definition of tactical planning and material on comparing and coordinating strategic and tactical planning, and the relationship between planning and levels of management.

Chapter 7
Chapter 7, "Plans and Planning Tools," explains various plans that should be made within an organization and the tools available to make the plans. A plan is defined as specific action proposed to help an organization achieve its objectives. Critical dimensions of plans that managers should scrutinize during plan development also are discussed in this chapter. These dimensions are the degree to which the plan is used over and over again (repetitiveness dimension); the amount of time the plan covers (time dimension); the portion of the organization the plan covers (scope dimension); and the level of the organization the plan addresses (level dimension). Based primarily upon the repetitiveness dimension, plans are categorized into standing plans (those used over and over again) and single-use plans (those used only a few times). A discussion of why plans fail and an explanation of plant facilities planning and human resources planning follow.

Chapter 7 also covers forecasting and scheduling. The specific, usable forecasting techniques presented are the jury of executive opinion method, the sales force estimation method, and the time series analysis method. Guidelines for choosing a particular forecasting method and information on the use of the product life cycle during the forecasting period also are explained. In discussing scheduling, Gantt charts and PERT (program evaluation and review techniques) are covered in detail.

FUNDAMENTALS OF PLANNING

STUDENT LEARNING OBJECTIVES

From studying this chapter, I will attempt to acquire:

1. A definition of planning and an understanding of the purposes of planning.
2. A knowledge of the advantages and potential disadvantages of planning.
3. Insights on how the major steps of the planning process are related.
4. An understanding of the planning subsystem.
5. A knowledge of how the chief executive relates to the planning process.
6. An understanding of the qualifications and duties of planners and how planners are evaluated.
7. Guidelines on how to get the greatest return from the planning process.

CHAPTER OUTLINE

RALPH AND HARVEY MOSS MUST PLAN

Ralph Moss was facing the most challenging task of his business career. His brother Louis Moss had died, leaving Ralph to be the chief executive officer of John Nageldinger & Sons, Inc. The company had been founded by Ralph's family and run by them for the last ninety-seven years. The company was in the business of manufacturing and selling compressed-gas regulators and portable oxygen equipment.

Ralph's business experience within the company was what made his new position such a challenge. For almost forty years, Ralph had worked primarily in the manufacturing area of the company. His experience was virtually limited to supervising the machine operators who manufactured company products. Most other responsibilities had been left to Ralph's brother Louis.

As the new chief executive officer, Ralph was struggling to solve one company problem after another, but his lack of experience made it very difficult. The longer Ralph functioned as Nageldinger & Sons' chief executive, the more frustrated he became. Finally, he realized that he was unable to manage the company alone.

Ralph convinced his thirty-nine-year-old son Harvey to help manage the family business. Although Harvey had recently begun his career as a management consultant, he decided to try to help his father.

One of the first things Harvey did upon arriving at Nageldinger & Sons was to tour the plant, a modest, one-story, concrete-and-brick building stashed in the far corner of a dead-end street. Although Harvey had worked at Nageldinger & Sons several years prior and somewhat knew what to expect on his tour, he was depressed with what he found.

Overall, the company's manufacturing operation hadn't changed in a long time. The company essentially was using machinery and operators that had been there thirty-five to forty years. In addition, the company was still marketing its products with a catalogue that Harvey had helped to design while attending college in 1960. Given this situation, it was not hard for Harvey to believe that Nageldinger & Sons had not made a profit for the last three years.

It was clear to Harvey that changes had to be made if Nageldinger & Sons was to be successful. A carefully developed plan would have to be designed and implemented.

Based on "A Compression of Old and New," by Leslie Schultz in *Inc.*, February 1983.

What's Ahead

The introductory case ends with Harvey Moss resolving to do a better job of planning at Nageldinger & Sons. The fundamentals of planning, as managers like Harvey Moss and Ralph Moss should understand them, are described in this chapter. Specifically, this chapter: (1) outlines the general characteristics of planning; (2) discusses steps in the planning process; (3) describes the planning subsystem; (4) elaborates on the relationship between planning and the chief executive; (5) summarizes the qualifications and duties of planners and how planners are evaluated; and (6) explains how to maximize the effectiveness of the planning process.

GENERAL CHARACTERISTICS OF PLANNING

Defining Planning

Planning is the process of determining how the organization can get where it wants to go. Chapter 3 emphasized the importance of organizational objectives and explained how to develop them. Planning is the process of determining exactly what the organization will do to accomplish its objectives. In more formal terms, planning has been defined as "the systematic development of action programs aimed at reaching agreed business objectives by the process of analyzing, evaluating, and selecting among the opportunities which are foreseen."[1]

As indicated above, plans are formulated to assist an organization in accomplishing its objectives. The Management in Action feature for this chapter emphasizes the importance of planning for a business venture of any size.

Planning determines how the organization can get where it wants to go.

Purposes of Planning

Over the years, management writers have presented several different purposes of planning. For example, C.W. Roney indicates that organizational planning has two purposes: protective and affirmative. The protective purpose of planning is to minimize risk by reducing the uncertainties surrounding business conditions and clarifying the consequences of related management action. The affirmative purpose of planning is to increase the degree of organizational success.[2] Still another purpose of planning is to establish a coordinated effort within the organization. An absence of planning is usually accompanied by an absence of coordination and, therefore, usually contributes to organizational inefficiency.

The fundamental purpose of planning, however, is to help the organization reach its objectives. As stated by Koontz and O'Donnell, the primary purpose of planning is to "facilitate the accomplishment of enterprise and objectives."[3] All other purposes of planning are simply spinoffs of this fundamental purpose.

The fundamental purpose of planning is to help the organization reach its objectives.

85

MANAGEMENT IN ACTION

GOT A GREAT IDEA?

You suspect that you're a budding entrepreneur. You have a great idea for a new product and want to set up a business to make you rich. Have you done any market research to gauge potential demand for your product? Have you met with manufacturers to find out about production? Have you developed cash flows and budgets and met with financial backers? Well, actually, no, you haven't, you're not really sure how to proceed. Besides, if you tell anyone about your great idea they'd steal it!

The cold truth is that if you don't have the skills and the planning it takes to turn ideas into commercial ventures your new company could join the 80 percent of new businesses that fail within five years of starting. However, there is help available for those with ideas and very little knowledge of how to turn those ideas into solid businesses plans. The inexperienced can turn to the expert help available at universities and government-sponsored small business centres that counsel entrepreneurs. These business centres have been set up in most provinces. The province of British Columbia, for instance, has established seventeen centres in the past two years at community colleges and universities through their Enterprise BC project. Counsellors are available to help a new business get started and remain functioning. They provide the basic skills essential to running a small business. The inexperienced learn what market research is necessary, where to get the data, and how to set up cash flows and budgets. And all of this help is free.

Greg Staple of Simon Fraser University Enterprise Centre at Burnaby, B.C., explains the basic service. "First of all we identify if you're the type of person who should be in the business you want to try. Do you have the energy, background, commitment?" Counsellors want to ensure that the budding entrepreneurs take a careful look at themselves, evaluating their strengths and weaknesses before the idea itself is evaluated. Then they help the entrepreneur look for any product or service the great idea may be modelled on and they evaluate how it's doing. If the idea looks viable, they put some figures together.

While the counsellors won't do the work for you, they can be relied on for direction. They will help you identify what information you need and where to go to get it, such as libraries, competitors, or suppliers. You also have to spend time researching your target market before going much further. Market research involves talking to people. You may be nervous about having your idea stolen, but the risk is small when compared with the need for proper research to launch a solid business. Meet with department store buyers, raw-materials suppliers, and

"The inexperienced learn what market research is necessary, where to get the data . . ."

future purchasers to get their opinions. Distribute questionnaires to a sample of your target market. Read some marketing texts. If your idea is an already established product or service, talk to people in the business and ask how they would package the idea, who their target market would be, and what pricing strategies they would use. Read up on your potential competitors, study annual reports and trade magazines, and check directories for the names and locations of other firms in your target industry.

The aim and result of all this work is a solid business plan. Says Staple: "You're going to have a document that lays out what the plan is, why it's a good idea, who's involved and what skills they have. And a set of numbers for the first five years of operation that show year by year how you stand financially, when you're going to need money, and how much." The business plan plays a vital role in obtaining financing for your business. While you may be able to forego a plan by financing a simple business yourself or with the help of family and friends, any other financial backer, from the bank to a government assistance program, will require a business plan. It should include the objectives for the business, the results from the market research, and the strategies to achieve your goals. Include financial statements, such as break-even figures for various strategies, and sets of budgets and cash flows. Discuss the personnel your business will need and the skills and abilities of those who may have already joined you.

The experts can help you package the business plan so as to ensure that financial backers will seriously consider your proposal. By developing a polished, detailed, and professional plan you can present your great idea more effectively. And in the end, a solid business plan presented effectively will help to sell your business and let you get on with the business of selling your great idea. Then your new business will be on its way toward a bright and successful future.

Based on "First Things First," by John Masters in *Canadian Business*, May 1987. Used with permission.

Planning: Advantages and Potential Disadvantages

A vigorous planning program has many advantages. One is that it helps managers to be future-oriented. They are forced to look beyond their normal everyday problems to project what may face them in the future. Decision coordination is a second advantage of a sound planning program. A decision should not be made today without some idea of how it will affect a decision that will have to be made tomorrow. The planning function assists managers in their efforts to coordinate their decisions. A third advantage to planning is that it emphasizes organizational objectives. Since organizational objectives are the starting points for planning, managers are constantly reminded of exactly what their organization is trying to accomplish.

Planning emphasizes the future, helps to coordinate decisions, and keeps the focus on objectives.

As a group, most managers feel that planning is extremely advantageous to the organization. In a study by Stieglitz, 280 managers were asked to assess the relative importance of such functions as public relations, organizational meetings, organizational planning, and organizational control. Over 65 percent of these managers ranked planning as the most important function.[4]

If the planning function is not well executed within the organization, however, planning can have several disadvantages. For example, an overemphasized planning program can take up too much managerial time. Managers must strike an appropriate balance between time spent on planning and time spent on organizing, influencing, and controlling. If they don't, some activities that are extremely important to the success of the organization may be neglected. Usually, the disadvantages of planning result from the planning function being used incorrectly.[5] Overall, planning's advantages generally outweigh its disadvantages.

If done incorrectly or excessively, planning can be disadvantageous.

Primacy of Planning

Planning is the primary management function—the function that precedes and is the foundation for the organizing, influencing, and controlling functions of managers. Only after managers have developed their plans can they determine

Planning is the foundation function.

FIGURE 4.1   Planning as the foundation for organizing, influencing, and controlling.

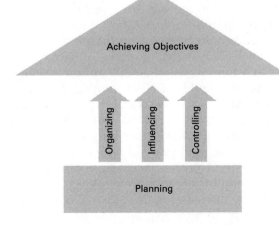

how they want to structure their organization, place their people, and establish organizational controls. As discussed in Chapter 1, planning, organizing, influencing, and controlling are interrelated. Planning is the foundation function and the first function to be performed. Organizing, influencing, and controlling are interrelated and based upon the results of planning. Figure 4.1 shows this relationship.

BACK TO THE CASE

It is obvious from the introductory case that little planning has occurred at Nageldinger & Sons in recent years. Harvey Moss, however, realizes that planning is the process of determining what Nageldinger & Sons should do to reach its objectives.

Because of the many related benefits of planning, Ralph Moss should encourage Harvey to pursue his resolution to plan more at Nageldinger & Sons. One particularly notable benefit is the probability of increased profits. To gain the benefits of planning, how-

ever, Ralph and Harvey must be careful that the planning function is well executed and not overemphasized.

They should also keep in mind that planning is the primary management function. Thus, as managers, they should not begin to organize, influence, or control until the planning process is complete. Planning is the foundation management function upon which all other functions at Nageldinger & Sons should be based.

STEPS IN THE PLANNING PROCESS

The six steps of the planning process are interrelated.

The planning process contains the following six steps:

1. *Stating organizational objectives*   A clear statement of organizational objectives is necessary for planning to begin since planning focuses on how the management system will reach those objectives.[6] Chapter 3 discusses how the objectives themselves are developed.
2. *Listing alternative ways of reaching objectives*   Once organizational objectives have been clearly stated, a manager should list as many available alternatives as possible for reaching those objectives.
3. *Developing premises upon which each alternative is based*   To a large extent, the feasibility of using any one alternative to reach organizational objectives is determined by the **premises**, or assumptions, upon which the alternative is based. For example, two alternatives a manager could generate to reach the organizational objective of increasing profit might be: (1) increase the sale of products presently being produced; or (2) produce and sell a completely new product. Alternative 1 would be based on the premise that the organization could get a larger share of an existing market. Alternative 2 would be based on the premise that a new product would capture a significant portion of a new market. A manager should list all of the premises for each alternative.
4. *Choosing the best alternative for reaching objectives*   An evaluation of alternatives must include an evaluation of the premises upon which the alternatives are based. A manager usually finds that the premises upon which some alternatives are based are unreasonable, and can therefore be excluded from further consideration. This elimination process helps in determining which alternative would be best to accomplish organizational objectives. The decision making required for this step is discussed more fully in Chapter 5.

FIGURE 4.2   Elements of the planning process.

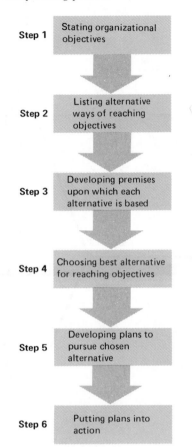

Step 1	Stating organizational objectives
Step 2	Listing alternative ways of reaching objectives
Step 3	Developing premises upon which each alternative is based
Step 4	Choosing best alternative for reaching objectives
Step 5	Developing plans to pursue chosen alternative
Step 6	Putting plans into action

5. *Developing plans to pursue the chosen alternative*   After an alternative has been chosen, a manager begins to develop strategic (long-range) and tactical (short-range) plans.[7] More information about strategic and tactical planning is presented in Chapter 6.

6. *Putting the plans into action*   Once plans have been developed, they are ready to be put into action. The plans should furnish the organization with both long-range and short-range direction for activity. Obviously, the organization does not directly benefit from the planning process until this step is performed.

Figure 4.2 shows how the six steps of the planning process relate to one another.

THE PLANNING SUBSYSTEM

Once managers understand the basics of planning, they can take steps to implement the planning process in their organization. This implementation is the key to a successful planning process. Even though managers might be experts on facts related to planning and the planning process, if they cannot transform

Implementation of the planning process is the key to success.

FIGURE 4.3   Relationship between overall management system and a subsystem.

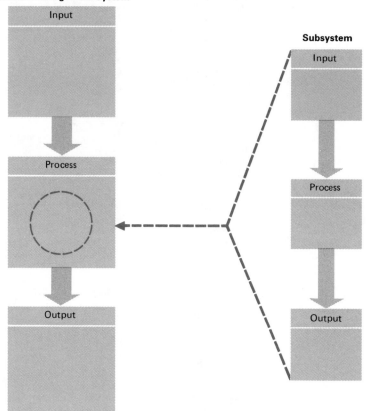

this understanding into appropriate action, they will not be able to generate useful organizational plans.

One way of approaching this implementation is to view planning activities as an organizational subsystem. A **subsystem** is a system created as part of the process of the overall management system. Figure 4.3 illustrates this relationship between the overall management system and a subsystem. Subsystems help managers to better organize the overall system and to enhance its success.

Figure 4.4 presents the elements of the planning subsystem. The purpose of this subsystem is to increase the effectiveness of the overall management system through more effective planning. The planning subsystem helps managers to better identify planning activities within the overall system and, therefore, to better guide and direct these activities.

The planning subsystem increases the effectiveness of the overall management system.

Obviously, only a portion of organizational resources are used as input in the planning subsystem. This input is allocated to the planning subsystem and transformed into output by following the steps of the planning process.

How planning subsystems are organized in the industrial world can be exemplified by the more informal planning subsystem at the Quaker Oats Company and the more formal planning subsystem at the Sun Oil Company.[8]

FIGURE 4.4   The planning subsystem.

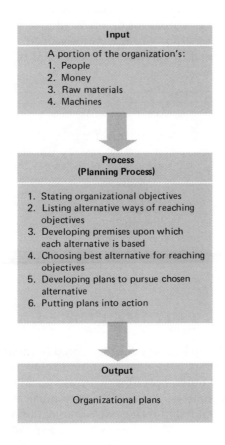

Input

A portion of the organization's:
1. People
2. Money
3. Raw materials
4. Machines

**Process
(Planning Process)**

1. Stating organizational objectives
2. Listing alternative ways of reaching objectives
3. Developing premises upon which each alternative is based
4. Choosing best alternative for reaching objectives
5. Developing plans to pursue chosen alternative
6. Putting plans into action

Output

Organizational plans

Quaker Oats Company

At Quaker Oats, speculations about the future are conducted, for the most part, on an informal basis. To help anticipate particular social changes in the future, the company has opened communication lines with various groups believed to be the harbingers of change. To spearhead this activity, a "non-committee" has been organized whose members represent a diversity of orientations. They listen to what is going on—monitor social changes—and thus augment the company's understanding of social change.

Quaker Oats plans on an informal basis.

Sun Oil Company

Several groups within Sun Oil Company are engaged in formal business planning and forecasting. Operational planning with a five-year horizon is done annually. The planning activity with the longest time horizon exists within the Sun Oil Company of Pennsylvania, the corporation's refining, transportation, and marketing arm. A centralized planning group, reporting to the vice-president of

Sun Oil plans on a formal basis.

development and planning, is responsible for assisting top management in setting the company's long-term objectives, developing plans to achieve these objectives, and identifying likely consumer needs and market developments of the future that might indicate business areas for diversification. Current efforts are focused on discussions of a series of long-range issues with the executive committee, a planning process designed to generate a restatement of long-term objectives.

BACK TO THE CASE

Harvey Moss believes that a plan needs to be designed and implemented for Nageldinger & Sons. The process of developing this plan should consist of six steps. It should begin with a statement of organizational objectives for Nageldinger & Sons and end with organizational plans being put into action.

To implement a planning process at Nageldinger & Sons, Ralph and Harvey should view planning as a subsystem that is part of the process of the overall management system. The Mosses would then use a portion of all of the organizational resources available at Nageldinger & Sons for the purpose of organizational planning. Naturally, the output of this subsystem would be the actual plans to be used in managing the company.

PLANNING AND THE CHIEF EXECUTIVE

The chief executive has many roles.

Henry Mintzberg of McGill University has pointed out that top managers or chief executives of organizations have many different roles to perform.[9] As organizational figureheads, they must represent their organizations in a variety of social, legal, and ceremonial matters. As leaders, they must ensure that organization members are properly guided in relation to organizational goals. As liaisons, they must establish themselves as links between their organizations and factors outside their organizations. As monitors, they must assess organizational progress. As disturbance handlers, they must settle disputes between organization members. And as resource allocators, they must determine where resources will be placed to benefit their organizations best.

The chief executive is also responsible for planning.

In addition to these many and varied roles, chief executives have the final responsibility for organizational planning. As the scope of planning broadens to include a larger portion of the management system, it becomes increasingly important for chief executives to become more involved in the planning process.

As planners, chief executives seek answers to the following broad questions:

1. In what direction should the organization be going?
2. In what direction is the organization going now?
3. Should something be done to change this direction?
4. Is the organization continuing in an appropriate direction?[10]

Keeping informed about social, political, and scientific trends is of utmost importance in helping chief executives to answer these questions.

Most chief executives obtain planning assistance from organization planners.

Given both the importance of top management participation in organizational planning and the importance of top management performing other time-consuming roles, more and more top managers obtain planning assistance by establishing a position for an organization planner.[11] Just as managers can ask others for help and advice in making decisions, so can they also involve others in formulating organizational plans.

Chief executives of most substantial organizations need help to plan.[12] The remainder of this chapter, therefore, assumes that the organization planner is an individual who is not the chief executive of the organization. The planner is presented as a manager responsible for giving assistance to the chief executive on organizational planning issues. If, by chance, the planner and the chief executive are the same person in a particular organization, the following discussion relating to the planner can be modified slightly to relate also to the chief executive.

THE PLANNER

Perhaps the most important input in the planning subsystem is the planner. This individual combines all other input and influences the subsystem process so that effective organizational plans become subsystem output. The planner is responsible not only for the plans that are developed but also for advising management about what action should be taken in relation to those plans.

Regardless of who actually does the planning, or the organization in which the planning is being done, the qualifications and duties of planners and how planners are evaluated are very important considerations in increasing the effectiveness of the planning subsystem.

Qualifications of Planners

Planners should have four primary qualifications. First, they should have considerable practical experience within their organization. Preferably, they should have been executives in one or more of the organization's major departments. This experience will help them develop plans that are practical and tailor-made for the organization.

Planners should be able to apply organizational experience,

Second, planners should be able to replace any narrow view of the organization (probably acquired while holding other organizational positions) with an understanding of the organization as a whole. They must know how all parts of the organization function and interrelate. In other words, they must possess an abundance of the conceptual skills mentioned in Chapter 1.

see the organization as a whole,

Third, planners should have some knowledge of and interest in the social, political, technical, and economic trends that could affect the future of the organization. They must be skillful in defining these trends and have the expertise to determine how the organization should react to them to maximize success. This particular qualification cannot be overemphasized.

detect and react to trends, and

The fourth and last qualification is that planners should be able to work well with others. They inevitably will work closely with several key members of the organization and should possess personal characteristics that are helpful in collaborating and advising effectively. The ability to communicate clearly, both orally and in writing, is one of the most important of these characteristics.[13]

get along with others.

Duties of Planners

Organizational planners have at least three general duties to perform: (1) overseeing the planning process; (2) evaluating developed plans; and (3) solving planning problems.[14]

Overseeing the Planning Process

First, and perhaps foremost, planners must see that planning gets done. To this end, they establish rules, guidelines, and planning objectives that apply to themselves and others involved in the planning process. In essence, planners must develop a plan for planning.

A plan for planning ensures that planning gets done.

Simply described, a **plan for planning** is a listing of all of the steps that must be taken to plan for an organization. A plan for planning generally includes such activities as evaluating an organization's present planning process in an effort to improve it, determining how much benefit an organization can gain as a result of planning, and developing a planning timetable to ensure that all of the steps necessary to plan for a particular organization are performed by some specified date.

Evaluating Developed Plans

Planners evaluate developed plans to see if they require modification.

The second general duty of planners is to evaluate plans that have been developed. Planners must decide if plans are sufficiently challenging for the organization, if plans are complete, and if plans are consistent with organizational objectives. If the developed plans do not fulfill these three requirements, they should be modified appropriately.

Solving Planning Problems

Planners recognize a problem, gather information, and then suggest solutions.

Planners also have the duty to gather information that will help solve planning problems. Sometimes, they may find it necessary to conduct special studies within the organization to obtain this information. They then can recommend what the organization should do in the future to deal with planning problems and forecast how the organization might benefit from related opportunities.

For example, a planner may observe that production objectives set by the organization are not being met. This is a symptom of a planning problem. The problem causing this symptom might be that objectives are unrealistically high or that plans developed to achieve production objectives are inappropriate. The planner must gather information pertinent to the problem and suggest to man-

---

FIGURE 4.5   Relationships among symptoms, problems, and opportunities that face the planner.

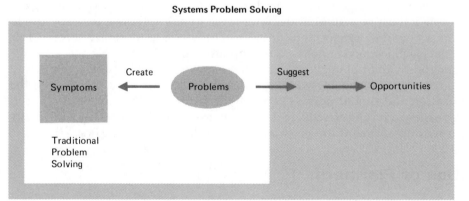

From William R. King and David I. Cleland, "A New Method for Strategic Systems Planning," *Business Horizons* (August 1975): 56. Copyright, 1975, by the Foundation for the School of Business at Indiana University. Reprinted by permission.

FIGURE 4.6   Responsibilities of an organization planner.

The planner has the responsibility to —

1. Provide information to assist management in formulating long- and short-range goals and plans of the company. Also assist in the updating of these goals plus general monitoring of attainment.
2. Coordinate activities and prepare special studies centring on acquisition, disposals, joint endeavours, manufacturing rights, and patents.
3. Serve as resource for determining the acquisition, disposal, and movement of physical properties.
4. Encourage the stimulation of ideas from management toward broadening company operations; extract these ideas and follow up on possibilities.
5. Develop, recommend, and obtain management approval of plans, procedures, and policies to be followed in implementing diversification program.
6. Perform basic research on diversification, using such sources as the Canadian Management Association, Conference Board of Canada, and others.
7. Perform internal and external economic studies to secure necessary information for overall planning.
8. Utilize staff service personnel plus line and committee persons in accumulating and evaluating data.
9. Analyze the company's physical properties and personnel capabilities to determine production spans.
10. In conjunction with staff services, periodically survey performance capabilities of sales, engineering, manufacturing, and service components of the company.
11. Conduct an initial survey of the manufacturing organization's physical properties (facilities, equipment, and tools) and keep information current.
12. Investigate and determine possibilities of other significant use for our basic products.
13. Assist in communicating and implementing the diversification decisions of management during transition periods.
14. Prepare necessary reports to keep management informed.

agement how the organization can solve its problem and become more successful. King and Cleland have presented the relationships among problems, symptoms, and opportunities in Figure 4.5.

The three duties of planners just discussed—overseeing the planning process, evaluating developed plans, and solving planning problems—are general comments on planners' activities. Figure 4.6 lists probable specific responsibilities of an organization planner at a large manufacturing company. As this list of responsibilities implies, the main focus of the planner's activities is to advise management on what should be done in the future. The planner assists management not only in determining appropriate future action but also in ensuring that the timing of that action is appropriate. In the end, the possibility always exists that the manager may not accept the planner's recommendations.

Planners advise management on what should be done in the future.

Evaluation of Planners

As with all other organization members, the planner's performance must be evaluated against the contribution made toward helping the organization achieve its objectives. The quality and appropriateness of the system for planning and the plans that the planner develops for the organization should be the primary considerations in this evaluation. Because the organizing, influencing, and controlling functions of the manager are based on the fundamental planning function, the evaluation of the planner becomes critically important.

Evaluation of the planner should be based on both an objective and subjective appraisal of performance.

Although assessment of the planner is somewhat subjective, a number of objective indicators do exist. For example, use of appropriate techniques is one objective indicator. If the planner is using appropriate techniques, it is probable that the planner is doing an acceptable job. The degree of objectivity displayed by the planner is another objective indicator. To a great extent, the planner's advice should be based on a rational analysis of appropriate information.[15] This is not to say that subjectivity and judgment should be excluded by the planner. This subjectivity and judgment, however, typically should be based on specific and appropriate information.

Z.A. Malik suggests that objective evidence that the planner is doing a reputable job exists if:

1. The organizational plan is in writing.
2. The plan is the result of all elements of the management team working together.
3. The plan defines present and possible future businesses of the organization.
4. The plan specifically mentions organizational objectives.
5. The plan includes future opportunities and suggestions on how to take advantage of them.
6. The plan emphasizes both internal and external environments.
7. The plan describes the attainment of objectives in operational terms when possible.
8. The plan includes both long- and short-term recommendations.[16]

These eight points furnish managers with some objective guidelines for evaluating a planner's performance. This evaluation, however, should never be completely objective. More subjective considerations include how well the planner gets along with key members of the organization, the amount of organizational loyalty displayed, and the planner's perceived potential.

BACK TO THE CASE

Technically, as chief executive officer of Nageldinger & Sons, Ralph Moss is responsible for organizational planning and performing such related time-consuming functions as keeping abreast of internal and external trends that could affect the future of the company. Because planning requires so much time, and because the chief executive officer of Nageldinger & Sons has many other responsibilities within the company in addition to organizational planning, Ralph might want to consider appointing a director of planning.

The organization planner at Nageldinger & Sons would need certain qualities. Ideally, the planner should have some experience at the company, be able to see it as an entire organization, have some ability to gauge and react to major trends that probably will af-

fect the company's future, and be able to work well with others. Ralph's son Harvey might be an ideal candidate.

If Harvey were to take over planning responsibilities at Nageldinger & Sons, he would be expected to oversee the planning process, evaluate developed plans, and solve planning problems. Perhaps the first problems he would have to tackle would be to develop plans for updating the company's manufacturing operations and for pointing Nageldinger & Sons in a profit-oriented direction.

Evaluation of Harvey as organization planner would be based on both an objective and subjective appraisal of his performance.

MAXIMIZING THE EFFECTIVENESS OF THE PLANNING PROCESS

Success in implementing a planning subsystem is not easily attainable. As the size of the organization increases, the planning task becomes more complicated, requiring more people, more information, and more complicated decisions.[17] Several safeguards, however, can ensure the success of an organizational planning effort. These safeguards include: (1) top management support; (2) an effective and efficient planning organization; (3) an implementation-focused planning orientation; and (4) inclusion of the right people.

Top Management Support

Top management in an organization must support the planning effort, or other organization members may not take the planning effort seriously.[18] Whenever possible, top management should actively help to guide and participate in planning activities. Furnishing the planner with whatever resources are needed to structure the planning organization, encouraging planning as a continuing process and not as a once-a-year activity, and preparing people for the changes that usually result from planning are clear signs that top management is solidly behind the planning effort. The chief executive must give continual and obvious attention to the planning process if it is to be successful.[19] He or she must not be so concerned about other matters that planning is not given the emphasis it deserves.[20]

All organization members should be aware that top management supports the planning effort.

An Effective and Efficient Planning Organization

A well-designed planning organization is the primary vehicle by which planning is accomplished and planning effectiveness is determined. The planner must take the time to design as efficient and effective a planning organization as possible.

The planning organization should have three built-in characteristics. First, it should be designed to use established management systems within the company. As expressed by Paul J. Stonich:

The planning organization should:

> Many organizations separate formal planning systems from the rest of the management systems that include organization, communication, reporting, evaluating, and performance review. These systems must not be viewed as separate from formal planning systems. Complex organizations need a comprehensive and coordinated set of management systems, including formal planning systems to help them toward their goals.[21]

1. Use established systems.

Second, the planning organization should be simple, yet complex enough to ensure a coordinated effort of all planning participants. Planning can be a complicated process requiring a somewhat large planning organization. The planner should strive to simplify the planning organization and make its complex facets as clearly understood as possible.

2. Be simple yet complex.

Lastly, the planning organization should be flexible and adaptable. Planning conditions are constantly changing, and the planning organization must be able to respond to these changing conditions.

3. Be flexible and adaptable.

An Implementation-Focused Planning Orientation

Planning should be aimed at implementation.

Because the end result of the planning process is some type of action that will help achieve stated organizational objectives, planning should be aimed at implementation.[22] As Peter Drucker points out, a plan is effective only if its implementation helps attain organizational objectives.[23] Plans should be developed and scrutinized after looking ahead to when they are to be implemented.[24] Ease of implementation is a positive feature of a plan that should be built in whenever possible.

Faulty implementation can doom plans.

The marketing plan of the Edsel automobile introduced by Ford in the 1950s is an example of how a sound plan can become unsuccessful simply because of ineffective implementation.[25] The rationale behind the Edsel was complete, logical, and defensible. Three consumer trends at that time solidly justified the automobile's introduction: (1) a trend toward buying higher-priced cars; (2) a general income increase for consumers had resulted in all income groups purchasing higher-priced cars; and (3) people who bought lower-priced Fords were trading them in on Buicks, Oldsmobiles, or Pontiacs after they became more affluent. Conceptually, these trends were so significant that Ford's plan to introduce the larger and more expensive Edsel appeared virtually risk-free.

Two factors in the implementation of this plan, however, turned the entire Edsel situation into a financial disaster. First, the network of controllers, dealers, marketing managers, and industrial relations managers created within Ford to get the Edsel to the consumer became very complicated and inefficient. Second, because Ford pushed as many Edsels as possible on the road immediately after introduction, the quality of the Edsel suffered, and consumers bought poorly manufactured products. Although the plan to make and market the Edsel was completely defensible, the long-term influence of the organization and manufacturing processes created to implement the plan doomed it to failure.

Inclusion of the Right People

Planners should seek input from various organization managers

Planning must include the right people.[26] Whenever possible, the planner should obtain input from the managers of the functional areas for which planning is being done. These managers are close to the everyday activity of their segments of the organization and can provide the planner with invaluable information. These managers probably also will be involved in implementing whatever plan develops and, therefore, can furnish the planner with feedback on how easily various plans are being implemented.

and also from individuals who will be directly affected by the plans.

Input from individuals who will be directly affected by the plans also can be helpful to the planner. These individuals actually do the work in the organization and can give opinions on how various alternative plans will influence work flow. Although it is extremely important that the planner involve others in the planning process, not all organization members can or should be involved. Stonich offers the following advice on the involvement of organization members in the planning process:

> In many corporations, the wrong sets of people participate in particular planning activities. Planning requires not only generation of information for making decisions, but decision making itself. The kinds of decisions and types of data needed should dictate the choice of who is involved in what aspects of planning within an organization.[27]

┌───┐
│ **BACK TO THE CASE** │
└───┘

Regardless of who actually ends up having primary responsibility for planning at Nageldinger & Sons, a number of safeguards can be taken to ensure that the planning efforts of this person will be successful. First, Ralph Moss and other top executives of the company should actively encourage planning activities and show support for the planning process. Second, the planning organization designed to implement the planning process should use established systems at the company, be simple yet complex, and be flexible and adaptable. Third, the entire planning process should be oriented toward easing the implementation of generated plans. Finally, all key people at Nageldinger & Sons should be included in the planning process.

Action Summary

Reread the learning objectives that follow. Each objective is followed by questions. Answering these questions accurately will help you to retain the most important concepts discussed in this chapter. After answering each question, check your answer with the answer key at the end of this chapter. (*Hint*: If you have doubt regarding the correct response, consult the page that follows the answer.)

From studying this chapter, I will attempt to acquire: **Circle:**

1. **A definition of planning and an understanding of the purposes of planning.**
   a. The affirmative purpose of planning is to increase the degree of organizational success.   T,F
   b. Which of the following is *not* one of the purposes of planning: (a) systematic; (b) protective; (c) affirmative; (d) coordination; (e) fundamental.   a, b, c, d, e

2. **A knowledge of the advantages and potential disadvantages of planning.**
   a. The advantages of planning include all of the following except: (a) helping managers to be future-oriented; (b) helping coordinate decisions; (c) requiring proper time allocation; (d) emphasizing organizational objectives; (e) all of the above are advantages of planning.   a, b, c, d, e
   b. The following is a potential disadvantage of planning: (a) too much time may be spent on planning; (b) an inappropriate balance between planning and other managerial functions may occur; (c) some important activities may be neglected; (d) incorrect use of the planning function could work to the detriment of the organization; (e) all of the above.   a, b, c, d, e

3. **Insights on how the major steps of the planning process are related.**
   a. The first major step in the planning process, according to the text, is: (a) developing premises; (b) listing alternative ways of reaching organizational objectives; (c) stating organizational objectives; (d) developing plans to pursue chosen alternatives; (e) putting plans into action.   a, b, c, d, e
   b. The assumptions on which alternatives are based are usually referred to as: (a) objectives; (b) premises; (c) tactics; (d) strategies; (e) probabilities.   a, b, c, d, e

4. **An understanding of the planning subsystem.**
   a. A subsystem is a system created as part of the process of the overall management system.   T,F
   b. The purpose of the planning subsystem is to increase the effectiveness of

the overall management system through which of the following: (a) systematizing the planning function; (b) more effective planning; (c) formalizing the planning process; (d) integrating the planning process; (e) none

a, b, c, d, e of the above.

5. **A knowledge of how the chief executive relates to the planning process.**
   a. The responsibility for organizational planning rests with middle manage-

T, F ment.
   b. The final responsibility for organizational planning rests with: (a) the planning department; (b) the chief executive; (c) departmental supervisors;

a, b, c, d, e (d) the organizational planner; (e) the entire organization.

6. **An understanding of the qualifications and duties of planners and how planners are evaluated.**
   a. The performance of the planner should be evaluated with respect to the contribution he or she makes toward helping the organization achieve its

T, F objectives.
   b. The organizational planner's full responsibilities are: (a) developing plans only; (b) advising about action that should be taken relative to the plans that the chief executive developed; (c) advising about action that should be taken relative to the plans of the board of directors; (d) selecting the

a, b, c, d, e person who will oversee the planning process; (e) none of the above.

7. **Guidelines on how to get the greatest return from the planning process.**

T, F a. Top management should encourage planning as an annual activity.
   b. Which of the following is *not* a built-in characteristic of an effective and efficient planning organization: (a) it should be designed to use established systems within a company; (b) it should be simple, yet complex enough to ensure coordinated effort; (c) it should cover an operating cycle of not more than one year; (d) it should be flexible and adaptable; (e) all of the above

a, b, c, d, e are characteristics of an effective and efficient planning organization.

INTRODUCTORY CASE WRAP-UP

"Ralph and Harvey Moss Must Plan" (p. 84) and its related back-to-the-case sections were written to help you better understand the management concepts contained in this chapter. Answer the following discussion questions about this introductory case to further enrich your understanding of the chapter content:

1. Do you think that Nageldinger & Sons has emphasized planning over the years? Explain.
2. What problems will Ralph and Harvey face in trying to make their company more of a planning organization?
3. Who would make a better planner for this organization—Ralph or Harvey? Explain.

Issues for Review and Discussion

1. What is planning?
2. What is the main purpose of planning?
3. List and explain the advantages of planning.
4. Why are the disadvantages of planning called *potential* disadvantages?
5. Explain the phrase *primacy of planning*.
6. List the six steps in the planning process.
7. Outline the relationships between the six steps in the planning process.
8. What is an organizational subsystem?

9. List the elements of the planning subsystem.
10. How do the many roles of a chief executive relate to his or her role as organizational planner?
11. Explain the basic qualifications of an organizational planner.
12. Give a detailed description of the general duties an organizational planner must perform.
13. How would you evaluate the performance of an organizational planner?
14. How can top management show its support of the planning process?
15. Describe the characteristics of an effective and efficient planning organization.
16. Why should the planning process emphasize the implementation of organizational plans?
17. Explain why the Edsel automobile failed to generate consumer acceptance.
18. Which people in an organization typically should be included in the planning process? Why?

Sources of Additional Information

Aguilar, F.J. *Scanning the Business Environment*. New York: Macmillan, 1967.

Alpander, Guvenc G. *Human Resources Management Planning*. New York: Amacom, 1982.

Belohlav, James A. "Long-Range Planning: Some Common Misconceptions." *Managerial Planning* 30 (September/October 1981): 41–43.

Belohlav, James A., and Herman A. Waggener. "Keeping the 'Strategic' in Your Strategic Planning." *Managerial Planning* (March/April 1980): 23–25.

Dilenschneider, R.L., and Richard C. Hyde. "Crisis Communications: Planning for the Unplanned." *Business Horizon* (January/February 1985): 35–41.

Donnelly, Robert M. *Guidebook to Planning: Strategic Planning and Budgeting Basics for the Growing Firm*. New York: Van Nostrand Reinhold, 1984.

Dyson, R.G., and M.J. Foster. "Making Planning More Effective." *Long-Range Planning* 16 (1983): 68–73.

Emery, J.C. *Organizational Planning and Control Systems*. New York: Macmillan, 1971.

Gluck, Frederick W., Stephen P. Kaufman, and A. Steven Walleck. "Strategic Management for Competitive Advantage." *Harvard Business Review* (July/August 1980): 154–61.

Hall, William K. "Survival Strategies in a Hostile Environment." *Harvard Business Review* (September/October 1980): 75–85.

Kaplan, Eileen E., and Jack M. Kaplan. "Career Planning: Gaining Managerial Commitment to the Planning Process." *Managerial Planning* 33 (July/August 1984): 48–50.

McConkey, Dale D. "If It's Not Broke—Fix It Anyway!" *Business Quarterly* 51 (Spring 1986): 50–52.

Naor, Jacob. "How to Make Strategic Planning Work for Small Business." *S.A.M. Advanced Management Journal* (Winter 1980): 35–39.

Nutt, Paul C. "Tactics of Implementation." *Academy of Management Journal* 29 (June 1986): 230–61.

Shim, Jae K., and Randy McGlade. "Current Trends in the Use of Corporate Planning Models." *Journal of Systems Management* 35 (September 1984): 24–31.

Steiner, G.A. *Managerial Long-Range Planning*. New York: McGraw-Hill, 1963.

Van Voorhis, Kenneth R. *Entrepreneurship and Small Business Management*. New York: Allyn & Bacon, 1980.

Yavitz, Boris, and William H. Newman. *Strategy in Action*. New York: Free Press, 1982.

Notes

1. Harry Jones, *Preparing Company Plans: A Workbook for Effective Corporate Planning* (New York: John Wiley & Sons, 1974), 3.
2. C.W. Roney, "The Two Purposes of Business Planning," *Managerial Planning* (November/December 1976): 1–6.
3. Harold Koontz and Cyril O'Donnell, *Management: A Systems and Contingency Analysis of Management Functions* (New York: McGraw-Hill, 1976), 130.
4. Harold Stieglitz, *The Chief Executive and His Job*, Personnel Policy Study no. 214 (New York: National Industrial Conference Board, 1969).
5. For a discussion of several of these disadvantages, see George R. Terry, *Principles of Management* (Homewood, Ill.: Irwin, 1972), 198–200.
6. George C. Sawyer, "The Hazards of Goal Conflict in Strategic Planning," *Managerial Planning* (May/June 1980): 11–13, 27.

7. For more detailed information on how strategic planning takes place, see Richard F. Vancil and Peter Lorange, "Strategic Planning in Diversified Companies," *Harvard Business Review* (January/February 1975): 81–90; and William R. King and David I. Cleland, "A New Method for Strategic Systems Planning," *Business Horizons* (August 1975): 55–64.

8. Excerpted, by permission of the publisher, from *1974–75 Exploratory Planning Briefs: Planning for the Future by Corporations and Agencies, Domestic and International,* © 1975 by AMACOM, a division of American Management Associations, pp. 10–11. All rights reserved.

9. Henry Mintzberg, "A New Look at the Chief Executive's Job," *Organizational Dynamics* (Winter 1973): 20–40.

10. Adapted from J.F.R. Perrin, *Focus on the Future* (London: Management Publications, 1971).

11. James M. Hardy, *Corporate Planning for Nonprofit Organizations* (New York: Association Press, 1972), 37.

12. Milton Leontiades, "The Dimensions of Planning in Large Industrialized Organizations," *California Management Review* 22 (Summer 1980): 82–86.

13. The section "Qualifications of Planners" is adapted from John Argenti, *Systematic Corporate Planning* (New York: John Wiley & Sons, 1974), 126.

14. These three duties are adapted from Walter B. Schaffir, "What Have We Learned About Corporate Planning?" *Management Review* (August 1973): 19–26.

15. Edward J. Green, *Wookbook for Corporate Planning* (New York: American Management Association, 1970).

16. Z.A. Malik, "Formal Long-Range Planning and Organizational Performance" (Ph.D. diss., Rensselaer Polytechnic Institute, 1974).

17. James Brian Quinn, "Managing Strategic Change," *Sloan Management Review* 21 (Summer 1980): 3–20.

18. Kamal E. Said and Robert E. Seiler, "An Empirical Study of Long-Range Planning Systems: Strengths—Weaknesses—Outlook," *Managerial Planning* 28 (July/August 1979): 24–28.

19. George A. Steiner, "The Critical Role of Management in Long-Range Planning," *Arizona Review*, April 1966.

20. Myles L. Mace, "The President and Corporate Planning," *Harvard Business Review* (January/February 1965): 49–62.

21. Paul J. Stonich, "Formal Planning Pitfalls and How to Avoid Them," *Management Review* (June 1975): 5–6.

22. Thomas A. Ratcliffe and David J. Logsdon, "The Business Planning Process—A Behavioral Perspective," *Managerial Planning* (March/April 1980): 32–37.

23. Peter F. Drucker, *Management: Tasks, Responsibilities, Practices* (New York: Harper & Row, 1973).

24. Bernard W. Taylor, III and K. Roscoe David, "Implementing an Action Program Via Organizational Change," *Journal of Economics and Business* (Spring/Summer 1976): 203–8.

25. William H. Reynolds, "The Edsel: Faulty Execution of a Sound Marketing Plan," *Business Horizons* (Fall 1967): 39–46.

26. To see how various management positions are typically involved in U.S. human resource planning, see Guvenc G. Alpander, "Human Resource Planning in U.S. Corporations," *California Management Review* 22 (Spring 1980): 24–32.

27. Stonich, "Formal Planning Pitfalls and How to Avoid Them," 5.

Action Summary Answer Key

1. a. T, p. 85
   b. a, p. 85
2. a. c, p. 87
   b. e, p. 87
3. a. c, p. 88
   b. b, p. 88
4. a. T, p. 90
   b. b, p. 90
5. a. F, p. 92
   b. b, p. 92
6. a. T, pp. 95–96
   b. e, p. 95
7. a. F, p. 97
   b. c, p. 97

INCREASES IN CRIME MEAN GROWTH FOR METROPOL

The Canadian security business is a growth industry. Vandalism, theft, and terrorism have created an $800 million market for security guards and security hardware. Sixty thousand Canadians are employed as security guards or investigators. Metropol Base-Fort Security Group of Winnipeg is the third-largest Canadian security firm and holds 7 percent of the Canadian market. The company's reputation for high quality has undoubtedly contributed to its rapid growth in the past few years.

Metropol was founded by a former RCMP officer in 1952. The current president, Pat Haney, joined Metropol in 1976 to run the Winnipeg operation. At that time, Winnipeg comprised 80 percent of the firm's business. Geographical expansion in the late 1970s and early 1980s and the late-1984 takeover of Alberta's leading security firm, Base-Fort Security Group, led to sales in 1985 of $30 million. Seventy percent of these sales were in Western Canada, where Metropol has offices in the four western provinces. The company also has offices in the Northwest Territories, Quebec, and Newfoundland.

In the spring of 1986, Haney was considering the firm's future. The security industry operates with low profit margins, and large multinational competitors, such as Pinkerton's Inc., were increasing their share of the market. Haney was concerned about Metropol's revenues: a full 90 percent came from security guard services. Haney believed that he had to find a way to distinguish Metropol's services from those of its competitors.

At the time, the demand for security services was expected to increase because of a rise in crime, higher insurance costs (thus encouraging loss prevention), and new security problems arising from technological innovations. Because start-up costs were low and there is no professional accreditation for those who work in the field, anyone could start a security firm simply by opening an office. The growing market also encouraged new competitors, who may have contributed to the security industry's already bad reputation; poor quality and a lack of reliability were common in the industry. The competition in the security guard business ran from small firms operated by former police officers to multinational corporations. Those in the security hardware business (alarms, fences, locks, electronic surveillance devices, and monitoring equipment) had to compete both with others selling the same goods and the security guard business, making the two businesses complementary and competitive at the same time.

"Metropol has managed to improve its main business activities with better security guard training."

Customers in the security business had little understanding of the industry. They often chose a security firm based on the lowest bid and were willing to switch companies to get a better deal. They would also bring the security function in-house if they thought it would save money. (Price-cutting in the security business is generally kept to a minimum by the low pre-tax profits of about 4 percent.) Another segment of the market, however, was well informed about security. Large companies with the potential for heavy losses from security breaches were choosing security firms based on reliability, reputation, and service quality, as well as price.

Taking these market and industry conditions into consideration, Haney believed that Metropol could succeed by offering superior services. He realized that some customers appreciated extra services and were willing to pay for them. Metropol was giving guards special training in handling emergencies such as bomb threats, hostage-taking incidents, and fires. To win loyalty from their customers, and to attract new clients, the firm was also running seminars on such topics as protection of proprietary

103

information. Metropol intended to maintain this high level of service and quality.

Metropol's size allowed for economies of scale when purchasing, which helped keep costs low. Because controlling costs is so important in a business with a low profit margin, Metropol was vigilant about monitoring all expenses.

Like other security firms, Metropol was experiencing an annual security guard turnover of about 100 percent. The firm was employing 1900 security guards and, since the work was low paying and boring, they could do little to reduce this high turnover.

Haney considered five possible alternatives for Metropol's future:

1. Continue the company operations with no changes in its current course.
2. Expand geographically to become a national firm.
3. Expand the range of products and services; for example, by developing Metropol brand security hardware.
4. Diversify into other services, such as nursing, secretarial, or janitorial services.
5. Enter the home security market as a supplier of such products and services as alarm systems, locks, mobile checks, and home sitting.

Haney decided to embark upon two of the alternatives; Metropol expanded geographically and moved into the home security market. In 1986, Toronto and Ottawa offices were opened and Metropol looked for an existing Ontario firm to buy in order to speed its entrance into that market. They also opened an office in Halifax. As well, Metropol Airport Security Services, a separate airport company, was established in May 1986. It now holds the contracts for security at every major Canadian airport.

A separate division of the parent firm, Metropol Emergency Response Centre, now handles the home security market. Two central stations, one in Winnipeg, the other in Edmonton, operate twenty-four hours a day monitoring houses equipped with alarm systems. Because the central stations are expensive to set up and run, Metropol uses long-distance telephone lines to monitor the houses and notify the local police when an alarm goes off. There are plans to open a central station in Toronto. To encourage potential customers, Metropol offers a financing program wherein alarm system payments can be spread out. Also, the company is advertising the home security service through newspaper ads and is planning a radio ad campaign.

Even with this expansion, Metropol has managed to improve its main business activities with better security guard training. Special training programs for guards working in different environments, such as hospitals and shopping malls, have been developed.

Not content with his firm's 4 to 6 percent growth each year, Pat Haney has ambitious plans for the future — including a possible expansion into the United States. Says the company's president, "We want to grow 20 percent, 30 percent, or 40 percent."

DISCUSSION ISSUES

1. Discuss the planning process at Metropol.
2. How does Pat Haney qualify as a planner? Elaborate.

Based on "Locking up profits," by Daniel Stoffman in *Canadian Business*, February 1987. Used with permission.

MAKING DECISIONS

STUDENT LEARNING OBJECTIVES

From studying this chapter, I will attempt to acquire:

1. A fundamental understanding of the term *decision*.
2. An understanding of each element of the decision situation.
3. An ability to use the decision-making process.
4. An appreciation for the various situations in which decisions are made.
5. An understanding of probability theory and decision trees as decision-making tools.

CHAPTER OUTLINE

INTRODUCTORY CASE 5

IMPORTANT DECISIONS AT TORO

Nearly everyone recognizes the name "Toro." The Toro Company is a leading manufacturer of outdoor power equipment. As such, Toro's product line includes lawn mowers, tillers, snowblowers, and chain saws. Since the Toro Company sells lawn mowers in the summer and snow-removal equipment in the winter, it was once considered to have an ideal product line.

Recently, however, two mild winters in a row reduced Toro's snowblower sales from $130 million to $6 million during a two-year period. Naturally, this drastic sales reduction trapped many retail outlets with excessive inventories of Toro snow-related equipment.

Ken Melrose, Toro's president, admits that some of the decisions made to overcome this undesirable financial picture were not the best. For example, Toro attempted to open up new sales avenues by extending its distribution of products to mass merchandisers. This move, however, primarily resulted in antagonizing Toro's long-established, independent distributors and dealers rather than opening up new sales avenues. As another example, Toro decided to bring out a new, less expensive lawn mower whose sales could help make up for the drop in sales of snow-related products. The quality of these mowers turned out to be inferior to Toro's usual products, however. For that reason, the mowers posed a real danger to Toro, since Toro customers rely very heavily upon product quality.

Finally, in response to the continued weakening demand for Toro's products and worsening financial condition of the company, Melrose decided to cut operating expenses. He reduced Toro's work force from 4000 to 1700 employees and temporarily closed the company's six snowblower and lawn mower plants. This cost-cutting tactic contributed significantly to Toro chalking up its first profit in nearly three years.

The future undoubtedly will challenge Melrose further by requiring him to make complicated decisions like: If weather conditions change so that demand for snow-related equipment skyrockets, how will Toro increase its manufacturing capability? If government regulations require new safety devices on Toro products, how will Toro handle the increased cost of these devices relative to product pricing? How will Toro best handle the seemingly increasing competition from companies like Sears and Honda?

While it is impossible to know exactly what decisions Melrose will have to make during his future years at Toro, it is certain that he will have to make many of them.

Based on "Another Mile to Go," by Jill Andresky in *Forbes*, April 25, 1983.

108

What's Ahead

The introductory case ends with the comment that Ken Melrose will undoubtedly have many difficult decisions to make during his future years as president of Toro. The purpose of this chapter is to assist individuals such as Melrose by discussing: (1) the fundamentals of decisions; (2) the elements of the decision situation; (3) the decision-making process; (4) various decision-making conditions; and (5) decision-making tools. These topics are critical to managers and other individuals who make decisions.

FUNDAMENTALS OF DECISIONS

Definition of a Decision

A **decision** is a choice made between two or more available alternatives. "Choosing the best alternative for reaching objectives," the fourth step of the planning process as presented in Chapter 4, is, strictly speaking, making a decision. Although decision making is covered in the planning section of this text, a manager also must make decisions when performing the other three managerial functions: organizing, controlling, and influencing.

> A decision is a choice between alternatives.

Everyone is faced with decision situations each day. Perhaps a decision situation simply involves choosing among studying, swimming, or golfing when considering alternative ways of spending the day. It does not matter which alternative is chosen, only that a choice is actually made.[1]

A practising manager must make numerous decisions every day.[2] Not all of these decisions are equal in significance to the organization. Some affect a large number of organization members, are costly to carry out, and/or have a long-term effect on the organization. These significant decisions can have a major impact not only on the management system itself but also on the career of the manager. Other decisions are fairly insignificant and affect only a small number of organization members, cost very little to carry out, and have only a short-term effect on the organization.

Types of Decisions

Decisions can be categorized by how much time a manager must spend in making them, what proportion of the organization must be involved in making them, and the organizational functions on which they focus.[3] Probably the most generally accepted method of categorizing decisions, however, is based on computer language and divides decisions into two basic types: programmed and nonprogrammed.[4]

FIGURE 5.1   Traditional and modern ways of handling programmed and non-programmed decisions.

Types of Decisions	Decision–Making Techniques	
	Traditional	*Modern*

Programmed:
Routine, repetitive decisions
Organization develops specific
    processes for handling them
	1. Habit
	2. Clerical routine:
	    Standard operating
	        procedures
	3. Organization structure:
	    Common expectations
	    A system of subgoals
	    Well–defined
	        informational channels
		1. Operations research:
		    Mathematical analysis
		    Models
		    Computer simulation
		2. Electronic data
		    processing

Nonprogrammed:
One–shot, ill–structured,
    novel, policy decisions
Handled by general problem–
    solving processes
	1. Judgment, intuition,
	    and creativity
	2. Rules of thumb
	3. Selection and training
	    of executives
		Heuristic problem–solving
		    techniques applied to:
		(a) training human
		        decision makers
		(b) constructing heuristic
		        computer programs

From Herbert A. Simon, *The Shape of Automation* (New York: Harper & Row, 1965) p. 62. Used with permission of the author.

Programmed decisions are routine and repetitive.

Programmed decisions are routine and repetitive, and the organization typically develops specific ways to handle them. A programmed decision might involve determining how products will be arranged on the shelves of a grocery store. This is a routine and repetitive problem for the organization, and standard arrangement decisions typically are made according to established management guidelines.

Non-programmed decisions are one-shot occurrences.

Non-programmed decisions, on the other hand, typically are one-shot occurrences and are usually less structured than programmed decisions. A non-programmed decision might involve whether or not a grocery store should carry an additional type of bread. This decision would be more of a "one-shot" occurrence and certainly would not be clear-cut. The manager must consider whether the new bread will stabilize bread sales by competing with existing bread carried in the store or increase bread sales by offering a choice of bread to the customer who has never bought bread in the store. These types of issues must be dealt with before the manager can finally decide whether or not to offer the new bread in the store. Figure 5.1 shows traditional and modern ways of handling programmed and non-programmed decisions.

Programmed and non-programmed decisions should be thought of as being at opposite ends of a programming continuum, as shown in Figure 5.2. The continuum also indicates that some decisions may not clearly be either programmed or non-programmed, but some combination of the two.

FIGURE 5.2   Continuum of extent of decision programming.

The Responsibility for Making Organizational Decisions

Many different kinds of decisions must be made within an organization—such as how to manufacture a product, how to maintain machines, how to ensure product quality, and how to establish advantageous relationships with customers. With varied decisions of this sort, some type of rationale must be developed that stipulates who within the organization has the responsibility for making which decisions.

One such rationale is based primarily on two factors: the scope of the decision to be made, and the levels of management. The **scope of the decision** refers to the proportion of the total management system that the decision will affect. The greater this proportion, the broader the scope of the decision is said to be. *Levels of management* simply refers to lower-level management, middle-level management, and upper-level management. The rationale for designating who makes which decisions is this: The broader the scope of a decision, the higher the level of the manager responsible for making that decision. Figure 5.3 illustrates this rationale.

> The broader the scope of a decision, the higher the level of the manager responsible for making that decision.

One example of this decision-making rationale is the manner in which E.I. DuPont de Nemours and Company handles decisions related to the research and development function.[5] As you can see from Figure 5.4, this organization has relatively narrow-scope research and development decisions, such as "which markets to test," made by lower-level managers, and relatively broad-scope research and development decisions, such as "authorize full-scale plant construction," made by upper-level managers.

Even though a manager may have the responsibility for making a particular decision, he or she can ask the advice of other managers, and/or subordinates. In fact, some managers advise having groups make certain decisions.

Consensus is one method a manager can use in getting a group to arrive at

---

FIGURE 5.3   Level of managers responsible for making decisions as decision scope increases from *A* to *B* to *C*.

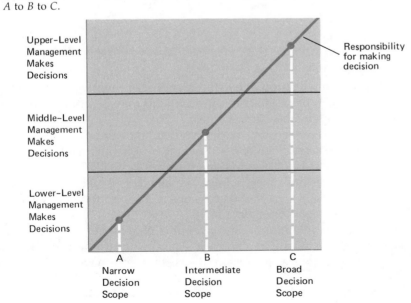

FIGURE 5.4 How scope of decision affects management level making decision at E. I. DuPont de Nemours and Company.

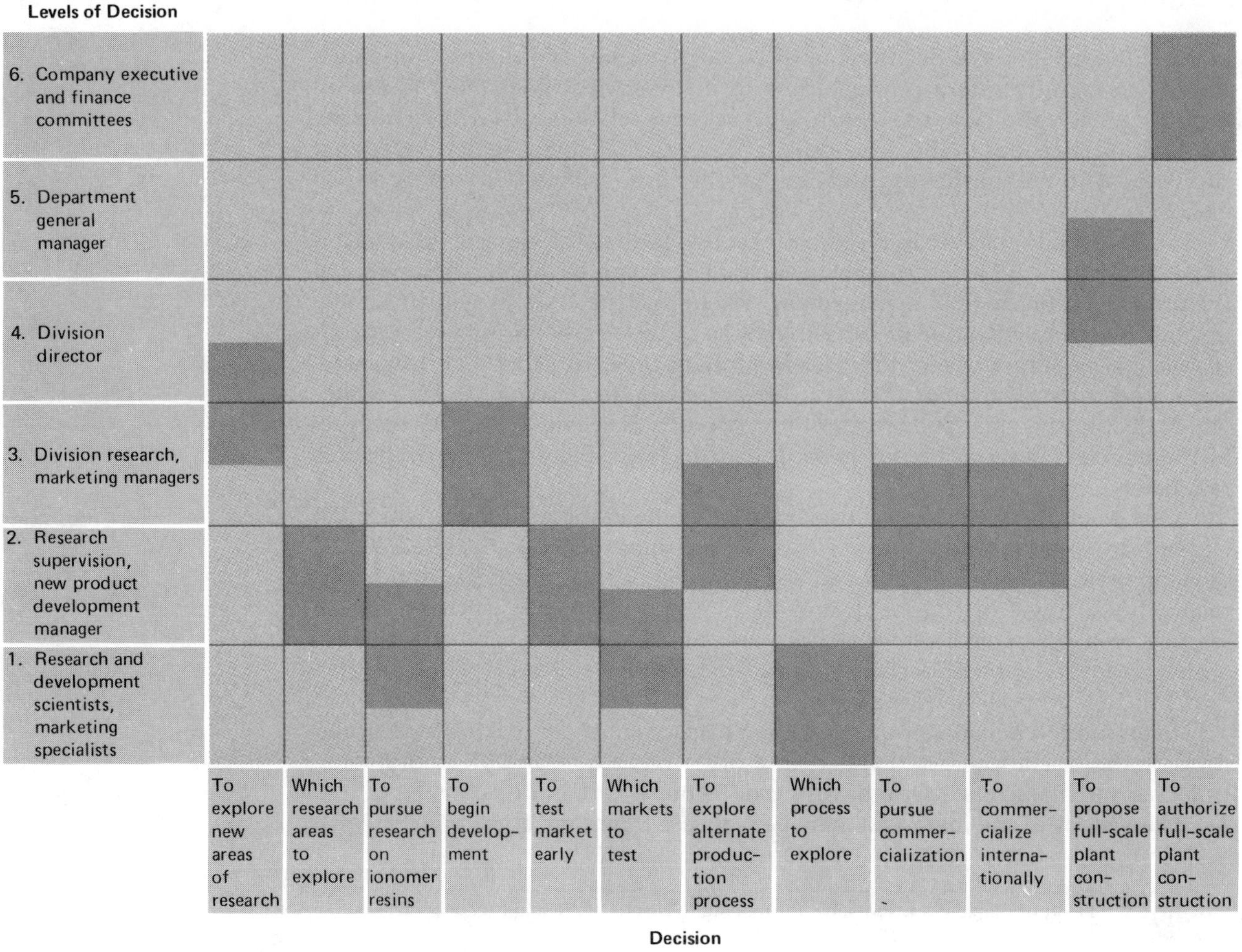

Levels of Decision

6. Company executive and finance committees
5. Department general manager
4. Division director
3. Division research, marketing managers
2. Research supervision, new product development manager
1. Research and development scientists, marketing specialists

Decisions (columns):
To explore new areas of research | Which research areas to explore | To pursue research on ionomer resins | To begin development | To test market early | Which markets to test | To explore alternate production process | Which process to explore | To pursue commercialization | To commercialize internationally | To propose full-scale plant construction | To authorize full-scale plant construction

Decision

Republished with permission of E. I. du Pont de Nemours & Company.

a particular decision.[6] Consensus is agreement on a decision by all individuals involved in making the decision. It usually occurs after lengthy deliberation and discussion by members of the decision group, who may be either all managers or a mixture of managers and subordinates.

Decisions through consensus have both advantages and disadvantages. One advantage is that managers can focus "several heads" on making a decision. Another is that individuals in the decision group are more likely to be committed to implementing a decision if they helped to make it. The main disadvantage to decisions through consensus is that discussions relating to the decisions tend to be quite lengthy and, therefore, very costly.

The Management in Action feature for this chapter focuses on Dofasco's decision-making orientation. The company's family atmosphere helps Dofasco remain among the top ten steelmakers in the world despite a worldwide decrease in the demand for steel.

Decisions through consensus: Everyone agrees.

DOFASCO DOES MORE THAN JUST COPE

The North American steel industry is in trouble. In the U.S., firms are experiencing serious problems. The second-largest integrated steelmaker, LTV Corporation, filed for bankruptcy in 1986. USX Corporation, the largest producer of steel in the U.S., is plagued with strikes and was the object of a takeover bid; this despite losses of US$183 million in the third quarter of 1986. Although we haven't seen the same occurrences in Canada, there are serious challenges for the industry as a whole and for individual Canadian steelmakers.

The market for steel in North America is shrinking and becoming highly competitive. Once-profitable firms considered to be secure employers are facing large financial losses and have been forced to lay off long-term employees. Algoma Steel Corporation Ltd. of Sault Ste. Marie, Ontario, hasn't made a profit since 1981 and has laid off 3500 workers since that time. With the first nine months of 1986 posting a $127 million loss, more layoffs are planned for the future. Since 1981, Canada's largest steelmaker, Stelco Inc., has let 4000 workers go from its one-time 12 000-strong labour force at its Hamilton steel works. Stelco's profit for the first nine months of 1986 was $56 million, down from $61.7 million the previous year.

But at Dofasco Inc., Stelco's neighbour in Hamilton, things are going a bit differently, and there are no plans to lay off any of the company's 11 800 employees. Although profits dropped to $101 million for the first nine months of 1986 from $104.4 million during the same period the year before, Dofasco's profit was almost double that of Stelco's. Dofasco is North America's most profitable integrated steelmaker and rates among the top ten in the world. In 1985, the firm produced one quarter of Canada's flat-rolled steel. The 1986 drop in profits was expected due to the scheduled shutdown of Dofasco's largest blast furnace for rebuilding.

Dofasco faces the same challenges that are effectively sinking other North American steelmakers. The demand for steel has decreased both in North America and worldwide. New competitors from countries such as Korea, Brazil, and Taiwan have joined more traditional rivals from Europe and Japan in the search for a fair share of a shrinking market. Costs in the steelmaking industry have increased tremendously while the North American economy is becoming more service based and less industrial. Some industry analysts are understandably pessimistic about the survival of Canadian steelmakers.

"one reason for Dofasco's success—a commitment to technological upgrading."

Others agree that the problems are severe, but not insurmountable. They believe that the steel industry is experiencing a down period in the demand cycle, and that smart Canadian steelmakers will rationalize their operations to remain competitive and take advantage of opportunities in the new U.S.-Canada trade relationship. In spite of industry forecasts, why has Dofasco not suffered the same fate as its rivals?

Dofasco traditionally has never overreacted to problems. The firm promotes an informal family atmosphere and shirt-sleeved management style. Dofasco's aim, despite industry problems, is to produce the highest quality steel possible. The company laid plans to lower costs and increase its efficiency in the mid-1970s. It then began a $2 billion capital spending program that is due for completion in the early 1990s. One way it will increase efficiency is by spending $750 million on a continuous-casting facility which will process molten steel directly into hot-rolled coils, thereby eliminating the ingot stage of steelmaking. Industry insiders see this as one reason for Dofasco's success—a commitment to technological upgrading. Another reason is Dofasco's No. 2 Melt Shop in Hamilton, which began operations in 1978. In this the last and largest of four shops that were built, a sophisticated computerized system runs the 200-tonne basic oxygen furnace which turns liquid iron, scrap metal, and elements such as carbon, silicon, and manganese into steel. Operators in the control room monitor video terminals which provide up-to-the-minute information on the temperature and chemical composition of the steel. Delicate sensing devices provide feedback on every stage of the process so that corrections can be made as the steel is produced, without stopping or slowing the process. This not only saves time and money but also helps to produce a high-end steel that is quickly becoming the market standard.

Dofasco's history of stable labour relations is also cited as a major reason for its success. The non-unionized firm has a reputation for reliability. Paternalism is a standard reinforced through the company slogan, "Our product is steel. Our strength is people." Dofasco commits considerable resources to promoting its family and community image. The idea of family is strong at Dofasco, and a significant portion of the labour force is comprised of fathers, sons, wives, and daughters. The 1986 Christmas party saw more than 30 000 employees and their families attend what Dofasco claims is one of the world's largest Christmas parties.

The firm's Employees Savings and Profit-Sharing Fund stands as a major example of the Dofasco way. The firm contributes 11 percent of pre-tax profits and all employees with more than three years of service are members, each receiving an equal share of the funds. Intended as a retirement fund, employees contribute up to $200 a year. An individual with forty years of service could leave with $350 000. Dofasco's Suggestion Program rewards employees with up to $30 000 for ideas that save or earn the company money. The firm also boasts of its "open-door policy," wherein employees can go right to Dofasco's president if they feel their complaints or concerns have not been adequately dealt with lower down.

Perhaps due to all these measures, there never has been—nor probably ever will be—a union at Dofasco. As early as the 1920s, the firm introduced some benefits and improved working conditions. The mid-1930s wave of industrial unionism saw the introduction of the profit-sharing and the suggestion programs, as well as other programs. These measures undoubtedly helped to head off the United Steelworkers of America's (USW) efforts to unionize the company. In addition, a relationship exists between the unionized workers at Stelco and Dofasco's non-unionized work force in that whenever Stelco workers settle a contract, their counterparts at Dofasco receive virtually the same terms and conditions. This has led Robert Storey, a professor in the Department of Labour Studies at McMaster University in Hamilton, to note, "Given the state of current industrial unionism in this country and the effectiveness of Dofasco's corporate style, there isn't much in the material sense that the USW can offer Dofasco workers right now. Still, what's missing for them, in my opinion, is a real part in the control of the

production process. On an intangible level, the question of a union at Dofasco comes down to a choice between things people have to struggle for and win versus things they're given by a paternalistic employer and so can be taken away." Should Dofasco ever take away jobs, its image and corporate philosophy would be severely challenged. Furthermore, the USW would take full advantage of such an event.

A third major reason for Dofasco's success in this difficult period is its ability to go out and sell its product; it has excellent sales and marketing skills. Dofasco knows the reason it makes steel is to make money, and it sells its steel just as efficiently as it produces it. A small sales and service staff located right in the middle of the company's grounds keeps operating costs down and ensures that orders are handled efficiently. Sales and service personnel can go right to the production supervisors and forepersons to discuss problems and customer orders. Ninety percent of the firm's sales are to the domestic market, the majority within a 480-kilometre radius of Hamilton. There are currently about 700 customers, including such giants as General Motors of Canada Ltd., Continental Group of Canada Ltd., and the auto-parts maker, Magna International Inc. Dofasco prides itself on taking care of its customers by listening to their problems and thanking them for their orders. When downswings occur in the steel market, Dofasco will use its good relations with its customers to go out and create new uses for its products. Also, anticipating future market conditions has meant that Dofasco has planned for and reacted more quickly to changing situations. During the 1982 recession, U.S. and other Canadian steelmakers were stuck with big inventories and substantial losses. Dofasco had to lay off 2000 workers that fall, but it was able to recall them all within one year. The firm also realized a $63.8 million profit on sales of $1.5 billion. Meanwhile, Stelco's 1982 sales were $2 billion, but its losses were $40.8 million.

What does the future hold for Dofasco? With mature economies needing less steel for power plants, pipelines, refineries, or chemical plants, steelmakers must look to other areas for growth. Since 1981, Dofasco has been investing in businesses other than steel. In that year, it acquired a 10 percent share of Calgary's Aberford Resources Ltd., an oil and gas exploration company. In 1985, Dofasco bought 20 percent of ITL Industries Ltd., a Windsor, Ontario company that makes plastic automotive parts and molding equipment. Dofasco is still clearly committed to the steelmaking industry; its emphasis on improved steelmaking efficiency is proof of that. But following the traditions that have built the firm, Dofasco is going about ensuring that its success extends long into the future.

Based on "Industrial Evolution," by Morton Ritts in *Canadian Business*, February 1987. Used with permission.

BACK TO THE CASE

If Ken Melrose, president of Toro Company, were forced to confront an issue such as increasing Toro's manufacturing capability for snow-related equipment, he would definitely be faced with a formal decision situation, a situation requiring him to pick one of a number of solutions. Melrose would need to scrutinize this decision carefully because of its significance to the organization and to Melrose himself. Technically, this decision would be non-programmed in nature and therefore would be characterized more by judgment than by simple quantitative data.

As the president of Toro, Melrose would probably have the ultimate responsibility for making such a broad-scope decision. This does not mean, however, that Melrose would have to make the decision by himself. He could ask for advice from Toro employees and perhaps even appoint a group of managers/employees to arrive at a consensus on which decision alternative should be implemented.

ELEMENTS OF THE DECISION SITUATION

Wilson and Alexis have indicated that there are six basic parts or elements to the decision situation.[7] These parts and their respective definitions follow.

State of Nature

State of nature refers to the aspects of the decision maker's environment that can affect the choice. Robert B. Duncan conducted a study in which he attempted to identify environmental characteristics that influenced decision makers. He grouped the characteristics into two categories: the internal environment and the external environment (see Figure 5.5).[8]

Environmental characteristics influence decision makers.

FIGURE 5.5   Environmental factors that can influence managerial decision making.

Internal Environment	External Environment

1. Organizational personnel component
   a. Educational and technological background and skills
   b. Previous technological and managerial skill
   c. Individual member's involvement and commitment to attaining system's goals
   d. Interpersonal behaviour styles
   e. Availability of human resources for utilization within the system
 	
2. Organizational functional and staff units component
   a. Technological characteristics of organizational units
   b. Interdependence of organizational units in carrying out their objectives
   c. Intraunit conflict among organizational functional and staff units
 	
3. Organizational level component
   a. Organizational objectives and goals
   b. Integrative process integrating individuals and groups into contributing maximally to attaining organizational goals
   c. Nature of the organization's product service
	4. Customer component
	   a. Distributors of product or service
	   b. Actual users of product or service
	
	5. Suppliers component
	   a. New materials suppliers
	   b. Equipment suppliers
	   c. Product parts suppliers
	   d. Labour supply
	
	6. Competitor component
	   a. Competitors for suppliers
	   b. Competitors for customers
	
	7. Sociopolitical component
	   a. Government regulatory control over the industry
	   b. Public political attitude towards industry and its particular product
	   c. Relationship with trade unions with jurisdiction in the organization
	
	8. Technological component
	   a. Meeting new technological requirements of own industry and related industries in production of product or service
	   b. Improving and developing new products by implementing new technological advances in the industry

Reprinted from "Characteristics of Organizational Environments and Perceived Environmental Uncertainty," by Robert B. Duncan. Published by *Administrative Science Quarterly*, Vol. 17, No. 3 (September 1972). By permission of *Administrative Science Quarterly*.

The Decision Makers

Decision makers are the individuals or groups who actually make the choice between alternatives. According to Ernest Dale, weak decision makers can have four different orientations: receptive, exploitation, hoarding, and marketing.[9]

Decision makers who have a receptive orientation feel that the source of all good is outside themselves, and therefore they rely heavily on suggestions from other organization members. Basically, they like others to make their decisions for them.

Decision makers with an exploitation orientation also believe that good is outside themselves, and they are willing to take ethical or unethical steps to steal ideas necessary to make good decisions. They build their organization on the ideas of others and typically extend little or no credit for the ideas to anyone but themselves.

The hoarding orientation is characterized by decision makers who preserve the status quo as much as possible. They accept little outside help, isolate themselves from others, and are extremely self-reliant. These decision makers emphasize maintaining their present existence.

Marketing-oriented decision makers consider themselves commodities that are only as valuable as the decisions they make. They try to make decisions that will enhance their value and are therefore conscious of what others think of their decisions.

> Ideal decision makers emphasize reason and sound judgment.

The ideal decision-making orientation is one that emphasizes trying to realize the potential of the organization as well as of the decision maker. Ideal decision makers try to use all of their talents and are influenced mainly by reason and sound judgment. They do not possess the qualities of the four undesirable decision-making orientations just described.

Goals to Be Served

> Goals are usually organizational objectives.

The goals that decision makers seek to attain are another element of the decision situation. In the case of managers, these goals should most often be organizational objectives. (Chapter 3 contains specifics about organizational objectives.)

Relevant Alternatives

> Relevant alternatives can be implemented to solve an existing problem.

The decision situation is usually comprised of at least two relevant alternatives. A **relevant alternative** is one that is considered feasible for implementation and also for solving an existing problem. Alternatives that cannot be implemented or will not solve an existing problem are irrelevant alternatives and should be excluded from the decision-making situation.

Ordering of Alternatives

> Decision makers rank alternatives.

The decision situation must have a process or mechanism that ranks alternatives from most desirable to least desirable. The process can be subjective, objective, or some combination of the two. Past experience of the decision maker is an example of a subjective process, and the rate of output per machine is an example of an objective process.

Choice of Alternatives

The last element of the decision situation is an actual choice between available alternatives. This choice establishes the fact that a decision is made. Typically, managers choose the alternative that maximizes long-term return for the organization.

The chosen alternative maximizes long-term return.

⊞ BACK TO THE CASE

If Ken Melrose had to make a decision about whether or not to increase Toro's manufacturing capability for snow-related equipment, he would need to be aware of all of the elements in the decision situation. Both the internal and external environments of Toro would be one focus of Melrose's analysis. For example, internally, does Toro have the human resources and equipment to increase its manufacturing capability? Externally, is there a customer market for snow-related equipment? Reason and sound judgment would need to character-

ize Melrose's orientation as a decision maker. Also, Melrose would have to keep Toro's organizational objectives in mind and list relevant alternatives to the increase in manufacturing capability of snow-related equipment. For example, one relevant alternative might be to increase Toro's manufacturing capability of lawn mowers. In addition, Melrose would need to list relevant alternatives in some order of desirability before choosing an alternative to implement.

⊞ THE DECISION-MAKING PROCESS

A decision is choosing one alternative from a set of available alternatives. The **decision-making process** is defined as the steps the decision maker takes to actually choose this alternative. Evaluation of a decision should be at least partially based on the process used to make the decision.[10]

A model of the decision-making process is presented in Figure 5.6. In order of occurrence, the decision-making steps this model suggests are: (1) identifying an existing problem; (2) listing possible alternatives to solve this problem; (3) selecting the most beneficial of these alternatives; (4) putting the selected alternative into action; and (5) gathering feedback to find out if the implemented alternative is solving the identified problem. The paragraphs that follow elaborate upon each of these steps and explain their interrelationships.

This model of the decision-making process is based on three primary assumptions.[11] First, the model assumes that humans are economic beings with the

The decision-making process makes three assumptions.

FIGURE 5.6   Model of the decision-making process.

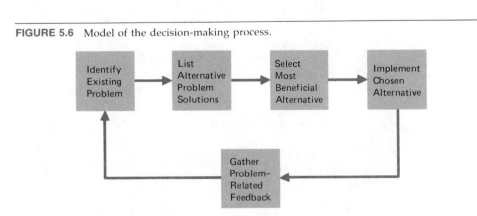

objective of maximizing satisfaction or return. Second, the model is based on the assumption that within the decision-making situation all alternative solutions as well as the possible consequences of each alternative are known. The last assumption is that decision makers have some priority system that allows them to rank the desirability of each alternative. If each of these assumptions is met in the decision-making situation, decision makers probably will make the best possible decision for the organization. In reality, one or more of these assumptions usually are not met, and related decisions, therefore, are usually something less than the best possible for the organization.

Identifying an Existing Problem

Problems are barriers to goal attainment and must be identified.

Decision making is essentially a problem-solving process that involves eliminating barriers to organizational goal attainment. Naturally, the first step in this elimination process is identifying exactly what these problems or barriers are. Only after the barriers have been adequately identified can management take steps to eliminate them. Chester Barnard has stated that organizational problems are brought to the attention of managers mainly through: (1) orders issued by managers' supervisors; (2) situations relayed to managers by their subordinates; and/or (3) the normal activity of the managers themselves.[12]

Listing Alternative Problem Solutions

Once a problem has been identified, managers should list the various alternative problem solutions. Very few organizational problems can be solved in only one way. Managers must search out the many alternative solutions that exist for most organizational problems.

A manager's decision alternatives are limited by various factors.

Before searching for alternative solutions, managers must be aware of five limitations on the number of problem-solving alternatives available: (1) authority factors (for example, a manager's superior may have told the manager that the alternative was feasible); (2) biological factors (for example, human factors within the organization may be inappropriate for implementing the alternatives); (3) physical factors (for example, physical facilities of the organization may be inappropriate for certain alternatives to be seriously considered); (4) technological factors (for example, the level of organizational technology may be inadequate

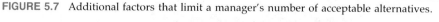

FIGURE 5.7   Additional factors that limit a manager's number of acceptable alternatives.

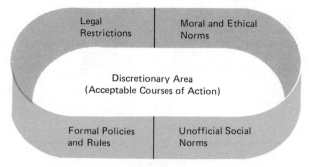

for certain alternatives); and (5) economic factors (for example, certain alternatives may be too costly for the organization).[13]

Figure 5.7 presents additional factors that can limit managers' decision alternatives. This figure uses the term *discretionary area* to designate feasible alternatives available to managers. Factors that limit this discretionary area are legal restrictions, moral and ethical norms, formal policies and rules, and unofficial social norms.[14]

Selecting the Most Beneficial Alternative

Decision makers can select the most beneficial solution only after they have evaluated each alternative very carefully. This evaluation should consist of three steps. First, decision makers should list, as accurately as possible, the potential effects of each alternative as if the alternative had already been chosen and implemented. Second, a probability factor should be assigned to each of these potential effects. This would indicate how probable the occurrence of the effect would be if the alternative was implemented. Third, keeping organizational goals in mind, decision makers should compare each alternative's expected effects and their respective probabilities. The alternative that seems to be most advantageous to the organization should be chosen for implementation.

Each alternative should undergo a three-step evaluation.

Implementing the Chosen Alternative

The next step is to actually put the chosen alternative into action. Decisions must be supported by appropriate action if they are to have a chance of being successful.

Gathering Problem-Related Feedback

After the chosen alternative has been implemented, decision makers must gather feedback to determine the effect of the implemented alternative on the identified problem. If the identified problem is not being solved, managers need to search out and implement some other alternative.

Decision action is evaluated through feedback.

BACK TO THE CASE

If Ken Melrose were facing a decision such as how to increase product safety, he would first need to identify the problem. For example, he would need to find out if customer injury was the result of faulty parts, inadequate safety devices, or poor operating instructions. Once he identified the problem, he would have to list all possible problem solutions—for example: Can the quality of parts be improved? Would better operating instructions reduce the risk of injury? Can additional safety devices be invented?

After eliminating infeasible solutions, Melrose would have to evaluate all remaining solutions, select

one, and implement it. If operating instructions were unreliable because of customer error or if better-quality parts were too expensive to manufacture, the best alternative might be to create new safety devices for Toro products. Melrose would then have to instruct his employees to design and manufacture such devices. Problem-related feedback would be extremely important once the safety devices were added. Melrose would need to find out if the new devices did, in fact, reduce customer injury. If they did not, he would need to decide what additional action should be taken to improve product safety.

⊞ DECISION-MAKING CONDITIONS

In most instances, it is impossible for decision makers to be sure of exactly what the future consequences of an implemented alternative will be. The word *future* is the key in discussing decision-making conditions. For all practical purposes, because organizations and their environments are constantly changing, future consequences of implemented decisions are not perfectly predictable.

In general, there are three different conditions under which decisions are made. Each of these conditions is based on the degree to which the future outcome of a decision alternative is predictable. These conditions are: (1) the complete certainty condition; (2) the complete uncertainty condition; and (3) the risk condition.[15] Figure 5.8 shows these three conditions on a continuum of predictability of organizational environment with complete certainty at one end and complete uncertainty at the other.

Complete Certainty Condition

The **complete certainty condition** exists when decision makers know exactly what the results of an implemented alternative will be. In this instance, managers have complete knowledge about a decision. All they have to do is list outcomes for alternatives and then pick the outcome with the highest payoff for the organization. For example, the outcome of an investment alternative based on buying government bonds is, for all practical purposes, completely predictable due to established government interest rates. Deciding to implement this alternative essentially would be making a decision in a complete certainty situation. Unfortunately, most organizational decisions are made outside of the complete certainty situation.

Complete Uncertainty Condition

The **complete uncertainty condition** exists when decision makers have absolutely no idea what the results of an implemented alternative will be. The complete uncertainty condition would exist, for example, if there were no historical data on which to base a decision. Not knowing what happened in the past makes it difficult to predict what will happen in the future. In this situation, decision makers usually find that sound decisions are merely a matter of chance. An example of a decision made in a complete uncertainty situation would be choosing to pull the candy machine lever labeled "Surprise of the Day" rather than choosing to pull a lever that would deliver a candy bar that looks delicious. It is fortunate that few organizational decisions are made in the complete uncertainty situation.

FIGURE 5.8   Continuum of decision-making conditions.

Complete Certainty Condition	Risk Condition		Complete Uncertainty Condition
(Low risk)	(Intermediate risk)	(High risk)	

Risk Condition

The primary characteristic of the **risk condition** is that decision makers have only enough information about the outcome of each alternative to estimate how probable the outcome will be if the alternative is implemented. Obviously, the risk condition is somewhere between the complete certainty situation and the complete uncertainty situation. For example, the manager who hires two extra salespeople to increase annual organizational sales is deciding in a risk situation. He may feel that the probability is high that these two new salespeople will increase total sales, but it is impossible to know for sure. Some risk is associated with this decision.

In reality, *degrees* of risk can be associated with decisions made in the risk situation. The lower the quality of information related to the outcome of an alternative, the closer the situation is to the complete uncertainty situation and the higher the risk associated with choosing that alternative. Most decisions made in organizations normally have some amount of risk associated with them.

Risk condition: Results of alternative are somewhat known.

BACK TO THE CASE

The introductory case reveals that, in the future, Ken Melrose probably will have to make a decision regarding how to handle increased competition from other companies. Melrose's decision-making condition for such a situation is somewhere between complete certainty and complete uncertainty about the outcome of his alternatives. He could decide, for example, to lower Toro's prices or to increase advertising to fight off the increasing competition, but he has no guarantee that such measures would produce the desired results. On the other hand, he *does* know what has worked in the past to stop competitors, and thus he is not dealing with a complete unknown. Therefore, any decision Melrose would make about handling increased competition would be made under the risk condition. In other words, Melrose would have to determine the outcome probability for each of his alternatives and base his decision on the alternative that looked most advantageous.

DECISION-MAKING TOOLS

Although some writers indicate that more subjective tools, such as extrasensory perception (ESP),[16] can be important to decision making, most managers tend to emphasize more objective decision-making tools, such as linear programming, queuing or waiting-line methods, and game theory.[17] (The cartoon illustrates that some situations can be influenced by both subjective and objective decision tools.)

"That, at any rate, is the situation as my coolly analytical left brain sees it. Now let me communicate, if I can, my right brain's gut reaction."
Reprinted by permission of J. B. Handelsman, Harvard Business Review *(September/October 1986).*

Perhaps the two most widely used of these more objective decision-making tools, however, are probability theory and decision trees.

Probability Theory

Probability theory is a decision-making tool used in risk situations—situations wherein decision makers are not completely sure of the outcome of an implemented alternative. Probability refers to the likelihood that an event or outcome will actually occur and allows decision makers to calculate an expected value for each alternative. The **expected value (EV)** for an alternative is the income (I) it would produce multiplied by its probability of making that income (P). In formula form, $EV = I \times P$. Decision makers generally choose and implement the alternative with the highest expected value.

An example will make the relationship between probability, income, and expected value more clear. A manager is trying to decide where to open a store that specializes in renting surfboards. He is considering three possible location alternatives (A, B, and C), all of which seem very feasible. For the first year of operation, the manager has projected that, under ideal conditions, he would earn $90 000 in Location A, $75 000 in Location B, and $60 000 in Location C. After studying historical weather patterns, however, he has determined that there is only a 20 percent chance or a 0.2 probability of ideal conditions during the first year of operation in Location A. Locations B and C have a 0.4 and a 0.8 probability, respectively, for ideal conditions during the first year. Expected values for each of these locations are as follows: Location A—$18 000; Location B—$30 000; Location C—$48 000. Figure 5.9 shows the situation this decision maker is faced with. According to this probability analysis, the manager should open a store in Location C, the alternative with the highest expected value.

Decision Trees

In the previous section, probability theory was applied to a relatively simple decision situation. Some decisions, however, are more complicated and involve a series of steps. These steps are interdependent; that is, each step is influenced

---

FIGURE 5.9   Expected values for locating surfboard rental store in each of three possible locations.

Alternative (Locations)	Potential Income	Probability of Income	Expected Value of Alternatives
A	$90 000	.2	$18 000
B	75 000	.4	30 000
C	60 000	.8	48 000
I	X	P	= EV

FIGURE 5.10   A basic decision tree illustrating the decision facing Stygian management.

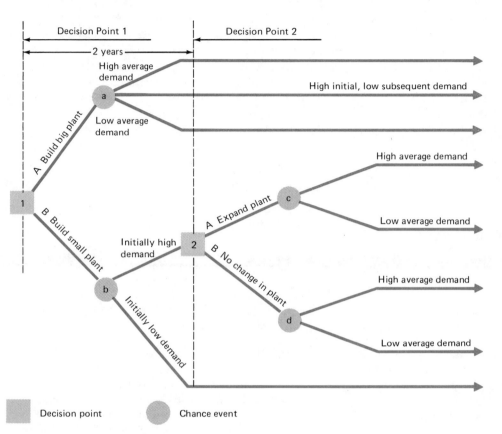

by the step that precedes it. A **decision tree** is a graphic decision-making tool typically used to evaluate decisions containing a series of steps.[18]

John F. Magee has developed a classic illustration that outlines how decision trees can be applied to a production decision.[19] In his illustration in Figure 5.10, the Stygian Chemical Company must decide whether to build a small or a large plant to manufacture a new product with an expected life of ten years. This figure clearly shows that management must decide (Decision Point 1) whether to build a small plant or a large one. If the choice is to build a large plant, the company could face product demands of high or low average demand, or high initial and then low demand. If, on the other hand, the choice is to build a small plant, the company could face either initially high or initially low product demand. If the small plant is built, however, and high product demand exists during an initial two-year period, management could then choose whether or not to expand its plant (Decision Point 2). Whether the decision is made to expand or not to expand, management could then face either high or low product demand.

Now that various possible alternatives related to this decision have been outlined, the financial consequence of each different course of action must be

A decision tree is a graphic decision-making tool for more complicated decisions.

compared. To adequately compare these consequences, management must: (1) study estimates of investment amounts necessary for building a large plant, for building a small plant, and for expanding a small plant; (2) weigh probabilities of facing different product demand levels for various decision alternatives; and (3) consider projected income yields per decision alternative.

Analysis of the expected values and net expected gain for each decision alternative helps management to decide on an appropriate choice. *Net expected gain* is defined in this situation as the expected value of an alternative minus investment cost. For example, if in Magee's example, building a large plant yields the highest net expected gain, Stygian management should decide to build the large plant.

BACK TO THE CASE

Ken Melrose has two tools he can use to make better decisions at Toro. First, he can use probability theory to obtain an expected value for various decision alternatives, and then implement the alternative with the highest expected value. For example, Melrose may need to decide whether to devote more of the company's resources to manufacturing snow removal or lawn equipment, a decision that would depend on such factors as manufacturing costs and expected weather conditions.

Second, with decisions that involve a series of steps related to each of several alternatives, Melrose could use a decision tree to assist him in picturing and

evaluating each alternative. For example, he could choose to design a new product or devote more resources to the improvement of existing products. Each of these alternatives would lead to different decision-making steps.

Melrose must remember, however, that business judgment is an essential component in the effective use of any decision-making tool. The purpose of the tool is to improve the quality of the judgment, not to replace it.[20] In other words, Melrose must not only choose alternatives based on probability theory and decision trees, but he must also use his own good judgment in deciding what is best for Toro.

Action Summary

Reread the learning objectives that follow. Each objective is followed by questions. Answering these questions accurately will help you to retain the most important concepts discussed in this chapter. After answering each question, check your answer with the answer key at the end of this chapter. (*Hint*: If you have doubt regarding the correct response, consult the page that follows the answer.)

Circle:

From studying this chapter, I will attempt to acquire:

1. **A fundamental understanding of the term** *decision.*

T,F
    a. A decision is a choice made between two or more alternatives.

    b. Decision making is involved in which of the following functions: (a) planning; (b) organizing; (c) controlling; (d) influencing; (e) all of the above.

a, b, c, d, e

2. **An understanding of each element of the decision situation.**
   a. Which type of decision-making orientation involves the feeling that the source of all good is outside oneself and that, therefore, one must rely heavily on suggestions from other organizational members: (a) exploitation; (b) hoarding; (c) marketing; (d) natural; (e) receptive.   a, b, c, d, e
   b. According to Wilson and Alexis, all of the following are elements of the decision situation except: (a) the state or nature of the decision environment; (b) the decision makers; (c) the goals to be served; (d) the timeliness of the decision; (e) the relevant alternatives.   a, b, c, d, e

3. **An ability to use the decision-making process.**
   a. After identifying an existing problem, the next major step in the decision-making process is: (a) defining the terminology in the problem statement; (b) listing possible alternatives to solve the problem; (c) investigating possible alternatives to determine their effect on the problem; (d) determining what parties will participate in the problem-solving process; (e) identifying sources of alternatives to solve the problem.   a, b, c, d, e
   b. After going through the decision-making process, if the identified problem is not being solved as a result of the implemented alternative, the manager should: (a) attempt to redefine the problem; (b) turn attention to another problem; (c) search out and implement some other alternative; (d) attempt to implement the alternative until the problem is solved; (e) accept the fact that the problem cannot be solved.   a, b, c, d, e

4. **An appreciation for the various situations in which decisions are made.**
   a. The risk condition exists when decision makers have absolutely no idea of what the results of an implemented alternative will be.   T, F
   b. When operating under the complete uncertainty condition, decision makers usually find that sound decisions are a matter of chance.   T, F

5. **An understanding of probability theory and decision trees as decision-making tools.**
   a. Expected value is determined by using the formula: (a) $EV = I \times P$; (b) $EV = I/P$; (c) $EV = I + P$; (d) $EV = P - I$; (e) $EV = 2P \times I$.   a, b, c, d, e
   b. In the case of the Stygian Chemical Company, the problem was solved through the use of: (a) executive experience; (b) decision tree technique; (c) queuing theory; (d) linear programming; (e) demand probability.   a, b, c, d, e

---

▤ INTRODUCTORY CASE WRAP-UP

"Important Decisions at Toro" (p. 108) and its related back-to-the-case sections were written to help you better understand the management concepts contained in this chapter. Answer the following discussion questions about this introductory case to further enrich your understanding of the chapter content:

1. List three alternatives that Melrose might want to consider before making a decision about increasing Toro's manufacturing capability.

2. What information would Melrose need to evaluate these three alternatives?

3. Do you think that you would enjoy making the kinds of decisions at Toro that Melrose must make? Explain.

Issues for Review and Discussion

1. What is a decision?
2. Describe the difference between a significant decision and an insignificant decision. Which would you rather make? Why?
3. List three programmed and three non-programmed decisions that the manager of a night-club would probably have to make.
4. Explain the rationale for determining which managers in the organization are responsible for making which decisions.
5. What is the consensus method of making decisions? When would you use it?
6. List and define the six basic elements of the decision-making situation.
7. How does the receptive orientation for decision making differ from the ideal orientation for decision making?
8. List as many undesirable traits of a decision maker as possible. (They are implied within the explanations of the receptive, exploitation, hoarding, and marketing orientations to decision making.)
9. What is a relevant alternative? An irrelevant alternative?
10. Draw and describe in words the decision-making process presented in this chapter.
11. What is meant by the term *discretionary area*?
12. List the three assumptions on which the decision-making process presented in this chapter is based.
13. Explain the difference between the complete certainty and complete uncertainty decision-making situations.
14. What is the risk decision-making situation?
15. Are there degrees of risk associated with various decisions? Why?
16. How do decision makers use probability theory? Be sure to discuss expected value in your answer.
17. What is a decision tree?
18. Under what conditions are decision trees usually used as decision-making tools?

Sources of Additional Information

Albert, Kenneth J. *Handbook of Business Problem Solving.* New York: McGraw-Hill, 1980.

Baker, Alan J. *Business Decision Making.* New York: St. Martin's Press, 1981.

Byrd, Jack, and L. Ted Moore. *Decision Models for Management.* New York: McGraw-Hill, 1982.

Cohen, Herb. "How You Can Get What You Want by Negotiation." *Nation's Business* 69 (May 1981): 87–90.

Einhorn, Hillel J., and Robin M. Hogarth. "Decision Making: Going Forward in Reverse." *Harvard Business Review* (January/February 1987): 66–70.

Einhorn, Hillel J., and Robin M. Hogarth. "Decision Making under Ambiguity." *Journal of Business* 59 (October 1986): S225–50.

Fox, Harold W. "The Frontiers of Strategic Planning: Intuition or Formal Models?" *Management Review* 70 (April 1981): 8–14.

Goldstein, Marilyn, David Scholthauer, and Brian H. Kleiner. "Management on the Right Side of the Brain." *Personnel Journal* (November 1985): 40.

Heyel, Carl. *The Manager's Bible/How To Resolve 127 Classic Management Dilemmas.* New York: Free Press, 1981.

Kepner, Charles, and Benjamin Tregoe. *The Rational Manager.* New York: McGraw-Hill, 1965.

Mustafi, Chandan Kumar. *Statistical Methods in Managerial Decisions.* Delhi, India: Macmillan India Limited, 1981.

Pickle, Hal B., and Royce L. Abrahamson. *Small Business Management*, 4th ed. New York: Wiley, 1986.

Qubein, Nido R. "How to Make Decisions—Fast." *Management World* (September 1985): 16–17.

Shull, Fremont, Andre Delbecq, and L.L. Cummings. *Organizational Decision Making.* New York: McGraw-Hill, 1970.

Simon, Herbert. *Administrative Behavior.* 3d ed. New York: Free Press, 1976.

Stephenson, Blair Y., and Stephen G. Franklin. "Better Decision Making for a 'Real World' Environment." *Administrative Management* 42 (July 1981): 24–26, 36, 38.

White, Kathy Brittain. "Dynamic Decision Support Teams." *Journal of Systems Management* 35 (June 1984): 26–31.

Wind, Yoram, and Vijay Mahajan. "Designing Product and Business Portfolios." *Harvard Business Review* (January/February 1981): 155–65.

Notes

1. Jack W. Duncan, *Decision Making and Social Issues* (Hinsdale, Ill.: Dryden, 1973), 1.
2. S.M. Perrone, "Understanding the Decision Process," *Administrative Management* (May 1968): 88–92.
3. Mervin Kohn, *Dynamic Managing: Principles, Process, Practice* (Menlo Park, Calif.: Cummings, 1977), 58–62.
4. Herbert A. Simon, *The New Science of Management Decision* (New York: Harper & Row, 1960), 5–8.
5. *The D of Research and Development* (Wilmington, Del.: E.I. DuPont de Nemours and Company, 1966), 28–29.
6. Jack J. Holder, Jr., "Decision Making by Consensus," *Business Horizons* (April 1972): 47–54.
7. Charles Wilson and Marcus Alexis, "Basic Frameworks for Decision," *Academy of Management Journal* 5 (August 1962): 151–64.
8. Robert B. Duncan, "Characteristics of Organizational Environments and Perceived Environmental Uncertainty," *Administrative Science Quarterly* 17 (September 1972): 313–27.
9. See Ernest Dale, *Management: Theory and Practice* (New York: McGraw-Hill, 1973), 548–49. This section of Dale's test is based on Erich Fromm, *Man for Himself* (New York: Holt, Rinehart & Winston, 1947), 62–117.
10. Douglas R. Emery and Francis D. Tuggle, "On the Evaluation of Decisions," *MSU Business Topics* (Spring 1976): 40–48.
11. These assumptions are adapted from James G. March and Herbert A. Simon, *Organizations* (New York: John Wiley & Sons, 1958), 137–38.
12. Chester I. Barnard, *The Function of the Executive* (Cambridge, Mass.: Harvard University Press, 1938).
13. For further elaboration on these factors, see Robert Tannenbaum, Irving R. Weschler, and Fred Massarik, *Leadership and Organization: A Behavioral Science Approach* (New York: McGraw-Hill, 1961), 277–78.
14. For more discussion of these factors, see F.A. Shull, Jr., A.L. Delbecq, and L.L. Cummings, *Organizational Decision Making* (New York: McGraw-Hill, 1970).
15. F.E. Kast and J.E. Rosenzweig, *Organization and Management: A Systems Approach* (New York: McGraw-Hill, 1970), 385.
16. John Mihalasky, "ESP in Decision Making," *Management Review* (April 1975): 32–37.
17. The scope of this text does not permit elaboration on these three decision-making tools. However, for an excellent discussion on how these tools are used in decision making, see Richard M. Hodgetts, *Management: Theory, Process and Practice* (Philadelphia: Saunders, 1975), 254–66.
18. William A. Spurr and Charles P. Bonini, *Statistical Analysis for Business Decisions* (Homewood, Ill.: Irwin, 1967), 202–17.
19. P.G. Moore, "Technique vs. Judgment in Decision Making," *Organizational Dynamics* 2 (1973–74): 69–79.
20. Charles H. Lang, "Decision Making," *Manage* (August 1959).

Action Summary Answer Key

1. a. T, p. 109
   b. e, p. 109
2. a. e, p. 116
   b. d, pp. 115–117

3. a. b, p. 118
   b. c, p. 119
4. a. F, p. 121
   b. T, p. 120

5. a. a, p. 122
   b. b, pp. 123–124

DECISIONS FOR LEE VALLEY TOOLS

Not everyone can turn their hobby into a successful business. But Leonard Lee did his homework before fulfilling his lifelong ambition to start his own company. After fourteen years with the federal government in several high-level positions, Lee quit the secure world of the civil service to start Lee Valley Tools Ltd.

Lee's research convinced him that there was a market in Canada for high-quality hand tools sold through the mail. He knew that as much as 5 percent of the Canadian population were cabinetmakers, woodcarvers, and other craftspersons and hobbyists. Lee also discovered that several U.S. companies were already profitably selling tools to this market by mail. Distribution by mail is economical and can be targeted to a specific group of potential customers. So Lee made arrangements with an American mail-order tool firm for access to its catalogue artwork and tool suppliers in return for a minority interest in Lee Valley Tools. By the end of 1978, with a loan of $50 000, Lee Valley Tools had a seventy-eight-page catalogue of 1000 items and a retail outlet in a rented Ottawa warehouse.

The catalogue is Lee Valley Tools' major competitive edge. In order to attract only serious customers, Lee Valley Tools' policy is to charge one dollar for its catalogue even though this covers only a portion of production costs. An advertisement in *Harrowsmith* magazine resulted in more than 2200 requests for the catalogue and doubled the mailing list. The colourful, detailed, and well-designed catalogue full of information has become Lee Valley Tools' major avenue for sales. It is also the best information source on hand tools available in Canada.

During a long postal strike in 1981 retail business at the Ottawa warehouse location was slow. Lee Valley Tools held an "André Ouellet Sale," named after the cabinet minister then responsible for the post office. An advertisement for the sale in an Ottawa newspaper generated interviews and network appearances for Leonard Lee and a huge increase in walk-in traffic at the retail outlet.

Originally, Lee Valley Tools had no direct competition. However, Lee believed in operating the business as if there were a major competitor waiting in the wings for the right opportunity. He devoted himself to plan-

"The catalogue is Lee Valley Tools' major competitive edge."

ning, product selection, and the catalogue and left the day-to-day operations to a general manager. (There is now a management team of five). In 1982, a rival Toronto store offering a smaller selection of tools was considering issuing a catalogue. This competition prompted Lee to open a second retail outlet in that city. It was successful from the first day, exceeding break-even sales volume in its first month.

Five years after opening its doors, Lee Valley Tools had thirty-two employees and more than 4000 products in the 162-page 1983-84 catalogue. Thirty percent of the products were made in Canada, 40 percent were from the U.S., and the rest came from countries such as West Germany and Japan. Lee Valley Tools had exclusive Canadian rights to several lines of tools and had reintroduced old ones that were manufactured for the company by independent suppliers. In addition, Lee Valley Tools branched out to sell complementary products such as woodworking books and magazines, building plans, antique tools, and adhesives. The company has since become known as the major source of hard-to-find antique hardware for cabinetmakers and has its own catalogue of these products.

Although the products seem expensive, their high quality and Lee Valley Tools' guarantee overcome any possible criticism. Any item can be returned for a full refund, including the cost of return parcel post, up to ninety days after purchase. No complaint against Lee Valley Tools has ever been registered with a better business bureau. In addition, Lee has been keeping prices down through purchasing in large quantities. The general price level in the 1983-84 catalogue was lower than in the previous year's. Also, Lee doesn't use shipping charges as a source of profits. To further cut costs, a computer system was introduced to reduce the order processing time and handle administrative tasks. On the whole, the company has an excellent reputation.

With the business profitable, Lee was considering several alternatives to ensure successful growth in the future:

1. Establish manufacturing facilities to produce the company's own tool design, work that is now contracted out.
2. Set up a separate wholesale operation to sell the company-designed products and imported lines to other retailers.
3. Establish more company-owned retail facilities.
4. Introduce new product categories, such as a line of power tools.
5. Increase marketing efforts in, and export sales to, the U.S.

Lee decided to go with four of the five alternatives, at least in part. The company did not establish manufacturing facilities but instead now has more of its products made-to-order. Staff has been increased to seventy-two full-time employees, including a product-development person, a manufacturing manager, and freelance craftspersons. Lee Valley Tools now has more control over the production of its items.

A separate wholesale distribution operation has not been set up due to a lack of retailers who specialize in many of Lee Valley Tools' products. The company has broadened distribution of its carving tools by sponsoring carving competitions to publicize the products.

The company's third retail outlet was opened in Vancouver in 1985. The operation is successful partly because the prices in British Columbia are the same as those in Ontario, an unusual pricing policy for a retailer. Although approached over one hundred times by interested franchisees, Lee has steered away from this option because "quality control is difficult enough when you have all the strings in your hand."

Pressure from both customers and the retail managers led Lee Valley Tools to add a line of power tools. The company has also added a catalogue of classic hardware to expand into this market.

Efforts have also paid off in the export market. A Canadian-made honing guide was licensed to a British firm which is selling it in eighty-one countries. A warehouse has been set up in the U.S. and Lee Valley Tools will incorporate in that country. Lee is unconcerned about possible retaliation from U.S. firms, as he believes that the Canadian market is too small to interest large American companies. But should it happen, Lee thinks that customers would remain loyal to his company because of Lee Valley Tools' high quality products, good service, and fair pricing.

The major challenge for the future is managerial in nature. The company has had to grow more slowly than the market demands due to a lack of management depth. Lee says that it is hard to find managers with the right combination of dedication and technical knowledge. "Our primary market strength is in knowledge of the product." The managers must have an in-depth knowledge of the product and not just try to increase sales through glib sales techniques.

With half of Lee Valley Tools' revenues now coming from retail operations, the company will continue to be successful only if customers are knowledgeable. To this end, the company is training customers through company-produced literature. For instance, the company sent every customer on its mailing list an eight-page brochure on adhesives. Lee believes that wise customers make sound purchasing decisions—the soundest being to buy their products from Lee Valley Tools.

DISCUSSION ISSUES

1. What types of decisions did Lee face? Should he have allowed other members of his management team to make these decisions? Explain.
2. Has Lee followed the model of the decision-making process in ensuring Lee Valley Tools' future success? According to the model, what should Lee do now?
3. Discuss the alternatives in terms of the three decision-making conditions.

Based on "Carving out a niche," by Daniel Stoffman in *Canadian Business*, August 1986. Used with permission.

CHAPTER

6

TYPES OF PLANNING: STRATEGIC AND TACTICAL

STUDENT LEARNING OBJECTIVES

From studying this chapter, I will attempt to acquire:

1. Definitions of both strategic planning and strategy.
2. An understanding of the strategy management process.
3. A knowledge of the impact of environmental analysis on strategy formulation.
4. Insights on how to use critical question analysis and SWOT analysis to formulate strategy.
5. An understanding of how to use business portfolio analysis to formulate strategy.
6. Insights on what tactical planning is, and how strategic and tactical planning should be coordinated.

CHAPTER OUTLINE

PLANNING FOR HOSPITAL CORPORATION OF AMERICA

Many changes are taking place in the health-care industry in the United States. Improvements in medical technology, surgical procedures, and hospital facilities are obvious examples. One change, however, may be apparent to neither the casual observer nor the hospital patient. More and more hospitals have changed from being operated as non-profit community organizations to being operated for profit.

The giant in this "hospitals for profit" movement is Hospital Corporation of America (HCA). It owns and manages approximately 400 hospital facilities throughout the world, cares for about 5 million patients a day, and has over 350 000 physicians affiliated with it. HCA has made outstanding progress since its founding in 1968. In 1982 its revenues rose nearly 50 percent, and in 1987 they reached $4.7 billion.

HCA is operated by Dr. Thomas Frist, Jr., the son of one of the co-founders. Although a surgeon by training, Dr. Frist sees himself more as a professional manager than as a physician. His professional reading probably focuses more on the latest management techniques than on the latest surgical techniques.

Profit-oriented hospitals and non-profit hospitals are presently at war. Profit-oriented hospitals have begun taking some non-traditional steps to compete for patient dollars. For example, some give birthday parties for babies born in their hospitals as a way of encouraging patients to return for future treatment. Others offer partial reductions on hospital bills if nurses do not respond to patient "call signals" within allotted amounts of time.

Non-profit hospitals, however, are putting up a good fight. Some are developing satellite treatment centres—small medical facilities in which physicians can perform minor surgery and deliver babies. Since these treatment centres do not require the full resources of the hospital, patient costs can be cut nearly in half.

Although Dr. Frist and HCA have been successful in recent years, the non-profit hospitals' promise of substantially cutting medical costs through satellite centres will undoubtedly draw a number of patients. It is difficult to forecast just how many patients might be lured away from HCA-run hospitals by these satellite centres. However, it certainly would seem advisable for Dr. Frist to develop a plan that would enable HCA to compete successfully with them.

Based on "Prescription for Profits," in *Time*, July 4, 1983.

What's Ahead

Dr. Thomas Frist, Jr., the head of Hospital Corporation of America discussed in the introductory case, is faced with developing a plan that will help his corporation compete favourably with non-profit satellite treatment centres. The material in this chapter suggests that Frist's efforts to meet this planning challenge should focus on the two basic types of organizational planning: strategic and tactical.

STRATEGIC PLANNING

For managers to be successful strategic planners, they must understand the fundamentals of strategic planning and how to formulate strategic plans.

Fundamentals of Strategic Planning

Defining Strategic Planning

Strategic planning is long-range planning that focuses on the organization as a whole.[1] Managers consider the organization as a total unit and ask themselves what must be done in the long term to attain organizational goals. *Long range* is usually defined as a period of time extending about three to five years into the future. Hence, in strategic planning, managers are trying to determine what their organization should do to be successful at some point three to five years in the future.

Managers may have a problem trying to decide exactly how far into the future they should extend their strategic planning. As a general rule, they should follow the **commitment principle**, which states that managers should commit funds for planning only if they can anticipate, in the foreseeable future, a return on planning expenses as a result of the long-range planning analysis. Realistically, planning costs are an investment and, therefore, should not be incurred unless a reasonable return on that investment is anticipated.

Strategic planning is long-range planning for attainment of organizational goals.

Defining Strategy

Strategy is defined as a broad and general plan developed to reach long-range objectives. Organizational strategy can, and generally does, focus on many different organizational areas,[2] such as marketing, finance, production, research and development, personnel,[3] and public relations.[4]

Actually, strategy is the end result of strategic planning. Although larger organizations generally tend to be more precise in their development of organizational strategy than smaller organizations,[5] every organization should have a

Strategy is the end result of strategic planning.

It must be consistent with organizational goals and purpose.

FIGURE 6.1   Examples of organizational objectives and related strategies for three organizations in different business areas.

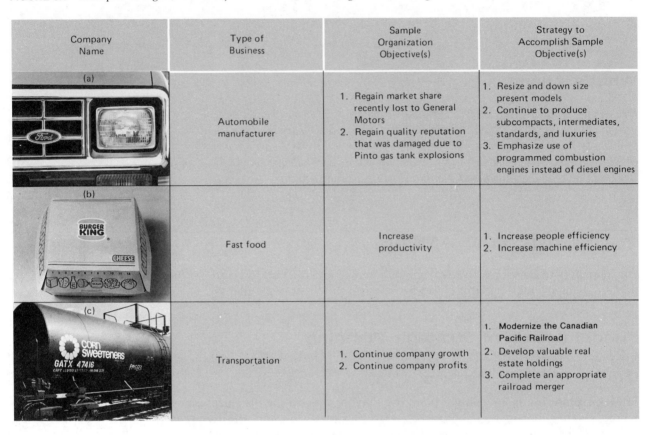

Company Name	Type of Business	Sample Organization Objective(s)	Strategy to Accomplish Sample Objective(s)
(a)	Automobile manufacturer	1. Regain market share recently lost to General Motors 2. Regain quality reputation that was damaged due to Pinto gas tank explosions	1. Resize and down size present models 2. Continue to produce subcompacts, intermediates, standards, and luxuries 3. Emphasize use of programmed combustion engines instead of diesel engines
(b)	Fast food	Increase productivity	1. Increase people efficiency 2. Increase machine efficiency
(c)	Transportation	1. Continue company growth 2. Continue company profits	1. Modernize the Canadian Pacific Railroad 2. Develop valuable real estate holdings 3. Complete an appropriate railroad merger

(a) and (b) based on E. Meadows, ''How Three Companies Increased Their Productivity,'' *Fortune*, March 10, 1980, pp. 92-101. (c) based on William B. Johnson, ''The Transformation of a Railroad,'' *Longe-Range Planning* 9 (December 1976): 18-23.

strategy of some sort.[6] For a strategy to be worthwhile, however, it must be consistent with organizational objectives, which, in turn, must be consistent with organizational purpose. Figure 6.1 illustrates this relationship between organizational objectives and strategy by presenting sample organizational objectives and strategies for three well-known business organizations.

Strategy Management

Strategy management is the process of ensuring that an organization possesses and benefits from the use of an appropriate organizational strategy. Within this definition, an appropriate strategy is a strategy best suited to the needs of an organization at a particular time.

The process of strategy management is generally thought to consist of four sequential and continuing steps: (1) strategy formulation; (2) strategy implementation; (3) strategy results measurement; and (4) strategy evaluation. The relationships and definitions of these steps are presented in Figure 6.2.

Strategy management consists of:
1. Strategy formulation.

FIGURE 6.2   The process of strategy management.

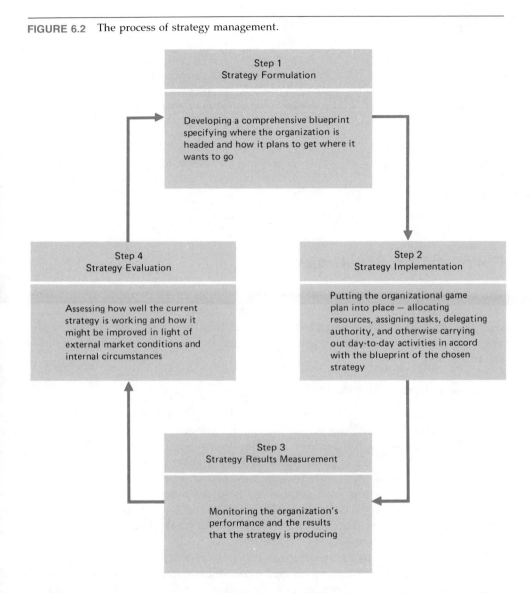

Step 1
Strategy Formulation

Developing a comprehensive blueprint specifying where the organization is headed and how it plans to get where it wants to go

Step 4
Strategy Evaluation

Assessing how well the current strategy is working and how it might be improved in light of external market conditions and internal circumstances

Step 2
Strategy Implementation

Putting the organizational game plan into place — allocating resources, assigning tasks, delegating authority, and otherwise carrying out day-to-day activities in accord with the blueprint of the chosen strategy

Step 3
Strategy Results Measurement

Monitoring the organization's performance and the results that the strategy is producing

From Arthur A. Thompson, Jr., and A. J. Strickland III, *Strategy and Policy: Concepts and Cases*, rev. ed., p. 24. Copyright © 1981 Business Publications, Inc. Reprinted by permission.

Perhaps the most important lesson to be learned from Figure 6.2 is that the actual making of a strategy is only one of four important steps in strategy management. For an organization to get maximum benefit from a strategy, the strategy must be implemented or put into action, constantly watched to see what effect it is having on the organization, and evaluated or examined to see if it is having the effect management desires. If the effect is desirable, perhaps the strategy could remain as is, with strategy results measurement and strategy evaluation continuing to determine if change will be necessary in the future. If the effect of a strategy is undesirable, however, management would probably start the entire strategy management process over again.

2. Strategy implementation.
3. Strategy results measurement.
4. Strategy evaluation.

BACK TO THE CASE

In developing a plan to compete with the non-profit satellite treatment centres, Dr. Thomas Frist, Jr., Hospital Corporation of America's manager, should probably begin by thinking strategically. That is, he should try to determine what can be done to ensure that HCA will be successful at some point three to five years in the future. Naturally, how to combat the satellite treatment centres will be a crucial part of this strategic focus. Dr. Frist must be careful, however, to spend funds on strategic planning only if he can anticipate a return on these expenses in the foreseeable future.

The end result of Dr. Frist's strategic planning will be a strategy, a broad plan that outlines what must be done to reach long-range objectives and carry out the organizational purpose of HCA. This strategy will focus on many organizational areas, one of which will be competing with satellite treatment centres. Once this strategy has been formulated, Dr. Frist must conscientiously carry out the remaining steps of the strategy management process: strategy implementation, strategy results measurement, and strategy evaluation.

Formulating Strategies

The preceding section discussed the fundamentals of strategic planning. This section builds upon that information by explaining how managers formulate strategy through environmental analysis and what tools managers use for developing organizational strategies. Several sample organizational strategies also are presented.

Environmental Analysis

Chapter 2 presented organizations as open management systems that are constantly interacting with their environment. In essence, an organization can be successful only if it is appropriately matched to its environment. **Environmental analysis** is the study of the organizational environment to pinpoint environmental factors that can significantly influence organizational operations. Managers commonly perform environmental analyses to help them understand what is happening both inside and outside their organization and to increase the probability that the organizational strategies they develop will appropriately reflect the organizational environment.

> Environmental analysis pinpoints factors that can influence operations.

> The three levels of the organizational environment are general, operating, and internal.

In order to perform an environmental analysis efficiently and effectively, a manager must thoroughly understand how organizational environments are structured.[7] For purposes of environmental analysis, the environment of an organization is generally divided into three distinct levels: the general environment, the operating environment, and the internal environment.[8] Figure 6.3 illustrates the relative positions of these levels to one another and to the organization; it also shows the important components of each level. Overall, managers must be aware of these three environmental levels, understand how each level affects organizational performance, and then formulate organizational strategies in response to this understanding.

The General Environment

> The general environment has broad long-term management implications; its components are economic, social, political, legal, and technological.

The level of an organization's external environment that contains components normally having broad long-term implications for managing the organization is the **general environment**. The components normally considered part of the general environment are economic, social, political, legal, and technological.

The *economic component* is the part of the general environment that indicates how resources are being distributed and used within the environment. This component is based on **economics**, the science that focuses on understanding

FIGURE 6.3   The organization, the levels of its environment, and the components of those levels.

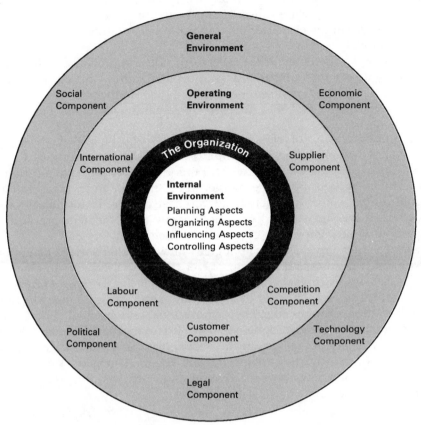

how people of a particular community or nation produce, distribute, and use various goods and services. Important issues considered in an economic analysis of an environment generally include the wages paid to labour, the taxes paid by labour and businesses, the cost of materials used during the production process, and the prices at which produced goods and services are sold to customers.[9]

Economic issues such as these can significantly influence the environment in which a company operates and the ease or difficulty the organization experiences in attempting to reach its objectives. For example, it should be somewhat easier for an organization to sell its products at higher prices if potential consumers in the environment are earning relatively high wages and paying relatively low taxes than if these same potential customers are earning relatively low wages and have significantly fewer after-tax dollars to spend.

Naturally, organizational strategy should reflect the economic issues in the organization's environment. To build on the preceding example, if the total amount of after-tax income that potential customers earn has significantly declined, an appropriate organizational strategy might be to lower the price of goods or services to make them more affordable. Such a strategy should be evaluated carefully, however, since it could have a serious impact on organizational profits.

The *social component* is the part of the general environment that describes the characteristics of the society in which the organization exists. Two important features of a society commonly studied during environmental analysis are demographics and social values.[10]

Wages, taxes, costs, and prices are examined in an economic analysis.

Economic issues can have an impact on attainment of objectives.

Organizational strategy should reflect economic issues.

Organizational strategy should reflect demographics.

Demographics is the statistical characteristics of a population. The characteristics include changes in number of people and income distribution among various population segments. These changes can influence the reception of goods and services within the organization's environment and thus should be reflected in organizational strategy.

For example, the demand for retirement housing probably would increase dramatically if both the number and the income of retirees in a particular market area doubled. Effective organizational strategy would include a mechanism for dealing with such a probable increase in demand within the organization's environment.

Demographics should also affect recruitment strategy.

An understanding of demographics can also be helpful in developing a strategy aimed at recruiting new employees to fill certain positions within an organization. Knowing that only a small number of people have a certain type of educational background, for example, would indicate to an organization that it should compete more intensely to attract these people. To formulate a recruitment strategy, managers need a clear understanding of the demographics of the groups from which employees eventually will be hired.

Organizational strategy should reflect social values.

Social values are the relative degrees of worth that society places on the ways in which it exists and functions. Over time, social values can change dramatically, causing obvious changes in the way people live. Figure 6.4 offers several brief examples of how changes in social values can cause changes in the way people live; these changes alter the organizational environment and, as a result, have an impact on organizational strategy. It is important for managers to remember that although changes in the values of a particular society may come either slowly or quickly, they are inevitable.[11] The Management in Action feature for this chapter illustrates how social values and demographics are reflected in organizational strategy.

FIGURE 6.4   Examples of how social values can affect strategy.

- At one time, it was thought that the normal thing for a family unit to do was to have two to four children. Today, not all accept this, and this value has a big impact on P&G (Pampers), Gerber (baby food), builders (houses versus condominiums), Mattel (toys), and others.

- It used to be common for retired people, single people, widows, and widowers to live with relatives. Now there is a trend toward living alone, and this has a big impact on builders, appliance manufacturers, food packers, magazine publishers, and others.

- For years, most married women stayed home. Now, most work. This has caused problems for firms that sold door-to-door (Avon and Fuller Brush) and has increased business for a variety of firms, such as those offering nursery school service, prepared foods, restaurants (two-employee families eat out more frequently), and home security systems, to name a few.

- At one time, people lived in one place. Now, there are thousands of people who are nomads—almost like the bedouins of Jordan. They live in campers and motor homes and move from place to place as jobs open up or as the spirit moves them. This provides opportunities for and threats to firms.

- Increased education has led to new attitudes on the part of employees about how many hours they wish to work, the quality of life they expect at work, and the kind of supervisory style they expect, which can affect how strategies are developed and implemented. New benefits programs are also needed for new life-styles.

- After the Three Mile Island nuclear plant incident, more people started to question the safety of nuclear power. New-plant construction and uranium mining in Canada, the United States, and Australia have been cut drastically, while coal operators are seeing new opportunities.

From William F. Glueck and Lawrence R. Jauch, *Business Policy and Strategic Management.* © 1984 McGraw-Hill Book Company, New York. Reprinted by permission.

BABIES ARE BIG BUSINESS

There's a baby boom going on in Canada today. It's different from the post-World-War-II baby boom, but it is real nonetheless. And for those business people with the abilities to take advantage of it, there are opportunities available and profits to be made.

The post-World-War-II baby-boom women are now having their children. One decade ago, the maternity market was small and quiet. Now with the baby-boom generation at the peak of their childbearing years, Canadian business people are responding with new products and services geared to this revived market. Already marketers have established profitable businesses catering to the children of baby boomers. Now many are realizing that the large number of pregnant women is a market in itself. In addition, this generation of pregnant women is affluent; they have more money to spend on themselves than their mothers did. Consequently, old and new businesses have targeted this market. They include maternity apparel shops, book publishers and sellers, drug manufacturers, childbirth educators, and fitness instructors.

The overall fertility rate has dropped by more than half from its high in 1959. Less children are being born, but the number of women of reproductive age has increased. While 3.4 million women between fifteen and forty-four produced 450 739 children in 1956, 6.1 million women in the same age range produced only 377 031 babies in 1984. Importantly, the number of first-born children is up sharply: 25.7 percent of all births were first-born children in 1956, while today these babies comprise 43 percent of all births. In addition, pregnant women in the 1980s are different from their predecessors. For one thing, they are older. Women aged thirty to thirty-four gave birth to 76 000 babies in 1984; in 1974, this same age bracket produced 48 000 babies. Also, a greater percentage of these women are employed: 54.3 percent of all women fifteen and over are in the labour force today, an increase from the 44.4 percent of ten years ago. These women are also earning more money than their younger counterparts: women aged twenty-five to thirty-four earn an average of $26 000 a year compared to $19 000 a year for the group aged eighteen to twenty-four, according to

"The childbirth classes and fitness industry have also boomed..."

139

Compusearch Market and Social Research Ltd. of Toronto. All this adds up to more affluent women willing to spend more on themselves while they are pregnant and buying more new products for their first child. Less money, however, is spent for the subsequent children. John Winter, a senior associate at Clayton Research Associates Ltd. in Toronto, estimates sales of goods and services aimed at pregnant women in Canada could add up to $1 billion a year.

In the past this specialized market was limited and dominated by a few. But in recent years new entrants have awakened to the opportunities this market presents and have gone after a share. Marketing consultants predict that this market boom could go on for another ten years or so before this generation passes out of its childbearing years. So there is still time to tap this market and cash in on some of the profits.

Maternity clothes manufacturers and retailers are the most obvious industries to take advantage of this market. Industry insiders estimate that a pregnant woman will spend $300 on maternity clothes. Various sources say that total maternity wear sales in Canada are between $100 million and $420 million a year. This is partly because working women who are pregnant have to spend more on maternity clothes than their stay-at-home predecessors. Maternity wear manufacturers are responding to this new baby-boom market by producing better-quality and more fashionable clothes. Welcome Additions Fashions Ltd. of Montreal has seen sales increase 40 percent in both 1984 and 1985. In retailing, the market has traditionally been dominated by a few chains, especially Shirley K Maternity (Canada) Ltd. Industry insiders say that the nation-wide chain garners at least a quarter of all maternity wear sales. Still there is room for smaller operators. Modmaster Ltd. of Ottawa operates Mom & Me maternity stores. They hope to grow through franchising to seventy-five stores nation-wide in the next ten years. Michel Friedman, president of the firm, claims: "The response has been tremendous. Six shopping centres have already asked me to go in. It's usually the other way around." Mom & Me is currently realizing $1 million in annual sales through three stores. Department stores are also refocusing on this market. The Hudson's Bay Co. Ltd. is developing plans to remerchandise and expand maternity wear departments in twenty-two of its fifty-nine Bay stores. Sears Canada Inc. changed the look and location of its maternity wear department in its "store-of-the-future" in Mississauga, Ontario. Sales in this department are 15 percent higher than the chain's national average.

Another group cashing in on the new baby boom are the book publishing and retailing industries. Since 1984, the book market aimed at pregnant women, especially those over thirty years old, has "exploded," according to Nigel Berrisford, Book Marketing Manager for W.H. Smith Canada Ltd. The average Smith-Classic outlet now stocks up to 175 different titles of books on prenatal and child care versus the half-dozen titles it carried ten years ago. Berrisford says that this is only a small fraction of the books being published in this area. Before 1981, these categories of books made up less than 1 percent of the chain's total sales; they now account for more than 4 percent. The entire Canadian industry for these books may be as high as $3 million in annual sales.

Although most pregnant women avoid taking drugs during their pregnancy, pharmaceutical companies are experiencing growth in their vitamin sales, especially their prenatal products. Dow (Canada) Inc. manufactures the market-leading Orifer F. The company estimates that Orifer F's share of the $8 million prenatal vitamin supplement market is 47 percent. Materna is the supplement produced by Toronto-based Lederle Laboratories, a division of Cyanamid Canada Inc. The company says that growth in this market was flat until the early 1980s. Since then, it has grown at 15 percent per year, a rate more than double the growth rate of the overall vitamin market. Materna came on the market in 1979 and now holds a 30 percent share of the market. The company expects the product's growth rate to be in double digits until at least the end of this decade.

The childbirth classes and fitness industry have also boomed along with the number of pregnant women. The new emphasis on health and fitness has spelled profits for those who can gear their services to this market. Prenatal and Parenthood Education Services runs prenatal education classes for the six Toronto-area health departments. Margaret McGovern, their executive director, says that 70 percent of all first-time pregnant women attended prenatal classes in 1985, up from 45 percent in 1981. The cost of such courses can run as high as $125. Preggae Woman runs thirty pre- and postnatal fitness courses at four locations in Toronto. It saw 600 women take classes in 1985, each spending between $300 and $450. It envisions nation-wide franchises. The firm also publishes a directory of pre- and post-natal services available in Toronto and has created an audio cassette tape of at-home exercises for pregnant women.

Many are already sharing in the profits from this new baby-boom market. The potential and opportunities are clearly there for more Canadian business people who are willing to provide products and services to an affluent market ready to spend money during this important period of their lives.

Based on "Maternity boom sparks retail battle," by Terry Brodie in *Financial Times of Canada*, July 7, 1986. Used with permission.

The *political component* is the part of the general environment that contains the elements related to government affairs. Examples include the type of government in existence, the government's attitude toward various industries, lobbying efforts by interest groups, progress on the passage of laws, and political party platforms and candidates.

The *legal component* is the part of the general environment that contains passed legislation. Simply stated, this component is the rules or laws that society's members must follow. Some examples of legislation specifically aimed at the operation of organizations are the federal Hazardous Products Act of 1969, provincial Occupational Health and Safety Act(s) (each province has its own), the Fisheries Act of 1970, the Ontario Environmental Protection Act of 1970, and the Clean Air Act of 1975. Naturally, over time, new laws are passed and some old ones are eliminated.

The *technology component* is the part of the general environment that includes new approaches to producing goods and services. These approaches can include new procedures as well as new equipment. The trend toward exploiting robots to improve productivity is an example of the technology component. The increasing use of robots in the next decade should vastly improve the efficiency of Canadian industry. Installation of these computer-controlled machines is expected to grow at an annual rate of 35 to 45 percent within the next ten years.[12]

The Operating Environment

The level of an organization's external environment that contains components normally having relatively specific and more immediate implications for managing the organization is the **operating environment**. As Figure 6.3 shows, major components of this environment level are generally thought to include customers, competition, labour, suppliers, and international issues.

The *customer component* is the operating environment segment that is composed of factors relating to those who buy goods and services provided by the organization. Profiles—detailed descriptions—of those who buy organizational products are commonly created by businesses. Developing such profiles helps management generate ideas for improving customer acceptance of organizational goods and services.

The *competition component* is the operating environment segment that is composed of those with whom an organization must battle in order to obtain resources. Since understanding competitors is a key factor in developing effective strategy, understanding the competitive environment is a fundamental challenge to management. Basically, the purpose of competitive analysis is to help management understand the strengths, weaknesses, capabilities, and likely strategy of existing and potential competitors.[13]

The *labour component* is the operating environment segment that is composed of factors influencing the supply of workers available to perform needed organizational tasks. Issues such as skill levels, trainability, desired wage rates, and average age of potential workers are important to the operation of the organization. Another important but often overlooked issue is potential workers' desire to work for a particular organization.

The *supplier component* is the operating environment segment that entails all variables related to the individuals or agencies that provide organizations with resources needed to produce goods or services. The individuals or agencies are called **suppliers**. Issues such as how many suppliers offer specified resources for sale, the relative quality of the materials offered by suppliers, the reliability of

---

The political component is related to government affairs.

The legal component involves passed legislation.

The technology component includes new approaches to production.

The operating environment includes relatively specific issues with more immediate implications.

Buyers of goods and services are profiled by organizations.

The organization must battle others to obtain resources.

The supply of workers is influenced by skill, trainability, wages, and age.

Suppliers are providers of organizational resources.

FIGURE 6.5   Important aspects of the international component of the organization's operating environment.

Legal Environment
Legal tradition
Effectiveness of legal system
Treaties with foreign nations
Patent and trademark laws
Laws affecting business firms

Economic Environment
Level of economic development
Population
Gross national product
Per capita income
Literacy level
Social infrastructure
Natural resources
Climate
Membership in regional economic blocks
  (EEC, LAFTA, etc.)
Monetary and fiscal policies
Nature of competition
Currency convertibility
Inflation
Taxation system
Interest rates
Wage and salary levels

Cultural Environment
Customs, norms, values, beliefs
Language
Attitudes
Motivations
Social institutions
Status symbols
Religious beliefs

Political System
Form of government
Political ideology
Stability of government
Strength of opposition parties and groups
Social unrest
Political strife and insurgency
Government attitude toward foreign firms
Foreign policy

Adapted from Arvind V. Phatak, *International Dimensions of Management* (Boston: Kent Publishing, 1983), p. 6.
© by Wadsworth, Inc. Reprinted by permission of PWS-Kent Publishing Co., a division of Wadsworth, Inc.

supplier deliveries, and the credit terms offered by suppliers all become important in managing an organization effectively and efficiently.

The *international component* is the operating environment segment that is composed of all the factors relating to the international implications of organizational operations. Although not all organizations must deal with international issues, the number is increasing dramatically and continually. Significant factors in the international component include other countries' laws, culture, economics, and politics.[14] Important variables within each of these four categories are presented in Figure 6.5.

International implications for organizations include other countries' laws, culture, economics, and politics.

The Internal Environment

The level of an organization's environment that exists inside the organization and normally has immediate and specific implications for managing the organization is the **internal environment**. In broad terms, the internal environment includes marketing, finance, and accounting. More specifically, from the viewpoint of management it includes planning, organizing, influencing, and controlling within the organization. Figure 6.6 contains these more management-specific factors in the internal environment and sample questions that managers can ask in exploring them.

The internal environment includes specific issues with immediate implications.

FIGURE 6.6   Several management-specific aspects of an organization's internal environment and questions related to exploring them.

Planning Aspects
• Are organizational plans clearly linked to organizational goals?
• Is the sequencing for the performance of specific tasks appropriate?
• Are plans developed for both the short term and the long term?

Organizing Aspects
• Are tasks assigned to the right people?
• Do organizing efforts put plans into action?
• Are tasks appropriately assigned to either individuals or groups?

Influencing Aspects
• Do the rewards offered employees actually motivate them?
• Are organization members encouraged to do work that actually contributes to organizational goal attainment?
• Is communication within the organization effective and efficient?

Controlling Aspects
• Is information gathered to measure recent performance?
• Is present performance compared to pre-established standards?
• Are organizational characteristics modified when necessary to ensure that pre-established standards are met?

BACK TO THE CASE

As part of his strategy development process, Dr. Frist should spend time analyzing the environment in which Hospital Corporation of America exists. Naturally, he should focus on his company's general, operating, and internal environments. Environmental factors that probably would be important for him to consider as he pursues strategic planning include levels of income and medical insurance possessed by potential patients in various areas, ages of potential patients within these areas, and social values regarding such issues as obtaining medical care in a traditional hospital versus a non-traditional satellite treatment centre. Obtaining information about environmental issues such as these will increase the probability that any strategy developed for HCA will be appropriate for the environment in which the firm operates and that the firm will be successful in the long term.

Tools for Developing Organizational Strategies

The preceding material emphasized that, since an organization must be well suited to its environment, the development of organizational strategy should include an environmental analysis. This section focuses on the special tools or techniques used to systematically develop organizational strategy that is based upon not only environmental analysis, but also a careful evaluation of the organization itself. These tools are: (1) critical question analysis; (2) SWOT analysis; and (3) business portfolio analysis.

Strategy development tools include critical question analysis, SWOT analysis, and business portfolio analysis.

These three strategy development tools are related but distinct. Managers should use whichever tool or combination of tools seems most appropriate for them and their organizations.

Critical Question Analysis

A synthesis of the ideas of several contemporary management writers suggests that formulating appropriate organizational strategy is a process of **critical question analysis**—answering the following four basic questions:[15]

What are the purpose and objectives of the organization? The answer to this question reveals where the organization wants to go. As stated earlier, appropriate strategy reveals organizational purpose and objectives. By answering this question during strategy formulation, managers are likely to remember this important point and thereby minimize inconsistencies among purposes, objectives, and strategies.

Where is the organization presently going? The answer to this question can tell managers if an organization is achieving organizational goals and, if so, whether or not the level of such progress is satisfactory. Whereas the first question focuses on where the organization wants to go, this one focuses on where the organization is actually going.

In what kind of environment does the organization now exist? Both internal and external environments—factors both inside and outside the organization— are covered in this question. For example, assume that a poorly trained middle-management team and a sudden influx of competitors in a market are factors that exist respectively in the internal and external environments of an organization. Any strategy formulated, if it is to be appropriate, probably should deal with these factors.

What can be done to better achieve organizational objectives in the future? The answer to this question actually results in the strategy of the organization. This question should only be answered, however, after managers have had adequate opportunity to reflect on the answers to the previous three questions. In other words, managers can develop appropriate organizational strategy only if they have a clear understanding of where the organization wants to go, where the organization is going, and the environment in which the organization exists.

SWOT Analysis

SWOT analysis is a strategic planning tool that matches internal organizational strengths and weaknesses with external opportunities and threats.[16] (SWOT is an acronym for a firm's Strengths and Weaknesses and its environmental Opportunities and Threats.) SWOT analysis is based upon the assumption that, if managers carefully review such strengths, weaknesses, opportunities, and threats, a useful strategy for ensuring organizational success in the future will become evident. Figure 6.7 contains several key considerations that managers should cover in performing a SWOT analysis.

Business Portfolio Analysis

Another strategy development tool that has gained wide acceptance is business portfolio analysis. **Business portfolio analysis** is the development of business-related strategy that is based primarily on market share of businesses and growth of markets in which businesses exist.[17] The philosophy upon which business portfolio analysis is based is that organizations should develop strategy much as they handle investment portfolios. Just as sound investments should be supported and unsound investments discarded, the essence of business portfolio analysis is that sound organizational activities should be emphasized, while unsound activities should be de-emphasized.

FIGURE 6.7 Important considerations for SWOT analysis.

Internal

Strengths	*Weaknesses*
A distinctive competence?	No clear strategic direction?
Adequate financial resources?	A deteriorating competitive position?
Good competitive skills?	Obsolete facilities?
Well thought of by buyers?	Subpar profitability because . . . ?
An acknowledged market leader?	Lack of managerial depth and talent?
Well-conceived functional area strategies?	Missing any key skills or competences?
Access to economies of scale?	Poor track record in implementing strategy?
Insulated (at least somewhat) from strong competitive pressures?	Plagued with internal operating problems?
Proprietary technology?	Vulnerable to competitive pressures?
Cost advantages?	Falling behind in R&D?
Competitive advantages?	Too narrow a product line?
Product innovation abilities?	Weak market image?
Proven management?	Competitive disadvantages?
Other?	Below–average marketing skills?
	Unable to finance needed changes in strategy?
	Other?

External

Opportunities	*Threats*
Enter new markets or segments?	Likely entry of new competitors?
Add to product line?	Rising sales of substitute products?
Diversify into related products?	Slower market growth?
Add complementary products?	Adverse government policies?
Vertical integration?	Growing competitive pressures?
Ability to move to better strategic group?	Vulnerability to recession and business cycle?
Complacency among rival firms?	Growing bargaining power of customers or suppliers?
Faster market growth?	Changing buyer needs and tastes?
Other?	Adverse demographic changes?
	Other?

From Arthur A. Thompson, Jr., and A. J. Strickland III, *Strategy Formulation and Implementation*, 3d ed. Copyright © 1986 Business Publications, Inc. Reprinted by permission.

The first step in performing a business portfolio analysis is identifying strategic business units (SBUs) that exist within an organization. A **strategic business unit** is defined as a significant organization segment that is analyzed to develop organizational strategy aimed at generating future "business" or revenue.

Exactly what constitutes an SBU varies from organization to organization. In larger organizations, an SBU could be a company division, a single product, or a complete product line. In smaller organizations, an SBU might be the entire company. Although SBUs vary drastically in form, each SBU has the common characteristics of: (1) being a single business or collection of related businesses; (2) having its own competitors; (3) having a manager who is accountable for its

Strategic business units (SBUs) vary in form

but have four common characteristics.

FIGURE 6.8   The business portfolio matrix.

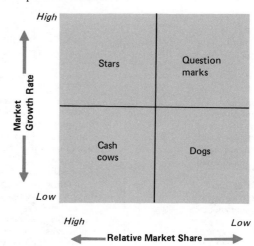

operation; and (4) being an area that can be independently planned for within the organization.[18]

After SBUs have been identified for a particular organization, the next step in a business portfolio analysis is to categorize the SBUs as being within one of the following four quadrants of the business portfolio matrix (see Figure 6.8):

SBUs are categorized as:

1. *"Stars"*   SBUs that are "stars" have a high share of a high-growth market. These SBUs typically need large amounts of cash to support their rapid and significant growth. "Stars" also generate large amounts of cash for the organization and are usually areas in which management can make additional investments and earn attractive returns.

"Stars"—high-growth market, high market share;

2. *"Cash cows"*   SBUs that are "cash cows" have a large share of a market that is growing only slightly. Naturally, these SBUs provide the organization with large amounts of cash. Since the market is not growing significantly, however, this cash is generally used to meet financial demands of the organization in other areas, such as in the expansion of a "star" SBU.

"Cash cows"—low-growth market, high market share;

3. *"Question marks"*   SBUs that are "question marks" have a small share of a high-growth market. These SBUs are called "question marks" because it is uncertain whether management should invest more cash in them to get a larger share of the market, or whether management should de-emphasize or eliminate them because such an investment would be ineffective. Naturally, through further investment, management attempts to turn "question marks" into "stars."

"Question marks"—high-growth market, small market share;

4. *"Dogs"*   SBUs that are "dogs" have a relatively small share of a low-growth market. These SBUs may barely support themselves, or they may even drain cash resources that other SBUs have generated. Examples of "dogs" are buggy whips and slide rules.

"Dogs"—low-growth market, low market share.

Companies like Canadian General Electric, Westinghouse, Canadian Tire, and Shell Canada Limited have used business portfolio analysis in their strategy management processes. There are, however, some possible pitfalls in this technique. For example, the business portfolio analysis model does not consider such factors as: (1) various types of risk associated with product development; (2) threats that inflation and other economic conditions can create in the future; and (3) social, political, and ecological pressures.[19] Managers must remember to weigh such factors carefully when designing organizational strategy based upon this model.

Various factors must be weighed carefully when using business portfolio analysis.

Sample Organizational Strategies

Analysis of the organizational environment and application of one or more of the strategy tools—critical question analysis, SWOT analysis, and business portfolio analysis—give managers a foundation on which to formulate an organizational strategy. Some of the organizational strategies that can evolve are growth, stability, retrenchment, and divestiture.

This discussion of sample organizational strategies tends to feature business portfolio analysis as the tool used to arrive at the strategy, but these same strategies could also result from critical question analysis or SWOT analysis.

Growth

Growth is a strategy adopted by management to increase the amount of business that an SBU is currently generating. The growth strategy is generally applied to "star" SBUs or to "question mark" SBUs that hold the potential of becoming "stars." Management generally invests substantial amounts of money to implement this strategy and may even sacrifice short-term profit to build long-term gain.[20]

Managers can also encourage growth by purchasing an SBU from another organization. For example, Black & Decker, not satisfied with being an international power in power tools, recently purchased General Electric's small appliance business. Through this purchase, Black & Decker hopes that the amount of business it currently enjoys will grow significantly over the long-term.[21]

Growth is a strategy to increase business.

Stability

Stability is a strategy adopted by management to maintain or slightly improve the amount of business that an SBU is generating. This strategy is generally applied to "cash cows" since these SBUs are already in an advantageous position. Management must be careful, however, that such a strategy doesn't turn "cash cows" into "dogs."

Stability is a strategy to maintain or slightly improve business.

Retrenchment

In this instance, *retrench* is used in the military sense, where it means to defend or fortify. Through **retrenchment** strategy, management attempts to strengthen or protect the amount of business an SBU is generating. The retrenchment strategy is generally applied to "cash cows" or "stars" that begin to lose market share.

Douglas D. Danforth, the chief executive of Westinghouse, is convinced that retrenchment is an important strategy for his company. According to Danforth, bigger profits at Westinghouse depend not only on the fast-growing new products, but also on revitalizing Westinghouse's traditional businesses of manufacturing motors and gears.[22]

Retrenchment is a strategy to strengthen or protect business.

"Divestiture is completed, sir."
Wall Street Journal, *March 27, 1984. From the* Wall Street
Journal–*Permission, Cartoon Feature Syndicate.*

Divestiture

Divestiture is a strategy adopted to eliminate an SBU.

Divestiture is a strategy generally adopted to eliminate an SBU that is not generating a satisfactory amount of business and has little hope of doing so in the near future. In essence, the organization sells or closes down the SBU in question. This strategy is generally applied to SBUs that are "dogs" or "question marks" that have failed to increase market share but still require significant amounts of cash. The cartoon humourously illustrates that divestiture means to discard or get rid of something.

BACK TO THE CASE

Dr. Frist has several tools available to assist him in formulating strategy for Hospital Corporation of America. To be effective, however, Frist must use these tools in conjunction with environmental analysis.

One of these tools, critical question analysis, would require Frist to analyze the purpose of Hospital Corporation of America, the direction in which HCA is going, the environment in which it exists, and how its goals might be better achieved.

SWOT analysis, another strategy development tool, would require Frist to generate information regarding the internal strengths and weaknesses of HCA as well as the opportunities and threats that exist within HCA's environment. Frist probably would classify the newly developing satellite treatment centres as an environmental threat and a significant factor to be

considered within his strategy development process.

Business portfolio analysis would require Frist to classify his SBUs as "stars," "cash cows," "question marks," or "dogs," depending upon the growth rate of the market in which the SBU exists and the market share the SBU possesses. Frist could decide, for example, to consider each of his hospitals as an SBU and categorize them according to the four classifications. As a result of this categorization process, he could develop strategies like growth, stability, retrenchment, or divestiture.

Frist should use whichever strategy development tool or combination of tools he thinks would be most useful to him. His objective, of course, is to develop an appropriate strategy for Hospital Corporation of America.

⊞ TACTICAL PLANNING

Tactical planning is short-range planning that emphasizes the current operations of various parts of the organization. *Short range* is defined as a period of time extending only about one year or less into the future. Managers use tactical planning to outline what the various parts of the organization must do for the organization to be successful at some point one year or less into the future.[23] Tactical plans usually are developed for organizations in the areas of production, marketing, personnel, finance, and plant facilities.

Tactical planning is short-range planning.

⊞ COMPARING AND COORDINATING STRATEGIC AND TACTICAL PLANNING

In striving to implement successful planning systems within organizations, managers must remember several basic differences between strategic planning and tactical planning. First, since upper-level managers generally have a better understanding of the organization as a whole than do lower-level managers, and since lower-level managers generally have a better understanding of the actual day-to-day organizational operations than do upper-level managers, strategic plans usually are developed by upper-level management and tactical plans usually are developed by lower-level management. Second, since strategic planning emphasizes analyzing the future and tactical planning emphasizes analyzing the everyday functioning of the organization, facts upon which to base strategic plans are usually more difficult to gather than facts upon which to base tactical plans. A third difference between strategic and tactical planning involves the amount of detail in the final plans. Since strategic plans are primarily based upon a prediction of the future and tactical plans are primarily based upon known circumstances that exist within the organization, strategic plans generally are less detailed than tactical plans. Lastly, since strategic planning focuses on the long-term and tactical planning focuses on the short-term, strategic plans cover a relatively long period of time while tactical plans cover a relatively short period of time. All of these major differences between strategic and tactical planning are summarized in Figure 6.9.

Tactical planning should reflect strategic planning.

There are four basic differences between strategic and tactical planning.

FIGURE 6.9   Major differences between strategic and tactical planning.

Area of Difference	Strategic Planning	Tactical Planning
Individuals involved	Mainly developed by upper-level management	Mainly developed by lower-level management
Facts upon which to base planning	Facts are relatively difficult to gather	Facts are relatively easy to gather
Amount of detail in plans	Relatively little detail found in plans	Plans contain substantial amount of detail
Length of time plans cover	Plans cover long periods of time	Plans cover short periods of time

In spite of their differences, tactical and strategic planning are integrally related. As Russell L. Ackoff states:

> In general, strategic planning is concerned with the longest period worth considering; tactical planning is concerned with the shortest period worth considering. Both types of planning are necessary. They complement each other. They are like the head and tail of a coin. We can look at them separately, even discuss them separately, but we cannot separate them in fact.[24]

In other words, managers need both tactical and strategic planning programs, but these programs must be closely related to be successful. Tactical planning should focus on what to do in the short term to help the organization achieve the long-term objectives determined by strategic planning.

PLANNING AND LEVELS OF MANAGEMENT

As managers move up in the organization, the time they spend on planning increases.

Top management of an organization has the primary responsibility for seeing that the planning function is carried out. Although all levels of management typically are involved in the planning process, upper-level managers usually spend more time planning than do lower-level managers. Lower-level managers are highly involved with the everyday operations of the organization and, therefore, normally have less time to contribute to planning than does top management. Middle-level managers usually spend more time planning than do lower-level managers, but less time than upper-level managers. Figure 6.10 shows the increase in planning time spent as managers move from lower-level to upper-level management positions. In small as well as large organizations, deciding on the amount of nature of work that managers should personally handle is extremely important.[25]

As managers move up in the organization, the scope of their planning broadens.

The type of planning managers do also changes as they move up in the organization. Typically, lower-level managers plan for the short-term; middle-level managers plan for a somewhat longer term; and upper-level managers plan

FIGURE 6.10 Increase in planning time as manager moves from lower-level to upper-level management positions.

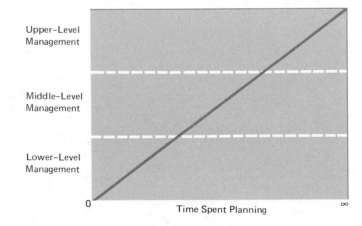

FIGURE 6.11   Movement of planning activities from a short-range to a long-range emphasis as a manager moves from a lower-level to an upper-level management position.

	Today	One Week Ahead	One Month Ahead	Three to Six Months Ahead	One Year Ahead	Two Years Ahead	Three to Four Years Ahead	Five to Ten Years Ahead
President	1%	2%	5%	17%	15%	25%	30%	5%
Vice-president	2%	4%	10%	29%	20%	20%	13%	2%
Works Manager	4%	8%	15%	38%	20%	10%	5%	
Superintendent	6%	10%	20%	43%	10%	9%	2%	
Department Manager	10%	10%	25%	39%	10%	5%	1%	
Section Supervisor	15%	20%	25%	37%	3%			
Group Supervisor	38%	40%	15%	5%	2%			

Reprinted with the special permission of *Dun's Review* from R. M. Besse, "Company Planning Must Be Planned," April 1957, p. 48. Copyright 1957, Dun & Bradstreet Publications Corporation.

for an even longer term. Lower-level managers' expertise with everyday operations makes them the best planners for what can be done in the short-term to reach organizational objectives—in other words, tactical planning. Upper-level managers usually have the best understanding of the organizational situation as a whole and are therefore better equipped to plan for the long-term—or to develop strategic plans. Figure 6.11 shows that as managers move from lower to upper management, they spend more time on strategic planning and less time on tactical planning. The total amount of time spent on strategic planning by lower-level managers, however, has been increasing.[26]

BACK TO THE CASE

In addition to developing strategic plans, Dr. Frist should consider tactical or short-range plans that would complement his strategic plans for Hospital Corporation of America. Tactical plans for HCA should emphasize what can be done within approximately the next year to reach the organization's three-to-five-year objectives. In essence, Frist should consider what shorter-range measures HCA can take to stem competition from non-profit satellite treatment centres.

In addition, Frist must closely coordinate strategic and tactical planning within HCA. He must keep in mind that strategic planning and tactical planning are different types of activities that may involve different people within the organization and result in plans with different degrees of detail. If designed correctly, his planning procedures for HCA probably will necessitate that upper-level managers spend more total time on planning—especially strategic planning—than lower-level managers and that lower-level managers concentrate on tactical planning.

Action Summary

Reread the learning objectives that follow. Each objective is followed by questions. Answering these questions accurately will help you to retain the most important concepts discussed in this chapter. After answering each question, check your answer with the answer key at the end of this chapter. (*Hint*: If you have doubt regarding the correct response, consult the page that follows the answer.)

Circle:

From studying this chapter, I will attempt to acquire:

1. **Definitions of both strategic planning and strategy.**
   a. Strategic planning is long-range planning that focuses on the organization as a whole.

T, F

   b. Strategy: (a) is a specific, narrow plan designed to achieve tactical planning; (b) is designed to be the end result of tactical planning; (c) is a plan designed to reach long-range objectives; (d) is timeless, and the same strategy can meet organizational needs anytime; (e) is independent of organizational objectives and therefore need not be consistent with them.

a, b, c, d, e

2. **An understanding of the strategy management process.**
   a. Which of the following is not one of the steps in strategy management: (a) strategy formulation; (b) strategy implementation; (c) strategy results measurement; (d) strategy evaluation; (e) all of the above are steps.

a, b, c, d, e

   b. Strategy evaluation includes: (a) looking at current strategy relative to market conditions; (b) allocating resources; (c) measuring results; (d) assigning tasks; (e) developing goals.

a, b, c, d, e

3. **A knowledge of the impact of environmental analysis on strategy formulation.**
   a. Environmental analysis is the strategy used to change an organization's environment to satisfy the needs of the organization.

T, F

   b. All of the following are factors to be considered in environmental analysis except: (a) organizational tactics; (b) economic issues; (c) demographics; (d) social values; (e) suppliers.

a, b, c, d, e

4. **Insights on how to use critical question analysis and SWOT analysis to formulate strategy.**
   a. Which of the following is not one of the four basic questions used in critical question analysis: (a) Where has the organization been? (b) Where is the organization presently going? (c) What are the purpose and objectives of the organization? (d) In what kind of environment does the organization now exist? (e) What can be done to better achieve organizational objectives in the future?

a, b, c, d, e

   b. SWOT is an acronym for "Strengths and Weaknesses, Objectives and Tactics."

T, F

5. **An understanding of how to use business portfolio analysis to formulate strategy.**
   a. Business portfolio analysis considers which of the following factors: (a) types of risk associated with product development; (b) threats that economic conditions can create in the future; (c) social factors; (d) market shares and growth of markets in which products are selling; (e) political pressures.

a, b, c, d, e

   b. Products that capture a high share of a rapidly growing market are sometimes known as: (a) "cash cows"; (b) milk products; (c) sweepstakes products; (d) "stars"; (e) dog products.

a, b, c, d, e

   c. Black and Decker's purchase of General Electric's small appliance business is an example of which of the following types of organizational strategies for General Electric; (a) growth; (b) stability; (c) retrenchment; (d) divestiture; (e) none of the above.

       a, b, c, d, e

6. **Insights on what tactical planning is and how strategic and tactical planning should be coordinated.**
   a. Tactical plans generally are developed for one year or less and usually contain fewer details than strategic plans.

       T, F

   b. Which of the following best describes strategic planning: (a) facts are difficult to gather, and plans cover short periods of time; (b) facts are difficult to gather, and plans cover long periods of time; (c) facts are difficult to gather, and the plans are mainly developed by lower-level managers; (d) facts are easy to gather, and the plans are mainly developed by upper-level managers; (e) facts are easy to gather, and the plans are mainly developed by lower-level managers.

       a, b, c, d, e,

INTRODUCTORY CASE WRAP-UP

"Planning for Hospital Corporation of America" (p. 132) and its related back-to-the-case sections were written to help you better understand the management concepts contained in this chapter. Answer the following discussion questions about this introductory case to further enrich your understanding of the chapter content:

1. Will Frist have to worry about competing with the satellite treatment centres in the short term or in the long term? Explain.

2. Assuming that Frist must do short-range and long-range planning to compete with the satellite treatment centres, which of these two types of planning must he do first? Explain.

3. How might patients' attitudes toward medical care enhance or diminish the success rate of the new satellite treatment centres?

Issues for Review and Discussion

1. What is strategic planning?
2. How does the commitment principle relate to strategic planning?
3. Define *strategy* and discuss its relationship with organizational objectives.
4. What are the major steps in the strategy management process? Discuss each step fully.
5. Why is environmental analysis an important part of strategy formulation?
6. List one major factor from each environmental level that could have significant impact on specific strategies developed for an organization. How could the specific strategies be affected by each factor?
7. Discuss the significance of the questions answered during critical question analysis.
8. Explain in detail how SWOT analysis can be used to formulate strategy.

9. What is business portfolio analysis?
10. Discuss the philosophy upon which business portfolio analysis is based.
11. What is an SBU?
12. Draw and explain the business portfolio matrix.
13. What potential pitfalls must managers avoid in using business portfolio analysis?
14. List and define four sample strategies that can be developed for organizations.
15. How do the strategies that you listed in Question 14 relate to "dogs," "question marks," "cash cows," and "stars"?
16. What is tactical planning?
17. How do strategic and tactical planning differ?
18. What is the relationship between strategic and tactical planning?
19. How do time spent planning and scope of planning vary as management level varies?

Sources of Additional Information

Certo, Samuel C., and J. Paul Peter. *Strategic Management: Concepts and Applications.* New York: Random House, 1988.

Christopher, William F. "Is the Annual Planning Cycle Really Necessary?" *Management Review* 70 (August 1981): 38–42.

Cotton, Donald B. *Organizing for Companywide Planning.* New York: Macmillan, 1969.

Feinberg, Mortimer R. "Preparing Contingency Plans." *Restaurant Business* 80 (May 1981): 3–8, 16.

Fennell, Mary L., and Jeffrey A. Alexander. "Organizational Boundary Spanning in Institutionalized Environments." *Academy of Management Journal* 30 (September 1987): 456–76.

Hall, George E. "Reflections on Running a Diversified Company." *Harvard Business Review* (January/February 1987): 84–92.

Heroux, Richard L. "How Effective Is Your Planning?" *Managerial Planning* 30 (September/October 1980): 3–8ff.

Hutchinson, J.D. *Management Strategy and Tactics.* New York: Holt, Rinehart & Winston, 1971.

Naylor, Thomas H. "Organizing for Strategic Planning," *Managerial Planning* 28 (July/August 1979): 3–9, 17.

Paul, Ronald N., and James W. Taylor. "The State of Strategic Planning." *Business* 36 (January/February/March 1986): 37.

Payne, B. *Planning for Company Growth.* New York: McGraw-Hill, 1963.

Pruchansky, Neal R., and William C. Scott. "Managing Strategy through an Interactionist Perspective." *Managerial Planning* (September/October 1984): 40–44, 50.

Ross, Joel E., and Michael J. Kami. *Corporate Management in Crisis: Why the Mighty Fall.* Englewood Cliffs, N.J.: Prentice-Hall, 1973.

Sawyer, George C. "The Hazards of Goal Conflict in Strategic Planning." *Managerial Planning* 28 (May/June 1980): 11–13, 27.

Scarborough, Norman M., and Thomas W. Zimmerer. "Strategic Planning for the Small Business." *Business* 37 (April/May/June 1987): 11–20.

Sord, Burnard H., and Glen A. Welsch. *Managerial Planning and Control.* Austin, Tex.: University of Texas, Bureau of Business Research, 1964.

Sweet, F.H. *Strategic Planning.* Austin, Tex.: University of Texas, Bureau of Business Research, 1964.

Warren, E.K. *Long-Range Planning: The Executive Viewpoint.* Englewood Cliffs, N.J.: Prentice-Hall, 1966.

Wortman, Leon A. *Successful Small Business Management.* New York: American Management Association, 1976.

Notes

1. Donald F. Harvey, *Strategic Management* (Columbus, Ohio: Merrill, 1982), 19.
2. Lawrence R. Jauch and Richard N. Osborn, "Toward an Integrated Theory of Strategy," *Academy of Management Review* 6 (July 1981): 491–98.
3. Charles R. Greer, "Counter–Cyclical Hiring as a Staffing Strategy for Managerial and Professional Personnel: Some Considerations and Issues," *Academy of Management Review* 9 (April, 1984): 324–30.
4. Yedzi M. Godiwalla, Wayne A. Meinhart, and William D. Warde, "How CEOs Form Corporate Strategy," *Management World* (May 1981): 28–29, 44.
5. Richard B. Robinson, Jr., and John A. Pearce II, "Research Thrust in Small Firm Strategic Planning," *Academy of Management Review* 9 (January 1984): 128–37.
6. George Sawyer, "Elements of Strategy," *Managerial Planning* (May/June 1981): 3–49.
7. Samuel C. Certo and J. Paul Peter, *Strategic Management: Concepts and Applications* (New York: Random House, 1988).
8. Philip S. Thomas, "Environment Analysis for Corporate Planning," *Business Horizons* (October 1974): 27–38.
9. For more information about several of these examples, see Abraham Katz, "Evaluating the Environment: Economic and Technological Factors," in *Handbook of Business Strategy,* ed. William D. Guth (Boston: Warren, Gorham & Lamont, 1985), 2–9.
10. This section is based on William F. Glueck and Lawrence R. Jauch, *Business Policy and Strategic Management* (New York: McGraw-Hill, 1984), 99–110.
11. D. Stanley Eitzen, *Social Structure and Social Problems in America* (Boston: Allyn & Bacon, 1974), 12–14.
12. "Robots for Greater Efficiency," *U.S. News & World Report,* September 5, 1983.
13. R.S. Wilson, "Managing in the Competitive Environment," *Long-Range Planning* 17 (1984): 50–63.
14. Peter Wright, "MNC—Third World Business Unit Performance: Application of Strategic Elements," *Strategic Management Journal* 5 (1984): 231–40.

15. Discussion in this section is based primarily on Thomas H. Naylor and Kristin Neva, "Design of a Strategic Planning Process," *Managerial Planning* (January/February 1980): 2–7; Donald W. Mitchell, "Pursuing Strategic Potential," *Managerial Planning* (May/June 1980): 6–10; Benton E. Gup, "Begin Strategic Planning by Asking Three Questions," *Managerial Planning* (November/December 1979): 28–31, 35; and L.V. Gerstner, Jr., "Can Strategic Planning Pay Off?" *Business Horizons.* 15 (1972): 5–16.

16. This section is based on Arthur A. Thompson and A.J. Strickland III, *Strategy Formulation and Implementation* (Plano, Tex.: Business Publications, 1983), 277–91.

17. Bruce D. Henderson, *Henderson on Corporate Strategy* (Cambridge, Mass.: ABT books, 1979).

18. Philip Kotler, *Marketing Management: Analysis, Planning and Control*, 4th ed. (Englewood Cliffs, N.J.: Prentice-Hall, 1980), 76.

19. Harold W. Fox, "The Frontiers of Strategic Planning: Intuition or Formal Models?" *Management Review* (April 1981): 8–14.

20. Ian C. MacMillan, Donald C. Hambrick, and Diana L. Day, "The Product Portfolio and Profitability—A PIMS-Based Analysis of Industrial-Product Businesses," *Academy of Management Journal* (December 1982): 733–55.

21. Bill Saporito, "Black & Decker's Gamble on Globalization," *Fortune*, May 14, 1984, 40–48.

22. Doron P. Levin, "Westinghouse's New Chief Aims to Push New Lines, Revitalize Traditional Ones," *Wall Street Journal*, November 28, 1983, 10.

23. For a detailed discussion of the characteristics of strategic and tactical planning, see George A. Steiner, *Top Management Planning* (Toronto, Canada: Collier-Macmillan, 1969), 37–39.

24. Russell L. Ackoff, *A Concept of Corporate Planning* (New York: Wiley, 1970), 4.

25. G.E. Tibbits, "Small Business Management: A Normative Approach," *MSU Business Topics* (Autumn 1979): 5–12.

26. "The New Breed of Strategic Planner," *Business Week*, September 17, 1984, 62–67.

Action Summary Answer Key

1. a. T, p. 133
   b. c, p. 133
2. a. e, p. 134
   b. a, p. 135

3. a. F, p. 136
   b. a, pp. 136–142
4. a. a, p. 144
   b. F, p. 144

5. a. d, p. 144
   b. d, p. 146
   c. d, pp. 147–148

6. a. F, p. 149
   b. b, p. 149

BELL CANADA: POISED FOR THE FUTURE

Despite decades of change in technology, regulatory structures, and business practices, Bell Canada's monopoly in key areas of communications remains unshaken. Such continuing dominance did not happen by accident. Unlike the railways, which were eclipsed by competing transport modes when technology and public works spending eluded their grasp, Bell Canada has held its dominance with a solid innovative thrust and a knack for keeping official opinion on its side when challenged on key issues.

The person who commands this tradition today is Léonce Montambault, the company's president and chief executive officer. "The future of communications in general and telecommunications in particular is a brilliant one—as long as we're prepared for it. And so we have to prepare ourselves. We are a company with high technological content. We have to make sure, though, that technology doesn't determine the future. Rather, it should be the market and the customer who determine what technology we'll need in the future."

Uncommunicative about what makes him "tick," Montambault prefers talking about some of the technological innovations the company is working on and its proposals for "rate rebalancing"—jargon for cheaper long-distance rates to be offset by high local ones. The

Montambault: "we have to prepare ourselves."

two strategies have a common thread: they are both aimed at outflanking potential competitors seeking to establish a firm footing in areas Bell has mapped out for itself.

According to Bell's plans, Montreal customers will soon be able to visit their friendly neighbourhood Téléboutique and walk away with computer terminals to be hooked into Bell's new Alex system (Alex, as in Alexander Graham Bell). Interactive computer systems, which allow customers to tap into remote databases for a fee, have been around for a few years. A phone, a home computer terminal, and a linking device called a modem can provide access to a range of information and entertainment services.

Following in the footsteps of the French telephone system's highly successful Minitel, Bell wants more of the action for itself. It hopes to have its own Alex terminals (to be rented for eight to ten dollars a month) in households throughout its territory and its own network of authorized service providers. So far, about forty-five companies have shown an interest in hooking up with Alex to sell services such as home shopping, home banking, electronic games, stock market quotes, and even college courses. Montreal was chosen for the launch, with Toronto to follow.

A Montreal company calling itself *Centre d'Excellence en Technologie Informatique* is offering the Minitel system in competition with Alex. However, Bell asserts that Alex gives faster responses and sharper pictures than Minitel, and meets North American technical standards. "There are very few trials going on in the United States for this type of service," says Montambault. "We're the first to develop a North American protocol, which will allow us to export our technology to the U.S. if it succeeds. It's a new angle, and there's no irrefutable proof it will take off."

Other areas of technological advance may be less evident to Bell customers, but will open the way to enhanced service in the future, especially for business users. Such is the case of ISDN (Integrated Services Digital Network), which provides more flexible use of existing lines and eliminates the need for separate networks for voice, data, and visual messages. It also allows access to digital services through ordinary wall jacks.

Montambault says 50 percent of Bell customers should be linked to digital exchanges by 1990 and 95 percent by 1995. Digital transmission is clearer and more versatile than traditional analogue transmission. "With ISDN you can concentrate everything on one line. The customer will determine what use he wants to make of it, for instance voice communications during the day and data transmission at night. Plenty of machines will be able to talk to each other without needing all sorts of different networks."

With 1987 revenues of $6.38 billion, profits of $731 million, and a territory covering most of Quebec, Ontario, and the Eastern Arctic, Bell is Canada's undisputed communications giant. Vertical integration of Bell with fellow BCE Inc. subsidiary Northern Telecom and jointly-owned Bell-Northern Research creates a mutually beneficial association that speeds technological advance, Montambault says.

While some have argued that Bell remains overly dependent on Northern Telecom as a supplier, the Re-strictive Trade Practices Tribunal in Ottawa has ruled that this vertical integration actually benefits customers in some respects. Montambault says exports of Northern Telecom products developed with Bell's collaboration provide economies of scale that bring down prices paid by Bell. While growing competition among suppliers means that Bell will turn to outside firms for a growing proportion of its needs, Northern Telecom is Bell's main supplier and will remain so as long as it serves the giant's needs.

DISCUSSION ISSUES

1. What would be the value of undertaking a critical analysis for Bell's Montambault? The value of a SWOT analysis? Discuss both.
2. Why has Bell's dominance not "happened by accident"? Discuss the current business strategy Bell has adopted.
3. What factors must Bell continue to monitor in order to stay on top strategically? Elaborate.
4. Does Bell engage in pure strategic planning, pure tactical planning, or a combination of both? Support your answer.

Based on "Bell Canada's Montambault poised to ring in future," by Eric Hamovitch in *This Week in Business*, March 19, 1988. Used with permission.

C H A P T E R

7

PLANS AND PLANNING TOOLS

STUDENT LEARNING OBJECTIVES

From studying this chapter, I will attempt to acquire:

1. A complete definition of a plan.
2. Insights regarding various dimensions of plans.
3. An understanding of various types of plans.
4. Insights on why plans fail.
5. A knowledge of various planning areas within an organization.
6. A definition of forecasting.
7. An ability to see the advantages and disadvantages of various methods of sales forecasting.
8. A definition of scheduling.
9. An understanding of Gantt charts and PERT.

CHAPTER OUTLINE

A PLANNING INCIDENT

Jane and Paul were partners in a small machine shop that did jobbing (contract) work predominantly for machine tool manufacturers. Because of a transportation strike, the shop was virtually shut down for a few days. The partners came in every day, of course, and one morning Jane mentioned that it had been months since both of them had sat down to discuss their business in general terms. The daily routine had kept them so busy that there hardly had been time to say, "Good morning."

Paul agreed and suggested that they get at it right then and there. During the next two hours, they discussed everything from how old their machines were to putting in new vending machines for coffee and sandwiches. What seemed to concern the partners most, however, was that most of their equipment was quite old, dating back to World War II days in many instances. This situation made matching the competition's quality and speed of output difficult.

Finally, Jane leaned back in her chair. "Paul, we've got to get our costs down. We can't do it overnight, but we can make that one of our major goals over the next few years. If we don't, we're just going to lose out on the bidding on new contracts."

Paul nodded his assent. "You're right, and there's something else too. For a long time, we've been preaching quality to our people, but it's really difficult for them with the equipment they've got to work with. We could lower costs and emphasize quality successfully if we could get some modern machinery in here. From what I've learned in the trade journals, with new machine tools, we could drop our cost 10 to 20 percent over the next five years."

From Earl F. Lundgren, *Organizational Management Systems and Process.* © 1974 Harper & Row, Publishers, Inc. Reprinted by permission of the author.

What's Ahead

Chapter 5 focused on the decision-making phase, or the evaluation-of-alternatives phase, of the planning process. Chapter 6 examined the two basic types of organizational planning—strategic and tactical. This chapter continues the discussion of the planning process by emphasizing additional fundamental issues about the plans that managers develop. Jane and Paul, the partners in the introductory case, need to formulate plans for their organization. In this chapter, fundamental facts about plans and the tools managers can use to develop them are presented.

 **PLANS**

The first half of this chapter covers the fundamental facts about plans by: (1) defining what a plan is; (2) outlining the dimensions of a plan; (3) listing various types of plans; (4) discussing why plans fail; and (5) explaining two major organizational areas in which planning usually takes place.

Plans: A Definition

A **plan** is a specific action proposed to help the organization achieve its objectives. According to Henry Sisk, "planning, the process of evaluating all relevant information and the assessment of probable future developments, results in the statement of a recommended course of action—a plan."[1] Regardless of how important experience-related intuition may be to managers, successful management action and strategy typically are based on reason. Rational managers are extremely important to the development of an organizational plan.[2]

A plan is a statement of recommended action.

Dimensions of Plans

Kast and Rosenzweig have indicated that a plan has four major dimensions: (1) repetitiveness, (2) time, (3) scope, and (4) level.[3] Each dimension is an independent characteristic of a plan and should be considered during plan development.[4]

In planning, managers should consider

The **repetitiveness dimension** describes the extent to which a plan is used time after time. Some plans are specially designed for one certain situation that is relatively short term in nature. Plans of this sort are essentially non-repetitive. On the other hand, some plans are designed to be used time after time for situations that exist continually over the long term. These plans are basically repetitive in nature.

the degree to which the plan is to be used over and over again,

161

the length of time the plan covers,

The **time dimension** of a plan is the length of the time period the plan covers. In Chapter 6, strategic planning was defined as being long term in nature, and tactical planning was defined as being short term. It follows, then, that strategic plans cover relatively long periods of time, while tactical plans cover relatively short periods of time.

the parts of the management system on which the plan focuses,

The **scope dimension** describes the portion of the total management system at which the plan is aimed. Some plans are designed to cover the entire open management system: the organizational environment, inputs, process, and outputs. A plan for the management system as a whole is often referred to as a master plan. Other plans, however, are developed to cover only a portion of the management system. An example would be a plan developed to cover the recruitment of new workers—a portion of the organizational input segment of the management system. The greater the portion of the management system that a plan covers, the broader the scope of the plan is said to be.

and the organizational level at which the plan is aimed.

The **level dimension** of a plan indicates the level of the organization at which the plan is aimed. Top-level plans are those designed for the top-management level of the organization, while middle-level and lower-level plans are designed for middle-level and lower-level management, respectively. Because all parts of the management system are interdependent, however, plans for any level of the organization have some effect on all other levels.

Figure 7.1 illustrates the four dimensions of an organizational plan. This figure stresses that when managers develop a plan, they should consider the degree to which the plan will be used over and over again, the period of time

FIGURE 7.1   Four major dimensions to consider when developing a plan.

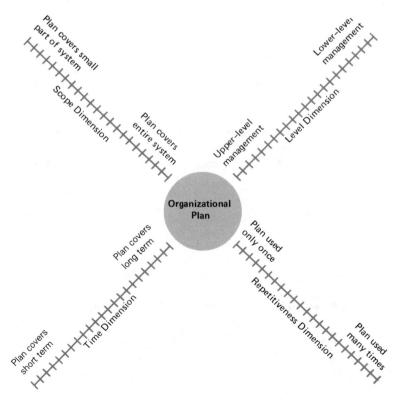

the plan will cover, the parts of the management system on which the plan focuses, and the organizational level at which the plan is aimed.

BACK TO THE CASE

Before Jane and Paul, the partners in the introductory case, develop plans for cutting costs and improving quality, they should understand that plans are recommendations for future actions and therefore should be action-oriented. Their plans should state precisely what they are going to do in order to achieve their goals.

In developing the plans, they should consider how often the plans will be used and the length of time they will cover. Will a plan be implemented only once, for a year, to address the quality issue, or be used on a long-term basis to handle the ongoing issue of quality control?

In addition, Jane and Paul should consider what part of the machine shop the plans will be aimed at and what level the plans will focus on. In other words, a plan to cut costs may encompass all shop operations, whereas a plan to improve quality may affect only one part of the production process. Similarly, a plan to cut costs may be aimed at top-level management, whereas a quality-control plan may be aimed at lower-level management and the machine operators themselves. Of course, Jane and Paul must realize that since management systems are interdependent, any plans they implement will affect the system as a whole.

Types of Plans

With the repetitiveness dimension as a guide, organizational plans usually are divided into two types: standing plans and single-use plans. **Standing plans** are used over and over again because they focus on organizational situations that occur repeatedly, while **single-use plans** are used only once or several times because they focus on dealing with relatively unique situations within the organization. Figure 7.2 illustrates that standing plans can be subdivided into policies, procedures, and rules, and that single-use plans can be subdivided into programs and budgets.[5]

Standing plans are used repeatedly, while single-use plans are used only once or several times.

Standing Plans: Policies, Procedures, and Rules

A **policy** is a standing plan that furnishes broad, general guidelines for channeling management thinking toward taking action consistent with reaching organizational objectives. For example, an organizational policy relating to personnel

Policies are broad, general guidelines for action.

FIGURE 7.2   Standing plans and single-use plans.

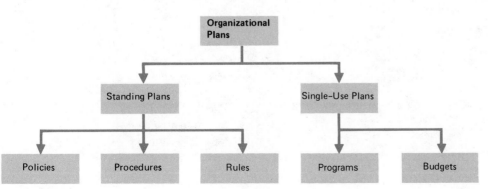

FIGURE 7.3 Organizational areas in which policy statements usually are written.

I. General Management

A. *Divisions and functional staffs*
1. Authority and responsibilities of divisions concerning pricing, capital authorization, interdivisional transfers, product areas, and authority retained in central headquarters
2. Functional staff relationships at headquarters and authority in divisions

B. *Growth*
1. Sales rate
2. Profit rate
3. Acquisitions

C. *Planning*
1. Budgets
2. Company basic lines of business
3. Comprehensive planning
4. Organization

D. *Policy authority and statements*

E. *Miscellaneous*
1. Acceptance of gifts or services by employees
2. Answering correspondence
3. Computer procurement
4. Disaster control
5. Employment of consultants
6. Gifts and gratuities to government and company personnel
7. Internal auditor reports
8. Political activities of managers
9. Records management

II. Marketing

A. *Products and services sold*
1. Types
2. Inventory of parts
3. Licensing
4. Modification
5. Quality
6. Warranty

B. *Customers*
1. Contract clearance
2. Export sales
3. Interdivisional transfers
4. Market areas
5. Market channels
6. Relations with customers, including dealers and distributors
7. Service for customers
8. Size of customers

C. *Pricing*
1. Authority to price
2. Compliance with antitrust laws
3. Discounting
4. Resale price maintenance
5. Timing of price change

D. *Sales promotion*
1. Advertising media
2. Product publicity

III. Production

A. *Assignments of products to divisions*

B. *Contracting*

C. *Manufacturing methods*

D. *Production control*

E. *Production planning*

F. *Quality control*

G. *Safety*

H. *Shipping*

I. *Size of production runs*

J. *Stabilization of production*

K. *Tooling*

IV. Procurement

A. *Make-or-buy decisions*

B. *Minimum procurement quantities*

C. *Purchasing channels*

D. *Relations with suppliers*

E. *Types of vendors*

V. Research

A. *Allocating funds*

B. *Basic research*

C. *Evaluating results*

D. *Inventions*

E. *Patents*

F. *Research areas*

G. *Research records*

H. *Trademarks*

VI. Finance

A. *Audit*

B. *Budget*
1. Developing
2. Controlling

C. *Credit*
1. Customers
2. Employees

D. *Dividend policy*
1. Size relative to profit
2. Stabilizing

E. *Expenditures*
1. Authority to spend company money
2. Contributions and donations

F. *Protecting capital*
1. Insurance
2. Reserves

G. *Structure*
1. Debt ratios
2. Long-term financing
3. Short-term financing

VII. Facilities

A. *Decision-making process for expenditure*

B. *Location*

C. *Maintenance*

D. *Replacement*

VIII. Personnel

A. *Collective bargaining and union relations*

B. *Communications systems*

C. *Employment and recruiting*

D. *Equal opportunities*

E. *Hours of work*

F. *Incentives and bonuses*

G. *Pensions*

H. *Selection*

I. *Services*
1. Food service
2. Health and safety
3. Insurance
4. Recreational and educational activities
5. Retirement
6. Sick leave
7. Transportation and parking

J. *Training and education*

K. *Wages and salaries*

L. *Working conditions*

IX. Public Relations

A. *Community*

B. *Conflict of interests*

C. *Contributions*

D. *Determining contents of communications*

E. *Extent of function*

F. *Role of executives*

G. *Selecting media for communications*

X. Legal

A. *Clearance of contracts*

B. *Compliance with law*

C. *Patents for employee inventors*

D. *Protection of proprietory rights*

E. *Reservation of rights and interests*

F. *Real property leases*

might be worded as follows: "Our organization will strive to recruit only the most talented employees." This policy statement is very broad and only gives managers a general idea of what to do in the area of personnel employment. The policy is intended to display the extreme importance management has attached to hiring competent employees and to guiding action accordingly. Other organizational areas in which policy statements usually are written are listed in Figure 7.3.

A **procedure** is a standing plan that outlines a series of related actions that must be taken to accomplish a particular task. In general, procedures outline more specific action than do policies. Organizations usually have many different sets of procedures that cover various tasks to be accomplished. The sample procedure in Figure 7.4 lists the series of steps recruiters take to interview prospective personnel at Indiana State University.

A **rule** is a standing plan that designates specific required action. In essence, a rule indicates what an organization member should or should not do and allows no room for interpretation. An example of a rule would be: "All students must be seated in silence immediately after the bell rings, signaling the beginning of class." The concept of rules may be more clear after thinking about the purpose

> Procedures outline specific actions to be performed sequentially.

> Rules designate specific, mandatory action.

FIGURE 7.4 Procedure for interviewing prospective personnel at Indiana State University.

1. Any candidate brought to campus for an interview should be a best prospect of at least three qualified persons whose credentials have been examined. Personnel supply in an academic field may reduce the number of possible candidates.

2. Before an invitation is extended to a candidate who must travel a distance greater than five hundred miles to reach Terre Haute, the department chairperson should:

   a. ascertain the existence of the vacancy or authorization by a call to the assistant vice-president for academic affairs.

   b. forward to the dean and assistant vice-president credentials which should include, if possible, parts d, e, f, and g, Item 6, below.

3. Any administrative person who is scheduled to interview a candidate should be forwarded credentials for the candidate prior to the interview.

4. Interviews with administrative personnel should be scheduled as follows:

   A candidate whose probable academic rank will be instructor or assistant professor should talk with the dean prior to the assistant vice-president. A candidate whose academic rank should probably be associate professor, in addition to the dean and assistant vice-president, should be scheduled for an interview with the vice-president for academic affairs. In addition to the above, a candidate for appointment as professor or department chairperson should also be scheduled for a meeting with the president.

5. Although courtesy to the candidate may demand that the interview schedule be maintained, the vice-president, at his or her discretion or in agreement with the suggestion by the chairperson, dean, or assistant vice-president, may cancel the interview for the candidate with the president.

6. A recommendation for appointment should contain the following:

   a. a letter from the department chairperson (or dean) setting forth the recommendation and proposing the academic rank and salary.

   b. a statement from the dean if the recommendation letter is prepared by the department chairperson.

   c. the completed university resume form. This can be completed by the candidate when on campus or returned to the chairperson by mail later, but must be included.

   d. vitae information.

   e. placement papers.

   f. official transcripts (especially important if placement papers are not current or prepared by a university bureau).

   g. as many as three letters of recommendation, one or two of these reflecting the candidate's current assignment. These letters are necessary if the placement materials have not been updated to contain current recommendations.

   h. a written report on any telephone conversations concerning the candidate made by the department chairperson.

7. Because of the difficulty in arranging interviews on Saturday, campus visits should occur during the week.

8. Whenever possible, accommodations at the Hulman Center should be limited to one overnight. The university cannot accept any charge for hotel accommodations other than at the Hulman Center. "Hotel accommodations" are defined to be lodging only, and not food, telephone, or other personal services.

9. Travel can be reimbursed in one of the following ways:

   a. a candidate traveling in-state will have mileage paid, at the rate of eight cents per mile. The official Indiana map is used to compute mileage rather than a speedometer reading.

   b. a candidate traveling from out-of-state can claim the cost of airfare (tourist class) or train fare (coach class).

   c. a candidate who may choose to drive from out-of-state cannot be paid a mileage cost. Instead, airfare and train-fare amounts are determined and the lesser of the two is paid as an automobile mileage reimbursement.

"In this organization, Challis, middle management uses only blue highlighting markers."

Wall Street Journal, *June 17, 1987. From the* Wall Street Journal—*permission, Cartoon Features Syndicate.*

and nature of rules in such games as Scrabble and Monopoly. Some organizations have too many rules, as the cartoon suggests.

Although policies, procedures, and rules are all standing plans, they are all defined differently and have different purposes within the organization. As Figure 7.5 illustrates, however, for the standing plans of an organization to be effective, policies, procedures, and rules must be consistent and mutually supportive.

FIGURE 7.5   A successful standing-plan program with mutually supportive policies, procedures, and rules.

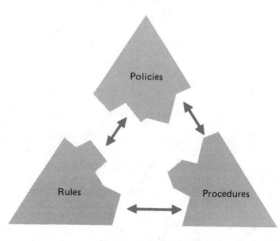

Single-Use Plans: Programs and Budgets

A **program** is a single-use plan designed to carry out a special project within an organization. The project itself typically is not intended to be in existence over the entire life of the organization. However, the program exists to achieve some purpose that, if accomplished, will contribute to the organization's long-term success.

A common example of a program is the management development program found in many organizations. This program exists to raise managers' skill level in one or more of the skills mentioned in Chapter 1: technical skills, conceptual skills, or human skills. Increasing the skill level of these managers, however, is not an end in itself. The purpose of the program is to produce competent managers who are equipped to help the organization be successful over the long term. Once managerial skills have been raised to a desired level, the management development program can be de-emphasized.

A **budget** is a single-use financial plan that covers a specified length of time. A firm's budget is a plan detailing how funds will be spent on labour, raw materials, capital goods, and so on, as well as how the funds for these expenditures will be obtained.[6] Although budgets are planning devices, they are also strategies for organizational control and are covered in more detail in Chapter 17.

Programs aid success indirectly.

Budgets are financial plans.

Why Plans Fail

If managers know why plans fail, they can take steps to eliminate the factors that cause failure and thereby increase the probability that their plans will be successful. A study by K.A. Ringbakk indicates that plans fail when:[7]

1. Corporate planning is not integrated into the total management system.
2. There is a lack of understanding of the different steps of the planning process.
3. Management at different levels in the organization has not properly engaged in or contributed to planning activities.
4. Responsibility for planning is wrongly vested solely in the planning department.
5. Management expects that plans developed will be realized with little effort.
6. In starting formal planning, too much is attempted at once.
7. Management fails to operate by the plan.
8. Financial projections are confused with planning.
9. Inadequate inputs are used in planning.
10. Management fails to see the overall planning process.

Planning Areas: Input Planning

As discussed earlier, organizational inputs, process, outputs, and environment are major factors in determining how successful a management system will be. Naturally, a comprehensive organizational plan should focus on each of these factors. The following two sections cover planning in two areas normally associated with the input factor: plant facilities planning and human resource plan-

Input planning: Plans
to provide organiza-
tional resources.

ning. Planning in areas such as these normally is called **input planning**—the development of proposed action that will furnish sufficient and appropriate organizational resources for reaching established organizational objectives.

Plant Facilities Planning

One facet of plant
facilities planning is
site selection.

Plant facilities planning involves determining the type of buildings and equipment an organization needs to reach its objectives. One major part of this determination is called **site selection**—deciding where a plant facility should be located. Figure 7.6 shows several major areas to be considered when selecting a plant site and sample questions that can be asked to begin exploring these areas. Naturally, the specifics of site selection vary from organization to organization.

One factor that can significantly influence site selection is whether a site is being selected in a foreign country. In a foreign country, management may face issues such as foreign governments taking different amounts of time to approve site purchases, and political pressures slowing down or preventing purchase of a site.

FIGURE 7.6   Major areas of consideration when selecting a plant site and sample exploratory questions.

Major Areas for Consideration in Site Selection	Sample Question to Begin Exploring Major Areas
Profit	
Market location	Where are our customers in relation to the site?
Competition	What competitive situation exists at the site?
Operating costs	
Suppliers	Are materials available near the site at reasonable cost?
Utilities	What are utility rates at the site? Are they sufficiently available?
Wages	What wage rates are paid in comparable organizations near the site?
Taxes	What are tax rates on income, sales, property, etc. for the site?
Investment costs	
Land/development	How expensive is land and construction at the site?
Others	
Transportation	Are airlines, railroads, highways, etc. available to the site?
Laws	What laws exist related to zoning, pollution, etc. that influence operations if the site is chosen?
Labour	Does an adequate labour supply exist around the site?
Unionization	What degree of unionization exists in the site area?
Living conditions	Are housing, schools, etc. appropriate around the site?
Community relations	Is the community supportive of the organization moving into the area?

Adapted from E. S. Groo, "Choosing Foreign Locations: One Company's Experience," *Columbia Journal of World Business* (September/October 1977): 77. Used with permission.

FIGURE 7.7   Results of weighing seven site variables for six countries.

Criteria	Maximum Value Assigned	Sites					
		Japan	Chile	Jamaica	Australia	Mexico	France
Living conditions	100	70	40	45	50	60	60
Accessibility	75	55	35	20	60	70	70
Industrialization	60	40	50	55	35	35	30
Labour availability	35	30	10	10	30	35	35
Economics	35	15	15	15	15	25	25
Community capability and attitude	30	25	20	10	15	25	15
Effect on company reputation	35	25	20	10	15	25	15
Total	370	260	190	165	220	275	250

Adapted from E. S. Groo, "Choosing Foreign Locations: One Company's Experience," *Columbia Journal of World Business* (September/October 1977): 77. Used with permission.

Many organizations use a weighting process to compare site differences among foreign countries. Basically, this weighting process involves: (1) deciding on a set of variables that are critical to obtaining an appropriate site; (2) assigning each of these variables a weight or rank of relative importance; and (3) ranking alternative sites, depending on how they reflect these different variables.

Site selection may involve a weighting process to compare site differences.

As an example, Figure 7.7 shows the results of such a weighting process for seven different site variables and six different countries. In this figure, "Living conditions" is worth 100 points and is the most important variable, while "Effect on company reputation" is worth 35 points and is the least important variable. Also in Figure 7.7, various countries are given a number of points for each variable, depending on the importance of the variable and how it exists within the country. The illustration shows that, given the established set of weighted criteria, Japan, Mexico, and France received more points and therefore are more desirable sites than Chile, Jamaica, or Australia.

Human Resource Planning

Human resources are another area with which input planners usually are concerned. Organizational objectives cannot be attained without appropriate personnel. Future needs for human resources are influenced mainly by employee turnover, the nature of the present work force, and the rate of growth of the organization.[8]

Personnel planners should try to answer such questions as: (1) What types of people does the organization need to reach its objectives? (2) How many of each type are needed? (3) What steps for the recruitment and selection of these people should the organization take? (4) Can present employees be further trained to fill future positions? (5) At what rate are employees lost to other organizations? These are not the only questions personnel planners should ask, but they are representative.

FIGURE 7.8   The human resource planning process.

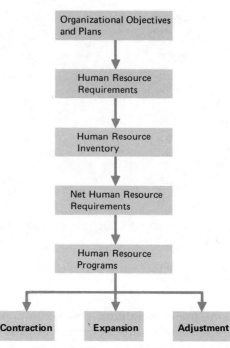

From Bruce Coleman, "An Integrated System for Manpower Planning," *Business Horizons* (October 1970): 89-95. Copyright, 1970, by the Foundation for the School of Business at Indiana University. Reprinted by permission.

The human resource planning process involves determining net human resource needs and finding people to meet those needs.

Figure 7.8 shows the human resource planning process as developed by Bruce Coleman. According to this model, **human resource planning** involves reflecting on organizational objectives to determine overall human resource needs, comparing these needs to the existing human resource inventory to determine net human resource needs, and, finally, seeking appropriate organization members to meet the net human resource needs.

BACK TO THE CASE

Jane and Paul probably should develop both standing plans and single-use plans for their machine shop. Standing plans include policies, procedures, and rules, and should be developed for situations that occur repeatedly. For example, one policy Jane and Paul could develop might focus on the product quality they want to emphasize with employees. Single-use plans include programs and budgets, and should be developed to help manage non-repetitive situations. For example, Jane and Paul might want to work on a budget that would allow them to purchase new machine tools. Jane and Paul also should become thoroughly aware of the reasons why plans fail and take steps to avoid these pitfalls.

Plant facilities planning and human resource plan-

ning are two additional areas Jane and Paul might want to discuss. Plant facilities planning entails developing the type of plant facility Jane and Paul would need to reach company objectives. Since they already have an operating plant, plant site location as a part of plant facilities planning probably is not too important to them. Modernization of equipment as a part of plant facilities planning, however, probably would be very interesting to them since they need to update their machinery to keep up with competitors. Human resource planning involves obtaining and/or developing the personnel the organization needs to reach its objectives. In this area, Jane and Paul might want to discuss additional skills their employees would need to run new machine tools.

PLANS TO MOVE SOUTH

The decision makers at Royal LePage Real Estate Services Ltd. see vast opportunities south of the border. In fact, they believe that the company can make more money in some U.S. cities than it can in all of Canada. The president of the firm's commercial division, Chris Davis, is in charge of turning around the unprofitable U.S. offices in Chicago and seven other cities. But this is just the first step in Royal LePage's plan to become a major presence in North American real estate. In addition to expanding its business in the U.S., the company wants to become known less as a real estate broker and more as an investment adviser.

Royal LePage firmly believes it has the potential to achieve its goal. While it offers a wide range of services, including mortgage lending, what the company is really banking on is its strong connection to its parent company, Royal Trustco. Royal Trustco is controlled by Trilon Financial Corporation, the growing financial services conglomerate of Peter and Edward Bronfman's Edper Investment Ltd. In fact, Trilon views Royal LePage as being part of its bid to become a "financial shopping centre."

If it wants to grow significantly, Royal LePage really does need the U.S. market. Davis calculates that the U.S. commercial properties market is roughly one hundred times larger than Canada's. This translates into annual commission revenues of $20 billion. Royal LePage would be happy with just a 1 percent share of this market. The company's immediate plans, however, are to turn around its existing U.S. commercial services and then expand into residential services. To finance these plans, Royal LePage intends to raise $25-to-$30 million in public share offerings.

The U.S. market presents certain challenges to Royal LePage. As in Canada, some cities have a surplus of commercial buildings due to overzealous development, and as a result prices are soft. Real estate analyst Frank Mayer of the Toronto-based investment dealer Brown Baldwin Nisher Ltd. predicts that commercial realtors will have to shift their attention from new projects to turning over existing properties. The U.S. real estate industry is seeing national firms consolidating and buying local realtors. Competition is increasing with huge financial service conglomerates, fast-moving specialty firms, and aggressive franchisers all vying for a share of the market.

"Royal LePage wants to increase its share of the Canadian real estate market . . ."

171

Another challenge is that Royal LePage's U.S. offices have lost several million dollars since they were acquired in 1982 from the Fuller Commercial Brokerage Company. To remedy this situation, Davis has sold off three offices in Texas that have been in decline along with the energy industry. The Los Angeles location was also closed. Offices were maintained in Tampa and North Palm Beach, Florida, as well as in Atlanta, Chicago, Denver, San Francisco, Oakland, and Santa Clara, California. The latter state even gained two offices, in San Jose and Walnut Creek. In early 1986, these U.S. offices took the Royal LePage name, shedding the Fuller Commercial Brokerage identification.

Since that time, Royal LePage has applied the same niche-carving technique that has been successful in Canada. In each office, staff determine one or two specialty commercial services that can be delivered at a profit. These might include appraisal, brokerage, and leasing work, land acquisition and development services, financing, and asset and investment management. Davis believes that "the U.S. market is so enormous that the Americans didn't have to specialize to the same extent we have. Canadians have the advantage of being in a very small market with intense competition among ourselves."

In addition to the niche-carving technique, Royal LePage is applying its hands-on management style south of the border. Davis monitors the divisions through weekly reports from the field. Royal LePage is also increasingly hiring newcomers to the real estate business, because they can more easily adopt the company's way of doing business.

When the existing U.S. offices break even, Royal LePage will then turn to expansion. Depending on local market conditions, the firm will follow one or both of two alternatives: open new offices, or buy existing realty firms. The Royal LePage board, which includes representatives from both Royal Trust and Trilon, will be responsible for making these decisions.

So far, the board has approved an investment of more than $1 million for the opening of five or six residential offices in one U.S. test market. This test market must show good growth potential. To control the test operation, there has to be a Royal LePage office nearby to provide marketing support, and it must be no further than a two-hour flight from the Royal LePage head office in Toronto. No moves will be made before research reports are thoroughly studied.

George Cormack, Royal LePage's president and CEO, insists that before this happens, however, the Canadian operation must be solid. Royal LePage wants to increase its share of the Canadian real estate market from its current 25 percent to 30 percent. The firm has many strengths with which to accomplish this. One is its residential computerized listing system, which links the company's offices and accesses the cross-Canada multiple listing service. The residential division's operating system is another strength. Offices are set up in clusters to provide support for each other, and each has a manager, a secretarial staff of three, and twenty-four sales representatives. When opening new residential offices, all the elements—from company policies and training methods to sales techniques and advertising budgets—can fall into place within four months.

One way Royal LePage has attracted new business is by offering their own residential mortgages. This service, introduced in the summer of 1985, has issued more than $1 billion in mortgages. The firm has begun negotiations with U.S. lenders to set up a similar service in the States.

The December 1984 merger of the real estate brokerage operations of A.E. LePage and Royal Trustco produced a major company with huge advantages over other brokers. Its parent, Royal Trustco, has assets of more than $13 billion and annual revenues of close to $2 billion. The combination of financial resources and superior planning suggest that Royal LePage's inroads into the U.S. market will meet with success.

Based on "Southern exposure," by Eva Varangu in *Canadian Business*, November 1986. Used with permission.

▦ PLANNING TOOLS

Planning tools are techniques managers can use to help develop plans. The remainder of this chapter discusses forecasting and scheduling, two of the most important of these tools.

Forecasting

Forecasting is the process of predicting future environmental happenings that will influence the operation of the organization. Although sophisticated forecasting techniques have been developed only rather recently, the concept of forecasting can be traced at least as far back in the management literature as Fayol.[9] The importance of forecasting lies in its ability to help managers better understand the future make-up of the organizational environment, which, in turn, helps them to formulate more effective plans.

William C. House, in describing the Insect Control Services Company, has developed an excellent illustration of how forecasting works. Figure 7.9 lists the primary factors that Insect Control Services attempts to measure in developing its forecast. In general, Insect Control Services forecasts by attempting to:[10]

1. Establish the relationships between industry sales and national economic and social indicators.
2. Determine the impact of government restrictions concerning the use of chemical pesticides on the growth of chemical, biological, and electromagnetic energy pest control markets.

> Forecasting involves predicting the future organizational environment.

FIGURE 7.9   Primary factors measured during Insect Control Services' forecasting process.

Gross National Product — Measure of total dollars available for industrial, commercial, institutional, and residential purchases of insect control units.

Personal Consumption Expenditures — Measure of dollars available for consumer purchases of:

1. *Services* — affect potential contract insect control services.
2. *Durables* — affect market potential for residential units.
3. *Nondurables* — affect sales of food, drugs, and other products that influence expansion of industrial and commercial users of insect control equipment.

Governmental Purchases of Goods, Services — Measure of spending for hospitals, government food services, other institutions that purchase insect control equipment.

Gross Private Domestic Investment in New Plant and Equipment — A measure of business expansion which indicates the size and nature of market potential for industrial and commercial purchases of insect control units in new or expanded existing establishments.

Industrial Production for Selected Industries — Measure of expansion of industrial output for industries that are users, potential users of insect control units, or materials suppliers for insect control services. Such expansion (or contraction) of output will likely affect:

1. Industrial and commercial purchases of insect control units.
2. Availability of materials used to manufacture insect control units.

Employment and Unemployment Levels — Indicates availability or scarcity of human resources available to augment Insect Control Services human resources pool.

Consumer, Wholesale Prices — Measure of ability, willingness of homeowners to purchase residential units and of the availability and cost of raw materials and component parts.

Corporate Profits — Indicates how trends in prices, unit labour costs, and productivity affect corporate profits. Size of total corporate profits indicates profit margins in present and potential markets and funds available for expansion.

Business Borrowings, Interest Rates — Measures of the availability and cost of borrowed funds needed to finance working capital needs and plant and equipment expansion.

Adapted, with permission, from W. C. House, "Environmental Analysis: Key to More Effective Dynamic Planning," *Managerial Planning* (January/February 1977): 27, published by the Planning Executive Institute, Oxford, Ohio 45046.

3. Evaluate sales growth potential, profitability, resources required, and risks involved in each of its market areas (commercial, industrial, institutional, governmental, and residential).
4. Evaluate the potential for expansion of marketing efforts in several geographic areas.
5. Determine the likelihood of technological breakthroughs that would make existing product lines obsolete.

Sales forecasting is the "key" organizational forecast.

In addition to the more general process of organizational forecasting illustrated by Insect Control Services are specialized types of forecasting, such as economic forecasting, technological forecasting, social trends forecasting, and sales forecasting. Although a complete organizational forecasting process can and usually should include all of these types of forecasting, sales forecasting is typically cited as the "key" organizational forecast. A sales forecast is a prediction of how high or how low sales will be over the period of time under consideration. It is the "key" forecast because it serves as the fundamental guideline for planning within the organization. Once the sales forecast has been completed, managers can decide, for example, if more salespeople should be hired, if more money for plant expansion must be borrowed, or if layoffs are upcoming and cutbacks in certain areas are necessary. The following section outlines various methods of sales forecasting.

Methods of Sales Forecasting

Jury of Executive Opinion Method

Jury of executive opinion: Executives predict sales.

The **jury of executive opinion method** of sales forecasting is very straightforward. A group of managers within the organization assemble to discuss their opinions on what will happen to sales in the future. Since these discussion sessions usually revolve around the hunches or experienced guesses of each of the managers, the resulting forecast is a blend of expressed opinions.

The delphi method of forecasting requires six steps.

A more recently developed forecasting method similar to the jury of executive opinion method is called the *delphi method*.[11] This method also gathers, evaluates, and summarizes expert opinions as the basis for a forecast.[12] The basic delphi method employs the following steps:

Step 1   Various experts are asked to answer independently, in writing, a series of questions about the future of sales or whatever other area is being forecasted.

Step 2   A summary of all answers is then prepared. No expert knows how any other expert answered the questions.

Step 3   Copies of the summary are given to the individual experts with the request that they modify their original answers if they think they should.

Step 4   Another summary is made of these modifications, and copies again are distributed to the experts. This time, however, expert opinions that deviate significantly from the norm must be justified in writing.

Step 5   A third summary is made of the opinions and justifications, and copies are distributed to the experts. Justification for all answers is now required in writing.

Step 6   The forecast is generated from all of the opinions and justifications that arise from Step 5.

Sales Force Estimation Method

The **sales force estimation method** requires the solicitation of the opinions of company salespeople instead of company managers. Salespeople interact with customers and can use this interaction as a basis for predicting future sales. As with the jury of executive opinion method, the resulting forecast generally is a compromise of the views of the salespeople as a group.

Sales force estimation: Salespeople predict sales.

Time Series Analysis Method

The **time series analysis method** predicts future sales by analyzing the historical relationship between sales and time. Information showing the relationship between sales and time typically is presented on a graph, as in Figure 7.10. This presentation clearly displays past trends, which can be used to predict future sales.

Time series analysis: Past sales predict future sales.

The time series analysis in Figure 7.10 indicates steadily increasing sales over time. However, since, in the long term, products generally go through what is

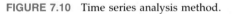

FIGURE 7.10   Time series analysis method.

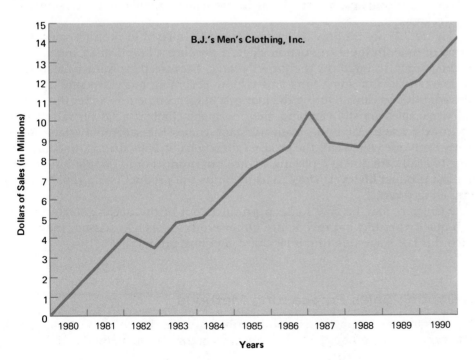

FIGURE 7.11   Stages of the product life cycle.

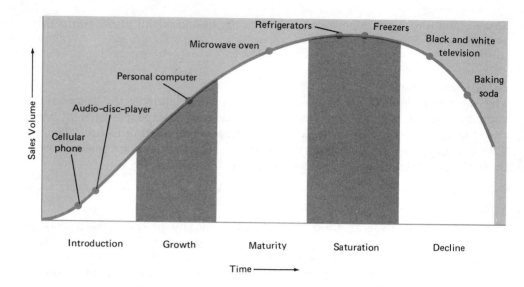

From Philip Kotler, *Marketing Management Analysis, Planning and Control,* © 1967, p. 291. Adapted by permission of Prentice-Hall, Inc., Englewood Cliffs, N.J.

Most new products and services go through a five-stage life cycle.

called a product life cycle, the increase predicted by Figure 7.10 probably is overly optimistic. A **product life cycle** is the five stages through which most new products and services pass. These five stages are introduction, growth, maturity, saturation, and decline.

Figure 7.11 shows how these five stages are related to product sales over a period of time. In the introduction stage, a product is brand-new, and sales are just beginning to build. In the growth stage, because the product has been in the marketplace for some time and is now becoming more accepted, product sales continue to climb. During the maturity stage, competitors enter the market, and while sales are still climbing, they normally climb at a slower rate than in the growth stage. After the maturity stage comes the saturation stage, when nearly everyone who wants the product already has it. Sales during the saturation stage typically are due to replacing a worn-out product or to population growth. The last product life cycle stage, decline, finds the product being replaced by a competing product.

Managers may be able to keep products out of the decline stage through high-quality product improvements. Other products, such as scissors, may never reach this last stage due to the lack of competing products.

The sales forecasting method chosen should be logical and adaptable and fit the organization's needs.

Evaluating Sales Forecasting Methods

The sales forecasting methods just described are not the only ones available to managers. Other methods include the statistical correlation method and the computer simulation method.[13] The methods just discussed, however, do provide a basic foundation for understanding sales forecasting.

In practice, managers find that each sales forecasting method has both advantages and disadvantages, as shown in Figure 7.12. Before deciding to use a particular sales forecasting method, a manager must carefully weigh the advantages and disadvantages as they relate to the organization. The decision may be to use a combination of these methods rather than just one. Whatever method is finally adopted, the framework should be logical, fit the needs of the organization, and be capable of adapting to changes in the environment.[14]

FIGURE 7.12 Advantages and disadvantages of three methods of sales forecasting.

Sales Forecasting Method	Advantages	Disadvantages
Jury of executive opinion	1. Can provide forecasts easily and quickly 2. May not require the preparation of elaborate statistics 3. Pools a variety of specialized viewpoints for experience and judgment 4. May be the only feasible means of forecasting, especially in the absence of adequate data	1. Is inferior to a more factual basis of forecasting since it is based so heavily on opinion 2. Requires costly executive time 3. Is not necessarily more accurate because opinion is averaged 4. Disperses responsibility for accurate forecasting 5. Presents difficulties in making breakdowns by products, time intervals, or markets for operating purposes
Sales force estimation	1. Uses specialized knowledge of people closest to the market 2. Places responsibility for the forecast in the hands of those who must produce the results 3. Gives sales force greater confidence in quotas developed from forecasts 4. Tends to give results greater stability because of the magnitude of the sample 5. Lends itself to the easy development of product, territory, customer, or sales representatives breakdowns	1. Sales representatives of some firms may be poor estimators, being either more optimistic or more pessimistic than conditions warrant 2. If estimates are used as a basis for setting quotas, sales representatives are inclined to understate the demand to make the goal easier to achieve 3. Sales representatives are often unaware of the broad economic patterns shaping future sales and are thus incapable of forecasting trends for extended periods 4. Since sales forecasting is a subsidiary function of the sales force, sufficient time may not be made available for it 5. Requires an extensive expenditure of time by executives and sales force 6. Elaborate schemes are sometimes necessary to keep estimates realistic and free from bias
Time series analysis	1. Forces the forecaster to consider the underlying trend, cycle, and seasonal elements in the sales series 2. Takes into account the particular repetitive or continuing patterns exhibited by the sales in the past 3. Provides a systematic means of making quantitative projections	1. Assumes the continuation of historical patterns of change in sales components without considering outside influences that may affect sales in the forecast period 2. Is often unsatisfactory for short-term forecasting, since, for example, the pinpointing of cyclical turning points by mechanical projections is seldom possible 3. May be difficult to apply in cases where erratic, irregular forces disrupt or hide the regularity of component patterns within a sales series 4. Requires technical skill, experience and judgment

Material in table adapted from *Sales Forecasting* (New York: The Conference Board, Inc., 1978), pp. 11–12, 31–44, 47–80.

BACK TO THE CASE

One of the planning tools available to Jane and Paul is forecasting, which involves predicting future environmental events that could influence the operation of their machine shop. Although various specific types of forecasting—such as economic, technological, and social trends—are available to them, Jane and Paul would probably use sales forecasting as their key forecast since it will predict for them how high or low their sales will be during the time period they are considering. Such a prediction can help Jane and Paul make decisions concerning hiring more employees, expanding the shop, and ordering the correct amount of raw materials.

In order to forecast sales, Jane and Paul could follow the jury of executive opinion method by discussing their opinions of future sales. Although this method would be quick and easy for them, it may not be as good as other methods because, in this case, it relies heavily on the opinions of only two people.

Jane and Paul could also ask their small sales force for opinions on predicted sales. Although the opinions of sales representatives may not be completely reliable, these people are closest to the market and must ultimately make the sales.

Finally, Jane and Paul could use the time series analysis method by analyzing the relationship between sales and time. Although this method takes into account the cyclical patterns and past history of sales, it also assumes the continuation of these patterns in the future without considering outside influences that could cause the patterns to change.

Since each sales forecasting method has both advantages and disadvantages, Jane and Paul should carefully analyze each of them before deciding which method or combination of methods should be used in their company.

Scheduling

Scheduling involves listing activities for reaching an objective.

Basically, **scheduling** is the process of formulating a detailed listing of activities that must be accomplished to attain an objective. This detailed listing is an integral part of an organizational plan. Two scheduling techniques are Gantt charts and the program evaluation and review technique (PERT).

Gantt Charts

The Gantt chart schedules resources.

The **Gantt chart**, a scheduling device developed by Henry L. Gantt, is essentially a bar graph with time on the horizontal axis and the resource to be scheduled on the vertical axis. Possible resources to be scheduled include management system inputs, such as human resources and machines.

Figure 7.13 shows a completed Gantt chart for a work period entitled "Workweek 28." The resources scheduled over the five workdays on this chart were human resources: Wendy Reese and Peter Thomas. During this workweek, both Reese and Thomas were scheduled to produce ten units a day for five days. Actual units produced, however, show a deviation from this planned production. There were days when each of these individuals produced more than ten units, as well as days when each produced fewer than ten units. Cumulative production on the chart shows that Reese produced forty units and Thomas produced forty-five units over the five days.

Gantt charts have many valuable uses.

Although a Gantt chart may seem quite simple at first glance, it can have many valuable uses for managers. First, managers can use the chart as a summary overview of how organizational resources are being used. From this summary, managers can detect such facts as which resources are consistently contributing to productivity. Second, managers can use the Gantt chart to help coordinate organizational resources. The Gantt chart can show which resources are not being

FIGURE 7.13 Completed Gantt chart.

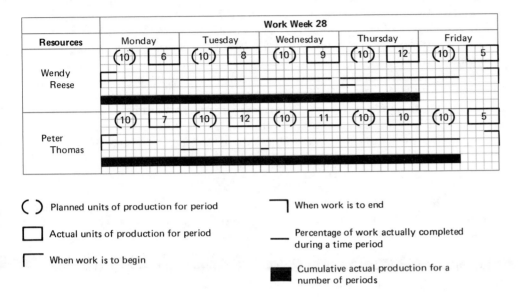

	Work Week 28				
Resources	Monday	Tuesday	Wednesday	Thursday	Friday
Wendy Reese	(10) 6	(10) 8	(10) 9	(10) 12	(10) 5
Peter Thomas	(10) 7	(10) 12	(10) 11	(10) 10	(10) 5

( ) Planned units of production for period

▢ Actual units of production for period

⌐ When work is to begin

⌐ When work is to end

— Percentage of work actually completed during a time period

▮ Cumulative actual production for a number of periods

used during specific periods and, therefore, can be scheduled to work on other production efforts. Third, the Gantt chart can be used to establish realistic worker output standards. For example, if workers are completing scheduled work too quickly, output standards may need to be raised so that workers are scheduled for more work per time period.

Program Evaluation and Review Technique (PERT)

The main weakness of the Gantt chart is that it does not contain any information about the interrelationship of tasks to be performed. All tasks to be performed are listed on the chart, but there is no way of telling if one task must be performed before another can be completed. The program evaluation and review technique (PERT), a technique that evolved partially from the Gantt chart, is a scheduling tool designed to emphasize the interrelationship of tasks.

PERT emphasizes the interrelationship of tasks.

Defining PERT

PERT is a network of project activities showing both estimates of time necessary to complete each activity within the project and the sequential relationship between activities that must be followed to complete the project. PERT was developed in 1958 for use in designing the Polaris submarine weapon system.[15] The individuals involved in managing this project felt that Gantt charts and other existing scheduling tools were of little use because of the complicated nature of the Polaris project and the interdependence of its tasks.[16]

PERT networks show both time estimates and sequential relationships.

The PERT network contains two primary elements: activities and events. **Activities** are specified sets of behaviour within a project, while **events** are the completions of major project tasks. Within the PERT network, each event is assigned corresponding activities that must be performed before the event can materialize.[17]

Activities and events are the primary elements of a PERT network.

A sample PERT network designed for the building of a house is presented in Figure 7.14. In this figure, events are symbolized by circles and activities are symbolized by arrows. To illustrate, Figure 7.14 indicates that after the event "Foundation Complete" (represented by a circle) has materialized, certain activities (represented by an arrow) must be performed before the event of "Frame Complete" (represented by another circle) can materialize.

Two other features of the network in Figure 7.14 should also be emphasized. First, the left-to-right presentation of events shows how events interrelate or the sequence in which they should be performed. Second, the numbers in parentheses above each arrow indicate the units of time necessary to complete each activity. These two features should help managers to ensure that only necessary work is being done on a project and that no project activities are taking too long.

Critical Path

The critical path is the sequence requiring the longest period of time.

Close attention should be paid to the critical path of a PERT network. The **critical path** is the sequence of events and activities requiring the longest period of time to complete. This path is called the critical path because a delay in the time necessary to complete this sequence results in a delay for the completion of the entire project. The critical path in Figure 7.14 is indicated by thick arrows, while all other paths are indicated by thin arrows. Managers try to control a project by keeping it within the time designated by the critical path.

FIGURE 7.14   PERT network designed for building a house.

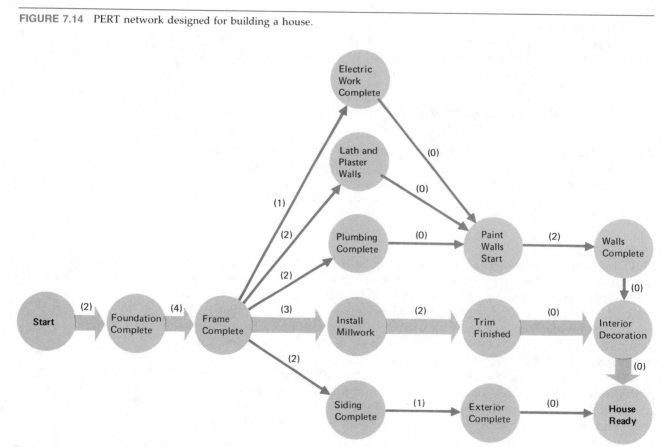

Reprinted by permission of the Sperry Rand Corporation.

Steps in Designing a PERT Network

When designing a PERT network, managers should follow four primary steps:

Step 1   List all the activities/events that must be accomplished for the project and the sequence in which these activities/events should be performed.
Step 2   Determine how much time will be needed to complete each activity/event.
Step 3   Design a PERT network that reflects all of the information contained in Steps 1 and 2.
Step 4   Identify the critical path.

BACK TO THE CASE

Scheduling is another planning tool available to Jane and Paul. It involves the detailed listing of activities that must be accomplished to reach an objective. For example, if Jane and Paul's goal is to have all of their employees working proficiently on new equipment within two years, they need to schedule activities such as installing the equipment, training the employees, and establishing new output standards.

Two scheduling techniques Jane and Paul could use are Gantt charts and PERT. To schedule their employee production output they might want to use Gantt charts—bar graphs with time on the horizontal axis and the resource to be scheduled on the vertical axis. They might also find these charts helpful for evaluating worker performance and setting new production standards.

If Jane and Paul want to see the relationship between tasks, they could use PERT to develop a flowchart showing activities, events, and the amount of time necessary to complete each task. For example, a PERT network would be helpful in scheduling the installation of new machines, since this type of schedule would allow Jane and Paul to see which equipment should be installed first, the amount of time each installation would require, and how other activities in the shop would be affected until the installation was complete.

PERT would also indicate to Jane and Paul the critical path they must follow for successful installation. This path represents the sequence of activities and events requiring the longest amount of time to complete, and it indicates the total time the project will take to finish. If new welding machinery takes longer to install than other types of equipment, Jane and Paul should target the completion of the entire equipment installation on the basis of this equipment's installation time.

Action Summary

Reread the learning objectives that follow. Each objective is followed by questions. Answering these questions accurately will help you to retain the most important concepts discussed in this chapter. After answering each question, check your answer with the answer key at the end of this chapter. (*Hint*: If you have doubt regarding the correct response, consult the page that follows the answer.)

From studying this chapter, I will attempt to acquire: **Circle:**

1. **A complete definition of a plan.**
   a. A plan is: (a) the company's buildings and fixtures; (b) a specific action proposed to help the company achieve its objectives; (c) a policy meeting; (d) a projection of future sales; (e) an experiment to determine the optimal distribution system.   a, b, c, d, e
   b. Which of the following is not generally an important component of a plan: (a) the evaluation of relevant information; (b) the assessment of probable

future developments; (c) a statement of a recommended course of action; (d) a statement of manager intuition; (e) strategy based on reason or rationality.

a, b, c, d, e

2. **Insights regarding various dimensions of plans.**

T, F

   a. Most plans affect top-management only.

a, b, c, d, e

   b. Which of the following is one of the four major dimensions of a plan: (a) repetitiveness; (b) organization; (c) time; (d) a and c; (e) b and c.

3. **An understanding of various types of plans.**

a, b, c, d, e

   a. Standing plans that furnish broad guidelines for channeling management thinking in specified directions are called: (a) procedures; (b) programs; (c) single-use plans; (d) policies; (e) rules.

a, b, c, d, e

   b. Programs and budgets are examples of: (a) single-use plans; (b) standing rules; (c) procedures; (d) Gantt chart components; (e) critical paths.

4. **Insights on why plans fail.**

a, b, c, d, e

   a. Which of the following is a reason why plans fail: (a) adequate inputs are used in planning; (b) corporate planning is integrated into the total management system; (c) management expects that plans developed will be realized with little effort; (d) management operates by the plan; (e) responsibility for planning is vested in more than just the planning department.

T, F

   b. The confusion of planning with financial projections will have no effect on the success of the plans.

5. **A knowledge of various planning areas within an organization.**

T, F

   a. Input planning includes only site selection planning.

a, b, c, d, e

   b. Personnel planners who reflect on organizational objectives to determine overall human resource needs and compare needs to existing human resource inventory are engaging in a type of planning called: (a) process layout; (b) plant facilities; (c) input; (d) life cycle; (e) delphi.

6. **A definition of forecasting.**

T, F

   a. Forecasting is the process of setting objectives and scheduling activities.

a, b, c, d, e

   b. According to the text, which of the following products is in the growth stage of the product life cycle: (a) microwave oven; (b) cellular phones; (c) black and white television; (d) personal computers; (e) refrigerators.

7. **An ability to see the advantages and disadvantages of various methods of sales forecasting.**

a, b, c, d, e

   a. The sales forecasting technique that utilizes specialized knowledge based on interaction with customers is: (a) jury of executive opinion; (b) sales force estimation; (c) time series analysis; (d) a and b; (e) b and c.

T, F

   b. One of the advantages of the jury of executive opinion method of forecasting sales is that it may be the only feasible means of forecasting, especially in the absence of adequate data.

8. **A definition of scheduling.**

a, b, c, d, e

   a. Scheduling can best be described as: (a) the evaluation of alternative courses of action; (b) the process of formulating goals and objectives; (c) the process of formulating a detailed listing of activities; (d) the calculation of the break-even point; (e) the process of defining policies.

b. Scheduling is the process of predicting future environmental happenings that will influence the operations of the organization.

T, F

9. **An understanding of Gantt charts and PERT.**
   a. Which of the following is *not* an acceptable use of a Gantt chart: (a) as a summary overview of how organizational resources are being used; (b) to help coordinate organizational resources; (c) to establish realistic worker output standards; (d) to determine which resources are consistently contributing to productivity; (e) none of the above (all are acceptable uses of Gantt charts).

a, b, c, d, e

   b. In a PERT network, the sequence of events and activities requiring the longest period of time to complete is: (a) called the network; (b) indicated by thin arrows; (c) the path that managers avoid; (d) the critical path; (e) eliminated from the rest of the project so that the project will not take too long.

a, b, c, d, e

INTRODUCTORY CASE WRAP-UP

"A Planning Incident" (p. 160) and its related back-to-the-case sections were written to help you better understand the management concepts contained in this chapter. Answer the following discussion questions about this introductory case to further enrich your understanding of the chapter content:

1. Given Jane and Paul's situation, list the kinds of plans they probably need.
2. Write some sample plans that could be developed, given the planning needs you listed in number 1.
3. What kind of information would Jane and Paul need to actually develop the plans you have written?

Issues for Review and Discussion

1. What is a plan?
2. List and describe the basic dimensions of a plan.
3. What is the difference between standing plans and single-use plans?
4. Compare and contrast policies, procedures, and rules.
5. What are the two main types of single-use plans?
6. Why do organizations have programs?
7. Of what use is a budget to managers?
8. Summarize the ten factors that cause plans to fail.
9. What is input planning?
10. Evaluate the importance of plant facilities planning to the organization.
11. What major factors should be involved in site selection?
12. Describe the human resource planning process.
13. What is a planning tool?
14. Describe the measurements usually employed in forecasting. Why are these taken?
15. Draw and explain the product life cycle.
16. Discuss the advantages and disadvantages of three methods of sales forecasting.
17. Elaborate on the statement that "all managers should spend some time scheduling."
18. What is a Gantt chart? Draw a simple chart to assist you in your explanation.
19. How can information related to the Gantt chart be used by managers?
20. How is PERT a scheduling tool?
21. How is the critical path related to PERT?
22. List the steps necessary to design a PERT network.

Sources of Additional Information

Allen, Louis A. "Managerial Planning: Back to Basics." *Management Review* (April 1981): 15–20.

Anderholm, Fred, III, James Gaertner, and Ken Milani. "The Utilization of PERT in the Preparation of Marketing Budgets." *Managerial Planning* 30 (July/August 1981): 18–23.

Brady, F. Neil. "Rules for Making Exceptions to Rules." *Academy of Management Review* (July 1987): 436–44.

Cartwright, T.J. "The Lost Art of Planning." *Long-Range Planning* 20 (April 1987): 92–99.

Clark, Thomas B., Walter E. Riggs, and Richard H. Deane, "Guidelines to Compressing Projects for Profit." *Business* (January/February/March 1985): 16–21.

Diven, David L. "Organizational Planning: The Neglected Factor in Merger and Acquisition Strategy." *Managerial Planning* 33 (July/August 1984): 4–8.

Germane, Gayton E. *The Executive Course: What Every Manager Needs to Know about the Essentials of Business.* Reading, Mass.: Addison-Wesley, 1986.

Levin, R.I., and C.A. Kirkpatrick. *Planning and Control with PERT/CPM.* New York: McGraw-Hill, 1966.

Lyneis, James M. *Corporate Planning and Policy Design: A System Dynamics Approach.* Cambridge, Mass.: MIT Press, 1980.

McLaughlin, Harold J. *Building Your Business Plan: A Step-by-Step Approach.* New York: Wiley, 1985.

Naylor, Thomas H. "Strategic Planning Models." *Managerial Planning* 30 (July/August 1981): 3–11.

Newman, William H., and James P. Logan. *Strategy, Policy, and Central Management.* Cincinnati: South-Western, 1981.

Rubin, Leonard R. "Planning Trees: A CEO's Guide through the Corporate Planning Maze." *Business Horizons* 27 (September/October 1984): 66–70.

Scott, Mel, and Richard Bruce. "Five Stages of Growth in Small Business." *Long-Range Planning* 20 (June 1987): 45–52.

Tagiuri, Renato. "Planning: Desirable and Undesirable." *Human Resource Management* (Spring 1980): 11–14.

Thompson, Stewart. *How Companies Plan.* New York: American Management Association, 1962.

Webb, Stan G. "Productivity through Practical Planning." *Administrative Management* 42 (August 1981): 47–50.

Welch, Jonathan B. "Strategic Planning Could Improve Your Share Price." *Long-Range Planning* 17 (April 1984): 144–47.

Notes

1. Henry L. Sisk, *Management and Organization* (Cincinnati: South-Western, 1973), 101.
2. Stewart Thompson, "What Planning Involves," American Management Association Research Study no. 54, 1962.
3. Fremont E. Kast and James E. Rosenzweig, *Organization and Management: A Systems Approach* (New York: McGraw-Hill, 1970), 443–49.
4. For discussion on expanding this list of four characteristics to thirteen, see P. LeBreton and D.A. Henning, *Planning Theory* (Englewood Cliffs, N.J.: Prentice-Hall, 1961), 320–44. These authors list the dimensions of a plan as (1) complexity, (2) significance, (3) comprehensiveness, (4) time, (5) specificity, (6) completeness, (7) flexibility, (8) frequency, (9) formality, (10) confidential nature, (11) authorization, (12) ease of implementation, and (13) ease of control.
5. For further discussion on each type of plan, see Herbert G. Hicks and C. Ray Gullett, *The Management of Organizations* (New York: McGraw-Hill, 1976), 271–78.
6. J. Fred Weston and Eugene F. Brigham, *Essentials of Managerial Finance* (New York: Holt, Rinehart & Winston, 1971), 107.
7. Kjell A. Ringbakk, "Why Planning Fails," *European Business*, July 1970.
8. Dale S. Beach, *Personnel: The Management of People at Work* (New York: Macmillan, 1975), 220.
9. Henri Fayol, *General and Industrial Management* (New York: Pitman, 1949).
10. William C. House, "Environmental Analysis: Key to More Effective Dynamic Planning," *Managerial Planning* (January/February 1977): 25–29.
11. Olfa Hemler, "The Uses of Delphi Techniques in Problems of Educational Innovations," no. 3499, RAND Corporation, December 1966.
12. A.R. Fusfeld and R.N. Foster, "The Delphi Technique: Survey and Comment," *Business Horizons* 14 (1971): 63–74.
13. For elaboration on these methods, see George A. Steiner, *Top Management Planning* (London: Collier-Macmillan, 1969), 223–27.

14. Gilbert Frisbie and Vincent A. Mabert, "Crystal Ball vs. System: The Forecasting Dilemma," *Business Horizons* 24 (September/October 1981): 72–76.

15. Willard Fazar, "The Origin of PERT," *The Controller*, December 1962.

16. Harold L. Wattel, *Network Scheduling and Control Systems CAP/PERT* (Hempstead, N.J.: Hofstra University, 1964).

17. R.J. Schonberger, "Custom-Tailored PERT/CPM Systems," *Business Horizons* 15 (1972): 64–66.

Action Summary Answer Key

1. a. b, p. 161
   b. d, p. 161
2. a. F, pp. 161–162
   b. d, pp. 161–162
3. a. d, p. 163
   b. a, p. 167

4. a. c, p. 167
   b. F, p. 167
5. a. F, p. 168
   b. c, pp. 169–170
6. a. F, p. 173
   b. d, p. 176

7. a. b, p. 175
   b. T, p. 177
8. a. c, p. 178
   b. F, p. 178
9. a. e, pp. 178–179
   b. d, p. 180

VAGUE EXPORTING PLANS AREN'T THE TICKET

Modern Homes Ltd. of Truro, Nova Scotia, thought it was on to something big: The manufacturer of modular wooden houses had just sold four units to a buyer in Saudi Arabia. Although the Saudi buyer had never seen the Modern Homes houses, he ordered four to be set up as model homes at an industrial exposition. At that time, in the late 1970s, the Middle East nations were rich in petrodollars. With the shortage of skilled labour and building materials in Saudi Arabia, the future sales of imported finished houses looked guaranteed. A buyer could purchase a house for $45 000, including freight and insurance, and reap a healthy profit by selling it in Saudi Arabia for $80 000 to $100 000.

Exporting seemed to suit Modern's needs as an avenue to long-term growth. A large export contract would also solve problems arising from idle manufacturing capacity due to the seasonal nature of production. In 1977, the firm sold 260 houses. Expected sales in 1978 were 450 units, a comfortable improvement in one year. Plant capacity was about 700 houses. Improved advertising, superior designs and components, and hard work by the new management team — on the job for less than a year — seemed to be the reason for the increased sales. The Saudi sale initially arose from a personal contact made by a member of the family that owned Modern Homes. A salesman, with the firm for just two days, completed the deal in only one and a half hours. The sale unloaded units that had been sitting unsold in the plant yard. For Modern Homes, this export contract seemed to be the ticket to future prosperity.

Although the sale was easily made, the completion of the deal proved to be a tough lesson in exporting for Modern's management, none of whom had any exporting experience. Shipping the units became the first challenge. The Saudi buyer arranged for a ship to pick up the houses at Saint John, New Brunswick. It arrived a week early with trucks and graders occupying the deck space intended for the houses. As well, one of the houses was designated to sit on a hatch cover over a hold that would not be filled until the ship made a later stop in Newfoundland. Then Modern found the ship's crew preparing to sail after only one and a half houses had been loaded. Several telephone calls later, Modern's plant manager had arranged to delay the sailing.

Due to the ship's early arrival in Saint John, the letter of credit for the sale had not been finalized. Modern nonetheless shipped the houses on the basis of good faith in the buyer's intention to pay. The company also had to ship the tools and equipment needed to erect and finish the houses. They could only assume these were needed, as they were unable to reach anyone at the buyer's Saudi office. Months after the shipment had left Canada, Modern's managers weren't sure where the units were. Eventually they traced them to their point of unloading at Jidda, but although agreeing with the buyer to provide a man to supervise the houses' assembly, they hadn't yet been asked to send him out.

With this experience behind them, Modern's managers realized that future export sales would have to be carried out differently. They also knew that the houses would need further work in order to sell successfully in Saudi Arabia. For example the electrical system would need to be converted to a 220-volt system and the houses would have to be termite-proofed. Modern also questioned the wisdom of shipping modular units. The shipping costs for what were basically large empty boxes would be considerably reduced if the design of the house were changed. Panelized units with walls that fold in would reduce shipping costs by 75 percent. However, these would take one month to erect versus the four days required to assemble a modular unit.

The plant manager and the marketing manager wanted to invest $50 000 to develop the Middle East market. However, Modern's controller believed that requests for sales literature were proof that a market already existed, and argued that all that was needed was a more easily shipped product. The two factions at Modern, one enthusiastic and the other cautious about exporting to the Middle East, couldn't reach a consensus. Although the firm was eventually paid for the units, it never did discover the whereabouts of the houses. Moreover, the assembly man was never called and the buyer didn't reorder.

In the end, Modern stayed out of exporting and tried to pursue other avenues of growth. For instance, it launched a new range of more stylish, upmarket houses. However, due to the recession in the early 1980s and the cyclical nature of the housing industry, the firm hasn't achieved much growth. It has also experienced a high turnover in management personnel, with few people staying long. Philip Rosson, associate professor at Dalhousie University's School of Business Administration, believes that Modern's exporting plans could have smoothed out the cyclical fluctuations in the Canadian market, but "this was a company that didn't have the will to plan for a move into overseas markets."

DISCUSSION ISSUES

1. Were Modern's exporting plans an example of standing plans or single-use plans? Elaborate.

2. How could PERT have been of value in planning the export sale?

3. What could Modern's management have done to ensure the success of the exporting sales?

Based on "Building blind," by Daniel Stoffman in *Canadian Business*, October 1986. Used with permission.

3

ORGANIZING

Organizing is one of the four major management functions that must be performed for organizations to have long-term success. The material in this section flows naturally from Section 2, "Planning," because organizing is the primary mechanism managers have for putting plans into action. In essence, organizing follows planning.

Chapter 8

Chapter 8, "Fundamentals of Organizing," defines organizing as the process of establishing orderly uses for all organizational resources. This process is presented as being comprised of five main steps: (1) reflecting on plans and objectives; (2) establishing major tasks; (3) dividing major tasks into subtasks; (4) allocating resources for subtasks; and (5) evaluating implemented organizing strategy. The organizing function is identified as a subsystem of the overall management system and is shown to be influenced by classical organizing principles concerning structure, division of labour, span of management, and scalar relationships.

Chapter 9

Chapter 9, "Organizing the Activity of Individuals," defines responsibility as the obligation to perform assigned activity and credits it with being the most fundamental ingredient for channeling the activity of individuals within organizations. The point is made in this chapter that once individuals are assigned some organizational responsibility, they also must be granted a corresponding amount of authority that will enable them to perform this obligation. Authority is defined as the right to perform or command. Delegation, another important management topic covered in this chapter, is explained as the process of assigning responsibility and authority to individuals within organizations. An organization is said to be centralized when its management delegates little authority, and decentralized when its management delegates significant amounts of authority.

Chapter 10

Chapter 10, "Providing Appropriate Human Resources," focuses on the task of furnishing people for the organization who will make desirable contributions to attaining organizational objectives. The process of furnishing such people is discussed as involving recruitment, selection, training, and performance evaluation. Recruiting entails screening the total supply of people available to fill a position, and selection involves choosing to hire one of those individuals. Once an individual has been selected or hired, she or he typically undergoes some type of training. Training is the process of developing in human resources qualities that ultimately will enable them to be more productive and thus contribute more to organizational goal attainment. This chapter also suggests that, for individuals to be made as productive as possible, their performance should be evaluated after they have been recruited, selected, and trained. This evaluation helps employees to know what they are doing right, what they are doing wrong, and how they can improve. Lastly, this chapter discusses the issue of women working in nontraditional jobs and the integration of these women into the organization as a special management problem in providing appropriate human resources for the organization.

Chapter 11

Over time, most managers find that they must make some changes in the way their organizations operate. The purpose of making such modifications, of course, is to increase organizational effectiveness—the extent to which an organization attains its organizational objectives. Chapter 11, "Organizational Change and Stress," defines changing an organization as the process of modifying an existing organization. How managers decide who will make the change, what should be changed, the type of change to make, what effect the change will have on people in the organization, and how to evaluate the change are discussed. The collective influence of all of these issues is presented as ultimately determining how successful a particular organizational change will be. The relationship between change and stress is emphasized, and the importance of studying and managing stress is discussed.

FUNDAMENTALS OF ORGANIZING

STUDENT LEARNING OBJECTIVES

From studying this chapter, I will attempt to acquire:

1. An understanding of the organizing function.
2. An appreciation for the complications of determining appropriate organizational structure.
3. Insights on the advantages and disadvantages of division of labour.
4. A working knowledge of the relationship between division of labour and coordination.
5. An understanding of span of management and the factors that influence its appropriateness.
6. An understanding of scalar relationships.

CHAPTER OUTLINE

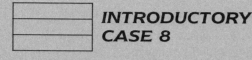

CONSOLIDATING BAKERIES

Ginette Dupont, a management consultant in Quebec City, is in a meeting with a client. The telephone rings and Dupont's secretary tells her that she has a long-distance call from Halifax. The individual placing the call is Ralph Zacarachy, the owner of a bakery. Dupont excuses herself for a moment and accepts the call privately. The following conversation takes place:

DUPONT: Hello, this is Ginette Dupont speaking.

ZACARACHY: Ms. Dupont, this is Ralph Zacarachy. A friend of mine, Wayne Chin, suggested that I call you for advice concerning a management problem I am presently facing. As you may recall, Wayne was one of your past clients.

DUPONT: Yes, I remember Wayne very well. He was trying to reorganize the departments in his housewares store and do some long-term planning. As I recall, we were able to solve his problem with minimum difficulty, and we also developed a very good working relationship. I'm glad you called. Is your situation similar to Wayne's?

ZACARACHY: No. I wish it were. My problem is a lot more difficult, or so it seems to me. You see, for several years I've owned a bakery in downtown Halifax. I've been doing well downtown, and I recently decided to purchase another bakery in a suburban shopping centre.

Now I'm faced with the problem of trying to organize the two bakeries. I don't really have a formal structure in either bakery. And since I've been a baker all my life, not a manager, I don't know how to coordinate the activities in the bakeries or organize my employees. I need to know what kinds of departments I should set up and how to divide up my employees' tasks. Also, it's difficult for me to manage both bakeries, since I obviously can't be in two places at once. I need the bakeries to be well organized, with their own managers, so they can function without me.

I'd really appreciate it if you could help me develop an organizing strategy. Do you think you can help?

DUPONT: Your situation is not all that difficult, though I'm sure it seems confusing to you right now. I've had experience handling this type of consolidation problem and would be happy to help you. Don't worry about the fee. I'm sure we can arrive at some mutually agreeable figure.

I have a list of standard questions regarding organizing that I usually ask clients with your kind of problem. Actually, these questions will only lay the rough groundwork for solving your problem. After you answer the questions, I should spend approximately a week thinking about your answers and then fly to Halifax to spend a couple of days with you to finalize your organizing strategy.

Since I am in a meeting right now, it would be difficult for me to talk too much longer. If you want, I'll call you back this afternoon to ask you these questions.

ZACARACHY: Your suggestion sounds fine, and I'm pleased you'll be able to work with me. I'll be in the downtown bakery all afternoon, so call at your convenience.

What's Ahead

The ending of the introductory case leaves Ralph Zacarachy, a bakery owner, waiting for a call from Ginette Dupont, a management consultant. Dupont will be calling to ask Zacarachy some questions. Zacarachy's answers will provide the basis for organizing his old bakery and a new one that he has just purchased. For these questions to be worthwhile, they must focus on the organizing function and furnish information that will help Dupont recommend a specific organizing strategy for Zacarachy's situation. The material in this chapter emphasizes both a definition of organizing and principles of classical organizing theory so that the types of questions Dupont should ask will be better understood.

A DEFINITION OF ORGANIZING

Organizing is the process of establishing orderly uses for all resources within the management system. These orderly uses emphasize the attainment of management system objectives and assist managers not only in making objectives apparent but also in clarifying which resources will be used to attain them.[1] *Organization*, as used in this chapter, refers to the result of the organizing process.

> Organizing is establishing orderly uses for all management system resources.

In essence, each organizational resource represents an investment from which the management system must get a return. Appropriate organization of these resources increases the efficiency and effectiveness of their use. Henri Fayol has developed sixteen general guidelines for organizing resources:[2]

1. Judiciously prepare and execute the operating plan.
2. Organize the human and material facets so that they are consistent with objectives, resources, and requirements of the concern.
3. Establish a single, competent, energetic, guiding authority (formal management structure).
4. Coordinate all activities and efforts.
5. Formulate clear, distinct, and precise decisions.
6. Arrange for efficient selection so that each department is headed by a competent, energetic manager and each employee is placed where she or he can render the greatest service.
7. Define duties.
8. Encourage initiative and responsibility.
9. Have fair and suitable rewards for services rendered.
10. Make use of sanctions against faults and errors.
11. Maintain discipline.
12. Ensure that individual interests are consistent with general interests of the organization.
13. Recognize the unity of command.
14. Promote both material and human coordination.
15. Institute and effect controls.
16. Avoid regulations, red tape, and paperwork.

The Importance of Organizing

The organizing function is extremely important to the management system because it is the primary mechanism with which managers activate plans. Organizing creates and maintains relationships between all organizational resources

> The organizing function is the mechanism to activate plans.

by indicating which resources are to be used for specified activities, and when, where, and how the resources are to be used. A thorough organizing effort helps managers to minimize costly weaknesses, such as duplication of effort and idle organizational resources.

Some management theorists consider the organizing function so important that they advocate the creation of an organizing department within the management system.[3] Typical responsibilities of this department would include: (1) developing reorganization plans that make the management system more effective and efficient; (2) developing plans to improve managerial skills to fit current management system needs; and (3) attempting to develop an advantageous organizational climate within the management system.[4]

The Organizing Process

The five main steps of the organizing process, as presented in Figure 8.1, are: (1) reflecting on plans and objectives; (2) establishing major tasks; (3) dividing major tasks into subtasks; (4) allocating resources and directives for subtasks; and (5) evaluating the results of implemented organizing strategy. As this figure implies, managers should continually repeat these steps. Through this repetition, they obtain feedback that will help them improve the existing organization.

The management of a restaurant can illustrate how the organizing process might work. The first step the manager would take to initiate the organizing process would be to reflect on the restaurant's plans and objectives. Since plans involve determining how the restaurant will obtain its objectives, and organizing involves determining how restaurant resources will actually be used to activate plans, the restaurant manager must start to organize by understanding planning.

The five-step organizing process should be continually repeated so that feedback will indicate potential improvements.

FIGURE 8.1   Five main steps of the organizing process.

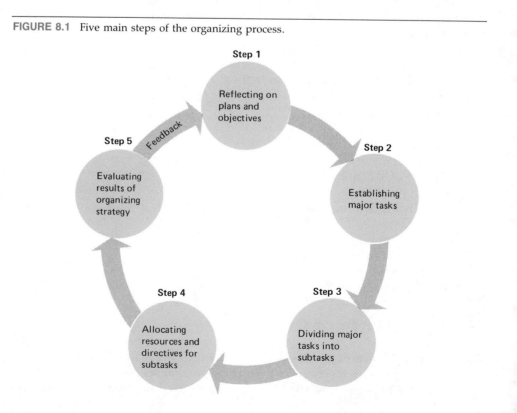

The second and third steps of the organizing process focus on tasks to be performed within the management system. The manager must designate major task areas or jobs to be performed within the restaurant. Two of these task areas might be waiting on customers and cooking food. Then the tasks must be divided into subtasks. For example, the manager might decide that waiting on customers includes the subtasks of taking orders and clearing the table.

The fourth organizing step the restaurant manager must perform is determining who will take orders, who will clear tables, and the details of the relationship between these individuals. The type of tables or booths and the type of silverware to be used also would be factors to be considered at this point.

Step five, evaluating the results of a particular organizing strategy, necessitates that the restaurant manager gather feedback on how well the implemented organizing strategy is working. This feedback should furnish information that can be used to improve the existing organization. For example, it may be that a particular type of table is not large enough and that larger ones must be purchased if the restaurant is to attain its goals.

The Organizing Subsystem

The organizing function, like the planning function, can be visualized as a subsystem of the overall management system (see Figure 8.2). The primary purpose

The output of the organizing subsystem is organization.

FIGURE 8.2 Relationships between overall management system and organizing subsystem.

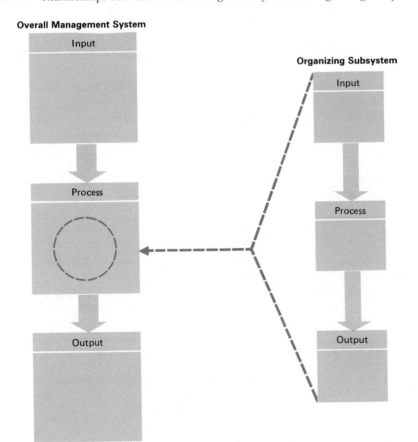

FIGURE 8.3   Organizing subsystem.

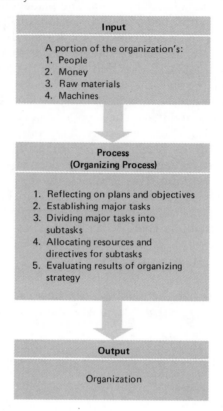

of the organizing subsystem is to enhance the goal attainment of the general management system by providing a rational approach for using organizational resources. Figure 8.3 presents the specific ingredients of the organizing subsystem. The input is comprised of a portion of the total resources of the organization, the process is made up of the steps of the organizing process, and the output is organization.

BACK TO THE CASE

Dupont's questions to Zacarachy in the introductory case "Consolidating Bakeries" should be aimed at establishing an orderly use of Zacarachy's organizational resources. Since these resources represent an investment on which he must get a return, Dupont's questions should be geared toward gaining information that will be used to maximize this return. In asking Zacarachy preliminary questions, Dupont should try to pinpoint exactly what Zacarachy is trying to accomplish with his bakeries, so they can be organized in the best way to achieve his goals.

Some preliminary questions Dupont could ask are as follows:

1. What objectives do you have for your bakeries? For example, do you want to be able to handle large orders in addition to small, individual ones? Do you want to be able to open more shops in the future?
2. What plans do you have to accomplish these objectives? Are you going to open more shops? Hire more employees?
3. What are the major tasks you go through to bake

your products? For example, how many steps are involved in making cakes to order?

4. Can these steps be broken down into smaller tasks, such as mixing the batter and decorating the cake?

5. What resources do you have to run your bakeries? I need as much information as you can give me regarding the number of employees, how much money you have, what types of supplies and ingredients you need, how many ovens are in each bakery, and so on.

Dupont should also begin thinking of some mechanism for evaluating the organizing strategy she develops for Zacarachy. Once the strategy is implemented, Zacarachy must be able to get feedback on how his two bakeries are functioning, so he can improve the organization. For example, he may find that he needs more ovens and employees in one bakery than in the other. With appropriate feedback, Zacarachy can continually improve the existing organizational system.

CLASSICAL ORGANIZING THEORY

Classical organizing theory is the cumulative insights of early management writers on how organizational resources can best be used to enhance goal attainment. Perhaps the one writer who had the most profound influence on classical organizing theory was Max Weber.[5] According to Weber, the main components of an organizing effort include detailed procedures and rules, a clearly outlined organizational hierarchy, and mainly impersonal relationships between organization members.

How can organizational resources best be used to reach goals?

Weber used the term **bureaucracy** to label the management system that contains these components. Although Weber firmly believed in the bureaucratic approach to organizing, he became concerned when managers seemed to overemphasize the merits of a bureaucracy.[6] He cautioned that a bureaucracy is not an end in itself but a means to the end of management system goal attainment. The main criticism of Weber's bureaucracy, as well as the concepts of other classical organizing theorists, is the obvious lack of concern for the human variable within the organization.[7] Considerable discussion on this human variable is presented in Section 4 ("Influencing") of this text.

Weber's bureaucracy contained detailed procedures and rules, an organizational hierarchy, and impersonal relationships.

The rest of this chapter summarizes four main considerations from classical organizing theory that all modern managers should include in their organizing efforts: (1) structure; (2) division of labour; (3) span of management; and (4) scalar relationships.[8]

Structure

In any organizing effort, managers must choose an appropriate structure.[9] **Structure** refers to designated relationships among resources of the management system. The purpose of structure is to facilitate the use of each resource, both individually and collectively, as the management system attempts to attain its objectives.[10]

Structure is designated relationships among organizational resources.

Organization structure is represented primarily by means of a graphic illustration called an **organization chart**. Traditionally, an organization chart is constructed in pyramid form, with individuals toward the top of the pyramid having more authority and responsibility than individuals toward the bottom.[11] The relative positioning of individuals within boxes on the chart indicates broad working relationships, while lines between boxes designate formal lines of communication between individuals.

An organization chart is a graphic illustration of authority and responsibility designations within the organization.

FIGURE 8.4   Sample organization chart for small restaurant.

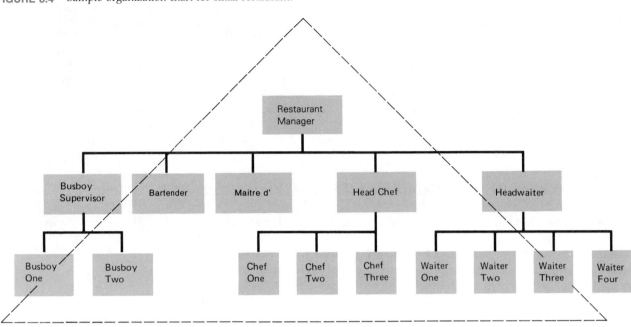

Figure 8.4 is an example of an organization chart. The dotted line in this figure is not part of the organization chart but has been added to illustrate the pyramid shape of the chart. Positions close to the restaurant manager's have more authority and responsibility; positions farther away have less authority and responsibility. Also, the location of positions on this chart indicates broad working relationships. For example, the positioning of the head chef over the three other chefs indicates that the head chef has authority over them and is responsible for their productivity. The lines between the individual chefs and the restaurant manager indicate that formal communication from chef one to the manager must go through the head chef.

Formal and Informal Structure

In reality, two basic types of structure exist within management systems: formal structure and informal structure. **Formal structure** is defined as relationships between organizational resources as outlined by management. Formal structure is represented primarily by the organization chart.

Informal structure, on the other hand, is defined as patterns of relationships that develop because of the informal existence of organization members. Informal structure evolves naturally and tends to be molded by individual norms, values, and/or social relationships. Informal structure co-exists with formal structure but is not necessarily identical to it.[12] The primary focus of this chapter is formal structure. More details on informal structure and how to manage it are presented in Chapter 15.

Formal structure: Relationships outlined by management.

Informal structure: Informal relationships that develop between organization members.

FIGURE 8.5   Organization structure based primarily on function.

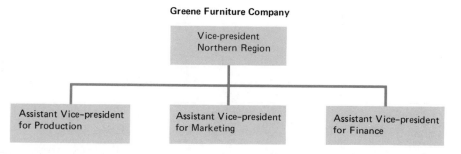

Departmentalization and Formal Structure: A Contingency Viewpoint

The most common method of establishing formal relationships between resources is by establishing departments. Basically, a **department** is a unique group of resources established by management to perform some organizational task. The process of establishing departments within the management system is called **departmentalization**. The creation of these departments typically is based on, or contingent upon, such situational factors as the work functions being performed, the product being assembled, the territory being covered, the customer being targeted, and the process designed to manufacture the product.*

Perhaps the most widely used base for establishing departments within the formal structure is the type of *work functions* (activities) being performed within the management system.[13] The major categories into which functions typically are divided are marketing, production, and finance. An organization chart based primarily on function for a hypothetical organization, Greene Furniture Company, is presented in Figure 8.5.

Organization structure based primarily on *product* departmentalizes resources according to the products being manufactured. As the management system manufactures more and more products, it becomes increasingly difficult to coordinate activities across products. Organizing according to product allows managers to logically group the resources necessary to produce each product. An organization chart showing Greene Furniture Company's structure based primarily on product is presented in Figure 8.6.

Departmentalization establishes formal relationships between resources.

Organizational design is contingent upon:
1. Type of activity.

2. Goods produced.

FIGURE 8.6   Organization structure based primarily on product.

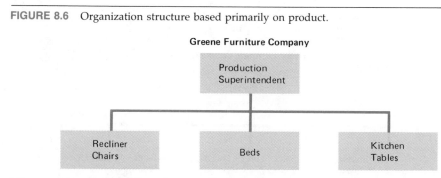

* For a quick review of the contingency approach to management, see page 46.

FIGURE 8.7   Organization structure based primarily on territory.

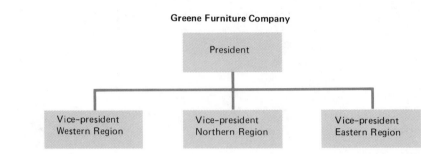

3. Work or market locations.

Structure based primarily on *territory* departmentalizes according to the place where the work is being done or the geographic market area on which the management system is focusing. As market areas and work locations expand, the physical distance between various places can make the management task extremely cumbersome. These distances can range from a relatively short span between two points in the same city to a relatively long span between two points in the same province or different provinces.[14] To minimize the effects of distances, resources can be departmentalized according to territory. An organization chart showing Greene Furniture Company's structure based primarily on territory is presented in Figure 8.7.

4. Who buys the products.

Structure based primarily on the *customer* establishes departments in response to major customers of the management system. This structure, of course, assumes that major customers can be identified and divided into logical categories. An organization chart showing Greene Furniture Company's structure based primarily on customers is shown in Figure 8.8. Greene Furniture obviously can clearly identify its customers and divide them into logical categories.

5. How the products are made.

Structure based primarily on *manufacturing process* departmentalizes according to the major phases of the process used to manufacture products. In the case of Greene Furniture Company, major phases of the manufacturing process might be woodcutting, sanding, gluing, and painting. An organization chart that would reflect these phases is presented in Figure 8.9.

Figures 8.5, 8.6, 8.7, 8.8, and 8.9 all use organization charts to illustrate a basis for establishing formal structure. If a situation warrants it, organization charts can be combined to use all of these factors for the benefit of the management

FIGURE 8.8   Organization structure based primarily on customers.

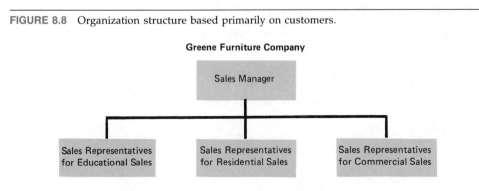

FIGURE 8.9   Organization structure based primarily on manufacturing process.

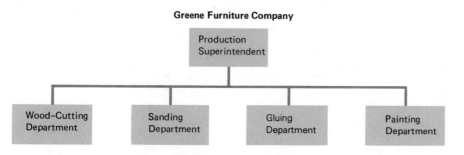

system. Figure 8.10 integrates the previous figures to show how all of these factors might be included on the same organization chart for the Greene Furniture Company.

FIGURE 8.10   Organization structure based primarily on function, product, territory, customers, and manufacturing process.

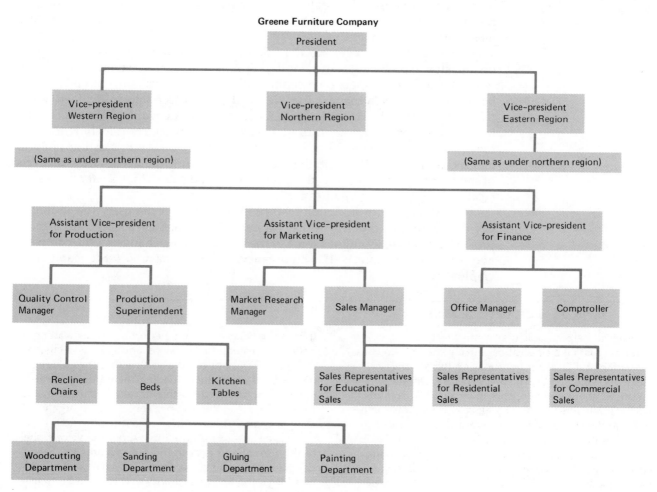

FIGURE 8.11   Forces influencing the evolution of organization structure.

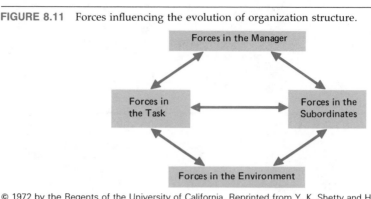

Forces Influencing Formal Structure

Forces in the manager, the task, the environment, and the subordinates influence the evolution of organizational structure.

According to Shetty and Carlisle, the formal structure of a management system is continually evolving. Four primary forces influence this evolution: (1) forces in the manager; (2) forces in the task; (3) forces in the environment; and (4) forces in the subordinates.[15] The evolution of a particular organization is actually the result of a complex and dynamic interaction among these forces, as Figure 8.11 illustrates.

Forces in the manager are the unique way in which a manager perceives organizational problems. Naturally, background, knowledge, experience, and values influence the manager's perception of how formal structure should exist or be changed. Forces in the task include the degree of technology involved in the task and the complexity of the task. As task activities change, a force is created to change the existing organization. Forces in the environment include the customers and suppliers of the management system, along with existing political and social structures. Forces in the subordinates include the needs and skill levels of subordinates. Obviously, as the environment and subordinates vary, forces are created to change the organization.

The Management in Action feature for this chapter discusses the strategies CN is adopting in order to restructure and reorganize itself back into a more profitable position. It outlines some of the factors forcing change on the company and the possible effects that reorganization may have on the company's employees.

BACK TO THE CASE

In order to help Zacarachy organize his bakeries, Dupont must take classical organizing theory into consideration and base her questions on its four major elements—the first of which is structure. Dupont's questions about structure should be aimed at creating working relationships among all bakery employees. In order to develop an effective organizational structure, Dupont should analyze situational factors in the bakeries, such as functions, products, geographic locations, customers, and processes involved in making the baked goods.

For example, Dupont could create departments in the bakery on the basis of the types of functions or ac-

tivities the bakery workers perform, such as waiting on customers, baking for the store, and baking to customer's orders. Dupont could also structure the bakeries on the basis of product, dividing them into the bread department, cookie department, cake department, and so on. Of course, the bakeries could also be organized using a combination of these structures.

Regardless of the structure Dupont develops, she could present and explain the departments to Zacarachy with an organization chart. This chart will allow him to see the line of authority and responsibility in his bakeries and to understand the broad working relationships among his employees.

ROUGH RIDE AHEAD: CN BRACES FOR DEREGULATION AND PRIVATIZATION

In his forty-six years working for CN, Ronald E. Lawless has done just about everything but drive the trains. His latest task, however, as the newly appointed CEO, may prove to be his most challenging. As the Montreal-based railway braces for deregulation and the prospect of being sold to the private sector, Lawless must find ways of rerouting a company that has been plagued by mammoth debt and dwindling business.

The company has already embarked on a course of streamlining its operations by selling assets, reducing staff, and pulling back on expansion plans in Western Canada. Suggestions that he is leading a stand-pat team elicits a very snappy "I don't wear a caretaker's shoes" from Lawless, who sees his primary responsibility as one of ensuring that all plans geared towards restoring the railway to prosperity are put in place. All signs suggest the trip will be anything but cushy.

CN's revenues in 1985 hit $5 billion, with a net income of $117.6 million, while net income in 1984 was $242 million. However, these figures turned into a loss of $75–$90 million in 1986. "We have to get ourselves in a position to carry that debt," says Lawless. In 1978, Ottawa, in an effort to ease the burden, had converted into equity $808 million of CN's obligations. Nonetheless, by 1986 the debt had risen to $3.4 billion, for a debt-equity ratio of 53:47. This ratio has to be reduced if CN hopes to borrow money at favourable rates.

Meanwhile, CN's standing with Standard and Poor's Corporation was cranked down two notches in the fall of 1986 to "AA". It was lowered because of "diminished" government support, falling revenues caused by low commodities traffic, and uncertainty surrounding proposed transportation deregulation. Philip Bates, a senior vice-president of the agency, points out that this is still a very high investment-grade rating. This evaluation is unlikely to be downgraded further unless "some change is in sight, like privatization." In fact, CN is considered to be a prime candidate in Ottawa's program of selling

"CN is now pulling back on its expansion plans."

203

Crown corporations. However, even Lawless recognizes that such a sale is unlikely to take place until the balance sheet has been put in order. "Given our financial situation at the moment, we are not a very suitable candidate," he concedes.

The strategy so far has been to streamline operations. The work force, which accounts for 50–60 percent of total costs, has been drastically reduced. In 1986 it was 54 000, compared with over 61 000 in 1985 and 131 000 in 1952. Additional decreases of 5–6 percent annually are expected over the next five years. Some of these cuts come from the sale of CN Route, the unprofitable trucking operation, and from the imminent closing of the maintenance shops in Moncton, New Brunswick. Other targets for divestment include the hotels, and exploration and communications activities. The next divestiture will likely be the hotels; from 1983 to 1985, CN hotels lost $11.6 million, and no improvement is in sight.

Besides the crushing debt, another factor which is bound to affect CN is deregulation. To shippers it is long overdue. "The new railway act will open up competition, which we don't have today," says Donald S. Wiersma, transportation manager of the Canadian Manufacturers' Association in Toronto. (The new act, Bill C-18, was passed early in 1988.) It is hoped that this will at least reduce, if not end, the monopoly the two railways—CN and CP— often exercise over captive shippers. Very often, transportation represents 40 to 50 percent of total costs for goods such as bulk commodities. Increased competition should trim some of these outlays, leading to substantial improvements in shippers' ability to compete in world markets. A pivotal aspect of C-18 concerns tariffs. Unlike in the U.S., where tariffs may be kept secret, CN and CP are currently obliged to make their rates known. The new bill, by allowing tariffs to be kept confidential, will help encourage deal making between shipper and carrier, thereby helping to block the growing flow of business to U.S. carriers.

In the early 1980s, CN and CP spent heavily to improve their western systems, as they were expecting substantial increases in the commodities business—a boom which never materialized. Having planned for growth which never came, CN is now pulling back on its expansion plans.

In the face of such setbacks, Lawless has given himself the job of boosting corporate morale, which has been sorely tried by seemingly endless layoffs, closings, and divestitures. "It's easy to get into a mode of downsizing, so they (employees) forget why they're here," he says. "I want them to know they've a good future with this company." The new CEO is carrying the message himself in meetings with key personnel across Canada. Behind the drumbeating, though, a sombre undertone rumbles in anticipation of deregulation and its emphasis on private enterprise. "I will meet personally with 1 000 employees, to make sure they understand the reason we're here is to service the marketplace, and that's the only reason for working here." If it works, CN may regain its winning ways, with a 1987 profit of $90 million. That, however, is still a long haul from 1984's net income of $242 million.

Based on "CN braces for deregulation, privatization," by Alan D. Gray in *Financial Times of Canada*, February 23, 1987. Used with permission.

204

Division of Labour

The second main consideration of any organizing effort is how to divide labour. The **division of labour** is the assignment of various portions of a particular task among a number of organization members. Rather than one individual doing the entire job, several individuals perform different parts of the total activity. Production is divided into a number of steps, with the responsibility for completion of various steps assigned to specific individuals.[16] In essence, individuals specialize in doing part of the task rather than the entire task.

Division of labour calls for specialization.

A commonly used illustration of division of labour is the automobile production line. Rather than one individual assembling an entire car, specific portions of the car are assembled by various individuals. The following sections discuss the advantages and disadvantages of division of labour and the relationship between division of labour and coordination.

Advantages and Disadvantages of Division of Labour

Several generally accepted explanations have been offered for why division of labour should be employed within an organizing strategy. First, since workers specialize in a particular task, their skill for performing that task tends to increase. Second, workers do not lose valuable time in moving from one task to another. Since they typically have one job and one place in which to do it, time is not lost changing tools or locations. Third, because workers concentrate on performing only one job, they naturally tend to try to make their job easier and more efficient. Lastly, division of labour creates a situation in which workers only need to know how to perform their part of the work task rather than the process for the entire product. The task of understanding their work, therefore, typically does not become too much of a burden.

Division of labour may be efficient and have economic benefits,

Arguments also have been presented, however, that seem to discourage the use of extreme division of labour or specialization.[17] Overall, these arguments stress that the advantages of division of labour focus solely on efficiency and economic benefit and overlook the human variable. Work that is extremely specialized tends to be very boring and therefore usually causes production rates to go down. Clearly, some type of balance is needed between specialization and human motivation. How to arrive at this balance is discussed further in Chapter 14.

but overspecialization is boring and may depress production rates.

Division of Labour and Coordination

In a division of labour situation with different individuals doing portions of a task, the importance of effective coordination within the organization becomes obvious. Mooney defines **coordination** as "the orderly arrangement of group effort to provide unity of action in the pursuit of a common purpose."[18] Coordination involves encouraging the completion of individual portions of a task in a synchronized order that is appropriate for the overall task. For example, part of the synchronized order for assembling an automobile entails installing seats only after the floor has been installed. Adhering to this order of installation is coordination.

Coordination involves encouraging the completion of individual portions of a task in an appropriate, synchronized order.

Establishing and maintaining coordination may, but does not always, involve close supervision of employees. Managers can also establish and maintain coordination through bargaining, formulating common purpose, and/or improving upon specific problem solutions.[19] Each of these roles can help achieve coordination and is considered a specific management tool. Managers should try to break away from the idea that coordination is only achieved through close employee supervision.

Mary Parker Follett has furnished concerned managers with valuable advice on how to establish and maintain coordination within the organization. First, Follett indicates that coordination can be attained with the least difficulty through direct horizontal relationships and personal communications. When a coordination problem arises, speaking with peer workers may be the best way to solve it. Second, Follett suggests that coordination be a discussion topic throughout the planning process. In essence, managers should plan for coordination. Third, maintaining coordination is a continuing process and should be treated as such. Managers cannot assume that because their management system shows coordination today it will show coordination tomorrow. Follett also says that managers should not leave the existence of coordination to chance. Coordination can be achieved only through purposeful managerial action. Lastly, according to Follett, the importance of the human element and the communication process should be considered when attempting to encourage coordination. Employee skill levels and motivation levels are primary considerations, as is the effectiveness of the human communication process used during coordination activities.[20]

BACK TO THE CASE

To help Zacarachy organize his employees, Dupont should make use of the second major element in classical organizing theory—division of labour. Dupont could propose that instead of one person doing all the work involved in making cakes or bread, the labour could be divided so that for each product, one person mixes dough, one person decorates or braids, and one person watches the ovens. In this way, employees could work more quickly and could specialize in one area of the baking process, such as cake decorating or bread braiding.

When Dupont makes suggestions for the division of labour, she should also consider a mechanism for enhancing coordination. Her questions to Zacarachy should allow her to gain a thorough understanding of how the baking process occurs, so that she can divide the tasks and maintain coordination within the departments. If, for example, the frosting on cakes must be a certain temperature before the cakes are decorated, Dupont must coordinate the frosting and decorating tasks so the cakes are frosted and chilled before the decorator is ready for them.

Dupont should stress to Zacarachy that precise coordination will require him to communicate with his employees. He will also need to continually plan for and take action toward maintaining such coordination.

Span of Management

The third main consideration of any organizing effort is span of management. **Span of management** refers to the number of individuals a manager supervises. The more individuals a manager supervises, the greater the span of management. Conversely, the fewer individuals a manager supervises, the smaller the span of management. Span of management is also called span of control, span of authority, span of supervision, and span of responsibility.

The central concern of span of management is a determination of how many individuals a manager can effectively supervise.[21] To use human resources efficiently, managers should supervise as many individuals as they can best guide toward production quotas. If they are supervising too few individuals, they are wasting a portion of their productive capacity. On the other hand, if they are supervising too many individuals, they necessarily lose part of their effectiveness.

Span of management: How many individuals can one manager effectively supervise?

Designing Span of Management: A Contingency Viewpoint

As reported by Harold Koontz, there are several important situational factors that influence the appropriateness of the size of an individual's span of management:[22]

Appropriate span of management is contingent upon:

Similarity of functions   is the degree to which activities performed by supervised individuals are similar or dissimilar. As the similarity of subordinates' activities increases, the span of management appropriate for the situation becomes wider. The converse is also generally accurate.

1. Likeness of subordinates' jobs.

Geographic contiguity   is the degree to which subordinates are physically separated. In general, the closer subordinates are physically, the more individual managers can supervise effectively.

2. Closeness of subordinates' jobs.

Complexity of functions   refers to the degree to which workers' activities are difficult and involved. The more difficult and involved these activities are, the more difficult it is to manage a large number of individuals effectively.

3. Difficulty of subordinates' jobs.

Coordination   refers to the amount of time managers must spend to synchronize the activities of their subordinates with the activities of other workers. The greater the amount of time managers must spend on coordination, the smaller their span of management should be.

4. Interdependence of subordinates' jobs.

Planning   refers to the amount of time managers must spend developing management system objectives and plans and integrating them with the activities of their subordinates. The more time they must spend on planning activities, the fewer individuals they can manage effectively.

5. Planning required for subordinates' jobs.

Figure 8.12 summarizes the factors that tend to increase and decrease span of management.

FIGURE 8.12   Major factors that influence the span of management.

Factor	Factor Has Tendency to Increase Span of Management When—	Factor Has Tendency to Decrease Span of Management When—
1. Similarity of functions	1. Subordinates have similar functions.	1. Subordinates have different functions.
2. Geographic contiguity	2. Subordinates are physically close.	2. Subordinates are physically distant.
3. Complexity of functions	3. Subordinates have simple tasks.	3. Subordinates have complex tasks.
4. Coordination	4. Work of subordinates needs little coordination.	4. Work of subordinates needs much coordination.
5. Planning	5. Manager spends little time planning.	5. Manager spends much time planning.

FIGURE 8.13   Geometric increase of possible management-subordinate relationships.

Number of Subordinates	Number of Relationships
1	1
2	6
3	18
4	44
5	100
6	222
7	490
8	1 080
9	2 376
10	5 210
11	11 374
12	24 708
18	2 359 602

From *Principles of Management*, p. 253, by Harold Koontz and Cyril O'Donnell. Copyright © 1972 by McGraw-Hill, Inc. Used with permission of McGraw-Hill Book Co.

Graicunas and Span of Management

Graicunas's formula determines the number of possible relationships between a manager and subordinates.

Perhaps the best-known contribution to span of management literature was made by V.A. Graicunas,[23] a management consultant.[24] His contribution was the development of a formula for determining the number of *possible* relationships between a manager and subordinates when the number of subordinates is known. **Graicunas's formula** is as follows:

$$C = n \left(\frac{2^n}{2} + n - 1 \right)$$

C is the total number of possible relationships between manager and subordinates, while n is the known number of subordinates. Figure 8.13 shows the results of what happens to the total possible number of manager-subordinate relationships as the number of subordinates increases from 1 to 18. As the number of subordinates increases arithmetically, the number of possible relationships between the manager and those subordinates increases geometrically. Figure 8.14 is an illustration of the six possible relationships between a manager and two subordinates.

A number of criticisms have been leveled at Graicunas's work. Arguments that Graicunas did not take into account a manager's relationships outside the organization and that he only considered potential relationships rather than actual relationships have some validity. The real significance of Graicunas's work, however, does not lie within the realm of these criticisms. His main contribution was pointing out that span of management is an important consideration that can have far-reaching organizational impact.[25]

FIGURE 8.14   Six possible relationships between manager *M* and two subordinates *X* and *Y*.

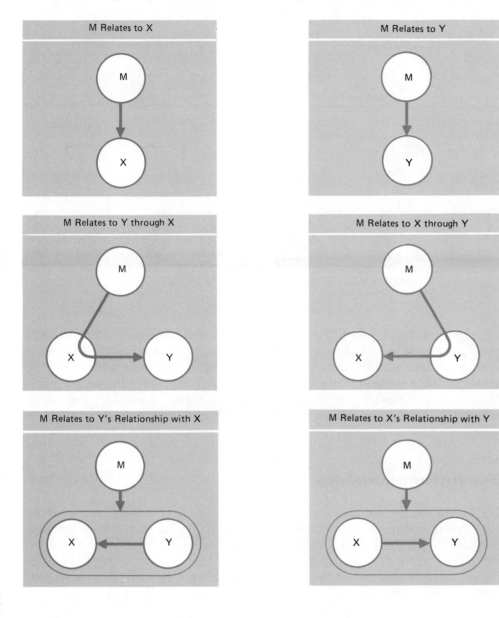

Height of Organization Chart

A definite relationship exists between span of management and the height of an organization chart. Normally, the greater the height of the organization chart, the smaller the span of management within that organization. It also follows that the lower the height of the organization chart, the greater the span of management. Organization charts with little height are usually referred to as **flat**, while organization charts with considerable height are usually referred to as **tall**.

A broad span of management indicates a flat organization chart, while a narrow span indicates a tall organization chart.

FIGURE 8.15 Relationship between organization chart height and span of management.

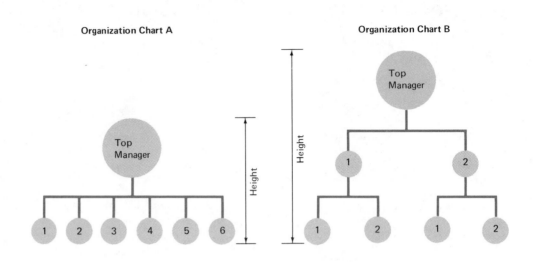

Figure 8.15 is a simple example of the relationship between organization chart height and span of management. Organization chart *A* has a span of management of six, and organization chart *B* has a span of management of two. As a result, chart *A* is flatter than chart *B*. Both charts *A* and *B* have the same number of individuals below the top manager. The larger span of management in *A* is reduced in *B* simply by adding a level to *B*'s organization chart.

Scalar Relationships

The fourth main consideration of any organizing effort is scalar relationships. **Scalar relationships** refer to a chain of command. Organization is built upon the premise that the individual at the top possesses the most authority and that other individuals' authority is scaled downward according to their relative position on the organization chart. The lower an individual's position on the organization chart, the less authority she or he possesses.

The scalar relationship concept, or chain of command, is related to the unity of command concept. The **unity of command** concept recommends that an individual should have only one boss. If too many bosses give orders, the most probable result is confusion, contradictory orders, and frustrated workers, a situation that usually results in ineffectiveness and inefficiency.

Fayol indicates that strict adherence to the chain of command is not always advisable.[26] Figure 8.16 serves to explain Fayol's rationale. If individual *F* needs information from individual *G* and follows the concept of scalar relationships or chain of command, *F* has to go through individuals *D, B, A, C,* and *E* before

FIGURE 8.16   Example organization chart showing that always adhering to the chain of command is not advisable.

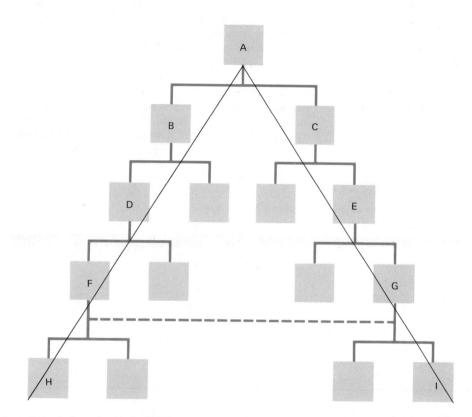

From H. Fayol, *General and Industrial Management*, trans. Constance Storrs (London: Sir Isaac Pitman & Sons, Ltd., 1963), p. 34. Used with permission.

reaching *G*. The information would get back to *F* only by going from *G* through *E*, *C*, *A*, *B*, and *D*. Obviously, this long and involved process can be very expensive for the organization in terms of time spent getting the information.

To decrease this expense, Fayol recommends that in some situations a bridge or "**gangplank**" should be used to allow *F* to go directly to *G* for information. This bridge is represented in Figure 8.16 by the dotted line that goes directly from *F* to *G*. Managers should use these organizational bridges with great care, however, because although *F* might get the information from *G* more quickly and cheaply, individuals *D*, *B*, *A*, *C*, and *E* are left out of the communication channel. This lack of information caused by using Fayol's bridge might be more costly in the long term than going through the established chain of command. If managers do use an organizational bridge, they must be extremely careful to inform all other appropriate individuals within the organization of the information they received.

Use of Fayol's "gang-plank" may be quicker, but it could be costly in the long term.

BACK TO THE CASE

The last two major elements in classical organizing theory are span of management and scalar relationships. Span of management is another of Dupont's major areas of recommendation to Zacarachy. It focuses on the number of subordinates managers can supervise in the bakeries. Dupont's questions to Zacarachy about span of management should cover several important situational factors, such as similarities among baking activities, the extent to which bakery workers are physically separated, and the complexity of baking functions.

For example, Dupont should know that baking cookies is fairly simple but baking bread is much more difficult. Therefore, the span of management for the bread department should probably be smaller than that for the cookie department. Other important factors Dupont should consider are the amount of time managers must spend coordinating bakery workers' activities and the amount of time managers spend planning. With all of this information, Dupont can suggest appropriate spans of management for the managers in Zacarachy's bakeries.

Dupont's recommendations should also relate to designating scalar relationships within the bakeries, such as determining that the manager of each department reports to the general manager of each bakery, who in turn reports to Zacarachy. Dupont must also consider when, if ever, this proposed chain of command should be bridged. For example, a bread baker who runs out of sugar and needs to borrow some from another department should be able to go directly to that department, rather than having to go through the chain of command. However, if sugar supplies in both departments are to be maintained, others in the chain of command, such as the bakery manager, would need to know, so more sugar could be ordered. Therefore, in making her recommendations to Zacarachy, it is important for Dupont to understand the relationships among the tasks being performed in the bakery and when it is necessary for an individual within the chain to know what others are doing.

Action Summary

Reread the learning objectives that follow. Each objective is followed by questions. Answering these questions accurately will help you to retain the most important concepts discussed in this chapter. After answering each question, check your answer with the answer key at the end of this chapter. (*Hint*: If you have doubt regarding the correct response, consult the page that follows the answer.)

Circle:

From studying this chapter, I will attempt to acquire:

1. **An understanding of the organizing function.**
   a. Of the five steps in the organizing process, which of the following is grossly out of order: (a) reflect on plans and objectives; (b) establish major tasks; (c) allocate resources and directives for subtasks; (d) divide major tasks into subtasks; (e) evaluate results of the implemented organizational strategy.

a, b, c, d, e

   b. Proper execution of the organizing function normally results in minimal duplication of effort.

T, F

2. **An appreciation for the complications of determining appropriate organizational structure.**
   a. The XYZ Corporation is organized as follows: it has (1) a president, (2) a vice-president in charge of finance, (3) a vice-president in charge of marketing, and (4) a vice-president in charge of human resources management. This firm is organized on the: (a) functional basis; (b) manufacturing process basis; (c) customer basis; (d) territorial basis; (e) production basis.

a, b, c, d, e

    b. All of the following forces are influences on the evolution of formal structure except: (a) forces in the manager; (b) forces in subordinates; (c) forces in the environment; (d) forces in the division of labour; (e) forces in the task.   a, b, c, d, e

3. Insights on the advantages and disadvantages of division of labour.

    a. Extreme division of labour tends to result in: (a) human motivation; (b) boring jobs; (c) non-specialized work; (d) decreased work skill; (e) all of the above.   a, b, c, d, e

    b. Which of the following is *not* a generally accepted advantage of division of labour within an organization: (a) workers' skills in performing their jobs tend to increase; (b) workers need to know only how to perform their specific work tasks; (c) workers do not waste time in moving from one task to another; (d) workers naturally tend to try to make their individual tasks easier and more efficient; (e) none of the above (all are advantages of the division of labour).   a, b, c, d, e

4. A working knowledge of the relationship between division of labour and coordination.

    a. Effective coordination is best achieved through close employee supervision.   T, F

    b. Mary Parker Follett contended that managers should plan for coordination.   T, F

5. An understanding of span of management and the factors that influence its appropriateness.

    a. Of the factors listed, which one would have a tendency to increase (expand) the span of management: (a) subordinates are physically distant; (b) subordinates have similar functions; (c) subordinates have complex tasks; (d) subordinates' work needs close coordination; (e) manager spends much time in planning.   a, b, c, d, e

    b. The concept of span of management concerns: (a) seeing that managers at the same level have equal numbers of subordinates; (b) employee skill and motivation levels; (c) supervision of one less than the known number of subordinates; (d) a determination of the number of individuals a manager can effectively supervise; (e) a and d.   a, b, c, d, e

6. An understanding of scalar relationships.

    a. The management concept that recommends that employees should have one and only one boss is termed: (a) departmentalization; (b) function; (c) unity of command; (d) scalar relationship; (e) none of the above.   a, b, c, d, e

    b. According to Fayol, under no circumstances should the chain of command be bypassed or circumvented.   T, F

INTRODUCTORY CASE WRAP-UP

"Consolidating Bakeries" (p. 192) and its related back-to-the-case sections were written to help you better understand the management concepts contained in this chapter. Answer the following discussion questions about this introductory case to further enrich your understanding of the chapter content:

1. How would you define *organizing*?
2. List as many questions as you can that you think Dupont will ask Zacarachy to lay the foundation for solving the organizing problem in the case.
3. Explain why it would be important for Dupont to ask each of the questions you listed.

Issues for Review and Discussion

1. What is organizing?
2. Explain the significance of organizing to the management system.
3. List the steps in the organizing process. Why should managers continually repeat these steps?
4. Can the organizing function be thought of as a subsystem? Explain.
5. Fully describe what Max Weber meant by the term *bureaucracy*.
6. Compare and contrast formal structure with informal structure.
7. List and explain three factors that management structure is based on, or contingent upon. Draw three sample portions of organization charts that illustrate the factors you listed.
8. Describe the forces that influence formal structure. How do these forces collectively influence structure?
9. What is division of labour?
10. What are the advantages and disadvantages of employing division of labour within a management system?
11. Define *coordination*.
12. Does division of labour increase the need for coordination? Why?
13. Summarize Mary Parker Follett's thoughts on how to establish and maintain coordination.
14. Is span of management an important management concept? Explain.
15. Do you think that similarity of functions, geographic contiguity, complexity of functions, coordination, and planning influence appropriate span of control in all management systems? Explain.
16. Summarize and evaluate Graicunas's contribution to span of management literature.
17. What is the relationship between span of management and *flat* and *tall* organizations?
18. What are scalar relationships?
19. Explain the rationale behind Fayol's position that always adhering to the chain of command is not necessarily advisable.
20. What caution should managers exercise when they use the "gangplank" Fayol described?

Sources of Additional Information

Allen, Louis A. "Managerial Planning: Back to Basics." *Management Review*, no. 4 (April 1981): 15–20.

Argyris, C. *Integrating the Individual and the Organization*. New York: Wiley, 1964).

Arnold, Mark R. "Unleashing Middle Managers." *Management Review*, no. 5 (May 1981): 58.

Brown, A. *Organization*. New York: Hibbert, 1945.

Chamberlain, Neil W. *Social Strategy and Corporate Structure*. New York: Macmillan, 1982.

Etzioni, A. *A Comparative Analysis of Complex Organizations*. Glencoe, Ill.: Free Press, 1961.

Fink, Stephen L., R. Stephen Jenks, and Robin D. Willits. *Designing and Managing Organizations*. Homewood, Ill.: Richard D. Irwin, 1983.

Ford, Jeffrey D., and David A. Baucus. "Organizational Adaptation to Performance Downturns: An Interpretation-Based Perspective." *Academy of Management Review* 12 (April 1987): 366–80.

Giblin, Edward J. "Differentiating Organizational Problems." *Business Horizons* 24 (May/June 1981): 60–64.

Goddard, Robert W. "The Rise of the New Organization." *Management World* 14 (January 1985): 7–11.

Jelinek, Mariann, Joseph A. Litterer, and Raymond E. Miles. *Organizations by Design: Theory and Practice*, 2d ed. Plano, Tex.: Business Publications, 1986.

Lorsch, J.W., and John J. Morse. *Organizations and Their Members: A Contingency Approach*. New York: Harper & Row, 1974.

Mintzberg, Henry. "Organization Design: Fashion or Fit?" *Harvard Business Review* (January/February 1981): 103–16.

Mitroff, Ian I. *Stakeholders of the Organizational Mind*. San Francisco: Jossey-Bass, 1983.

Mondy, R. Wayne, and Robert M. Noe III. *The Management of Human Resources*, 3d ed. Boston: Allyn & Bacon, 1987.

Putnam, Linda L., and Michael E. Pacanowsky. *Communication and Organizations: An Interpretive Approach*. Beverly Hills, Calif.: Sage, 1983.

Ritchie, J.B., and Paul Thompson. *Organization and People: Readings, Cases, and Exercises in Organizational Behavior*, 3d ed. St. Paul, Minn.: West Publishing, 1984.

Robbins, Stephen P. *Organization Theory: The Structure and Design of Organizations*. Englewood Cliffs, N.J.: Prentice-Hall, 1983.

Skibbins, Gerald J. *Organizational Evolution*. Seaside, Calif.: Intersystems Publications, 1981.

Notes

1. Douglas S. Sherwin, "Management of Objectives," *Harvard Business Review* (May/June 1976): 149–60.

2. Henri Fayol, *General and Industrial Management* (London: Sir Isaac Pitman and Sons, 1949), 53–54.

3. William F. Glueck, "Who Needs an Organization Department?" *California Management Review* 4 (Winter 1972): 77–82.

4. Burt K. Scanlan, "Managerial Leadership in Perspective: Getting Back to Basics," *Personnel Journal* (March 1979): 168–70.

5. Max Weber, *Theory of Social and Economic Organization*, trans. and ed. by A.M. Henderson and Talcott Parsons (London: Oxford University Press, 1947).

6. Richard Bendix, *Max Weber: An Intellectual Portrait* (New York: Doubleday, 1960).

7. Charles Perrow, "The Short and Glorious History of Organizational Theory," *Organizational Dynamics* (Summer 1973): 2–15.

8. William G. Scott, "Organization Theory: An Overview and Appraisal," *Academy of Management Journal* (April 1961): 7–26.

9. George H. Rice, Jr., "A Set of Organizational Models," *Human Resource Management* 19 (Summer 1980): 21.

10. Lyndall Urwich, *Notes on the Theory of Organization* (New York: American Management Association, 1952).

11. For an interesting discussion of a non-traditional organization structure, see Pamela M. Banks and David W. Ewing, "It's Not Lonely Upstairs," *Harvard Business Review* (November/December 1980): 111–32.

12. Fred A. Katz, "Explaining Informal Work Groups in Complex Organizations: The Case for Autonomy of Structure," *Administrative Science Quarterly* 10 (September 1965): 204–23.

13. Gerald C. Werner, "Organizing for Innovation: Does a Product Group Structure Inhibit Technological Developments?" *Management Review* (March 1981): 47–51.

14. For information regarding steps to handle international organizing problems, see Gilbert H. Clee and Wilber M. Sachtjen, "Organizing a Worldwide Business," *Harvard Business Review* (November/December 1964): 55–67.

15. Y.K. Shetty and Howard M. Carlisle, "A Contingency Model of Organization Design," *California Management Review* 15 (1972): 38–45.

16. Adam Smith, *The Wealth of Nations* (New York: Random House, 1937).

17. C.R. Walker and R.H. Guest, *The Man on the Assembly Line* (Cambridge, Mass.: Harvard University Press, 1952).

18. J. Mooney, "The Principles of Organization," in *Ideas and Issues in Public Administration*, ed. D. Waldo (New York: McGraw-Hill, 1953), 86.

19. George D. Greenberg, "The Coordinating Roles of Management," *Midwest Review of Public Administration* 10 (1976): 66–76.

20. Henry C. Metcalf and Lyndall F. Urwich, eds., *Dynamic Administration: The Collected Papers of Mary Parker Follett* (New York: Harper & Row, 1942), 297–99.

21. Gerald G. Fisch, "Stretching the Span of Management," *Harvard Business Review*, no. 5 (1963): 74–85.

22. Harold Koontz, "Making Theory Operational: The Span of Management," *The Journal of Management Studies* (October 1966): 229–43.

23. V.A. Graicunas, "Relationships in Organization," *Bulletin of International Management Institute* (March 1933): 183–87.

24. For more on the life of Graicunas, see Arthur C. Bedeian, "Vytautas Andrius Graicunas: A Biographical Note," *Academy of Management Journal* 17 (June 1974): 347–49.

25. Lt. Col. L.F. Urwick, "V.A. Graicunas and the Span of Control," *Academy of Management Journal* 17 (June 1974): 349–54.

26. Henri Fayol, *General and Industrial Administration* (Belmont, Calif: Pitman, 1949).

Action Summary Answer Key

1. a. c, p. 194
   b. T, pp. 193–194
2. a. a, p. 199
   b. d, p. 202
3. a. b, p. 205
   b. e, p. 205
4. a. F, pp. 205–206
   b. T, p. 206
5. a. b, p. 207
   b. d, pp. 206–207
6. a. c, p. 210
   b. F, pp. 210–211

CROWN LIFE'S BUMPY TURNAROUND RIDE

The future is looking good. Michael Burns, president of Crownx Inc., is pleased with the turnaround at Crown Life Insurance over the past few years. Crown Life is the biggest star in the corporate universe of Crownx Inc., a Toronto-based conglomerate with a bevy of other subsidiaries in the nursing home, information technology, and financial services businesses.

Crown Life is but one of several companies in the Crown Financial Group, a Crownx subsidiary formed to oversee the conglomerate's financial subsidiaries, and whose objective is to build an integrated financial services empire. At the end of 1985, Crown Life had assets of $5.9 billion, and $76.5 billion worth of life insurance spread over Canada, the U.S., the U.K., the Caribbean, and the Pacific Rim.

When Crown Life began its existence in June 1900, life insurance appeared to be a lucrative business for anyone with the capital and know-how to start a company; the average family at that time owned only $450 worth of life insurance, just enough to take care of unexpected burial expenses. Early on, control of the company landed in the hands of the Burns and Jodrey families, two prominent business clans with origins in the Maritimes. Throughout the 1950s and 1960s, business grew at a tremendous rate, and company managers had to bend over backwards not to make money.

But by 1971, changes were in store. Attempts to modernize the company were made, and productivity improvement programs along with monthly financial reports were introduced—all efforts designed to focus more attention on the bottom line. But it was to no avail. By the early 1980s, a crisis had developed. "Our profits were eroding," says president Alan Morson, "especially in the U.S. health insurance market, which was a large bucket of business." According to Morson, Crown Life was suffering because management was continuing in its timeworn, outdated ways. The man who undertook to change all that was Michael Burns.

In 1980, Crown Life was courting potential investors when it suddenly switched its strategy and launched plans to acquire Extendicare, the fourth-largest nursing home operator in North America. The reasons were simple: growth, and an opportunity to use Extendicare as

Michael Burns "is pleased with the turnaround at Crown Life."

an upstream holding company for Crown Life through which it could launch takeover raids. (As an insurer, Crown Life was limited by federal law to a 30 percent stake in other companies.) The deal was consummated with an exchange of shares. The Burns and Jodrey families handed their Crown Life holdings to Extendicare in exchange for 6 million shares in the nursing home giant, thereby acquiring control of Extendicare. After the deal, Extendicare owned 35 percent of Crown Life, but an immediate follow-up offer to Crown Life shareholders and other transactions since then have boosted that holding to 94 percent. In 1983, the name of the holding company was changed from Extendicare Ltd. to Crownx Inc.

Meanwhile, unbeknownst to Crown's management, Michael Burns held private conversations with McKinsey and Co. Inc., a New York-based management consulting firm, asking for a team to review Crown's operations and to make proposals for wholesale changes. Apart from proposing drastic measures to improve Crown's management methods and operating efficiency, McKinsey recommended that Crown's executive suites be cleaned out. It was decided that an outsider be hired for the job: enter Robert Bandeen, president of CN and a director of Crown Life. Even before he took over at Crown, Bandeen had become familiar with some of the company's deficiencies while sitting on its board of directors. "The whole company wasn't run in an entrepreneurial spirit," he says.

"I tried to give people a sense of responsibility and accountability." The people he kept on, that is.

Between 1982 and 1985, the eighty-six-year-old life insurance company was gutted like a tumbledown building and then rebuilt from the inside out. Lifelong employees and executives filed out of Crown Life's doors in numbed disbelief as Robert Bandeen fired 25 percent of the payroll in a two-year period, brought in new executive talent, and generally modernized the way the company's affairs were managed.

A total of 750 employees were lopped from the payroll between June 1982 and November 1985. Crown Life was reorganized into seven profit centres based on geography and product line. Operations in the U.S. and Canada were split, with each country having a separate profit centre for group and individual insurance. Profit centres were also established for Britain and elsewhere, as was the company's reinsurance business. The company raised its health insurance premiums in the U.S. and became more selective in the quality of business it wrote. Besides slashing the number of staff and reorganizing operations, Bandeen began to transform Crown Life into a performance-oriented workplace. He introduced an annual training course for middle management at a Quebec university where lecturers taught thirty to forty staff for four weeks each June. To further reinforce the idea that productivity pays, bonuses were introduced for managers who reached yearly profit targets.

Bandeen believed his mandate to be one of building a dynamic financial services empire based on Crown Life. To that end, he acquired the titular power to perform the role of empire builder by assuming the presidencies of Crown Financial Services when it was created, and of Crownx after it was formed in 1983, (at that time, Michael Burns was chairman of the board at Crownx). But it was becoming increasingly obvious that Bandeen wanted greater power to run all of Crownx's affairs. That, as he discovered, didn't sit too well with Burns and David Hennigar, the other major stakeholder in Crown Life. Exit one Robert Bandeen.

When Bandeen quit as Crown Life's chairman in the fall of 1985, he left behind a company poised to make record profits but saddled with a shellshocked work force with abysmal morale. Says a CEO from a competing company, "It wasn't what Bandeen did. It was the way he did it. I don't know if Crown Life will ever recover."

Crown Life is currently a company concentrating on the hard future and trying to forget the past. But in-house surveys show that morale remains at subterranean levels, indicating that scars still exist a year after Bandeen's departure. According to Morson, however, there has been some improvement. But, while Bandeen's methods may have been harsh, their impact on Crown Life's bottom line has been substantial. In 1982, Crown Life's common shareholders made a meagre 6.16 percent return on their investment. In 1985, the rate of return was 19.39 percent. Net income rose from $4.6 million in 1982 to $71.6 million in 1985. More than $56 million of that 1985 profit flowed through to Crown Life's 94-percent owner, Crownx, helping to boost the parent company's profit to $66.1 million for the year.

And what about the future? More than just a cash cow for Crownx and its shareholders, Crown Life has been spruced up and recharged to provide a solid base for Crownx's further expansion in the financial services sector. Shares were issued by Crownx to reduce its debt-to-equity ratio from an unhealthy 1.2:1 at year-end 1984 to 0.5:1 in 1986. "We have the capital to do some fairly major things," Hennigar says. Future possibilities include acquiring another life insurer in the $200 million range, if not in Canada then in the U.S. The company has already acquired an interest in merchant banking, and mutual funds are another possibility. Burns finds the idea of buying a property and casualty insurer the less interesting course. Noting that federal regulations may be changed to allow insurance companies to control trust companies, Burns states: "If we decide we should get into the deposit-taking business, we will do so." The company will not, however, move too far too fast, preferring instead a cautious acquisition strategy. This will likely lead to more cross-selling of products among Crownx's subsidiaries—an activity which has already begun at Crown Life.

DISCUSSION ISSUES

1. According to what factors is the new structure as recommended by Bandeen being organized? How is this influenced by the current structure and the nature of the business? Discuss.
2. What forces led to the reorganization of Crown Life's structure in the early 1980s? Explain.
3. How is the reorganization of Crown Life in the early 1980s, and currently, an example of organizing as a subsystem of overall management system? Elaborate on your answer.

Based on "Crown Life's bumpy turnaround ride," by James Fleming in *Financial Times of Canada*, November 24, 1986. Used with permission.

CHAPTER

9

ORGANIZING THE ACTIVITY OF INDIVIDUALS

STUDENT LEARNING OBJECTIVES

From studying this chapter, I will attempt to acquire:

1. An understanding of the relationship between responsibility, authority, and delegation.
2. Information on how to divide and clarify job activities of individuals within an organization.
3. Knowledge of the differences between line authority, staff authority, and functional authority.
4. An appreciation for the issues that can cause conflict in line and staff relationships.
5. Insights on the value of accountability to the organization.
6. An understanding of how to delegate.
7. A strategy for eliminating various barriers to delegation.
8. A working knowledge of when and how an organization should be decentralized.

CHAPTER OUTLINE

REDESIGNING JOB ACTIVITIES

Leo Mercier was recently appointed manager of the student employment department in the financial aid division of Concordia University. The purpose of the student employment department is to help students who need part-time work to compete effectively in the community labour market. This help includes such activities as assistance in finding a position, guidance in writing résumés, and suggestions on how to prepare for an interview. Mercier graduated from the school of business administration at Carleton University six months ago.

During his first week on the job, Mercier's only official responsibility was reading a policy manual that familiarized him with the student financial aids division. According to this manual, Mercier was under the direct supervision of the manager of the student financial aid division and at the same level as the manager of student

loans and the manager of scholarships and grants. The formal relationship between these four individuals is presented in Case Figure 9.1.

On the first day of Mercier's second week on the job, he called a meeting with his eight subordinates to introduce himself and to begin orienting himself to his new position. During the meeting, Mercier admitted that to do his job well he would have to become familiar with the job each individual was performing, the relationship of the student employment department to other departments in the student financial aid division, and the student employment situation within the community.

The meeting ended with Mercier stressing that his first priority was to learn how the student employment department operated. To this end, Mercier asked each person at the meeting to submit within two weeks a detailed, written summary of his or her activities during a normal workweek.

At the end of two weeks, Mercier was pleased to discover that all eight performance summaries had been submitted. After analyzing the summaries, however, he was somewhat puzzled that no one was responsible for performing certain job activities that seemed fundamental to a student employment department. For example, no one from the student employment department ever followed up to see how well a student performed in a job. Mercier reasoned that this follow-up could be of significant help in convincing certain employers of the value of student employees. If this follow-up and the other neglected fundamental activities that Mercier found were to be added to the present normal operation of the student employment department, some individuals within the department would have an increased work load.

CASE FIGURE 9.1 The formal relationship between managers of the financial aids division.

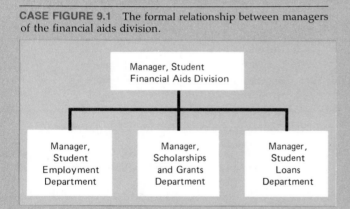

What's Ahead

Leo Mercier, the lower-level manager in the introductory case, is faced with the task of modifying the job activities of certain individuals within the student employment department. In essence, Mercier must change the way in which his department operates. The information in this chapter should be of great value to Mercier or to anyone confronted with a similar task since organizing the job activities of individuals within an organization is the principal topic of the chapter. Three major elements of organizing are presented: (1) responsibility; (2) authority; and (3) delegation.

Chapter 8 dealt with using principles of organizational structure, division of labour, span of management, and scalar relationships to establish an orderly use of resources within the management system. Productivity within any management system, however, results from specific activities performed by various individuals within the organization. An effective organizing effort, therefore, includes not only a rationale for the orderly use of management system resources, but also three other elements of organizing that specifically channel the activities of organization members. These three elements are responsibility, authority, and delegation.

RESPONSIBILITY

Responsibility is perhaps the most fundamental method of channeling the activity of individuals within an organization. **Responsibility** is the obligation to perform an assigned activity. It is a person's self-assumed commitment to handle a job to the best of his or her ability. The source of this responsibility lies within the individual. If a person accepts a job, he or she agrees to carry out a series of duties or activities or to see that someone else carries them out. The act of accepting the job means that the person is obligated to a superior to see that job activities are successfully completed. Since responsibility is an obligation that a person *accepts*, there is no way it can be delegated or passed on to a subordinate.

A summary of an individual's job activities within an organization is usually in a formal statement called a job description. A **job description** is simply a listing of specific activities that must be performed by whoever holds the position. Unclear job descriptions can confuse employees and may cause them to lose interest in their jobs.[1]

Job activities, of course, are delegated by management to enhance the accomplishment of management system objectives. Management analyzes its objectives and assigns specific duties that will lead to reaching those objectives. A sound organizing strategy includes specific job activities for each individual within the organization. As objectives and other conditions within the management system change, however, individual job activities within the organization may have to be changed.

Three areas related to responsibility are: (1) dividing job activities; (2) clarifying job activities of management; and (3) being responsible. Each of these topics is discussed in the sections that follow.

Responsibility is the obligation to complete assigned activities.

A job description summarizes a person's job activities.

Job activities are related to organizational objectives.

Dividing Job Activities

Since, typically, many individuals work within a given management system, organizing necessarily involves dividing job activities among a number of people. One individual cannot be obligated or responsible for performing all of the activities within an organization. Some method of distributing job activities and thereby channeling the activities of several individuals is needed.

The phrase *functional similarity* refers to what many management theorists believe to be the most basic method of dividing job activities. Stated simply, the **functional similarity method** suggests that management should take four basic interrelated steps to divide job activities. These steps and the sequence in which they should be taken are: (1) management examines management system objectives; (2) management designates appropriate activities that must be performed to reach those objectives; (3) management designs specific jobs by grouping similar activities; and (4) management makes specific individuals responsible for performing those jobs. Figure 9.1 illustrates the sequence of activities suggested by the functional similarity method.

Thierauf, Klekamp, and Geeding have indicated that at least three additional guides can be used to supplement the functional similarity method.[2] The first of these supplemental guides suggests that overlapping responsibility should be avoided when making job activity divisions. **Overlapping responsibility** exists when more than one individual is responsible for the same activity. Generally speaking, only one individual should be responsible for completing any one activity. The second supplemental guide is to avoid responsibility gaps. A **responsibility gap** exists when certain tasks are not included in the responsibility area of any individual. In essence, a responsibility gap creates a situation in which nobody within the organization is obligated to perform certain necessary activities. The third supplemental guide is that creating job activities for accomplishing tasks that do not enhance goal attainment should be avoided. Organization members should be obligated to perform only those activities that lead to goal attainment.

Functional similarity method: four interrelated, sequential steps for dividing job activities.

In dividing job activities, managers should avoid overlapping responsibility, responsibility gaps, and job activities that do not enhance goal attainment.

FIGURE 9.1   Sequence of activities for the similarity of function method of dividing responsibility

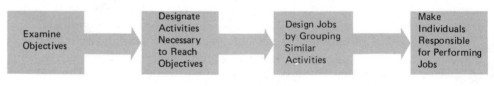

Examine Objectives → Designate Activities Necessary to Reach Objectives → Design Jobs by Grouping Similar Activities → Make Individuals Responsible for Performing Jobs

---

BACK TO THE CASE

Leo Mercier is faced with modifying required activities of various individuals within the student employment department. These activity modifications should help his department to become more successful if he derives them directly from student employment objectives. Mercier's specific steps to make these modifications should include the analysis of departmental objectives, the outlining of specific student employment activities that must be performed to reach those objectives, the designing of student employment jobs by grouping similar activities, and the assigning of these jobs to student employment personnel. To supplement these steps, Mercier must be careful not to create overlapping responsibilities, responsibility gaps, or responsibilities for activities that do not lead directly to goal attainment.

Clarifying Job Activities of Managers

Clarification of the job activities of managers is as important, if not more important, than dividing the job activities of non-managers since managers affect greater portions of the resources within the management system. Hence, such factors as responsibility gaps usually have a more significant impact on the management system when they relate to managers as opposed to non-managers.

One process used to clarify management job activities "enables each manager to actively participate with his or her superiors, peers, and subordinates in systematically describing the managerial job to be done and then clarifying the role each manager plays in relationship to his or her work group and to the organization."[3] The purpose of this interaction is to assure that no overlaps or gaps in perceived management responsibilities exist and that managers are performing only those activities that lead to the attainment of management system objectives. Although this process typically has been used to clarify the responsibilities of managers, it may also be effective in clarifying the responsibilities of non-managers.

A specific tool developed to implement this interaction process is the **management responsibility guide**.[4] The management responsibility guide assists organization members in describing the various responsibility relationships that exist in their organization and summarizing how the responsibilities of various managers within their organization relate to one another.

The seven main organizational responsibility relationships described by this tool are listed in Figure 9.2. Once organization members have decided which of these management responsibility relationships exist within their organization, they then define the relationships between these responsibilities.

Figure 9.3 contains a sample completed management responsibility guide for a division of an aerospace company. This sample exhibit summarizes existing management responsibility relationships within the division and shows how these

The job activities of managers can be clarified with a management responsibility guide.

FIGURE 9.2 Seven responsibility relationships between managers, as used in the management responsibility guide.

1. *General Responsibility* — The individual guides and directs the execution of the function through the person accepting operating responsibility.
2. *Operating Responsibility* — The individual is directly responsible for the execution of the function.
3. *Specific Responsibility* — The individual is responsible for executing a specific or limited portion of the function.
4. *Must Be Consulted* — The individual, if the decision affects his or her area, must be called upon before any decision is made or approval is granted, to render advice or relate information, but not to make the decision or grant approval.
5. *May Be Consulted* — The individual may be called upon to relate information, render advice, or make recommendations.
6. *Must Be Notified* — The individual must be notified of action that has been taken.
7. *Must Approve* — The individual (other than persons holding general and operating responsibility) must approve or disapprove.

FIGURE 9.3 Sample page of management responsibility guide for division of aerospace company.

Number	Function	Vice-president Aerospace	Vice-president Manufacturing	Director Engineering	Manager Industrial Technology	Manager Quality Assurance	Manager Marketing	Manager Contracts	Manager Master Scheduling	Manager Financial Services			Relationship Code
101	Coordinate division budgeting and financial planning activities and communicate financial information to division management	A	E-F	E-F	E-F	E-F	E-F	E-F	E	B			**Relationship Code**
		A-F	D-F	E	F	F	E-F	E	D				
102	Develop project and program schedule requirements; establish, coordinate, and control schedules and report on status	A	E-F	E-F	E-F	E-F	E-F	E-F	B				
		A	D	D	D-F	C	D	D		F			**A** General Responsibility
103	Direct contract activities and evaluate and approve contract provisions of all division sales proposals and contract documents	A					E-F	B	E-F	F			
		A		E			D		D-F	C			**B** Operating Responsibility
104	Plan and coordinate divisional marketing activities so as to secure the business necessary to maximize division's capabilities	A	E-F	E-F	E-F		B	D-F	E-F	F			
		A-D	F			E		C-G	C-D	F			**C** Specific Responsibility
105	Develop and design new and improve existing electronic and electromechanical aerospace products and processes	A	F	B			E						
		A-F	E		E		D-G						**D** Must Be Consulted
106	Secure materials and tools, coordinate human resources, and manufacture products to specified quantity, quality, time, and cost requirements	A	B			F		E-F		E-F			
		A		E	E	C-D		E	F	E			**E** May Be Consulted
107	Establish quality assurance policies, procedures, and controls to insure that products meet applicable standards and specifications	A	D-F	D-F	E	B	F	E-F	E-F				
		A	D-G	E-F	E		E	D		F			**F** Must Be Notified
108	Develop and design propriety products and processes utilizing proven technology specifically adapted to industrial automation	A	D-F	C	B	E	E	D	F	F			
		A-F	E-F	B	D-F			E	E	F			**G** Must Approve
		A	E				E-F	D-F	F				

Organization identification Aerospace Aerospace division	Number 200	Management responsibility guide Approval	Date	Page No. 1 of 1

relationships complement one another. The actual members of this aerospace division, of course, were the individuals who completed this management responsibility guide.

FIGURE 9.4   Four key dimensions of responsible management behaviour.

Behaviour with Subordinates	Behaviour with Upper Management	Behaviour with Other Groups	Personal Attitudes and Values
Responsible managers — 1. Take complete charge of their work groups. 2. Pass praise and credit along to subordinates. 3. Stay close to problems and activities. 4. Take action to maintain productivity and are willing to terminate poor performers if necessary.	Responsible managers — 1. Accept criticism for mistakes and buffer their groups from excessive criticism. 2. Ensure that their groups meet management expectations and objectives.	Responsible managers make sure that any gaps between their areas and those of other managers are securely filled.	Responsible managers — 1. Identify with the group. 2. Put organizational goals ahead of personal desires or activities. 3. Perform tasks for which there is no immediate reward but which help subordinates, the company, or both. 4. Conserve corporate resources as if the resources were their own.

Being Responsible

Managers can be described as responsible if they perform the activities they are obligated to perform.[5] Since managers typically have more impact on an organization than non-managers, responsible managers are a prerequisite for management system success. Several recent studies have shown that responsible management behaviour is highly valued by top executives because the responsible manager guides many other individuals within the organization in performing their duties appropriately.

The degree of responsibleness that managers possess can be determined by analyzing their: (1) attitude toward and conduct with subordinates; (2) behaviour with upper management; (3) behaviour with other groups; and (4) personal attitudes and values. Figure 9.4 summarizes what each of these dimensions includes for the responsible manager.

Performance of obligated activities is a measure of managerial responsibleness.

BACK TO THE CASE

Mercier must recognize that his own job activities within the student employment department, not only those of his subordinates, are a major factor in determining departmental success. Because Mercier's actions have an impact on all personnel within the student employment department, his job activities must be well defined. From the viewpoint of the student financial aids division as a whole, Mercier's job activities should be coordinated with those of the manager of scholar-

ships and grants and the manager of student loans. Perhaps the manager of the student financial aids division could use the management responsibility guide process to achieve this coordination of responsibilities.

Overall, for Mercier to be a responsible manager, he must perform the activities he is obligated to perform, and he must respond appropriately to his subordinates, the manager of the student financial aids division, and his peer managers.

AUTHORITY

Individuals are delegated job activities to channel their behaviour appropriately. Once they have been delegated these activities, however, they also must be delegated a commensurate amount of authority to perform the obligations.

Authority is the right to perform or command. Authority allows its holder to act in certain designated ways and to directly influence the actions of others through orders that she or he issues.

The following example illustrates the relationship between job activities and authority. Two primary tasks for which a Petro-Canada manager is responsible are pumping gasoline and repairing automobiles. In this example, the manager has the complete authority necessary to perform either of these tasks. If this manager chooses, however, he can delegate the activity of automobile repair to the assistant manager. Along with this activity of repairing, however, the assistant should also be delegated the authority to order parts, to command certain attendants to help, and to do anything else necessary to perform the obligated repair jobs. Without this authority, the assistant manager may find it impossible to complete the delegated job activities.

Practically speaking, authority is a factor that only increases the probability that a specific command will be obeyed.[6] The following excerpt emphasizes that authority does not always exact obedience:

> People who have never exercised power have all kinds of curious ideas about it. The popular notion of top leadership is a fantasy of capricious power: the top man presses a button and something remarkable happens; he gives an order as the whim strikes him, and it is obeyed. Actually, the capricious use of power is relatively rare except in some large dictatorships and some small family firms. Most leaders are hedged around by constraints—tradition, constitutional limitations, the realities of the external situation, rights and privileges of followers, the requirements of team work, and most of all, the inexorable demands of large-scale organization, which does not operate on capriciousness. In short, most power is wielded circumspectly.[7]

As shown in Chapter 8, the positioning of individuals on an organization chart indicates the relative amount of authority delegated to each individual. Individuals toward the top of the chart possess more authority than individuals toward the bottom. Chester Barnard writes, however, that in reality the source of authority is not determined by decree from the formal organization but by whether or not authority is accepted by those existing under the authority. According to Barnard, authority exists and will exact obedience only if it is accepted.

In line with this rationale, Barnard defines *authority* as the character of communication by which it is accepted by an individual as governing the actions the individual takes within the system. Barnard indicates that authority will be accepted only if: (1) an individual can understand the order being communicated; (2) an individual believes that the order is consistent with the purpose of the organization; (3) an individual sees the order as compatible with his or her personal interests; and (4) an individual is mentally and physically able to comply with the order. The fewer of these four conditions that exist, the smaller the probability that authority will be accepted and that obedience will be exacted.

Barnard also offers some guidance on what action managers can take to raise the odds that their commands will be accepted and obeyed. According to Barnard, more and more of a manager's commands will be accepted over the long term if:[8]

1. Formal channels of communication are used by the manager and are familiar to all organization members.
2. Each organization member has an assigned formal communication channel through which he or she receives orders.

Marginal notes:

Authority is the right to perform or command.

Authority must reflect responsibility.

Commands may not be obeyed.

For commands to be obeyed, authority must be accepted.

Acceptance of authority can be increased if managers follow certain guidelines.

3. The line of communication between manager and subordinate is as direct as possible.
4. The complete chain of command is used to issue orders.
5. Managers possess adequate communication skills.
6. Managers use formal communication lines only for organizational business.
7. A command is authenticated as coming from a manager.

BACK TO THE CASE

Mercier must be sure that any individuals within the student employment department who are delegated additional job activities are also delegated a commensurate amount of authority to give related orders and to accomplish their obligated activities. Student employment personnel must recognize, however, that authority must be accepted if it is to exact obedience. To increase the probability of acceptance, care should be taken to ensure that individuals understand internal orders, see orders as being consistent with both the objectives of the student employment department and the student financial aids division, perceive orders as being compatible with their individual interests, and see themselves as being mentally and physically able to follow the orders.

Types of Authority

Three main types of authority can exist within an organization: (1) line authority; (2) staff authority; and (3) functional authority. Each type exists only to enable individuals to carry out different types of responsibilities with which they have been charged.

Line and Staff Authority

Line authority is the most fundamental authority within an organization and reflects existing superior-subordinate relationships. **Line authority** is the right to make decisions and to give orders concerning the production, sales, or finance-related behaviour of subordinates. Overall, line authority pertains to matters directly involving management system production, sales, and finance and, as a result, the attainment of objectives. Individuals directly responsible for these areas within the organization are delegated line authority to assist them in performing their obligated activities.

> Line authority reflects existing superior-subordinate relationships.

Whereas line authority involves giving orders concerning production activities, **staff authority** is the right to advise or assist those who possess line authority and other staff personnel. Staff authority exists to enable those responsible for improving the effectiveness of line personnel to perform their required tasks. Examples of organization members with staff authority are members of accounting and personnel departments. Obviously, line and staff personnel must work closely together to improve the efficiency and effectiveness of the organization. The relationship that exists between line and staff personnel in most organizations is presented in Figure 9.5.

> Staff authority is the right to advise or assist those with line authority.

Size is perhaps the most significant factor in determining whether or not staff personnel are used within an organization. Generally, the larger the organization, the greater the need for staff personnel. As an organization grows, management generally finds a greater need for more expertise in more diversified areas. Although the small organization may also need this expertise, hiring part-

> The need for staff personnel is greater in large organizations.

FIGURE 9.5 Basic relationships between line and staff personnel in most organizations.

1. The units that are designated as line have ultimate responsibility for successful operation of the company. Therefore, the line must also be responsible for operating decisions.
2. Staff elements contribute by providing advice and service to the line in accomplishing the objectives of the enterprise.
3. Staff is responsible for providing advice and service to appropriate line elements when requested to do so. However, staff also has the responsibility of proffering advice and service where it is not requested, but where it believes it is needed.
4. The solicitation of advice and the acceptance of suggestions and counsel is usually at the option of the line organization. However, in some cases, it must be recognized that only the top level of the line organization has this option and that its decision on the use of staff advice or service is binding throughout lower levels. In these cases, subordinate levels in the line may have no option in the use of specialized staff services, but may be required to use them.

   For example, the engineering department may analyze the use of machines, tools, jigs, and fixtures and present recommendations to the line. The operating line organization does not ask for this advisory service. Higher management provides it as a means of improving operations by bringing to the problem the most highly skilled and best informed specialists.

   In this case, it is the line managers' responsibility to make most effective use of this advice. If they disagree with it, they should have the opportunity to appeal to higher authority.

   The same holds true with certain services. Because line managers cannot possibly equip themselves to perform highly specialized parts of their job, staff units may perform these services for them. For example, the services of cost accountants are provided to help line managers determine their costs. If the line managers disagree with the methods of collecting this data or with the figures themselves, they may appeal to higher authority. But since they are not equipped to gather and analyze this data themselves, and since cost standards are necessary to effective operation, they must use the services of the accountants.
5. Line should give serious consideration to offers of advice and service made by staff units and should follow it if it is to the company's best interest to do so. However, except in those cases where the use of staff advice and service is compulsory and subject only to appeal to higher authority, it is not mandatory that the advice of staff should be followed unfailingly. Except as noted above, line managers have the authority to modify, reject, or accept such advice.
6. Both line and staff should have the right of appeal to higher authority in case of disagreement as to whether staff recommendation should be followed. However, this right to appeal should not be permitted to supersede the line's responsibility for making immediate decisions when required by the operating situation.

From Louis A. Allen, "Developing Sound Line and Staff Relationships," from *Studies in Personnel Policy* No. 153. National Industrial Conference Board, 1956. Used with permission.

time consultants when a need arises may be more practical than hiring a full-time staff individual who may not always be kept busy.

Figure 9.6 shows how line-staff relationships can be presented on an organization chart. The plant manager on this chart has line authority over each immediate subordinate—personnel manager, production manager, and sales manager. The personnel manager also has staff authority in relation to the plant manager. This simply means that the personnel manager possesses the right to advise the plant manager on personnel matters. Final decisions concerning personnel matters, however, are in the hands of the plant manager, the individual holding line authority. Similar relationships exist between the sales manager and the sales research specialist, as well as between the production manager and the quality control manager. To carry the example of the personnel manager's staff authority one step further, Figure 9.7 contains a detailed listing of the types of decision

FIGURE 9.6   Possible line-staff relationships in selected organizational areas.

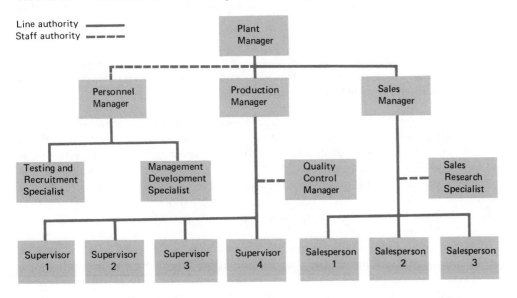

FIGURE 9.7   Typical decision areas for a personnel director.

Personnel records/reports Personnel research Insurance benefits administration Unemployment compensation administration EEO compliance/affirmative action	Employee communications/publications Executive compensation administration Human resource planning Safety programs/OSHA compliance Management development
Wage/salary/administration Workers' compensation administration Tuition aid/scholarships Job evaluation Health/medical services	Food services Performance evaluation, nonmanagement Community relations/fund drives Suggestion systems Thrift/savings plan administration
Retirement preparation programs Pre-employment testing Vacation/leave processing Induction/orientation Promotion/transfer/separation processing	Security/plant protection Organization development Management appraisal/MBO Stock plan administration Skill training, nonmanagement
Counseling/employee assistance programs Pension/profit-sharing plan administration College recruiting Recreation/social/recognition programs Recruiting/interviewing/hiring	Public relations Administrative services (mail, PBX, phone, messengers, etc.) Payroll processing Travel/transportation services administration Library Maintenance/janitorial services
Attitude surveys Union/labor relations Complaint/disciplinary procedures Relocation services administration Supervisory training	

Adapted from ASPA-BNA Survey No. 47, "Personnel Activities, Budgets, and Staffs: 1983–1984," *Bulletin to Management* No. 1785—Part II, June 21, 1984. Reprinted by permission.

areas over which a personnel manager generally has jurisdiction. These decision areas are not directly related to production but could ultimately have a favourable influence on it.

Roles of Staff Personnel

Harold Stieglitz has pinpointed the following three roles that staff personnel typically perform to assist line personnel:[9]

1. *The advisory or counseling role*   The professional expertise of staff personnel in this role is aimed at solving organizational problems. In this role, staff personnel are seen as internal consultants, with the relationship between line and staff being similar to that between a professional and a client. An example of this role might be the staff quality control manager who advises the line production manager on possible technical modifications to the production process that would help to maintain the quality of products produced.
2. *The service role*   Staff personnel in this role provide services that can more efficiently and effectively be provided by a single centralized staff group than by many individuals within the organization attempting to provide these services themselves. This role can probably best be understood by viewing staff personnel as suppliers and line personnel as customers. For example, members of a personnel department recruit, employ, and train workers for all organizational departments. In essence, they are the suppliers of workers, and the various organizational departments needing workers are their customers.
3. *The control role*   In this role, staff personnel help to establish a mechanism for evaluating the effectiveness of organizational plans. Staff personnel exercising this role are seen as representatives or agents of top management.

These three are not the only roles performed by staff personnel within organizations, but they do represent the main ones. In the final analysis, the role of staff personnel in any organization should be specially designed to best meet the needs inherent within that organization. It is entirely possible that to meet the needs of a particular organization, staff personnel must perform some combination of the three main roles.

Conflict in Line-Staff Relationships

Most management practitioners readily admit that a noticeable amount of conflict usually centres around line-staff relationships.[10] From the viewpoint of line personnel, conflict is created between line and staff personnel because staff personnel tend to assume line authority, do not give sound advice, steal credit for success, do not keep line personnel informed, and do not see the whole picture. From the viewpoint of staff personnel, conflict is created between line and staff personnel because line personnel do not make proper use of staff personnel, resist new ideas, and do not give staff personnel enough authority.

To overcome these potential conflicts, staff personnel must strive to emphasize the objectives of the organization as a whole, encourage and educate line personnel in the appropriate use of staff personnel, obtain needed skill if it is not already possessed, and deal with resistance to change rather than view this

The staff relationship to the line can be as:

professional to client;

supplier to customer

or as an agent of top management.

Conflicts arise between line and staff personnel for many reasons.

Overcoming these conflicts requires a serious and continuous effort.

resistance as an immovable barrier. Line personnel's effort in minimizing line-staff conflict should include using staff personnel wherever possible, making proper use of the abilities of staff personnel, and keeping staff personnel appropriately informed.[11]

BACK TO THE CASE

Assuming that the main objective of the student employment department is to help students to compete more effectively in the community labour market, student employment personnel who are directly responsible for achieving this objective must possess line authority to perform their responsibilities. For example, individuals responsible for contacting prospective employers must be given the right to do everything necessary to develop these contacts to the best benefit of students.

Although the student employment department is relatively small, it may be possible that at least one individual is charged with the responsibility of assisting the line in a staff position. Perhaps this individual is responsible for advising Mercier on various surveys that could be conducted to convince prospective employers that university students do make good part-time workers. Any individuals responsible for advising the line should be delegated appropriate staff authority.

As in all organizations, the potential for conflict between student employment line and staff personnel probably would be significant. Mercier should be aware of this potential and encourage both line and staff personnel to minimize it.

Functional Authority

Functional authority is the right to give orders within a segment of the organization in which this right is normally non-existent. This authority usually is assigned to individuals to complement the line or staff authority already possessed. Functional authority generally covers only specific task areas and is operational only for designated amounts of time. It typically is possessed by individuals who, in order to meet their responsibilities, must be able to exercise some control over organization members in other areas.

The vice-president for finance in an organization could be an example of someone with functional authority. Among her basic responsibilities, she is obligated to monitor the financial situation within the management system. To accomplish this monitoring, however, she must have appropriate financial information continually flowing to her from various segments of the organization. The vice-president for finance usually is delegated the functional authority to order various departments to furnish her with the kinds and amounts of information she needs to perform her analysis. In reality, the functional authority this vice-president possesses allows her to give orders to personnel within departments in which she normally cannot give orders.

From the previous discussion on line authority, staff authority, and functional authority, it is reasonable to conclude that, although authority can exist within an organization in various forms, these forms should be used in a combination that will best enable individuals to carry out their assigned responsibilities and

Functional authority allows an individual to exert control in areas of the organization where this person usually has no authority.

Line, staff, and functional authority can be combined for the overall benefit of the organization.

FIGURE 9.8   Advantages and disadvantages of line authority, staff authority, and functional authority.

Advantages	Disadvantages
Line Authority	
Maintains simplicity Makes clear division of authority Encourages speedy action	Neglects specialists in planning Overworks key people Depends on retention of a few key people
Staff Authority	
Enables specialists to give expert advice Frees the line executive of detailed analysis Affords young specialists a means of training	Confuses organization if functions are not clear Reduces power of experts to place recommendations into action Tends toward centralization of organization
Functional Authority	
Relieves line executives of routine specialized decisions Provides framework for applying expert knowledge Relieves pressure of need for large numbers of well-rounded executives	Makes relationships more complex Makes limits of authority of each specialist a difficult coordination problem Tends toward centralization of organization

Reprinted with permission of Macmillan Publishing Company from *The New Management* by Robert M. Fulmer. Copyright © 1974 by Robert M. Fulmer.

FIGURE 9.9   Proposed design for incorporating three types of authority in a hospital.

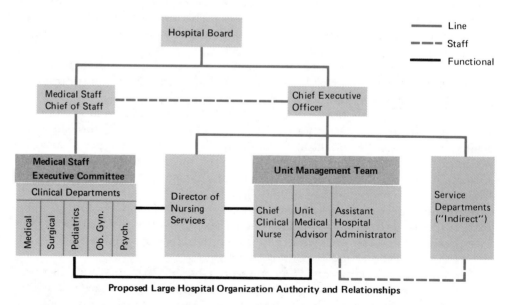

Proposed Large Hospital Organization Authority and Relationships

From David B. Starkweather, "The Rationale for Decentralization in Large Hospitals," *Hospital Administration* 15 (Spring 1970): 139. Courtesy of Dr. P. N. Ghei, Secretary General, Indian Hospital Association, New Delhi.

thereby best help the management system to accomplish its objectives. When trying to decide what authority combination is best for a particular organization, managers must keep in mind that the use of each type of authority naturally has both advantages and disadvantages. (See Figure 9.8.) Figure 9.9 is an organization chart that shows how these three types of authority could be combined for the overall benefit of a hospital management system.

Accountability

Accountability is a management philosophy whereby individuals are held liable or accountable for how well they use their authority and live up to their responsibility of performing predetermined activities.[12] The concept of accountability implies that, if predetermined activities are not performed, some type of penalty or punishment is justifiably forthcoming.[13] One company executive has summed up the punishment theme of accountability with the statement, "Individuals who do not perform well simply will not be around too long."[14] Also implied within the accountability concept, however, is the notion that some kind of reward follows if predetermined activities are performed well.

The accountability concept implies rewards and punishments.

BACK TO THE CASE

Functional authority and accountability are two additional factors that Leo Mercier must consider when modifying responsibilities within the student employment department. Some student employment personnel may have to be delegated functional authority to supplement the line or staff authority already possessed. The staff person who advises Mercier on conducting possible surveys to support the hiring of students may need information from various student employment personnel on what types of students seem to be performing well in certain kinds of jobs. Functional authority would enable this staff individual to command that this information be channeled to him or her.

Student employment personnel also should understand the accountability concept—that living up to assigned responsibilities brings rewards, while not living up to assigned responsibilities brings punishments.

DELEGATION

Previous sections of this chapter have discussed responsibility and authority as complementary factors that channel activity within the organization. **Delegation** is the actual process of assigning job activities and corresponding authority to specific individuals within the organization. This section focuses on the delegation process by discussing: (1) steps in the delegation process; (2) obstacles to the delegation process; (3) elimination of obstacles to the delegation process; and (4) centralization and decentralization.

Delegation is assigning jobs and authority to others.

Steps in the Delegation Process

The three-step delega-
tion process involves
assigning duties,

granting authority,

and creating an
obligation.

According to Newman and Warren, there are three steps in the delegation process, any of which may be either observable or implied.[15] The first of the three steps is assigning specific duties to the individual. In all cases, the manager must be sure that the subordinate has a clear understanding of what these duties entail. Whenever possible, the activities should be stated in operational terms so that a subordinate knows exactly what action must be taken to perform the assigned duties. The second step of the delegation process involves granting appropriate authority to the subordinate. The subordinate must be given the right and power within the organization to accomplish the duties assigned. The last step of the delegation process involves creating the obligation for the subordinate to perform the duties assigned. The subordinate must be aware of the responsibility to complete the duties assigned and his or her acceptance of that responsibility. Figure 9.10 offers several suggestions that managers can follow to ensure the success of the delegation process.

FIGURE 9.10   Guidelines for making delegation effective.

- Give employees freedom to pursue tasks in their own way
- Establish mutually agreed-upon results and performance standards related to delegated tasks
- Encourage an active role on the part of employees in defining, implementing, and communicating progress on tasks
- Entrust employees with completion of whole projects or tasks whenever possible
- Explain relevance of delegated tasks to larger projects or to department or organization goals
- Give employees the authority necessary to accomplish tasks
- Allow employees the not ordinarily available access to information, people, and departments necessary to perform delegated task
- Provide training and guidance necessary for employees to complete delegated tasks satisfactorily
- When possible, delegate tasks on basis of employee interests

The Management in Action feature which follows describes the appointment of Claude Brochu as president of the Montreal Expos, reviewing in brief his background and managerial philosophy as it relates to delegation and functional orientation.

BASEBALL DID YOU SAY?

"Know anybody who could be president of my baseball team?" Almost three months from the day the question was posed, Charles Bronfman, principal owner of the Montreal Expos, found his man. He came in the guise of one Claude Brochu, the former executive vice-president of Joseph E. Seagram and Sons Ltd. Working for deputy chairman Bronfman at Seagram, Brochu had had four promotions in ten years, climbing the corporate ladder in a multinational empire which had earned $319 million on sales of $2.97 billion in 1985. From a perennial winner, Brochu has now gone to a fourth-place ball club with total sales of about $40 million and $5 million worth of red ink in 1986 alone.

"As a manager, (Brochu) believes in working by consensus . . ."

This is definitely not a move many would contemplate. Although baseball gets a great deal of publicity, in dollar terms it is only a minor industry. Erratic hours, fickle consumers, high labour costs, and a tradition of promoting from within are but a few of the industry's constants. So why did Brochu make the move?

Excitement. "My marketing job at Seagram, really I could do with my eyes closed. And I'm still at an age where I could take a chance in my career," the new man says. Brochu replaces John J. McHale, a former player who became president when the club was founded in 1968. Although McHale will be around as chief executive for another year, Brochu is now in charge.

The son of an army officer, Brochu studied Roman and Greek history at the University of Ottawa; spent three years in the Canadian Forces; went back to school and got a master's degree in business; and once out, rose quickly through the ranks in the marketing world. Although this sounds like a tightly focused and very straight-arrow career path, there have been some surprising turns: MBA instead of an army career and marketing instead of industrial relations. He attributes his entrepreneurial spirit to his parents' influence. "I was always the kid with the Kool-Aid stand and the paper route."

With the completion of his MBA at McMaster University in Hamilton, Brochu moved back to Quebec in 1971, and, aside from a three-year stint in Toronto, has lived in Montreal ever since. Before joining Seagram in 1976, Brochu was with three different cosmetics firms in five years. According to him, this is absolutely typical for an MBA graduate. "I broadened my skills in marketing, in sales, and in personnel." When he took the Expos' job, some of Montreal's francophone media crowed that Bronfman had finally chosen "un petit gars de chez nous."

He is, however, undeniably a specimen of the New Canadian—a citizen equally at home in both cultures. When asked about a political career, Brochu shrugs and maintains that he is more comfortable with the profit motive.

Brochu denies setting himself any fixed sojourn with the Expos. "Maybe five years, maybe ten, maybe a lifetime. I do think, however, that it will take at least five years to reach the standards that I want." As a manager, he believes in working by consensus, with very short lines of command and authority centralized in a key group of decision makers who review almost every issue. "I'm basically a hands-on guy. I like to know everything." This means working long hours; he is usually at work by seven-thirty every morning.

Until this latest career switch, Brochu's involvement with baseball had been limited to family trips to spring training. Next year, he'll get down to West Palm Beach, Florida again, although not for the whole six weeks of training camp. "The team is important, but that's in such good hands . . .," says Brochu. The new president will leave baseball decisions to general manager Murray Cook and the club's other baseball men. "I'll be back and forth. Here, we've got sponsors, suppliers, our whole ticket program, plenty of things to deal with." Brochu, with help from Cook and the players, must win back the fans who've stayed away in recent years. Home attendance was 1.128 million in 1986, just half of 1982's total. But true to the master marketer's previous track record, Brochu had already made two converts before he even took over the position: his two sons, aged thirteen and eleven. Baseball did you say? OK!

Based on "How a francophone from the fast track found himself in charge of the ballclub," by Brian Kappler in *The Gazette* (Montreal), October 4, 1986. Used with permission.

Obstacles to the Delegation Process

Obstacles that can make delegation within an organization difficult or even impossible can be classified in three general categories: (1) obstacles related to the supervisor; (2) obstacles related to subordinates; and (3) obstacles related to organizations.

Some obstacles to delegation are supervisor-related.

One supervisor-related obstacle to delegation is that some supervisors resist delegating their authority to subordinates because they find using their authority very satisfying. Two other such obstacles are that supervisors may be afraid that their subordinates will not do a job well or that surrendering some of their authority may be seen by others as a sign of a weak manager. Also, if supervisors are insecure in their job or see specific activities as being extremely important to their personal success, they may find it difficult to put the performance of these activities into the hands of others. The supervisor in the cartoon has no trouble delegating: The problem is the task he is choosing to delegate. Dislike of a task is not a sufficient reason for delegating it.

"I hate to fire people, so I'm ordering you two to fire each other."

Wall Street Journal, *September 11, 1987. From the* Wall Street Journal–*permission, Cartoon Features Syndicate.*

Some obstacles are subordinate-related.

Even if supervisors wish to delegate to subordinates, they may encounter several subordinate-related roadblocks. First, subordinates may be reluctant to accept delegated authority for fear of failure or because of a lack of self-confidence. These two obstacles probably will be especially apparent if subordinates have not experienced the use of delegated authority previously. Other obstacles include the feeling that the supervisor will not be available for guidance once the delegation is made or that being a recipient of additional authority may complicate comfortable working relationships that presently exist.

Some obstacles are organization-related.

Characteristics of the organization itself also may make delegation difficult. For example, a very small organization may present the supervisor with only a minimal number of activities to be delegated. In addition, if very few job activities and little authority have been delegated over the history of the organization, attempting to initiate the delegation process could make individuals very reluctant and apprehensive. In essence, the supervisor would be introducing a change in procedure that some members of the organization might resist very strongly.[16]

Eliminating Obstacles to the Delegation Process

Since delegation usually results in several organizational advantages, eliminating obstacles to delegation is important to managers. Advantages of delegation include improved subordinate involvement and interest, more free time for the supervisor to accomplish tasks, and, as the organization gets larger, assistance from subordinates in completing tasks the manager simply wouldn't have time for otherwise. Although delegation also has potential disadvantages, such as the possibility of the manager losing track of the progress of a task once it has been delegated,[17] the potential advantages of some degree of delegation generally outweigh the potential disadvantages.

What can managers do to minimize the effect of obstacles to the delegation process? First of all, they must continually strive to uncover any obstacles to delegation that exist in their organization. Next, they should approach specific action to minimize the effect of these obstacles with the understanding that the obstacles may be deeply ingrained in the situation and may, therefore, require long-term time and effort. Specific managerial actions usually necessary to overcome obstacles include building subordinate confidence in the use of delegated authority, minimizing the impact of delegated authority on established working relationships, and helping the delegatee with problems whenever necessary.

Koontz, O'Donnell, and Weihrich imply that for managers to overcome obstacles to delegation, they also must possess certain critical characteristics. These characteristics include the willingness to consider seriously the ideas of others, the insight to allow subordinates the free rein necessary to carry out their responsibilities, trust in the abilities of subordinates, and the ability to allow people to learn from their mistakes without suffering unreasonable penalties for making them.[18]

Good delegators uncover obstacles to delegation and take specific action to minimize the obstacles' effects.

BACK TO THE CASE

To delegate effectively within the student employment department, Mercier must assign specific duties to individuals, grant corresponding authority to these individuals, and create the awareness within these individuals that they are obligated to perform these activities.

Mercier also must be aware that obstacles to delegation may exist within himself, his subordinates, or the student employment department. Discovering which obstacles exist and then taking steps to eliminate them is a prerequisite for successful delegation. If Mercier is to be a successful delegator, he also must be willing to consider the ideas of his subordinates, allow them the free rein necessary to perform their assigned tasks, trust them, and help them to learn from their mistakes without suffering unreasonable penalties.

Centralization and Decentralization

Noticeable differences exist in the relative number of job activities and the relative amount of authority delegated to subordinates from organization to organization. In practice, it is not a case of delegation either existing or not existing within an organization. Delegation exists in most organizations, but in varying degrees.

FIGURE 9.11   Centralized and decentralized organizations on delegation continuum.

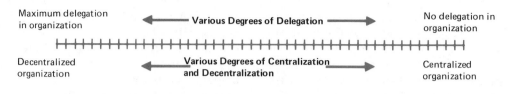

The terms **centralization** and **decentralization** describe the general degree to which delegation exists within an organization. These terms can be visualized at opposite ends of a delegation continuum (see Figure 9.11). From Figure 9.11 it is apparent that centralization implies that a minimal number of job activities and a minimal amount of authority have been delegated to subordinates by management, while decentralization implies the opposite.

The problems usually facing practicing managers are determining whether to further decentralize an organization and deciding how to decentralize if that course of action is advisable. The section that follows contains practical suggestions on whether an organization should be decentralized and how decentralization should take place.

Centralization implies minimal delegation; decentralization implies maximum delegation.

Decentralizing an Organization: A Contingency Viewpoint

The degree of decentralization managers should employ depends on, or is contingent upon, their own unique organizational situation. Specific questions to determine the amount of decentralization appropriate for a situation include:

The amount of decentralization is determined by:

1. The size of the organization.

1. *What is the present size of the organization?*   As indicated earlier, the larger the organization, the greater the likelihood that decentralization would be advantageous. As an organization increases in size, managers have to assume more and more responsibility and different types of tasks. Delegation is typically an effective means of helping managers keep up with this increased workload.

2. The location of customers.

2. *Where are the organization's customers located?*   As a general rule, the more physically separated the organization's customers, the more viable the situation for a significant amount of decentralization. Decentralization places appropriate management resources close to the customers and thereby allows for quicker customer service.

3. The homogeneity of the product line.

3. *How homogeneous is the product line of the organization?*   As the product line becomes more heterogeneous or diversified, the appropriateness of decentralization generally increases. Different kinds of decisions, talents, and resources are needed to manufacture different products. Decentralization usually minimizes the potential confusion that can result from diversification by separating organizational resources by product and keeping pertinent decision making close to the manufacturing process.

4. The location of suppliers.

4. *Where are organizational suppliers?*   The location of raw materials from which organization products are manufactured is another important consideration. Time loss and perhaps even transportation costs associated with shipping raw materials over great distances from supplier to manufacturer could support the need for decentralization of certain functions.

For example, the wood necessary to manufacture a certain type of bedroom set may only be available from tree growers in certain western provinces. If the bedroom set is an important enough product line for a furniture company and if the costs of transporting the lumber are substantial, a sound basis for a decision to decentralize probably exists. The effects of this decision might be the building of a plant that produces only bedroom sets in a western province close to where the necessary wood is readily available. The advantages of such a costly decision, of course, would only accrue to the organization over the long term.

5. *Is there a need for quick decisions in the organization?* If there is a need for speedy decision making within the organization, a considerable amount of decentralization is probably in order. Decentralization avoids red tape and allows the subordinate to whom authority has been delegated to make on-the-spot decisions if necessary.[19] This delegation is advisable only if the delegatees in question have the ability to make sound decisions. If they don't, the increased decision-making speed via delegation has no advantage. Quick or slow, a decision cannot reap benefits for the organization if it is unsound.

6. *Is creativity a desirable feature of the organization?* If the answer to this question is yes, then some decentralization probably is advisable. Decentralization allows delegatees the freedom to find better ways of doing things. The mere existence of this freedom can encourage the incorporation of new and more creative techniques within the task process.[20]

5. The need for quick decisions.

6. The desire for creativity.

BACK TO THE CASE

Centralization implies that few job activities and little authority have been delegated to subordinates, while decentralization implies that many job activities and much authority have been delegated. Mercier will have to determine the degree of delegation best for the student employment department. For guidelines, he can use the rule of thumb that greater degrees of delegation probably will be appropriate for the student employment department as the department becomes larger, as potential employers and student clients become more dispersed and diversified, and as the needs for quick decision making and creativity increase.

Decentralization at Massey-Ferguson

Positive decentralization is decentralization that is advantageous for the organization in which it is being implemented, while negative decentralization is the opposite. Perhaps the best way to ascertain how an organization should be decentralized is to study the efforts of an organization with positive decentralization: Massey-Ferguson.[21]

Massey-Ferguson is a worldwide farm equipment manufacturer that has enjoyed noticeable success with decentralization over the past several years.[22] At Massey-Ferguson, there are three guidelines for determining the degree of decentralization of decision making appropriate for a situation:[23]

Positive decentralization is advantageous, while negative decentralization is not.

Massey-Ferguson follows guidelines for the decentralization of decision making.

1. The competence to make decisions must be possessed by the person to whom authority is delegated. A derivative of this is that the superior must have confidence in the subordinate to whom authority is delegated.

2. Adequate and reliable information pertinent to the decision is required by the person making the decision. Decision-making authority, therefore, cannot be pushed below the point at which all information bearing on the decision is available.

3. If a decision affects more than one unit of the enterprise, the authority to make the decision must rest with the manager accountable for the most units affected by the decision.

Massey-Ferguson also encourages a definite attitude toward decentralization. The organization manual of Massey-Ferguson indicates that delegation is not delegation in name only but a frame of mind that includes both what a supervisor says to subordinates and the way he or she acts toward them. Managers at Massey-Ferguson are encouraged to allow subordinates to make a reasonable number of mistakes and to help subordinates learn from these mistakes.

At Massey-Ferguson, centralization comple-ments decentralization.

Another feature of the positive decentralization at Massey-Ferguson is that decentralization is complemented with centralization:

> The organization plan that best serves our total requirements is a blend of centralized and decentralized elements. Marketing and manufacturing respon-sibilities, together with supporting service functions, are located as close as possible to local markets. Activities that determine the long-range character of the company, such as the planning and control of the product line, the plan-ning and control of facilities and money, and the planning of the strategy to react to changes in the patterns of international trade, are highly centralized.[24]

Massey-Ferguson management recognizes that decentralization is not necessarily an either/or decision and uses the strengths of both centralization and decen-tralization to its advantage.

Some activities at Massey-Ferguson can-not be delegated.

Not all activities at Massey-Ferguson, however, are eligible for decentrali-zation consideration. Only management is allowed to follow through on the following responsibilities:[25]

1. The responsibility for determining the overall objectives of the enterprise.
2. The responsibility for formulating the policies that guide the enterprise.
3. The final responsibility for the control of the business within the total range of the objectives and policies, including control over any changes in the nature of the business.
4. The responsibility for product design, where a product decision affects more than one area of accountability.
5. The responsibility for planning for the achievement of overall objectives and for measuring actual performance against those plans.
6. The final approval of corporate plans or budgets.
7. The decisions pertaining to the availability, and the application, of general company funds.
8. The responsibility for capital-investment plans.

BACK TO THE CASE

The Massey-Ferguson decentralization situation could give Mercier many valuable insights on what character-istics the decentralization process in the student em-ployment department should assume. First, Mercier should use definite guidelines to decide whether or not his situation warrants added decentralization. In general, additional delegation probably is warranted in the student employment department as the compe-tence of subordinates increases, as Mercier's confidence in the subordinates increases, and as more adequate and reliable decision-making information becomes available to subordinates. For delegation to be advanta-geous for the student employment department, Mercier also must help subordinates to learn from their mistakes, and he may want to consider supplementing decentralization with centralization.

Action Summary

Reread the learning objectives that follow. Each objective is followed by questions. Answering these questions accurately will help you to retain the most important concepts discussed in this chapter. After answering each question, check your answer with the answer key at the end of this chapter. (*Hint*: If you have doubt regarding the correct response, consult the page that follows the answer.)

From studying this chapter, I will attempt to acquire: **Circle:**

1. **An understanding of the relationship between responsibility, authority, and delegation.**
   a. Responsibility is a person's self-assumed commitment to handle a job to the best of his or her ability.   T, F
   b. Which of the following elements is *not* an integral part of an effective organizing effort: (a) rationale for the orderly use of management system resources; (b) responsibility; (c) authority; (d) delegation; (e) none of the above (they are all important).   a, b, c, d, e

2. **Information on how to divide and clarify job activities of individuals within an organization.**
   a. Which of the following is *not* one of the four basic steps for dividing responsibility by the functional similarity method: (a) designing specific jobs by grouping similar activities; (b) examining management system objectives; (c) formulating management system objectives; (d) designating appropriate activities that must be performed to reach objectives; (e) making specific individuals responsible for performing activities.   a, b, c, d, e
   b. A management responsibility guide can assist organization members in which of the following ways: (a) by describing the various responsibility relationships that exist in their organization; (b) by summarizing how the responsibilities of various managers within the organization relate to one another; (c) by identifying manager work experience; (d) a and b; (e) none of the above.   a, b, c, d, e

3. **Knowledge of the differences between line authority, staff authority, and functional authority.**
   a. The production manager mainly has: (a) functional authority; (b) staff authority; (c) line authority; (d) a and c; (e) all of the above.   a, b, c, d, e
   b. An example of functional authority is the vice-president of finance being delegated the authority to order various departments to furnish him or her with the kinds and amounts of information needed to perform an analysis.   T, F

4. **An appreciation for the issues that can cause conflict in line and staff relationships.**
   a. From the viewpoint of staff personnel one reason for line-staff conflict is that line personnel: (a) do not make proper use of staff personnel; (b) resist new ideas; (c) do not give staff personnel enough authority; (d) a and c; (e) all of the above.   a, b, c, d, e

a, b, c, d, e

b. From the viewpoint of line personnel, conflicts between line and staff can occur for which of the following reasons: (a) staff may assume line authority; (b) staff may not offer sound advice; (c) staff may steal credit for success; (d) staff may fail to keep line informed; (e) all of the above.

5. **Insights on the value of accountability to the organization.**

T, F

    a. Accountability is how well individuals live up to their responsibility for performing predetermined activities.

    b. Rewarding employees for good work is most closely related to: (a) simplicity; (b) a clear division of authority; (c) centralization; (d) decentralization; (e) accountability.

a, b, c, d, e

6. **An understanding of how to delegate.**

T, F

    a. The correct ordering of the steps in the delegation process is the assignment of duties, the creation of responsibility, and the granting of authority.

    b. Which of the following are obstacles to the delegation process: (a) obstacles related to supervisors; (b) obstacles related to subordinates; (c) obstacles related to the organization; (d) all of the above; (e) none of the above.

a, b, c, d, e

7. **A strategy for eliminating various barriers to delegation.**

    a. Eliminating obstacles to delegation usually results in which of the following advantages: (a) improved subordinate involvement and interest; (b) more free time for supervisor; (c) assistance for supervisor to accomplish tasks he or she wouldn't be able to do otherwise; (d) all of the above; (e) none of the above.

a, b, c, d, e

    b. Generally, the potential advantages of some degree of delegating outweigh the disadvantages.

T, F

8. **A working knowledge of when and how an organization should be decentralized.**

    a. A high degree of centralization within an organization would be most advisable under which of the following conditions: (a) the organization is relatively small; (b) the organization is relatively large; (c) creativity is important to the firm's success; (d) the delegatees have the ability to make sound decisions; (e) the product line is diversified.

a, b, c, d, e

    b. According to the management philosophy that exists at Massey-Ferguson, the responsibility for formulating the policies that guide the organization should be highly decentralized.

T, F

INTRODUCTORY CASE WRAP-UP

"Redesigning Job Activities" (p. 220) and its related back-to-the-case sections were written to help you better understand the management concepts contained in this chapter. Answer the following discussion questions about this introductory case to further enrich your understanding of the chapter content:

1. The introductory case ends with Mercier discovering

that certain basic job activities are not covered in his department. What should he do now?

2. Assuming that certain fundamental functions have been excluded from the present job activities of the subordinates, what mistakes probably were made by the previous manager that allowed such exclusions to exist?

Issues for Review and Discussion

1. What is responsibility, and why does it exist in organizations?
2. Explain the process a manager would go through to divide responsibility within an organization.
3. What is a management responsibility guide, and how is it used?
4. List and summarize the four main dimensions of responsible management behaviour.
5. What is authority, and why does it exist in organizations?
6. Describe the relationship between responsibility and authority.
7. Explain Barnard's notion of authority and acceptance.
8. What steps can managers take to increase the probability that subordinates will accept their authority? Be sure to explain how each of these steps increases the probability.
9. Summarize the relationship that generally exists between line and staff personnel.
10. Explain three roles that staff personnel can perform in organizations.
11. List five possible causes of conflict in line-staff relationships and suggest appropriate action to minimize the effect of these causes.
12. What is functional authority?
13. Give an example of how functional authority actually works in an organization.
14. Compare the relative advantages and disadvantages of line, staff, and functional authority.
15. What is accountability?
16. Define *delegation* and list the steps of the delegation process.
17. List three obstacles to the delegation process and suggest action for eliminating them.
18. What is the relationship between delegation and decentralization?
19. What is the difference between decentralization and centralization?

Sources of Additional Information

Chandler, A.D., Jr. *Strategy and Structure.* Garden City, New York: Anchor Books, Doubleday, 1966.

Clark, P.A. *Organizational Design: Theory and Practice.* London: Tavistock, 1972.

Fotilas, Panagiotis N. "Semi-Autonomous Work Groups: An Alternative in Organizing Production Work?" *Management Review* 70 (July 1981): 50–54.

Griffin, Ricky W. *Task Design: An Integrative Approach.* Glenview, Ill.: Scott, Foresman, 1982.

Hage, Jerald. *Theories of Organizations/Form, Process, and Transformation.* New York: Wiley, 1980.

Hutton, Thomas J. "Human Resources or Management Resources?" *Personnel Administrator* 32 (January 1987): 66–79.

Janz, Tom, Lowell Hellervik, and David C. Gilmore. *Behavior Description Interviewing.* Boston: Allyn and Bacon, 1986.

Kelly, Marcia M. "Exploring the Potentials of Decentralized Work Settings." *Personnel Administrator* 29 (February 1984): 48–52.

Leana, Carrie R. "Predictors and Consequences of Delegation." *Academy of Management Journal* 29 (December 1986): 715–26.

Leavitt, Harold J., William R. Dill, and Henry B. Eyring. *The Organizational World.* New York: Harcourt Brace Jovanovich, 1973.

Levinson, Robert E. *The Decentralized Company.* New York: Amacom, 1983.

Reich, Robert B. "The Team as Hero." *Harvard Business Review* (May/June 1987): 77–83.

Roos, Leslie L., Jr., and Roger I. Hall. "Influence Diagrams and Organizational Power," *Administrative Science Quarterly* 25 (March 1980): 57–71.

Sabl, Robert J. "Succession Planning—A Blueprint for Your Company's Future." *Personnel Administrator* 32 (September 1987): 101–108.

Scott, William G., and Terence R. Mitchell. *Organization Theory.* Homewood, Ill.: Richard D. Irwin, 1972.

Shrode, William A., and Dan Voich, Jr. *Organization and Management: Basic Systems Concepts.* Homewood, Ill.: Richard D. Irwin, 1974.

Smith, Howard R. "The Uphill Struggle for Job Enrichment." *California Management Review* 23 (Summer 1981): 33–38.

Tavernier, Gerard. "Awakening a Sleeping Giant: Ford's Employee Involvement Program." *Management Review* 70 (June 1981): 15–20.

Notes

1. Stephen X. Doyle and Benson P. Shapiro, "What Counts Most in Motivating Your Sales Force?" *Harvard Business Review* (May/June 1980): 133–40. See also G.F. Scollard, "Dynamic Descriptions: Job Descriptions Should Work for You," *Management World* (May 1985): 34–35.
2. Robert J. Thierauf, Robert C. Klekamp, and Daniel W. Geeding, *Management Principles and Practices: A Contingency and Questionnaire Approach* (New York: Wiley, 1977), 334.
3. Robert D. Melcher, "Roles and Relationships: Clarifying the Manager's Job," *Personnel* 44 (May/June 1967): 34–41.
4. For more information on management responsibility guides, see Melcher, "Roles and Relationships."
5. This section is based primarily on John H. Zenger, "Responsible Behavior: Stamp of the Effective Manager," *Supervisory Management* (July 1976): 18–24.
6. Max Weber, "The Three Types of Legitimate Rule," trans. Hans Gerth, *Berkeley Journal of Sociology* 4 (1953): 1–11.
7. John Gardner, "The Anti-Leadership Vaccine," *Carnegie Foundation Annual Report*, 1965.
8. Chester I. Barnard, *The Functions of the Executive* (Cambridge, Mass.: Harvard University Press, 1938).
9. Harold Stieglitz, "On Concepts of Corporate Structure," *Conference Board Record* 11 (February 1974): 7–13.
10. For a classic discussion of this area, see Louis A. Allen, "Developing Sound Line and Staff Relationships," in *Studies in Personnel Policy*, no. 153, National Industrial Conference Board, 1956, 70–80. See also Wendell L. French, *The Personnel Management Process: Human Resource Administration and Development* (Boston: Houghton Mifflin, 1987), 66–68.
11. Derek Sheane, "When and How to Intervene in Conflict," *Personnel Management* (November 1979): 32–36; John M. Ivancevich and Michael T. Matteson, "Intergroup Behavior and Conflict," in their *Organizational Behavior and Management* (Plano, Tex.: Business Publications, 1987), 305–45. For additional information on how to handle conflict, see Andrew K. Hoh, "Consensus Building: A Creative Approach to Resolving Conflicts," *Management Review* (March 1981): 52–54.
12. Robert Albanese, *Management* (Cincinnati: South-Western Publishing, 1988), 313.
13. For an excellent review of the punishment literature, see Henry P. Sims, Jr., "Further Thoughts on Punishment in Organizations," *Academy of Management Review* 5 (January 1980): 133.
14. "How Ylvisaker Makes 'Produce or Else' Work," *Business Week*, October 27, 1973, 112.
15. William H. Newman and E. Kirby Warren, *The Process of Management: Concepts, Behavior, and Practice*, 4th ed. (Englewood Cliffs, N.J.: Prentice-Hall, 1977), 39–40.
16. For organizational barriers unique to a family business, see Louis B. Barnes and Simon A. Hershon, "Transferring Power in the Family Business," *Harvard Business Review* (July/August 1976): 105–14.
17. Ted Pollock, "You Must Delegate . . . but You're Still Responsible," *Industrial Supervision* (February 1976): 10–11.
18. Harold Koontz, Cyril O'Donnell, and Heinz Weihrich, *Essentials of Management*, 8th ed. (New York: McGraw-Hill, 1986), 231–33.
19. Ernest Dale, "Centralization versus Decentralization," *Advanced Management Journal* (June 1955): 11–16.
20. Donald O. Harper, "Project Management as a Control and Planning Tool in the Decentralized Company," *Management Accounting* (November 1968): 29–33.
21. For further discussion on positive and negative centralization and decentralization, see Terence R. Mitchell and James R. Larson, Jr., *People in Organizations* (New York: McGraw-Hill, 1987), 49–50.
22. Information for this section is mainly from John G. Staiger, "What Cannot Be Decentralized," *Management Record* 25 (January 1963): 19–21. At the time the article was written, Staiger was vice-president of administration, North American Operations, Massey-Ferguson, Limited.
23. Staiger, "What Cannot Be Decentralized," 19.
24. Staiger, "What Cannot Be Decentralized," 21.
25. Staiger, "What Cannot Be Decentralized," 21.

Action Summary Answer Key

1. a. T, p. 221
   b. e, p. 221
2. a. c, p. 222
   b. d, p. 223
3. a. c, p. 227
   b. T, p. 231
4. a. e, p. 230
   b. e, p. 230
5. a. F, p. 233
   b. e, p. 233
6. a. F, p. 234
   b. d, p. 236
7. a. d, p. 237
   b. T, p. 237
8. a. a, p. 238
   b. F, pp. 239–240

DIVERSIFICATION ON THE WATERFRONT

Walter Oster, the forty-seven-year-old president of The Whaler's Group, a Toronto-based restaurateur and developer, is busy these days poring over blueprints and tramping through the gravelly construction site of the $36 million hotel and condominium project his company is building. The 157-room Admiral Hotel, with its 20 000 square feet of ground-level commercial space and underground parking for 378 cars, will carry the nautical theme that has become Oster's trademark. His company's symbol, in fact, features a little gold whale.

The Whaler's Group operates more than 2 200 restaurant seats in the Toronto area. Their establishments include October's nightclub, the waterfront Pier 4 Storehouse Restaurant, and three Whaler's Wharf seafood outlets. This hotel venture is the first thrust by The Whaler's Group into the risky business of hotel management. The move leaves some analysts wondering if the company that will make $15 million in gross revenues in 1986 from its food services operations has the financial wherewithal to challenge established hotel giants in a highly competitive marketplace. "Hotels run by the large hotel management firms, which manage or own huge blocks of hotel rooms around the globe, have the edge logistically over a one-hotel operation," says Harry Rannala, real estate analyst for Merrill Lynch Canada Inc.

Oster, however, remains undaunted by the challenge. He believes the management skills required to run a successful restaurant aren't much different from those needed to run a hotel. "In a hotel, it's the food service section that creates the most problems," says Oster, who is treasurer of the Canadian Restaurant and Foodservices Association. "It carries the highest overhead and requires the most attention. We have been running restaurants for 13 years."

Oster is confident that Whaler's management style will transfer itself successfully to the running of the hotel. "We're hands-on operators," says Oster, who has applied this hands-on philosophy to every facet of his company. It is common to find him personally shopping for kitchen equipment and linens, or flying to France with his vice-president of restaurant operations to sample wines that will fill the 100 000 bottles Whaler's will use in its restaurant operations this year. Walter Oster's modus operandi is to know everything that's going on. But, adds Tony Georgis, vice-president of restaurant operations, "he delegates too, and has great trust in his managers."

This need to delegate comes out of necessity. As a small company run by Oster and his partners, Marcello Gasparetto and Albert Oliva, Whaler's has outgrown it-

Oster: "We're hands-on operators."

self. The result is that the partners have turned increasingly to hiring specialized managers.

One of these is Cy Massey, who will be the Hotel Admiral's general manager. He was hired earlier in the year because of his strong background in the hotel business, most recently as executive assistant manager with CN Hotels Inc.'s L'Hotel in Toronto. Don Adamson, who spent twenty-seven years supervising construction work for Redfern Construction Toronto Ltd., is another key player recently brought aboard as project manager. Oster has also hired a staff lawyer, a controller, and a beverage expert. These managers run the day-to-day business under his direction. "We're putting more professionalism into our management," he says, adding that by the time the new hotel opens, Whaler's will have twenty-six people in its administrative offices. The company currently employs 540 people, but when the hotel opens it will hire an additional 400.

Whaler's also encourages employees who show the aptitude to enter management ranks. Says Georgis, who joined the company as a waiter in 1977 and became its new vice-president of operations in January 1986: "We like our people to grow along with us, like I did."

DISCUSSION ISSUES

1. How are the current company's management skills appropriate for its new hotel venture? Explain.
2. With regard to delegation, what is Oster's management style most appropriately called? Elaborate.
3. As the company diversifies its business, will delegation and decentralization be necessary? How is Oster's management style an advantage here? Explain.

Based on "Restaurant group makes splash on waterfront," by Bruce Gates in *The Financial Post*, May 31, 1986. Used with permission.

PROVIDING APPROPRIATE HUMAN RESOURCES

STUDENT LEARNING OBJECTIVES

From studying this chapter, I will attempt to acquire:

1. An overall understanding of how appropriate human resources can be provided for the organization.
2. An appreciation for the relationship among recruitment efforts, an open position, sources of human resources, and the law.
3. Insights on the use of tests and assessment centres in employee selection.
4. An understanding of how the training process operates.
5. A concept of what performance appraisals are and how they can best be conducted.
6. An appreciation for the complex situation involving women who are working in non-traditional jobs.

CHAPTER OUTLINE

SPECIAL TRAINING AT FAIRCHILD INDUSTRIES

Charlie Collis still gets hot under the collar when he describes the worst mistake of his thirty-six-year career at Fairchild Industries. Collis, who had retired as executive vice-president one year earlier, was talking about the incident with younger managers at Fairchild who were still on the job.

According to Collis, his big mistake occurred when he was president of the U.S. Company Fairchild Republic, Fairchild Industries' airplane manufacturing division. Fairchild Republic had just won a U.S. government contract to build the A-10 Thunderbolt attack plane. This contract was especially important to the company because the Thunderbolt project would catapult Fairchild into billion-dollar-a-year-corporation status.

All seemed well with the Thunderbolt project until a U.S. Air Force analyst began pressuring Collis. The analyst wanted Collis to move all work other than the Thunderbolt out of the Fairchild plant in Farmingdale, New York, and into a Fairchild plant in Hagerstown, Maryland. The analyst believed that, over the long term, this move would lower the manufacturing costs of the Thunderbolt project.

At the time, Collis resisted the pressure. He believed the Air Force was going well beyond its authority by trying to tell him how to run his business. Because of Collis's uncooperativeness in this area, the Air Force analyst informed his supervisor that Fairchild was not willing to take the steps necessary to carry out the Thunderbolt project appropriately. Quickly, several Air Force investigators were "swarming" all over the company.

Collis admitted that he made a mistake: "I got mad and didn't organize the problem. I had to go." As a result of this friction with the Air Force, Edward G. Uhl, Fairchild's no-nonsense president, yanked Collis back to corporate headquarters and named a new president of Fairchild Republic.

Collis's frank discussion of his mistake was taking place at company headquarters as part of a special training program through which the retired Collis was expected to pass his accumulated wisdom along to the next generation of Fairchild managers. Fairchild Industries believes that retired executives who are free from corporate politics and pressure on the job can impart some of their experience to present managers, thereby helping them become better corporate leaders in the future.

Based on "Handing Down the Old Hands' Wisdom," by Joel Dreyfuss in *Fortune*, June 13, 1983.

What's Ahead

Charlie Collis, the retired manager in the introductory case, was assisting Fairchild Industries in one facet of the process of providing appropriate human resources for the organization—training. This chapter focuses on the complete process of providing appropriate human resources by first defining appropriate human resources and then examining the steps to be followed in providing them.

The emphasis in Chapter 9 was on organizing the activity of individuals within the management system. To this end, responsibility, authority, and delegation were discussed in detail. This chapter continues to explore the relationship between individuals and organizing by discussing how appropriate human resources can be provided for the organization.

DEFINING APPROPRIATE HUMAN RESOURCES

The phrase **appropriate human resources** refers to those individuals within the organization who make a valuable contribution to management system goal attainment. This contribution, of course, is a result of productivity in the positions they hold. The phrase *inappropriate human resources* refers to those organization members who do not make a valuable contribution to the attainment of management system objectives. In essence, these individuals are ineffective in their jobs.

Productivity in all organizations is determined by how human resources interact and combine to use all other management system resources. Such factors as background, age, job-related experience, and level of formal education all have some role in determining the degree of appropriateness of the individual to the organization. Although the process of providing appropriate human resources for the organization is involved and somewhat subjective, the following section offers insights on how to increase the success of this process.

> Appropriate human resources are those individuals who contribute to the attainment of management system objectives.

STEPS IN PROVIDING APPROPRIATE HUMAN RESOURCES

To provide appropriate human resources to fill either managerial or non-managerial openings, managers follow four sequential steps: (1) recruitment; (2) selection; (3) training; and (4) performance appraisal. Figure 10.1 illustrates the relationship among these steps.

FIGURE 10.1 Four sequential steps to provide appropriate human resources for an organization.

Step 1	Step 2	Step 3	Step 4
Recruitment	Selection	Training	Performance appraisal

Recruitment

Recruitment is the initial screening of prospective employees.

Recruitment is the initial screening of the total supply of prospective human resources available to fill a position. The purpose of recruitment is to narrow a large field of prospective employees to a relatively small group of individuals from which someone eventually will be hired. To be effective, recruiters must know: (1) the job they are trying to fill; (2) where potential human resources can be located; and (3) how the law influences recruiting efforts.

Knowing the Job

Job analysis entails determining a job description and a job specification.

Recruitment activities must begin with a thorough understanding of the position to be filled so that the broad range of potential employees can be narrowed intelligently. **Job analysis** is a technique commonly used to gain an understanding of a position. Basically, job analysis is aimed at determining a **job description**—the activities a job entails—and a **job specification**—the characteristics of the individual who should be hired for the job. Figure 10.2 shows the relationship between job analysis, job description, and job specification. Figure 10.3 shows the procedure for performing a job analysis.

Numerous laws—both federal and provincial—have been passed to prohibit the use of job specifications that limit employment to one sex. Employers are not allowed to exclude persons of either sex from job consideration, though physical requirements such as strength may, in practice, bar many women from some jobs.

One result of job specification laws is the elimination of sex distinctions in the "help wanted" sections of newspapers. A second result is the change in job

---

FIGURE 10.2 Relationship between job analysis, job description, and job specification.

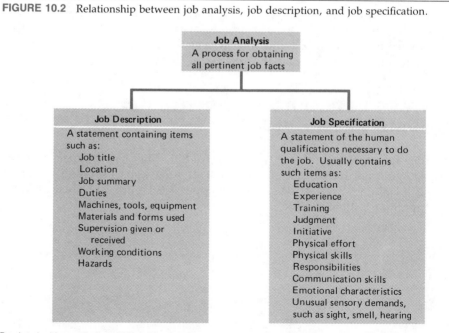

Reprinted with permission of Macmillan Publishing Company from *Personnel: The Management of People at Work* by Dale S. Beach. Copyright © 1970 by Dale S. Beach.

FIGURE 10.3   Information to obtain when performing a job analysis.

Identifying Information (Such as):
   Name of incumbent
   Organization/unit
   Title and series
   Date
   Interviewer

Brief Summary of Job: (This statement will include the primary duties of the job. It may be prepared in advance from class specifications, job descriptions, or other sources. However, it should be checked for accuracy using the task statements resulting from the analysis.)

Job Tasks:
   What does the worker do? How does the worker do it? Why? What output is produced?
   What tools, procedures, aids are involved? How much time does it take to do the task?
   How often does the worker perform the task in a day, week, month, or year?

Knowledge, Skills, and Abilities Required:
What does it take to perform each task in terms of the following?
1. Knowledge required
   a. What subject matter areas are covered by the task?
   b. What facts or principles must the worker have an acquaintance with or understand in these subject matter areas?
   c. Describe the level, degree, and breadth of knowledge required in these areas or subjects.
2. Skills required
   a. What activities must the worker perform with ease and precision?
   b. What are the manual skills required to operate machines, vehicles, equipment, or to use tools?
3. Abilities required
   a. What is the nature and level of language ability, written or oral, required of the worker on the job? Are there complex oral or written ideas involved in performing the task, or simple instructional materials?
   b. What mathematical ability must the worker have? Will the worker use simple arithmetic, complex algebra?
   c. What reasoning or problem-solving ability must the worker have?
   d. What instructions must the worker follow? Are they simple, detailed, involved, abstract?
   e. What interpersonal abilities are required? What supervisory or managing abilities are required?
   f. What physical abilities such as strength, coordination, visual acuity must the worker have?

Physical Activities:
   Describe the frequency and degree to which the incumbent is engaged in such activities as:
   pulling, pushing, throwing, carrying, kneeling, sitting, running, crawling, reaching, climbing.

Environmental Conditions:
   Describe the frequency and degree to which the incumbent will encounter working under
   such conditions as these: cramped quarters, moving objects, vibration, inadequate ventilation.

Typical Work Incidents:
1. Situations involving the interpretation of feelings, ideas, or facts in terms of personal viewpoint
2. Influencing people in their opinions, attitudes, or judgments about ideas or things
3. Working with people beyond giving and receiving instructions
4. Performing repetitive work, or continuously performing the same work
5. Performing under stress when confronted with emergency, critical, unusual, or dangerous situations; or in situations in which work speed and sustained attention are make-and-break aspects of the job
6. Performing a variety of duties often changing from one task to another of a different nature without loss of efficiency or composure
7. Working under hazardous conditions that may result in: violence, loss of bodily members, burns, bruises, cuts, impairment of senses, collapse, fractures, electric shock

Worker Interest Areas:
   Identify from the list below, the preferences for work activities suggested by each task.
   A preference for activities:
      1. Dealing with things and objects
      2. Concerning the communication of data
      3. Involving business contact with people
      4. Involving work of a scientific and technical nature
      5. Involving work of a routine, concrete, organized nature
      6. Involving work of an abstract and creative nature
      7. Involving work for the presumed good of people
      8. Relating to process, machine, and technique
      9. Resulting in prestige or the esteem of others
      10. Resulting in tangible, productive satisfaction

From U.S. Civil Service Commission.

FIGURE 10.4   Changes in job titles.

Former Job Title	New Job Title
Brakeman	Brake Worker
Cameraman	Camera Operator
Cowboy	Cowhand
Driver-Salesman	Route Driver
Egg Poultryman	Egg Farmer
Longshoreman	Longshore Worker
Mail Boy	Mail Clerk
Nursemaid	Nursery Attendant
Policeman	Police Officer
Prison Matron	Correctional Officer
Public Relations Man	Public Relations Agent
Repairman	Repairer
Saleswoman	Salesperson
Sound Effects Man	Sound Effects Technician
Stewardess	Flight Attendant

Manual of Sex-free Occupational Titles, Occupational and Career Analysis Branch, Department of Employment and Immigration, 1976.

titles. Employment and Immigration Canada has updated its *Canadian Classification and Dictionary of Occupations* with a *Manual of Sex-free Occupational Titles*. Figure 10.4 shows some of the changes.

BACK TO THE CASE

In the training session at Fairchild Industries in the introductory case, Charlie Collis was using his knowledge and experience as a manager to help the current managers at Fairchild understand that they must be concerned with obtaining appropriate human resources—the people who will make a valuable contribution to the attainment of Fairchild's organizational objectives. During the Thunderbolt project, for example, Collis should have considered hiring people to work solely on the attack plane in order to meet Fairchild's goal of producing attack planes for the Air Force. In finding appropriate human resources, Collis would have had to follow four basic steps: (1) recruitment; (2) selection; (3) training; and (4) performance appraisal.

Basically, recruitment would entail the initial screening of individuals available to fill open positions at Fairchild. For recruitment efforts to be successful at Fairchild, recruiters would have to know the jobs they were trying to fill, where potential human resources could be located, and how the law might influence recruiting efforts.

Recruiters could acquire an understanding of an open position at Fairchild by performing a job analysis. The job analysis would force them to determine the job description of the open position—the activities of a draftsperson, engineer, maintenance supervisor, or accountant, for example—and the job specification of the position, including the type of individual who should be hired to fill that position.

Knowing Sources of Human Resources

The labour supply is constantly in flux.

Besides a thorough knowledge of the position the organization is trying to fill, recruiters must be able to pinpoint sources of human resources. A barrier to this pinpointing is the fact that the supply of individuals from which to choose in the labour market is continually changing; there are times when finding appropriate human resources is much harder than other times. For example, an article that appeared over twenty years ago indicated that organizations should prepare for a frantic scramble to obtain managers from a very low supply in the labour market.[1] In discussing the same managerial recruitment issue, however, a more recent article indicates that the situation has changed dramatically:

> For the past couple of years, a few thoughtful observers of new business trends have been warning that a glut of corporate executives is imminent. The reason, of course, is the . . . baby boom of the late 1940s and 1950s.[2]

Overall, sources of human resources available to fill a position can be categorized in two ways: sources inside the organization, and sources outside the organization.

Sources Inside the Organization

The existing pool of employees presently within an organization is one source of human resources. Individuals already within an organization may be well qualified for an open position. Although existing personnel sometimes are moved laterally within an organization, most internal movements are promotions. Promotion from within typically has the advantages of building morale, encouraging employees to work harder in hopes of being promoted, and making individuals inclined to stay with a particular organization because of possible future pro-

Promoting from within has a number of advantages.

FIGURE 10.5   Management inventory card.

Name	Age	Employed
Murray, Mel	47	1977

Present Position	On Job
Manager, sales (House Fans division)	6 years

Present Performance
Outstanding—exceeded sales goal in spite of stiffer competition.

Strengths
Good planner—motivates subordinates very well—excellent communication.

Weaknesses
Still does not always delegate as much as situation requires. Sometimes does not understand production's problems.

Efforts to Improve
Has greatly improved in delegating in last two years; also has organized more effectively after taking a management course on own time and initiative.

Could Move to	When
Vice-president, marketing	1989

Training Needed
More exposure to problems of other divisions (attend top staff conference?) Perhaps university program stressing staff role of corporate marketing versus line sales.

Could Move to	When
Manager, House or Industrial Fans division	1990 1991

Training Needed
Course in production management; some project working with production people; perhaps a good business game somewhere.

From Walter S. Wikstrom, "Developing Managerial Competence: Concepts, Emerging Practices," *Studies in Personnel Policy*, No. 189, pp. 9, 14. Used with permission.

motions.[3] Companies like Esso and Canadian General Electric find it very rewarding to train managers themselves for promotion within the organization.[4]

Some type of **human resources inventory** usually is helpful to a company to keep current with possibilities for filling a position from within. The inventory should indicate which individuals within an organization would be appropriate for filling a position if it became available. Walter S. Wikstrom has suggested three types of records that can be combined to maintain a useful human resources inventory within an organization.[5] Although Wikstrom focuses on filling managerial positions, slight modifications to his inventory forms would make his records equally applicable to non-managerial positions.

The first of Wikstrom's three record-keeping forms for a human resources inventory is a **management inventory card** (Figure 10.5). The management inventory card in Figure 10.5 has been completed for a fictional manager named Mel Murray. The card indicates Murray's age, year of employment, present position and length of time held, performance ratings, strengths and weaknesses, the positions to which he might move, when he would be ready to assume these positions, and additional training he would need to fill these positions. In short, this card is both an organizational history of Murray and an explanation of how he might be used in the future.

Figure 10.6 shows Wikstrom's second human resources inventory form—a **position replacement form**. This form focuses on maintaining position-centred information, rather than the people-centred information on the management inventory card. This particular form, therefore, indicates very little about Murray as a person but a great deal about individuals who could replace him. The position replacement form is helpful in determining what would happen to Murray's present position if he were selected to be moved within the organization or if he left the organization altogether.

> The management inventory card contains people-centred information.

> The position replacement form contains job-centred information.

FIGURE 10.6   Position replacement form.

Position			
Manager, sales (House Fans division)			
Performance	**Incumbent**	**Salary**	**May Move**
Outstanding	Mel Murray	$44 500	1 year
Replacement 1		**Salary**	**Age**
Earl Renfrew		$39 500	39
Present Position		**Employed:**	
Field sales manager, House Fans		Present job 3 years	Company 10 years
Training Needed Special assignment to study market potential for air conditioners to provide forecasting experience.			**When ready** now
Replacement 2		**Salary**	**Age**
Bernard Storey		$38 500	36
Present Position		**Employed:**	
Promotion manager, House Fans		Present Job 4 years	Company 7 years
Training Needed Rotation to field sales. Marketing conference in fall, 1989.			**When ready** 2 years

From Walter S. Wikstrom, "Developing Managerial Competence: Concepts, Emerging Practices," *Studies in Personnel Policy*, No. 189, pp. 9, 14. Used with permission.

FIGURE 10.7   Management manpower replacement chart.

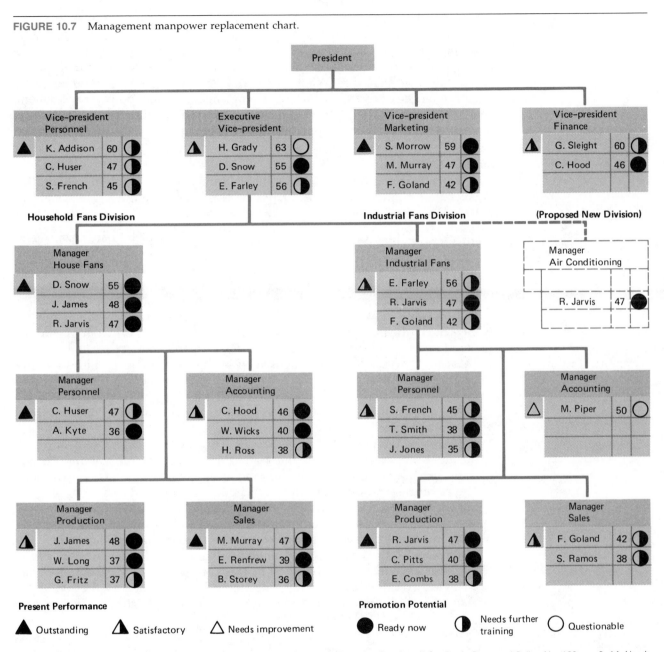

Present Performance

▲ Outstanding   ◭ Satisfactory   △ Needs improvement

Promotion Potential

● Ready now   ◐ Needs further training   ○ Questionable

From Walter S. Wikstrom, "Developing Managerial Competence: Concepts, Emerging Practices," *Studies in Personnel Policy*, No. 189, pp. 9, 14. Used with permission.

Wikstrom's third sample human resources inventory form is called a **management manpower replacement chart** (Figure 10.7). This chart presents a composite view of those individuals that management considers significant for human resources planning. The performance rating and promotion potential of Murray can be easily compared with those of other human resources when trying to determine which individual would most appropriately fill a particular position.

The management inventory card, the position replacement form, and the management manpower replacement chart are three separate record-keeping devices for a human resources inventory. Each form, however, furnishes different

A management manpower replacement chart compares individuals who might be considered for promotion.

All inventory information should be considered collectively.

data upon which to base a hiring-from-within decision. The questions these forms help to answer are: (1) What is the organizational history of an individual, and what potential does he or she possess? (management inventory card); (2) If a position becomes vacant, who might be eligible to fill that position? (position replacement form); and (3) What are the relative merits of one individual filling the position as compared to another? (management manpower replacement chart). Considering the answers to these three questions collectively should help to ensure the success of hiring-from-within decisions.

Sources Outside the Organization

If for some reason a position cannot be filled by someone presently within the organization, numerous sources of prospective human resources are available outside the organization. Several of these sources are:

Obtaining human resources from outside the organization involves:

1. Recruiting from the competition.

1. *Competitors*   One commonly tapped external source of human resources is competing organizations. Since there are several advantages to luring human resources away from competitors, this type of piracy has become a common practice. Among the advantages are: (1) the competitor will have paid for the individual's training up to the time of hire; (2) the competing organization will probably be weakened somewhat by the loss of the individual; and (3) once hired, the individual becomes a valuable source of information regarding how to best compete with his or her former organization.

2. Recruiting from public and private employment agencies.

2. *Employment agencies*   Employment agencies help people to find jobs and organizations to find people. Employment agencies can be either public or private. Public employment agencies do not charge fees, while private agencies collect a fee from either the person hired or the organization once a hiring has been finalized.

3. Recruiting through advertising.

3. *Readers of certain publications*   Perhaps the most widely addressed source of potential human resources is the readership of certain publications. To tap this source, recruiters simply place an advertisement in a suitable publication. The advertisement describes the open position in detail and announces that the organization is accepting applications from qualified individuals. The type of position to be filled determines the type of publication in which the advertisement will be placed. The objective is to advertise in a publication whose readers are likely to be interested in filling the position. An opening for a top-level executive might be advertised in *The Financial Post* or *The Globe and Mail*, whereas a training director opening might be advertised in the *Journal of Training and Development*, and an educational opening might be advertised in the *Chronicle of Higher Education*.

4. Recruiting of new graduates.

4. *Educational institutions*   Several recruiters go directly to schools to interview students close to graduation. Liberal arts schools, business schools, engineering schools, junior colleges, and community colleges all have somewhat different human resources to offer. Recruiting efforts should focus on those schools with the highest probability of providing human resources appropriate for the open position.

The Management in Action for this chapter features the recent growth of Employee Assistance Programs within the business community, outlining the various trends and issues connected to their implementation. In many cases, companies have turned increasingly to these programs as a way of ensuring for themselves the distinctive advantage of having contented and productive employees.

SHOW YOU CARE: EAPS REDUCE STRESS AND INCREASE PROFITS

On a scale of one to *Hill Street Blues*, it wasn't much of a robbery. A lone thief entered a busy suburban Toronto branch of the Bank of Montreal one Friday afternoon and fled a richer man. The police came and the financial damages incurred were tallied. That was the easy part. The other cost, the kind that can give employees post-robbery night sweats, would be more difficult to calculate.

How does one compute the emotional and psychological backlash to such an event? Similarly, how does one decipher the behaviour of an employee whose mild-mannered demeanor slowly grows surly? How can one tell when gnawing job-related resentments are threatening to explode? All these and similar questions point to the need to demystify stress for employees, and to make it easy for them to get help when they need it. The solution: Employee Assistance Programs, otherwise known as EAPs. Nowadays many companies are adopting programs to help employees overcome stress in coping with their jobs or dealing with personal problems, such as marital strife or alcoholism.

In the past half year or so, the Bank of Montreal's supervisory staff has started to understand precisely how employees may react if they're caught in any of the bank's 175 (on average) annual robberies. Guidelines developed include teaching management that holdup victims often need more than a pat on the back and the rest of the day off to recover. A number may require long-term counselling, and all deserve some evidence that the bank's concerns extend beyond an empty cash drawer.

Post-crime trauma counselling, however, is only one of the services available to the bank's 26 000 employees and their families. Ray Johnston, a trained social worker who is the Bank of Montreal's employee assistance manager, and his staff of four professional counsellors also provide confidential help and assistance in dealing with a wide variety of problems, from alcohol and drug abuse to on-the-job stress and marriage difficulties. To tap this free service, employees have only to call one of the bank's three EAP offices (in Montreal, Toronto, and Calgary) from anywhere in the country. Since its inception four years ago, hundreds of employees have sought help from the program.

The Bank of Montreal's EAP is not unique, nor is the propelling spirit behind it new. Since the Second World War, many employers have at least been aware that workplace stress costs money and that there is a direct correlation between a company's profit margin and its rate

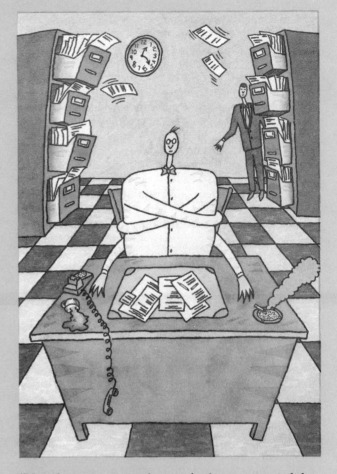

"Nowadays many companies are adopting programs to help employees overcome stress . . ."

of absenteeism. But it is only recently that EAPs have become a popular method of aiding troubled employees through confidential counselling and referral services. A survey of top Canadian companies indicates that almost two thirds have some form of assistance plan, ranging from substance-abuse counselling to the "broad brush" approach available at the Bank of Montreal. This represents a 54 percent increase since 1980.

All this means that staff who perhaps would have faced dismissal even a decade ago are now being given a second chance and, consequently, are becoming better employees. Al Bates, a Bank of Montreal senior vice-president, says, "We're convinced that anything you can do to help an employee feel good by proving your concern has to positively impact productivity." Aubrey Peterson, Imperial Oil Ltd.'s vice-president of general services, makes much the same point about his company's EAP, which has been in place since 1980. Furthermore, he maintains that its current EAP is not a new phenomenon, but merely a more sophisticated reflection of the company's concern for its employees. Both executives contend, however, that it is important to remember that neither the

257

program nor its practitioners are in the "hand-holding business"; rather, they are problem solvers whose job it is to help employees lead full, productive lives.

While both the Bank of Montreal and Imperial Oil have chosen to operate their own plans, other companies are turning to outside firms to design and run their EAPs, paying an average of thirty-five dollars per employee per year. Psychologist Jack Santa-Barbara, president of six-year-old Corporate Health Consultants of Mississauga, Ontario, reports that his company has doubled its business since 1985, today counting the likes of Northern Telecom (Bramalea) Ltd., Confederation Life Insurance Co., and the Canadian Broadcasting Corporation among its twenty-four clients. In Toronto, David Wright, the employee services director of the Family Service Association, heads a staff of eight counsellors who design and market EAPs; since 1979, when this service was first introduced, his department has guided program installations in twenty-five organizations, including Rothman's Canada Inc., Xerox Canada Inc., Union Carbide Canada, and Molson Ontario Breweries Ltd. Wright attributes the 400 percent increase in his agency's EAP business since 1980 to a fresh wave of enlightened self-interest on the part of corporations and to the 1982 recession: "In the aftermath of cutbacks and layoffs, companies were asking us about their remaining employees, who were now going to be challenged to do a lot more. They wanted help to deal with the inevitable increase in stress and its potential impact on overall company performance."

EAPs come in a wide variety of styles, which initially may seem confusing to newcomers. At the Bank of Montreal, Al Johnston employs a straight assessment-referral approach; employees' problems are assessed, and then employees are referred to whichever resources within the community are best equipped to help. At Imperial Oil, however, troubled employees at two of the company's locations are seen by on-staff counsellors (at all other locations health staff make referrals to community services). Imperial's EAP director, Dr. S. Klarreich, administers an annual EAP budget of $130 000 and runs "the equivalent of a private practice within the company," working closely with the company's health staff of sixteen nurses and thirteen doctors. Air Canada offers an example of yet another EAP model. In operation since 1978, Air Canada's program is jointly administered by 150 volunteers from the company and the four unions that represent its staff of 22 000. With a B.A. in social work, Sally Barker earns a living as a passenger sales agent in Toronto, but regularly doubles as an EAP counsellor. Barker, who is from the Canadian Autoworkers Union, is entitled to give the EAP only half a day per week although she "lives with it twenty-four hours a day." Given the limited time officially sanctioned for her EAP involvement, Barker usually doesn't counsel but instead simply directs employees to appropriate outside help.

Outside EAP providers with on-call counsellors who either visit a company's premises or counsel employees in their outside offices naturally favour their own approach, called case management, over assessment-referral and direct counselling. "It's a much more intense engagement with the employee's problem and subsequent recovery process," says Jack Santa-Barbara. "You're not just a traffic cop directing problems to this or that agency. What you do is establish needs and objectives with your client and then match them to community resources. But you stay involved with the case and share responsibility for recovery."

There are still a number of companies who shun the notion of EAPs altogether. Part of this resistance stems from the typical Canadian organizational reluctance to get involved with someone's personal problems, even though it can be demonstrated that these problems have a direct effect on job performance and may even have been exacerbated by the job itself. It is easier and less messy to fire an alcoholic after several warnings than it is to assume some responsibility for getting that person help, because that may be an implicit admission of guilt. Another factor is the subtle contempt held for anyone with a psychological problem; it's as though it is viewed as a weakness that indicates the person just can't cut it in the tough world of post-recession business. Jack Santa-Barbara, however, counters that one of the demonstrable benefits of an EAP is the way it can help managers side-step the potential minefield of personal issues: "If an EAP is properly marketed within a company, middle management will realize it's a handy resource that frees them to concentrate on assessing the performance aspects of a job. They no longer have to get embroiled in all those personal problems that should rightly be handled by professional counsellors."

Yet Santa-Barbara is quick to acknowledge that the underlying spirit of benign self-interest that drives EAPs has to be there. "Among companies with successful EAPs," he says, "there's an explicit assumption that people are important and that the company must support them if demands are made." As companies introduce new services and new products in an increasingly competitive and stressful environment, there is a growing realization that EAPs provide an inexpensive source of support for the very people who make or break an organization. Still to be measured are those intangible benefits which follow any successful EAP: improved relationships, improved self-esteem, improved problem-handling abilities, and improved productivity in general.

But no matter how well used they are, EAPs are often considered vulnerable within the corporate arena precisely because program leaders can't produce the kind of "annual numbers show" that consoles accountants. Many programs are deemed to exist at the fickle pleasure of a benevolent management. Even the most charitable and enlightened executive can be forgiven for asking some tough questions about what kind of return on an EAP investment can be expected. It does not help that answers vary according to the quality of the projects and companies. According to Santa-Barbara, the current methodology used in calculating investment return is suspect because it's imprecise. "We only know that these programs pay for themselves," he concludes.

Helen Krafchik, who is responsible for Warner-Lambert's (Canada) EAP, flatly refuses to equate dollars and cents with people's lives; to her the bottom line involves helping the hurting person. Developed for the 1 400-employee company by Metro Toronto's Family Service and the Canadian Mental Health Association, Warner-Lambert's program has been in place since 1976. According to Wayne Britt, vice-president of human resources, the company's EAP has been well used from the beginning. Calculating investment return, on the other hand, has never been a priority with them. "The program costs $36 000 a year," he explains. "Our absenteeism rate is down under 2 percent and our turnover rate is around 5 percent or about half the industry's norm. Other than that, we don't know what our payback is and nobody around here spends much of their time worrying about it." As for Krafchik, who runs the program with the help of an on-call Family Service counsellor, Britt says, "She's the most trusted person in the company. Her work is completely confidential."

In point of fact, trust and confidentiality are the blood and oxygen of EAPs. However well-intentioned, lofty initial promises of trust and confidentiality become meaningless if they're betrayed even once. The issues can and do get tricky. An employee may seek confidential counselling from an EAP person for on-the-job stress. Does management have the right to know if it's exerting too much pressure on the employee? Other controversies generated by EAPs frequently arise as well. Program offices located on company premises, for instance, are convenient to visit and enable employees to discuss their problems in familiar surroundings. However, anyone seen entering or leaving is assumed to have a problem, which might generate workplace gossip. Debate continues about the ethical implications of the mandatory referral method used by some EAP practitioners, by which an employee is ordered to get help or face dismissal. Critics believe it is a form of economic blackmail that serves no one except the company.

As companies wrestle over whether or not they need an EAP, their values are being tested. For some an EAP is a natural move because they have always prized their people and they have good employee-handling records to prove it. For others it's a little like "the Tin Man trying to find a heart." To be successful, EAPs must be part of a total caring environment. Those who think otherwise run the danger of creating a machine which just recycles people; what is really needed is a concerted effort to educate employees and provide them with the option of an alternative lifestyle. EAPs make a very clear statement about who and what a company stands for. More important still, EAPs make a very clear statement about how companies want to be judged by their own employees. In the final analysis, this is not necessarily a question of altruism, but rather a recognition that healthy human resources are an important asset to any company. In this sense, EAPs are simply good business policy.

Based on "Show You Care," by Patrick Conlon in *Canadian Business*, April 1987. Used with permission.

Knowing the Law

Legislation has an impact on organizational recruitment practices in Canada because:

> every individual should have an equal opportunity with other individuals to make for himself or herself the life that he or she is able and wishes to have, consistent with his or her duties and obligations as a member of society, without being hindered in or prevented from doing so by discriminatory practices based on race, national or ethnic origin, colour, religion, age, sex, or marital status, or conviction for an offense for which a pardon has been granted or by discriminatory employment practices based on physical handicaps. *The Canadian Human Rights Act*, paragraph 2, subsection (a)

Personnel managers must not be influenced by a prospective employee's sex, religion, race, national origin, or age. The legislation governing human rights is a combination of federal and provincial acts with the goal of providing equal employment opportunities for all. This legislation does allow employers to reward outstanding performance and not reward mediocre productivity. The basis for rewards, however, must be directly related to the work and not to an individual's age, sex, race, or other irrelevant issues.

The Canadian Human Rights Act of 1977 permits the Canadian Human Rights Commission to enforce the act by improving equal employment opportunities for special groups. The act encourages affirmative action programs as a legal way to improve opportunities for a special group that may previously have suffered discrimination. Companies often voluntarily develop affirmative action programs in order to correct earlier discriminatory practices and also to avoid any future infractions. The existence of such a program helps guard against both intentional and unconscious discrimination.

Equal employment opportunity legislation and affirmative action plans affect the activities of personnel departments in the following ways:

1. Job descriptions cannot contain irrelevant requirements that are only intended to exclude certain individuals.
2. Human resource plans must state the firm's affirmative action commitment.
3. Performance evaluation cannot contain biases intended to discriminate against special individuals.
4. The recruitment process cannot exclude any prospective applicants and must attract all.
5. The selection process cannot use screening mechanisms that are not related to the job.
6. Compensation must be related to performance, skills, and seniority, and must not discriminate against individuals in special classifications.
7. Training must be available to all individuals without regard to factors external to the work.

For a look at the human rights issues involved in hiring practices, it is important to understand the human rights legislation governing hiring practices.

There is a guideline drawn up by the federal government entitled *Bona Fide Occupational Requirements Guidelines*. The document clarifies the Canadian Human Rights Act as it applies to employment practices for all federal government departments and agencies, Crown corporations, and businesses under federal jurisdiction such as banks, airlines, and some railway companies. This covers about 10 percent of Canada's labour force.

Other businesses follow their own provincial codes, which are broadly similar to the federal law. But federal practices have a habit of finding their way into provincial law.

Nearly every employer knows that he or she cannot deny work to anyone on the basis of race, colour, national or ethnic origin, religion, or age. But marital status and conviction for an offense for which a pardon has been granted are also deemed irrelevant. Questions of sex and physical requirements can be even murkier. According to the guidelines, hypothesized assumptions about employment suitability are not allowed for all employers under federal jurisdiction. They need solid, proven reasons for turning down women, short people, tall people, deaf people, blind people, or epileptics, for example.

The guidelines focus on three central areas: essential tasks, reasonable accommodation for employees' needs, and individual ability. At the federal employment level, the Public Service Commission also ensures that applicants with physical handicaps or those who have a criminal record are not discriminated against. It is those applicants who best meet the professional and linguistic requirements who are hired to fill vacant public service positions.

The primary responsibility of the Public Service Commission is to ensure that appointments to and within the public service are based on merit (i.e., on processes designed to ensure an objective evaluation of a person's qualifications for the job to be performed) and that selections are free from discrimination on the basis of sex, race, national origin, religion, colour, marital status, or age. In 1986 this led the Commission to establish an umbrella organization under which the various affirmative action programs (with the sole exception of the Women's Career Counselling and Referral Bureau) could be coordinated in an efficient and results-oriented manner across the country. In order to ensure that the Commission was empowered to carry out its mandate effectively, Parliament granted it the exclusive authority to make appointments under the Public Service Employment Act, and directed that its staffing systems meet specific requirements designed to protect certain rights of candidates and employees, and generally to ensure fair treatment in all staffing practices. In recent years the Commission has made more explicit certain other basic principles, in addition to merit and quality, to be served by its staffing system: namely, the efficiency and effectiveness of departmental operations, the sensitivity and responsiveness of the administration machinery of government to the public it serves, and effective equality of access to the Public Service of Canada for all Canadians.

In addition, the Public Service Commission has assumed various responsibilities in support of government policies related to employment in the public service. These include areas such as managerial and professional training, official language policies, and programs aimed at increasing the participation in the public service of certain groups such as francophones, women, Native people and handicapped persons. In performing its statutory responsibilities, the Commission touches on all of these areas. This responsibility has been a top priority in recent years, leading to the establishment of more affirmative action programs for women, Native people, disabled people, and members of visible minority groups. This commitment includes fostering activities and delivering programs to increase the participation and equitable distribution of members of target groups at all levels of the Public Service.[6] The Commission, however, has agreed to carry out certain activities related to various aspects of these programs, recognizing that the government (and more specifically the Treasury Board of Canada), as employer, is the locus of responsibility and accountability. For example, equal opportunity and training and development programs, including language training, are performed in accordance with terms and conditions established by Treasury Board policies. In these areas the Public Service Commission is expected to and does participate in policy development.

Finally, the Canadian Charter of Rights and Freedoms, with its section on equality rights (designed to provide individuals with protection from discrimination), further guarantees that protection of human rights in employment will be at the forefront of all employment-related activities. It guarantees an individual the right to an equal opportunity in employment, and a legal as well as moral basis for action should the individual be discriminated against. Effective since April 1985, the Charter's effect on human rights and employment in the long term have yet to be determined.

BACK TO THE CASE

A successful recruitment effort at Fairchild Industries would require recruiters to know where to locate the human resources needed to fill open Fairchild positions. These sources might be both within Fairchild and outside of it.

While handling the Thunderbolt project, Charlie Collis should have recognized that he needed to allocate more human resources to the project in order to satisfy the Air Force. To do this, Collis could have kept current on the possibility of filling positions from within by maintaining some type of human resource inventory. This inventory would have helped him organize information about: (1) the organizational histories and potential of various Fairchild employees; (2) the employees at Fairchild who might be eligible to fill the positions needed to complete the Thunderbolt

project; and (3) the relative abilities of various Fairchild employees to fill the necessary openings. Some of the sources of potential human resources outside of Fairchild that Collis should have been aware of were competitors, public and private employment agencies, the readers of industry-related publications, and various types of educational institutions.

In the training session, Collis should have made the current Fairchild managers aware of how the law influences their recruitment efforts. Basically, the law says that Fairchild recruitment practices cannot discriminate on the basis of race, colour, religion, sex, or national origin. If recruitment practices at Fairchild were to be found discriminatory, the company would be subject to prosecution.

Selection

The second major step involved in furnishing appropriate human resources for the organization is selection. **Selection** is choosing an individual to hire from all those who have been recruited. Hence, selection is dependent upon and follows recruitment. As the cartoon shows, however, providing appropriate human resources involves more than just selecting what are thought to be the best people.

The selection process typically is represented as a series of stages through which prospective employees must pass to be hired.[7] Each successive stage reduces the total group of prospective employees until, finally, one individual is hired. Figure 10.8 lists specific stages of the selection process, indicates reasons for eliminating prospective employees at each stage, and illustrates how the group of potential personnel for an organization is narrowed down to the individual who ultimately becomes the employee. Two tools often used in the selection process are testing and assessment centres.

"I pick the best people I can find, and I don't try to second-guess them."

Reprinted by permission of James Stevenson from Harvard Business Review *(September/October 1987).*

FIGURE 10.8 Summary of major factors involved in the selection process.

Stages of the Selection Process	Reasons for Elimination	
Preliminary screening from records, data sheets, etc.	Lack of adequate educational and performance record	Available potential personnel from inside or outside company
Preliminary interview	Obvious misfit from outward appearance and conduct	
Intelligence test(s)	Failure to meet minimum standards	
Aptitude test(s)	Failure to have minimum necessary aptitude	
Personality test (s)	Negative aspects of personality	Rejection of potential employees
Performance references	Unfavorable or negative reports on past performance	
Diagnostic interview	Lack of necessary innate ability, ambition, or other qualities	
Physical examination	Physically unfit for job	
Personal judgment	Remaining candidate placed in available position	Employee

Reprinted by permission from L. C. Megginson, *Providing Management Talent for Small Business* (Baton Rouge, La. Division of Research, College of Business Administration, Louisiana State University, 1961), p. 108.

Testing

Tests are used to measure:

1. Potential.

2. Skill level.

3. Vocational interests.

4. Personality.

Testing can be defined as examining human resources for qualities relevant to performing available jobs.[8] Although many different kinds of tests are available for organizational use, they generally can be divided into four categories:[9]

1. *Aptitude tests*   These tests measure the potential of an individual to perform some task. Aptitude tests are diversified in that some measure general intelligence while others measure special abilities, such as mechanical, clerical, or visual abilities. Figure 10.9 describe the eleven information areas covered by one aptitude test, the Wechsler Adult Intelligence Scale.
2. *Achievement tests*   Tests that measure the level of skill or knowledge an individual possesses in a certain area are called achievement tests. This skill or knowledge may have been acquired through various training activities or actual experience in the area.
3. *Vocational interest tests*   These tests attempt to measure an individual's interest in performing various kinds of activities and are administered on the assumption that certain people perform jobs well because the job activities are interesting to them. The basic purpose of this type of test is to help select those individuals who find certain aspects of an open position interesting.
4. *Personality tests*   Personality tests attempt to describe an individual's personality dimensions, such as emotional maturity, subjectivity, or objectivity. Personality tests can be used advantageously if the personality characteristics needed to do well in a particular job are well defined and if individuals possessing those characteristics can be pinpointed and selected.

FIGURE 10.9   The eleven information areas covered by the Wechsler Adult Intelligence Scale.

Verbal

1. Information. A series of open-ended questions dealing with the kinds of factual data people normally pick up in their ordinary contacts.
2. Comprehension. Another series of open-ended questions covering the individual's understanding of the need for social rules.
3. Arithmetic. All the questions are of the story or problem type. Scoring is for correctness of solutions and time to respond.
4. Digit Span. A group of numbers is read and the subject repeats them from memory, sometimes backward.
5. Similarities. Pairs of terms are read and a common property or characteristic must be abstracted.
6. Vocabulary. A series of words must be defined in the subject's own terms.

Performance

7. Picture Completion. A number of pictures are presented in which the subject must identify the missing component.
8. Picture Arrangement. Items require that a series of pictures be arranged as rapidly as possible in the order that makes the most sense.
9. Object Assembly. Jigsaw puzzles must be put together within a given time limit.
10. Block Design. Working with a set of small blocks having red, white, or red and white faces, the subject attempts to duplicate various printed designs as quickly as possible.
11. Digit Symbol. The subject is given a series of paired symbols and numbers as a code. The subject is then to write as many correct numbers as he or she can for each of a series of scrambled symbols within a set time period.

Reprinted from John B. Miner, *Personnel Psychology* (New York: Macmillan, 1969). Courtesy John B. Miner.

Several guidelines should be observed when using tests as part of the selection process. First, care should be taken to ensure that the test being used in both valid and reliable. A test is valid if it measures what it is designed to measure and reliable if it measures similarly time after time. Second, tests results should not be used as the sole source of information to determine whether or not to hire someone. People change over time, and someone who doesn't score well on a particular test might still develop into a productive employee. Such factors as potential and desire to obtain a position should be assessed subjectively along with test scores in making the final selection decision. A third guideline is that care should be taken to determine that tests used are non-discriminatory in nature. "Many tests contain language or cultural biases which may discriminate against minorities."[10]

Tests must be used correctly.

Assessment Centres

Another tool often used to help increase the success of employee selection is the assessment centre. Although the assessment centre concept is discussed in this chapter primarily as an aid to selection, it also has been used as an aid in such areas as human resources training and organization development. The first industrial use of the assessment centre is usually credited to AT & T.[11] Since AT & T's initial efforts, the assessment centre concept has been growing quickly and has been adopted by such companies as Merrill Lynch, Prudential Life Insurance, IBM, and Canadian General Electric.[12]

"An **assessment centre** is a program, not a place, in which participants engage in a number of individual and group exercises constructed to simulate important activities at the levels to which participants aspire."[13] These exercises might include such activities as participating in leaderless discussions, giving some type of oral presentation, or leading a group in solving some assigned problem. Individuals performing these activities are observed by managers or trained observers who evaluate both their ability and potential.[14] In general, participants are assessed on the basis of: (1) leadership; (2) organizing and planning; (3) decision making; (4) oral and written communication skills; (5) initiative; (6) energy; (7) analytical ability; (8) resistance to stress; (9) use of delegation; (10) behaviour flexibility; (11) human relations competence; (12) originality; (13) controlling; (14) self-direction; and (15) overall potential.[15]

Assessment centres simulate tasks to be performed at specific levels of the organization.

BACK TO THE CASE

After the initial screening of potential human resources, Fairchild Industries will be faced with the task of selecting the individuals to be hired from those who have been screened. Two tools that Charlie Collis could suggest to help in this selection process are testing and assessment centres.

For example, after screening potential employees for positions on the Thunderbolt project, Collis could have used aptitude tests, achievement tests, vocational interest tests, or personality tests to see if any of the individuals he had screened had the qualities necessary to work on the attack plane project. In using these

tests, however, Collis would have had to make sure that the tests were both valid and reliable, and that they were non-discriminatory.

Collis also could have used assessment centres to simulate the tasks necessary to build the Thunderbolt attack plane. Individuals who performed well on these tasks would probably be more appropriate for the project than those who did poorly.

Over all, in the training session Charlie Collis should encourage Fairchild managers to use testing and assessment centres in selecting individuals for open positions.

Training

After recruitment and selection, the next step in providing appropriate human resources for the organization is training. **Training** is the process of developing qualities in human resources that ultimately will enable them to be more productive and, thus, contribute more to organizational goal attainment. Hence, the purpose of training is to increase the productivity of individuals in their jobs by influencing their behaviour. "Governmental agencies, industrial firms, volunteer organizations, educational institutions, and other segments of our society are placing more and more emphasis on the need to train human resources."[16] Figure 10.10 provides an overview of the types and popularity of training being offered by organizations.

The training of individuals is essentially a four-step process: (1) determining training needs; (2) designing the training program; (3) administering the training program; and (4) evaluating the training program. The relationship among these steps is presented in Figure 10.11. Each of these steps is described in more detail in the sections that follow.

Determining Training Needs

The first step of the training process is determining the organization's training needs. **Training needs** are the information areas or skill areas of an individual or group that require further development to increase the organizational productivity of that individual or group. Only if training focuses on these needs can it be of some productive benefit to the organization.

FIGURE 10.10   Types and popularity of training offered by organizations.

Types of Training	Percentage of Surveyed Companies That Offer This Type of Training
1. Management skills and development	74.3
2. Supervisory skills	73.4
3. Technical skills/knowledge updating	72.7
4. Communication skills	66.8
5. Customer relations/services	63.8
6. Executive development	56.8
7. New methods/procedures	56.5
8. Sales skills	54.1
9. Clerical/secretarial skills	52.9
10. Personal growth	51.9
11. Computer literacy/basic computer skills	48.2
12. Employee/labor relations	44.9
13. Disease prevention/health promotion	38.9
14. Customer education	35.7
15. Remedial basic education	18.0

FIGURE 10.11   Steps of the training process.

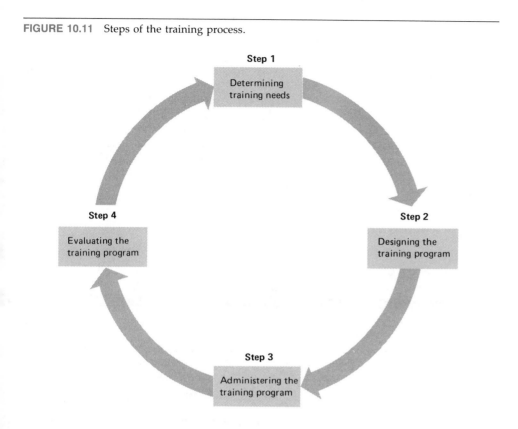

Training of organization members is typically a continuing activity. Even individuals who have been with an organization for some time and who have undergone initial orientation and skills training need continued training to improve skills.

Several methods of determining which skills to focus on for more established human resources are available. The first method is evaluating the production process within the organization. Such factors as excessive rejected products, deadlines that are not met, and high labour costs are clues to existing levels of production-related expertise. Another method for determining training needs is direct feedback from employees on what they feel are the organization's training needs. Organization members may be able to verbalize clearly and accurately exactly what types of training they need to help them do a better job. A third way of determining training needs involves looking into the future. If the manufacture of new products or the use of newly purchased equipment is foreseen, some type of corresponding training almost certainly will be needed.

Training needs can be determined by evaluating the production process,

requesting employee feedback,

and looking into the future.

Designing the Training Program

Once training needs have been determined, a training program aimed at meeting those needs must be designed. Basically, designing a program entails assembling various types of facts and activities that will meet the established training needs. Obviously, as training needs vary, the facts and activities designed to meet those needs vary.

Training ingredients must be assembled.

BACK TO THE CASE

After hiring, Fairchild Industries must train new employees to be productive organization members. To train effectively, Fairchild must determine training needs, design a corresponding training program, and administer and evaluate the training program.

Designing a training program requires that Fairchild assemble facts and activities that address specific company training needs. These needs are simply information or skill areas that need to be further developed in Fairchild employees to make them more productive.

Over the long term, training at Fairchild should focus on more established employees as well as newly hired employees.

Charlie Collis, the retired Fairchild manager discussed in the introductory case, was conducting a training session for upwardly mobile managers at Fairchild. The company has determined that training by such an instructor helps managers become "more appropriate"—in other words better able to help Fairchild achieve its objectives.

Administering the Training Program

The next step of the training process is administering the training program, or actually training the individuals. Various techniques exist for both transmitting necessary information and developing needed skills in training programs. Several of these techniques are discussed in the sections that follow.

Techniques for Transmitting Information

Two techniques for transmitting information in training programs are lectures and programmed learning. Although it probably could be argued that these techniques develop some skills in individuals as well as transmit information to them, they are primarily devices for the dissemination of information.

Lectures involve one-way communication,

Lectures   Perhaps the most widely used technique for transmitting information in training programs is the lecture. Bass and Vaughn define the **lecture** as a primarily one-way communication situation in which an instructor presents information to a group of listeners.[17] The instructor typically does most of the talking in this type of training situation. Trainees participate primarily by listening and note taking.

and have both advantages and disadvantages.

An advantage of the lecture is that it allows the instructor to expose trainees to a maximum amount of information within a given time period. The lecture, however, also has its disadvantages:

> The lecture generally consists of one-way communication: the instructor presents information to the group of passive listeners. Thus, little or no opportunity exists to clarify meanings, to check on whether trainees really understand the lecture material, or to handle the wide diversity of ability, attitude, and interest that may prevail among the trainees. Also, there is little or no opportunity for practice, reinforcement, knowledge of results, or overlearning.
>
> Ideally, the competent lecturer should make the material meaningful and intrinsically motivating to his or her listeners. However, whether most lectures achieve this goal is a moot question.
>
> These limitations, in turn, impose further limitations on the lecture's actual content. A skillful lecturer may be fairly successful in transmitting conceptual knowledge to a group of trainees who are ready to receive it; however, all the evidence available indicates that the nature of the lecture situation makes it of minimal value in promoting attitudinal or behavioural change.[18]

Programmed learning is learning independently.

Programmed Learning   Another commonly used technique for transmitting information in training programs is called programmed learning. According to Leonard Silvern, **programmed learning** is a technique for instructing without the presence or intervention of a human instructor.[19] Small parts of information that necessitate related responses are presented to individual trainees. Trainees can determine from the accuracy of their responses whether their understanding of the obtained information is accurate. The types of responses required of trainees vary from situation to situation but usually are multiple-choice, true-false, or fill-in-the-blank. Figure 10.12 shows a portion of a programmed learning training

---

FIGURE 10.12   Portion of a programmed learning training package emphasizing PERT.

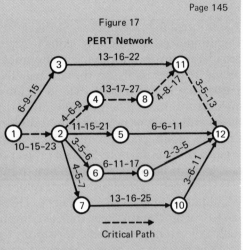

Frame 3²⁴   Page 145

Program evaluation and review technique, PERT, is performed on a set of time-related activities and events which must be accomplished to reach an objective. The evaluation gives the expected completion time and the probability of completing the total work within that time. By means of PERT, it is possible not only to know the exact schedule, but also to control the various activities on a daily basis. Overlapping and related activities are reviewed. PERT is more practical for jobs involving a one-time effort than for repeat jobs. It is a planning-controlling medium designed to: (1) focus attention on key components, (2) reveal potential problem areas, (3) provide a prompt reporting on accomplishments, and (4) facilitate decision making.

The time-related activities and events are set forth by means of a PERT network (see figure 17). In this illustration, the circles represent events that are sequential accomplishment points; the arrows represent activities or the time-consuming elements of the program. In this type of network, an arrow always connects two activities. All of the activities and events must be accomplished before the end objective can be attained. The three numbers shown for each arrow or activity represent its estimated times, respectively, for the optimistic, most likely, and pessimistic times. The program starts with event no. 1 and ends with event no. 12. From calculations for the time required for each path

Figure 17

PERT Network

from no. 1 to no. 12, it is found that path 1–2–4–8–11–12 requires the *longest time* and, hence, is the *critical path* because it controls the time required to complete the program. Toward it, managers would direct their attention in order to: (1) ensure that no breakdowns occur in it; (2) better the current times required, if possible; and (3) trade off time from the noncritical paths to the critical path, if the net effect is to reduce total time of the critical path.

Indicate whether each of the following statements is true or false by writing "T" or "F" in the space provided.

_____1. PERT centers its attention on social constraints.
_____2. PERT is best applied to assembly-line operations.
_____3. In PERT, the *critical path* is the path that requires the longest time.
_____4. In the PERT network, circles represent events and the arrows represent activities.
Now turn to Answer Frame 3²⁴, page 146.

Answer frame 3²⁴   Page 146

1. False. PERT centers its attention on *time* constraints.
2. False. PERT is more practical for jobs involving a one-time effort than for repeat jobs.
3. True. In PERT, the critical path is the path that requires the *longest* time. If this path can be shortened, the program can be completed in a shorter time period.
4. True. Circles represent events that are sequential accomplishment points, and arrows represent activities or the time-consuming elements for the program.
You have completed chapter 24. Now turn to chapter 25.

package that could be used to familiarize trainees with PERT (program evaluation and review technique).

As with the lecture method, programmed learning has both advantages and disadvantages. Among the advantages are that students can learn at their own pace, know immediately if they are right or wrong, and participate actively. The primary disadvantage of this method is that there is nobody to answer a question for the learner should a question arise.

Techniques for Developing Skills

Techniques for developing skills in training programs can be divided into two broad categories: on-the-job techniques and classroom techniques. Techniques for developing skills on the job usually are referred to as **on-the-job training**. These techniques reflect a blend of job-related knowledge and experience and include coaching, position rotation, and special project committees. Coaching is direct critiquing of how well an individual is performing a job. Position rotation involves moving an individual from job to job to obtain an understanding of the organization as a whole. Special project committees involve assigning a particular task to an individual to furnish him or her with experience in a designated area.[20]

Classroom techniques for developing skills also reflect a blend of both job-related knowledge and experience. The skills addressed via these techniques can range from technical skills, such as computer programming, to interpersonal skills, such as leadership. Specific classroom techniques aimed at developing skills include various types of management games and a diversity of role-playing activities. The most common format for management games requires small groups of trainees to make and then evaluate various management decisions. The role-playing format typically involves acting out and then reflecting upon some people-oriented problem that must be solved in the organization. A good example of this is the application of these techniques to orientation training for new recruits.

Contrary to the typical one-way communication role in the lecture situation, the skills instructor in the classroom encourages high levels of discussion and interaction among trainees; develops a climate in which trainees learn new behaviour from carrying out various activities; acts as a resource person in clarifying related information; and facilitates learning via job-related knowledge and experience in applying that knowledge.[21] The difference between the instructional role used in information dissemination and the instructional role used in skill development is dramatic.[22]

Evaluating the Training Program

After the training program has been completed, management should evaluate its effectiveness. Because training programs represent a cost investment—costs include materials, trainer time, and production loss due to individuals being trained rather than doing their jobs—a reasonable return is required.

Basically, management must evaluate the training program to determine if it meets the needs for which it was designed. Answers to questions such as the following help to determine training program effectiveness:

1. Has the excessive reject rate declined?
2. Are deadlines being met more regularly?
3. Are labour costs per unit produced decreasing?

If the answer to questions such as these is yes, the training program is at least somewhat successful, but perhaps its effectiveness could be enhanced through certain selective changes. If, on the other hand, the answer is no, some significant modification to the training program is warranted.

BACK TO THE CASE

After training needs at Fairchild Industries have been determined and programs have been designed to meet those needs, the programs must be administered and evaluated.

Charlie Collis was participating in a training program involving the lecture technique; Fairchild Industries could also use the programmed learning technique for transmitting information to trainees. For actually developing skills in trainees, Fairchild could use on-the-job training methods, such as coaching, position rotation, or special project committees. For developing skills in a classroom setting, it could use instructional techniques, such as role-playing activities. For example, lower-level Fairchild supervisors could be asked to act out the roles of managers handling various kinds of employee problems. These situations could then be analyzed from the viewpoint of how to improve supervisor-worker relationships.

Once a Fairchild training program has been completed, it must be evaluated to determine if it met the training need for which it was designed. Training programs aimed at specific motor skills such as typing would be much easier to evaluate than would training programs such as the one Charlie Collis was conducting, which was aimed at developing managerial decision-making skills. The evaluation of any training program at Fairchild, of course, should emphasize how to improve the program the next time it is implemented.

Performance Appraisal

Even after individuals have been recruited, selected, and trained, the task of making them productive individuals within the organization is not finished. The fourth step in the process of providing appropriate human resources for the organization is performance appraisal. **Performance appraisal** is the process of reviewing individuals' past productive activity to evaluate the contribution they have made toward attaining management system objectives. As with training, performance appraisal is a continuing activity and focuses on the more established human resources within the organization as well as on the relatively new human resources. One of its main purposes is to furnish feedback to organization members about how they can become more productive. Performance appraisal also has been called performance review or performance evaluation. Names and descriptions of several methods of performance appraisal are given in Figure 10.13.

Performance appraisals evaluate individuals' contributions to the attainment of management system objectives.

Why Use Performance Appraisals?

Most firms in Canada and the United States use some type of performance appraisal system.[23] Douglas McGregor has suggested the following three reasons for performance appraisals in an organization:[24]

1. They provide systematic judgments to support salary increases, promotions, transfers, and sometimes demotions or terminations.
2. They are a means of telling a subordinate how he or she is doing and of suggesting needed changes in behaviour, attitudes, skills, or job knowledge; they let the subordinate know where he or she stands with the boss.

FIGURE 10.13   Descriptions of several methods of performance appraisal.

Name of Appraisal Method	Description
Rating scale	Individuals appraising performance use a form containing several employee qualities and characteristics to be evaluated (e.g., dependability, initiative, leadership). Each evaluated factor is rated on a continuum or scale ranging, for example, from one to seven or more points.
Employee comparisons	Appraisers rank employees according to such factors as job performance and value to the organization. Only one employee can occupy a particular ranking.
Free-form essay	Appraisers simply write down their impressions of employees in paragraph form.
Critical–form essay	Appraisers write down particularly good or bad events involving employees as these events occur. Records of all documented events for any one employee are used to evaluate his or her performance.

Compiled from *Personnel Administration and Human Resource Management* by Andrew F. Sikula (New York: John Wiley & Sons, 1976), pp. 208–211.

3. They also are being used increasingly as a basis for the coaching and counseling of the individual by the superior.

Handling Performance Appraisals

Four guidelines can help to maximize the benefits of performance appraisals.

If performance appraisals are not handled well, their benefit to the organization is minimized. Several guidelines can assist in increasing the appropriateness with which performance appraisals are conducted.[25] The first of these guidelines is that performance appraisals should stress both performance within the position the individual holds and the success with which the individual is attaining objectives. Performance and objectives should become inseparable topics of discussion during performance appraisals. As a second guideline, appraisals should emphasize the individual in the job and not the evaluator's impression of observed work habits. In other words, emphasis should be more on an objective analysis of performance than on a subjective evaluation of habits. The third guideline is that the appraisal should be acceptable to both the evaluator and the evaluatee. Both individuals should agree that the appraisal can be of some benefit both to the organization and the worker. The last guideline is that performance appraisals should be used as the basis for improving individuals' productivity within the organization[26] by making them better equipped to produce.[27]

Potential Weaknesses of Performance Appraisals

To maximize the potential payoff of performance appraisals to the organization, managers must avoid several potential weaknesses of the appraisal process. As indicated by George A. Rider, these potential weaknesses are: (1) that individuals involved in performance appraisals could view them as a reward-punishment situation; (2) that the emphasis of performance appraisal could be put on completing paperwork rather than critiquing individual performance; and (3) that some type of negative reaction from a subordinate could be generated when the evaluator offers any unfavourable comments.[28]

To avoid these potential weaknesses, supervisors and employees should view the performance appraisal process as an opportunity to increase the worth of the individual through constructive feedback, not as a means of rewarding or punishing the individual through positive or negative comments. Paperwork should be seen only as an aid in providing this feedback and not as an end in itself. Also, care should be taken to make appraisal feedback as tactful and objective as possible to help minimize any negative reactions of the evaluatee.[29]

Management must avoid potential weaknesses of the appraisal process.

INTEGRATING WOMEN IN NON-TRADITIONAL JOBS: A SPECIAL PROBLEM

Women are being hired in increasing numbers to fill positions in organizations that, traditionally, they have not held.[30] These non-traditional jobs include lower-level positions like construction worker as well as upper-level positions like plant manager. One reason women want to fill such jobs is that pay for performing them is typically well above pay for performing jobs more traditionally held by women. Naturally, organizations are increasing their hiring of women to fill such positions for many reasons. One may be that the federal government through the Advisory Council for the Status of Women has set a mandatory guideline that requires that a proportion of women must work on all federally financed construction projects.[31]

Regardless of the reasons for this emerging movement of women working in jobs that traditionally were held by men, managers must cope with the problem of how to integrate female workers successfully into the organization. According to Nancy R. Brunner, a program aimed at handling this problem should include two primary phases: pre-hire preparation and post-hire activities.[32]

Programs that integrate women holding non-traditional jobs into the organization should include both pre-hire preparation and post-hire activities.

Pre-hire Preparation

Pre-hire preparation involves getting the women ready to come into the organization as well as making the organization ready for the women's entry. Included in this preparation are:[33]

Pre-hire activities get women and organizations ready.

Job analysis   To define job responsibilities clearly, identify specific training needs, and develop job-proficiency guides. The guides outline expected increases in performance competence and the skills that must be demonstrated at each successive level of improvement.

Interview/selection training   To prepare managers for involvement in the selection of women and enable them to help define the job-related dimensions that candidates capable of performance and growth in the organization should have.

Workshops for the male supervisors as well as peers   To begin to dispel myths about women workers and develop positive solutions for overcoming barriers.

Pre-selection counselling and tour for women candidates   To familiarize women with the specific nature of the work, to show them the areas in which they would be working, and to provide them an opportunity for self-assessment of their readiness for entering the positions.

Planning for technical training and for follow-up   To provide women with structured training experiences immediately upon reporting to work and to prepare to offer them needed support services.

Post-hire Activities

Phase two of Brunner's program to integrate women workers successfully into the organization—post-hire activities—is aimed at helping newly hired female workers to adapt to their new environment. Management designs these activities and requires the involvement of both men and women from various organizational positions and levels. These activities include:[34]

Orientation for women selected   To orient them to the job environment, connect them with women already in non-traditional work, and acquaint them with available support services (such as counselling).

General technical training   To enable the women to meet basic job requirements.

On-the-job training   To facilitate the development of task-specific job skills needed to improve performance at each stage or skill level.

Periodic counselling for the women   To monitor the progress of their entry into the workplace and to provide guidance as needed.

Follow-up sessions with the men   To monitor adaptation of male workers to having women on board and to provide guidance as needed.

Rap sessions with both men and women   To discuss and solve possible tensions between male and female workers and other problems as needed.

Periodic management discussions with the women, their trainers, and supervisors   To monitor individual and group progress and to demonstrate ongoing support.

Periodic evaluation and revision   To measure results and identify program elements that need to be changed or strengthened.

The main focus of this chapter has been on explaining the generally accepted steps in providing appropriate human resources for the organization: (1) recruitment; (2) selection; (3) training; and (4) performance appraisals. This section implies that managers periodically face special human resource problems, such as integrating female workers holding non-traditional jobs, that force them to complement these steps with additional activities.

BACK TO THE CASE

The last step in providing appropriate human resources at Fairchild Industries is performance appraisal. This means that the contributions that Fairchild employees make to the attainment of management system objectives must be evaluated. As with the training effort, performance appraisal at Fairchild should focus on more established employees as well as on new employees.

Charlie Collis probably would have benefited from a performance appraisal from company president Edward Uhl during the Thunderbolt project. Collis's appraisal would have stressed his activities on the job and his effectiveness in accomplishing job objectives—namely, building the Thunderbolt attack plane to the Air Force's satisfaction. An objective appraisal would have provided Collis with tactful, constructive criticism that might have helped increase his productivity. Handled properly, Collis's appraisal would have been not

a reward or a punishment but rather an opportunity to make him more valuable to Fairchild. Had Collis been given an objective, productive analysis of his performance, he might have been able to complete the Thunderbolt contract to the satisfaction of Fairchild and the Air Force, rather than being taken off the project.

In addition to giving performance appraisals to their employees as a means of maintaining appropriate human resources, Fairchild Industries will probably have to take special pre-hire and post-hire steps to achieve maximum organizational benefits from women working in non-traditional jobs. If Fairchild addresses these issues, in addition to following the generally accepted steps of recruitment, selection, and training discussed earlier, it will be better able to provide appropriate human resources within the company.

Action Summary

Reread the learning objectives that follow. Each objective is followed by questions. Answering these questions accurately will help you to retain the most important concepts discussed in this chapter. After answering each question, check your answer with the answer key at the end of this chapter. (*Hint*: If you have doubt regarding the correct response, consult the page that follows the answer.)

From studying this chapter, I will attempt to acquire: **Circle:**

1. **An overall understanding of how appropriate human resources can be provided for the organization.**
   a. An appropriate human resource is an individual whose qualifications are matched to job specifications.   T, F
   b. The term *appropriate human resources* refers to: (a) finding the right number of people to fill positions; (b) individuals being satisfied with their jobs; (c) individuals who help the organization to achieve management system objectives; (d) individuals who are ineffective; (e) none of the above.   a, b, c, d, e

2. **An appreciation for the relationship among recruitment efforts, an open position, sources of human resources, and the law.**
   a. The process of narrowing a large number of candidates to a smaller field is: (a) rushing; (b) recruitment; (c) selection; (d) enlistment; (e) enrollment.   a, b, c, d, e
   b. The characteristics of the individual who should be hired for the job are indicated by the: (a) job analysis; (b) job specification; (c) job description; (d) job review; (e) job identification.   a, b, c, d, e

3. **Insights on the use of tests and assessment centres in employee selection.**
   a. The level of skill or knowledge an individual possesses in a particular area is measured by: (a) aptitude tests; (b) achievement tests; (c) acuity tests; (d) assessment tests; (e) vocational interest tests.   a, b, c, d, e
   b. Which of the following guidelines does *not* apply when tests are being used in selecting potential employees: (a) the tests should be both valid and reliable; (b) the tests should be non-discriminatory in nature; (c) the tests should not be the sole source of information for determining whether or not someone is to be hired; (d) such factors as potential and desire to obtain a position should not be assessed subjectively; (e) none of the above—all are important guidelines.   a, b, c, d, e

4. **An understanding of how the training process operates.**
   a. Four steps involved in training individuals are: (1) designing the training program; (2) evaluating the training program; (3) determining training needs; (4) administering the training program. The correct sequence for taking these steps is:
   (a) 1, 3, 2, 4
   (b) 3, 4, 1, 2
   (c) 2, 1, 3, 4
   (d) 3, 1, 4, 2
   (e) none of the above   a, b, c, d, e
   b. The lecture offers learners an excellent opportunity to clarify meanings and ask questions since communication is two-way.   T, F

5. **A concept of what performance appraisals are and how they can best be conducted.**

   a. Performance appraisals are important in an organization because they: (a) provide systematic judgments to support promotions; (b) provide a basis for coaching; (c) provide a basis for counselling; (d) let the subordinate know where he or she stands with the boss; (e) all of the above.

   b. To achieve the maximum benefit from performance evaluations, a manager should: (a) focus only on the negative aspects of performance; (b) punish the worker with negative feedback; (c) be as subjective as possible; (d) focus only on the positive aspects of performance; (e) use only constructive feedback.

6. **An appreciation for the complex situation involving women who are working in non-traditional jobs.**

   a. Pre-hire preparation focuses on helping hired female workers adapt to their new environment.

   b. One of the steps in phase two of the program to integrate women workers into the organization successfully is: (a) planning for technical training and for follow-up; (b) interview/selection training; (c) rap sessions with both men and women; (d) job analysis; (e) none of the above.

INTRODUCTORY CASE WRAP-UP

"Special Training at Fairchild Industries" (p. 248) and its related back-to-the-case sections were written to help you better understand the management concepts contained in this chapter. Answer the following discussion questions about this introductory case to further enrich your understanding of the chapter content:

1. How important is the training of employees to an organization such as Fairchild Industries? Explain.

2. What actions besides training must an organization like Fairchild take to make employees as productive as possible?
3. How easy would it be to evaluate the effectiveness of the training program that Charlie Collis was conducting at Fairchild Industries? Explain.

Issues for Review and Discussion

1. What is the difference between appropriate and inappropriate human resources?
2. List and define the four major steps in providing appropriate human resources for the organization.
3. What is the purpose of recruitment?
4. How are job analysis, job description, and job specification related?
5. List the advantages of promotion from within.
6. Compare and contrast the management inventory card, the position replacement form, and the management manpower replacement chart.

7. List three sources of human resources outside the organization. How can these sources be tapped?
8. Does the Canadian Human Rights Act influence organizational recruitment practices? If so, how?
9. Describe the role of the Public Service Commission.
10. Can affirmative action programs be useful in recruitment? Explain.
11. Define *selection*.
12. What is the difference between aptitude tests and achievement tests?
13. Describe three guidelines for using tests in the selection process.
14. What are assessment centres?
15. List and define the four main steps of the training process.
16. Explain two possible ways of determining organizational training needs.
17. What are the differences between the lecture and programmed learning as alternative methods of transmitting information in the training program?
18. On-the-job training methods include coaching, position rotation, and special project committees. Explain how each of these methods works.
19. What are performance appraisals, and why should they be used?
20. If someone asked your advice on how to conduct performance appraisals, describe in detail what you would say.
21. What pre-hire preparation and post-hire activities can be performed to integrate female workers holding non-traditional jobs into the organization?

Sources of Additional Information

Alpander, Guvenc G. *Human Resources Management Planning*. New York: Amacom, 1982.

Brinkerhoff, Derick W., and Rosabeth Moss Kanter. "Appraising the Performance of Performance Appraisal." *Sloan Management Review* (Spring 1980): 3–16.

Chan, Dr. K.H. "Decision Support System for Human Resource Management." *Journal of Systems Management* 35 (April 1984): 17–25.

Cummings, William Theodore, and Mark R. Edwards. "How to Evaluate Your Sales Force." *Business* 34 (April/May/June 1984): 30–36.

Drucker, Peter F. *The Effective Executive*. New York: Harper & Row, 1967.

Franklin, William H., Jr. "Why Training Fails." *Administrative Management* 42 (July 1981): 42–43, 72–74.

Friedman, Martin G. "Ten Steps to Objective Appraisals." *Personnel Journal* 65 (June 1986): 66–71.

Gordon, Judith R. *Human Resource Management: A Practical Approach*. Boston: Allyn and Bacon, 1986.

Hollmann, Robert W., and Mary Ellen Campbell. "Communications Strategies for Improving HRM Effectiveness." *Personnel Administrator* 29 (July 1984): 93–98.

Lebreton, Preston. "The Management Awareness Concept: A Missing Link in the Evolving Science of Management." *Managerial Planning* 30 (July/August 1981): 12–17.

Lopez, Felix M., Jr. *Personnel Interviewing: Theory and Practice*. New York: McGraw-Hill, 1965.

Lowe, Terry R. "Eight Ways to Ruin a Performance Review." *Personnel Journal* 65 (January 1986): 60.

O'Callaghan, John C., Jr. "Human Resource Development." *Managerial Planning* 30 (July/August 1981): 38–42.

"Regaining the Competitive Edge." *Personnel Administrator* 31 (July 1986): 34–45.

Regel, Roy W., and Robert W. Hollmann. "Gauging Performance Objectively." *Personnel Administrator* 32 (June 1987): 74–81.

Rowland, Kendrith M., Gerald R. Ferris, and Jay L. Sherman. *Current Issues in Personnel Management*. Boston: Allyn & Bacon, 1983.

Teel, Kenneth S. "Performance Appraisal: Current Trends, Persistent Progress." *Personnel Journal* (April 1980): 296–301, 316.

Wallace, Marc J. *Administering Human Resources*. New York: Random House, 1982.

Wexley, Kenneth N., and Gary A. Yukl. *Organizational Behavior and Personnel Psychology*. Homewood, Ill.: Richard D. Irwin, 1984.

Notes

1. Arch Patton, "The Coming Scramble for Executive Talent," *Harvard Business Review* (May/June 1967): 155–71.

2. Thomas J. Murray, "The Coming Glut in Executives," *Dun's Review* (May 1977): 64. An even more recent article pointing out this trend is "Slackening in Executive Demand," *Personnel Management* 17 (September 1985): 74.

3. Fred K. Foulkes, "How Top Nonunion Companies Manage Employees," *Harvard Business Review* (September/October 1981): 90.

4. John Perham, "Management Succession: A Hard Game to Play," *Dun's Review* (April 1981): 54–55, 58.

5. Walter S. Wikstrom, "Developing Managerial Competence: Concepts, Emerging Practices," *Studies in Personnel Policy*, no. 189, National Industrial Conference Board, 95–105.

6. Public Service Commission of Canada, *Annual Report 1986*, 21.

7. For more discussion on the stages of the selection process, see David J. Cherrington, *Personnel Management: The Management of Human Resources* (Dubuque, Iowa: Wm. C. Brown Publishers, 1987), 186–231.

8. This section is based on Andrew F. Sikula, *Personnel Administration and Human Resource Management* (New York: Wiley, 1976), 188–90.

9. For information on various tests available, see O.K. Buros, ed., *The Seventh Mental Measurements Yearbook* (Highland Park, N.J.: Gryphon Press, 1978).

10. Gene E. Burton, Dev S. Pathak, and David B. Burton, "Recruiting, Testing and Selecting: Delicate EEOC Areas," *Management World* (October 1976): 30.

11. D.W. Bray and D.L. Grant, "The Assessment Centre in the Measurement of Potential for Business Management," *Psychological Monographs* 80, no. 17 (1966): 1–27.

12. James C. Hyatt, "More Concerns Use 'Assessment Centers' to Gauge Employees' Managerial Abilities," *Wall Street Journal*, January 3, 1974, 15.

13. Barry M. Cohen, "Assessment Centres," *Supervisory Management* (June 1975): 30. See also T.J. Hanson and J.C. Balestreri-Sepro, "An Alternative to Interviews: Pre-employment Assessment Process," *Personnel Journal* (June 1985): 114.

14. For information about strengths and weaknesses of assessment centres, see C.W. Millard and Sheldon Pinsky, "Assessing the Assessment Center," *Personnel Administrator* (May 1980): 85–88.

15. Ann Howard, "An Assessment of Assessment Centers," *Academy of Management Journal* 17 (March 1974): 117.

16. Gordon L. Lippitt, "Criteria for Evaluating Human Resource Development," *Training and Development Journal* (October 1976): 3.

17. Bernard Bass and James Vaughn, *Training in Industry: The Management of Learning* (Belmont, Calif.: Wadsworth, 1966).

18. Bass and Vaughn, *Training in Industry*.

19. Leonard Silvern, "Training: Man-Man and Man-Machine Communications," in *Systems Psychology*, ed. Kenyon DeGreen (New York: McGraw-Hill, 1970), 383–405.

20. For more information on training techniques, see Cherrington, *Personnel Management*, 304–36.

21. Samuel C. Certo, "The Experiential Exercise Situation: A Comment on Instructional Role and Pedagogy Evaluation," *Academy of Management Review* (July 1976): 113–16.

22. For more information on instructional roles in various situations, see Bernard Keys, "The Management of Learning Grid for Management Development," *Academy of Management Review* (April 1977): 289–97.

23. For more information on the performance appraisal process, see Robert L. Mathis and John H. Jackson, "Appraisal of Human Resources," in their *Personnel: Human Resource Management* (St. Paul, Minn.: West Publishing, 1985), 337–66.

24. Douglas McGregor, "An Uneasy Look at Performance Appraisal," *Harvard Business Review* (September/October 1972): 133–34.

25. Harold Koontz, "Making Managerial Appraisal Effective," *California Management Review* 15 (Winter 1972): 46–55.

26. Thomas L. Whisler, "Appraisal as a Management Tool," in *Performance Appraisal: Research and Practice*, ed. Thomas L. Whisler and Shirley F. Harper (New York: Holt, Rinehart & Winston, 1962).

27. William J. Birch, "Performance Appraisal: One Company's Experience," *Personnel Journal* (June 1981): 456–60.

28. George A. Rider, "Performance Review: A Mixed Bag," *Harvard Business Review* (July/August 1973): 61–67.

29. John D. Colby and Ronald L. Wallace, "The Art of Leveling with Subordinates about Their Performance," *Supervisory Management* (December 1975): 26–29.

30. Women's Bureau, New York City, U.S. Department of Labor, 1980.

31. "The Hardships That Blue-Collar Women Face," *Business Week*, August 14, 1978, 88.

32. The remainder of this section is based primarily on Nancy R. Brunner, "Blue-Collar Women," *Personnel Journal* (April 1981): 279–82.

33. Brunner, "Blue-Collar Women."

34. Brunner, "Blue-Collar Women."

Action Summary Answer Key

1. a. F, p. 249
   b. c, p. 249
2. a. b, p. 250
   b. b, p. 250

3. a. b, p. 264
   b. d, p. 265
4. a. d, p. 266
   b. F, p. 268

5. a. e, pp. 271–272
   b. e, pp. 272–273
6. a. F, p. 273
   b. c, p. 274

UNIONS: FRIEND OR FOE?

To join or not to join? This is very often the question employees are confronted with, especially when the going gets tough in the workplace. More than just a signature on a card, the decision to join a union often involves a multitude of issues connected to the employee's work situation. Seeing what can happen when workers join a union, one sometimes wonders why anyone does. First-contract strikes, for example, are becoming increasingly predictable catastrophes. It is the tense early days of unionization, however, which provide the best place to look for an understanding of the whole process. Why do workers join unions when strife has become a likely, if not inevitable, outcome?

Financial reward, although the most obvious reason, may not necessarily be the most important. According to Cameron Nelson, business agent for the Brewery, Malt and Softdrink Workers, whose unionized members often make double the wages of those who are unorganized, says, "If you go in cold, where there are no complaints or disillusion with management, you'll probably get turned down. But if the company has been mismanaged, has promised something and not come through and so forth, then they'll be ready and will probably come to you."

"To join or not to join?"

So why do employees join? Two phrases consistently come up as a response: "We want to stand up," and "We want to have a voice." The genesis for such sentiments may come from poor treatment from a supervisor, anger about favouritism and unwarranted promotions, or from being told once too often, "If you don't like it, there's the door." It could even be a matter of workers feeling they're being taken for granted; in response they want to stand up and be noticed, to speak up and be heard. Finally, underneath it all may be the fundamental indignity of being the ones who are hired and fired at the behest—if not the whim—of an employer over whom they have little or no comparable power.

The motives people have for joining unions frequently have little to do with unions themselves. Some workers might even be hostile to the unions. "We don't want to join a union, you know," they'll often say. "We just want to get together and stand up to the company. A union though, that's something else. They take your money and force you to go on strike." Thus the issue is not unionization per se. Management attitudes often reflect the same understanding. The most bitter negotiations are frequently not over money but over management rights and prerogatives. Many a company has been prepared to give far more in dollars than it is ready to cede in control. The self-assertion on both sides is implicitly at stake.

Furthermore, there are those who maintain that joining a union is simply a reflection of the workers' desire to exercise their democratic, or perhaps even political rights in a broad sense. Whatever impels such an action, joining a union is a simple act in itself. The long-range implications connected to unionization, however, are more complex—for both workers and management. A popular anecdote on just this issue concerns a real-life incident which occurred during one of Canada's most horrendous first-contract strikes—that by Toronto's Artistic Woodwork in 1973: Two policemen cruising in a patrol car called over one of the strikers, a Greek immigrant known as Zizi. "How smart are you?" asked one of them. "Why?" asked Zizi. "Well, how much money have you lost already in this strike? Don't you see no matter what you get in a settlement you'll never make up what you've lost?" (This is very probably a calculation that has passed through the mind of anyone who ever struck for weeks, not to say months.) "I know," said Zizi. "So?" needled the officer. "But I think for the future," he replied.

To join or not to join? The choice lies not only in the hands of workers, but also within the jurisdiction of employers. Consequently, if dignity and self-respect are the real reasons workers join unions, could employers circumvent unionization by treating their work force with more dignity and respect? This thought has probably occurred to many a manager. But the situation is like the dependent neurotic who decides to behave independently in order to please his therapist: somehow he misses the point. Similarly, if employers confer dignity and respect on workers simply in order to prevent them from asserting their dignity and respect (by joining a union), is the gesture worth anything? Why *do* employees join unions anyway?

DISCUSSION ISSUES

1. What should unions and workers' attempts to organize them tell management? How does this relate to an organization's policy on human resources? Explain.
2. How does an organizing attempt and a union's presence affect the organization's performance? Elaborate on the possible advantages and disadvantages for the company connected to the existence of a union.
3. Based on what has been given in the case, how can organizations pre-empt an organizing drive? Explain.

Based on "A Dignified Response," by Rick Salutin in *Canadian Business*, October 1986. Used with permission.

ORGANIZATIONAL CHANGE AND STRESS

STUDENT LEARNING OBJECTIVES

From studying this chapter, I will attempt to acquire:

1. A working definition of *changing an organization*.
2. An understanding of the relative importance of change and stability to an organization.
3. Some ability to know what type of change should be made within an organization.
4. An appreciation for why individuals affected by a change should be considered when the change is being made.
5. Some facility in evaluating change.
6. An understanding of how organizational change and stress are related.

CHAPTER OUTLINE

GM'S GREAT DIVIDE

Roger B. Smith got off to a rocky start in his first year as the chairman of General Motors Corporation. Early in his reign, GM made some strategic goofs in crucial labour negotiations with the United Auto Workers, and Smith himself alienated a number of company VIPs by attempting to limit an annual shareholders' meeting to only three hours. On the positive side, however, Smith guided the giant automaker through a bruising recession and in recent years has helped the company reach profits of over $3.5 billion.

Soon, however, the soft-spoken Smith is expected to make a move even more stunning than his company's recent record profits. He will propose the most revolutionary change in the way GM runs its business since the company was restructured in the 1920s by organizational genius Alfred P. Sloan.

At an upcoming meeting in New York, Smith will ask the GM board of directors to approve a carefully crafted proposal to reduce the company's five famous car divisions—Chevrolet, Pontiac, Oldsmobile, Buick, and Cadillac—to only two, each larger than either the Ford Motor Company or the Chrysler Corporation. Smith's ideas calls for the new Chevrolet-Pontiac division to pro-

duce and sell only GM's smaller cars and the Buick-Oldsmobile-Cadillac division to handle the larger models.

Beyond this merging of names for the new divisions, Smith's proposal will change the corporate face of General Motors in other important ways. Since the early 1920s, such key activities as design, engineering, and marketing were directed essentially by staffs at the top corporate level. Under Smith's new proposal, these activities will be handled by separate and independent staffs at the two new divisions. For each division, the buck will stop at the two new executive vice-presidents—the individuals who will head each division and be strictly accountable to GM's top brass for the division's profits and performance.

Smith's proposal calls for these organizational changes to be implemented over a three-year period. If the proposed organizational structure is adopted, most experts agree, the "new" General Motors will be a leaner, tougher competitor in a domestic market that it already dominates. This would be bad news not only for Ford and Chrysler, but for Japan as well.

Based on "GM Plans a Great Divide," in *Newsweek*, January 9, 1984.

What's Ahead

Roger B. Smith, the General Motors chairman in the introductory case, has the main role in deciding what changes to make within his company. Smith also is held accountable for implementing changes successfully. In this regard, Smith and other managers facing the task of modifying an organization could use the information in this chapter on the fundamentals of changing an organization, the factors to consider when changing an organization, and organizational change and stress.

FUNDAMENTALS OF CHANGING AN ORGANIZATION

Thus far, discussion in this "Organizing" section of the text has centred on the fundamentals of organizing, furnishing appropriate human resources for the organization, authority, delegation, and responsibility. This chapter focuses on changing an organization. The fundamental principles involved in changing an organization are discussed in the paragraphs that follow.

Defining "Changing an Organization"

Changing an organization is the process of modifying an existing organization. The purpose of organizational modifications is to increase organizational effectiveness; that is, the extent to which an organization accomplishes its objectives. These modifications can involve virtually any organizational segment and typically include changing the lines of organizational authority, the levels of responsibility held by various organization members, and the established lines of organizational communication.

Most managers agree that, if an organization is to be successful, it must change continually in response to significant developments, such as changes in customer needs, technological breakthroughs, and new government regulations. The study of organizational change is extremely important because all managers at all organizational levels are faced throughout their careers with the task of changing their organization. According to a study by Ronald Daniel, large North American manufacturers make major changes in their organizations approximately once every two years.[1] Managers who can make changes successfully are highly valued in organizations of all types.[2]

Many managers consider change to be so critical to the success of the organization that they encourage employees to continually search for areas in which beneficial organizational change can be made. At General Motors, for example, employees are provided with a "think list" to encourage them to develop ideas for organizational change and to remind them that change is extremely important to the continued success of GM. The "think list" contains the following questions:[3]

1. Can a machine be used to do a better or faster job?
2. Can the fixture now in use be improved?
3. Can materials handling for the machine be improved?

Existing organizations are often modified to increase organizational effectiveness.

Organizations must change continually.

Employees can provide ideas for change.

4. Can a special tool be used to combine the operations?
5. Can the quality of the part being produced be improved by changing the sequence of the operation?
6. Can the material used be cut or trimmed differently for greater economy or efficiency?
7. Can the operation be made safer?
8. Can paperwork regarding this job be eliminated?
9. Can established procedures be simplified?

Change Versus Stability

Stability should complement change.

In addition to organizational change, some degree of stability is a prerequisite for long-term organizational success. Figure 11.1 presents a model developed by Hellriegel and Slocum that shows the relative importance of change and stability to organizational survival. Although these authors use the word *adaptation* in their model rather than *change*, the two terms are essentially synonymous. This model stresses that the greatest probability of organizational survival and growth exists when both stability and adaptation are high within the organization (number 3 on the model). The organization without stability to complement or supplement change is at a definite disadvantage. When stability is low, the probability for organizational survival and growth declines. Change after change without stability typically results in confusion and employee stress.[4]

FIGURE 11.1   Adaptation, stability, and organizational survival.

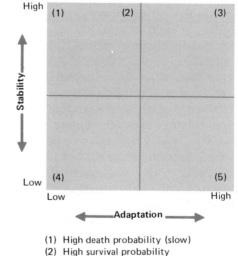

(1) High death probability (slow)
(2) High survival probability
(3) High survival and growth probability
(4) Certainty of death (quick)
(5) Certainty of death (quick)

BACK TO THE CASE

If Roger Smith, in his deliberations on changing General Motors, followed the recommendations made in this first section of the chapter, then he considered only those modifications that would further facilitate the accomplishment of GM's objectives. Smith probably realized that, if GM was to have continued success, he would have to modify the organization a number of times over the long term. In fact, appropriate change is so important to GM that Smith may have considered initiating some type of program that would encourage employees to submit their ideas on increasing the effectiveness of the company. When considering possible changes, however, Smith undoubtedly realized that some level of stability was also necessary if his company was to survive and grow over the long term.

FACTORS TO CONSIDER WHEN CHANGING AN ORGANIZATION

How managers deal with the major factors to be considered when changing an organization determines to a great extent how successful an organizational change will be. These major factors are: (1) the change agent; (2) determining what should be changed; (3) the type of change to make; (4) individuals affected by the change; and (5) evaluation of change. Although the following sections discuss each of these factors individually, Figure 11.2 makes the point that their collective influence ultimately determines the success of a change.

FIGURE 11.2   The collective influence of five major factors on the success of changing an organization.

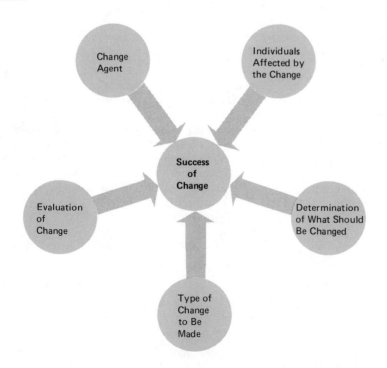

The Change Agent

A change agent is an individual inside or outside the organization who tries to effect change.

Perhaps the most important factor to be considered by managers when changing an organization is determining who will be the change agent. The term **change agent** refers to anyone inside or outside the organization who tries to effect change.[5] The change agent might be a self-designated manager within the organization or possibly an outside consultant hired because of a special expertise in a particular area. Although in reality the change agent may not be a manager, the terms *manager* and *change agent* are used synonymously throughout this chapter.

A change agent needs special skills to be successful.

Several special skills are necessary to be a successful change agent, including the ability to determine how a change should be made, to solve change-related problems, and to use behavioural science tools to influence people appropriately during the change. Perhaps the most overlooked skill necessary to be a successful change agent is deciding how much change organization members can withstand. As indicated by the following excerpt, too much change can be very disturbing:

> Millions of psychologically normal people will experience an abrupt collision with the future when they fall victim to tomorrow's most menacing malady— the disease of change. Unable to keep up with the supercharged pace of change, brought to the edge of breakdown by insistent demands to adapt to novelty, many will plunge into future shock. For them, the future will arrive too soon.[6]

Overall, managers should choose change agents who possess the most expertise in the areas suggested by the special skills. A potentially beneficial change for the organization might not result in any advantages if the wrong person is designated to make the change.

BACK TO THE CASE

Since Roger Smith has the main role in deciding what changes to make at General Motors as well as actually implementing these changes, he is a change agent. Smith probably designated himself change agent because of his ability to determine how the particular type of change within his company should be made and how to solve organizational problems that could arise as a result of it. In order to implement his plan, Smith must recognize that one thing he needs to do is form new, independent departments to handle design, engineering, and marketing. He also must realize that he will need to deal with problems that arise when the two new divisions, each with its own executives, are formed.

As change agent, Smith also has the ability to use behavioural science tools to influence organization members during the change and to determine how much change these members can withstand. Smith should know how to influence his staff so members learn to work together in their new divisions, and he also must realize that his plan should be implemented gradually so employees will not be overwhelmed by the change. Over all, Smith probably believes that these abilities will enable him to make successful changes at General Motors.

Determining What Should Be Changed

Another major factor managers should consider is exactly what should be changed within the organization. In general, managers should make changes that increase organizational effectiveness.

FIGURE 11.3 Determination of organizational effectiveness by interrelationship between people, technological, and structural factors.

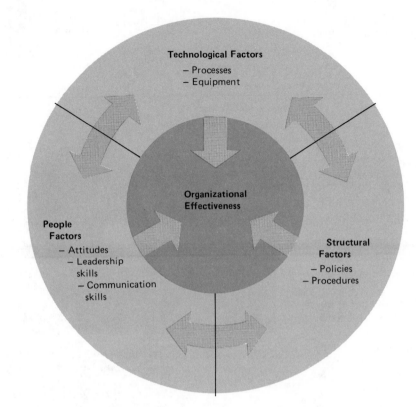

According to Giegold and Craig, organizational effectiveness is primarily the result of organizational activities centring around three main classes of factors: (1) people; (2) structure; and (3) technology.[7] **People factors** are defined as attitudes, leadership skills, communication skills, and all other characteristics of the human resources within the organization. Organizational controls, such as policies and procedures, constitute **structural factors**, while **technological factors** are any types of equipment or processes that assist organization members in the performance of their jobs.

For an organization to maximize effectiveness, appropriate people must be matched with appropriate technology and appropriate structure. Thus, people factors, technological factors, and structural factors are not independent determinants of organizational effectiveness. Instead, as Figure 11.3 shows, organizational effectiveness is determined by the relationship among these three factors.

Two commonly used steps managers can take to help determine what changes would increase the appropriateness of the people-structure-technology relationship are conducting an internal organizational diagnosis and conducting an external organizational diagnosis.

The Management in Action feature for this chapter illustrates the factors and processes involved in determining and responding to a changing environment. It provides an overview of the various types of changes which can occur in an organization, both internal and external.

People, structural, and technological factors must be appropriately matched to maximize organizational effectiveness.

MANAGING IN A CHANGING ENVIRONMENT

*Some ideas of John A. Brindle, President
of Sun Life Assurance Co. (Canada)*

CORPORATE PROFILE

Sun Life Assurance Company of Canada was incorporated under the laws of Canada and opened for business in 1871. It is a mutual life insurance company which offers a broad range of financial services and products for groups and individuals through the parent company and its subsidiaries. These include life and health insurance, disability insurance, dental plans, annuities, pension and investment management, savings and investment instruments, financial planning, and related services. Sun Life also provides funds for private placements, mortgages, and loans.

The company is active in the retrocession market on an international basis as well. It has more than 3 100 field representatives and more than 4 500 staff in its international organization. Sales and service offices are located in major cities in its principal countries of operation — Canada, the United States, and Great Britain — and in Bermuda, Hong Kong, Ireland, and the Philippines. With assets of nearly $16 billion, additional assets under management of $13.6 billion, and $123 billion of life insurance in force, Sun Life is one of the largest life insurance companies in the world.

INTRODUCTION

Sun Life president John A. Brindle concedes that his experience with the company has certainly convinced him of change's inevitability. Not so its constancy, however: "The rate and scope of change in our environment in the mid-1980s seems if anything to be accelerating." Accordingly, the dominant factor affecting much of management thinking is the need to develop a more responsive, sophisticated, and less traditional approach to managing a large multinational corporation, as the company operates with increasing frequency within a turbulent world where it can no longer be confident that established trends will continue. Like most companies, Sun Life has found it necessary to adapt itself to the new realities and to come to some new understanding both of itself and of the world in which it functions. There is no question that Sun Life has changed substantially over the past few years.

The single most significant thing top management has found in shaping Sun Life's responses to the evolving

"Sun Life president John A. Brindle concedes that his experience with the company has certainly convinced him of change's inevitability."

environment is a change in management's perception of planning itself. According to Brindle, "We had previously worked with the implicit assumption that there was an ideal world to which we should respond with an ideal plan. We now recognize that the world will not stand still long enough for us to describe it definitely, let alone ideally." Thus it is not possible to devise a single, appropriate, corporate response. As a result, management has come to expect both more and less from their planning processes: certainty is out, but quicker and more varied responses are in. Sun Life management has been forced to move from the comfort and security of a planning concept meant to show the company how to extend its business trend lines into the future, to the more complex and sophisticated concept of quickly identifying significant internal and external trends and providing profitable responses.

The following sections present a number of important issues that Sun Life is facing and must necessarily respond to. An issue in this instance is defined as "a condition or pressure, either internal or external to an organization, that, if it continues, will have a significant effect on the functioning of the organization or its future interests."

IMPACT OF CHANGING CONDITIONS ON PROFITABLE GROWTH

Given that insurance is a relatively mature sector in the fast-growing financial services industry, with the likelihood of real economic growth in the region of 2 to 3 percent only, Sun Life has had to take a closer look at the nature of its business than it had previously. Its resulting analysis indicates two distinct sectors of corporate business, each with its own characteristics and each requiring different management responses.

The traditional core businesses consist of individual life insurance, group life and health insurance, and group pensions. Accounting for about 90 percent of Sun Life's business and assets, these absorb most of the company's management time and attention. Brindle classifies these as "momentum" kinds of business: "We have them rolling well at the moment, but we need to ensure that nothing gets in the way to impede their progress and slow them down." Continued success in this sector requires almost compulsive attention to detail. To maintain or increase momentum, the company must ensure that the businesses are staffed with skilled, high-energy, results-oriented executive and sales personnel. An ability to detect and counter initiatives by competitors, and resources that encourage and support new and continuing business will be necessary and essential. The same applies to cost-effectiveness and productivity.

Meanwhile, the second sector of Sun Life's businesses contains the new areas into which it has been moving in response to the need for growth and the opportunities which have been available. Here the new markets and new product lines provide diversification and a new way of doing business. Skills required to identify and establish Sun Life in these new areas are somewhat different from those required for the core businesses; overall, greater attention to factors external to the basic insurance industry and a more flexible view of the world and Sun Life's role in it are required. As well, long-standing policies that have guided the company must be questioned.

Having two distinct sectors in its business has led Sun Life to divide management attention more clearly than before, the prime reason being the recognition that nothing must dilute the crucial efforts of the managers in the core businesses to maintain the required momentum. This recognition has also trickled into the company's planning process, which is now divided into three distinct but related parts:

1. **Directional planning** is a long-range, high-level planning procedure that looks at the company's businesses, expansion opportunities, and long-term goals. It assesses the company's overall mission, competitive advantages and disadvantages, main areas of business interest, and the ways in which the company must strengthen itself for success.

2. **Strategic planning** involves "figuring out" how the company can achieve its agreed-upon direction. Strategic planning occurs both at the corporate and national levels. In this process, the company's business development planning is quite separate from the planning for the on-going, core business.

3. **Operational planning** refers to the development of the company's annual fiscal plan, which is aimed at setting up and funding the principal projects and programs necessary to maintain momentum in the core businesses.

These are but some of the ways by which Sun Life has learned to look after itself in response to the need to maintain profitability in the future and thereby increase effectiveness.

SHIFTING PATTERNS OF DEMAND FOR FINANCIAL SERVICES

A number of macro-social factors—such as the increased urbanization of populations, emerging minorities, the growth of two-income and single-parent households, changing attitudes, values, and family economics—have led to a distinct change in the pattern of financial services that consumers are looking for today. They've also led to changes in the regulations governing the industry. Such environmental changes take on even greater importance given the competitive nature of the business.

In general, there is now a greater demand for products that place more emphasis on savings and investment rather than on the insurance element. This has led Sun Life to develop more products that have a large investment component, to enter the mutual fund arena, and to emphasize annuity and pension products. John Brindle recognizes, however, that it is insufficient merely to introduce new products; what is more important is to ensure the company's position in the marketplace. As a result, top management has had to refocus and reposition the company with these changing conditions in mind, re-evaluating the company's basic activities and policies with regard to its after-sales service, marketing approaches, and all the organizational and managerial factors which affect the company's responsiveness and flexibility.

SHIFT IN DEMAND TO LOW-MARGIN/HIGH-VOLUME PRODUCTS

New products with lower margins, combined with strong competition in the markets, dictate that more attention is paid to the company's organization and practices, specifically, economy and efficiency. Since selling is one of the largest components of product cost, all aspects of product distribution have come under close scrutiny. Not content with just revising long-standing policies, Sun Life has also looked at various elements (compensation practices, training, point-of-sale support, after sales service, supervision) that contribute to an effective, high-yielding sales force, and more care is now being placed on productivity improvement. In the process, professional advice has been sought, employees have been surveyed, and certain productivity measures (such as automation) have been introduced.

PROSPECTS OUTSIDE OF CANADA

Given the company's history of international expansion and the significant growth opportunities represented by the substantially larger markets outside of Canada, Sun Life is looking to its foreign operations to provide major growth for the company in the future. The turbulent nature of markets everywhere, however, has led to an increased need to monitor international economic and political trends. For instance, good economic opportunities are to be had in various Pacific Rim countries. Many are the inducements encouraging Western companies to export jobs to those lower-wage areas. Continuous monitoring and assessment, however, is required to adjust Sun Life's posture in each of these markets in order to match the company's needs and abilities with the opportunities available.

According to John Brindle, top management's response to these factors has led to a revision (to some degree) in the way it looks at Sun Life. "We are changing our perspective and management structure from that of an international company to that of a decentralized multinational." As a consequence, head office is now concentrating more on gathering and analyzing information and on long-range planning, while devolving more operational autonomy to its various national companies around the world. Local operations have been restructured along business-unit lines to facilitate market and financial-performance measurements. Heavy emphasis has been put on training to improve the ability of local managers to identify business opportunities and respond accordingly. Whenever appropriate, and wherever their contribution will enhance the results, head office will involve local managers in the strategic planning process, thereby effectively helping to stimulate and support local operations rather than running the company's international businesses from Canada.

ADVANCES IN TECHNOLOGY

Adequate current information is of key importance in an industry such as insurance where one is dealing with intangible products and from which customers derive delayed gratification. Information is the common ingredient in all aspects of the business and an ability to communicate and use the information is essential to profitability. This being the case, the development of the new computer technologies has had an enormous impact on the industry. Data processing development, for instance, has helped Sun Life stay on top of its increasing business and the workflow that results from it. It helped mechanize various administrative processes and thereby increase productivity.

This use of technology to contain costs is an ongoing and growing feature of the industry. Given the importance of information technology in determining the health of the organization, Sun Life has given it a high priority throughout the company and has formulated a senior management "systems steering committee" to ensure that this subject receives executive attention. Responsibilities include the setting of priorities in systems development, strategy and strategic planning, and reevaluating the way the company is currently organized to handle the development, maintenance, and enhancement of systems.

THE EVOLVING LEGISLATIVE AND REGULATORY ENVIRONMENT

Since financial institutions, by their very nature, are entrusted with the custody and management of other people's money, it is only natural that governments have taken a keen interest in the way the industry operates, and has, through legislation and regulations, laid down a number of guidelines and prohibitions that define both the universe within which companies work and the way they may conduct their business. In particular, governments regulate two major aspects of financial institutions: (1) **corporate powers**, which are the range of activities in which a company may engage, the scope of products it may offer, and the sorts of subsidiaries or related businesses it may own; and (2) **financial management**, which concerns the reserves and capitals that must be maintained, the kinds of investment instruments that may be purchased and the relative proportion of each, and restrictions on the proportion of ownership allowed in certain other companies. Other government actions, such as changes in personal and corporate taxation, as well as changes in certain social legislation, can also have an immediate effect on the industry.

All of this has led Sun Life to put greater emphasis on its government relations activities. The company is closely monitoring and participating in the consultation process which the government of Canada has instituted in an active attempt to control its environment. Elsewhere, the company has increased its political gathering capabilities and has started looking at itself through the eyes of government in an attempt to anticipate action to come.

CONCLUSION

The above are but some responses to the important external issues with which Sun Life must deal. They involve an increased emphasis on information, longer-range planning, and decentralized activity, and a true reevaluation of the company from a particular perspective. The multidimensional nature of Sun Life's activities brings added complexity to the organization, a complexity which is well understood by its executives. "At Sun Life, we recognize that maintaining our position in the industry and serving the best interests of our policyholders require constant change and adaptation to the evolving world in which we find ourselves," says John Brindle. "There is no question that challenges will continue to arise: those who can change in response are those who will prosper. We are determined to prosper."

Based on "Managing in a Changing Environment: The Sun Life Experience," by John A. Brindle in *Business Quarterly*, Spring 1986. Used with permission of *Business Quarterly*, published by School of Business Administration, The University of Western Ontario, London.

The Type of Change to Make

People change, structural change, and technological change are three types of organizational changes.

The type of change to make is a third major factor managers should consider when changing an organization. Although managers can choose to change an organization in many different ways, most changes can be categorized as one of three types: (1) people change; (2) structural change; or (3) technological change. These three types obviously correspond to the three main determinants of organizational effectiveness. Each change is named for the one determinant that the change emphasizes over the other two. For example, **technological change** emphasizes modifying the level of technology within a management system. Since technological change often involves outside experts and highly technical language, structural change and people change are the two types discussed in more detail here.

Structural Change

Structural change primarily emphasizes increasing organizational effectiveness by changing controls that influence organization members during the performance of their jobs. The following sections further describe this approach and discuss matrix organizations (organizations modified to complete a special project) as an example of structural change.

Describing Structural Change

Structural change focuses on modifying organizational structure.

Structural change is aimed at increasing organizational effectiveness through modifications to existing organizational structure. These modifications can take several forms: (1) clarifying and defining jobs; (2) modifying organizational structure to fit the communication needs of the organization; and (3) decentralizing the organization to reduce the cost of coordination, increase the controllability of subunits, increase motivation, and gain greater flexibility.[8] Although structural change must include some consideration of people and technology to be successful, its primary focus is obviously on changing organizational structure. In general, managers choose to make structural changes within the organization if information gathered from internal and external organizational diagnoses indicates that the present organizational structure is the main cause of organizational ineffectiveness. The precise structural change managers make varies from situation to situation, of course.

Matrix Organizations

Matrix organizations are created to complete special projects.

Perhaps structural change is best illustrated by describing matrix organizations. According to C.J. Middleton, a **matrix organization** is a more traditional organization that is modified primarily for the purpose of completing some type of special project.[9] For this reason, matrix organizations are also called project organizations. The project itself may be either long term or short term, with employees needed to complete the project borrowed from various organizational segments.

John F. Mee has developed an excellent example showing how a more traditional organization can be changed into a matrix organization.[10] Figure 11.4 presents a portion of a traditional organizational structure divided primarily according to product line. Although this organizational design might be generally

FIGURE 11.4   Portion of a traditional organizational structure based primarily on product.

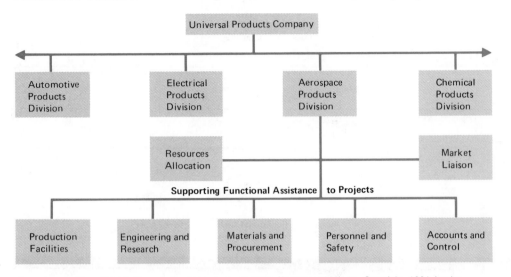

From John F. Mee, "Matrix Organization," *Business Horizons* (Summer 1964): 71. Copyright, 1964, by the Foundation for the School of Business at Indiana University. Reprinted by permission.

useful, managers could learn through internal organizational diagnosis that this design makes it impossible for organization members to give adequate attention to three government projects of extreme importance to long-term organizational success.

Figure 11.5 presents one way of changing this more traditional organizational structure into a matrix organization to facilitate completion of these three government projects. A manager would be appointed for each of the three projects and allocated personnel with appropriate skills to complete the project. The three project managers would have authority over personnel assigned to them and be accountable for the performance of those personnel. Each of the three project managers would be placed on the chart in Figure 11.5 in one of the three boxes labeled Pacific Project, Prairie Project, and Atlantic Project. As a result, work flow related to each project would go from right to left on the chart. After the projects were completed, the organization chart could be changed back to its original design, if that design is more advantageous.

There are several advantages and disadvantages to making structural changes such as those reflected by the matrix organization. Among the major advantages are the claims that such structural changes generally result in better control of a project, better customer relations, shorter project-development time, and lower project costs. Accompanying these advantages, however, are the claims that such structural changes also generally create more complex internal operations, encourage inconsistency in the application of company policy, and result in a more difficult situation to manage.[11] One point, however, is clear. For a matrix organization to be effective and efficient, organization members must be willing to learn and execute somewhat different organizational roles.[12] The significance of these advantages and disadvantages relative to the success of changing a specific organization obviously varies from situation to situation.

The significance of the advantages and disadvantages of matrix organizations varies from situation to situation.

FIGURE 11.5   Traditional organization chart transformed into matrix organization.

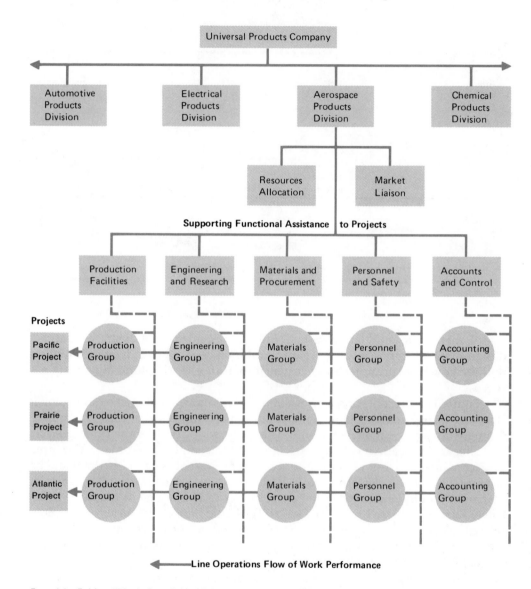

From John F. Mee, "Matrix Organization," *Business Horizons* (Summer 1964): 71. Copyright, 1964, by the Foundation for the School of Business at Indiana University. Reprinted by permission.

People Change

Although successful people change also involves some consideration of structure and technology, primary emphasis is on people. The following sections discuss people change and examine grid organization development, one commonly used means of attempting to change organization members.

Describing People Change

People change emphasizes increasing organizational effectiveness by changing organization members. The focus of this type of change is on such factors as modifying employees' attitudes and leadership skills. In general, managers should attempt to make this type of change when the results of organizational diagnoses indicate that human resources are the main cause of organizational ineffectiveness.

The process of people change can be referred to as **organization development (OD)**. Although OD focuses mainly on changing people, these changes are based on an overview of structure, technology, and all other organizational ingredients.[13] To demonstrate this organizational overview approach, Figure 11.6 shows both overt and covert organizational components considered during OD efforts. Overt factors are generally easily detectable and pictured as the tip of an organizational iceberg, while covert factors are usually more difficult to assess and therefore displayed as that part of the organizational iceberg that is "under water."

Organizational effectiveness can be increased by changing people's attitudes and leadership skills.

Organization development is the process of people change.

FIGURE 11.6   The organizational iceberg.

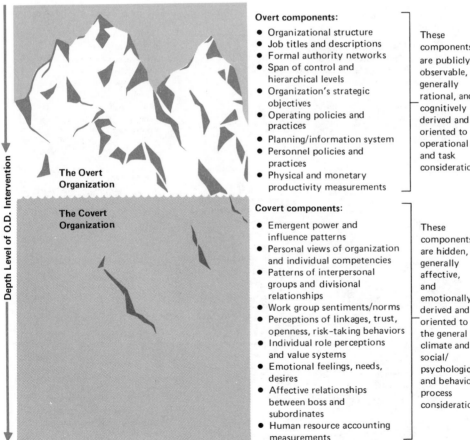

Depth Level of O.D. Intervention

The Overt Organization

The Covert Organization

Overt components:
- Organizational structure
- Job titles and descriptions
- Formal authority networks
- Span of control and hierarchical levels
- Organization's strategic objectives
- Operating policies and practices
- Planning/information system
- Personnel policies and practices
- Physical and monetary productivity measurements

These components are publicly observable, generally rational, and cognitively derived and oriented to operational and task considerations.

Covert components:
- Emergent power and influence patterns
- Personal views of organization and individual competencies
- Patterns of interpersonal groups and divisional relationships
- Work group sentiments/norms
- Perceptions of linkages, trust, openness, risk–taking behaviors
- Individual role perceptions and value systems
- Emotional feelings, needs, desires
- Affective relationships between boss and subordinates
- Human resource accounting measurements

These components are hidden, generally affective, and emotionally derived and oriented to the general climate and social/psychological and behavioral/process considerations.

From Richard J. Selfridge and Stanley I. Sokolik, "A Comprehensive View of Organization Development," p. 47, *MSU Business Topics* (Winter 1975). Reprinted by permission of the publishers, Division of Research, Graduate School of Business Administration, Michigan State University.

BACK TO THE CASE

In researching his proposal to restructure General Motors, Roger Smith probably considered changing technological factors, people factors, and structural factors at GM that could increase organizational effectiveness. He must have decided that the needed change concerned primarily structured factors. As a result, he decided to propose to GM's board of directors that the company's five divisions be reduced to two. In addition, Smith's thoughts probably included placing such key functions as design, engineering, and marketing at the divisional level rather than at the corporate level, where they had been in the past. In essence, the executive vice-presidents for each division would be accountable for divisional profits. Smith's proposal called for these changes to be made over a three-year period.

Grid OD

One commonly used OD technique for changing people in organizations is called **Grid OD**.[14] The managerial grid is a basic model describing various managerial styles and is used as the foundation for grid OD. The **managerial grid** is based on the premise that various managerial styles can be described by means of two primary attitudes of the manager: concern for people and concern for production.

FIGURE 11.7   The managerial grid.

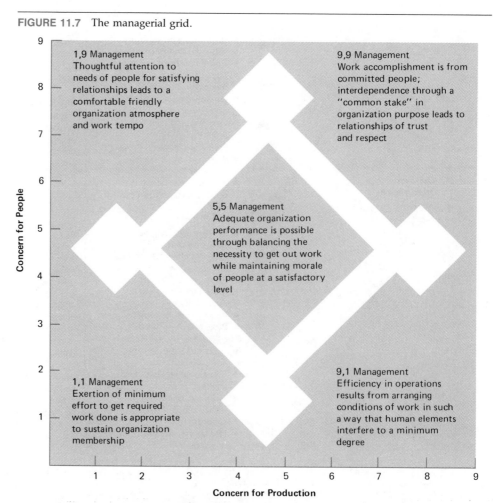

Within this model, each attitude is placed on an axis scaled 1 through 9 and is used to generate five managerial styles. Figure 11.7 shows the managerial grid, its five managerial styles, and the factors that characterize each of these styles.

The central theme of this managerial grid is that 9,9 management (as shown on the grid) is the ideal managerial style. Managers using this style have both high concern for people and high concern for production. Managers using any other style have lesser degrees of concern for people or production and are thought to reduce organizational success accordingly. The purpose of grid OD is to change organization managers so that they approximate the 9,9 management style.

How is a grid OD program actually conducted? The program itself has six main training phases conducted for all managers within the organization. The first two of these phases focus on acquainting managers with the managerial grid concept and assisting them in determining which managerial style they most commonly use. The last four phases of the grid OD program concentrate on encouraging managers to adopt the 9,9 management style and showing them how to use this style within their specific job situation. Emphasis throughout the program is on developing teamwork within the organization.

Some evidence suggests that grid OD is a useful technique because it is effective in enhancing profit, positively changing managerial behaviour, and positively influencing managerial attitudes and values.[15] Grid OD probably will have to undergo more rigorous testing for an extended period of time, however, before conclusive statements can be made.[16]

> Grid OD focuses on encouraging managers to adopt the 9,9 management style.

The Status of Organization Development (OD)

If the entire OD area is taken into consideration, changes that emphasize both people and the organization as a whole seem to have inherent strength. There are, however, several commonly voiced weaknesses of OD efforts. These weaknesses indicate that: (1) the effectiveness of an OD program is difficult to evaluate; (2) OD programs are generally too time consuming; (3) OD objectives are commonly too vague; (4) total costs of an OD program are difficult to pinpoint at the time the program starts; and (5) OD programs are generally too expensive.[17]

> Managers should be aware of the weaknesses of OD and how to work around them.

Despite these weaknesses, however, the use of OD techniques probably will grow in the future.[18] Therefore, these weaknesses should not eliminate OD but indicate areas to perfect within it. Common guidelines that managers can use to improve the quality of OD efforts are: (1) systematically tailoring OD programs to meet the specific needs of the organization; (2) continually demonstrating as part of the program exactly how people should change their behaviour; and (3) conscientiously changing organizational reward systems so that organization members who change their behaviour as suggested by an OD program are rewarded.[19]

BACK TO THE CASE

If the General Motors board of directors approves Roger Smith's plan, the changes he will implement will not be classified as people change. Although the people involved in the change must be considered to some extent, the main emphasis of the proposed change is on structural change.

If, however, Smith had found that problems with human resources were the main cause of organizational ineffectiveness, he might have proposed organization development rather than structural change. In fact, Smith may find that later on he needs to use a grid OD in order to modify management styles and produce more cooperative team effort once the proposed structural changes are implemented.

Individuals Affected by the Change

A fourth major factor to be considered by managers when changing an organization is the people affected by the change. A good assessment of what to change and how to make the change probably will be wasted if organization members do not support the change. To increase the chances of employee support, managers should be aware of: (1) the usual employee resistance to change; (2) how this resistance can be reduced; and (3) the three phases usually present when behavioural change occurs.

Resistance to Change

Resistance to change within an organization is as common as the need for change. After managers decide on making some organizational change, they typically meet with employee resistance aimed at preventing the change from occurring. This resistance generally exists because organization members fear some personal loss, such as a reduction in personal prestige, a disturbance of established social and working relationships, and personal failure due to an inability to carry out new job responsibilities.

Resistance to change is often based on feared personal loss.

Reducing Resistance to Change

Since resistance typically accompanies proposed change, managers must be able to reduce the effects of this resistance to ensure the success of needed organizational modifications. Resistance usually can be reduced by following several generally accepted guidelines:[20]

Resistance to change can be reduced if managers:

1. Avoid surprises.

1. *Avoid surprises*   People typically need time to evaluate proposed change before management implements it. Elimination of this time to evaluate how proposed change may affect individual situations usually results in automatic opposition to change. Whenever possible, individuals who will be affected by a change should be kept informed of the type of change being considered and the probability that the change will be adopted.

2. Promote understanding.

2. *Promote real understanding*   When fear of personal loss related to a proposed change is reduced, opposition to the proposed change is reduced.[21] Most managers would agree that having organization members thoroughly understand a proposed change is a major step in reducing this fear. This understanding may even generate support for the proposed change by focusing attention on possible individual gains that could materialize as a result of the change. Individuals should receive information that will help them to answer the following change-related questions that they invariably will be asking themselves:

- Will I lose my job?
- Will my old skills become obsolete?
- Am I capable of producing effectively under the new system?
- Will my power and prestige decline?
- Will I be given more responsibility than I care to assume?
- Will I have to work longer hours?
- Will it force me to betray or desert my good friends?[22]

3. Present a positive attitude toward change.

3. *Set the stage for change*   Perhaps the most powerful tool for reducing resistance to change is management's positive attitude toward change. This attitude should be displayed openly by top and middle management as well as by

lower management. In essence, management should demonstrate its appreciation for change as one of the basic prerequisites necessary for a successful organization. Management also should strive to be seen not as encouraging change for the sake of change, but as encouraging change only to increase organizational effectiveness. To emphasize this attitude toward change, some portion of organizational rewards should be earmarked for those organization members most instrumental in implementing constructive change.

4. *Make tentative change* Resistance to change also can be reduced by making changes on a tentative basis. This approach establishes a trial period during which organization members spend some time working under a proposed change before voicing support or non-support of the change. Tentative change is based on the assumption that a trial period during which organization members "live under" a change is the best way of reducing feared personal loss. Arnold Judson has summarized the benefits of using the tentative approach:

4. Implement change on a tentative basis.

- Those involved are able to test their reactions to the new situation before committing themselves irrevocably.
- Those involved are able to acquire more facts on which to base their attitudes and behaviour toward the change.
- Those involved with strong preconceptions are in a better position to regard the change with greater objectivity. Consequently, they could review their preconceptions and perhaps modify some of them.
- Those involved are less likely to regard the change as a threat.
- Management is better able to evaluate the method of change and make any necessary modifications before carrying it out more fully.[23]

The Behavioural Side of Change

Almost any change requires that organization members modify the way in which they are accustomed to behaving or working. Therefore, managers must not only be able to decide upon the best people-structure-technology relationship for the organization but also to make corresponding changes in such a way that related human behaviour is changed most effectively. Positive results of any change will materialize only if organization members change their behaviour as necessitated by the change.

According to Kurt Lewin, behavioural change is caused by three distinct but related conditions experienced by an individual: (1) unfreezing; (2) changing; and (3) refreezing.[24] The first condition, **unfreezing**, is a state in which individuals become ready to acquire or learn new behaviours—they experience the ineffectiveness of their present mode of behaviour and are ready to attempt to learn new behaviour that will make them more effective. It may be especially difficult for individuals to "thaw out" because of positive attitudes they traditionally associated with their past behaviour.

Unfreezing is the state in which people are ready to change.

Changing, the second of Lewin's conditions, is a situation in which individuals, now unfrozen, begin experimenting with new behaviour. They try new behaviours they hope will increase their effectiveness. According to Edgar Schein, this changing is best effected if it involves both identification and internalization.[25] *Identification* is a process in which individuals performing new behaviours pattern themselves after someone who already has expertise in those behaviours; that is, individuals model themselves after an expert. *Internalization* is a process in which individuals performing new behaviours attempt to use those behaviours

Changing is the state in which people experiment with new behaviours.

as part of their normal behavioural pattern. In other words, individuals consistently try to make the new behaviours useful over an extended period of time.

Refreezing, the third of Lewin's conditions, is a situation in which individuals see that the new behaviour they have experimented with during "changing" is now part of themselves. They have developed attitudes consistent with performing the new behaviour and now see that behaviour as part of their normal mode of operations. Rewards individuals receive as a result of performing the new behaviour are very instrumental in refreezing.

For managers to increase their success as change agents, they must be able to make their changes in such a way that individuals who will be required to modify their behaviour as a result of the change live through Lewin's three conditions. A manager might do this in the following way:

A middle-level manager named Sara Clark has gathered information through an internal organizational analysis that indicates that Sandor Xstris, a lower-level manager, must change his technique for transmitting memos within the organization. Clark knows that Xstris firmly believes he can save time and effort by writing out his intracompany memos longhand rather than having them typed, proofread, corrected if necessary, and then sent out. Xstris also believes that an added benefit to this strategy is the fact that it frees his secretary to do other kinds of tasks.

Clark, however, has been getting several requests for help in reading Xstris's sometimes illegible handwriting and knows that some of Xstris's memos are written so poorly that words and sentences are misinterpreted. Clearly, some change seems necessary. As his superior, Clark could simply mandate change by telling Xstris to write more clearly or to have his memos typed. This strategy, however, may not have enough impact to cause a lasting behavioural change and could conceivably result in the additional problem of personal friction between the two managers.

Clark could increase the probability of Xstris changing his behaviour in a more lasting way if she helps Xstris to experience unfreezing, changing, and refreezing. To encourage unfreezing Xstris, Clark could direct all questions she receives concerning Xstris's memos back to Xstris himself and make sure that Xstris is aware of all memo misinterpretations and resulting mistakes. This should demonstrate to Xstris that there is some need for change.

Once Xstris recognizes this need for changing the way in which he writes his memos, he will be ready to try alternative memo-writing methods. Clark could then suggest methods to Xstris, taking special care to give him examples of what others do to write intracompany memos (identification). Over time, Clark could also help Xstris to develop the method of transmitting memos that best suits his talents (internalization).

After Xstris has developed an effective method of writing memos, Clark should take steps to ensure that positive feedback about his memo writing reaches Xstris. This feedback, of course, will be instrumental in refreezing Xstris's new method. The feedback can come from Clark, Xstris's subordinates and peers, and from Xstris's own observations.

Evaluation of Change

As with all other action managers take, they should spend some time evaluating the changes they make. The purpose of this evaluation is not only to gain insights on how the change itself might be modified to further increase organizational

Refreezing is the state in which people see their new behaviour as part of themselves.

Evaluation of change may increase the organizational benefit from the change.

effectiveness, but also to determine if the steps taken to make the change can be modified to increase organizational effectiveness the next time they are used.

According to Margulies and Wallace, making this evaluation may be difficult because outcome data from individual change programs may be unreliable.[26] Regardless of the difficulty, however, managers must do their best to evaluate change to increase the organizational benefit from the change.

Evaluation of change often involves watching for symptoms that indicate that further change is necessary. For example, if organization members continue to be oriented more to the past than to the future, if they recognize the obligations of rituals more than the challenges of current problems, or if they owe allegiance more to departmental goals than to overall company objectives, the probability is relatively high that further change is necessary.[27]

A word of caution, however, is needed at this point. Although symptoms such as those listed in the preceding paragraph generally indicate that further change is warranted, this is not always the case. The decision to make additional changes should not be made solely on the basis of observing symptoms; more objective information resulting from repeated and well-executed internal and external organizational diagnoses also should be considered. In general, additional change is justified if it: (1) further improves the means for satisfying someone's economic wants; (2) increases profitability; (3) promotes human work for human beings; or (4) contributes to individual satisfaction and social well-being.[28]

Certain symptoms may indicate that further change is warranted.

BACK TO THE CASE

Roger Smith must realize that even though he has formulated a change that would be very beneficial to General Motors, his attempt to implement this change could prove unsuccessful if he does not appropriately consider the people affected by the change. For example, because Smith is proposing a reduction of the number of GM divisions from five to two, many organization members may fear that this change will eliminate their jobs. As a result, they may subtly resist the change.

To overcome this resistance, Smith could use such strategies as giving affected employees enough time to fully evaluate and understand the change, presenting a positive attitude about the change, and if resistance is very strong, suggesting that the proposed change will

be tentative to truly evaluate its impact on the organization. In addition, Smith probably would find Lewin's unfreezing-changing-refreezing theory very helpful in implementing the proposed change.

Smith's proposed change at GM needs to be evaluated after implementation to discover if further organizational change is necessary and if the process used by Smith to make the change might be improved for future use. This evaluation process could result, for example, in a suggestion that marketing should be moved from the divisional level back to the company level, or that implementation of future changes should put more emphasis on assisting individuals affected by the change to experience unfreezing, changing, and refreezing.

CHANGE AND STRESS

This chapter has focused on changing an organization to make it more effective, efficient, and successful. When managers implement changes, however, they should also be concerned about the stress they may be creating. Such stress could be significant enough to eliminate the improvement that was intended to be the result of the change. In fact, stress could result in the organization being less effective than it was before the change was attempted. This section defines stress and discusses the importance of studying and managing stress.

Change can cause stress.

Defining Stress

Stress is strain.

The bodily strain that an individual experiences as a result of coping with some environmental factor is **stress**. Hans Selye, perhaps the most well-known authority on this subject, says that stress is simply the rate of wear and tear on the body.[29] In organizations, this wear and tear is caused primarily by the body's unconscious mobilization of energy when an individual is confronted with organizational or work demands.[30]

The Importance of Studying Stress

Stress should be studied because it can harm employees, cause absenteeism and turnover, and affect safety.

There are at least three sound reasons for studying stress.[31] First, stress can have damaging psychological and physiological effects on employees' health and on employees' contributions to the effectiveness of the organization. It can cause heart disease, and it can keep employees from being able to concentrate or to make decisions. A second important reason to study stress is that it is a major cause of employee absenteeism and turnover. Certainly, such factors severely limit the potential success of an organization. The third reason it is important to study stress is that stress experienced by an employee can affect the safety of other workers or even the public. For example, the stress felt by commercial airline pilots represents a potential danger not only to the co-pilots and attendants but also to the passengers.

Managing Stress in Organizations

Since stress is felt by virtually all employees in all organizations, insights about managing stress are valuable to all managers. This section is built on the assumption that in order to appropriately manage stress in organizations, managers must: (1) understand how stress influences worker performance; (2) identify where unhealthy stress exists in organizations; and (3) help employees handle stress.

"I suspect your problem is stress-related."
Wall Street Journal, *February 25, 1987. From the* Wall Street Journal–*permission, Cartoon Features Syndicate.*

FIGURE 11.8   The relationship between worker stress and the level of worker performance.

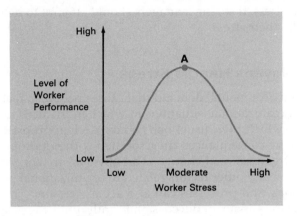

Understanding How Stress Influences Worker Performance

To deal with stress in an organization, managers must understand the relationship between the amount of stress felt by a worker and the worker's performance. This relationship is shown in Figure 11.8. According to this figure, extremely high and extremely low levels of stress tend to have negative effects on production. Additionally, increasing stress tends to increase performance up to some point (point A in the figure). If the level of stress increases beyond this point, performance will begin to deteriorate. In sum, from a performance viewpoint, having individuals experience some stress is generally considered advantageous because it tends to increase production; however, having individuals feel too much or too little stress is generally considered disadvantageous because it tends to decrease production.

Stress can be too high or too low.

Identifying Unhealthy Stress in Organizations

After managers understand the impact of stress on performance, they must be able to identify where stress exists within the organization. Once the existence of stress is pinpointed, the managers must determine if the stress is at an appropriate level or if it is too high or too low. Since most stress-related organizational problems involve too much stress, rather than too little, the remainder of this section focuses on undesirably high levels of stress.

High stress causes more organizational problems than low stress.

It can be difficult for managers to identify the people in the organization who are experiencing detrimentally high levels of stress. Part of the difficulty is that people often respond to high stress in different ways. Another part of the difficulty is that physiological reactions to stress are hard, if not impossible, for managers to observe and monitor. Such reactions include high blood pressure, pounding heart, and gastrointestinal disorders.

Stress can be hard to detect.

Despite the difficulty, there are several observable symptoms of undesirably high stress levels that managers can look for.[32] (The cartoon shows one very obvious—though unlikely—symptom.) These symptoms are as follows:[33]

- Constant fatigue.
- Low energy.
- Moodiness.
- Increased aggression.
- Excessive use of alcohol.
- Temper outbursts.
- Compulsive eating.
- High levels of anxiety.
- Chronic worrying.

Managers who observe one or more of these symptoms in employees should investigate further to determine if employees exhibiting the symptoms are indeed under too much stress. If so, the managers should attempt to help the employees reduce or handle their stress.

Helping Employees Handle Stress

A **stressor** is an environmental demand that causes people to feel stress. Stressors are common in organizational situations in which individuals are confronted by circumstances in which their usual behaviours are inappropriate or insufficient and where negative consequences are associated with not properly dealing with the situation.[34] Organizational change is an obvious stressor. As Figure 11.9 indicates, however, many other factors related to organizational policies, structure, physical conditions, and processes can also act as stressors.

In general, stress is not reduced significantly until the stressors causing it have been coped with satisfactorily or withdrawn from the environment. For example, if too much organizational change is causing undesirably high levels of stress, management may be able to reduce stress by improving organizational training aimed at preparing workers to deal with the job demands resulting from the change. Management might also deal with such stress by not making further organizational changes. Such action would be aimed at reducing the significance of organizational change as a stressor and thereby reducing stress levels.

In addition to working in a focused manner on organizational change and other organizational stressors after they are observed, management can adopt several strategies to help prevent the development of unwanted stressors in organizations. Three such strategies follow:[35]

1. *Create an organizational climate that is supportive of individuals*   Organizations today commonly seem to evolve into large bureaucracies with formal, inflexible, impersonal climates. This type of set-up can lead to considerable job stress. Making the organizational environment less formal and more supportive of employee needs will help prevent the development of unwanted organizational stressors.

2. *Make jobs interesting*   In general, routine jobs that do not allow employees some degree of freedom often result in undesirable employee stress. Management's focus on making jobs as interesting as possible should help prevent the development of unwanted stressors related to routine, boring jobs.

3. *Design and operate career counselling programs*   Considerable stress can be generated when employees do not know what their next career step might be or when they might take it. If management can show employees what the next step will probably be and when it realistically can be achieved, the development of unwanted organizational stressors in this area can be discouraged.

IBM is an example of a company that has focused on career planning for its employees.[36] IBM has a corporation-wide program to encourage supervisors to conduct voluntary career planning sessions with employees on an annual basis. These sessions result in one-page career action plans. At the end of the sessions, the employees have a clear idea of where their careers are headed. The development of undesirable career-related stressors at IBM has been discouraged as a result of this program.

FIGURE 11.9   Additional organizational stressors.

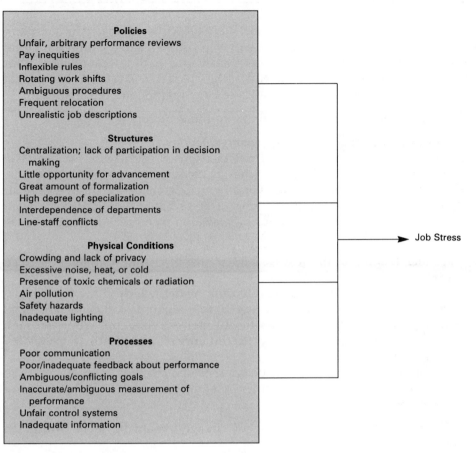

Policies
Unfair, arbitrary performance reviews
Pay inequities
Inflexible rules
Rotating work shifts
Ambiguous procedures
Frequent relocation
Unrealistic job descriptions

Structures
Centralization; lack of participation in decision
  making
Little opportunity for advancement
Great amount of formalization
High degree of specialization
Interdependence of departments
Line-staff conflicts

Physical Conditions
Crowding and lack of privacy
Excessive noise, heat, or cold
Presence of toxic chemicals or radiation
Air pollution
Safety hazards
Inadequate lighting

Processes
Poor communication
Poor/inadequate feedback about performance
Ambiguous/conflicting goals
Inaccurate/ambiguous measurement of
  performance
Unfair control systems
Inadequate information

→ Job Stress

Reprinted by permission of the authors from Arthur P. Brief, Randall S. Schuler, and Mary Van Sell, *Managing Job Stress* (Boston: Little, Brown, 1981), p. 66.

BACK TO THE CASE

Roger Smith should be careful not to create too much stress on other organization members as a result of his planned change. Such stress could be significant enough to eliminate any planned improvement at GM and could eventually result in such stress related effects on employees as heart disease and the inability to make sound decisions.

Although some additional stress on organization members as a result of Smith's planned change at GM could enhance productivity, too much stress could have a negative impact on production. Signs that Smith could look for include constant fatigue, increased aggression, temper outbursts, and chronic worrying.

If Smith determines that undesirably high levels of stress have resulted from his changes at GM, he should try to reduce the stress. He may be able to do so through training programs aimed at better equipping organization members to execute new job demands resulting from the change. Or he may want to simply slow the rate of his planned change.

It would probably be wise for Smith to take action that would prevent unwanted stressors from developing as a result of his planned change. In this regard, Smith could ensure that the organizational climate at GM is supportive of individual needs and that jobs resulting from the planned change are as interesting as possible.

Action Summary

Reread the learning objectives that follow. Each objective is followed by questions. Answering these questions accurately will help you to retain the most important concepts discussed in this chapter. After answering each question, check your answer with the answer key at the end of this chapter. (*Hint*: If you have doubt regarding the correct response, consult the page that follows the answer.)

Circle:

From studying this chapter, I will attempt to acquire:

1. **A working definition of** *changing an organization.*

T, F

   a. The purpose of organizational modifications is to increase the extent to which an organization accomplishes its objectives.

   b. Organizational modifications typically include changing: (a) overall goals and objectives; (b) established lines of organizational authority; (c) levels of responsibility held by various organization members; (d) b and c; (e) all

a, b, c, d, e

    of the above.

2. **An understanding of the relative importance of change and stability to an organization.**

   a. According to the Hellriegel and Slocum model, which of the following is the most likely outcome when both adaptation and stability are high: (a) high probability of slow death; (b) high survival probability; (c) high survival and growth probability; (d) certainty of quick death; (e) possibility

a, b, c, d, e

    of slow death.

   b. According to Hellriegel and Slocum, repeated changes in an organization without stability typically results in employees with a high degree of

T, F

    adaptability.

3. **Some ability to know what type of change should be made within an organization.**

   a. Although managers can choose to change an organization in many ways, most changes can be categorized as one of three types: (1) people change;

T, F

    (2) goal or objective change; and (3) technological change.

   b. Decentralizing an organization is a structural change aimed at: (a) reducing the cost of coordination; (b) increasing the controllability of subunits; (c)

a, b, c, d, e

    increasing motivation; (d) all of the above; (e) a and b.

4. **An appreciation for why individuals affected by a change should be considered when the change is being made.**

   a. All of the following are examples of personal loss that organization members fear as a result of change except: (a) possibility of a reduction in personal prestige; (b) disturbance of established social relationships; (c) reduction in overall organizational productivity; (d) personal failure due to an inability to carry out new job responsibilities; (e) disturbance of established working

a, b, c, d, e

    relationships.

   b. Support for a proposed change may be altered by focusing attention on

T, F

    possible individual gains that could materialize as a result of the change.

5. **Some facility in evaluating change.**

   a. Symptoms indicating that further change is necessary are that organization members: (a) are oriented more to the future than to the past; (b) recognize the challenge of current problems more than the obligations of rituals;

(c) owe allegiance more to overall company goals than to departmental goals; (d) none of the above; (e) a and b.

a, b, c, d, e

b. Change is an inevitable part of management and considered so important to organizational success that some managers encourage employees to suggest needed changes.

T, F

6. **An understanding of how organizational change and stress are related.**
   a. Stress is simply the rate of wear and tear on the body.

T, F

   b. From a managerial viewpoint, stress on employees can be either too high or too low.

T, F

   c. Stressors are the factors within an organization that reduce employee stress.

T, F

INTRODUCTORY CASE WRAP-UP

"GM's Great Divide" (p. 284) and its related back-to-the-case sections were written to help you better understand the management concepts contained in this chapter. Answer the following discussion questions about this introductory case to further enrich your understanding of the chapter content.

1. How complicated would it be for Roger Smith to actually implement his plan? Explain.
2. Assuming that Smith gets GM board approval to make his proposed changes, do you think that certain employees will subtly resist the changes? Why or why not?
3. What reasons would Smith give to the GM board to explain why his changes must take so long (three years) to fully implement?
4. What elements of Smith's plan would cause organization members to experience stress, and what could Smith do to help alleviate this stress? Be specific.

Issues for Review and Discussion

1. What is meant in this chapter by the phrase *changing an organization*?
2. Why do organizations typically undergo various changes?
3. Does an organization need both change and stability? Explain.
4. What major factors should a manager consider when changing an organization?
5. Define *change agent* and list the skills necessary to be a successful change agent.
6. Explain the term *organizational effectiveness* and describe the major factors that determine how effective an organization will be.
7. Describe the relationship between "determining what should be changed within an organization" and "choosing a type of change for the organization."
8. What is the difference between structural change and people change?
9. Is matrix organization an example of a structural change? Explain.
10. What is the difference between the overt and covert factors considered during organizational development?
11. Draw and explain the managerial grid.
12. Is grid OD an example of a technique used to make structural change? Explain.
13. What causes resistance to change?
14. List and explain the steps managers can take to minimize resistance to change.
15. Explain the significance of unfreezing, changing, and refreezing to changing the organization.
16. How and why should managers evaluate changes they make?
17. Define *stress* and explain how it influences performance.
18. List three stressors that could exist within an organization. For each stressor, discuss a specific management action that could be aimed at eliminating the stressor.
19. What impact can career counselling have on employee stress? Explain.

Sources of Additional Information

Argyris, C. *Management and Organization Development.* New York: McGraw-Hill, 1972.

Appelbaum, S.H. *Stress Management For Health Care Professionals.* Rockville, Maryland: Aspen Publication, 1981.

Barnes, Louis B. "Managing the Paradox of Organizational Trust." *Harvard Business Review* (March/April 1981): 107–16.

Chapman, Elwood N. *Your Attitude Is Showing: A Primer of Human Relations.* 5th ed. Chicago: Science Research Associates, 1987.

Dubinsky, Alan J. "Managing Work Stress." *Business* 35 (July/August/September 1985): 3–10.

Dyer, William G. *Contemporary Issues in Management and Organization Development.* Reading, Mass.: Addison-Wesley, 1983.

Goodman, Paul S. *Change in Organizations.* San Francisco: Jossey-Bass, 1982.

Harvey, Donald F., and Donald R. Brown. *An Experiential Approach to Organization Development.* Englewood Cliffs, N.J.: Prentice-Hall, 1982.

Janger, Allen J. *Matrix Organization of Complex Businesses.* New York: Conference Board, 1979.

Leavitt, Harold. "Applied Organization Change in Industry." In *Handbook on Organizations,* edited by James March. Chicago: Rand McNally, 1965.

Linder, Jane C. "Computers, Corporate Culture and Change." *Personnel Journal* 64 (September 1985): 48–55.

McLean, A.J., D.B.P. Sims, I.L. Mangham, and D. Tuffield. *Organization Development in Transition.* Chichester, England: Wiley, 1982.

Marchington, Mick. "Employee Participation—Consensus or Confusion?" *Personnel Management* 13 (April 1981): 38–41.

Pearson, Andrall E. "Muscle-Build the Organization." *Harvard Business Review* (July/August 1987): 49–55.

Umstot, Denis D. "Organization Development Technology and the Military: A Surprising Merger?" *Academy of Management Review* 5 (1980): 189–201.

Vancil, Richard F. "A Look at CEO Succession." *Harvard Business Review* (March/April 1987): 107–17.

Zierden, William E. "Managing Workplace Innovations: A Framework and a New Approach." *Management Review* 70 (June 1981): 57–61.

Notes

1. Ronald D. Daniel, "Reorganization for Results," *Harvard Business Review* (November/December 1966): 96–104.
2. Bridgford Hunt, "Managers of Change: Why They Are in Demand," *S.A.M. Advanced Management Journal* (Winter 1980): 40–44.
3. John S. Morgan, *Managing Change: The Strategies of Making Change Work for You* (New York: McGraw-Hill, 1972), 99.
4. Oliver L. Niehouse and Karen B. Massoni, "Stress—An Inevitable Part of Change," *S.A.M. Advanced Management Journal* (Spring 1979): 17–25.
5. Warren C. Bennis, K.D. Benne, and R. Chin, eds., *The Planning of Change: Readings in the Applied Behavioral Sciences* (New York: Holt, Rinehart & Winston, 1961), 69.
6. Alvin Toffler, *Future Shock* (New York: Bantam Books, 1971).
7. William C. Giegold and R.J. Craig, "Whatever Happened to OD?" *Industrial Management* (January/February 1976): 9–12.
8. W.F. Glueck, "Organization Change in Business and Government," *Academy of Management Journal* 12 (1969): 440–41.
9. C.J. Middleton, "How to Set Up a Project Organization," *Harvard Business Review* (March/April 1967): 73.
10. John F. Mee, "Matrix Organization," *Business Horizons* (Summer 1964).
11. Middleton, "How to Set Up a Project Organization," 74.
12. Harvey F. Kolodny, "Managing in a Matrix," *Business Horizons* 24 (March/April 1981): 17–24.
13. John C. Alpin and Duane E. Thompson, "Successful Organizational Change," *Business Horizons* (August 1974): 61–66.
14. This section is based primarily on R. Blake, J. Mouton, and L. Greiner, "Breakthrough in Organization Development," *Harvard Business Review* (1964): 133-55. For a discussion of other methods for implementing OD change, see William F. Glueck, *Organization Planning and Development* (New York: American Management Association, 1971).
15. Blake, Mouton, and Greiner, "Breakthrough in Organization Development."
16. L.G. Malouf, "Managerial Grid Evaluated," *Training Development Journal* 20 (1966): 6–15.
17. W.J. Heisler, "Patterns of OD in Practice," *Business Horizons* (February 1975): 77–84.

18. William E. Halal, "Organization Development in the Future," *California Management Review* 16 (Spring 1974): 35–41.
19. Martin G. Evans, "Failures in OD Programs—What Went Wrong," *Business Horizons* (April 1974): 18–22.
20. This strategy for minimizing the resistance to change is based on "How Companies Overcome Resistance to Change," *Management Review* (November 1972): 17–25.
21. John P. Kotter and Leonard A. Schlesinger, "Choosing Strategies for Change," *Harvard Business Review* (March/April 1979): 106–13.
22. "How Companies Overcome Resistance," 25.
23. Arnold S. Judson, *A Manager's Guide to Making Changes* (New York: Wiley, 1966), 118.
24. Kurt Lewin, "Frontiers in Group Dynamics: Concept, Method, and Reality of Social Sciences—Social Equilibria and Social Change," *Human Relations* 1 (June 1947): 5–14.
25. Edgar H. Schein, "Management Development as a Process of Influence," *Industrial Management Review* (May 1961): 59–76.
26. Newton Margulies and John Wallace, *Organizational Change: Techniques and Applications* (Chicago: Scott, Foresman, 1973), 14.
27. Larry E. Greiner, "Patterns of Organizational Change," *Harvard Business Review* (May/June 1967): 119–30.
28. Edgar C. Williams, "Changing Systems and Behavior: People's Perspectives on Prospective Changes," *Business Horizons* 12 (August 1969): 53.
29. Hans Selye, *The Stress of Life* (New York: McGraw-Hill, 1956).
30. James C. Quick and Jonathan D. Quick, *Organizational Stress and Preventive Management* (New York: McGraw-Hill, 1984).
31. Richard M. Steers, *Introduction to Organizational Behavior*, (Glenview, Ill.: Scott, Foresman, 1981), 340–41.
32. For more discussion of this area, see Keith Davis and John W. Newstrom, *Human Behavior at Work: Organizational Behavior* (New York: McGraw-Hill, 1985), 469–70.
33. J. Clifton Williams, *Human Behavior in Organizations* (Cincinnati: South-Western, 1982), 212–13.
34. John M. Ivancevich and Michael T. Matteson, "Organizations and Coronary Heart Disease: The Stress Connection." *Management Review* 67 (October 1978): 14–19.
35. Fred Luthans, *Organizational Behavior* (New York: McGraw-Hill, 1985), 146–48.
36. Donald B. Miller, "Career Planning and Management in Organizations," *S.A.M. Advanced Management Journal* 43 (Spring 1978): 33–43.

Action Summary Answer Key

1. a. T, p. 285
   b. d, p. 285
2. a. c, p. 286
   b. F, p. 286
3. a. F, p. 294
   b. d, p. 294
4. a. c, p. 300
   b. T, p. 300
5. a. d, p. 303
   b. T, p. 285
6. a. T, p. 304
   b. T, p. 305
   c. F, p. 306

CTV UNDER SIEGE

CTV Television, the most popular network with Canadian viewers, is facing the worst crisis in its twenty-five-year history. Owned by sixteen affiliate stations which share in the network's revenues and costs, CTV is struggling to cope with an ownership and power-sharing structure that is proving to be inefficient and, perhaps, ultimately unworkable. Insiders are betting that its biggest and most powerful member, Toronto's Baton Broadcasting, Inc., is running short on patience with the system and may pull out entirely—a move some think could prove fatal to the network. Though Baton management denies that scenario, some network affiliates' fears were recently reinforced when Baton decided to open a new station in Ottawa, where it will compete directly with a CTV affiliate.

Meanwhile, CTV is experiencing its worst-ever public relations difficulties. In early 1987, CTV management decimated the network's highly regarded news and public affairs division. It did not help when André Bureau, chairman of the Canadian Radio-television and Telecommunications Commission (CRTC), told CTV he would renew its five-year broadcasting licence only if the network produced more and better programming.

Despite declining network revenues, which, in 1987, were expected to fall more than $10 million from 1986's take of $135 million, Bureau ordered CTV to spend at least $403 million on Canadian programming over the next five years. (CTV sells original programming to advertisers, with the net revenue shared among the affiliates who carry the shows. Other programs, such as U.S. comedies, are bought by CTV and sold to the affiliates, which insert local ads.) The CRTC's spending order represents a 75 percent increase over the five-year period ending in 1986. Bureau made clear his disappointment that Canada's only privately owned national television system lacked long-term strategies and objectives.

CTV, however, doesn't need to be told it's short on plans. Troubled from top to bottom, the network is virtually certain to undergo structural and ownership changes over the next couple of years. Because of its size and wealth, Baton will likely have the greatest influence over what the new CTV will look like. The company already owns three CTV affiliates, including Toronto's huge CFTO, which has the largest revenue and cost-sharing stake in the network (see Case Figure 11.1).

It's well known that Baton would like to own, or at least control CTV. If Baton decides it can't attain control or decides not to, it's rumoured the company will take itself out of the network and operate independently. Pull-

"Bureau made clear his disappointment that (CTV) lacked long-term strategies and objectives."

ing out would mean an end to fights with smaller stations over cost and revenue sharing and a host of other money-related annoyances. Observers point out that Baton television operations are integrated to the point where the company could turn itself into a network virtually overnight.

More importantly, however, Baton—through Toronto's CFTO—is the dominant player in the biggest market in Canada. It is also represented in Regina and Saskatoon, and soon will be in Ottawa as well. But if Baton leaves CTV, another affiliate owner might be tempted, or encouraged by the CRTC, to start a new station in Toronto to fill the void, thereby competing with CFTO. CTV sources say that that risk alone could be enough to keep Baton within the fold.

Beyond the question of Baton's future participation, the network's biggest headache is its unusual ownership structure—the prime cause of the perennial bickering between CTV and its affiliates. The problem is there are too many bosses calling the shorts. CTV is the only television network in North America that is owned by its affiliates—sixteen of them, held by eleven private and publicly traded communications companies. The key is that affiliates under common ownership have only one vote. Thus Newfoundland Broadcasting, owner of tiny CJON in St. John's, has the same say on the CTV board

CASE FIGURE 11.1 CTV affiliates and their revenue and cost-sharing percentage in the network.

Owner	Affiliate	Percentage
Baton Broadcasting	CFTO (Toronto) CKCK (Regina) CFQC (Saskatoon)	24.3
British Columbia Television	CHAN (Vancouver) CHEK (Victoria)	16.5
CFCF	CFCF (Montreal)	14.2
CHUM	CJCH (Halifax) CKCW (Moncton) CJCB (Sydney)	8.0
Standard Broadcasting	CJOH (Ottawa)	7.8
Sanwapta Broadcasting	CFRN (Edmonton)	7.3
Maclean Hunter	CFCN (Calgary)	7.2
CAP Communications	CKCO (Kitchener)	6.9
Moffat Communications	CKY (Winnipeg)	4.4
Mid-Canada Communications	CICI (Sudbury)	2.0
Newfoundland Broadcasting	CJON (St. John's)	1.4

as CHUM, which has three television stations and an 8 percent share in ad revenues and network costs.

The affiliates divide network revenues and expenses among themselves according to their size, as measured by advertising sales, not their viewership. On the basis of their percentage of ad sales in the network, any profit (the amount remaining after all network programming, operating, and administrative costs are paid) is spread among the affiliates as a dividend for carrying about thirty-five hours a week of network programming. Similarly with the shortfalls, which are making their presence known with increasing frequency. CTV forecasted revenue for 1987 at about $122 million, or 7.6 percent less than the year before.

One possibility for a CTV overhaul is to copy the U.S. networks, which have a single, controlling shareholder. Such a move would make a number of affiliates happy. "The way it is now, we lack a single, strong coherent voice running the network," says CTV chairman Bill McGregor, who runs CTV's Kitchener affiliate. Baton is studying the controlling shareholder idea. Some affiliates, however, may oppose the proposal because it would lessen their influence over what programs are produced. Another alternative within the network is to give the smaller affiliates less than one full vote each.

McGregor feels that a more likely event would be the consolidation of network power among fewer owners, perhaps three or four instead of the current eleven. This would require that some of the affiliates be sold to the wealthier operations like Baton, BCTV, or Maclean Hunter Ltd. of Calgary. If the affiliates were for sale, they would be expensive. Currently, all CTV stations are profitable; six of them are among the ten most profitable in Canada. The problem then: no CTV affiliates for sale. How could this be solved?

DISCUSSION ISSUES

1. What must Baton do before undertaking any changes within CTV? Given an organizational diagnosis, what factors will Baton be likely to use to support its quest for greater control?

2. Given the possibility of people, structural, and technological change, which would be most appropriate for CTV's current predicament? How might this be accomplished? Explain.

3. What kinds of resistance will Baton—and CTV overall—meet in attempting to make any changes? How could this resistance be reduced or eliminated?

Based on "CTV under siege," by Eric Reguly, in *The Financial Post*, March 30, 1987. Used with permission.

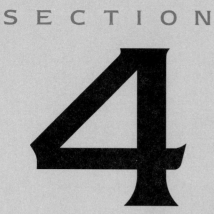

INFLUENCING

Influencing is the third of the four major management functions that must be performed for organizations to have long-term success. The previous two sections—"Planning" and "Organizing"—dealt with determining how the organization gets where it wants to go and establishing working relationships among organizational resources that will help the organization to get there. This section focuses on people variables managers must consider to get organization members to become and remain productive within the organization. Major topics in this section include communication, leadership, motivation, and management of groups, as well as a definition of influencing.

Chapter 12

Chapter 12, "Fundamentals of Influencing and Communication," defines influencing as the process of guiding the activities of organization members in appropriate directions. Influencing is presented as a subsystem of the overall management system. This subsystem is discussed as involving issues primarily relating to communication, motivation, leadership, and consideration of groups. Communication is defined in Chapter 12 as the process of sharing information with other individuals. Such topics as the elements of the interpersonal communication situation, the interpersonal communication process, successful and unsuccessful communication attempts, and verbal and non-verbal communication are discussed. Interpersonal communication that takes place in organizations is called organizational communication, which is presented as being either formal or informal.

Chapter 13

Chapter 13, "Leadership," defines leadership as the process of directing the behaviour of others toward the accomplishment of some objective and emphasizes that leadership is not another word for management. The point also is made in this chapter that individuals' ability to appropriately match their leadership style with both the leadership situation and their followers is a primary determinant of successful leadership. Specific leadership strategies as they relate to managerial decision making, the level of follower maturity, and engineering a situation to fit leadership style are discussed in detail.

Chapter 14

Chapter 14, "Motivation," defines motivation state of an individual that causes him or have in a way that ensures the accomplishment of some goal. Three models used to discuss motivation are the needs-goal model, the Vroom expectancy model, and the Porter-Lawler model. Human needs, an integral part of motivation theory, are described through Maslow's hierarchy of needs, Argyris's maturity-immaturity continuum, and McClelland's achievement theory. Strategies presented in this chapter that managers can use to motivate organization members include appropriate managerial communication, Theory Y, job enrichment, flextime, behaviour modification, and Likert's management systems.

Chapter 15

Chapter 15, "Managing Groups," stresses that, for managers to influence organization members successfully, they must be able to manage groups of people. A group is defined as any number of people who interact with one another, are psychologically aware of one another, and perceive themselves to be a group. Organizational groups are explained as being divided into two types: formal groups and informal groups. Formal groups are work groups established by management decree, while informal groups develop naturally as organization members interact with one another. Chapter 15 suggests that managers can maximize the effectiveness of a work group by understanding and appropriately applying concepts regarding the relationship between work group productivity and: (1) the size of a work group; (2) the cohesiveness of a work group; (3) work group norms; and (4) the status of work group members.

CHAPTER

12

FUNDAMENTALS OF INFLUENCING AND COMMUNICATION

STUDENT LEARNING OBJECTIVES

From studying this chapter, I will attempt to acquire:

1. An understanding of influencing.
2. An understanding of interpersonal communication.
3. A knowledge of how to use feedback.
4. An appreciation for the importance of non-verbal communication.
5. Insights on formal organizational communication.
6. An appreciation for the importance of the grapevine.
7. Some hints on how to encourage organizational communication.

CHAPTER OUTLINE

TROUBLES AT MATTEL

In the beginning, the Barbie doll was Mattel, Inc. Now, after several unwieldy years of acquisitions and sometimes explosive growth, Barbie and the toy division she spawned may be all that survive.

Mattel has proclaimed itself a victim of the collapse of the video-game and low-cost-computer markets. Former Mattel officials, other industry executives, and even suppliers, however, say that Mattel's problems are much more severe than this market collapse. These individuals blame an isolated, lacklustre management that got too greedy, moved too slowly, and never did understand some of Mattel's new ventures.

There are indeed several signs that Mattel's problems are complex and extensive. The company reported a loss of $176.5 million for only half of one operating year. Hundreds of employees, some hired not long before, were fired. The much-promoted Aquarius home computer system was abandoned, and a line of personal security products was sold to liquidators at a price much below cost. Profit margins were cut drastically on the Intellivision video game, and the entire Intellivision system itself faced an uncertain future. Even a longtime head of the toy division quit in frustration. Some people say that this crisis at Mattel was the company's worst in about twelve years.

Much of the crisis was blamed on Arthur S. Spear, Mattel's chief executive officer and past vice-president of operations. Even those who believe that Spear restored a vital level of confidence to the company admit that his management style is at least partly to blame for the problems. "Spear is something of a recluse," says a former top executive. Communicating with him is difficult.

To compound this communication problem with Spear, another former official at Mattel indicated there are communication problems relating to divisional management. Division managers have always had a free rein in running their own units. Some believe that this freedom contributes to a lack of communication among divisions and between them and the corporate staff. According to a former executive, "There has always been this view at the division level to shut out the corporate staff and not let corporate know what was really happening."

Mattel officials have not been eager to respond to these comments. One corporate spokesperson, however, did say that former executives and outsiders certainly are neither knowledgeable nor unbiased sources of information regarding the appropriateness of management activities at Mattel.

Based on "Troubles at Mattel Seen Extending Beyond Fallout in Electronics Line," by Stephen J. Sansweet in *The Wall Street Journal*, May 6, 1983.

What's Ahead

Arthur S. Spear, Mattel's chief executive officer mentioned in the introductory case, has been accused of having a management style that is characterized by poor communication. The case raises two important questions: First, can poor communication be the major cause of Mattel's problems? Second, how can communication effectiveness be increased within an organization like Mattel? The information in this chapter is designed to help a manager such as Spear answer these questions. The chapter is divided into two main parts: (1) fundamentals of influencing; and (2) communication.

⊞ FUNDAMENTALS OF INFLUENCING

The four basic managerial functions—planning, organizing, influencing, and controlling—were introduced in Chapter 1. *Influencing* follows *planning* and *organizing* to be the third of these basic functions covered in this text. A definition of *influencing* and a discussion of the influencing subsystem follow.

Defining "Influencing"

Influencing is the process of guiding the activities of organization members in appropriate directions. Appropriate directions, of course, are those that lead to the attainment of management system objectives. Influencing involves focusing on organization members as people and dealing with such issues as morale, arbitration of conflicts, and the development of good working relationships among individuals.

Influencing is guiding activities in appropriate directions.

The Influencing Subsystem

As with the planning and organizing functions, the influencing function can be viewed as a subsystem that is part of the overall management system process (Figure 12.1). The primary purpose of the influencing subsystem is to enhance the attainment of management system objectives by guiding the activities of organization members in appropriate directions.

Figure 12.2 shows the specific ingredients of the influencing subsystem. Input of this subsystem is comprised of a portion of the total resources of the overall management system, and output is appropriate organization member behaviour. The process of the influencing subsystem involves the performance of four primary management activities: (1) leading; (2) motivating; (3) considering groups; and (4) communicating. Managers transform a portion of organizational resources into appropriate organization member behaviour mainly by performing these four activities.

Managers guide activities by leading, motivating, considering groups, and communicating.

FIGURE 12.1   Relationship between overall management system and influencing subsystem.

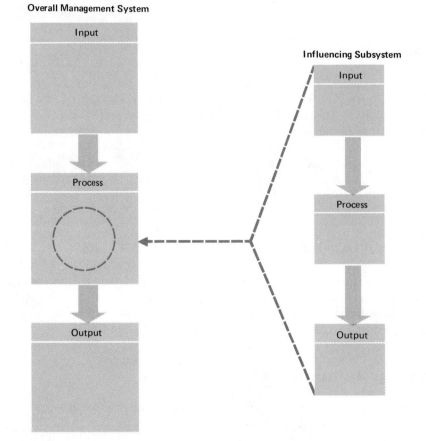

As Figure 12.2 shows, leading, motivating, and considering groups are related influencing activities, each of which is accomplished, to some extent, by managers communicating with organization members. For example, managers decide what kind of leader they should be only after they analyze the characteristics of various groups with which they will interact and how these groups can best be motivated. Then, regardless of the strategy they adopt, their leading, motivating, and working with groups will be accomplished, at least to some extent, by communicating with other organization members.

In fact, as Figure 12.3 implies, essentially all management activities are at least partially accomplished through communication or communication-related endeavours.[1] Since communication is used repeatedly by managers, communication skills are often referred to as the fundamental management skill.

Supporting the notion that communication is the fundamental management skill are the results of a recent survey of chief executives. The results (which appear in Figure 12.4) show communication skills as the most important skills (along with interpersonal skills) to be taught to management students.

Communication is discussed further in the remainder of this chapter, while leading, motivating, and considering groups are discussed in Chapters 13, 14, and 15, respectively.

Communication is the fundamental management skill.

FIGURE 12.2   The influencing subsystem.

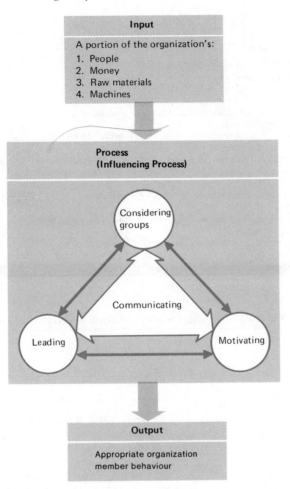

FIGURE 12.3   Management tasks and possible communication-related behaviour used to help accomplish those tasks.

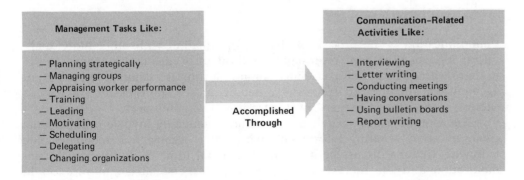

FIGURE 12.4   Chief executives rank importance of skills to be taught to management students.

Rank*	Key Learning Area	Frequency Indicated
1	Oral and written communication skills	25
1	Interpersonal skills	25
3	Financial/managerial account skills	22
4	Ability to think, be analytical, and make decisions	20
5	Strategic planning and goal setting—concern for long-term performance	13
6	Motivation and commitment to the firm—to give 110%	12
7	Understanding of economics	11
8	Management information systems and computer applications	9
8	To know all you can about your business, culture, and overall environment	9
8	Marketing concept (the customer is king) and skills	9
11	Integrity	7
11	To know yourself: Setting long- and short-term career objectives	7
13	Leadership skills	6
13	Understanding of the functional areas of the business	6
15	Time management: Setting priorities—how to work smart, not long or hard	1

*1 is most important.

Reprinted by permission from Stephen C. Harper, "Business Education: A View from the Top," *Business Forum* (Summer 1987): 25.

BACK TO THE CASE

One of the primary functions of Mattel's Arthur S. Spear is influencing—guiding the activities of Mattel employees so that the accomplishment of organizational objectives is enhanced. Spear could perform this function by leading such individuals as division managers or perhaps corporate market research staff, by motivating them to do better jobs, by working well with various groups of Mattel employees, and by communicating successfully with Mattel employees.

Of all these influencing activities, however, communication should be especially important to Spear since communication is the main tool through which he, at least to some extent, should accomplish his duties as chief executive officer. Although more facts would be needed before a final determination could be made, the introductory case suggests that Spear's lack of effective communication could be contributing substantially to problems at Mattel.

COMMUNICATION

Communication is sharing thoughts or ideas with others.

Communication is the process of sharing information with other individuals. Information, as used here, represents any thought or idea that managers desire to share with other individuals. Since communication is a commonly used management skill and often is cited as the one ability most responsible for a manager's success, prospective managers must learn how to communicate.[2]

The communication activities of managers generally involve interpersonal communication—sharing information with other organization members. The following sections discuss both the more general topic of interpersonal communication and the more specific topic of interpersonal communication in organizations.

Interpersonal Communication

To be a successful interpersonal communicator, a manager must understand: (1) how interpersonal communication works; (2) the relationship between feedback and interpersonal communication; and (3) the importance of verbal versus non-verbal interpersonal communication. A discussion of each of these topics follows.

How Interpersonal Communication Works

Interpersonal communication is the process of sharing information with other individuals.[3] To be complete, the interpersonal communication process must have the following three basic elements:

Interpersonal communication has three elements:

1. *The source/encoder*   The **source/encoder** is that person in the interpersonal communication situation who originates and encodes information that he or she desires to share with another person. Encoding is the process of putting information in some form that can be received and understood by another individual. Putting thoughts into a letter is an example of encoding. Until information is encoded, it cannot be shared with others. In subsequent discussion, the source/encoder is referred to simply as the source.

   1. The source/encoder of information.

2. *The signal*   Encoded information that the source intends to share constitutes a **message**. A message that has been transmitted from one person to another is called a **signal**.

   2. The signal.

3. *The decoder/destination*   The **decoder/destination** is that person with whom the source is attempting to share information. This individual receives the signal and decodes or interprets the message to determine its meaning. Decoding is the process of converting messages back into information. In all interpersonal communication situations, message meaning is a result of decoding. The decoder/destination is referred to as the destination throughout the remainder of this chapter.

   3. The decoder/destination.

The classic work of Wilbur Schramm helps us to understand the role that each of the three elements of the interpersonal communication process plays. As implied in Figure 12.5, the source determines what information he or she intends to share, encodes this information in the form of a message, and then transmits the message as a signal to the destination. The destination decodes the transmitted message to determine its meaning and then responds accordingly.

FIGURE 12.5   Role of the source/encoder, signal, and decoder/destination in the communication process.

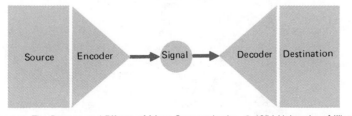

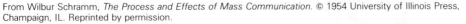

From Wilbur Schramm, *The Process and Effects of Mass Communication.* © 1954 University of Illinois Press, Champaign, IL. Reprinted by permission.

A manager who desires to assign the performance of a certain task to a subordinate would use the communication process in the following way: First, the manager would determine exactly what task she wanted the subordinate to perform. Then she would encode and transmit a message to the subordinate that would accurately reflect this assignment. The message transmission itself could be as simple as the manager telling the subordinate what the new responsibilities include. Next, the subordinate would decode the message transmitted by the manager to ascertain its meaning and then respond to it appropriately.

Successful and Unsuccessful Interpersonal Communication

Successful communication is an interpersonal communication situation in which the information the source intends to share with the destination and the meaning the destination derives from the transmitted message are the same. Conversely, **unsuccessful communication** is an interpersonal communication situation in which the information the source intends to share and the meaning the destination derives from the transmitted message are different.

To increase the probability that communication will be successful, a message must be encoded to ensure that the source's experience concerning the way in which a signal should be decoded is equivalent to the destination's experience of the way it should be decoded. If this situation exists, the probability is high that the destination will interpret the signal as intended by the source. Figure 12.6 illustrates these overlapping fields of experience that ensure successful communication.

Barriers to Successful Interpersonal Communication

Factors that decrease the probability that communication will be successful commonly are called communication barriers. A clear understanding of these barriers is helpful to managers in their attempt to maximize communication success. The following sections discuss both communication macrobarriers and communication microbarriers.

If the message is decoded as the source intended, communication is successful.

FIGURE 12.6   Overlapping fields of experience that ensure successful communication.

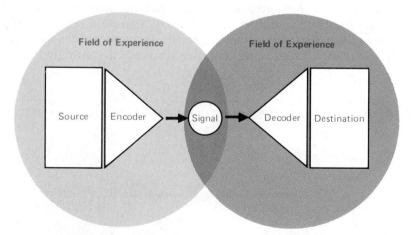

From Wilbur Schramm, *The Process and Effects of Mass Communication.* © 1954 University of Illinois Press, Champaign, IL. Reprinted by permission.

Communication Macrobarriers   **Communication macrobarriers** are those that hinder successful communication in a general communication situation.[4] These factors relate primarily to the communication environment and the larger world in which communication takes place. Among these macrobarriers are:[5]

1. *The increasing need for information*   Because society is constantly and rapidly changing, individuals have a greater and greater need for information. This increased information need tends to overload communication networks, and as a result, communication is distorted. To minimize the effects of this barrier, managers should take steps to ensure that organization members are not overloaded with too much information. Only information critical to the performance of their jobs should be transmitted to them.

2. *The need for increasingly more complex information*   With today's rapid technological advances, most people are faced with more complex communication situations in their everyday lives. If managers take steps to emphasize simplicity in communication, the effects of this barrier can be lessened. Also, furnishing organization members with adequate training to deal with more technical areas might be another strategy for overcoming this barrier.

3. *The reality that individuals in Canada are increasingly coming in contact with individuals using other languages besides English and French*   As business becomes international in scope and as organization members travel more, this trend will accelerate. The potential communication barrier of this multilanguage situation is obvious. Moreover, when dealing with foreigners it is important to be familiar not only with their language but also their culture. Knowledge of a foreign language may be of little value if individuals don't know which words, phrases, and actions are culturally acceptable.

Communication Microbarriers   **Communication microbarriers** are those that hinder successful communication in a specific communication situation.[6] These factors relate directly to such variables as the communication message, the source, and the destination. Among these microbarriers are:[7]

1. *The source's view of the destination*   The source in any communication situation has a tendency to view a destination in a specific way and to influence the messages by this view. For example, individuals tend to speak differently to people they think are informed about a subject than to those they think are uninformed. The destination can sense these source attitudes, which often block successful communication. Managers should keep an open mind about the people with whom they communicate and be careful not to imply any negative attitudes through their communication behaviour.

2. *Message interference*   Stimuli that compete with the communication message for the attention of the destination are called **message interference**, or noise.[8] An example of message interference is a manager talking to his secretary while the secretary is trying to correct a typing mistake. Correcting the mistake is message interference because it competes with the manager's communication message for the secretary's attention. Managers should attempt to communicate only when they have the total attention of the individual or individuals with whom they wish to share information.

3. *The destination's view of the source*   The destination can have certain attitudes toward the source that can also hinder successful communication. If, for example, a destination believes that the source has little expertise in the area about which the source is communicating, the destination may filter out much

---

To minimize communication macrobarriers, managers can:

1. Limit the amount of communication transmitted to subordinates.

2. Make messages to subordinates as simple as possible.

3. Encourage subordinates to learn and understand foreign languages and cultures.

To minimize communication microbarriers, managers can:

1. Be aware of their attitudes toward the destination.

2. Try to monopolize their subordinates' attention.

3. Be aware of their attitudes toward the source.

of the source's message and only slightly consider the part of the message actually received. When communicating, managers should attempt to consider the worth of messages transmitted to them independent of their personal attitudes toward the source. They may lose many valuable ideas if personal feelings toward others influence which messages they listen to carefully.

4. Make messages specific.

4. *Perception* **Perception** is an individual's interpretation of a message. Different individuals can perceive the same message in very different ways. The two primary factors that influence the way in which a stimulus is perceived are the level of the destination's education and the destination's amount of experience. To minimize the negative effects of this perceptual factor on interpersonal communication, managers should try to send messages with precise meanings. Ambiguous words generally tend to magnify negative perceptions. The cartoon shows how a different interpretation of a message can result in unsuccessful communication.

5. Define their words in messages.

5. *Multi-meaning words* Because many words in the English language have several different meanings, a destination may have difficulty deciding which meaning should be attached to the words of a message. A manager should not assume that a word means the same thing to all people who use it.

A study by Lydia Strong substantiates this point. Strong concluded that for the 500 most common words in our language, there are 4 070 different dictionary definitions. On the average, each of these words has over eighteen usages. The word *run* is an example:[9]

Babe Ruth scored a *run*.
Did you ever see Jesse Owens *run*?
I have a *run* in my stocking.
There is a fine *run* of salmon this year.
Are you going to *run* this company or am I?
You have the *run* of the place.
What headline do you want to *run*?
There was a *run* on the bank today.
Did he *run* the ship aground?
I have to *run* (drive the car) downtown.
Who will *run* for president this year?
Joe flies the New York–Chicago *run* twice a week.
You know the kind of people they *run* around with.
The apples *run* large this year.
Please *run* my bath water.

When encoding information, managers should be careful to define the terms they use whenever possible. They should also try to use words in the same way they see their destination use them.

BACK TO THE CASE

In discussing Arthur S. Spear's ability to communicate, we are actually discussing his ability to share ideas with other Mattel employees. For Spear to be a successful communicator, he must concentrate on the three essential elements of the communication process. The first element is the source, or the individual who wishes to share information with another. In this case, the source is Spear. The second element is the signal, or the message transmitted by Spear. The third element is the destination, or that Mattel employee with whom Spear wishes to share information. Spear should communicate with Mattel employees by determining what information he wants to share, encoding the information, and then transmitting the message. The subordinates would then interpret the message and respond accordingly. Spear's communication would be successful if subordinates interpreted messages as Spear intended.

If Spear is to be a successful communicator, he must minimize the impact of numerous communication barriers. These barriers include Mattel employees' needs to have more information, and also more complex information to do their jobs; message interference; Spear's view of the destination as well as the destination's view of Spear; the perceptual process of people involved in the communication attempt; and multi-meaning words.

Feedback and Interpersonal Communication

Feedback is the destinations' reaction to a message. In general, feedback can be used by the source to ensure successful communication.[10] For example, if the destination's message reaction is inappropriate, the source can conclude that communication was not successful and that another message should be transmitted. On the other hand, if the destination's message reaction is appropriate, the source can conclude that communication was successful. This, of course, assumes that the appropriate reaction did not happen merely by chance. Because of the potentially high value of feedback, managers should encourage feedback whenever possible and evaluate this feedback very carefully.

Feedback can be either verbal or non-verbal.[11] For example, to gather verbal feedback, the source could simply ask the destination pertinent message-related questions. The destination's answers would probably indicate to the source whether or not the message was perceived as intended. To gather non-verbal feedback, the source would have to observe the destination's non-verbal response to a message. An example would be a manager who has transmitted a message to a subordinate indicating new steps that must be taken in the normal performance of the subordinate's job. Assuming that no other problems exist, if the steps are not followed accurately the manager has non-verbal feedback that indicates he should further clarify the initial message.

Robert S. Goyer has suggested other uses for feedback besides determining if a message is perceived as intended.[12] For example, over time the source can use feedback to evaluate his personal communication effectiveness by determining the proportion of the destination's message reactions that actually were

Feedback is the destination's reaction to a message.

Feedback can be either verbal or non-verbal.

The communication effectiveness index evaluates personal communication effectiveness.

FIGURE 12.7   Calculation of communication effectiveness index.

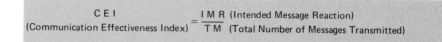

$$\text{C E I} \atop \text{(Communication Effectiveness Index)} = \frac{\text{I M R}}{\text{T M}} \frac{\text{(Intended Message Reaction)}}{\text{(Total Number of Messages Transmitted)}}$$

intended by the source. A formula illustrating how this evaluation, the **communication effectiveness index**, can be calculated is shown in Figure 12.7. The higher this proportion, the greater the communication effectiveness of the source.

One communication problem may be a confusing vocabulary.

If managers discover that their communication effectiveness index is relatively low over an extended period of time, they should assess their situation to determine how to improve their communication skills. One problem they may discover is that they are repeatedly using a vocabulary confusing to the destination. For example, a study conducted by Group Attitudes Corporation found that if managers tended to use certain words repeatedly in communicating with steelworkers, the steelworkers almost certainly became confused.[13] Figure 12.8 shows thirty words that Group Attitudes Corporation found to be misunderstood frequently by steelworkers and suggested phrases or words that managers should use instead.

The "ten commandments of good communications" are:

Besides analyzing their vocabulary, managers should attempt to increase their communication effectiveness by following the "ten commandments of good communication" as closely as possible. These commandments are:[14]

1. Clarify ideas.

1. *Seek to clarify your ideas before communicating* The more systematically you analyze the problem or idea to be communicated, the clearer it becomes. This is the first step toward effective communication. Many communications fail

FIGURE 12.8   Thirty words frequently misunderstood by steelworkers and suggested words or phrases to be used in their place.

1. Accrue — *pile up; collect*	15. Fortuitously — *by chance; accidentally; luckily*
2. Compute — *figure*	16. Generate — *create; build; produce*
3. Concession — *giving up (something)*	17. Impediment — *barrier; roadblock*
4. Contemplate — *think about; expect*	18. Inadequate — *not enough*
5. Delete — *cancel; take out; remove*	19. Increment — *raise; increase*
6. Designate — *name; appoint*	20. Inevitably — *in the end; finally*
7. Deterioration — *breaking down; wearing away*	21. Initiate — *begin; start*
8. Detriment — *hurt; damage; harm*	22. Injurious — *damaging; harmful*
9. Economic problem — *a cost problem*	23. Jeopardy — *danger*
10. Efficiency — *the way it should be (e.g., operating a machine the way it should be operated)*	24. Magnitude — *size*
	25. Modify — *change; alter*
11. Embody — *contain; include; hold*	26. Objectivity — *fairness*
12. Equitable — *fair; just*	27. Pursuant — *in agreement with*
13. Excerpt — *section; part*	28. Perpetuate — *keep alive; continue*
14. Facilitate — *help along*	29. Subsequently — *later*
	30. Ultimate — *final; end*

because of inadequate planning. Good planning must consider the goals and attitudes of those who will receive the communication and those who will be affected by it.

2. *Examine the true purpose of each communication* Before you communicate, ask yourself what you really want to accomplish with your message—obtain information, initiate action, change another person's attitude? Identify your most important goal and then adapt your language, tone, and total approach to serve that specific objective. Don't try to accomplish too much with each communication. The sharper the focus of your message, the greater its chances of success.

2. Examine the purpose.

3. *Consider the total physical and human setting whenever you communicate* Meaning and intent are conveyed by more than words alone. Many other factors influence the overall impact of a communication, and managers must be sensitive to the total setting in which they communicate. Consider, for example, your sense of timing, that is, the circumstances under which you make an announcement or render a decision; the physical setting—whether you communicate in private or otherwise, for example; the social climate that pervades work relationships within the company or a department and sets the tone of its communications; custom and practice—the degree to which your communication conforms to, or departs from, the expectations of your audience. Be constantly aware of the total setting in which you communicate. Like all living things, communication must be capable of adapting to its environment.

3. Consider the total setting.

4. *Consult with others, when appropriate, in planning communications.* Frequently, it is desirable or necessary to seek the participation of others in planning a communication or in developing the facts on which to base the communication. Such consultation often lends additional insight and objectivity to your message. Moreover, those who have helped you plan your communication will give it their active support.

4. Consult with others.

5. *Be mindful, while you communicate, of the overtones as well as the basic content of your message* Your tone of voice, your expression, your apparent receptiveness to the responses of others—all have tremendous impact on those you wish to reach. Frequently overlooked, these subtleties of communication often affect a listener's reaction to a message even more than its basic content. Similarly, your choice of language—particularly your awareness of the fine shades of meaning and emotion in the words you use—predetermine in large part the reactions of your listeners.

5. Consider the overtones.

6. *Take the opportunity, when it arises, to convey something of help or value to the receiver* Consideration of the other person's interests and needs—trying to look at things from the other person's point of view—frequently points up opportunities to convey something of immediate benefit or long-range value to the other person. Subordinates are most responsive to managers whose messages take the subordinates' interests into account.

6. Offer the receiver something of value.

7. *Follow up your communication* Your best efforts at communication may be wasted, and you may never know whether you have succeeded in expressing your true meaning and intent if you do not follow up to see how well you have put your message across. You can do this by asking questions, by encouraging the receiver to express his or her reactions, by follow-up contacts, and by subsequent review of performance. Make certain that every important

7. Follow up the communication.

communication has feedback so that complete understanding and appropriate action result.

8. Be aware of future needs.

8. *Communicate for tomorrow as well as today*   While communications may be aimed primarily at meeting the demands of an immediate situation, they must be planned with the past in mind if they are to maintain consistency in the receiver's view. Most important, however, communications must be consistent with long-range interests and goals. For example, it is not easy to communicate frankly on such matters as poor performance or the shortcomings of a loyal subordinate, but postponing disagreeable communications makes these matters more difficult in the long run and is actually unfair to your subordinates and your company.

9. Have actions support communication.

9. *Be sure your actions support your communications*   In the final analysis, the most persuasive kind of communication is not what you say, but what you do. When your actions or attitudes contradict your words, others tend to discount what you have said. For every manager, this means that good supervisory practices—such as clear assignment of responsibility and authority, fair rewards for effort, and sound policy enforcement—serve to communicate more than all the gifts of oratory.

10. Be a good listener.

10. *Last, but by no means least: Seek not only to be understood but to understand—be a good listener*   When you start talking you often cease to listen, at least in that larger sense of being attuned to the other person's unspoken reactions and attitudes. Even more serious is the occasional inattentiveness you may be guilty of when others are attempting to communicate with you. Listening is one of the most important, most difficult, and most neglected skills in communication. It demands that you concentrate not only on the explicit meanings another person is expressing, but also on the implicit meanings, unspoken words, and undertones that may be far more significant. Thus, you must learn to listen with the inner ear if you are to know the inner person.

Verbal and Non-verbal Interpersonal Communication

Interpersonal communication is generally divided into two types: verbal and non-verbal. Up to this point, the main emphasis of the chapter has been on **verbal communication**—communication that uses either spoken or written words to share information with others.

Non-verbal communication is encoding without words.

Non-verbal communication is sharing information without using words to encode thoughts. Factors commonly used to encode thoughts in non-verbal communication include gestures, vocal tones, and facial expressions. In most interpersonal communication, verbal and non-verbal communications are not either-or occurrences. Instead, the destination's interpretation of a message generally is based not only on the words in the message but also on such factors as the source's gestures and facial expressions.

Non-verbal communication may influence the impact of a message more than verbal communication.

In an interpersonal communication situation in which both verbal and non-verbal factors are present, non-verbal factors may have more influence on the total impact of a message than verbal factors. Albert Mehrabian has developed a formula that shows the relative contributions of both verbal and non-verbal factors to the total impact of a message. This formula is as follows: Total message impact = .07 words + .38 vocal tones + .55 facial expressions.[15] Of course, both vocal tones and facial expressions are non-verbal factors. Besides vocal tones and facial expressions, gestures,[16] gender,[17] and dress[18] can influence the impact of a verbal message. Given the great potential influence of non-verbal factors on the impact of a message, managers should use non-verbal message ingredients to complement verbal message ingredients whenever possible.[19]

Non-verbal messages also can be used to add new content to a verbal message. To this end, a head might be nodded or a voice might be toned to show either agreement or disagreement.

Regardless of how managers decide to combine verbal and non-verbal factors, they must be sure that the two do not unknowingly present contradictory messages. For instance, the words of a message might express approval while the non-verbal factors express disapproval. This type of situation creates message ambiguity and leaves the destination frustrated.

> Managers must avoid contradictory verbal and non-verbal messages.

BACK TO THE CASE

Mattel employees' reactions to Arthur S. Spear's messages provide Spear with perhaps his most useful tool in making communication successful—feedback. When feedback does not seem appropriate, Spear should transmit another message to clarify the meaning of his first message. Spear must be alert for both verbal and non-verbal feedback. Over time, if feedback indicates that Spear is a relatively unsuccessful communicator, he should analyze his situation carefully to improve his communication effectiveness. Spear might find, for instance, that he is using a vocabulary that is generally inappropriate for certain employees or that he is not following one or more of the ten commandments of good communication.

In addition, Spear must remember that he can communicate to others without using words. His facial expressions, gestures, and even the tone of his voice say things to people. Most of Spear's communication situations involve the simultaneous sending of both verbal and non-verbal messages to Mattel employees. Since the total impact of a message may be generated mostly by its non-verbal components, Spear must be certain that his non-verbal messages complement his verbal messages.

Interpersonal Communication in Organizations

To be effective communicators, managers must not merely understand the more general interpersonal communication concepts discussed previously but also the characteristics of interpersonal communication within organizations, called **organizational communication**. Organizational communication directly relates to the goals, functions, and structure of human organizations,[20] and organizational success, to a major extent, is determined by the effectiveness of organizational communication.[21]

Although organizational communication is often referred to by early management writers, the topic began to receive systematic study and attention only after World War II.[22] From World War II to the 1950s, organizational communication as a discipline made significant advances in such areas as mathematical communication theory and behavioural communication theory.[23] In more recent times, emphasis on organizational communication has grown in colleges of business throughout the nation.[24] The following information focuses on three fundamental organizational communication topics: (1) formal organizational

> Organizational communication is interpersonal communication within organizations.

communication; (2) informal organizational communication; and (3) the encouragement of formal organizational communication.

Formal Organizational Communication

Formal organizational communication follows the organization chart.

In general, organizational communication that follows the lines of the organization chart is called **formal organizational communication**.[25] As discussed in Chapter 8, the organization chart depicts relationships between people and jobs and shows the formal channels of communication between them.

Types of Formal Organizational Communication

In general, there are three basic types of formal organizational communication: (1) downward; (2) upward; and (3) lateral.

Downward organizational communication concerns the direction and control of employees.

Downward Organizational Communication   Communication that flows from any point on an organization chart downward to another point on the organization chart is called **downward organizational communication**. This type of formal organizational communication primarily relates to the direction and control of employees. Job-related information that focuses on what activities are required, when the activities should be performed, and how the activities should be coordinated with other activities within the organization must be transmitted to employees. This downward communication typically includes a statement of organizational philosophy, management system objectives, position descriptions, and other written information relating to the importance, rationale, and interrelationships of various departments.[26]

Upward organizational communication provides organizational feedback.

Upward Organizational Communication   Communication that flows from any point on an organization chart upward to another point on the organization chart is called **upward organizational communication**. This type of organizational communication primarily contains information managers need to evaluate the organizational area for which they are responsible and to tell them if something is going wrong within the organization. For example, upward communication generally contains information that relates to production reports, shipping reports, and customer complaints.[27] Organizational modifications based on this feedback enable the organization to be more successful in the future.

Lateral organizational communication involves planning and coordinating.

Lateral Organizational Communication   Communication that flows from any point on an organization chart horizontally to another point on the organization chart is called **lateral organizational communication**. Communication that flows across the organization usually focuses on coordinating the activities of various departments and developing new plans for future operating periods. Within the organization, all departments are related to all other departments. Only through lateral communication can these departmental relationships be coordinated well enough to enhance the attainment of management system objectives.

The Management in Action feature which follows outlines the potential influencing and coordination problems which may arise with the presence of lateral relationships in an organization. It provides a guideline for anticipating and handling these problems.

HOW TO WIN FRIENDS AND INFLUENCE CO-MANAGERS

Most of the power gaps one finds in professional, managerial, and technical jobs are associated with relationships outside the formal chain of command. This makes the jobholders' performances dependent on people other than the jobholders' own bosses and subordinates, while giving them little or no formal control over these same people. This situation is often complicated by the existence of several other factors: the large number of lateral relationships that may be associated with such jobs; the geographic dispersion of the parties involved; the possible differences in goals and beliefs among the parties; and ambiguity with regard to where all the relevant lateral relationships exist. These and other factors make managing such relationships a complicated, and very important, leadership task.

The costs associated with these difficult-to-manage lateral relationships can be large; very often, good product ideas are abandoned because of resistance from colleagues. The amount of frustration connected with these situations is correspondingly large, resulting in lower productivity, apathy, and even resignations. In situations such as these, it is essential that the employees recognize the relational aspect of work. Unfortunately, however, most don't. Consequently, the leadership and managerial responsibility of influencing and communicating demands that attention be given to: (1) identifying where all the relevant lateral relationships exist, including the almost-invisible ones; (2) assessing who among these may resist cooperation, and determining why and how strongly; (3) developing, whenever possible, a good relationship with these people to facilitate the communication, education, or negotiation process required to reduce or overcome most kinds of resistance; and (4) carefully selecting and implementing more subtle or forceful methods to deal with the resistance when these other steps don't work.

Effective leadership in a job that includes a complicated set of lateral relationships requires, first and foremost, a keen sense of where these relationships are. This is often not an easy task. For a number of reasons, lateral relationships are frequently not very visible. For example, few lateral dependencies are identified on organization charts or in job descriptions. More fluid in nature, they

"very often, good product ideas are abandoned because of resistance from colleagues."

333

tend to change more often than relationships within the chain of command. Coping with this reality requires constant sensitivity to the issue of whose cooperation or compliance may be necessary in the future. This, in turn, depends on where one is going, what may have to be accomplished, who will need to be involved if these tasks are to be accomplished effectively and responsibly, and finally, who may want to block these actions. Problems such as these are avoidable, but they require routine consideration of the following questions: (1) What am I trying to achieve in my work? What is my vision of the future? (2) What are key tasks I need to accomplish this year? This month? This week? Today? (3) For each of these, whose cooperation will definitely be necessary? Whose cooperation may be necessary? and (4) Whose compliance will definitely be necessary? That is, who can block or retard the accomplishment of these tasks? Whose compliance may be necessary.

The next step involves diagnosing who may resist cooperation, why, and how strongly. Many are the reasons why otherwise reasonable people may resist cooperation. They may not cooperate because they have different priorities, or limitations on their abilities. Their resistance may be due to different assessments of how they can best contribute, or they may simply be unaware of what is needed. There may be little trust, or they may be angry. Finally, and perhaps most important of all, they may not cooperate because they believe they have a different stake in the action and do not want to lose something they value. The central theme here is one of diversity: significant differences in stakes, abilities, priorities, and assessments of the situation can easily lead to conflict instead of cooperation. To resolve these problems, it is essential to realize that: (1) these conflicts are rooted in the complex differences involved; and (2) these differences are created by strong formal and informal forces. Differences among departments, for example, are primarily a function of the organizational structure which created these departments. Those insensitive to these differences and the powerful underlying forces often assume that an impassioned speech on "unity of purpose" will automatically induce cooperation. They are wrong.

Armed with a sense of where problems may develop because of lateral relationships, effective leadership then requires the selection and implementation of strategies geared towards eliminating or overcoming these problems. The most commonly used strategy here is relationship development. Effective managers work to develop a personal relationship with the relevant persons, using that relationship to facilitate the communication, education, or negotiation process required to reduce or overcome most kinds of resistance to cooperation. While some may find this insincere and manipulative, others smile knowingly and maintain that all interaction at work is like this. But both miss the point, for neither sees how certain circumstances may call for this "carefully planned" and executed interaction for the good of all concerned. However, a good relationship coupled with good communication can overcome only some of the resistance which may be encountered in a lateral relationship. In some cases the use of more complicated and more forceful methods, such as indirect pressure and influencing through another (who is well received), may be called for.

The basic approach here applies to a wide variety of situations. But there does come a point when the number of such relationships and the differences involved become so great that the situation becomes unmanageable. When this happens, the only solution to the problem involves reducing the number of lateral relationships or the diversity of the parties involved. For an organization, this often means breaking large, highly specialized, functionally structured units into smaller, more self-contained, and more autonomous units. Dozens of large corporations have been attempting to do exactly this, calling the change "decentralization" or "divisionalization."

Based on "How to win friends and influence comanagers," by John P. Kotter in *Canadian Business*, October 1985. Used with permission of The Free Press, a Division of Macmillan, Inc. from *Power and Influence* by John P. Kotter. Copyright © 1985 by John P. Kotter.

Patterns of Formal Organizational Communication

By nature, organizational communication creates patterns of communication among organization members. These patterns essentially evolve from the repeated occurrence of various serial transmissions of information. According to William Haney, a **serial transmission** involves passing information from one individual to another. A serial transmission of information occurs when:

> A communicates a message to B; B then communicates A's message (or rather his or her interpretation of A's message) to C; C then communicates his or her interpretation of B's interpretation of A's message to D; and so on. The originator and the ultimate recipient of the message are separated by middle people.[28]

A serial transmission occurs when one person tells another, who tells another, and so on.

Of course, one of the obvious weaknesses of a serial transmission is that messages tend to become distorted as the length of the serial transmission increases. Research has shown that in a serial transmission message details may be omitted, altered, or added.[29]

As presented in a classic article by Alex Bavelas and Dermot Barrett,[30] the potential inaccuracy of messages transmitted is not the only weakness of a serial transmission. A serial transmission can also influence morale, the emergence of a leader, and the degree to which individuals involved in the transmission are organized and efficient. Three basic organizational communication pattern studies and their corresponding effects on the variables just mentioned are shown in Figure 12.9.

FIGURE 12.9   Relationship between three patterns of organizational communication and group characteristics of speed, accuracy, organization, emergence of leader, and morale.

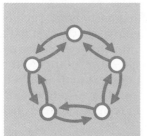 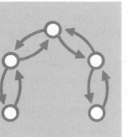 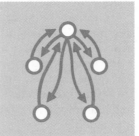

Speed	Slow	Fast	Fast
Accuracy	Poor	Good	Good
Organization	No stable form of organization	Slowly emerging but stable organization	Almost immediate and stable organization
Emergence of Leader	None	Marked	Very pronounced
Morale	Very good	Poor	Very poor

BACK TO THE CASE

As chief executive officer at Mattel, Arthur S. Spear must strive to understand the intricacies of organizational communication—interpersonal communication as it takes place within the organization. The success of organizational communication at Mattel is an important factor in determining the company's level of success. Spear should communicate with his people in one of two basic ways; formally or informally.

In general, Spear's formal communication should follow the lines on the organization chart. Spear can communicate downward to, for example, divisional managers or upward to, for example, Mattel's board of directors. Spear's downward communication should focus on the activities subordinates should be performing, while his upward communication should indicate how well the company is doing. Since Spear is chief executive officer and has no one at his same level within the organization, he would not communicate laterally. He should, however, take steps to ensure that lateral communication does occur at other organizational levels to enhance planning and coordination at Mattel.

Informal organizational communication ignores the organization chart.

Informal Organizational Communication   Organizational communication that does not follow the lines of the organization chart is called **informal organizational communication**. This type of communication typically follows the pattern of personal relationships among organization members. One friend communicates with another friend, regardless of their relative positions on the organization chart. Informal organizational communication networks generally exist because organization members have a desire to know information that formal organizational communication does not furnish.

The grapevine is the network of informal organizational communication.

The informal organizational communication network, or **grapevine**, has several distinctive characteristics: (1) the grapevine springs up and is used irregularly within the organization; (2) it is not controlled by top executives, who may not even be able to influence it; and (3) it is used largely to serve the self-interests of the people within it.

Another characteristic of the grapevine is that it usually transmits information very quickly. One study of more than four thousand employees of a U.S. naval ordnance test station focused on the speed at which information passed by use of grapevines. The employees were asked the following question: "Suppose that management made an important change in the way the organization would be run—through what channel or means of communication would you get the word first?" Employees ranked seven communication sources in response to this question as follows:[31]

1. Grapevine, 38 percent.
2. Supervisor, 27 percent.
3. Official memo, 17 percent.
4. Station newspaper, 7 percent.
5. Station directive system, 4 percent.
6. Bulletin boards, 4 percent.
7. Other, 3 percent.

The grapevine usually follows one of four patterns.

As with formal organizational communication, informal organizational communication involves serial transmissions. Organization members involved in these transmissions, however, are more difficult for managers to identify than those in the formal communication network. As Figure 12.10 illustrates, four different patterns of grapevines generally tend to exist in organizations:[32]

1. *The single-strand grapevine*   A tells B, who tells C, who tells D, and so on. This type of grapevine generally tends to distort messages more than any other.

FIGURE 12.10 Four types of organizational grapevines.

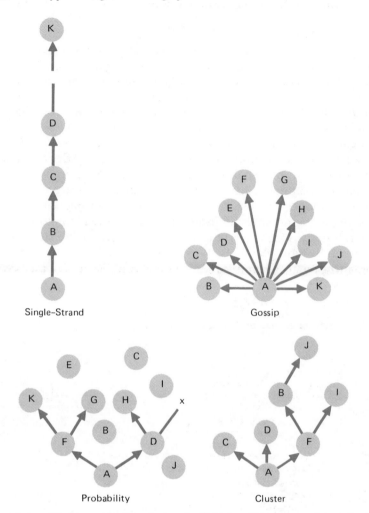

Single-Strand

Gossip

Probability

Cluster

2. *The gossip grapevine*   A informs everyone else on the grapevine.
3. *The probability grapevine*   A communicates randomly, for example, to F and D. F and D then continue to inform other grapevine members in the same way.
4. *The cluster grapevine*   A selects and tells C, D, and F. F selects and tells I and B, and B selects and tells J. Information in this grapevine travels only to selected individuals.

Clearly, the grapevine is a factor with which managers must deal since a grapevine can and often does generate rumours that can be detrimental to organizational success.[33] To minimize the development of such rumours, some managers advise distributing maximum information through formal communication channels.[34] Some writers argue, however, that managers should encourage the development of grapevines and strive to become grapevine members to gain information feedback that could be very valuable in improving the organization.[35]

Should grapevines be discouraged or encouraged?

Exactly how individual managers should deal with the grapevine, of course, depends on the specific organizational situation in which the managers find themselves.

Encouraging Formal Organizational Communication Organizational communication often is called the "nervous system" of the organization. The organization acts only as its "nervous system," or organizational communication, directs it. Since formal organizational communication is generally the most important type of communication that takes place within the organization, managers must encourage its free flow if the organization is to be successful.

Managers can use many different strategies to encourage the flow of formal organizational communication. One strategy is listening attentively to messages that come through formal channels. This listening shows organization members that managers are interested in what subordinates have to say and, as a result, encourages employees to use formal communication channels in subsequent situations. General guidelines for listening are presented in Figure 12.11. Another managerial strategy is to support the flow of clear and concise statements through formal communication channels. Receiving an ambiguous message through a formal organizational communication channel can discourage members from us-

Strategies for encouraging formal organizational communication include:

1. Listening.

2. Sending clear messages.

FIGURE 12.11 Ten commandments for good listening.

1. *Stop talking!*
   You cannot listen if you are talking.
   Polonius (*Hamlet*): "Give every man thine ear, but few thy voice."
2. *Put the talker at ease.*
   Help the talker feel free to talk.
   This is often called a permissive environment.
3. *Show the talker that you want to listen.*
   Look and act interested. Do not read your mail while he or she talks.
   Listen to understand rather than to oppose.
4. *Remove distractions.*
   Don't doodle, tap, or shuffle papers.
   Will it be quieter if you shut the door?
5. *Empathize with the talker.*
   Try to put yourself in the talker's place so that you can see his or her point of view.
6. *Be patient.*
   Allow plenty of time. Do not interrupt the talker.
   Don't start for the door or walk away.
7. *Hold your temper.*
   An angry person gets the wrong meaning from words.
8. *Go easy on argument and criticism.*
   This puts the talker on the defensive. He or she may "clam up" or get angry.
   Do not argue: even if you win, you *lose*.
9. *Ask questions.*
   This encourages the talker and shows you are listening.
   It helps to develop points further.
10. *Stop talking!*
   This is first and last, because all other commandments depend on it.
   You just can't do a good listening job while you are talking.

   Nature gave us two ears but only one tongue,
   which is a gentle hint that we should listen more than we talk.

From *Human Behavior at Work*, p. 396, by Keith Davis. Copyright © 1972 by McGraw-Hill, Inc. Used with permission of McGraw-Hill Book Company.

ing that channel again. A third strategy managers can use is taking care to ensure that all organization members have free access to the use of formal communication channels within the organization. Obviously, organization members cannot communicate formally within the organization if they don't have access to the formal communication network. A fourth strategy is assigning specific communication responsibilities to staff personnel. In this capacity, for example, staff personnel could be of enormous help to line personnel in spreading important information throughout the organization.

3. Providing access to channels.

4. Using staff personnel.

BACK TO THE CASE

If the charge against Spear in the introductory case—that he is difficult to communicate with—is true, a very extensive and often-used grapevine probably has developed at Mattel. Although the company grapevine must be dealt with, Spear may not be able to influence it significantly. Mattel employees, as well as employees in any company, typically are involved in grapevines for self-interests and because the formal organization has not furnished them with the information they feel they need.

By developing various social relationships, Spear could, conceivably, become part of the grapevine and obtain valuable feedback from it. Also, because grapevines generate rumours that could have a detrimental

effect on Mattel's success, Spear should try to ensure that Mattel personnel are given all the information they need to do their jobs well through formal organizational communication, thereby reducing the need for a grapevine.

Since formal organizational communication is vitally important to Mattel, Spear should try to encourage its flow as much as possible. He can do this by listening intently to messages that come to him over formal channels, supporting the flow of clear messages through formal channels, and making sure that all Mattel employees have access to formal communication channels.

Action Summary

Reread the learning objectives that follow. Each objective is followed by questions. Answering these questions accurately will help you to retain the most important concepts discussed in this chapter. After answering each question, check your answer with the answer key at the end of this chapter. (*Hint*: If you have doubt regarding the correct response, consult the page that follows the answer.)

From studying this chapter, I will attempt to acquire:

Circle:

1. **An understanding of influencing.**
   a. The influencing function can be viewed as coercing the activities of organization members in appropriate directions.   T, F
   b. Which of the following activities is *not* a major component of the influencing process: (a) motivating; (b) leading; (c) communicating; (d) correcting; (e) considering groups.   a, b, c, d, e

2. **An understanding of interpersonal communication.**
   a. Communication is best described as the process of: (a) sharing emotion; (b) sharing information; (c) sending messages; (d) feedback formulation; (e) forwarding information.   a, b, c, d, e
   b. The basic elements of interpersonal communication are: (a) source/encoder, signal, decoder/destination; (b) sender/message, encoder, receiver/decoder; (c) signal, source/sender, decoder/destination; (d) signal, source/decoder, encoder/destination; (e) source/sender, signal, receiver/destination.   a, b, c, d, e

3. A knowledge of how to use feedback.

T, F

a. Feedback is only verbal.

b. Robert S. Goyer has suggested using feedback: (a) as a microbarrier; (b) as a way for the source to evaluate his or her communication effectiveness; (c) to ensure that instructions will be carried out; (d) to evaluate the decoder;

a, b, c, d, e

(e) all of the above.

4. An appreciation for the importance of non-verbal communication.

T, F

a. In interpersonal communication, non-verbal factors may play a more influential role than verbal factors.

T, F

b. Non-verbal messages can contradict the verbal message, which can create frustration in the destination.

5. Insights on formal organizational communication.

a. Which of the following is *not* upward communication: (a) cost accounting reports; (b) purchase order summary; (c) production reports; (d) corporate

a, b, c, d, e

policy statement; (e) sales reports.

b. The primary purpose served by lateral organizational communication is:

a, b, c, d, e

(a) coordinating; (b) organizing; (c) direction; (d) evaluation; (e) control.

6. An appreciation for the importance of the grapevine.

a. Which of the following statements concerning the grapevine is *not* correct: (a) grapevines are irregularly used in organizations; (b) a grapevine can and often does generate harmful rumours; (c) the grapevine is used largely to serve the self-interests of the people within it; (d) some managers use the grapevine to their advantage; (e) in time, and with proper pressure, the

a, b, c, d, e

grapevine can be eliminated.

T, F

b. The grapevine is much slower than formal communication channels.

7. Some hints on how to encourage organizational communication.

a. To encourage formal organizational communication, managers should: (a) support the flow of clear and concise statements through formal channels; (b) ensure free access to formal channels for all organization members; (c) assign to staff personnel specific communication responsibilities; (d) a

a, b, c, d, e

and b; (e) all of the above.

b. Since formal organizational communication is the most important type of communication within an organization, managers must restrict its flow if

T, F

the organization is to be successful.

▤ INTRODUCTORY CASE WRAP-UP

"Troubles at Mattel" (p. 318) and its related back-to-the-case sections were written to help you better understand the management concepts contained in this chapter. Answer the following discussion questions about this introductory case to further enrich your understanding of the chapter content:

1. List three problems that could be caused at Mattel because of Spear's being a poor communicator.

2. Explain how the problems that you listed in number 1 can be caused by Spear's being a poor communicator.

3. If Spear is a poor communicator as charged, could he be contributing to the communication problems relating to divisional management? Explain.

Issues for Review and Discussion

1. What is influencing?
2. Describe the relationship between the overall management system and the influencing subsystem.
3. What factors make up the input, process, and output of the influencing subsystem?
4. Explain the relationship between the factors that comprise the process section of the influencing subsystem.
5. What is communication?
6. How important is communication to managers?
7. Draw the communication model presented in this chapter and explain how it works.
8. How does successful communication differ from unsuccessful communication?
9. Summarize the significance of "field of experience" to communication.
10. List and describe three communication macro-barriers and three communication micro-barriers.
11. What is feedback, and how should managers use it when communicating?
12. How is the communication effectiveness index calculated, and what is its significance?
13. Name the ten commandments of good communication.
14. What is non-verbal communication? Explain its significance.
15. How should managers use non-verbal communication?
16. What is organizational communication?
17. How do formal and informal organizational communication differ?
18. Describe three types of formal organizational communication, and explain the general purpose of each type.
19. Can serial transmissions and other formal communication patterns influence communication effectiveness and also the individuals using the patterns? If so, how?
20. Draw and describe the four main types of grapevines that exist in organizations.
21. How can managers encourage the flow of formal organizational communication?

Sources of Additional Information

Arnold, Hugh J., and Daniel C. Feldman. *Organizational Behavior*. New York: McGraw-Hill, 1986.

Barnlund, Dean. *Interpersonal Communication: Survey and Studies*. Boston: Houghton Mifflin, 1968.

Bosmajian, H.A., ed. *The Rhetoric of Nonverbal Communication*. Chicago: Scott, Foresman, 1971.

Dunham, Randall B. *Organizational Behavior: People and Processes in Management*. Homewood, Ill.: Richard D. Irwin, 1984.

Ebenstein, Michael, and Leonard I. Krauss. "Strategic Planning for Information Resource Management." *Management Review* 70 (June 1981): 21–26.

Eisenberg, Abne M., and Ralph R. Smith. *Nonverbal Communication*. Indianapolis: Bobbs-Merrill, 1972.

French, Wendell L., Fremond E. Kast, and James E. Rosenzweig. *Understanding Human Behavior in Organizations*. New York: Harper & Row, 1985.

Friedman, Selma. "Where Employees Go for Information (Some Surprises!)." *Administrative Management* 42 (September 1981): 72–73.

Goldhaber, Gerald M. *Organizational Communication*, 4th ed. Dubuque, Iowa: Wm. C. Brown, 1983.

Gordon, William I., and John R. Miller. *Managing Your Communication*. Prospect Heights, Ill.: Waveland, 1983.

Gruneberg, Michael, and Toby Wall. *Social Psychology and Organizational Behavior*. New York: Wiley, 1984.

Lesikar, Raymond. *Business Communication*. Homewood, Ill.: Richard D. Irwin, 1972.

Micheli, Linda, Frank V. Cespedes, Donald Byker, and Thomas J.C. Raymond. *Managerial Communication*. Glenview, Ill.: Scott, Foresman, 1984.

Montgomery, Robert L. "Are You a Good Listener?" *Nation's Business* 69 (October 1981): 65–68.

Penrose, John. "Telecommunication, Teleconferencing, and Business Communication." *Journal of Business Communication* 21 (Winter 1984): 93–112.

Reinsch, N.L. and Phillip V. Lewis. "Communication Apprehension as a Determinant of Channel Preferences." *Journal of Business Communication* 21 (Summer 1984): 53–62.

Shatshat, H.M., and Bong-Gon P. Shin. "Organizational Communication—A Key to Successful Strategic Planning." *Managerial Planning* 30 (September/October 1981): 37–40.

Timm, Paul R. "Driving Out the Devils of Communication," *Management World* 13 (July 1984): 27–29.

Umstot, Denis D. *Understanding Organizational Behavior: Concepts and Applications*. New York: West Publishing, 1984.

Notes

1. See the following articles for insights into and examples of how communication is related to the performance of management activities: Larry Penley and Brian Hawkins, "Studying Interpersonal Communication in Organizations: A Leadership Application," *Academy of Management Journal* (June 1985): 309–26; Richard C. Huseman, Elmore R. Alexander III, and Russell W. Driver, "Planning for Organizational Change: The Role of Communication," *Managerial Planning* 28 (May/June 1980): 32–36; H.M. Shatshat and Bong-Gon P. Shin, "Organizational Communication—A Key to Successful Strategic Planning," *Managerial Planning* 30 (September/October 1981): 37–40.

2. James B. Strenski, "Two-Way Communication—A Management Necessity," *Personnel Journal* (January 1970): 29–35. See also Stephen C. Harper, "Business Education: A View from the Top," *Business Forum* (Summer 1987): 24–27.

3. This section is based on the following classic article on interpersonal communication: Wilbur Schramm, "How Communication Works," *The Process and Effects of Mass Communication*, ed. Wilbur Schramm (Urbana: University of Illinois Press, 1954), 3–10.

4. This section is based primarily on David S. Brown, "Barriers to Successful Communication: Part I, Macrobarriers," *Management Review* (December 1975): 24–29.

5. James K. Weekly and Raj Aggarwal, *International Business: Operating in the Global Economy* (New York: Dryden Press, 1987).

6. This section is based primarily on David S. Brown, "Barriers to Successful Communication: Part II, Microbarriers," *Management Review* (January 1976): 15–21.

7. Sally Bulkley Pancrazio and James J. Pancrazio, "Better Communication for Managers," *Supervisory Management* (June 1981): 31–37.

8. Gene E. Burton, "Barriers to Effective Communication," *Management World* (March 1977): 4–8.

9. Lydia Strong, "Do You Know How to Listen?" in *Effective Communications on the Job*, ed. M. Joseph Dooher and Vivienne Marquis (New York: American Management Association, 1956), 28.

10. Robert E. Callahan, C. Patrick Fleenor, and Harry R. Knudson, *Understanding Organizational Behavior: A Managerial Viewpoint* (Columbus, Ohio: Charles E. Merrill, 1986).

11. For more on non-verbal issues, see I.T. Sheppard, "Silent Signals," *Supervisory Management* (March 1986): 31–33; S. Strecker, "Opening Moves and Winning Plays: An Interview with Ken Delmar," *Executive Female* (January/February 1985): 24–48.

12. Robert S. Goyer, "Interpersonal Communication and Human Interaction: A Behavioral View," paper presented at the 138th annual meeting of the American Association for the Advancement of Science, 1971. For an article that complements this orientation toward feedback, see R. Abrams, "Do You Get What You Ask For?" *Supervisory Management* (April 1986): 32–34.

13. Verne Burnett, "Management's Tower of Babel," *Management Review* (June 1961): 4–11.

14. Reprinted by permission of the publisher, from *Management Review* (October 1955). © 1955 American Management Association, Inc. All rights reserved.

15. Albert Mehrabian, "Communication without Words," *Psychology Today* (September 1968): 53–55.

16. For a practical article emphasizing the role of gestures in communication, see S.D. Gladis, "Notes Are Not Enough," *Training and Development Journal* (August 1985): 35–38.

17. Nicole Steckler and Robert Rosenthal, "Sex Differences in Nonverbal and Verbal Communication with Bosses, Peers, and Subordinates," *Journal of Applied Psychology* (February 1985): 157–63.

18. Andrew J. DuBrin, *Contemporary Applied Management* (Plano, Tex.: Business Publications, 1982), 127–34.

19. W. Alan Randolph, *Understanding and Managing Organizational Behavior* (Homewood, Ill.: Richard D. Irwin, 1985), 349–50.

20. Gerald M. Goldhaber, *Organizational Communication* (Dubuque, Iowa: Wm. C. Brown, 1983).

21. Don J. Baxter, "Employee Communication . . . A Matter of Organizational Survival," *Journal of Organizational Communication* 4, no. 1 (1974): 5–7.

22. Paul H. Pietri, "Organizational Communication: The Pioneers," *Journal of Business Communication* 11, no. 4 (1974): 3–6.

23. Kenneth R. Van Voorhis, "Organizational Communication: Advances Made during the Period from World War II through the 1950s," *Journal of Business Communication* 11, no. 4 (1974): 11–18.

24. Phillip J. Lewis, "The Status of 'Organizational Communication,' in Colleges of Business," *Journal of Business Communication* 12, no. 4 (1975): 25–28.

25. This section is based primarily on Paul Preston, "The Critical 'Mix' in Managerial Communications," *Industrial Management* (March/April 1976): 5–9.

26. Arnold E. Schneider, William C. Donaghy, and Pamela J. Newman, "Communication Climate within an Organization," *Management Controls* (October/November 1976): 159–62.

27. Schneider, Donaghy, and Newman, "Communication Climate within an Organization."

28. William V. Haney, "Serial Communication of Information In Organizations," in *Concepts and Issues in*

Administrative Behavior, ed. Sidney Mailick and Edward H. Van Ness (Englewood Cliffs, N.J.: Prentice-Hall, 1962), 150.

29. Haney, "Serial Communication," 150.

30. Alex Bavelas and Dermot Barrett, "An Experimental Approach to Organizational Communication," *Personnel* 27 (1951): 366–71.

31. Eugene Walton, "Communicating Down the Line: How They Really Get the Word," *Personnel* (July/August 1959): 78–82.

32. Keith Davis, "Management Communication and the Grapevine," *Harvard Business Review* (January/February 1953): 43–49.

33. Linda McCallister, "The Interpersonal Side of Internal Communications," *Public Relations Journal* (February 1981): 20–23.

34. Eugene Walton, "How Efficient Is the Grapevine?" *Personnel* (March/April 1961): 45–49.

35. For an article defending the value of grapevines, see W. Kiechel, "In Praise of Office Gossip," *Fortune*, August 19, 1985, 253–54.

Action Summary Answer Key

1. a. F, p. 319
   b. d, p. 319
2. a. b, p. 322
   b. a, p. 323

3. a. F, p. 327
   b. b, pp. 327–328
4. a. T, pp. 330–331
   b. T, p. 331

5. a. d, p. 332
   b. a, p. 332
6. a. e, pp. 336–337
   b. F, p. 336

7. a. e, pp. 338–339
   b. F, p. 338

FAILURE TO COMMUNICATE AT SOFTWARE SERVICES LTD.

John Stevens, director of the international division of Software Services Ltd., was almost bowled over in the corridor one day by Paul Horn, a project leader at the Toronto-based company. Horn was in a rage. "You're just the man I wanted to see," he erupted. Horn then went on to recount his problem with Yulan Sun, a visiting expert from the People's Republic of China. Sun had just deliberately erased an important piece of software that the company had been developing, and it would take several months to reconstruct the work. Not only that: the firm might miss a trade show at which it had planned to launch the software.

Horn knew that Sun had saved a floppy-disk copy of the program, which dealt with work-shift scheduling. This meant that the situation could still be salvaged. But Sun had adamantly refused to turn over the floppy disk when approached first by Horn's assistant and then by Horn himself. She told Horn she wanted a guarantee that he would give her credit for the program and see that it was presented at an upcoming trade show. When he said he couldn't promise anything, she became even more insistent, saying that the work was hers and that she had the right to do anything she wanted with it. As he told it, Horn replied that Sun's work could not have been done without Software's facilities and that the project was a team effort.

Stevens, who fancied himself a China hand and was the person responsible for the educational program through which Sun had been placed at Software, was stunned. While he knew that language and cultural problems can ruin both business and personal dealings with people from other countries, in Sun's case he thought he had done a good job at overcoming them; until this incident, her stay at the company had been a big success.

Stevens realized he would have to talk to Sun, but he agreed with Horn that he should wait until he returned from a week-long trip to the U.S. While Stevens was away, Horn sent Sun a memo, again setting out his view of the matter and again insisting that she turn over her copy. Stevens, who asked his secretary to read him the memo over the phone, learned that Sun had refused to reply; she wanted to meet first with Stevens. As he mulled over the situation in his Chicago hotel room, Stevens shuddered at the possible consequences, not only for Horn's project but for Software's agreement with China. In his mind he reviewed the events of Sun's stay in Canada, trying to figure out what had gone wrong.

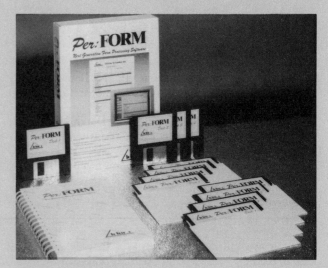

"Sun had just deliberately erased an important piece of software . . ."

Yulan Sun was the first of twenty-two Chinese, including ten advanced specialists and twelve inexperienced programmers, who were each to spend a year at Software during the four-year educational program. The objective of the program, sponsored by the Canadian International Development Agency (CIDA), was to update experienced people, like Sun, who had fallen behind during the Cultural Revolution and to expose inexperienced programmers to the latest equipment and techniques. In return for facilities and management, the company received the free services of the visiting Chinese.

This was Sun's first exposure to life outside China. Before the Cultural Revolution, she had been a member of the computer engineering department at the prestigious Huszhong University. While there, she had written two books and several articles on computers. During the revolution, the university was closed and Sun was separated from her family and sent to do agricultural labour. Three years later she was pronounced "rehabilitated." Following her return home, her husband (also an engineering professor) was subjected to two years of the same treatment. After the revolution, Sun returned to the university and eventually became director of the economic information laboratory of the economic management engineering department. It was in this capacity that she was chosen as the university's first visitor to Canada under the CIDA program.

On arrival in Canada, she spent six weeks in an orientation program in Vancouver. During this period, Stevens stopped off in Vancouver on his way to China and invited Sun to breakfast at his hotel. Once he arrived in China, Stevens was invited to lunch at the home of Sun's family, where he was offered a sumptuous meal of his favourite Chinese specialties.

Sun plunged enthusiastically into life in Toronto. She was invited to several homes, including Stevens', during her first weeks. At work, she immersed herself in the activities of two different project groups to learn the computer languages and familiarize herself with the hardware. She made it clear that she was a very capable professional who could make a significant contribution to the company.

About halfway through her one-year stay, Sun joined Paul Horn's group, which was working on a system for scheduling several shifts of workers. She had a keen interest in the problem because many Chinese enterprises were three-shift operations. She knew they spent a great deal of time on scheduling, often with disappointing results.

As she pushed ahead with her project, Sun made good progress. Her completed program enabled a scheduler to make adjustments to several variables with ease and to see the results in graphic form instantly. Work that used to take a scheduler a month to complete could be converted into an hour-long task using the software. At this point, Sun demonstrated her work for Stevens and Lindsay Tan, a systems analyst and Hong Kong native who had become her good friend. Stevens was impressed both with the work and the Chinese visitor's display of material perspective.

However, Stevens had also heard about a few problems, mostly related to language. Sun seemed to understand very little casual conversation, but was reluctant to admit it. Horn had told Stevens what happened after he first introduced Sun to the project. Horn took her to the research site—a hospital—to meet the supervisor who handled the scheduling of nurses. Horn discussed the problem with the scheduler, all the while trying to include Sun in the conversation. When Horn thought they were finished, he asked Sun if she had any comments. She then proceeded to ask the scheduler what the problem was— the very thing they had just discussed for forty-five minutes.

In another incident a few weeks before she erased the scheduling program, Stevens was worried by a meeting he had with Sun. She said she felt overwhelmed by all the work she had to do, including the scheduling project and the short time available for it before her return to China. In addition to various projects at Software, she wanted to spend some time at the University of Waterloo's computing centre and visit several Canadian and U.S. cities. Stevens said he would try to set up the Waterloo visit but suggested that Sun work on the project a bit more until she was satisfied that her part of the work could be passed on to other members of Horn's team.

Two weeks later, Sun still hadn't been sufficiently satisfied with her progress to pass the project on, but Horn said that if she would brief his assistant and the person she had been working with, they would be able to complete it. Stevens, Horn, and Sun had also tried to discuss Horn's plans to prepare the company's presentation to the upcoming trade show. Several times during the meeting, however, Stevens had noticed Sun's apparent blankness at Horn's comments. When this happened, Horn would repeat his comments rather than trying to clarify them. Similarly, Sun had seemed oblivious to Horn's puzzlement at her pronunciation. To his dismay, Stevens had found himself acting as a translator during the meeting.

In addition, when her wishes were thwarted, Sun became impatient and didn't hesitate to raise her voice in anger. She also seemed aggressive in dealings with individuals she saw as lower in status than herself. Stevens, too, had several run-ins with her. Sun was angry that her Waterloo visit hadn't been arranged, insisting that Stevens had guaranteed it would take place; Stevens, on the other hand, recalled that he had promised only to try to arrange something. They also had a shouting match over Stevens' refusal to cover all her expenses for proposed trips to Montreal and Ottawa. However, such problems seemed minor, especially since the supervisor at the hospital had reacted enthusiastically to a demonstration by Sun of the scheduling program. (Curiously, Sun had dismissed compliments about her presentation, denying that it had gone well.)

Stevens knew that if Sun refused to turn over the program it would take at least three months to reconstruct the model, and Software would miss some critical deadlines. He considered threatening to cancel his firm's agreement with China in order to indicate to Sun the gravity of the situation. Yet, despite the loyalty he felt to the company and to Horn, Stevens also felt committed to the program with China and to Sun's success as the first visitor. How should he have handled the situation?

DISCUSSION ISSUES

1. Which communication macro- and microbarriers would you suspect had the greatest impact on the exchanges between Yulan Sun and her colleagues at Software Services Ltd., Paul Horn and John Stevens?
2. Which of the basic "ten commandments of good communication" are relevant to the situation at Software Services? Explain.
3. How should Stevens have handled the situation? How would you?

Based on "Failure to communicate," by Daniel Stoffman in *Canadian Business*, April 1986. Used with permission.

LEADERSHIP

STUDENT LEARNING OBJECTIVES

From studying this chapter, I will attempt to acquire:

1. A working definition of leadership.
2. An understanding of the relationship between leading and managing.
3. An appreciation for the trait and situational approaches to leadership.
4. Insights on how to make decisions as a leader.
5. A strategy for using the life cycle theory of leadership.
6. An understanding of alternatives to leader flexibility.

CHAPTER OUTLINE

347

BECOMING A SUCCESSFUL LEADER

Gordon Toms is a dietitian and manager of a hospital food services department in a large metropolitan hospital. One of Toms' strengths as a manager is that he continually reads management-related articles to improve his managerial effectiveness. Last week he read an article that compared successful and unsuccessful organizational leaders in the United States. A summary of the main theme of this article is presented in Case Figure 13.1.

Toms was somewhat disturbed because, as he attempted to evaluate himself in relation to the two profiles, he seemed to have more of the characteristics of the less successful leader than the more successful leader. Toms developed a strategy, based on this article, for becoming a more successful leader. The strategy required that he change his interests and attitudes to be more consistent with the profile of the more successful leader. Toms reasoned that, as his interests and attitudes came closer to those of more successful leaders, he would become a more successful leader himself.

CASE FIGURE 13.1   A comparison of successful and unsuccessful organization leaders in the United States.

Profile of More Successful Leaders

People who were usually in the upper 10 percent of their school class.

Their favorite subject was probably one of the social sciences or English, even though they may have majored in engineering or business.

They read the *New York Times*, are familiar with the Bible, and prefer French impressionist paintings and Tchaikovsky's music.

Their TV habits tend towards news programs and sports, with occasional mixing of such programs as "All in the Family."

Their most admired leader is Winston Churchill, although Richard M. Nixon rated high with them before Watergate. Dwight D. Eisenhower and John F. Kennedy are lesser choices, but in the top four.

Their average annual income is around $75 000, although their range might be as low as $25 000 or as high as $1 000 000. Their age range is the mid-fifties. More often than not they are Republicans rather than Independents or Democrats (3 to 2).

Successful executives place a high priority on moral standards and integrity, on a sense of fairness to others, and a sense of personal worthfulness. They are less interested in defeating communism or advancing capitalism than in being happy.

In their scale of values, they place power and economics at the top of the list. However, they are significantly higher than less successful executives in their concern for people.

Profile of Less Successful Leaders

Less successful people tend to be from the middle or lower half of their school class.

Their favorite subject was science or math.

They read the *New York Times* less than their successful counterparts and the *Wall Street Journal* more.

They prefer sports to news on TV and have limited interest in art and music.

They are politically more independent or neutral than successful people, and three times more often a Republican than a Democrat.

Their average income is $16 000, and their rate of salary growth over the past ten years was half that of the successful executives. Their choice of a leader was Nixon (pre-Watergate), almost three times over Churchill or Eisenhower.

They place survival and return on investments on the same par as integrity. They are less interested in helping humanity than helping themselves. They no longer have their hearts set on making a fortune, but are more willing to settle for improving their financial security and their work situation.

They place a great value on intelligence and place economics at the top of their list of values.

From Henry A. Singer, "Human Values and Leadership," *Business Horizons* (August 1975): 85–88. Copyright, 1975, by the Foundation for the School of Business at Indiana University. Reprinted by permission.

What's Ahead

Gordon Toms, the dietitian-manager in the introductory case, is attempting to become a more successful leader by changing his interests and attitudes. The information in this chapter would be helpful to an individual like Toms as the basis for developing a more useful leadership strategy. This chapter discusses: (1) how to define leadership; (2) the difference between a leader and a manager; (3) the trait approach to leadership; and (4) the situational approach to leadership.

DEFINING LEADERSHIP

Leadership is the process of directing the behaviour of others toward the accomplishment of some objective. Directing, in this sense, means causing individuals to act in a certain way or to follow a particular course. Ideally, this course of action is perfectly consistent with such factors as established organizational policies, procedures, and job descriptions. The central theme of leadership is getting things accomplished through people. As indicated in Chapter 12, leadership is one of the four main interdependent activities of the influencing subsystem and is accomplished, at least to some extent, by communicating with others. Leadership is of such great importance to organizational success that some management writers recommend that, when interviewing candidates to fill an open management position, the interviewer should try to find out the candidate's leadership style to see if it is appropriate for the needs of the organization.[1]

> Leadership is guiding the behaviour of others.

LEADER VERSUS MANAGER

Leading is not the same as managing.[2] Although some managers are leaders and some leaders are managers, leading and managing are not identical activities.[3] According to Theodore Levitt, management consists of:

> the rational assessment of a situation and the systematic selection of goals and purposes (what is to be done); the systematic development of strategies to achieve these goals; the marshalling of the required resources; the rational design, organization, direction, and control of the activities required to attain the selected purposes; and, finally, the motivating and rewarding of people to do the work.[4]

Leadership, on the other hand, as one of the four primary activities comprising the influencing function, is a subset of management. Managing is much broader in scope than leading and focuses on behavioural as well as non-behavioural issues. Leading emphasizes mainly behavioural issues. Figure 13.1 makes the point that, although all managers are not necessarily leaders, the most effective managers, over the long term, are. Figure 13.2 is a list of the primary activities that effective managers/leaders perform.

> Leadership is part of management.

349

FIGURE 13.1   Most effective managers over the long term are also leaders.

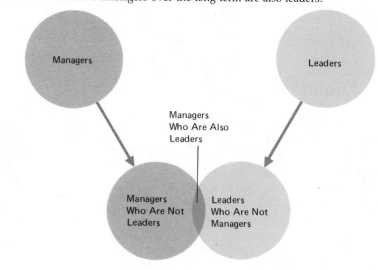

FIGURE 13.2   Primary activities of the effective manager/leader.

1. *In Terms of Attitudes toward Subordinates:*
   a. Has confidence in subordinates and conveys this confidence.
   b. Is approachable and friendly.
   c. Is eager to help subordinates to be more effective and works at removing obstacles to achievement.
   d. In dealing with subordinates, is emotionally supportive and is careful to avoid ego-threatening behaviour.
   e. Tries to minimize stress in relationships with subordinates to avoid diminishing subordinates use of intellectual capabilities.
   f. Permits subordinates to have latitude in the solution of work problems where the subordinate's ingenuity can result in gains and where standardization in method is not imperative.
   g. Is cognizant of the need for leadership styles to be somewhat different in different technological settings, for example, that it is easily possible to overstructure and be too directive in a laboratory setting and to understructure and be too participative in some factory settings.
   h. Encourages the participation of subordinates but only on the basis of a genuine interest in utilizing constructive suggestions and only where subordinates perceive participation as being legitimate.
2. *In Terms of Technology, Planning, and Selection:*
   a. Utilizes and encourages subordinates to utilize the appropriate technology in attaining these goals — e.g., work simplification, appropriate tools, proper layout, and so on.
   b. Is an effective planner in terms of both short-range and long-range goals and contingencies.
   c. Selects subordinates with appropriate qualifications.
3. *In Terms of Performance Standards and Appraisal:*
   a. Works with subordinates in establishing attainable but high performance standards and high goals — which are consistent with the goals of the enterprise.
   b. Appraises subordinates as nearly as possible on objective, measurable performance but makes compensation and promotion judgments on the basis of total performance.
4. *In Terms of the Linking-Pin Function:*
   a. Is an effective link with higher management and other groups within the enterprise in facilitating task performance.
5. *In Terms of Rewards and Correction:*
   a. Gives recognition to good work.
   b. Uses subordinates' mistakes as an educational opportunity rather than an opportunity for punishment.

THE TRAIT APPROACH TO LEADERSHIP

The **trait approach to leadership** is based on early leadership research that seemed to assume that a good leader is born and not made. The mainstream of this research attempted to describe successful leaders as precisely as possible. The reasoning was that, if a complete profile of the traits of a successful leader could be summarized, it would be fairly easy to pinpoint those individuals who should and should not be placed in leadership positions.

Many of the studies that attempted to summarize the traits of successful leaders have been documented.[5] One of these summaries concludes that successful leaders tend to possess the following characteristics:[6]

1. Intelligence, including judgment and verbal ability.
2. Past achievements in scholarship and athletics.
3. Emotional maturity and stability.
4. Dependability, persistence, and a drive for continuing achievement.
5. The skill to participate socially and adapt to various groups.
6. A desire for status and socioeconomic position.

An evaluation of a number of these trait studies, however, concludes that their findings generally tend to be inconsistent.[7] One researcher says that fifty years of study have failed to produce one personality trait or set of qualities that can be used consistently to discriminate leaders from non-leaders.[8] It follows, then, that no trait or combination of traits guarantees that a leader will be successful. Leadership is apparently a much more complex issue than simply describing the traits of successful leaders.

Traits cannot predict leadership success.

BACK TO THE CASE

From the preceding material, Gordon Toms should be able to see that his leadership activities in the hospital involve directing the behaviour of food services employees so that hospital goals are reached. Toms also should recognize that leading and managing are not the same thing. When managing, Toms is involved with planning, organizing, influencing, and controlling within the food services area. When leading, Toms actually is performing an activity that is part of the influencing function of management. To maximize his long-term success, Toms should strive to be both a manager and a leader.

The introductory case concludes with Toms attempting to increase his success as a leader by changing his interests and attitudes. Studies based on the trait approach to leadership should indicate to Toms that merely changing his individual characteristics will not guarantee his success as a leader.

THE SITUATIONAL APPROACH TO LEADERSHIP

The emphasis of leadership study has shifted from the trait approach to the situational approach. The more modern **situational approach to leadership** is based on the assumption that all instances of successful leadership are somewhat different and require a unique combination of leaders, followers, and leadership situations. This interaction commonly is expressed in formula form: $SL = f(L,F,S)$. In this formula, SL is *successful leadership*, f stands for *function of*, and L,F, and S are, respectively, the *leader*, the *follower*, and the *situation*. A translation of this formula would be that successful leadership is a function of the leader, the

The situational approach to leadership in formula form is $SL = f(L,F,S)$.

follower, and the situation. In other words, the leader, the follower, and the situation must be appropriate for one another if a leadership attempt is to be successful.

Leadership Situations and Decisions

Tannenbaum and Schmidt wrote one of the first and perhaps most well-known discussions on the situational approach to leadership. Their discussion emphasizes situations in which a leader makes decisions.[9] Since one of the most important tasks of a leader is making sound decisions, practical and legitimate leadership thinking should contain some emphasis on decision making. Figure 13.3 presents Tannenbaum and Schmidt's model of leadership behaviour that contains such a decision-making emphasis.

The model presented in Figure 13.3 is actually a continuum, or range, of leadership behaviour available to managers in making decisions. Each type of decision-making behaviour on this model has both a corresponding degree of authority used by the manager and a related amount of freedom available to subordinates. Management behaviours at the extreme left of the model characterize the leader who makes decisions by maintaining high control and allowing little subordinate freedom, while those at the extreme right characterize the leader who makes decisions by exercising little control and allowing much subordinate freedom and self-direction. Behaviour between the extreme left and right of the model reflects a gradual change from autocratic to democratic leadership, or vice versa. Managers displaying leadership behaviour toward the right of the model are more democratic and called subordinate-centred leaders, while managers displaying leadership behaviour toward the left of the model are more autocratic and called boss-centred leaders. Each type of leadership behaviour in this model is explained in more detail in the following paragraphs:

The manager makes the decision and announces it   This behaviour is characterized

> Leadership decision-making behaviour can range from autocratic to democratic.

FIGURE 13.3   Continuum of leadership behaviour that emphasizes decision making.

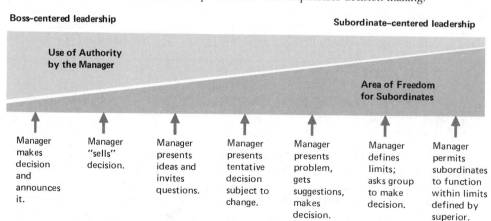

Boss-centered leadership

Subordinate-centered leadership

Use of Authority by the Manager

Area of Freedom for Subordinates

| Manager makes decision and announces it. | Manager "sells" decision. | Manager presents ideas and invites questions. | Manager presents tentative decision subject to change. | Manager presents problem, gets suggestions, makes decision. | Manager defines limits; asks group to make decision. | Manager permits subordinates to function within limits defined by superior. |

Wall Street Journal, *February 5, 1987. From the Wall
Street Journal—permission, Cartoon Features Syndicate.*

by the manager: (1) identifying a problem; (2) analyzing various alternatives
available to solve the problem; (3) choosing the alternative that will be used
to solve the problem; and (4) requiring followers to implement the chosen
alternative. The manager may or may not use coercion, but the followers
have no opportunity to participate directly in the decision-making process.
(The cartoon depicts a manager who made a decision and announced it. As
the Tannenbaum and Schmidt model implies, however, this is not *always*
the best way to handle decision making.)

The manager "sells" the decision   As before, the manager identifies the problem
and independently arrives at a decision. Rather than announce the decision
to subordinates for implementation, however, the manager tries to persuade
subordinates to accept the decision.

The manager presents ideas and invites questions   Here, the manager makes the
decision and attempts to gain acceptance through persuasion. One additional
step is taken, however, since subordinates are invited to ask questions about
the decision.

The manager presents a tentative decision subject to change   The manager actually
allows subordinates to have some part in the decision-making process. The
manager retains, however, the responsibility for identifying and diagnosing
the problem and arrives at a tentative decision that is subject to change based
upon subordinate input. The final decision is made by the manager.

The manager presents the problem, gets suggestions, and then makes the decision   This
is the first leadership activity described thus far that allows subordinates the
opportunity to offer problem solutions before the manager offers a problem
solution. The manager still, however, identifies the problem in the first place.

The manager defines the limits and requests the group to make a decision   This behaviour
is characterized by the manager first defining the problem and setting the
boundaries within which a decision must be made. The manager then indicates that he and the group are partners in making an appropriate decision.
However, if the group does not perceive the manager as genuinely desiring
a serious group decision-making effort, it will tend to arrive at conclusions
that reflect what the group thinks the manager wants rather than what the
group actually thinks.

The manager permits the group to make decisions within prescribed limits   Here the manager actually becomes an equal member of a problem-solving group. The entire group identifies and assesses the problem, develops alternative problem solutions, and chooses an alternative to be implemented. Everyone within the group understands that the group's decision will be implemented.

BACK TO THE CASE

The situational approach to leadership can give Gordon Toms more insight on how to develop his leadership skill than can the trait approach. The situational approach would suggest that successful leadership within the hospital is determined by the appropriateness of a combination of three factors: (1) Toms as a leader; (2) the food services employees as followers; and (3) the situation within the food services department. Each of these factors plays a significant role in determining whether or not Toms is successful.

One of the most important activities Toms performs as a leader is making decisions. He can make decisions in any number of ways, ranging from authoritarian to democratic. For example, Toms could make the decision to improve the hospital menu, announce to his employees how the menu will change, and require them to implement the change. Or Toms could define the changes that are needed on the menu, discuss them with the food services staff, and allow the staff to come up with an improved menu.

Of course, Toms could also be less extreme in his decision making, in that his leadership behaviour could fall in the middle of the continuum. For example, he could suggest to his employees that a new menu is needed, ask them to develop ideas for improvement, and then make the decision on the basis of his own ideas and those of the staff.

Determining How to Make Decisions as a Leader

The true value of the model developed by Tannenbaum and Schmidt can be realized only if a leader can use it to make practical and desirable decisions. According to these authors, the three primary factors or forces that influence a manager's determination of which leadership behaviour to use to make decisions are: (1) forces in the manager; (2) forces in subordinates; and (3) forces in the leadership situation.

Forces in the Manager

Forces in the manager include:
1. Values of the manager.

Managers should be aware of four forces within themselves that influence their determination of how to make decisions as a leader. The first of these forces is a manager's values, such as the relative importance to the manager of organizational efficiency, personal growth, growth of subordinates, and company profits. For example, if subordinate growth is valued very highly a manager may want to give the group members the valuable experience of making a decision, even though she could have made the same decision much more quickly and efficiently alone.

2. Confidence in subordinates.

The second force within the manager is her level of confidence in subordinates. In general, the more confidence a manager has in subordinates, the more likely her style of decision making will be democratic, or subordinate-centred. The reverse is also true. The less confidence a manager has in subordinates, the more likely her style of decision making will be autocratic, or boss-centred.

3. Strengths of the leader.

The third force within the manager that influences her determination of how to make decisions as a leader are her personal leadership strengths. Some managers are more effective in issuing orders than leading a group discussion and vice versa. A manager must be able to recognize her personal leadership strengths and to capitalize on them.

The fourth influencing force within a manager is tolerance for ambiguity. As a manager moves from a boss-centred style to a subordinate-centred style, she loses some certainty about how problems should be solved. If this reduction of certainty is disturbing to a manager, it may be extremely difficult for her to be successful as a subordinate-centred leader.

4. Tolerance for ambiguity.

Forces in Subordinates

A manager also should be aware of forces within subordinates that influence his determination of how to make decisions as a leader.[10] To understand subordinates adequately, a manager should keep in mind that each subordinate is both somewhat different and somewhat alike. Any cookbook approach for deciding how to lead all subordinates is therefore impossible. Generally speaking, however, a manager probably could increase his success as a leader by allowing subordinates more freedom in making decisions if:[11]

1. The subordinates have relatively high needs for independence. (People differ greatly in the amount of direction they desire.)
2. The subordinates have a readiness to assume responsibility for decision making. (Some see additional responsibility as a tribute to their ability; others see it as "passing the buck.")
3. They have a relatively high tolerance for ambiguity. (Some employees prefer to have clear-cut directives given to them; others prefer a wider area of freedom.)
4. They are interested in the problem and feel that it is important.
5. They understand and identify with goals of the organization.
6. They have the necessary knowledge and experience to deal with the problem.
7. They have learned to expect to share in decision making. (Persons who have come to expect strong leadership and who suddenly are confronted with the request to share more fully in decision making are often upset by this new experience. On the other hand, persons who have enjoyed a considerable amount of freedom resent the boss who begins to make all the decisions alone.)

There are seven forces in subordinates that indicate the type of decision-making approach a manager should take.

If these characteristics of subordinates do not exist in a particular situation, a manager probably should move toward a more autocratic or boss-centred approach to making decisions.

Forces in the Situation

The last group of forces that influence a manager's determination of how to make decisions as a leader are forces in the leadership situation. The first such situational force involves the type of organization in which the leader works. Such organizational factors as the size of working groups and their geographical distribution become especially important in deciding how to make decisions as a leader. Extremely large work groups or a wide geographic separation of work groups, for example, could make a subordinate-centred leadership style impractical.

Forces in the situation include:
1. The organization.

Another such force in the leadership situation is the effectiveness of group members working together. To this end, a manager should evaluate such issues as the experience of the group in working together and the degree of confidence

2. The effectiveness of groups.

FIGURE 13.4 Collective influence of forces in the manager, subordinates, and the situation on the leadership style adopted for decision making.

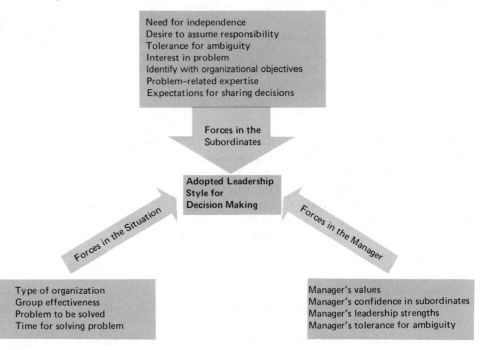

group members have in their ability to solve problems as a group. As a general rule, a manager should only assign decision-making responsibilities to effective work groups.

3. The problem to be solved.

A third situational force that influences a manager's determination of how to make decisions as a leader is the problem to be solved. Before acting as a more subordinate-centred leader, a manager should be sure that a group possesses the expertise necessary to make a decision about the existing problem. As a group loses the necessary expertise to solve a problem, a manager generally should move toward more boss-centred leadership.

4. The time available to solve the problem.

A fourth situational force involves the time available to make a decision. As a general guideline, the less time available to make a decision, the more impractical it becomes to have that decision made by a group. Typically, it takes a group more time to reach a decision than an individual.

Figure 13.4 summarizes the main forces that influence a manager's determination of how to make decisions as a leader and stresses that this determination is the result of the collective influence of all of these forces. As the situational approach to leadership implies, a manager will be successful as a decision maker only if the method used to make those decisions appropriately reflects the leader, the followers, and the situation.

The following Management in Action feature profiles the Montreal Citizens Movement executive committee president, Michael Fainstat. It outlines his philosophy on the processes of political decision making and democracy, and reveals the various forces that helped shape his beliefs.

MICHAEL FAINSTAT: QUITE POSSIBLY THE MOST POWERFUL MAN IN MONTREAL

One day Michael Fainstat is working out of a small room in his home, with only the phone and a few walls to talk to. The next he's in room 202 at Montreal's City Hall, with secretaries, assistants, security guards, and guys with tool belts running in and out. There are ladders and fluorescent tubes to dodge, word processors, photocopiers, typewriters, and a Centrex system to master. The light switch gives him trouble. Opening the curtains intimidates him. "It's a dream," says Fainstat. "Sometimes it feels like a dream."

The history of Michael Fainstat is the history of democracy in Montreal. As a leading member of the Montreal Citizens Movement (MCM), a political party favouring an open, democratic style of government, Fainstat was the conscience of the city for a dozen years, prodding and pulling the plantation mentality of Mayor Jean Drapeau's long-reigning Civic Party administration into the twentieth century. In touch with the times, Fainstat tried to turn the "me decade" into the "we decade." He lobbied the provincial government to jam democracy down Drapeau's throat and succeeded. He championed causes both big and small and did it with such conviction and stridency that in 1982 a fellow politician told a journalist that Fainstat couldn't tell the difference between "a traffic ticket and a mass genocide." He pounced on every transgression, from a seventy-five-cent increase in bicycle permits to a water filtration plant that came in about $165 million over budget.

His resolve was so great that he compiled a library of information on the machinations of the city. His basement became the MCM's *Centre du Documentation*, a few walls of files in which, he tells all comers, he can find any dossier within thirty seconds. It takes him an hour a day just to keep it up to date. As the only easily accessible source of information about city administration, he became partners with the press—Fainstat trying to spread the word, the media looking for any word. Fainstat returned phone calls and gave good quotes. Better yet, he knew what he was talking about. And people trusted him.

With its resounding victory in the 1986 municipal election—winning all but one of the council seats—the MCM changed the face of Montreal politics. Friend of the press, friend of the civil service, ally of the right, the left

"Michael Fainstat's legacy lies in his tremendous belief in people and society."

and most points in between, the MCM is eerily reminiscent of the Parti Québécois at its ascendancy. The person who will have to ensure that the party doesn't follow the PQ's downward spiral is Fainstat, President of the Executive Committee and the party's senior statesman. Those in the intimate circle call him "The Senator." Others call him "The Teacher," "The Conciliator," everything but "The Great Helmsman."

At the swearing-in ceremony in the church-like council chambers, with its crucifix, stained glass, and sombre lighting, Fainstat received a standing ovation from his party and invited guests. Speeches were made in his honour, including one by Civic Party survivor Germain Prégent. Fainstat had already volunteered to assist Prégent through the bewildering and lonely shoals of being a solitary opposition voice.

So now there's no Fainstat in the opposition to keep tabs on abuses of power, no one to hand the media stories of scandal. But when the strafing starts, as it invariably will, the party that was so good at criticism will have to learn how to administer while it tries to avoid debating itself to death. "Switching from opposition to administration is a whole change of character, a change of personality," says Fainstat. But for Fainstat, the city's second most powerful man (after Mayor Jean Doré), the problems will be minimized through the not-so-simple process of

357

democracy. Executive Committee members will circulate and talk to their constituents. There will be commissions, special committees, and district meetings. "People are going to feel that it is the level of government closest to the people," said Fainstat. "We're going to consult and consult and consult."

Fainstat is at his most animated getting into a rap on social democracy, community participation, and citizen consultation—watchwords of the Fainstat philosophy, by way of a mother and father who came to Canada from Lithuania and Poland and worked as a seamstress and a presser, respectively. His mother worked for the union, organizing sweatshops. At the Fainstat family table, he tells friends, the daily bread was union made, even though it cost seven cents and a non-union loaf was five cents. "We'll eat union bread or we won't eat," his mother would say.

Another enduring lesson came with middle age, after he resigned from the presidency of Combustion and Power Equipment Ltd., where he was a minority partner. The company had made him wealthy, designing anti-pollution gear for natural gas and oil-burning systems, but the American buyers, Peabody International, didn't share Fainstat's humanistic approach to management. "There was constant consultation with all the staff, participation in decision making and direction . . . and a very important profit-sharing scheme," he remembers. "Once we became a subsidiary of this American company I found that there was a conflict in management approaches."

So in 1973 he resigned and took his pension, his wife, Ruth, took a sabbatical from social work, and they hit the road. They travelled for about a year, hopping from one repressed state to another in the Second and Third Worlds. They visited about fifty different countries, most of them poverty stricken, and found spots of utter destitution. In some, people still smiled, laughed, and seemed to enjoy life. In others, no one would look them in the eye; people were depressed, without hope. "The difference was the level of local involvement in decision making," he says. Warming up to a favourite topic, he recalls that in Bali and Nepal, in spite of military rule and too little to eat, "the tradition of having local meetings at a local house in the centre of the village where everyone gets together—men, women, and kids—to sit around and argue about their problems . . . the level of cultural expression was just unbelievable."

Having a say in what went on in their streets fuelled the energies of a community. "The most important thing in politics, that transcends the federal international situation is what happens locally, right in the community,

right on the streets, right in the village," he says. "What happens locally is so terribly important in terms of the way people relate to each other, how they smile, how they dance, how they play and have fun in spite of the economic and military oppression."

To the disenchanted on the far left like Dimitrios Roussopoulos, a political writer and activist, letting people talk about their problems or even recommend solutions is not the same as resolving problems and improving the quality of life. "Michael Fainstat puts a tremendous amount of importance on changing the form," says Roussopoulos, "not enough consideration to the contents. Historically that's wrong." But Fainstat believes otherwise, favouring a step-by-step approach in a city where universal suffrage arrived only in 1970. He says people are not in the habit of participating. "We can't impose democracy on these people," Fainstat says. "We need to animate, act as catalysts." He says it's too easy for neighbourhood councils to become dominated by elitist cliques.

MCM councillor Marvin Rohand says, "The MCM is a party of the centre. The program is somewhat left." But according to him, the party doesn't have the political will to fulfill it. However, if anyone can accommodate the various elements pushing and pulling at the party, he says, Fainstat can. "He has the political credibility for the left to respect him and the management capacities for the right to respect him."

During the internal debates of 1978, when the party started its shift from movement to political party—bleaching its blue collar white—Fainstat stayed out of the line of fire and survived unscathed to begin four years as the sole opposition to the Civic Party. It was four years of hell, banging his head against Drapeau's debate-halting bell, enduring a telephone that never stopped ringing, and trying to keep house and home together while Ruth worked with sexually assaulted children.

Although neither Fainstat nor his wife ever saw the job of solitary MCM councillor leading to anything like being the second most powerful man in Montreal—some might argue the most powerful—it was a dark-horse cause and both were used to that. They had met at McGill University during the early years of the Second World War, when Hitler was squashing Europe and Maurice Duplessis was beating up unions and padlocking doors in Quebec. Fainstat was president of the Student Labour Club and Ruth was the secretary. Together they later fought for daycare, helped start a cooperative nursery school, worked with the New Democrats, and marched to ban the bomb and stop the war in Southeast Asia. Ruth calls it applying "basic values" to specific situations. City politics—she helped organize her husband's campaign—is but "another arena of expression for the things we believe in."

But clearly leadership is not something Fainstat aspired to; in fact, he "dropped his hat" quite by accident. After returning from his travels abroad, he attended an MCM meeting and found himself one of the only people who didn't have a reason not to run for office. Says a friend: "He filled all the requirements. I think he was forced into it. He had to run."

Regardless of his political genesis, Michael Fainstat's legacy lies in his tremendous belief in people and society.

Friends and opposition members alike acknowledge his humanistic approach to life. "He really, really believes in those basic principles of democracy and social justice," says Loyola councillor Sharon Leslie. And so his work at City Hall has become but another instance of applying "basic values" to a specific situation. For Michael Fainstat, it is as simple as that.

Based on "Michael Fainstat: Quite Possibly the Most Powerful Man in Montreal," by David Sherman in *Montreal Magazine*, January/February 1986. Used with permission.

Determining How to Make Decisions as a Leader: An Update

Forces within the manager, subordinates, and situation are increasingly inter-related and complex.

Tannenbaum and Schmidt's original article on leadership decision making was so widely accepted that these two authors were invited by *Harvard Business Review* to update their original work.[12] This update stresses that in modern organizations the relationship among forces within the manager, subordinates, and situation is becoming more complex and more interrelated than ever. As this relationship becomes increasingly complicated, it obviously becomes more difficult for the leader to determine how to lead.

The decision environment is also a force to be considered.

This update also stresses both societal and organizational environments as more modern forces to consider when determining how to lead. Such societal and organizational values as the development of minority groups and pollution control should have some influence on the decision making of leaders.

BACK TO THE CASE

In trying to decide exactly how to make his decisions as a leader, Gordon Toms should consider forces in himself as manager, forces in his food services subordinates, and forces in the situation of the food services department. Forces within Toms include his own ideas about how to lead and his level of confidence in the food services staff. If Toms believes he is more knowledgeable about diet and food costs than his staff is, he will be likely to make boss-centred decisions about what items to put on the hospital's menu.

Forces within the food services subordinates, such as the need for independence, the readiness to assume responsibility, and the knowledge of and interest in the issues to be decided, also affect Toms's decisions as a leader. If Toms's staff is relatively independent and responsible and its members feel strongly that an improved menu is important to meeting the hospital's ob-

jectives, then Toms will be inclined to allow his employees more freedom in deciding how to change the hospital menu.

Forces within the food services department include the number of people making decisions and the problem to be solved. For example, if Toms's staff is small, he will be more likely to use a democratic decision-making style, allowing his employees to become involved in such decisions as improving the hospital menu. He will also be likely to use a subordinate-centred leadership style if his staff is knowledgeable about the problem at hand, such as how to more efficiently serve hospital patients. In changing the hospital menu, however, Toms might use an autocratic style, since his employees may not be as knowledgeable as he is about dietary issues.

Leadership Situations in General

Decision-making behaviour is a stream of leadership thought that focuses on leadership situations in more general terms. This stream of thought usually is discussed as beginning with a series of leadership studies affiliated with the Bureau of Business Research at Ohio State University. These studies are called the OSU studies.[13]

The OSU Studies

Structure behaviour restricts the self-guidance of subordinates.

The OSU studies are a series of leadership investigations that concluded that leaders exhibit two main types of behaviour. The first type of behaviour, called **structure behaviour**, is any leadership activity that delineates the relationship between the leader and the leader's followers or establishes well-defined pro-

FIGURE 13.5 Four fundamental leadership styles based on structure behaviour and consideration behaviour.

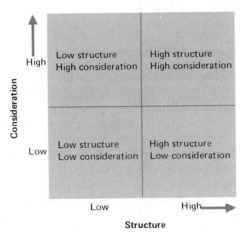

cedures that followers should adhere to in performing their jobs. Overall, structure behaviour limits the self-guidance of followers in the performance of their tasks. Although it would be correct to conclude that structure behaviour can be, and sometimes is, relatively firm, it would be incorrect to assume that it is rude and malicious.[14]

The second main type of leadership behaviour described by the OSU studies, **consideration behaviour**, is leadership behaviour that reflects friendship, mutual trust, respect, and warmth in the relationship between the leader and the followers. Consideration behaviour generally is aimed at developing and maintaining a more human relationship between the leader and the followers.

The OSU studies resulted in a model that depicts four fundamental leadership styles (Figure 13.5). A **leadership style** is the behaviour a leader exhibits while guiding organization members in appropriate directions. Each of the four leadership styles in Figure 13.5 is a different combination of structure behaviour and consideration behaviour. For example, the high structure/low consideration leadership style represents a leader who emphasizes structure behaviour and deemphasizes consideration behaviour.

Effectiveness of Various Leadership Styles

One investigation of high school superintendents concluded that desirable leadership behaviour seems to be associated with high leader emphasis on both structure and consideration, while undesirable leadership behaviour tends to be associated with low leader emphasis on both dimensions.[15] Similarly, the managerial grid covered in Chapter 11 implies that the most effective leadership style is characterized by high consideration and high structure.

One should be extremely careful, however, in concluding that any one leadership style is more effective than any other.[16] The overall leadership situation is so complex that pinpointing one leadership style as the most effective seems to be an oversimplification. In fact, a successful leadership style for managers in one situation may be ineffective for them in another situation. Recognizing the need to link leadership styles to appropriate situations. A.K. Korman indicates that a worthwhile contribution to leadership literature would be a rationale for

Consideration behaviour emphasizes a more human relationship.

A leadership style is the behaviour exhibited by the leader.

Which leadership style is best depends on the situation.

systematically linking appropriate styles with various situations so as to ensure effective leadership.[17] The life cycle theory of leadership, which is covered in the next section, provides such a rationale.

The Life Cycle Theory of Leadership

The life cycle theory of leadership links style and situations,

The **life cycle theory of leadership** is a rationale for linking leadership styles with various situations so as to ensure effective leadership. This theory uses essentially the same two types of leadership behaviour as the OSU leadership studies, but calls these dimensions "task" rather than structure, and "relationships" rather than consideration.

and is based on follower maturity, leader task behaviour, and leader relationship behaviour.

Life cycle theory is based primarily on the relationship between follower maturity, leader task behaviour, and leader relationship behaviour. In general terms, according to this theory, leadership style primarily should reflect the maturity level of the followers. **Maturity** is defined as the ability of the followers to perform their job independently, their ability to assume additional responsibility, and their desire to achieve success. The more of each of these characteristics that followers possess, the more mature they are said to be. Maturity, as used in life cycle theory, is not necessarily linked to chronological age.

Figure 13.6 shows the life cycle theory of leadership model. The curved line in this model indicates the maturity level of the followers. As the maturity curve runs from right to left, the followers' maturity level increases. In more specific terms, life cycle theory suggests that effective leadership behaviour should shift

---

FIGURE 13.6 The life cycle theory of leadership model.

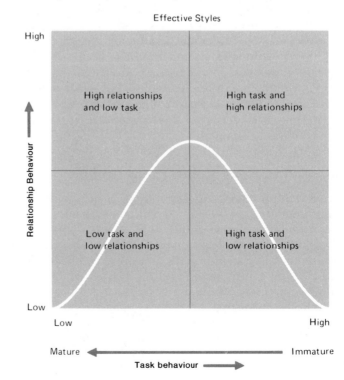

From Paul Hersey, Kenneth H. Blanchard, *Management of Organizational Behavior: Utilizing Human Resources*, 3rd ed., © 1977, p. 103. Reprinted by permission of Prentice-Hall, Inc., Englewood Cliffs, New Jersey.

FIGURE 13.7   How basic leadership styles are perceived by others as effective and ineffective.

Basic Styles	Effective	Ineffective
High task and low relationships	Often seen as knowing what he or she wants and imposing personal methods for accomplishing this without creating resentment.	Often seen as having no confidence in others, unpleasant, and interested only in short–run output.
High task and high relationships	Often seen as satisfying the needs of the group for setting goals and organizing work, but also providing high levels of socioemotional support.	Often seen as initiating more structure than is needed by the group and spends more time on socioemotional support than necessary.
High relationships and low task	Often seen as having implicit trust in people and as being primarily concerned with developing their talents.	Often seen as primarily interested in harmony and being seen as "a good person," and being unwilling to risk disruption of a relationship to accomplish a task.
Low task and low relationships	Often seen as appropriately permitting subordinates to decide how the work should be done and playing only a minor part in their social interaction.	Often seen as uninvolved and passive, as a "paper shuffler," who cares little about the task at hand or the people involved.

From Paul Hersey, Kenneth H. Blanchard, *Management of Organizational Behavior: Utilizing Human Resources*, 3d ed., © 1977 by Prentice-Hall, Inc., Englewood Cliffs, New Jersey. Used with permission of Dr. W. J. Reddin, University of New Brunswick.

from "(1) high task/low relationships behaviour to (2) high task/high relationships behaviour to (3) high relationships/low task behaviour to (4) low task/low relationships behaviour, as one's followers progress from immaturity to maturity."[18]

Life cycle theory suggests, therefore, that a style of leadership will be effective only if it is appropriate for the maturity level of the followers. Figure 13.7 indicates how each of the four main leadership styles is perceived when it is both effective and ineffective, or appropriate and inappropriate, for followers' maturity levels.

There are some exceptions to the general philosophy of life cycle theory. For example, if there is a short-term deadline to meet, a leader may find it necessary to accelerate production through a high task/low relationships style rather than a low task/low relationships style, even though the leader's followers may be extremely mature. A high task/low relationships leadership style carried out over the long term with such followers, however, typically results in a poor working relationship between leader and followers.

There are exceptions to the life cycle theory.

The following is an example of how life cycle theory would apply in an actual leadership situation: A man has just been hired as a salesperson in a men's clothing store. At first, this individual is extremely immature, or in other words, unable to solve task-related problems independently. According to life cycle theory, the appropriate style for leading this salesperson at his level of maturity is high task/low relationships. The leader should tell the salesperson exactly what should be done and how it should be done. The salesperson should be shown how to make cash and charge sales and how to handle merchandise returns. The leader also should begin laying some of the groundwork for developing a personal relationship with the salesperson. Too much relationships behaviour at this point, however, should be avoided since it easily can be misinterpreted as permissiveness.

As time passes and the salesperson increases somewhat in job-related maturity, the next appropriate style for leading him is high task/high relationships. Although the salesperson's maturity has increased somewhat, the leader needs to watch him closely because he still needs some guidance and direction at various times. The main difference between this leadership style and the first leadership style is the amount of relationships behaviour displayed by the leader. Building on the groundwork laid during the period of the first leadership style, the leader is now ready to start developing an atmosphere of mutual trust, respect, and friendliness between him and the salesperson.

As more time passes, the salesperson's maturity level increases still further. The next style appropriate for leading this individual is high relationships/low task. The leader can now de-emphasize task behaviour because the salesperson is now of above-average maturity in his job and usually can solve job-related problems independently. As with the previous leadership style, the leader still emphasizes the development of a human relationship with his follower.

As the salesperson's maturity level approximates its maximum, the appropriate style for leading him is low task/low relationships. Again, the leader can de-emphasize task behaviour because the follower is thoroughly familiar with the job. The leader also can de-emphasize relationships behaviour because he now has a good working relationship with the follower. Here, task behaviour is seldom needed, and relationships behaviour is used primarily to nurture the good working rapport that has developed between the leader and the follower. The salesperson, then, is left to do his job without close supervision, knowing that he has a positive working relationship with a leader who can be approached for additional guidance.

Recently, the life cycle theory of leadership has become widely accepted as a useful rationale upon which to base leader behaviour. The theory has served as the basis for leadership training in various organizations and has also appeared in numerous management textbooks. Although at first glance life cycle theory seems like a worthwhile leadership concept, some care probably should be exercised in its application due to the lack of scientific investigation verifying its worth.[19]

BACK TO THE CASE

The OSU leadership studies should furnish Gordon Toms with insights on leadership behaviour in general situations. According to these studies, Toms can exhibit two general types of leadership behaviour: structure and consideration. Toms will be using structure behaviour if he tells food services personnel what to do—for example, to work more quickly in serving meals to hospital patients. He will be using consideration behaviour if he attempts to develop a more human rapport with his employees by discussing their concerns and developing friendships with them.

Of course, depending on how Toms emphasizes these two behaviours, his leadership style can reflect a combination of structure and consideration ranging from high structure/low consideration to low structure/high consideration. For example, if Toms stresses giving orders to employees and de-emphasizes develop-

ing relationships, he will be exhibiting high structure/low consideration. If he emphasizes a good rapport with his staff and allows its members to function mostly independently of him, his leadership style will be termed low structure/high consideration.

Although no single leadership style is more effective than any other in all situations, the life cycle theory of leadership furnishes Toms with a strategy for using various styles in various situations. According to this theory, Toms should make his style consistent primarily with the maturity level of the food services personnel. As Tom's followers progress from immaturity to maturity, his leadership style should shift systematically from (1) high task/low relationships behaviour to (2) high task/high relationships behaviour to (3) high relationships/low task behaviour to (4) low task/low relationships behaviour.

Leader Flexibility

Situational theories of leadership such as life cycle theory are based on the concept of **leader flexibility**—that successful leaders must change their leadership style as they encounter different situations. Can leaders be so flexible as to span all major leadership styles? The only answer to this question is that some leaders can be flexible and some cannot. After all, a leadership style may be so ingrained in a leader that it takes years to even approach flexibility. Also, some leaders may have experienced such success in a basically static situation that they believe flexibility is unnecessary. Unfortunately, there are numerous obstacles to leader flexibility.

One strategy, proposed by Fred Fiedler, for overcoming these obstacles is changing the organizational situation to fit the leader's style, rather than changing the leader's style to fit the organizational situation.[20] Relating this thought to the life cycle theory of leadership, it may be easier to shift various leaders to situations appropriate for their leadership styles than to expect leaders to change styles as situations change. It probably would take three to five years to train managers to effectively use a concept such as life cycle theory.[21] Changing the situation a particular leader faces, however, can be done in the short term simply by exercising organizational authority.

According to Fiedler and his **contingency theory of leadership**, leader-member relations, task structure, and the position power of the leader are the three primary factors that should be used for moving leaders into situations more appropriate for their leadership styles. *Leader-member relations* is the degree to which the leader feels accepted by his or her followers. *Task structure* is the degree to which goals—the work to be done—and other situational factors are outlined clearly. *Position power* is determined by the extent to which the leader has control over rewards and punishments the followers receive. How these three factors can be arranged in eight different combinations is presented in Figure 13.8. Each of these eight combinations is called an octant.

Figure 13.9 shows how effective leadership varies with these eight octants. From an organizational viewpoint, this figure implies that management should attempt to match permissive, passive, and considerate leaders with situations reflecting the middle of the continuum containing the octants. Figure 13.9 also implies that management should try to match a controlling, active, and structuring

Leader flexibility is adapting leadership style to the situation.

However, it may be easier to change the situation to fit the leader's style.

The contingency theory of leadership emphasizes changing:

FIGURE 13.8   Eight combinations, or octants, of three factors: leader-member relations, task structure, and leader position power.

Octant	Leader–Member Relations	Task Structure	Leader Position Power
I	Good	High	Strong
II	Good	High	Weak
III	Good	Weak	Strong
IV	Good	Weak	Weak
V	Moderately poor	High	Strong
VI	Moderately poor	High	Weak
VII	Moderately poor	Weak	Strong
VIII	Moderately poor	Weak	Weak

From *A Theory of Leadership Effectiveness* by F. E. Fiedler, p. 34. Copyright © 1967 by McGraw-Hill, Inc. Used by permission of McGraw-Hill Book Company.

FIGURE 13.9   How effective leadership style varies with Fiedler's eight octants.

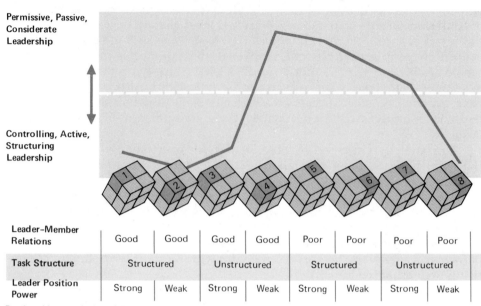

Leader–Member Relations	Good	Good	Good	Good	Poor	Poor	Poor	Poor
Task Structure	Structured		Unstructured		Structured		Unstructured	
Leader Position Power	Strong	Weak	Strong	Weak	Strong	Weak	Strong	Weak

leader with the extremes of this continuum. Possible actions that Fiedler suggests to modify the leadership situation are:[22]

1. Task structure.

1. In some organizations, we can change the individual's task assignment. We may assign to one leader very structured tasks which have implicit or explicit instructions telling him what to do and how to do it, and we may assign to another the tasks that are nebulous and vague. The former are the typical production tasks; the latter are exemplified by committee work, by the development of policy, and by tasks which require creativity.

2. The leader's position power.

2. We can change the leader's position power. We not only can give him a higher rank and corresponding recognition, we also can modify his position power by giving him subordinates who are equal to him in rank and prestige or subordinates who are two or three ranks below him. We can give him subordinates who are experts in their specialties or subordinates who depend upon the leader for guidance and instruction. We can give the leader the final say in all decisions affecting his group, or we can require that he make decisions in consultation with his subordinates, or even that he obtain their concurrence. We can channel all directives, communications, and information about organizational plans through the leader alone, giving him expert power, or we can provide these communications concurrently to all his subordinates.

3. Leader-member relations.

3. We can change the leader-member relations in this group. We can have the leader work with groups whose members are very similar to him in attitude, opinion, technical background, race, and cultural background. Or we can assign him subordinates with whom he differs in any one or several of these important aspects. Finally, we can assign the leader to a group in which the members have a tradition of getting along well with their supervisors or to a group that has a history and tradition of conflict.

Overall, Fiedler's work helps to destroy the myths that there is one best leadership style and that leaders are born, not made. Further, Fiedler's work supports the theory that almost every manager in an organization can be a successful leader if placed in a situation appropriate for his or her leadership style. This, of course, assumes that someone within the organization has the ability to assess the characteristics of the organization's leaders and of other important organizational variables and then match the two accordingly.[23] Although criticism of Fiedler's work can be found,[24] his leadership research is probably the most rigorous to date, and his works are highly recommended to anyone seeking insights on the challenges and "how-to's" of leadership.

Leaders can be successful in situations that suit their leadership styles.

BACK TO THE CASE

Life cycle theory suggests that Gordon Toms should be flexible enough to behave as the situation requires. If Toms finds it extremely difficult to be flexible, however, he should attempt to structure his situation so as to make it appropriate for his style. As suggested by Fiedler, if Toms's leadership style is more high task in nature, he generally will be a more successful leader in situations best described by octants 1, 2, 3, and 8 in Figures 13.8 and 13.9. On the other hand, if Toms's leadership style is more relationships oriented, he will be a more successful leader in situations representative of octants 4, 5, 6, and 7 in these figures. Overall, Fiedler's work provides Toms with insights on how to engineer situations within the food services department so that they are appropriate for his leadership style.

Action Summary

Reread the learning objectives that follow. Each objective is followed by questions. Answering these questions accurately will help you to retain the most important concepts discussed in this chapter. After answering each question, check your answer with the answer key at the end of this chapter. (*Hint*: If you have doubt regarding the correct response, consult the page that follows the answer.)

From studying this chapter, I will attempt to acquire: **Circle:**

1. **A working definition of leadership.**
   a. The process of directing others toward the accomplishment of some objective is: (a) communication; (b) controlling; (c) leadership; (d) managing; (e) none of the above.   a, b, c, d, e
   b. Directing must be consistent with which of the following: (a) organizational policies; (b) procedures; (c) job descriptions; (d) none of the above; (e) all of the above.   a, b, c, d, e

2. **An understanding of the relationship between leading and managing.**
   a. Leading and managing are the same process.   T, F
   b. In the relationship between managers and leaders, one could say that: (a) all managers are leaders; (b) all leaders are managers; (c) some leaders are not managers; (d) managers cannot be leaders; (e) management is a subset of leadership.   a, b, c, d, e

3. **An appreciation for the trait and situational approaches to leadership.**
    a. Which of the following is true about the conclusions drawn from the trait approach to leadership: (a) the trait approach identifies traits that consistently separate leaders from non-leaders; (b) there are certain traits that guarantee that a leader will be successful; (c) the trait approach is based on early research that assumes that a good leader is born, not made; (d) leadership is a simple issue of describing the traits of successful leaders; (e) none of the above is true.

a, b, c, d, e

    b. The situational approach to leadership takes which of the following into account: (a) the leader; (b) the follower; (c) the situation; (d) a and b; (e) a, b, and c.

a, b, c, d, e

4. **Insights on how to make decisions as a leader.**
    a. Forces in the manager that determine his or her leadership behaviour include: (a) the manager's values; (b) the manager's confidence in subordinates; (c) the manager's strengths; (d) the manager's tolerance for ambiguity; (e) all of the above.

a, b, c, d, e

    b. Limiting the self-guidance of the follower and specifically defining procedures for the follower's task performance is called: (a) initiating behaviour; (b) structure behaviour; (c) maturity behaviour; (d) consideration behaviour; (e) relationships behaviour.

a, b, c, d, e

5. **A strategy for using the life cycle theory of leadership.**
    a. The ability of followers to perform their jobs independently and to assume additional responsibility in their desire to achieve success is called: (a) maturity; (b) authority; (c) aggressiveness; (d) assertiveness; (e) consideration.

a, b, c, d, e

    b. Usually upon entrance into an organization, an individual is unable to solve task-related problems independently. According to life cycle theory, the appropriate style of leadership for this person is: (a) high task/low relationships; (b) high task/high relationships; (c) high relationships/low task; (d) low task/low relationships; (e) none of the above.

a, b, c, d, e

6. **An understanding of alternatives to leader flexibility.**
    a. According to Fiedler, the three primary factors that should be used as a basis for moving leaders into more appropriate situations are: (a) task behaviour, consideration behaviour, maturity; (b) maturity, job knowledge, responsibility; (c) the worker, the leader, the situation; (d) leader-member relations, task structure, position power; (e) task structure, leadership style, maturity.

a, b, c, d, e

    b. Fiedler's studies have proven true the myths that leaders are born, not made and that there is one best leadership style.

T, F

⬚ INTRODUCTORY CASE WRAP-UP

"Becoming a Successful Leader" (p. 348) and its related back-to-the-case sections were written to help you better understand the management concepts contained in this chapter. Answer the following discussion questions about this introductory case to further enrich your understanding of the chapter content:

1. Evaluate Gordon Toms's strategy.
2. How would you have reacted to the article summarized in Case Figure 13.1 if you were Toms?

Issues for Review and Discussion

1. What is leadership?
2. How does leadership differ from management?
3. Explain the trait approach to leadership.
4. What relationship exists between successful leadership and leadership traits?
5. Explain the situational approach to leadership.
6. Draw and explain Tannenbaum and Schmidt's leadership model.
7. List the forces in the manager, subordinates, and the situation that ultimately determine how a manager should make decisions as a leader.
8. What contribution did the OSU studies make to leadership theory?
9. Can any one of the major leadership styles resulting from the OSU studies be called more effective than the others? Why?
10. What is meant by *maturity* as used in the life-cycle theory of leadership?
11. Draw and explain the life cycle theory of leadership model.
12. What is meant by *leader flexibility*?
13. Describe some obstacles to leader flexibility.
14. In general, how might obstacles to leader flexibility be overcome?
15. In specific terms, how does Fiedler suggest that obstacles to leader flexibility be overcome?

Sources of Additional Information

Beggs, James M. "Leadership—The NASA Approach," *Long-Range Planning* 17 (April 1984): 12–24.

Culligan, Matthew J., Suzanne Deakins, and Arthur H. Young. *Back-to-Basics Management: The Lost Craft of Leadership.* New York: Facts on File, 1983.

Davis, Stanley M. *Managing Corporate Culture.* Cambridge, Mass.: Ballinger Publishing, 1984.

Derr, C. Brooklyn, "What Value Is Your Management Style?" *Personnel Journal* 66 (June 1987): 74–83.

Fiedler, Fred, and Martin Chemers. *Leadership and Effective Management.* Glenview, Ill.: Scott, Foresman, 1974.

Ford, Jeffrey D. "The Management of Organizational Crises." *Business Horizons* 24 (May/June 1981): 10–16.

Groocock, John M., and Richard A. Beaumont. "How Sound Employee Relations Contribute to Profitability." *AMA Forum* 71 (October 1982): 29–47.

Guest, David, and Robert Horwood. "Characteristics of the Successful Performance Manager." *Personnel Management* 13 (May 1981): 18–23.

Hayes, James L. *Memos for Management Leadership.* New York: Amacom, 1983.

Kleiner, Brian H. "Tracing the Evolution of Leadership Styles." *Management World* (March 1981): 18–20.

Lattimer, Robert L., and Marvin L. Winitsky. "Unleashing Creativity." *Management World* 13 (April/May 1984): 22–24.

McGregor, Douglas. *Leadership and Motivation.* Cambridge, Mass.: M.I.T. Press, 1966.

Mintzberg, Henry. *The Nature of Managerial Work.* New York: Harper & Row, 1980.

Peters, Thomas J. "Leadership: Sad Facts and Silver Linings." *Harvard Business Review* (November/December 1979): 164–72.

Plachy, Roger J. "Leading vs. Managing: A Guide to Some Crucial Distinction." *Management Review* 70 (September 1981): 58–61.

Schein, Edgar H. *Organizational Culture and Leadership.* San Francisco, Calif.: Jossey-Bass Publishers, 1985.

Stogdill, R. M. *Handbook of Leadership.* New York: Free Press, 1974.

Vroom, Victor, and Philip Yetton. *Leadership and Decision Making.* Pittsburgh: University of Pittsburgh Press, 1973.

White, Donald D., and David A. Bednar. *Organizational Behavior: Understanding and Managing People at Work.* Boston: Allyn and Bacon, 1986.

Notes

1. Thomas J. Neff, "How to Interview Candidates for Top Management Positions," *Business Horizons* (October 1980): 47–52.

2. For more discussions on leader vs. manager, see Joseph L. Massie and John Douglas, *Managing: A Contemporary Introduction* (Englewood Cliffs, N.J.: Prentice-Hall, 1977), 372–73.

3. Abraham Zaleznik, "Managers and Leaders: Are They Different?" *Harvard Business Review* (May/June 1977): 67–78.

4. Theodore Levitt, "Management and the Post-Industrial Society," *The Public Interest* (Summer 1976): 73.

5. As an example, see R. D. Mann, "A Review of the Relationship between Personality and Performance in Small Groups," *Psychological Bulletin* 56, no. 4 (1959): 241–70.

6. Ralph M. Stogdill, "Personal Factors Associated with Leadership: A Survey of the Literature," *Journal of Psychology* 25 (January 1948): 35–64.

7. Cecil A. Gibb, "Leadership," in *Handbook of Social Psychology*, ed. Gardner Lindzey (Reading, Mass: Addison-Wesley, 1954).

8. Eugene E. Jennings, "The Anatomy of Leadership," *Management of Personnel Quarterly* 1 (Autumn 1961).

9. Robert Tannenbaum and Warren H. Schmidt, "How to Choose a Leadership Pattern," *Harvard Business Review* (March/April 1957): 95–101.

10. William E. Zierden, "Leading Through the Follower's Point of View," *Organizational Dynamics* (Spring 1980): 27–46.

11. Tannenbaum and Schmidt, "How to Choose a Leadership Pattern," 95–101.

12. Robert Tannenbaum and Warren H. Schmidt, "How to Choose a Leadership Pattern," *Harvard Business Review* (May/June 1973): 162–80.

13. Roger M. Stogdill and Alvin E. Coons, eds., "Leader Behavior: Its Description and Measurement," Research Monograph no. 88 (Columbus, Ohio: Ohio State University Bureau of Business Research, 1957).

14. "How Basic Management Principles Pay Off: Lessons in Leadership," *Nation's Business*, March 1977, 46–53.

15. Andrew W. Halpin, *The Leadership Behavior of School Superintendents* (Chicago: University of Chicago Midwest Administration Center, 1959).

16. W.J. Reddin, "The Tridimensional Grid," *Training and Development Journal* (July 1964).

17. A.K. Korman, " 'Consideration,' 'Initiating Structure,' and Organizational Criteria—A Review," *Personnel Psychology: A Journal of Applied Research* 19 (Winter 1966): 349–61.

18. P. Hersey and K. H. Blanchard, "Life Cycle Theory of Leadership," *Training and Development Journal* (May 1969): 26–34.

19. Claude L. Graeff, "The Situational Leadership Theory: A Critical View," *Academy of Management Review* 8, no. 2 (1983): 285–91.

20. Fred E. Fiedler, "Engineer the Job to Fit the Manager," *Harvard Business Review* 43 (September/October 1965): 115–22. See also Fred E. Fiedler, *A Theory of Leadership Effectiveness* (New York: McGraw-Hill, 1967).

21. Rensis Likert, *New Patterns of Management* (New York: McGraw-Hill, 1961).

22. From A Theory of Leadership Effectiveness by F.E. Fiedler. Copyright © 1967 by McGraw-Hill, Inc. Used with permission of McGraw-Hill Book Company.

23. Fred E. Fiedler, "How Do You Make Leaders More Effective: New Answers to an Old Puzzle," *Organizational Dynamics* (Autumn 1972): 3–18.

24. Timothy McMahon, "A Contingency Theory: Logic and Method Revisited," *Personnel Psychology* 25 (Winter 1972): 697–710.

Action Summary Answer Key

1. a. c, p. 349
   b. e, p. 349
2. a. F, p. 349
   b. c, p. 349
3. a, c, p. 351
   b. e, pp. 351–352
4. a. e, pp. 354–355
   b. b, pp. 360–361
5. a. a, p. 362
   b. a, pp. 362–363
6. a. d, p. 365
   b. F, p. 367

BILLY DIAMOND: BUILDING AN AIRLINE AND A SENSE OF PROSPERITY FOR HIS PEOPLE

All successful careers receive their launch somewhere, generally without much notice, but there may not be another with a beginning quite so humble as that of Billy Diamond, one of Canada's most extraordinary negotiators. In the fall of 1957 he was eight years old, a skinny Cree kid from Rupert House in Northern Quebec who had been put aboard a float plane by the village chief, his father, while his mother wept for a child who did not even know English, let alone where he was headed. Eighty miles across James Bay he arrived at the Moose Fort Indian Residential School, where Georgie Visitor welcomed the newcomer by taking away his toy helicopter. The proposition: Billy could have the helicopter back if he agreed to steal bread from the dining room. "I kept up my end of the bargain," Diamond remembers, "I got back what was mine and I never let it go again."

In 1974, the Grand Chief of the Cree Council, the same Billy Diamond, negotiated the $135-million James Bay and Northern Quebec Agreement with the Quebec and federal governments. This landmark agreement eventually came to serve as the foundation for the first experiment in self-government, when the 9 000 Crees of James Bay began to appreciate the joys and frustrations of being in charge of their own destiny.

Twice each year, Billy Diamond returns to the same hunting territory where his father first brought him as a child. Near the mouth of the Broadback River, he waits behind a canvas blind for the snow geese to pass over. Fifteen years ago on one of these hunts, he and his father listened on a portable radio as Quebec Premier Robert Bourassa announced the James Bay hydro-electric project. Billy Diamond knew then that it would also become his project. As he again sat waiting in the blind, he was struck by what those fifteen years had brought. Sitting where his father had once called down the geese was Isao Toyama, technical engineer of overseas projects for Yamaha Motor Co. Ltd. And where once Malcolm Diamond would have had a sled to get them back home to Rupert House (now called Waskaganish), now a chartered helicopter came for them, hurrying Diamond and Toyama off to yet another meeting in the remarkable economic swirl created by Billy Diamond, the kid with a toy helicopter who became a man with his own airline.

" 'Leadership,' says Diamond, 'is stretching creativity.' "

The deal that Diamond engineered in March 1986 between the Waskaganish Enterprise Development Corporation (WEDCO) and Yamaha was worth only $200 000, yet it became front-page news. The massive Japanese conglomerate—its world sales in 1985 were roughly $4 billion—had never entered into a North American joint venture until Diamond approached it to see if the Japanese might be interested in redesigning the centuries-old Hudson's Bay canoe. Acting as president of WEDCO, a holding company whose shareholders are the citizens of Rupert House, Diamond engineered a scheme that, less than twelve months after his initial approach, saw the first redesigned fibreglass boat come out of the Waskaganish shop. The joint venture—60 percent WEDCO, 30 percent Yamaha Motor Canada Ltd. and 10 percent Yamaha of Japan—had plans to be producing 500 boats a year within a few years, generating revenues of approximately $500 000.

One soon begins to understand why Diamond jokingly refers to himself as "the corporate Indian," why he once went to Brian Craik, who studied the Cree language before going to work for Indian and Northern Affairs in Ottawa, and asked for a Cree equivalent of "compound interest." Though Diamond chose not to run for Grand Chief in 1984, he continues to be the key person in the economy of Northern Quebec. Currently he heads the Cree School Board; sits on the board of directors of Cree Co., the holding company the Crees established for their commercial ventures; and is president of Air Creebec, a

Val d'Or-based regional airline that has tripled its growth since the James Bay Cree went into 51 percent—49 percent partnership with Austin Airways Ltd. of Timmins, Ont. in 1979. From two small airplanes, Air Creebec has expanded to seven, with three new Dash-8 aircraft on order. "The Crees are now a major impact in the whole economy of Quebec," says Robert Epstein, an American-educated lobbyist who works full-time for the Crees in Ottawa. "And for Billy to have done that from zero is just absolutely amazing." Adds Kent Minam, the Yamaha executive who negotiated the boat-building project: "You cannot help but be impressed with him. It is as if Billy Diamond has a mission for the Cree people."

"Leadership," says Diamond, "is stretching creativity." In one small but highly symbolic example, Diamond decided to take on the local Hudson's Bay store, the dominant force in Rupert House for centuries. He formed a small business that began selling produce from a basement, dreaming of reaching perhaps $350 000 in revenues in the first year. Instead, villagers flocked to pay $2.25 for a dozen eggs that, before competition, had sold for $3.50. Sales in the first year surpassed $1 million.

According to Diamond, what is important to Cree society and to Northern Quebec is to keep that dollar circulating. Currently, 80 percent of revenues leave the community within twenty-four hours. "Our aim is to keep the money in the villages, to build an economic base," he says. "You can have all the constitutional conferences about self-government you want, but unless you have economic self-sufficiency, it doesn't matter. You know, we were indoctrinated to think that we couldn't do anything, that we were failures. The church told us that, the Bay store told us, Indian Affairs told us." Billy Diamond intends to change this myth. "He is a great chief," says Masafumi (Mark) Aoba, president of Yamaha's Canadian operations. "I was so impressed with his personality, by the way he always thinks about his people and their development."

The Cree themselves realize that Billy Diamond is their Chief. They realize that everything he has touched so far has been blessed. And they know, too, that he plans to maintain his hands-on approach, battling the mercury that threatens their fish and the government officials who threaten their agreement. But in his own son he sees that much of the fight has already been won. Last Christmas Philip Diamond cuddled up to the man who once did whatever was necessary to get his toy helicopter back, and asked his father if Santa Claus could bring him a Hawker-Siddeley-748—"and I mean a real one, not a toy." Billy Diamond knew then that he had passed on what his father had bequeathed earlier: the right to reach for the impossible.

DISCUSSION ISSUES

1. Would you consider Billy Diamond to be a manager or a leader? Support your answer by contrasting both roles.
2. Describe Billy Diamond's leadership style in accordance with:
   (a) The Trait Approach.
   (b) The Situational Approach.
   (c) The Life Cycle Theory of Leadership.
3. Can a person actually change his or her managerial style? Explain. Using the life cycle theory of leadership, explain how it might be necessary for Billy Diamond to change his leadership style.

Based on "Billy Diamond: Building an airline for himself and a new sense of prosperity for his people," by Roy MacGregor in *Canadian Business*, August 1986. Used with permission.

CHAPTER 1

MOTIVATION

STUDENT LEARNING OBJECTIVES

From studying this chapter, I will attempt to acquire:

1. A basic understanding of human motivation.
2. Insights on various human needs.
3. An appreciation for the importance of motivating organization members.
4. An understanding of various motivation strategies.

CHAPTER OUTLINE

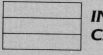

INTRODUCTORY CASE 14

NORTH AMERICAN TOOL & DIE, INC.

Shortly after purchasing a small manufacturing company—North American Tool & Die, Inc., a manufacturer of computer components on a contract basis—Thomas H. Melohn and Garner Beckett realized that they had only a slightly profitable company and a relatively unenthusiastic work force. Even longtime employees were looking around for better jobs.

Since a concerned and involved work force is generally a prerequisite for a significant company turnaround, the new owners decided to concentrate on motivating the employees. In formulating their strategy, Melohn and Beckett probably asked themselves questions such as: (1) Why are we the only ones to initiate new ideas? (2) Why do our people avoid confronting tough situations facing our business? (3) Why do our middle managers seem to resist innovation? (4) Why are our employees cleaned up and ready to leave the plant fifteen minutes early?

Unfortunately, purchasers of operating companies often inherit problems created by prior owners and managers. Regardless of who created the problems at North American Tool & Die, however, disgruntled employees probably were asking themselves questions such as: (1) Why don't managers ever listen to my suggestions or ideas? (2) How is it that my job has become so boring?

(3) For thirty years I have kept quiet and done my job, and for what?

Three years after Melohn and Beckett began their efforts to develop a motivated work force, a much different situation existed at North American Tool & Die. Company sales had tripled, and profits had grown six times. In addition, turnover of the company's seventy employees were almost non-existent. A few employees told a visitor during a plant tour that they had never imagined that the company could become such a challenging and exciting place to work.

Explaining why he and Beckett were so successful in turning their company around, Melohn indicated that when they took over the company, they had four objectives: expanding the company, increasing profits, sharing the wealth with employees, and having everyone experience satisfaction—and even fun—in performing the jobs. Furthermore, Melohn said, he and Beckett decided that the only way to attain these goals was to develop a feeling of trust between themselves and employees. According to Melohn, it was the successful creation of this trust that led to the turnaround in employee morale and, ultimately, to the financial turnaround at North American Tool & Die.

Based on "How to Build Employee Trust and Productivity," by Thomas H. Melohn in *Harvard Business Review*, January-February 1983.

What's Ahead

Melohn and Beckett, the new owners of North American Tool & Die in the introductory case, were faced with an unmotivated work force. In three years, they were able to transform dissatisfied, disillusioned workers into an involved, interested, motivated group of employees. The ability to motivate a work force is a skill that is extremely valuable to virtually all managers. The material in this chapter discusses the motivation process and the steps that can be taken to motivate organization members, and explains how Melohn and Beckett could have accomplished this employee transformation.

THE MOTIVATION PROCESS

To be successful in working with other people, managers first need a thorough understanding of the motivation process. To this end, a definition of motivation, various motivation models, and descriptions of people's needs are the main topics of discussion in this section of the chapter.

Defining Motivation

Motivation is the inner state that causes an individual to behave in a way that ensures the accomplishment of some goal.[1] In other words, motivation explains why people behave the way they do. The more managers understand organization members' behaviour, the better able they should be to influence that behaviour and make it more consistent with the accomplishment of organizational objectives. Since productivity in all organizations is a result of the behaviour of organization members, influencing this behaviour is a manager's key to increasing productivity.

Motivation influences productivity.

Motivation Models

Three models that describe how motivation occurs are: (1) the needs-goal model; (2) the Vroom expectancy model; and (3) the Porter-Lawler model. These three models build on one another to furnish a description of the motivation process that begins at a relatively simple and easily understood level but culminates at a somewhat more intricate and realistic level.

FIGURE 14.1   The needs-goal model of motivation.

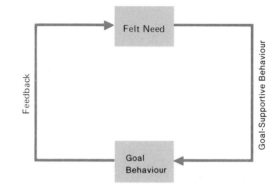

The Needs-Goal Model of Motivation

In the needs-goal model, goal behaviour reduces felt needs.

The **needs-goal model** of motivation (Figure 14.1) is the most fundamental of the three motivation models discussed in this chapter. As its name implies, needs and goals are the two primary components of this model. As Figure 14.1 indicates, motivation begins with an individual feeling a need. This need is then transformed into behaviour directed at supporting, or allowing, the performance of goal behaviour to reduce the felt need. Theoretically, goal-supportive behaviour and goal behaviour continue until a felt need has been reduced significantly.

For example, when an individual feels a hunger need, this need typically is transformed first into behaviour directed at supporting the performance of the goal behaviour of eating. Examples of this supportive behaviour could include such activities as buying, cooking, and serving the food to be eaten. Goal-supportive behaviours such as these and the goal behaviour itself of eating typically continue until the individual's felt hunger need substantially subsides. Once the individual experiences the hunger need again, however, the entire cycle is repeated.

The Vroom Expectancy Model of Motivation

The Vroom expectancy model addresses motivation strength — the intensity of a desire to perform a behaviour.

In reality, the motivation process is a more complex situation than depicted by the needs-goal model of motivation. The **Vroom expectancy model** handles some of these additional complexities.[2] As with the needs-goal model, the Vroom expectancy model is based on the premise that felt needs cause human behaviour. In addition, however, the Vroom model addresses the issue of motivation strength. **Motivation strength** is an individual's degree of desire to perform a behaviour. As this desire increases or decreases, motivation strength is said to fluctuate correspondingly.

Vroom's expectancy model is shown in equation form in Figure 14.2. According to this model, motivation strength is determined by: (1) the perceived value of the result of performing a behaviour; and (2) the perceived probability that the behaviour performed will cause the result to materialize. As both of these

FIGURE 14.2   Vroom's expectancy model of motivation in equation form.

$$\begin{array}{c}\text{Motivation} \\ \text{Strength}\end{array} = \begin{array}{c}\text{Perceived value of result} \\ \text{of performing behaviour}\end{array} \times \begin{array}{c}\text{Perceived probability that} \\ \text{result will materialize}\end{array}$$

factors increase, the motivation strength, or the individual's desire to perform the behaviour, increases. In general, individuals tend to perform those behaviours that maximize personal rewards over the long term.

An illustration of how Vroom's model applies to human behaviour could be a college student who has been offered the summer job of painting three houses at the rate of two hundred dollars a house. Assuming that the student has a need for money, his motivation strength or desire to paint the houses is determined by two major factors; (1) his perceived value of six hundred dollars; and (2) the perceived probability that he actually could paint the houses satisfactorily and, thus, receive the six hundred dollars. As the perceived value of the six-hundred-dollar reward and the probability that the houses could be painted satisfactorily increase, the student's motivating strength to paint the houses increases, and vice versa.

The Porter-Lawler Model of Motivation

Porter and Lawler developed a motivation model that presents a more complete description of the motivation process than either the needs-goal model or the Vroom expectancy model.[3] The **Porter-Lawler model** of motivation (Figure 14.3) is consistent with the prior two models in that it accepts the premises that felt

The Porter-Lawler model is a more complete model because it stresses:

FIGURE 14.3   The Porter-Lawler model of motivation.

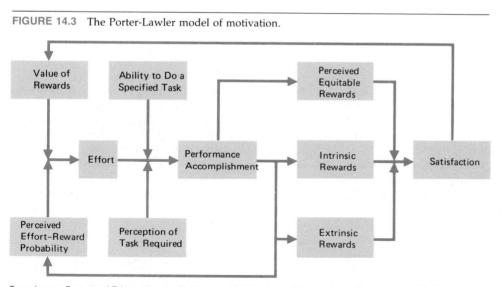

From Lyman Porter and Edward Lawler III, *Managerial Attitudes and Performance*. Copyright © 1968 Richard D. Irwin, Inc. Reprinted by permission.

needs cause human behaviour and that effort expended to accomplish a task is determined by the perceived value of rewards that will result from the task and the probability that the rewards actually will materialize. In addition, however, the Porter-Lawler motivation model stresses three other characteristics of the motivating process:

1. Intrinsic and extrinsic rewards.

1. The perceived value of a reward is determined by both intrinsic and extrinsic rewards that result in need satisfaction when a task is accomplished. **Intrinsic rewards** come directly from performing a task, while **extrinsic rewards** are extraneous to the task. For example, when a manager counsels a subordinate about a personal problem, the manager may get some intrinsic reward in the form of personal satisfaction simply from helping another individual. In addition to this intrinsic reward, however, the manager also would receive some extrinsic reward in the form of the overall salary the manager is paid.[4]

2. Task requirements and ability.

2. The extent to which an individual effectively accomplishes a task is determined primarily by two variables: the individual's perception of what is required to perform the task and the individual's ability to perform the task. Naturally, an individual's effectiveness at accomplishing a task increases as perception of what is required to perform the task becomes more accurate and as ability to perform the task increases.

3. The perceived fairness of rewards.

3. The perceived fairness of rewards influences the amount of satisfaction produced by those rewards. In general, the more equitable an individual perceives rewards to be, the greater the satisfaction the individual will experience as a result of receiving those rewards.

The Management in Action feature for this chapter discusses the increasing popularity of pay-for-performance systems and outlines the various considerations which must be reviewed before the implementation of such programs.

BACK TO THE CASE

Motivation is an inner state that causes individuals to act in certain ways that ensure the accomplishment of some goal. Melohn and Beckett obviously had an accurate understanding of the motivation process in that they were able to influence the behaviour of their employees to make it more consistent with the objectives of North American Tool & Die.

To motivate their employees, Melohn and Beckett probably kept five specific principles of human motivation clearly in mind: (1) felt needs cause behaviour aimed at reducing those needs; (2) the degree of desire to perform a particular behaviour is determined by an individual's perceived value of the result of performing the behaviour and the perceived probability that the behaviour actually will cause the result to materialize; (3) the perceived value of a reward for a particular behaviour is determined by both intrinsic and extrinsic rewards that result in need satisfaction when the behaviour is accomplished; (4) individuals can effectively accomplish a task only if they understand what the task requires and have the ability to perform the task; and (5) the perceived fairness of a reward influences the degree of satisfaction generated when the reward is received.

PAY FOR PERFORMANCE: A RUN FOR THEIR MONEY

During the recession of the early 1980s, many employers were forced to cut staff or curb salary increases to ride out the storm. Those employees who survived were happy enough just to have their jobs. But not anymore. Many of these employees are now beginning to show signs of discontent because the tight-fisted management style of the recession has remained. Most are being asked to take on heavier loads while being rewarded with smaller hikes in pay. A study by Hewitt Associates, an international compensation and benefits consulting firm, indicates a tremendous and continual decline in annual salary increases in Canada: 12 percent in 1981, 10 percent in 1982, 6 percent in 1983, and 5 percent or less in 1987. It's becoming a challenge to motivate employees in this climate.

Given this situation, employers can either ignore the problem or do what most of their staunchest competitors are doing—turn to pay for performance. A form of compensation that gives employees attractive incentives to work harder and more effectively, pay for performance is more than just a loose practice of annual raises: it links pay increases to the quality of work done. For the employees, this provides an opportunity to improve their incomes by meeting specific performance standards. For the employers, it provides a link between individual employee goals and business goals.

There are several ways to provide this link. To reward individual performance, some companies offer a year-end merit raise only if an employee has met certain goals. Others offer a "re-earnable bonus"—a one-time bonus that rewards individual performance without increasing base salary and that may be earned again in the next performance review. Many have turned to profit-sharing plans to reward team effort. Some offer gain-sharing plans, by which employees are rewarded if the company meets goals in areas such as customer service or productivity—even if there are no profits earned. And then there are companies that offer combinations of these schemes.

Pay-for-performance systems don't work for every company or every job, and even when they do work they're no corporate cure-all. But a significant number of companies are beginning to recognize that these systems may yield substantial benefits. "Compensation is now regarded as one of the means by which a company achieves its objectives," says Peter Larson, a senior research associate with the Conference Board of Canada.

"pay for performance . . . gives employees attractive incentives to work harder and more effectively . . ."

Companies are eager to find out how pay for performance can be used to communicate and reinforce what they want from employees. Many managers are in fact rankled by traditional salary systems involving regular, across-the-board salary increases, feeling that they're based on the assumption that everyone in a given job functions at the same level.

Before initiating a pay-for-performance system, a company should know that all systems are not alike; a system has to be custom-made to the company's need. Some companies ask their own human resource people to plan and install a suitable system; others go to outside consultants, paying fees that can range from $5000 to $50 000. Regardless of where the initiative comes from, several key decisions and critical points must be considered prior to the implementation stage. The company must identify exactly what sort of performance it wants to encourage in each job and it must ensure that the system does indeed encourage it. For example, is the employer willing to sacrifice product quality while giving a reward for higher-level production? Or is product quality more important?

Secondly, employees will want to know what is expected of them and will only accept a pay-for-performance system if it treats them equitably and rewards goals they can reach. If it doesn't, it may end up demoralizing

381

rather than motivating them. The company must define very precisely the reasons why a certain employee might receive a performance bonus when others do not. An important way to ensure that employees feel their goals are attainable is to inform them regularly about how they are doing, so they always have the finish line in sight. Thirdly, companies should give out performance rewards as soon as possible. The shorter the time between when a person does well and when he or she gets the reward, the more "psychologically visible" the reward will be. Fourthly, the pay incentive that's up for grabs must be big enough. Most human resource professionals believe that good employee motivation is achieved by annual incentives of at least 20 percent of salary for white-collar workers and lower-to-middle management, and up to 34 percent for senior management. Currently, the figures are about 10 percent and 20 percent, respectively. Finally, the system must be tailored to the general nature of the company. In an entrepreneurial environment, for example, where growth is the only goal, target-related and MBO systems would be inappropriate. In this instance, open-ended incentives such as gain sharing and profit sharing would be more motivating.

While it's important to determine what sort of pay-for-performance plan can work best for a particular company and its employees, it's also important to know when it may not work at all. In a unionized setting, union cooperation may be a problem, since pay for performance may be inapplicable to some unionized jobs. There are other jobs, professional or pseudo-professional, where pay for performance won't work because performance can't easily be measured or quantifiably improved. Human resources management is an example.

There are some critics who don't believe in pay for performance for any job, in any company. They see such incentive programs as tools that can be used to harass the employees. "They are usually put together to drum somebody out of the place, or they are used to develop personal loyalty to the manager who is doing the ap-

praisal," says Kevin Hayes, a national representative and researcher for the Canadian Labour Congress and a former management-level employee. Others share labour's reservations about performance-pay incentives. Alexander Mikalachki, Associate Dean of Programs at the University of Western Ontario's business school, has great reservations, particularly concerning jobs in which performance is hard to measure or there is a lot of team effort. "Everybody wants pay for performance—there is no argument against it because it's so appealing. The problem is you can't do it for most jobs. What you're doing through performance appraisal is trying to enforce a scheme that really falls apart because of your inability to apply it fairly." When this happens, the system can fail to achieve its goal of increasing motivation. According to Mikalachki, should a company misdirect its efforts on an ineffective pay-for-performance system, it may be at the expense of other, more basic motivational tools, such as making positive comments to employees about their work. The importance, however, of recognizing an employee's good work is something that people on both sides of the incentive pay question agree on. Often job satisfaction and motivation can be treated in employees by such forms of recognition as symbolic awards or promotions, not just pay hikes.

In the final analysis, companies must remember that pay for performance does not replace the good management practice of stroking people, even according to those who tout it as effective. But does pay for performance make workers perform? Does it increase productivity? Or does it just keep workers happy? Answers, especially dollars-and-cents answers, are difficult to come by. But, in the end, if pay incentives at least hold the promise of keeping an organization's best workers from drifting away to the competition, they may be worth looking at for that reason alone.

Based on "A Run For Their Money," by David Silbert in *Canadian Business*, May 1987. Used with permission.

Human Needs

The motivation models discussed thus far imply that a thorough understanding of motivation is based on a thorough understanding of human needs. There is some evidence that people in the general population typically possess strong needs for self-respect, respect from others,[5] promotion, and psychological growth.[6] Although the task of precisely pinpointing all human needs is impossible; several theories have been developed to help managers better understand these needs: (1) Maslow's hierarchy of needs; (2) Argyris's maturity-immaturity continuum; and (3) McClelland's achievement motivation.

Understanding motivation requires understanding human needs.

Maslow's Hierarchy of Needs

Perhaps the most widely accepted description of human needs of the general population is the hierarchy of needs concept developed by Abraham Maslow.[7] Maslow states that human beings possess five basic needs: (1) physiological needs; (2) security needs; (3) social needs; (4) esteem needs; and (5) self-actualization needs. He theorizes that these five basic needs can be arranged in a hierarchy of importance or order in which individuals generally strive to satisfy them. Each need and its relative positioning on the hierarchy of importance are shown in Figure 14.4.

Maslow's hierarchy reflects a sequence of satisfaction of such needs as

  Physiological needs relate to the normal functioning of the body and include needs for water, rest, sex, and air. Until these needs are met, a significant portion of an individual's behaviour is aimed at satisfying them. If these needs are satisfied, behaviour becomes aimed at satisfying the security needs on the next level of Maslow's hierarchy.

body needs,

  Security, or safety needs are the needs individuals feel to keep themselves free from harm, including both bodily and economic disaster. Management probably can best help employees to satisfy their physiological and security needs through employee salaries, since it is with these salaries that employees can buy

freedom from harm,

FIGURE 14.4 Maslow's hierarchy of needs.

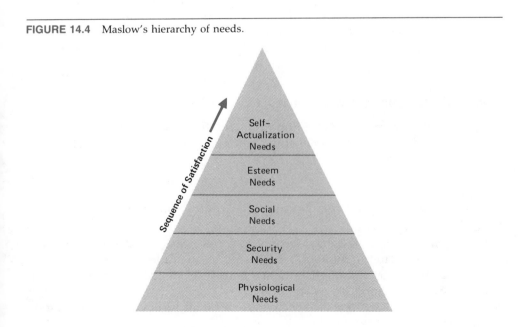

such things as food and housing.[8] As security needs are satisfied, behaviour tends to be aimed at satisfying social needs.

a sense of belonging,

Social needs include an individual's desire for love, companionship, and friendship. Overall, these needs reflect a person's desire to be accepted by others. As these needs are satisfied, behaviour shifts to satisfying esteem needs.

respect,

Esteem needs are an individual's desire for respect and generally are divided into two categories: self-respect and respect from others. Once esteem needs are satisfied, an individual emphasizes satisfying self-actualization needs.

and maximization of potential.

The need to **self-actualize** is the desire to maximize whatever potential an individual possesses. For example, a high school principal who seeks to satisfy self-actualization needs would strive to become the best principal possible. Self-actualization needs are the highest level of Maslow's hierarchy.

Although many management theorists admit that Maslow's hierarchy can be useful in understanding human needs, many concerns about the hierarchy have also been expressed. Maslow himself said:

Maslow's hierarchy should be used cautiously.

> I of all people should know just how shaky this foundation for the theory is as a final foundation. My work on motivation came from the clinic, from a study of neurotic people. The carryover of this theory to the industrial situation has some support from industrial studies, but certainly I would like to see a lot more studies of this kind before feeling finally convinced that this carryover from the study of neurosis to the study of labour in factories is legitimate. The same thing is true of my studies of self-actualizing people — there is only this one study of mine available. There were many things wrong with the sampling, so many in fact that it must be considered to be, in the classical sense anyway, a bad or poor or inadequate experiment, I am quite willing to concede this — because I'm a little worried about this stuff which I consider to be tentative being swallowed whole by all sorts of enthusiastic people who really should be a little more tentative in the way that I am.[9]

Other concerns related to Maslow's hierarchy include a re-emphasis on its lack of a research base,[10] a questioning of whether or not Maslow has pinpointed accurately five basic human needs for his hierarchy,[11] and doubt as to whether human needs actually are arranged in a hierarchy.[12] Despite such concerns, Maslow's hierarchy probably remains the most popular conceptualization of human needs to date. The concerns mentioned, however, indicate that Maslow's hierarchy should be considered more a subjective statement than an objective description of human needs.

Argyris's Maturity-Immaturity Continuum

Argyris has proposed a natural maturation process

Argyris's maturity-immaturity continuum also furnishes insights on human needs.[13] According to Argyris, as people naturally progress from immaturity to maturity, they move:[14]

1. From a state of passivity as an infant to a state of increasing activity as an adult.
2. From a state of dependence on others as an infant to a state of relative independence as an adult.
3. From being capable of behaving only in a few ways as an infant to being capable of behaving in many different ways as an adult.
4. From having erratic, casual, shallow, and quickly dropped interests as an infant to having deeper interests as an adult.
5. From having a short time perspective as an infant to having a much longer time perspective as an adult.

6. From being in a superordinate position as an infant to aspiring to occupy an equal and/or subordinate position as an adult.
7. From a lack of awareness of self as an infant to awareness and control over self as an adult.

Thus, according to Argyris's continuum, as individuals mature, they have increasing needs for: more activity, a state of relative independence, behaving in many different ways, deeper interests, considering a relatively long time perspective, occupying an equal position with other mature individuals, and more awareness of themselves and control over their own destiny. Unlike Maslow's hierarchy, Argyris's needs are not arranged in a hierarchy. Similar to Maslow's hierarchy, however, Argyris's continuum primarily represents a subjective position on the existence of human needs.

that produces specific maturity needs.

McClelland's Achievement Motivation

Another theory about human needs focuses on the need for achievement. This theory, popularized primarily by David C. McClelland, defines the **need for achievement ("n Ach")** as the desire to do something better or more efficiently than it has ever been done before.[15] McClelland claims that in some businesspeople the need to achieve is so strong that it is more motivating than a quest for profits.[16] To maximize their satisfaction, individuals with high achievement needs tend to set goals for themselves that are challenging yet achievable.[17] Although these individuals do not avoid risk completely, they assess risk very carefully. Individuals motivated by the need to achieve do not want to fail and will avoid tasks that involve too much risk. Individuals with a low need for achievement generally avoid challenges, responsibilities, and risk.

McClelland's "need for achievement" is the desire to do something better than before.

BACK TO THE CASE

Even though Melohn and Beckett undoubtedly understood the basic motivation principle that felt needs cause behaviour, they still had to be thoroughly familiar with the various human needs of their employees at North American Tool & Die before they could motivate them.

According to Maslow, people generally possess physiological needs, security needs, social needs, esteem needs, and self-actualization needs arranged in a hierarchy of importance. Argyris suggests that, as people mature, they have increasing needs for activity, independence, flexibility, deeper interests, analyses of longer time perspectives, a position of equality with other mature individuals, and control over personal destiny. McClelland believes that the need for achievement—the desire to do something better or more efficiently than it has ever been done before—is a strong human need.

MOTIVATING ORGANIZATION MEMBERS

People are motivated to perform behaviour to satisfy personal needs. Therefore, from a managerial viewpoint, motivation is the process of furnishing organization members with the opportunity to satisfy their needs by performing productive behaviour within the organization. As discussed in Chapter 12, motivating is one of the four primary interrelated activities of the influencing function performed by managers to guide the behaviour of organization members toward attainment of organizational objectives. The following sections discuss the importance of motivating organization members and strategies for motivating organization members.

Motivation of organization members requires satisfying human needs through work.

The Importance of Motivating Organization Members

Motivation increases appropriate behaviour, thereby increasing productivity.

Figure 14.5 makes the point that unsatisfied needs of organization members can lead to either appropriate or inappropriate organization member behaviour. Managers who are successful at motivating organization members minimize inappropriate organization member behaviour and maximize appropriate organization member behaviour. Correspondingly, these managers raise the probability that organization member productivity will increase and lower the probability that organization member productivity will decrease. Successful motivation of organization members is extremely important to managers.

Strategies for Motivating Organization Members

Managers have various strategies for motivating organization members. Each strategy is aimed at satisfying organization members' needs (consistent with those described by Maslow's hierarchy of needs, Argyris's maturity-immaturity continuum, and McClelland's achievement motive) through appropriate organization member behaviour.[18] These managerial motivation strategies are: (1) managerial communication; (2) Theory X-Theory Y; (3) job design; (4) behaviour modification; and (5) Likert's management systems. Each strategy is discussed further in the sections that follow.

It is important to remember, however, that no one of these strategies will necessarily always be more effective for a manager than any other. In fact, a manager may find that some combination of all or any number of these strategies is the most effective strategy in an organizational situation.

FIGURE 14.5   Unsatisfied needs of organization members resulting in either appropriate or inappropriate behaviour.

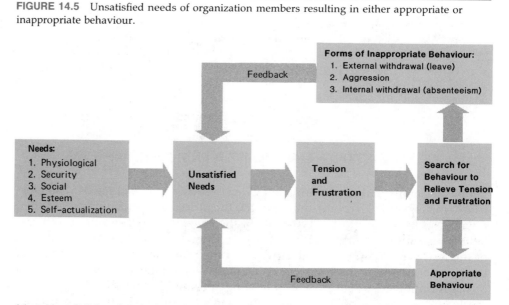

Adapted from B. Kolasa, *Introduction to Behavioral Science in Business* (New York: Wiley, 1969), p. 256. Used with permission.

Managerial Communication

Perhaps the most basic motivation strategy for managers is simply to communicate with organization members. This manager-subordinate communication can satisfy such basic human needs as recognition, a sense of belonging, and security.[19] For example, such a simple action as a manager attempting to become better acquainted with subordinates could contribute substantially to the satisfaction of each of these three needs. As another example, a communication message from a manager to a subordinate that praises the subordinate for a job well done can help to satisfy recognition and security needs of the subordinate. As a general rule, managers should strive to communicate often with other organization members, not only because communication is the primary means of conducting organizational activities, but also because it is a basic tool for satisfying the human needs of organization members.

Motivation through communication is one of the simplest strategies.

Theory X-Theory Y

Another motivation strategy involves a manager's assumptions about the nature of people. Douglas McGregor identified two sets of these assumptions: **Theory X** involves assumptions that McGregor feels managers often use as the basis for dealing with people, while **Theory Y** represents the assumptions that McGregor feels management should strive to use.[20] Theory X and Theory Y assumptions are presented in Figure 14.6.

McGregor implies that managers who use Theory X assumptions are "bad" and that those who use Theory Y assumptions are "good." Reddin, however, argues that production might be increased by using either Theory X or Theory Y assumptions, depending on the situation the manager faces:

Theory X involves negative assumptions about people, while Theory Y involves positive assumptions.

> Is there not a strong argument for the position that any theory may have desirable outcomes if appropriately used? The difficulty is that McGregor had

FIGURE 14.6 McGregor's Theory X—Theory Y assumptions about the nature of people.

Theory X Assumptions	Theory Y Assumptions
The average person has an inherent dislike for work and will avoid it if he or she can. Because of this human characteristic of dislike of work, most people must be coerced, controlled, directed, and threatened with punishment to get them to put forth adequate effort toward the achievement of organizational objectives. The average person prefers to be directed, wishes to avoid responsibility, has relatively little ambition, and wants security above all.	The expenditure of physical and mental effort in work is as natural as play or rest. People will exercise self-direction and self-control in the service of objectives to which they are committed. Commitment to objectives is a function of the rewards associated with achievement. The average person learns, under proper conditions, not only to accept but to seek responsibility. The capacity to exercise a relatively high degree of imagination, ingenuity, and creativity in the solution of organizational problems is widely, not narrowly, distributed in the population.

From *The Human Side of Enterprise* by Douglas McGregor. Copyright © 1960 by McGraw-Hill, Inc. Used with permission of McGraw-Hill Book Company.

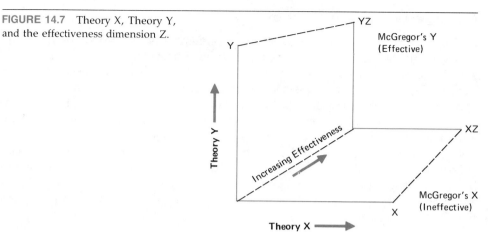

FIGURE 14.7   Theory X, Theory Y, and the effectiveness dimension Z.

From W. J. Reddin, "The Tri-Dimensional Grid." Reproduced by special permission from the July 1967 *Training and Development Journal.* Copyright 1964 by the American Society for Training and Development Inc.

considered only the ineffective application of Theory X and the effective application of Theory Y.[21]

Reddin proposes a **Theory Z**—an effectiveness dimension that implies that managers who use either Theory X or Theory Y assumptions when dealing with people can be successful, depending on their situation. Figure 14.7 shows Z as an effectiveness dimension relating to Theory X and Theory Y.

The basic rationale for using Theory Y rather than Theory X in most situations is that managerial activity that reflects Theory Y assumptions generally is more successful in satisfying the human needs of most organization members than management activities that reflect Theory X assumptions. Therefore, management activities based on Theory Y assumptions generally are more successful in motivating organization members than management activities based on Theory X assumptions.

Theory Z is the effectiveness dimension.

Theory Y is more successful in most cases.

BACK TO THE CASE

Once Melohn and Beckett's managers understood that felt needs cause behaviour and were aware of people's different types of needs, they were ready to apply this information to motivating their work force at North American Tool & Die. From Melohn and Beckett's viewpoint, motivating the employees meant furnishing them with the opportunity to satisfy their human needs by performing their jobs. This was very important to Melohn and Beckett because successful motivation tends to increase employee productivity. If Melohn and Beckett had not furnished their employees with an opportunity to satisfy their human needs while working, low morale within the company probably would have continued. Few employees would have continued to initiate new ideas, people would have continued to avoid confronting tough situations, and middle management would have continued to resist innovation.

What could Melohn and Beckett actually do to motivate North American Tool & Die workers? One strategy they might have followed is merely taking time to communicate with their employees. Manager-employee communication can help satisfy employee needs for recognition, belonging, and security. Another of Melohn and Beckett's strategies might have been based on McGregor's Theory X-Theory Y concept. In following this concept when dealing with employees, Melohn and Beckett would have assumed that work was as natural as play; that employees could be self-directed in goal accomplishment; that the granting of rewards encouraged the achievement of North American Tool & Die objectives; that employees sought and accepted responsibility; and that most employees were creative, ingenious, and imaginative. The adoption of such assumptions by Melohn and Beckett could have led to the satisfaction of many of the needs defined by Maslow, Argyris, and McClelland.

Job Design

A third strategy managers can use to motivate organization members relates to the design of jobs organization members perform. The following two sections discuss earlier and more recent job design strategies.

Earlier Job Design Strategies

A movement has existed in the more recent history of American business to make jobs simpler and more specialized to increase worker productivity. Theoretically, this movement is aimed at making workers more productive by enabling them to be more efficient. Perhaps the best example of this movement is the development of the automobile assembly line. A negative result that generally accompanies this work simplification and specialization, however, is job boredom, as the cartoon suggests. As work becomes simpler and more specialized, it typically becomes more boring and less satisfying to individuals performing the jobs. As a result productivity suffers.

Work simplification and specialization has produced job boredom.

Perhaps the earliest major attempt to overcome this job boredom was job rotation. **Job rotation** entails moving individuals from job to job, or not requiring individuals to perform only one simple and specialized job over the long term. For example, rather than constantly mowing lawns, a gardener would be shifted to other activities, such as trimming bushes, raking grass, and sweeping sidewalks. Although job rotation programs have been known to increase organizational profitability, they typically are ineffective because, over time, individuals become bored with all the jobs they are rotated into.[22] Job rotation programs, however, usually are more effective in achieving other objectives, such as the training objective of providing individuals with an overview of how various units of an organization function.

With job rotation, individuals move from job to job.

Job enlargement is another strategy developed to overcome the boredom of more simple and specialized jobs. **Job enlargement** advocates claim that jobs become more satisfying as the number of operations an individual performs increases. According to the job enlargement concept, then, the gardener's job would become more satisfying as such activities as trimming bushes, raking grass, and sweeping sidewalks were added to the gardener's initial job responsibility of mowing grass. Some research supports[23] the theory that job enlargement makes jobs more satisfying, while some does not.[24] Job enlargement programs, however, generally have been more successful in increasing job satisfaction than job rotation programs.

Job enlargement increases the number of tasks an individual performs.

More Recent Job Design Strategies

A number of other job design strategies have evolved since the development of job rotation and job enlargement programs. Two of these more recent strategies are job enrichment and flextime.

Job Enrichment   Frederick Herzberg concludes from his research that the degrees of satisfaction and dissatisfaction that organization members feel as a result of performing a job are two different variables determined by two different sets of items.[25] The set of items that influence the degree of job satisfaction are called **motivating factors**, or motivators, while the set of items that influence the degree of job dissatisfaction are called **hygiene, or maintenance factors**. Hygiene factors relate to the work environment, while motivating factors relate to work itself. Items that make up Herzberg's motivating and hygiene factors are presented in Figure 14.8.

Motivating factors influence job satisfaction, while hygiene factors influence job dissatisfaction.

FIGURE 14.8   Herzberg's hygiene factors and motivators.

Dissatisfaction: Hygiene or Maintenance Factors	Satisfaction: Motivating Factors
1. Company policy and administration 2. Supervision 3. Relationship with supervisor 4. Relationship with peers 5. Working conditions 6. Salary 7. Relationship with subordinates	1. Opportunity for achievement 2. Opportunity for recognition 3. Work itself 4. Responsibility 5. Advancement 6. Personal growth

Reprinted by permission of the *Harvard Business Review*, from "One More Time: How Do You Motivate Employees?" by Frederick Herzberg (January/February 1968). Copyright © 1968 by the President and Fellows of Harvard College; all rights reserved.

Herzberg indicates that, if hygiene factors are undesirable in a particular job situation, organization members will become dissatisfied. Making these factors more desirable by, for example, increasing salary generally will not motivate organization members to do a better job, but it will keep them from becoming dissatisfied. On the other hand, if motivating factors are high in a particular job situation, organization members generally are motivated to do a better job. In general, organization members tend to be more motivated and productive as more motivators are built into their job situation.

Job enrichment entails incorporating motivators into the job situation.

The process of incorporating motivators into a job situation is called **job enrichment**. Although such companies as Texas Instruments Incorporated[26] and the Volvo Company[27] have reported notable success in motivating organization members through job enrichment programs, experience indicates that, for a job enrichment program to be successful, it must be designed and administered very carefully.[28] An outline of a successful job enrichment program is presented in Figure 14.9.

Herzberg's overall findings indicate that the most productive organization members are involved in work situations characterized by desirable hygiene factors and motivating factors. The respective needs on Maslow's hierarchy of needs that desirable hygiene factors and motivating factors generally satisfy are shown in Figure 14.10. Esteem needs can be satisfied by both types of factors. An example of esteem needs satisfied by a hygiene factor could be a private parking space—a status symbol and working condition evidencing the importance of the organization member. An example of esteem needs satisfied by a motivating factor could be an award received for outstanding performance—a display of importance through recognition for a job well done.

Flextime   Another more recent job design strategy for motivating organization members is based on a concept called flextime. Perhaps the most common traditional characteristic of work performed in North America is that jobs are performed within a fixed eight-hour workday. Recently, however, this tradition has been challenged. Faced with motivation problems and absenteeism, many managers are turning to scheduling innovations as a possible solution.[29]

The main purpose of these scheduling innovations is not to reduce the total number of hours during which organization members perform jobs but to provide workers with greater flexibility in the exact hours during which they must perform their jobs. The main thrust of **flextime**, or flexible working hours programs, is that it allows workers to complete their jobs within a forty-hour workweek that they arrange themselves.[30] The choices of starting and finishing times can be as flexible as the organizational situation allows.

FIGURE 14.9 Outline of successful job enrichment program.

Specific Changes Aimed at Enriching Jobs	"Motivators"—These Changes Are Aimed at Increasing
1. Removing some controls while retaining accountability	Responsibility and personal achievement
2. Increasing the accountability of individuals for own work	Responsibility and recognition
3. Giving a person a complete natural unit of work (module, division, area, and so on)	Responsibility, achievement, and recognition
4. Granting additional authority to an employee in his or her activity; job freedom	Responsibility, achievement, and recognition
5. Making periodic reports directly available to the worker rather than to the supervisor	Internal recognition
6. Introducing new and more difficult tasks not previously handled	Growth and learning
7. Assigning individuals specific or specialized tasks, enabling them to become expert	Responsibility, growth, and advancement

Reprinted by permission of the *Harvard Business Review*, from "One More Time: How Do You Motivate Employees?" by Frederick Herzberg (January/February 1968). Copyright © 1968 by the President and Fellows of Harvard College; all rights reserved.

FIGURE 14.10 Needs on Maslow's hierarchy that desirable hygiene factors and motivating factors generally satisfy.

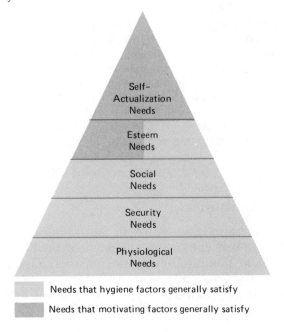

Self-Actualization Needs

Esteem Needs

Social Needs

Security Needs

Physiological Needs

Needs that hygiene factors generally satisfy

Needs that motivating factors generally satisfy

FIGURE 14.11   Advantages and disadvantages of using flextime programs.

Advantages	Disadvantages
Improved employee attitude and morale	Lack of supervision during some hours of work
Accommodation of working parents	Key people unavailable at certain times
Decreased tardiness	Understaffing at times
Fewer traffic problems—workers can avoid congested streets and highways	Problem of accommodating employees whose output is the input for other employees
Accommodation of those who wish to arrive at work before interruptions begin	Employee abuse of flextime program
Increased production	Difficulty in planning work schedules
Facilitation of employee scheduling of medical, dental, and other types of appointments	Problem of keeping track of hours worked or accumulated
Accommodation of leisure-time activities of employees	Inability to schedule meetings at convenient times
Decreased absenteeism	Inability to coordinate projects
Decreased turnover	

Reprinted by permission from Edward G. Thomas, ''Workers Who Set Their Own Time Clocks,'' *Business and Society Review* (Spring 1987): 50.

and appears to produce higher motivation levels.

Various kinds of organizational studies have indicated that flextime programs seem to have some positive organizational effects. Douglas Fleuter, for example, has reported that flextime contributes to greater job satisfaction, which typically results in greater productivity.[31] Other research concludes that flextime programs can result in higher motivation levels of workers.[32] (A listing of the advantages and disadvantages of flextime programs appears in Figure 14.11.) Although many well-known companies, such as Scott Paper, Sun Oil, and Samsonite, have adopted flextime programs,[33] more research must be conducted to conclusively assess its true worth.

BACK TO THE CASE

Melohn and Beckett could have used two major job design strategies to motivate their employees at North American Tool & Die. With job enrichment, Melohn and Beckett could have incorporated into employee jobs such motivating factors as opportunities for achievement, recognition, and personal growth. However, for maximum success, hygiene factors at North American Tool & Die—company policy and administration, supervision, salary, and working conditions, for

example—also would have had to be perceived as desirable by employees.

The second major job design strategy that Melohn and Beckett could have used to motivate their employees is flextime. With flextime, the employees would have some freedom in scheduling the beginning and ending of workdays. Of course, this freedom would have been somewhat limited by such organizational factors as seasonal demand or peak selling seasons.

Behaviour Modification

Behaviour modification focuses on the consequences of behaviour.

A fourth strategy that managers can use in motivating organization members is based primarily on a concept known as behaviour modification. As stated by B.F. Skinner, **behaviour modification** focuses on encouraging appropriate behaviour as a result of the consequences of that behaviour.[34] According to the law of effect,[35] behaviour that is rewarded tends to be repeated, while behaviour that is punished tends to be eliminated. Although behaviour modification programs typically involve the administration of both rewards and punishments, the rewards generally are emphasized since they typically have more effective influence on behaviour than punishments. Obviously, the main theme of behaviour modification is not new.[36]

Behaviour modification theory asserts that if managers want to modify subordinates' behaviour, they must ensure that appropriate consequences occur as a result of that behaviour.[37] For example, if a particular activity such as a worker arriving on time for work is positively reinforced, or rewarded, the probability increases that the worker will begin arriving on time with greater frequency. In addition, if the worker experiences some undesirable outcome related to arriving late for work, such as a verbal reprimand, the worker is negatively reinforced when this outcome is eliminated due to the worker arriving on time. According to behaviour modification, positive reinforcement and negative reinforcement are both rewards that increase the likelihood that behaviour will continue. **Positive reinforcement** is a desirable consequence of a behaviour, while **negative reinforcement** is the elimination of an undesirable consequence of behaviour.

Punishment is the presentation of an undesirable behavioural consequence and/or the removal of a desirable behavioural consequence that decrease the likelihood of a behaviour continuing.[38] Extending the earlier example given, managers could punish employees for arriving late for work by exposing employees to some undesirable consequence, such as a verbal reprimand, and/or by removing the desirable consequence of salary by refusing to pay employees wages for the amount of time they are late.[39] Although this punishment probably would quickly cause workers to come to work on time, it might be accompanied by undesirable side effects, such as employee turnover and absenteeism, if emphasized by managers over the long term.

Behaviour modification programs have been applied both successfully and unsuccessfully in a number of different organizations.[40] The behaviour modification efforts of Emery Air Freight Company, now called Emery Worldwide, resulted in the finding that the establishment and use of an effective feedback system is extremely important in making a behaviour modification program successful.[41] This feedback should be aimed at keeping employees informed of the relationship between various behaviours and the consequences associated with them. Other ingredients that successful behaviour modification programs include are: (1) giving different levels of rewards to different workers depending on the quality of their performance; (2) telling workers what they are doing wrong; (3) punishing workers privately so as not to embarrass them in front of others; and (4) always giving rewards and punishments when earned to emphasize that management is serious about behaviour modification efforts.[42]

Likert's Management Systems

Another strategy that managers can use for motivating organization members is based on the work of Rensis Likert.[43] As a result of studying several types and sizes of organizations, Likert concludes that management styles in organizations can be categorized into the following systems:[44]

System 1 This style of management involves having no confidence or trust in subordinates. Subordinates do not feel free to discuss their job with superiors and are motivated by fear, threats, punishments, and occasional rewards.

Positive and negative reinforcement both support appropriate behaviour.

Punishment involves enforcing undesirable consequences or removing desirable consequences.

According to Likert, as management style moves from

treating people poorly,

"I'm just a number here, like you, Caswell—but a higher number."
New Yorker, *May 4, 1987, p. 134. Drawing by Vietor; © 1987 The New Yorker Magazine, Inc.*

Information flow primarily is directed downward, with upward communication viewed with great suspicion. The bulk of all decision making is at the top of the organization. (The cartoon shows how a manager with a system 1 management style might interact with a subordinate.)

System 2   This style of management involves having condescending confidence and trust (such as master to servant) in subordinates. Subordinates do not feel very free to discuss their job with superiors and are motivated by rewards and some actual or potential punishment. Information flows mostly downward, while upward communication may or may not be viewed with suspicion. While policies primarily are made at the top of the organization, decisions within a prescribed framework are made at lower levels.

System 3   This style of management involves having substantial, but not complete, confidence in subordinates. Subordinates feel rather free to discuss their job with superiors and are motivated by rewards, occasional punishment, and some involvement. Information flows both up and down. Upward communication is often accepted but at times may be viewed with suspicion. While broad policies and general decisions are made at the top of the organization, more specific decisions are made at lower levels.

System 4   This style of management involves having complete trust and confidence in subordinates. Subordinates feel completely free to discuss their job with superiors and are motivated by such factors as economic rewards based on a compensation system developed through participation and involvement in goal setting. Information flows upward, downward, and horizontally. Upward communication is generally accepted; however, if it is not, related questions are asked candidly. Decision making is spread widely throughout the organization and is well coordinated.

Likert suggests that, as management style within an organization moves from system 1 to system 4, the human needs of individuals within that organization tend to be more effectively satisfied over the long term. Thus, as management style within an organization moves toward system 4, the organization tends to become more productive over the long term.

to treating people less poorly,

to treating people fairly well,

to treating people extremely well,

productivity increases.

FIGURE 14.12 Comparative long-term and short-term effects of system 1 and system 4 on organizational production.

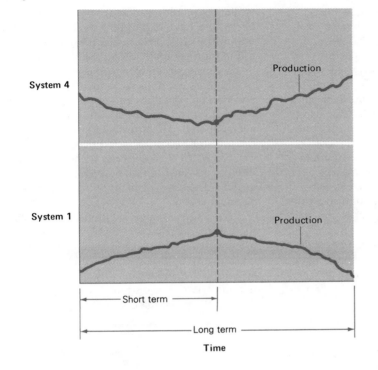

Figure 14.12 illustrates the comparative long- and short-term effects of both system 1 and system 4 on organizational production. Managers may increase production in the short term by using a system 1 management style, since motivation by fear, threat, and punishment is generally effective in the short term. Over the long term, however, this style usually causes production to decrease, primarily because of the long-term non-satisfaction of organization members' needs and poor working relationships that develop between managers and subordinates.

Conversely, managers who attempt to initiate a system 4 management style probably face some decline in production initially, but an increase in production over the long term. This trend exists over the short term because managers must implement a new system to which organization members must adapt. The production increase over the long term materializes as a result of organization members becoming adjusted to the new management system, greater satisfaction of the human needs of organization members, and good working relationships that tend to develop between managers and subordinates.

Likert offers his **principle of supportive relationships** as the basis for management activity aimed at developing a system 4 management style. This principle states:

> The leadership and other processes of the organization must be such as to ensure a maximum probability that in all interactions and in all relationships within the organization, each member in light of his or her background, values, desires, and expectations will view the experience as supportive and one which builds and maintains his or her sense of personal worth and importance.[45]

Likert's principle of supportive relationships emphasizes personal worth and importance.

BACK TO THE CASE

Melohn and Beckett could have applied behaviour modification to their situation at North American Tool & Die by rewarding appropriate employee behaviour and punishing inappropriate employee behaviour. Punishment would have had to have been used very carefully, however. If used continually, the working relationship between Melohn and Beckett and their employees would have been destroyed. For the behaviour modification program to have been successful, Melohn and Beckett would have had to furnish employees with feedback on which behaviours were appropriate and inappropriate, give workers different rewards depending on the quality of their performance, to tell workers what they were doing wrong, to punish workers privately, and to consistently give rewards and punishments when earned.

To have used Likert's system 4 management style to motivate employees over the long term, Melohn and Beckett would have had to demonstrate complete confidence in their workers and to encourage workers to feel completely free to discuss problems with them. In addition, communication at North American Tool & Die would have had to flow freely in all directions within the organization structure, with upward communication generally discussed candidly. Melohn and Beckett's decision-making process under system 4 would have had to involve many employees. Melohn and Beckett could have used the principle of supportive relationships as the basis for their system 4 management style. Melohn stated in the introductory case that he and Beckett believed that the development of a real feeling of trust between themselves and their employees was critical to the attainment of organizational goals. This statement definitely reflects a system 4 management style.

No single strategy mentioned in this chapter for motivating organization members would necessarily be more valuable to managers such as Melohn and Beckett than any of the other strategies. In reality, Melohn and Beckett could have easily found that some combination of all of these strategies was most useful in motivating the work force at North American Tool & Die.

Action Summary

Reread the learning objectives that follow. Each objective is followed by questions. Answering these questions accurately will help you to retain the most important concepts discussed in this chapter. After answering each question, check your answer with the answer key at the end of this chapter. (*Hint*: If you have doubt regarding the correct response, consult the page that follows the answer.)

Circle:

From studying this chapter, I will attempt to acquire:

1. **A basic understanding of human motivation.**

   a, b, c, d, e

   T, F

   a. An individual's inner state that causes him or her to behave in such a way as to ensure accomplishment of a goal is: (a) ambition; (b) drive; (c) motivation; (d) need; (e) leadership.
   b. According to the needs-goal model, a fulfilled need is a motivator.
   c. Which of the following most comprehensively describes how motivation takes place: (a) the Vroom expectancy model; (b) the needs-goal model; (c) the Porter-Lawler model; (d) all of the above; (e) none of the above.

   a, b, c, d, e

2. **Insights on various human needs.**

   a, b, c, d, e

   a. Which of the following is a rank-ordered listing of Maslow's hierarchy of needs from lowest to highest: (a) self-actualization, social, security, physiological, esteem; (b) social, security, physiological, self-actualization; (c) esteem, self-actualization, security, social, physiological; (d) physiological, security, social, esteem, self-actualization; (e) physiological, social, esteem, security, self-actualization.
   b. According to Argyris, as individuals mature, they have an increasing need for: (a) greater dependence; (b) a shorter-term perspective; (c) more inactivity; (d) deeper interests; (e) youth.

   a, b, c, d, e

c. The desire to do something better or more efficiently than it has ever been done before is known as the need for: (a) acceleration; (b) achievement; (c) acclamation; (d) actualization; (e) none of the above.   a, b, c, d, e

3. **An appreciation for the importance of motivating organization members.**
   a. From a managerial viewpoint, motivation is the process of furnishing organization members with the opportunity to satisfy their needs by performing productive behaviour within the organization.   T, F
   b. The concepts of motivation and appropriate behaviour are closely related.   T, F

4. **An understanding of various motivation strategies.**
   a. Which of the following is a Theory Y assumption: (a) the average person prefers to be directed; (b) most people must be threatened and coerced before they will put forth adequate effort; (c) commitment to objectives is a function of the rewards associated with achievement; (d) the average person seeks no responsibility; (e) all of the above.   a, b, c, d, e
   b. The process of incorporating motivators into the job situation is called: (a) job enlargement; (b) flextime; (c) satisfying; (d) job enrichment; (e) Theory X.   a, b, c, d, e
   c. Successful behaviour modification programs can include: (a) giving rewards and punishments when earned; (b) giving rewards according to performance quality; (c) telling workers what they are doing wrong; (d) punishing workers privately; (e) all of the above.   a, b, c, d, e

INTRODUCTORY CASE WRAP-UP

"North American Tool & Die, Inc." (p. 376) and its related back-to-the-case sections were written to help you better understand the management concepts contained in this chapter. Answer the following discussion questions about this introductory case to further enrich your understanding of the chapter content:

1. Do you think it is unusual for managers like Melohn and Beckett to be faced with the challenge of motivating a work force? Explain.

2. What could the previous owners have done to alienate their employees to the extent indicated by the case?

3. It took three years for Melohn and Beckett to develop their motivated work force. Could they have realistically expected to accomplish this task sooner? Why or why not?

Issues for Review and Discussion

1. Define *motivation* and explain why managers should understand it.
2. Draw and explain the needs-goal model of motivation.
3. Summarize Vroom's expectancy model of motivation.
4. List and explain three characteristics of the motivation process contained in the Porter-Lawler motivation model that are not contained in either the needs-goal model or Vroom's expectancy model.
5. What does Maslow's hierarchy of needs tell us about people's needs?
6. What concerns have been expressed about Maslow's hierarchy of needs?
7. Describe Argyris's maturity-immaturity continuum.
8. What is the need for achievement?
9. Summarize the characteristics of individuals who have a high need for achievement.
10. Define motivating of organization members.
11. Is the process of motivating organization members important to managers? Why?
12. How can managerial communications be used to motivate organization members?
13. What are Theory X, Theory Y, and Theory Z?

What does each of these theories tell us about motivating organization members?

14. What is the difference between job enlargement and job rotation?
15. Describe the relationship between hygiene factors, motivating factors, and job enrichment.
16. Define *flextime*.
17. Define *behaviour modification*.
18. What basic ingredients are necessary to make a behaviour modification program successful?
19. In your own words, summarize Likert's four management systems.
20. What effect do Likert's systems 1 and 4 generally have on organizational production in both the short and long term? Why do these effects occur?

Sources of Additional Information

Argyris, C. *Integrating the Individual and the Organization.* New York: Wiley, 1964.

Arnold, Hugh J. "A Test of the Validity of the Multiplicative Hypothesis of Expectancy-Valence Theories of Work Motivation." *Academy of Management Journal* 24 (March 1981): 128–41.

Davis, Keith, and John W. Newstrom, *Human Behavior at Work: Organizational Behavior.* 7th ed. New York: McGraw-Hill, 1985.

Freedman, Sara M., and John R. Montanari. "An Integrative Model of Managerial Reward Allocation." *Academy of Management Review,* 5, no. 3 (1980): 381–90.

Gardner, Jerry. "Creating Motivating Workplaces." *Personnel Journal* (May 1981): 406–408.

Glatthorn, Allan A., and Herbert R. Adama. *Listening Your Way to Management Success.* Glenview, Ill.: Scott, Foresman, 1983.

Hanna, John B. "Assessing Your People Potential." *Management World* 13 (April/May 1984): 30–31.

Kanter, Rosabeth Moss, and Barry A. Stein. "Ungluing the Stuck: Motivating Performance and Productivity through Expanding Opportunity." *Management Review* 70 (July 1981): 45–49.

Lawler, E.E. *Pay and Organizational Effectiveness.* New York: McGraw-Hill, 1971.

Locke, Edwin A. "The Nature and Causes of Job Satisfaction." In *Handbook of Industrial and Organizational Psychology,* edited by M.D. Dunnette. Chicago: Rand McNally, 1976.

Magnus, Margaret, "Employee Recognition: A Key to Motivation." *Personnel Journal* (February 1981): 103–107.

Miner, John B. *Organizational Behavior: Performance and Productivity.* New York: Random House, 1988.

Mischkind, Louis A. "Is Employee Morale Hidden behind Statistics?" *Personnel Journal* 65 (February 1986): 74–79.

Ryans, Adrian B., and Charles B. Weinberg. "Improving Productivity in the Sales Force — Learning from Our Own Experience: A Company-Focused Approach." *Business Quarterly* (Spring 1984): 67–69.

Seybolt, John W. "Dealing with Premature Employee Turnover." *California Management Review* 25 (Spring 1983): 107–17.

Skinner, B.F. *Beyond Freedom and Dignity.* New York: Knopf, 1971.

Steers, Richard M., and Lyman W. Porter, eds. *Motivation and Work Behavior,* 3rd ed. New York: McGraw-Hill, 1983.

Vroom, Victor H. *Work and Motivation.* New York: Wiley, 1982.

Notes

1. Bernard Berelson and Gary A. Steiner, *Human Behavior: An Inventory of Scientific Findings* (New York: Harcourt, Brace, and World, 1964), 239–40.
2. Victor H. Vroom, *Work and Motivation* (New York: Wiley, 1964).
3. L.W. Porter and E.E. Lawler, *Managerial Attitudes and Performance* (Homewood, Ill.: Richard D. Irwin, 1968).
4. For more information on intrinsic and extrinsic rewards, see H.J. Arnold, 'Task Performance, Perceived Competence, and Attributed Causes of Performance as Determinants of Intrinsic Motivation," *Academy of Management Journal* 28 (December 1985): 876–88.
5. *Work in America: Report of the Special Task Force to the Secretary of Health, Education, and Welfare* (Cambridge, Mass.: M.I.T. Press, 1972).
6. H. Sheppard and N. Herrick, *Where Have All the Robots Gone?* (New York: Free Press, 1972).
7. Abraham Maslow, *Motivation and Personality,* 2d ed. (New York: Harper & Row, 1970).
8. Allen Flamion, "The Dollars and Sense of Motivation," *Personnel Journal* (January 1980): 51–53.
9. Abraham Maslow, *Eupsychian Management* (Homewood, Ill.: Richard D. Irwin, 1965).

10. Jack W. Duncan, *Essentials of Management* (Hinsdale, Ill.: Dryden Press, 1975), 105.

11. C.P. Adlerfer, "An Empirical Test of a New Theory of Human Needs," *Organizational Behavior and Human Performance* 4, no. 2 (1969): 142–75.

12. D.T. Hall and K. Nougaim, "An Examination of Maslow's Need Hierarchy in an Organizational Setting," *Organizational Behavior and Human Performance* 3, no. 1 (1968): 12–35.

13. Chris Argyris, *Personality and Organization* (New York: Harper & Bros., 1957).

14. Argyris, *Personality and Organization.*

15. David C. McClelland, "Power Is the Great Motivator," *Harvard Business Review* (March/April 1976): 100–10.

16. David C. McClelland and David B. Winter, *Motivating Economic Achievement* (New York: Free Press, 1969).

17. Burt K. Scanlan, "Creating a Climate for Achievement," *Business Horizons* 24 (March/April 1981): 5–9.

18. William H. Franklin, Jr., "Why You Can't Motivate Everyone," *Supervisory Management* (April 1980): 21–28.

19. Edwin Timbers, "Strengthening Motivation through Communication," *Advanced Management Journal* 31 (April 1966): 64–69.

20. Douglas McGregor, *The Human Side of Enterprise* (New York: McGraw-Hill, 1960).

21. W.J. Reddin, "The Tri-Dimensional Grid," *Training and Development Journal* (July 1964).

22. For more discussion on the implications of job rotation in organizations, see Alan W. Farrant, "Job Rotation Is Important," *Supervision* (August 1987): 14–16.

23. L.E. Davis and E.S. Valfer, "Intervening Responses to Changes in Supervisor Job Designs," *Occupational Psychology* (July 1965): 171–90.

24. M.D. Kilbridge, "Do Workers Prefer Larger Jobs?" *Personnel* (September/October 1960): 45–48.

25. This section is based on Frederick Herzberg, "One More Time: How Do You Motivate Employees?" *Harvard Business Review* (January/February 1968): 53–62.

26. Scott M. Meyers, "Who Are Your Motivated Workers?" *Harvard Business Review* (January/February 1964): 73–88.

27. John M. Roach, "Why Volvo Abolished the Assembly Line," *Management Review* (September 1977): 50.

28. Richard J. Hackman, "Is Job Enrichment Just a Fad?" *Harvard Business Review* (September/October 1975): 129–38.

29. E.G. Thomas, "Flexible Work Keeps Growing," *Management World* 15 (April/May 1986): 43–45.

30. D.A. Bratton, "Moving Away from Nine to Five," *Canadian Business Review* 13 (Spring 1986): 15–17.

31. Douglas L. Fleuter, "Flextime—A Social Phenomenon," *Personnel Journal* (June 1975): 318–19.

32. Lee A. Graf, "An Analysis of the Effect of Flexible Working Hours on the Management Functions of the First-Line Supervisor" (Ph.D. diss., Mississippi State University, 1976).

33. William Wong, "Rather Come in Late or Go Home Earlier? More Bosses Say OK," *Wall Street Journal*, July 12, 1973, 1.

34. B.F. Skinner, *Contingencies of Reinforcement* (New York: Appleton-Century-Crofts, 1969).

35. E.L. Thorndike, "The Original Nature of Man," *Educational Psychology* 1 (1903).

36. Keith E. Barenklaw, "Behavior Reinforcement," *Industrial Supervisor* (February 1976): 6–7.

37. Fred Luthans and Robert Kreitner, *Organizational Behavior Modification and Beyond* (Glenview, Ill.: Scott, Foresman, 1985).

38. Richard D. Arvey and John M. Ivancevich, "Punishment in Organizations: A Review, Proposal, and Research Suggestions," *Academy of Management Journal* (January 1980): 123–32; P.M. Padsokaff, "Relationships between Leader Reward and Punishment Behavior and Group Process and Productivity," *Journal of Management* 11 (Spring 1985): 55–73.

39. For another practical discussion on punishment, see Bruce R. McAfee and William Poffenberger, *Productivity Strategies: Enhancing Employee Job Performance* (Englewood Cliffs, N.J.: Prentice-Hall, Spectrum, 1982).

40. Ricky W. Griffin and Gregory Moorhead, *Organizational Behavior* (Boston: Houghton Mifflin, 1986), 183–89.

41. "New Tool: Reinforcement for Good Work," *Psychology Today* (April 1972): 68–69.

42. W. Clay Hamner and Ellen P. Hamner, "Behavior Modification on the Bottom Line," *Organizational Dynamics* 4 (Spring 1976): 6–8.

43. Rensis Likert, *New Patterns of Management* (New York: McGraw-Hill, 1961).

44. These descriptions are based on the table of organizational and performance characteristics of different management systems in Rensis Likert, *The Human Organization* (New York: McGraw-Hill, 1967), 4–10.

45. Likert, *New Patterns of Management*, 103.

Action Summary Answer Key

1. a. c, p. 377
   b. F, p. 378
   c. c, pp. 379–380

2. a. d, pp. 383–384
   b. d, pp. 384–385
   c. b, p. 385

3. a. T, p. 385
   b. T, p. 386

4. a. c, p. 387
   b. d, pp. 389–390
   c. e, pp. 392–393

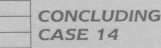
NORTHERN ASKS A LOT— AND GETS IT

Change, turbulence, aggression, conflict, challenge, stimulus: these are some of the qualities that drive Canada's telecommunications giant, Northern Telecom Ltd. Northern is a fascinating place to work, *if* you're prepared to take on the challenges it offers. In 1985, revenues were expected to top $5 billion—a far cry from the $450 million of ten years ago—and the company expects continued growth of 25 percent annually. This remarkable pace means that change is inevitable. The corporate drive for new products, in an industry on the forefront of technology, creates an additional impetus for change. Northern employees have to be flexible and, above all, adaptable in order to cope with the constant diversity.

John Rankin, vice-president of human resources, thinks Northern's corporate climate starts with the engineers—"the wild ones who have the most fun." (They also have the heaviest workload.) Northern is populated by a wide variety of people who provide the basis for a unique climate. This climate consists of a constant state of competitiveness, a dash of constructive conflict, and a heavy dose of work. The following quotes exemplify how Northern's employees feel about their jobs:

- I like it here because every day is so different from the day before. If you can cope with the lifestyle, it's a really fun place to work—crazy, chaotic, confusing, but lots of fun.

"The way the senior staff has managed growth is very effective—it stops a person from stagnating."

- The way the senior staff has managed growth is very effective—it stops a person from stagnating. I work long, hard hours here because I enjoy it, not because I have to. I like the pressures; I don't see it as stress, rather it's a challenge to work out how to manage it, how to find the best solution.
- The company encourages conflict. Its decentralized structure means conflicting priorities. We just work them out to a conclusion, which usually results in a better end product. It's not a confrontational kind of conflict—rather, it is constructive in nature.

- Most people here love the stress. They want to be stretched, to know where the limits are. And you do have to sacrifice things—like taking the kids to the hockey game. If the work pressure's there, you stay at work and get the job done.
- Those unwilling to let work cut into home life need not apply. Unless you're willing to make those sacrifices, you might end up not having a job.

It is interesting to note that almost everyone at Northern has a story about prospective employees being asked to come for a job interview at 9 a.m. on a Sunday—one way of weeding out undedicated applicants.

With demands on people that are unusually strenuous, the company tries to compensate by taking the worry out of the financial area. To achieve its goal of being a winner, Northern's salaries are at the top of the compensation scale. "We want people to worry about their jobs, not their pay, or their pensions," says Rankin. "So we look after them with a range of comprehensive benefits. It's not paternalism—we just want them to worry about working night and day for Northern Telecom." The benefits program is generous, containing an excellent medical/dental plan, an unusually generous non-contributory pension plan, and maternity benefits which top up the Unemployment Insurance Commission payments to 75 percent of salary. The firm's ample investment plan also allows workers to participate in the company's success through a form of share ownership. Options also exist for a wide range of possible investment vehicles, including a registered retirement savings plan and a deferred profit-sharing plan. Tuition refunds are available to employees wishing to upgrade educational skills, while fitness classes and coping-with-stress programs are held at some locations during lunch hours.

Paradoxically, the disadvantages of working at Northern Telecom also centre on its tremendous pressures: long hours, stress, not enough time for extracurricular activities. The size of the firm can also be a problem—it's easy to get lost in the shuffle. Meanwhile, Northern's emphasis on educational qualifications makes any big leap of levels almost impossible without a university degree. But for the energetic, ambitious risk-taker who's looking for challenges and doesn't mind the constant flux or heavy workload, Northern Telecom provides a great work environment. Through its network of subsidiaries, the firm also provides the lure of opportunities for international postings. And the monetary rewards are substantial—if you can find the time to spend what you make.

DISCUSSION ISSUES

1. What do you feel motivates Northern's employees to work under such demanding conditions? Using Maslow's hierarchy of needs, what level seems to be motivating the employees at Northern? Support your answers.
2. From the perspective of the Porter-Lawler model, explain how Northern's employees are motivated.
3. How can you explain Northern's employees in terms of McClelland's achievement motivation theory? Be precise.

Based on "Northern asks a lot—and gets it," by Eva Innes in *The Financial Post*, April 26, 1986. Used with permission.

MANAGING GROUPS

STUDENT LEARNING OBJECTIVES

From studying this chapter, I will attempt to acquire:

1. A definition of the term *group* as used within the context of management.
2. A thorough understanding of the difference between formal and informal groups.
3. Knowledge of the types of formal groups that exist in organizations.
4. An understanding of how managers can determine which groups exist in an organization.
5. An appreciation for how managers must simultaneously evaluate formal and informal groups to maximize work group effectiveness.

CHAPTER OUTLINE

A MEETING ABOUT MANAGING GROUPS

All five vice-presidents of the Crutch Athletic Equipment Company were gathered for a special meeting. From the conversation taking place, it was easy to tell that none of the five knew what the meeting was about. Each had received a memo about the meeting from Jesse Flick, the president of the company, but the memo had given no hint as to the meeting's purpose.

Flick walked into the room, greeted everyone present, sat down, and then began the following speech:

As you know, ladies and gentlemen, our company over the past two years has shown only moderate success. After considerable thought as to how we might excel over the next few years, I have determined that a sound strategy should include improving our use of groups within the company. Lately, I've noticed that though we are very structured in the sense that we have our design departments, marketing departments, production departments, and so on, but these groups aren't working as well as they should. I don't think each group alone is as effective as it could be, and there's not enough communication among the different departments.

I'd also like to see the development of some new groups. For example, I think there's a need to get a special group together to address the idea of manufacturing athletic clothes. Since this is a big step for us, I don't want to rely solely on our regular channels to handle it. I think we need to look at some new avenues for handling this type of situation.

I'd also like to see some more informal interaction among the people in your respective departments. I don't think the attitudes of our employees are as good as they could be, and I think the overall work environment could benefit from more informal interactions. Of course, we need ways to get these groups going, and we will need to learn some management skills so these groups will be effective.

What I'd like to do for the remainder of this meeting is to open the floor to all of you and hear some of your ideas about managing groups. Anyone want to start?

What's Ahead

Jesse Flick, the company president in the introductory case, is advising his vice-presidents on how to manage work groups. The material in this chapter develops a foundation for group management theory by: (1) defining groups; (2) discussing the kinds of groups that exist in organizations; and (3) explaining what steps managers should take to manage groups appropriately.

The previous chapters in this section have dealt with three primary activities of the influencing function: (1) communication; (2) leadership; and (3) motivation. This chapter focuses on managing groups, the last major influencing activity to be discussed in this text. As with the other three activities, managing work groups requires guiding the behaviour of organization members so as to increase the probability of reaching organizational objectives.

DEFINING GROUPS

To deal with groups appropriately, managers must have a thorough understanding of the nature of groups in organizations.[1] As used in management-related discussions, a **group** is not simply a gathering of people, but "any number of people who (1) interact with one another, (2) are psychologically aware of one another, and (3) perceive themselves to be a group."[2] Such a group is characterized by its members communicating with one another over time and being small enough so that each group member is able to communicate with all other members on a face-to-face basis.[3] As a result of this communication, each group member influences and is influenced by all other group members.[4]

Group members interact, are aware of one another, and perceive themselves as a group.

    The study of groups is important to managers since the common ingredient of all organizations is people, and since the most common technique for accomplishing work through these people is dividing them into work groups. Cartwright and Lippitt list four additional reasons for the importance of studying groups:[5]

1. Groups exist in all kinds of organizations.
2. Groups inevitably form in all facets of organizational existence.
3. Groups can cause either desirable or undesirable consequences within the organization.
4. Understanding groups can assist managers in increasing the probability that groups with which they work will cause desirable consequences within the organization.

KINDS OF GROUPS IN ORGANIZATIONS

Groups that exist in organizations typically are divided into two basic types: formal and informal.

Formal Groups

Formal groups are established by management.

A **formal group** is one that exists within an organization by virtue of management decree to perform tasks that enhance the attainment of organizational objectives.[6] Figure 15.1 shows an example of a formal group. Placement of organization members in such areas as marketing departments, personnel departments, or production departments involves establishing formal groups.

"Linking pins" belong to two formal groups.

Organizations are made up of a number of formal groups that exist at various organizational levels. The coordination of and communication among these formal groups is the responsibility of managers or supervisors commonly called "linking pins." Figure 15.2 shows the various formal groups that can exist within an organization and the linking pins associated with those groups. The linking pins are organization members who belong to two formal groups.

Formal groups are clearly defined and structured. The following sections discuss: (1) the basic kinds of formal groups; (2) examples of formal groups as they exist in organizations; and (3) the four stages of formal group development.

Kinds of Formal Groups

Command groups handle routine activities.

Formal groups are commonly divided into command groups and task groups.[7] **Command groups** are formal groups that are outlined on the chain of command on an organization chart. In general, command groups typically handle the more routine organizational activities.

Task groups tackle non-routine tasks.

Task groups, on the other hand, are formal groups of organization members who interact with one another to accomplish most non-routine organizational tasks. Although task groups are commonly considered to be made up of members on the same organizational level, they can consist of people from different levels of the organizational hierarchy. For example, a manager could establish a task group to consider the feasibility of manufacturing some new product. Representatives from various levels of such organizational areas as production, market research, and sales probably would be included as task group members.

FIGURE 15.1   A formal group.

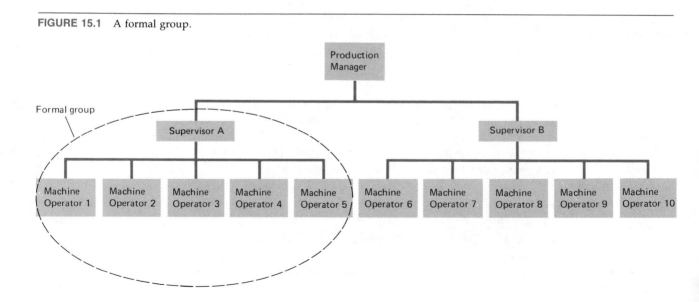

FIGURE 15.2   Formal groups that can exist within an organization and related linking pins.

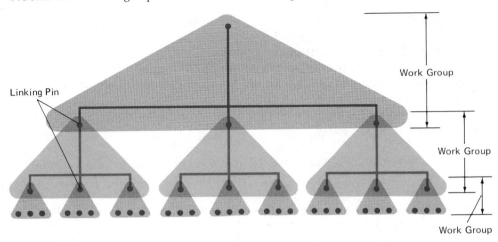

From *New Patterns of Management* by Rensis Likert, p. 104. Copyright © 1961 by McGraw-Hill, Inc. Used with permission of McGraw-Hill Book Company.

BACK TO THE CASE

When Jesse Flick of Crutch Athletic Equipment finished his introduction, there were a few minutes of silence while the vice-presidents considered what he had just said. Richard Simmons, the vice-president for design, was the first to respond:

> First of all, everyone, I think we need to define the term *group* and understand that there are several types of groups before we address how to handle these groups. To refresh your memories, a *group* is any number of people who interact, are psychologically aware of each other, and who perceive themselves as a group. Crutch Athletic is currently made up of formal groups—you know, the groups that appear on the company's organization charts, such as my design department, Susan Jamieson's

> marketing department, and so on. Since we vice-presidents act as the "linking pins" among these departments, our ability to coordinate and communicate with these groups, as well as our success in dealing with our own departments, is certainly important to the success of the company as a whole.

> Also, as Jesse mentioned, we can form new groups to handle some of our non-routine challenges. I propose that we form a task group; that is, we should each choose two people from our own department and get them together on the athletic clothing concept. Then, of course, there are the informal groups Jesse mentioned, which we need to consider also. But I don't want to do all the talking. Perhaps we can get back to that subject later.

Examples of Formal Groups

Committees and work teams are two formal groups that can be established in organizations. Committees are a more traditional formal group, while work teams only recently have begun to gain popular acceptance and support. Since the organizing section of this text emphasized command groups, the examples in this section emphasize task groups.

Committees

A **committee** is a group of individuals that has been charged with performing some type of activity. A committee, therefore, usually is classified as a task group.

Committees are
established for
specific reasons.

From a managerial viewpoint, the major reasons for establishing committees are: (1) to allow organization members to exchange ideas; (2) to generate suggestions and recommendations that can be offered to other organizational units; (3) to develop new ideas for solving existing organizational problems; and (4) to assist in the development of organizational policies.[8]

Committees typically exist within all organizations and at all organizational levels. As Figure 15.3 suggests, the larger organization, the greater the probability that committees are used within that organization on a regular basis. The following two sections discuss why managers should use committees and what makes committees successful.

Why Managers Should Use Committees   Managers generally agree that committees have several uses in organizations. One is that committees can improve the quality of decision making.[9] Generally speaking, as more people become involved in making a decision, the strengths and weaknesses of that decision are discussed in more detail, and the quality of the decision tends to increase.

Another reason for committees is that they encourage honest opinions. Committee members feel protected because the group output of a committee logically cannot be totally associated with any one member of that group.

Committees also tend to increase organization member participation in decision making and thereby enhance support of committee decisions. Also, as a result of this increased participation, committee work creates the opportunity for committee members to satisfy their social or esteem needs.

Larger organizations use committees more regularly.

Committees tend to increase the quality of decision making,

encourage honest opinions,

enhance decision support,

provide needs satisfaction,

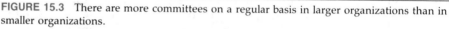

FIGURE 15.3   There are more committees on a regular basis in larger organizations than in smaller organizations.

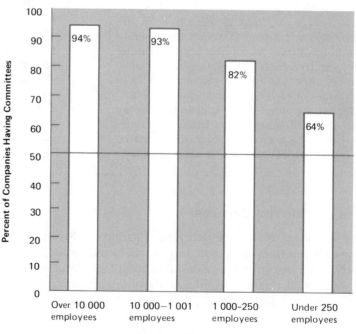

Finally, committees ensure the representation of important groups in the decision-making process. Managers must choose committee members wisely, however, to achieve this representation.

Executives vary somewhat in their opinions about using committees in organizations. A study reported by McLeod and Jones indicates that most executives favour using committees in organizations.[10] According to this study, although executives claim to get significantly more information from organizational sources other than committees, they find that the information from committees is more valuable to them than the information from any other source (see Figure 15.4).

and ensure group representation.

FIGURE 15.4   Comparing volume and value of information to executives from several organizational sources. *In each rectangle, the number* above *the diagonal is the percentage of overall volume for that source. The number* below *the diagonal is the average value, from 0 (no value) to 10 (maximum value), assigned the transaction. Figures may not total 100 percent because of rounding.*

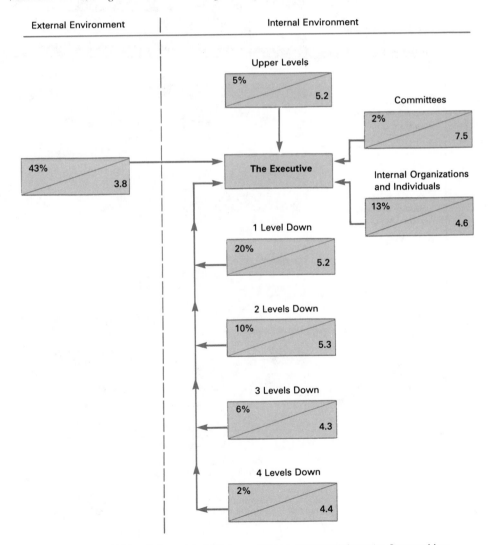

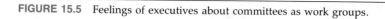

FIGURE 15.5   Feelings of executives about committees as work groups.

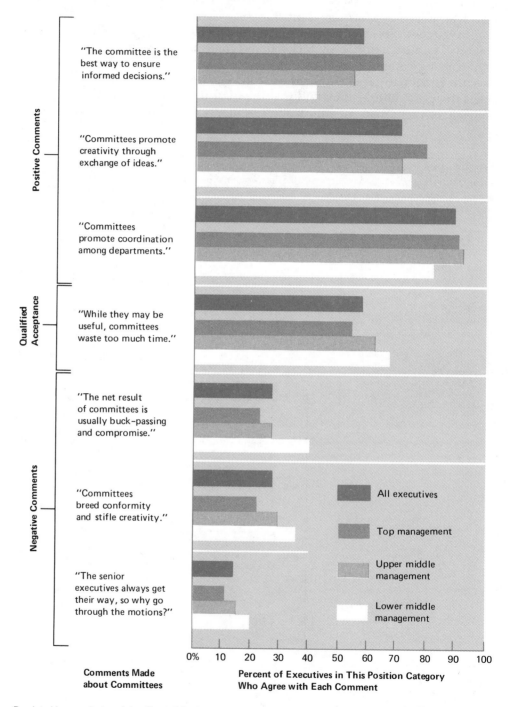

However, some top executives show only qualified acceptance of committees as work groups, and others express negative feelings. Figure 15.5 indicates that, in general, the executives who are negative about using committees are fewer in number than those who are positive about them or who display qualified acceptance of them.

What Makes Committees Successful   Although committees have become a commonly accepted management tool, managerial action taken to establish and run committees is a major variable in determining a committee's degree of success. Procedural steps that can be taken to increase the probability that a committee will be successful are:[11]

1. The committee's goals should be clearly defined, preferably in writing. This focuses the committee's activities and reduces the time devoted to discussing what the committee is supposed to do.
2. The committee's authority should be specified. Can the committee merely investigate, advise, and recommend, or is it authorized to implement decisions?
3. The optimum size of the committee should be determined. With fewer than five members, the advantages of group work may be diminished. With more than ten or fifteen members, the committee may become unwieldy. While size varies with the circumstances, the ideal number of committee members for many tasks seems to range from five to ten.
4. A chairperson should be selected on the basis of the ability to run an efficient meeting—that is, an individual's ability to keep the participation of all committee members from getting bogged down in irrelevancies and to see that the necessary paperwork gets done.
5. Appointing a permanent secretary to handle communications is often useful.
6. The agenda and all supporting material for the meeting should be distributed before the meeting. When members have a chance to study each item beforehand, they are more likely to stick to the point and be ready with informed contributions.
7. Meetings should be started on time, and the time at which they will end should be announced at the outset.

In addition to these procedural steps there are a number of more people-oriented guidelines managers can follow to increase the probability of a committee's success. In this regard, a manager can increase the quality of discussion in committees by:[12]

1. *Rephrasing ideas already expressed*   This rephrasing makes sure that the manager as well as other individuals in the committee have a clear understanding of what has been said.
2. *Bringing a member into active participation*   All committee members represent possible sources of information, and the manager should serve as a catalyst to spark individual participation whenever appropriate.
3. *Stimulating further thought by a member*   The manager should encourage committee members to think ideas through carefully and thoroughly. Only this type of analysis generates high-quality committee output.

Managers should also help the committee to avoid a phenomenon called "groupthink."[13] **Groupthink** is the mode of thinking that people engage in when seeking agreement becomes so dominant in a group that it tends to override

Managers should take procedural steps to increase the probability of a committee's success.

Managers can also strive to improve the quality of committee discussion.

Groupthink involves a desire for unanimous agreement.

the realistic appraisal of alternative problem solutions. Groups operate under groupthink when group members are so concerned with being too harsh in their judgments of other group members that objective problem solving is lost. Such groups tend to adopt a softer line of criticism and seek complete support on every issue, with little conflict generated to endanger the "we-feeling" atmosphere.

Work Teams

Work teams are another example of task groups used in organizations. A more recently developed management tool than committees, work teams generally are established to achieve greater organizational flexibility or to cope with rapid growth.

A case in point would be a situation faced by William W. George, a corporate vice-president of Litton Industries. George created work teams within the Litton microwave cooking division to manage rapid growth.[14] One such team described by George included members from new product development, manufacturing, marketing, cost-reduction, facilities planning, and new business ventures. As designed by George, the team had a designated leader, representation from several functional departments, and involvement by top management on an "as required" basis.

Work teams help organizations to be flexible and to cope with rapid growth.

BACK TO THE CASE

When Richard Simmons had finished his explanation of formal groups, Susan Jamieson, the vice-president for marketing, expanded on his ideas about forming a task group:

> I agree with Richard. I think we should form a committee to develop the athletic clothing idea, the reason being that a committee would allow the departments to exchange ideas and generate suggestions. I feel that a committee would improve our decision making and encourage honest opinions in this new, unexplored area. We need to get some fresh ideas, and a committee would encourage member participation. Also, I think it is essential to represent all of the departments in this decision. When we introduce a new product, we must consider every angle, including design, production, marketing, sales, and so on.
>
> Then, when this new athletic line takes off, we can organize a different type of task group, a work team, to handle the company's tremendous growth. After all, we want to make sure we can produce these clothes as quickly as my department can market them!

Everyone smiled at Jamieson's enthusiasm. Then Henry Reed, the vice-president for production, interjected:

> Excuse me, Susan, but to get back to your committee idea, I think we need to consider what steps to take to make this committee successful. After all, while committees can be useful, a poorly run committee wastes a lot of time.
>
> First of all, we should clearly define this committee's goals and state its authority. Is the committee just going to come up with ideas and do some market research, or should it also take the initial steps toward manufacturing the clothes? And with two people from each department, as Richard suggested, we'd have a twenty-member committee. Perhaps one person from each department would be better. Of course, we need to address issues such as appointing a secretary to handle communications and appointing a chairperson who is good with people-oriented issues. We need someone who can rephrase ideas clearly to ensure that everyone understands and who can get members to participate and think about the issues while avoiding "groupthink." We want original ideas to come out of this committee, not a unanimous opinion because everyone is avoiding conflict.
>
> But before we get that far, I think we must first understand how to develop the committee from scratch. Anyone have any thoughts on this?

Stages of Formal Group Development

Another facet to managing formal groups is understanding the stages of formal group development. Bernard Bass has suggested that group development is a four-stage process influenced primarily by groups learning how to use their resources.[15] Although these stages may not occur sequentially, for purposes of clarity the discussion that follows assumes that they do. The four stages can be labeled and defined as follows:

Groups develop in four stages:

1. *The acceptance stage*   It is relatively common for members of a new group initially to mistrust each other somewhat. The acceptance stage occurs only after the initial mistrust within a group has been transformed into mutual trust and the general acceptance of group members by one another.

1. Acceptance.

2. *The communication and decision-making stage*   Once the acceptance stage has been passed, group members are better able to communicate frankly with one another. This frank communication provides the basis for establishing and using effectively some type of group decision-making mechanism.

2. Communication and decision-making.

3. *The group solidarity stage*   The group solidarity stage comes naturally as the mutual acceptance of group members increases and communication and decision making continue within the group. This stage is characterized by members becoming more involved in group activities and cooperating, rather than competing, with one another. Group members find being a member of the group extremely satisfying and are committed to enhancing the group's overall success.

3. Group solidarity.

4. *The group control stage*   A natural result of the group solidarity stage is the group control stage. This stage involves group members attempting to maximize group success by matching individual abilities with group activities and by assisting each other. Flexibility and informality tend to characterize this group development stage.

4. Group control.

In general terms, as a group passes through each of these four stages, it tends to become more mature, more effective, and, therefore, more productive. The group that reaches maximum maturity and effectiveness is characterized by:[16]

Mature groups are more productive and can be identified by five characteristics.

1. *Members functioning as a unit*   The group works as a team. Members do not disturb each other to the point of interfering with their collaboration.
2. *Members participating effectively in group effort*   Members work hard when there is something to do. They usually do not loaf even if they get the opportunity.
3. *Members being oriented toward a single goal*   Group members work for common purposes and thereby do not waste group resources by moving in different directions.
4. *Members having the equipment, tools, and skills necessary to attain the group's goals*   Group members are taught various parts of their jobs by experts and strive to acquire whatever resources are needed to attain group objectives.
5. *Members asking and receiving suggestions, opinions, and information from each other*   If a member is uncertain about something, he or she stops working and asks another group member for information. Group members generally talk to each other openly and frequently.

The following Management in Action feature looks at the conditions and steps necessary for ensuring an effective process for managing teamwork, especially at the top. Impediments to good teamwork often come from the top of an organization, flowing down to negatively affect the lower levels.

TEAMWORK AT THE TOP

How can one tell when good teamwork exists? Or doesn't exist? Some common symptoms of poor teamwork include: department heads telling other department heads how to manage their operations; people withholding information; a failure to follow up or meet commitments to the group effort; and team members who are generally unwilling to compromise. Given the potentially negative effects these may have on an organization's performance, it is important that top management communicate the importance of good teamwork to its managers. But very often an important impediment to good teamwork resides with the CEOs themselves. Strong CEOs have little need to be cooperative in the usual way, and it's not uncommon for such leaders to feel that "nobody can do it as well as I can."

Although a group takes time to become a well integrated and effective team, it is essential that CEOs realize they can help manage this process. Without a personal commitment from the CEO, directives such as "get it together" or "fix the problem" will often be ineffective. Chief executives have a pivotal role since they are both a member of the team and the person leading it. In any organization it is the CEO who sets the tone for the others to follow. Aloofness from the participatory process of good teamwork creates an unpredictable work environment for the senior staff, an environment of ambiguity that invites gossip, scapegoating, and hostility. CEOs should also have the courage to subject their actions to scrutiny, and should generate discussion, ask questions, and listen to answers. The focus, however, should always be on work.

There is a fairly straightforward process to developing teamwork once the basic agreement to do so has been reached. But each member of the group must be willing to change some aspect of his or her own behaviour in order to obtain the objective. Teamwork is a two-way trade. Once the reason for the team's existence has been established, the CEO should define each individual manager's contribution to the solution of the problem. Then each person should be given the opportunity to review the ways in which he or she can contribute, indicating to the other members of the team the cooperation that will be needed. In this way, every member of the team "trades" with the other members, including the CEO. The reward system used to encourage teamwork plays an important motivator role here. Some form of group incentive is needed—profit sharing, for instance—along

"Chief executives have a pivotal role since they are both a member of the team and the person leading it."

with more informal and personal rewards that only the CEO can give.

Overall, it is essential for the CEO to realize that it is impossible to be a team player and still be the boss. An effective leader understands the impact his or her power has on others and tends to think through the consequences before exercising this power. Finally, it is essential that the CEO remain alert to any signs suggesting that one or more of the team members is becoming too individualistic, i.e., letting a personal need for recognition get in the way of team play. Such problems need to be turned into assignments for cooperation by the department head involved. Keeping the importance of "teamwork at the top" in mind when reviewing candidates for senior positions is one way of ensuring a good management team.

Based on "Teamwork at the Top: Suggestions for the CEO," in *Newsletter—For CEOs Only* (Rohrer, Hibler & Replogle, Ltd.), Vol. 2, no. 1, 1987.

BACK TO THE CASE

In response to Henry Reed's question on how to develop a committee, Alan Green, vice-president for sales, spoke up about the stages of group development:

> We must understand that it's going to take some time for a new group to develop into a productive working unit. The different department members in any new committee must start by trusting and accepting one another and then begin communicating and exchanging ideas. Once this acceptance and communication increases, group solidarity and control come naturally. In other words, the group members get involved, cooperate, and try to maximize the group's success.
>
> So with this new committee we've been talking about, we must be patient and let the group mature before we can expect maximum effectiveness and productivity. Hopefully, if given time to grow, the group will function as a unit, members will participate willingly and effectively, and the group will reach some decisions about what we need to do to be productive and competitive in the athletic clothing market.

Informal Groups

Informal groups are the second major kind of group that can exist within an organization. **Informal groups** are those that develop naturally as people interact. As shown in Figure 15.6, informal group structures can deviate significantly from formal group structures. As in the case of Supervisor A in Figure 15.6, an organization member can belong to more than one informal group at the same time. In

Informal groups develop naturally as people interact.

FIGURE 15.6   Three informal groups that deviate significantly from formal groups within the organization.

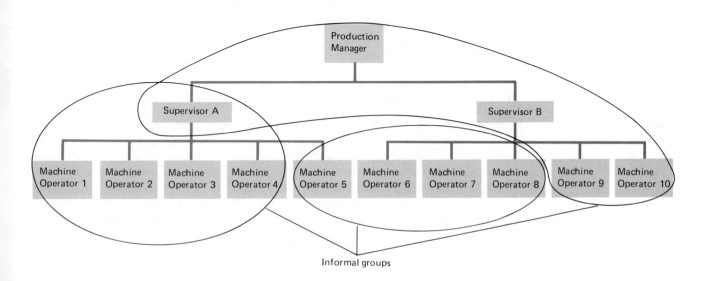

contrast to formal groups, informal groups typically are not highly structured in terms of procedure and are not formally recognized by management.

The following sections discuss: (1) various kinds of informal groups that can exist in organizations; (2) the benefits usually reaped by membership in informal groups; and (3) encouraging the development of informal groups.

Kinds of Informal Groups

Interest groups have issues of common concern.

Informal groups generally are divided into two types: interest groups and friendship groups. **Interest groups** are informal groups that gain and maintain membership primarily because of a special concern each member possesses about a specific issue. An example might be a group of workers pressing management for better pay or working conditions. In general, once the interest or concern that caused this informal group to form has been eliminated, the group tends to disband.

Friendship groups are basically social relationships.

As its name implies, **friendship groups** are informal groups that form in organizations because of the personal affiliation members have with one another. As with interest groups, the membership of friendship groups tends to change over time. Here, however, group membership changes as friendships dissolve or new friendships are made.

Benefits of Informal Group Membership

Informal group membership has many rewards.

Informal groups tend to develop in organizations because of various benefits that group members obtain. These benefits include: (1) perpetuation of social and cultural values that group members consider important; (2) status and social satisfaction that might not be enjoyed without group membership; (3) increased ease of communication between group members; and (4) increased desirability of the overall work environment.[17] These benefits may be one reason why employees who are on fixed shifts or who continually work with the same groups are sometimes more satisfied with their work than employees whose shifts are continually changing.[18]

Encouraging the Development of Informal Groups

Quality circles may help to establish manager/worker informal groups.

One tool managers may be able to use to assist in the development of informal groups is called a quality circle. **Quality circles** are simply small groups of factory workers who meet regularly with management to discuss quality-related problems. Naturally, during these meetings management has opportunities to nurture relationships with various informal groups. In fact, quality circles may actually result in some managers and workers becoming members of the same informal groups. Although managers report good success with the use of quality circles, the circles are so new that research has not yet been able to assess their long-term impact on the organization.

BACK TO THE CASE

The vice-presidents of Crutch Athletic Equipment continued to share ideas about managing formal groups, until Jesse Flick again took control of the discussion:

At this point, I would like to address the other issue I mentioned at the beginning of the meeting—working with informal groups in your departments. As you all know, employees group together at times because of certain issues. Remember last year, for example, when the non-smokers in the company got together to pressure us into creating non-smoking areas in their departments? And, of course, employees form friendship groups, which ease communication and provide feelings of satisfaction in the company. In general, these informal groups can improve the work environment for everyone involved, and I strongly suggest that you encourage their development.

Perhaps we could even try quality circles, where each manager in your department meets with subordinates on a regular basis. In fact, why don't each of you arrange for your managers to try a quality circle sometime in the next month? Have the managers report back to you about whether the effort was successful, and we can discuss the results at our next meeting. Now, let's get back to discussing how we can effectively manage our work groups.

MANAGING WORK GROUPS

To manage work groups effectively, managers must simultaneously consider the impact of both formal and informal group factors on organizational productivity. This consideration requires three steps: (1) determining group existence; (2) understanding the evolution of informal groups; and (3) maximizing work group effectiveness.

Determining Group Existence

Perhaps the most important step that managers should take in managing work groups is determining what groups exist within the organization and who constitutes the membership of those groups. **Sociometry** is an analytical tool that managers can use to help determine such information. Sociometry also can provide information on the internal workings of an informal group, such as who leads the group, the relative status level of various members within the informal group, and the informal group's communication networks.[19] This information on informal groups, along with an understanding of the established formal groups as shown on an organization chart, gives managers a complete picture of the group structure with which they must deal.

> A sociometric analysis determines what groups exist and the membership of those groups.

The procedure involved in performing a sociometric analysis in an organization is quite basic.[20] Various organization members simply are asked, either through an interview or questionnaire, to state several other organization members with whom they would like to spend some of their free time. A sociogram is then constructed to summarize the informal relationships among group members that were uncovered. **Sociograms** are diagrams that visually link individuals within the group according to the number of times they were chosen and whether or not the choice was reciprocal.

> A sociogram is a graphic summary of the sociometric analysis.

FIGURE 15.7   Sample sociograms.

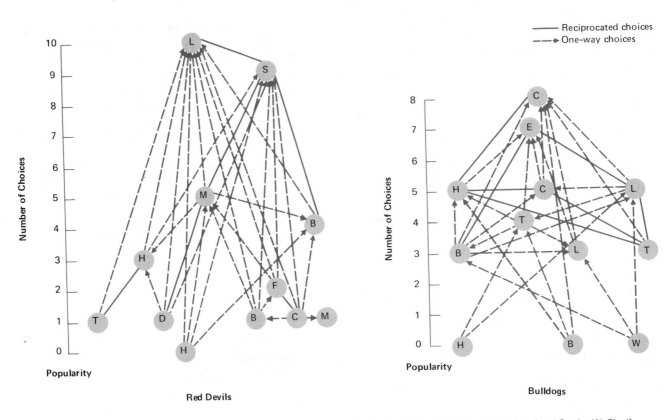

Figure 15.7 shows two sample sociograms based on a study of two groups of boys in a summer camp—the Bulldogs and the Red Devils.[21] An analysis of these sociograms results in several interesting observations. For example, more boys within the Bulldogs than within the Red Devils were chosen as being desirable to spend time with. This probably implies that the Bulldogs are a closer-knit informal group than the Red Devils. Also, communication between L and most other Red Devils members is likely to occur directly, while communication between C and other Bulldogs is likely to pass through other group members. Lastly, the greater the number of times an individual is chosen, the more likely that individual will be the group leader. Thus, individuals C and E would tend to be Bulldog leaders, while individuals L and S would tend to be Red Devil leaders.

Sociometric analysis can give managers many useful insights on the existence of informal groups within an organization. Although managers may not desire to perform a formal sociometric analysis within an organization, they can casually gather information that would indicate what form a sociogram might take in a particular situation. This information can be gathered through inferences made in normal conversations that managers have with other organization members and observations of how various organization members relate to one another.

Understanding the Evolution of Informal Groups

Obviously, knowing what groups exist within an organization and what characterizes the membership of those groups is an extremely important prerequisite for managing groups effectively. A second prerequisite is understanding how informal groups evolve, since this gives managers some insights on how to encourage informal groups to develop appropriately within an organization. Naturally, encouraging these groups to develop appropriately and maintaining good relationships with work group members can help to ensure that organization members support management in the process of attaining organizational objectives.[22]

Perhaps the most widely accepted framework for explaining the evolution of informal groups was developed by George Homans.[23] Figure 15.8 broadly summarizes his theory. According to Homans, the sentiments, interactions, and activities that emerge as part of an informal group actually result from the sentiments, interactions, and activities that exist within a formal group. In addition, Homans says that the informal group exists to obtain the consequences of satisfaction and growth for informal group members. Feedback on whether or not these consequences are achieved can result in forces that attempt to modify the formal group so as to increase the probability that the informal group achieves these consequences.

An example to illustrate Homan's concept would be twelve factory workers who are members of a formal work group that manufactures toasters. According to Homans, as these workers interact to assemble toasters, they discover common personal interests that encourage the evolution of informal groups. In turn, these informal groups tend to maximize the satisfaction and growth of informal group members. Once established, these informal groups will probably resist changes or established segments of formal groups that threaten the satisfaction and growth of informal group members.

According to Homans, informal groups evolve from the sentiments, interactions, and activities of formal groups.

FIGURE 15.8   Homan's ideas on how informal groups develop.

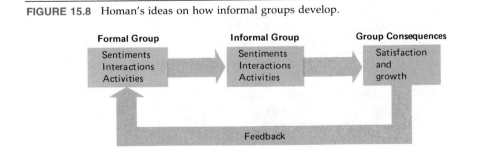

BACK TO THE CASE

After Jesse Flick finished offering suggestions about informal groups, Henry Reed continued the discussion of managing groups:

> I think that, in order to be successful managers, we need to consider how both formal and informal groups affect our productivity. I think we need to determine what informal groups exist and who the group members are and then try to understand how these groups form. With this information, we can strive to make our groups more effective.

> One way we can get information about the groups in our departments is to use sociometry. We can design a questionnaire asking our employees whom they spend time with and then construct a sociogram to summarize this information. Of course, we can do a more casual analysis by just talking to our employees and observing how they interact with one another.

> We should also try to understand how the informal groups evolve and should realize that our formal structure in the company influences the informal groups that develop. For example, in my department, I've got thirty men who work on baseball equipment. Needless to say, many of them love baseball, have become friends because of their common interest, and work well together as a result. If I needed to make some changes in the department, I would try to accommodate these friendship groups to keep everyone satisfied. I'd try not to do anything to threaten any one member, such as pull one guy off the baseball line and put him on something else. In other words, these informal groups are the result of the way we force people to interact. Therefore, the best way to influence these groups is to make appropriate changes within the formal dimensions of the company.

Maximizing Work Group Effectiveness

Once managers determine which groups exist within an organization and understand how informal groups evolve, they should strive to maximize work group effectiveness. As the following discussion emphasizes, maximizing work group effectiveness requires that managers continue to consider both formal and informal dimensions of the organization.[24]

Figure 15.9 indicates the four factors primarily responsible for collectively influencing work group effectiveness: (1) size of work group; (2) cohesiveness

FIGURE 15.9   Primary determinants of work group effectiveness.

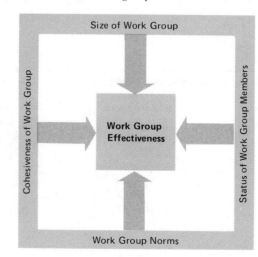

of work group; (3) work group norms; and (4) status of work group members. The terms *work group* and *formal group* are used synonymously in the sections that follow.

Size of Work Group

As work group size (the number of members in a work group) increases, forces usually are created within that group that can either increase or decrease its effectiveness.[25] The ideal number of members for a work group depends primarily on the group's purpose.[26] For example, the ideal size for a fact-finding work group usually is set at about fourteen members, while the maximum size for a problem-solving work group is approximately seven members.[27]

Work group size is a significant determinant of group effectiveness because it has considerable impact on three major components of a group: (1) leadership; (2) group members; and (3) group processes. A summary of how these three factors can be influenced by group size is presented in Figure 15.10.

When attempting to maximize group effectiveness by modifying formal group size, managers also should consider informal group factors. For example, a manager may decide that a formal work group should be reduced in size to make it more effective. Before making this reduction, however, the manager should consider the existence of informal groups within that formal group. If the manager reduces the size of the formal group by transferring the informal group leader, the effectiveness of the work group could diminish considerably due to the loss of its informal leader. The slight ineffectiveness of the overly large formal work group might be more advantageous than the greater ineffectiveness that

Work group size influences group effectiveness.

Managers should consider both formal and informal group factors when evaluating group size and effectiveness.

FIGURE 15.10   Possible effects of group size on group leadership, group members, and group processes.

Dimensions	2–7 Members	Group Size 8–12 Members	13–16 Members
Leadership			
1. Demand on leader	Low	Moderate	High
2. Differences between leaders and members	Low	Low to moderate	Moderate to high
3. Direction of leader	Low	Low to moderate	Moderate to high
Members			
4. Tolerance of direction from leader	Low to high	Moderate to high	High
5. Domination of group interaction by a few members	Low	Moderate to high	High
6. Inhibition in participation by ordinary members	Low	Moderate	High
Group processes			
7. Formalization of rules and procedures	Low	Low to moderate	Moderate to high
8. Time required for reaching decisions	Low to moderate	Moderate	Moderate to high
9. Tendency for subgroup to form	Low	Moderate to high	High

could result from reducing the formal group size and possibly transferring the informal group leader.

Cohesiveness of Work Group

Group cohesiveness is based on a strong desire to remain a group member.

Another factor that can influence work group effectiveness is the degree of cohesiveness within the group. **Group cohesiveness** is the attraction group members feel for one another in terms of desires to remain a member of the group and resist leaving it.[28] The greater these desires, the greater the cohesiveness within the group. In general, the cohesiveness of a work group is determined by the cohesiveness of the informal groups that exist within that work group. Therefore, to manage the degree of cohesiveness that exists within a work group, managers must manage the degree of cohesiveness that exists within the informal group or groups that constitute that work group.

Cohesiveness tends to increase productivity.

Group cohesiveness is extremely important to managers since the greater the cohesiveness that exists within a group, the greater the probability the group will accomplish its objectives. In addition, some evidence indicates that groups whose members have positive feelings toward one another tend to be more productive than groups whose members have negative feelings toward one another.[29]

Indicators of high group cohesiveness include:[30]

1. The members have a broad, general agreement on the goals and objectives of the informal group.
2. A significant amount of communication and interaction is evident among participating members.
3. There is a satisfactory level of homogeneity in social status and social background among the members.
4. Members are allowed to participate fully and directly in the determination of group standards.
5. The size of the group is sufficient for interaction but is not so large as to stymie personal attention. Normally, the optimum size range of an informal group is from four to seven members.
6. The members have a high regard for their fellow members.
7. The members feel a strong need for the mutual benefits and protection the group appears to offer.
8. The group is experiencing success in the achievement of its goals and in the protection of important values.

Managers must consider the formal and informal dimensions of group cohesiveness.

Since the cohesiveness of informal groups is such an influential determinant of cohesiveness within work groups and, as a result, of work group effectiveness, management should assist in the development of informal group cohesiveness whenever possible. This, of course, assumes that the informal group is attempting to make a constructive contribution to organizational goal attainment. To this end, managers should attempt to enhance the prestige of existing informal group members, design the overall organization to encourage informal group development, and eliminate organizational barriers to continuing informal group membership over an extended period of time.

If, however, managers determine that an informal group is attempting to attain objectives that are counterproductive to those of the organization, an appropriate strategy would be to attempt to reduce informal group cohesiveness. For example, managers could take action to limit the prestige of existing group members and design the overall organization to discourage further group co-hesiveness. This type of action, however, could result in a major conflict between management and various informal groups that exist within the organization. Overall, managers must keep in mind that the greater the cohesiveness within informal groups with non-productive objectives, the greater the probability that those non-productive objectives will be attained.

Work Group Norms

Group norms are a third major determinant of work group effectiveness. **Group norms**, as used in this chapter, apply only to informal groups and can be defined as appropriate or standard behaviour that is required of informal group members. These norms, therefore, significantly influence informal group members' behaviour as members of their formal group. According to J.R. Hackman group norms: (1) are structured characteristics of groups that simplify the group-influence processes; (2) apply only to behaviour and not to private thoughts and feelings of group members; (3) generally develop only in relation to those matters that most group members consider important; (4) usually develop slowly over time; and (5) sometimes apply only to certain group members.[31]

Group norms are required behaviour of group members.

Systematic study of group norms has revealed that there is generally a close relationship between group norms and the profitability of the organization of which that group is a part.[32] Although it would be impossible to state all possible norms that might develop in a group, most group norms relate to one or more of the following ten categories: (1) organizational pride; (2) performance; (3) profitability; (4) teamwork; (5) planning; (6) supervision; (7) training; (8) innovation; (9) customer relations; and (10) honesty or security.

Norms usually are divided into two general types: negative norms and positive norms. **Negative norms** are required informal group behaviour that limits organizational productivity, while **positive norms** are required informal group behaviour that contributes to organizational productivity. Examples of both positive and negative norms are presented in Figure 15.11. The cartoon illustrates a negative norm that allows informal group members to agree on which nights they will leave work earlier so they can take turns looking good to the boss.

Negative norms limit organizational productivity, while positive norms contribute to organizational productivity.

"Come on Scott, be a buddy—look, if you leave the office before me tonight, I'll leave before you any two times you say."

U.S. News & World Report, *June 1, 1987. William Hamilton's cartoon is reprinted by permission of Chronicle Features, San Francisco.*

FIGURE 15.11   Examples of positive and negative group norms.

Negative Norms	
Factory Workers	Keep your mouth shut when the boss is around.
Factory Workers	We stop working fifteen minutes before quitting time to wash up.
Utility Workers	We always take a nice long coffee break in the morning before climbing those poles.
Typing Pool	Don't rush the work — they'll just give you more to do.
Salesclerks	Don't hurry to wait on a customer — they'll keep.

Positive Norms	
Factory Workers	Do it right the first time.
Typing Pool	Make certain it looks nice — we want to be proud of our work.
Car Salespeople	We want to sell more cars than anyone else in the city.
Grocery Clerks	Go out of your way to satisfy customers — we want them to come back.
Factory Workers	Don't waste materials — they cost money.

From T. W. Johnson & J. E. Stinson, *Managing Today and Tomorrow*, © 1978, Addison-Wesley Publishing Co., Inc., Reading Massachusetts. Figure on page 69. Reprinted with permission.

Normative profiles indicate norm variations.

Some managers consider group norms to be of such great importance to the organization that they develop profiles of group norms to assess the norms' organizational impact. Figure 15.12 shows a normative profile developed by one company manager. This particular normative profile is characterized by a number of norm differences. For example, a high level of organizational pride and good customer relations contrasts with a lower concern for profitability. What actually happened in this company was that employees placed customer desires at such a high level that they were significantly dwindling organizational profitability to please customers. Once these norms were discovered, management took steps to make the situation more organizationally advantageous.

Characteristics of formal work groups can spawn negative norms in the informal group.

As the preceding information suggests, a key to managing the behaviour within a formal work group is managing the norms of the informal group or groups that exist within that formal group. More specifically, Homans's framework for analyzing group behaviour indicates that informal group norms are mainly the result of the characteristics of the formal work group of which the informal group is a part. As a result, to change existing norms within an informal group, characteristics of the formal work group of which that informal group is a part must be changed.

FIGURE 15.12   Sample normative profile.

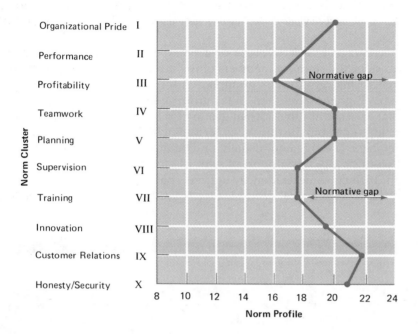

For example, an informal group could have the negative norm: "Don't rush the work—they'll just give you more to do." For a manager to change this norm, the factor in the formal work group from which this norm probably arose should be eliminated. The manager might find that this norm is a direct result of the fact that workers are formally recognized within the organization through pay and awards, regardless of the amount of work performed. Changing this formal policy so that the amount of work accomplished is considered in formal organizational recognition should help to dissolve this negative norm. In some situations, norms may be extremely difficult, if not impossible, to change.

Status of Work Group Members

Status is the position of a group member in relation to other group members. Overall, an individual's status within a group is determined not only by the person's work or role within the group but also by the non-work qualities the individual brings into the group.[33] Work-related determinants of status include titles, work schedules, and, perhaps most commonly, amounts of pay group members receive.[34] Non-work-related determinants of status include education

Status is a group member's position within the group.

Status in formal groups

level, race, age, and sex. Figure 15.13 is an entertaining but realistic treatment of how status symbols vary within formal groups of an organizational hierarchy. These status symbols generally are used within formal work groups to reward individual productivity and to show the different levels of organizational importance.

and also in informal groups within that formal group

can affect productivity.

To maximize the effectiveness of a work group, however, managers also should consider the status of members of the informal group or groups that exist within that formal group. For example, within a formal group, formal group leaders have higher status than other group members. The informal group or groups that exist within that formal group also have informal leaders, who generally are different from the formal leader and of higher status than other informal group members. Management usually finds that, to increase productivity within a formal work group, the support of both the formal and informal leaders must be gained. In fact, some evidence suggests that production is more associated with support from informal group leaders than from formal group leaders.[35]

FIGURE 15.13   How status symbols vary with various levels of the organizational hierarchy.

Visible Appurtenances	Top Dogs	V.I.P.s	Brass	No. 2s	Eager Beavers	Hoi Polloi
Briefcases	None—they ask the questions	Use backs of envelopes	Someone goes along to carry theirs	Carry their own—empty	Daily—carry their own—filled with work	Too poor to own one
Desks, office	Custom-made (to order)	Executive style (to order)	Type A, "Director"	Type B, "Manager"	Castoffs from No. 2s	Yellow oak— or castoffs from eager beavers
Tables, office	Coffee tables	End tables or decorative wall tables	Matching tables, type A	Matching tables, type B	Plain work table	None—lucky to have own desk
Carpeting	Nylon— one-inch pile	Nylon— one-inch pile	Wool-twist (with pad)	Wool-twist (without pad)	Used wool pieces—sewed	Asphalt tile
Plant stands	Several—kept filled with strange, exotic plants		Two—repotted whenever they take a trip	One medium-sized —repotted annually during vacation	Small—repotted when plant dies	May have one in the department or bring their own from home
Vacuum-water bottles	Silver	Silver	Chromium	Plain painted	Coke machine	Water fountains
Library	Private collection	Autographed or complimentary books and reports	Selected references	Impressive titles on covers	Books everywhere	Dictionary
Shoe-shine service	Every morning at 10:00	Every morning at 10:15	Every day at 9:00 or 11:00	Every other day	Once a week	Shine their own
Parking space	Private—in front of office	In plant garage	In company garage —if enough seniority	In company properties— somewhere	On the parking lot	Anywhere they can find a space —if they can afford a car

Reprinted, by permission of the publisher, from "What Raises a Man's Morale," by Morris S. Viteles, *Personnel* (January 1954): 305.

BACK TO THE CASE

After the vice-presidents had discussed ways to better understand group existence and evolution, Diane Lewis, the vice-president for customer relations, turned their attention to another component of managing work groups—maximizing group effectiveness:

> Now that we understand more about our formal and informal groups, we should consider the four major factors that influence their effectiveness, so we can implement some changes. First, of all, the size of the work group can be important to its productivity. As we noted earlier about the clothing committee, a twenty-person group for this type of committee could hamper the group's effectiveness. Also, we must consider informal groups before making changes in group size. As Henry alluded to earlier, he would not pull a few men, especially the more respected members, from his baseball group in order to reduce its size. The group could end up being less productive without its respected members than it would be if it were slightly too large.

> This brings me to the second factor—group cohesiveness. Since a more cohesive group will tend to be more effective, we should try to increase the cohesiveness of our groups. Again, informal groups are very important here. We can increase the cohesiveness of our formal groups by doing such things as allowing members to take breaks together or rewarding informal group members for a job well done.

> The group norms, or appropriate behaviours required within the informal group, are a third factor that affects the quality of formal group behaviour. Since these norms affect our profitability, we must be aware of them and understand how to influence them within the formal group structure. For example, if the men in Henry's baseball group really care about the quality of the bats they produce and, as a result, are taking too much time to manufacture them, Henry could reward this positive norm by giving bonuses to group members who produce the best-quality bats in the shortest amount of time. This reward would increase the formal group productivity while encouraging a positive norm within the informal group.

> Status within the informal groups comes into play here too. If Henry wants to increase his bat production, he should try to encourage the informal group's leaders, as well as the group's formal manager. Chances are that Henry's baseball group will be successful in producing more bats if its informal high-status members support that objective.

> Overall, if we want to maximize group effectiveness, we must remember both the formal and informal dimensions of our groups while considering the four main factors I've just mentioned.

At this point in the discussion, Jesse Flick interjected:

> Thank you, Diane. I think we've covered enough material for today. This has been a very productive meeting, and you have all expressed important ideas about managing groups. Now, if there are no questions, I'd like you to think about and review what we've discussed here today. Any questions? Well then, this meeting is adjourned!

Action Summary

Reread the learning objectives that follow. Each objective is followed by questions. Answering these questions accurately will help you to retain the most important concepts discussed in this chapter. After answering each question, check your answer with the answer key at the end of this chapter. (*Hint*: If you have doubt regarding the correct response, consult the page that follows the answer.)

Circle:

From studying this chapter, I will attempt to acquire:

1. **A definition of the term** *group* **as used within the context of management.**

T, F
   a. A group is made up of people who interact with one another, perceive themselves to be a group, and are primarily physically aware of one another.
   b. According to Cartwright and Lippitt, it is *not* true to say that: (a) groups exist in all kinds of organizations; (b) groups inevitably form in all facets of organizational existence; (c) groups cause undesirable consequences within the organization so their continued existence should be discouraged; (d) understanding groups can assist managers in increasing the probability that groups with which they work will cause desirable consequences within
a, b, c, d, e   the organization; (e) all of the above are true.

2. **A thorough understanding of the difference between formal and informal groups.**

T, F
   a. An informal group is a group that exists within an organization by virtue of management decree.

T, F
   b. A formal group is one that exists within an organization by virtue of interaction among organization members in proximity to one another.

3. **Knowledge of the types of formal groups that exist in organizations.**

a, b, c, d, e
   a. The type of group that generally handles more routine organizational activities is the: (a) informal task group; (b) informal command group; (c) formal task group; (d) formal command group; (e) none of the above.
   b. Managers should be encouraged to take which of the following steps to increase the success of a committee: (a) clearly define the goals of the committee; (b) rephrase ideas that have already been expressed; (c) select a chairperson based on the ability to run an efficient meeting; (d) a and b;
a, b, c, d, e   (e) a, b, and c.

4. **An understanding of how managers can determine which groups exist in an organization.**

T, F
   a. The technique of sociometry involves asking people with whom they would like to manage.
   b. A sociogram is defined in the text as: (a) a letter encouraging group participation; (b) a diagram that visually illustrates the number of times that the individuals were chosen within the group and whether or not the choice was reciprocal; (c) a composite of demographic data useful in determining informal group choices; (d) a computer printout designed to profile psychological and sociological characteristics of the informal group;
a, b, c, d, e   (e) none of the above.

5. **An appreciation for how managers must simultaneously evaluate formal and informal groups to maximize work group effectiveness.**

a. Which of the following factors has the least influence on the effectiveness of a work group: (a) age of the work group; (b) size of the work group; (c)
a, b, c, d, e   cohesiveness of the work group; (d) norms of the work group; (e) a and d.
   b. Knowing what informal groups exist within an organization and how in-
T, F   formal groups evolve are prerequisites for managing groups effectively.

INTRODUCTORY CASE WRAP-UP

"A Meeting about Managing Groups" (p. 404) and its related back-to-the-case sections were written to help you better understand the management concepts contained in this chapter. Answer the following discussion questions about this introductory case to further enrich your understanding of the chapter content:

1. Do you think that Flick chose an important topic on which to hold a meeting? Explain.
2. Do you think that the vice-presidents had good ideas for managing their groups? What additional suggestions could they have given?

Issues for Review and Discussion

1. How is the term *group* defined in this chapter?
2. Why is the study of groups important to managers?
3. What is a formal group?
4. Explain the significance of "linking pins" to formal groups in organizations.
5. List and define two types of formal groups that can exist in organizations.
6. Why should managers use committees in organizations?
7. What steps can managers take to ensure that a committee will be successful?
8. Explain how work teams can be valuable to an organization.
9. Describe the stages a group typically goes through as it becomes more mature.
10. What is an informal group?
11. List and define two types of informal groups in organizations.
12. What benefits generally accrue to members of informal groups?
13. What is the relationship between quality circles and informal groups?
14. Are formal groups more important to managers than informal groups? Explain.
15. Describe the sociometric procedure used to study informal group membership. What can the results of a sociometric analysis tell managers about members of an informal group?
16. Explain Homans's concept of how informal groups develop.
17. List and define the primary factors that influence work group effectiveness.
18. What is the relationship among formal groups, informal groups, and increasing work group effectiveness?

Sources of Additional Information

Brightman, Harvey J., and Penny Verhoeven. "Why Managerial Problem-Solving Groups Fail." *Business* 36 (January/February/March 1986): 24–29.

Collins, B.E., and H. Guetzkow. *A Special Psychology of Group Processes for Decision Making.* New York: Wiley, 1964.

Delbecq, A., A.H. Van de Ven, and D.H. Gustafson. *Group Techniques for Program Planning.* Glenview, Ill.: Scott, Foresman, 1975.

Earl, Michael J. *Perspectives on Management: A Multidisciplinary Analysis.* New York: Oxford University Press, 1983.

Ferraro, Vincent L., and Sheila A. Adams. "Interdepartmental Conflict: Practical Ways to Prevent and Reduce It." *Personnel* (July/August 1984): 12–23.

Franecki, Dennis J., Ralph F. Catalanello, and Curtiss K. Behrens, "Employee Committees: What Effect Are They Having?" *Personnel* (July/August 1984): 67–78.

Gordon, Judith R. *A Diagnostic Approach to Organizational Behavior,* 2d ed. Boston: Allyn and Bacon, 1987.

Halal, William E., and Bob S. Brown. "Participative Management: Myth and Reality." *California Management Review* 23 (Summer 1981): 20–32.

Hare, A.P. *Handbook of Small Group Research*. New York: Free Press, 1962.

Homestead, Michael S. *The Small Group*. New York: Random House, 1969.

Luthans, Fred. *Organizational Behavior*. New York: McGraw-Hill, 1973.

Marsh, Arthur. "Employee Relations—From Donovan to Today." *Personnel Management* 13 (June 1981): 34–36, 47.

Napier, R.W. and M.K. Gershenfeld. *Groups: Theory and Experience*. Boston: Houghton Mifflin, 1973.

Quible, Dr. Zane K. "Quality Circles: A Well-Rounded Approach to Employee Involvement." *Management World* 10 (September 1981): 10–11, 38.

Scanlon, Burt, and Bernard Keys. *Management and Organizational Behavior*. New York: Wiley, 1983.

Schweiger, David M., William R. Sandberg, and James W. Ragan. "Group Approaches for Improving Strategic Decision Making: A Comparative Analysis of Dialectical Inquiry, Devil's Advocacy, and Consensus." *Academy of Management Journal* 29 (March 1986): 51–71.

Seashore, W.E. *Group Cohesiveness in the Industrial Work Group*. Ann Arbor, Mich.: Institute for Social Research, 1964.

Steele, Fred I. *Physical Settings and Organization Development*. Reading, Mass.: Addison-Wesley, 1973.

Wanous, John P., and Margaret A. Youtz. "Solution Diversity and the Quality of Group Decisions." *Academy of Management Journal* 29 (March 1986): 149–158.

Notes

1. Robert L. Masson and Edward Jacobs, "Group Leadership: Practical Points for Beginners," *Personnel and Guidance Journal* (September 1980): 52–55.

2. Edgar H. Schein, *Organizational Psychology* (Englewood Cliffs, N.J.: Prentice-Hall, 1965), 67.

3. George C. Homans, *The Human Group* (New York: Harcourt, Brace & World, 1950), 1.

4. Marvin E. Shaw, *Group Dynamics: The Psychology of Small Group Behavior* (New York: McGraw-Hill, 1971), 10.

5. Dorwin Cartwright and Ronald Lippitt, "Group Dynamics and the Individual," *International Journal of Group Psychotherapy* 7 (January 1957): 86–102.

6. Edgar H. Schein, *Organizational Psychology*, 2d ed. (Englewood Cliffs, N.J.: Prentice-Hall, 1970), 82.

7. For more information on these groups, see Leonard R. Sayles, "Research in Industrial Human Relations," in *Industrial Relations* (New York: Harper & Bros., 1957).

8. For a discussion of individual versus group decision making, see George P. Huber, *Managerial Decision Making* (Glenview, Ill.: Scott, Foresman, 1980), 140–48.

9. Ethel C. Glenn and Elliott Pood, "Groups Can Make the Best Decisions, if You Lead the Way," *Supervisory Management* (December 1978): 2–6.

10. Raymond McLeod, Jr., and Jack W. Jones, "Making Executive Information Systems More Effective," *Business Horizons* (September/October 1986): 29–37.

11. Cyril O'Donnell, "Ground Rules for Using Committees," *Management Review* 50 (October 1961): 63–67. See also "Making Committees Work," *Infosystems* (October 1985): 38–39.

12. These guidelines are taken from "How Not to Influence People," *Management Record* (March 1958): 89–91. This article also can be consulted for additional guidelines.

13. Irving L. Janis, *Groupthink* (Boston: Houghton Mifflin, 1982).

14. For more information on the use of task teams in the Litton microwave cooking division, see William W. George, "Task Teams for Rapid Growth," *Harvard Business Review* (March/April 1977): 71–80.

15. Bernard Bass, *Organizational Psychology* (Boston: Allyn & Bacon, 1965), 197–98.

16. Bass, *Organizational Psychology*, 199.

17. Keith Davis and John W. Newstrom, *Human Behavior at Work: Organizational Behavior* (New York: McGraw-Hill, 1985), 310–12.

18. Muhammad Jamal, "Shift Work Related to Job Attitudes, Social Participation, and Withdrawal Behavior: A Study of Nurses and Industrial Workers," *Personnel Psychology* 34 (Autumn 1981): 535–47.

19. J.L. Moreno, "Contributions of Sociometry to Research Methodology in Sociology," *American Psychological Review* 12 (June 1947): 287–92.

20. J.H. Jacobs, "The Application of Sociometry to Industry," *Sociometry* 8 (May 1954): 181–98.

21. Muzafer Sherif, "A Preliminary Experimental Study of Intergroup Relations," in *Social Psychology at the Crossroads*, ed. John H. Rohrer and Muzafer Sherif (New York: Harper & Bros., 1951).

22. Edgar H. Schein, "SMR Forum: Improving Face-to-Face Relationships," *Sloan Management Review* 22 (Winter 1981): 43–52.

23. Homans, *The Human Group*.

24. For an interesting attempt to analyze characteristics of work groups in a small business, see James Curran and John Stanworth, "The Social Dynamics of the Small Manufacturing Enterprise," *Journal of Management Studies* 18 (April 1981): 141–58.

25. W. Alan Randolph, *Understanding and Managing Organizational Behavior* (Homewood, Ill.: Richard D. Irwin, 1985), 398–99.

26. Davis and Newstrom, *Human Behavior at Work*, 218.

27. Don Hellriegel and John W. Slocum, Jr., *Management* (Reading, Mass.: Addison-Wesley, 1986), 539–42.

28. Stanley E. Seashore, *Group Cohesiveness in the Industrial Work Group* (Ann Arbor: University of Michigan Press, 1954).

29. Raymond A. Van Zelst, "Sociometrically Selected Work Teams Increase Production," *Personnel Psychology* 4 (Autumn 1952): 175–85.

30. O. Jeff Harris, *Managing People at Work* (New York: Wiley, 1976), 122.

31. J.R. Hackman, "Group Influence on Individuals," in *Handbook for Industrial and Organizational Psychology*, ed. M.P. Dunnette (Chicago: Rand McNally, 1976).

32. This section is based primarily on P.C. André De la Porte, "Group Norms: Key to Building a Winning Team," *Personnel* (September/October 1974): 60–67.

33. A. Mazur, "A Cross-Species Comparison of Status in Small Established Groups," *American Sociological Review* 38, no. 5 (1973): 513–30.

34. Peter F. Drucker, "Is Executive Pay Excessive?"*Wall Street Journal*, May 23, 1977, 22.

35. T.N. Whitehead, "The Inevitability of the Informal Organization and Its Possible Value," in *Readings in Management*, ed. Ernest Dale (New York: McGraw Hill, 1970).

Action Summary Answer Key

1. a. F, p. 405
   b. c, p. 405
2. a. F, p. 415
   b. F, p. 406

3. a. d, p. 406
   b. e, p. 411
4. a. F, p. 417
   b. b, p. 417

5. a. a, pp. 420–421
   b. T, p. 419

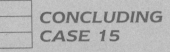
GM: TURNAROUND AT STE. THÉRÈSE

For more than ten years, operations at General Motors' sole assembly plant in Quebec were characterized by low quality, high turmoil, and labour mistrust. "People on the line wanted to get better, but there was no way of getting their message across. Nobody gave a damn," says Paul Morin, chairman of the Canadian Auto Workers (CAW) local 1163.

They do now. Just thirteen months after being told their plant was in imminent danger of being shut down, workers and managers have won a two-year reprieve. Although Ste. Thérèse's long-term future is still in doubt, the company and the local union have jointly forged a turnaround of remarkable proportions. A major factor has been management's decision to replace its tradition of negotiating sensitive local issues once every three years with a more consultative, ongoing approach. The results have been extremely positive: during GM's most recent quality survey in January 1987, the plant posted the best rating ever for a GM plant in Canada. "It's the fifth time in a row we have surpassed our goal," plant manager Gary Henson says.

While obviously complex, Ste. Thérèse's rebound is most closely linked to the arrival of two key people late in 1985: Henson, who came to Ste. Thérèse after spending three years researching a GM plant in Atlanta; and Morin, who was elected the union's new plant chairman just weeks before Henson's arrival. At a time when the plant was nearing rock bottom, that new start for both union and management proved a blessing. Both agreed Ste. Thérèse needed one change more than any other: better communication between workers and management.

For Henson, this led immediately to meetings with his staff, then with union leaders. His message: only through cooperation, with managers setting an example for the workers, did the plant have any hope for a future. "I told them that if we could try to work together, to manage our problems better, it would go down onto the floor."

Eager to learn more about employees' frustrations, Henson spent much of the next three months meeting each employee personally. Besides talking, he also handed out a small plastic card bearing his picture and his goals as plant manager. Since many workers suspected he'd been brought to Ste. Thérèse to close it down, Henson says the card communicated that he was there to help provide a quality workplace and that, rather than closing the plant down, he wanted to ensure continued employment. "That was the first time in a long while that people had physically come into contact with their plant manager," says Gary Charron, a supervisor in the plant's sheet metal and chassis department. "It also sent a message that we, as supervisors, had to come out of our offices, too."

But quality was still an issue. At the Montreal Auto Show in January 1986, Henson warned an audience that beyond 1987 Ste. Thérèse's future was in doubt. This prompted CAW president Bob White to visit the site for a first-hand look at the problems. This in turn led to a February 1 meeting in Montreal between members of the CAW and the local union, as well as the plant's management and senior people from GM's office in Oshawa, Ontario.

At the meeting, the union communicated its desire to solve the quality problems, but felt it needed more information. The two sides agreed to form a steering committee that would meet monthly to examine problem areas at the plant and suggest ways to improve quality. Soon after the committee was launched, workmanship in troubled spots began improving. Since then, the plant has consistently improved in its absenteeism, grievance, quality, and productivity levels. According to Morin, this turnaround was due solely to improvements in communication: "We're talking, they're listening. They're talking, we're listening."

Today both groups have plenty of opportunity for both. In addition to weekly meetings, there are smaller talks on the plant floor every morning. Led by Henson, workers are encouraged to discuss plant quality, ask questions, or prepare for upcoming changes. Each area supervisor also conducts regular lunch-hour sessions on a range of topics. All of these changes have had a dramatic effect not only on employees, but on supervisors as well. According to one, "We've gone from being foremen to motivators and communicators."

According to Henson, the union's agreement to renegotiate its contract symbolizes all that has changed in the attitude of workers and management at Ste. Thérèse. Besides reducing the number of worker classifications from fifty-five to thirteen, the new contract will group workers into six-member "teams" with broader responsibilities; specifically, to assure accountability and improve quality. Besides simple assembly, for example, the teams will be responsible for inspecting their own work and making repairs. "People still set in their minds that something good for the company is necessarily bad for workers, haven't reached that point of understanding," Morin adds. "Sometimes, what's good for the company is also good for the employees."

DISCUSSION ISSUES

1. How is Henson's management style symbolic of a good understanding of group management? How might the union's role be a factor here?

2. How does his management style tie in with his emphasis on communication?
3. Would you expect the individual work teams at Ste. Thérèse to be highly cohesive? Explain.

Based on "Turnaround at GM's Ste. Thérèse plant reflects new labor-management attitude," by Brian Banks in *The Gazette* (Montreal), February 17, 1987. Used with permission.

CONTROLLING

Controlling is the fourth and last management function that must be performed for organizations to have long-term success. Sections 2 through 4 have dealt, respectively, with determining how the organization will get where it wants to go, establishing working relationships between resources that will help the organization to get there, and guiding the activities of organization members toward goal accomplishment. Section 5 points out that, in addition to planning, organizing, and influencing, managers must control, or modify, existing organizational variables to ensure organizational success.

Chapter 16

Chapter 16, "Principles of Controlling," defines the control function as making something happen the way it was planned to happen and defines controlling as the process that must be carried out to control. Controlling is presented in this chapter as a subsystem of the overall management system and as entailing three main steps: (1) measuring performance; (2) comparing performance to standards; and (3) taking corrective action. The three major types of control—precontrol, concurrent control, and feedback control—are discussed. The job of a controller also is covered in detail. The major topics that conclude this chapter are the importance of power to managers attempting to control, the potential barriers to successful controlling, and how to make controlling successful.

Chapter 17

Chapter 17, "Production Management and Control," presents production as an area that must be carefully controlled within organizations. Operations management, or managing the production process, is also emphasized. Production is defined as the transformation of organizational resources into products. The relationship between productivity and robotics, as well the relationship between production and the production facility, are stressed. Control tools discussed in this chapter that relate directly to production control are management by exception, break-even analysis, materials requirements planning and control, and quality control. This chapter also discusses two control tools that relate more indirectly to production control: budgets and ratio analysis.

Chapter 18

Chapter 18, the last chapter in this section, discusses information as it relates to the control function. Information is defined as conclusions derived from data analysis. The value of this information is discussed in terms of its appropriateness, quality, timeliness, and quantity. This chapter also describes how managers can use computers as electronic tools for generating and analyzing organizational information. The last major topic covered in this chapter is the management information system (MIS). An MIS is defined as an organizational network established to provide managers with information that will assist them in decision making. Planning, designing, implementing, and improving an MIS are discussed in detail. Management decision support systems are also discussed.

CHAPTER

16

PRINCIPLES OF CONTROLLING

STUDENT LEARNING OBJECTIVES

From studying this chapter, I will attempt to acquire:

1. A definition of *control*.
2. A thorough understanding of the controlling subsystem.
3. An appreciation for various kinds of control and how each kind can be used advantageously by managers.
4. Insights on the relationship between power and control.
5. Knowledge of the various potential barriers that must be overcome for successful control.
6. An understanding of steps that can be taken to increase the quality of a controlling subsystem.

CHAPTER OUTLINE

HOSPITAL SERVICES, INC.

In the 1960s, considerable interest was generated in hospital care. The aged and the poor were heavily subsidized by government programs aimed, among other things, at helping those in need to get adequate hospital care. During the same time, the cost of hospital services doubled, and still there were not enough beds for patients. Federal and state governments saw the need to distinguish between the types of care that were most suitable. It was clear that not everyone needed the full service care of general hospitals. The law contemplated that, once patients were discharged from such a facility, they would be sent for a limited time to a convalescent hospital, where the service level and costs were much lower. And, theoretically, having completed the allowed time, or as much of it as was needed, in this institution, patients would be returned to their homes, where they could receive needed services.

Jules McDonald was among several people who had the idea of building or buying a chain of convalescent hospitals to serve the growing needs for beds. He thought that a chain probably could achieve some economies of operation that a single hospital would not find possible. He intended to broaden his business by purchasing land, securing a mortgage to take care of the hospitals, and selling the whole package to investors. He would place his own optical stores and drugstores within each hospital, have his own wholesalers in drugs and hospital equipment, and create his own construction companies.

McDonald needed money to do these things. He knew that the stocks of convalescent hospital chains were being traded in multiples from 60 to 200 times earnings, and so he determined to tap the investment market for capital. He got together a few scattered assets, packaged them attractively, and took his business public. It could not be said that he could show any earnings, but he stressed his prospective earnings per share. Amazingly, the idea sold, and he raised about $15 million.

With cash in the bank and an attractive vision in his head, McDonald was ready to go with his Hospital Services, Inc. Plush offices came first. Then a group of lawyers and tax accountants was added. A salesman sold him a computer. Convalescent hospitals were purchased at high prices. Land was bought across the country, and construction was begun. Acquisitions were eagerly sought. McDonald did not do this all by himself. He was specially gifted in his public relations, government relations, and negotiations skills and tended to specialize in them. Managers were hired to take care of construction, hospital management, and finance.

As the months passed, the cash raised from the public issue was fast used. On paper, the cash flow from operations should have been adequate, but it did not actually materialize. No one, it seemed, was able to get a reading on hospital finances. In some cases, there were no profits; in other cases, the individual institution kept its own cash balance; and in others, there was a heavy drain of funds to cover expenses. The government did not help either. Its agencies were new at this activity; interpretations were being made in the law so frequently that no one knew what practice to follow.

Throughout this period of operation, there was no slowdown in activity. McDonald was in his element, but his controller failed to warn him of imminent bankruptcy. There did come a day when he ran out of money. This occurred at a time when bankers were tightening up credit and the stock market was falling fast.

As he looked over his wreck, he inquired, "What control system should I have had?"

From *Essentials of Management* by Harold Koontz. Copyright © 1978 by McGraw-Hill Book Company. Used with permission of McGraw-Hill Book Co.

What's Ahead

Perhaps the most significant managerial weakness of Jules McDonald, the president in the introductory case, was his failure to design and implement an effective control system for Hospital Services Inc. The material in this chapter would help a manager such as McDonald overcome this weakness. The chapter emphasizes four main topics: (1) fundamentals of controlling; (2) the controller and control; (3) power and control; and (4) performing the control function.

FUNDAMENTALS OF CONTROLLING

Prospective managers need a working knowledge of the essentials of the controlling function.[1] To this end, the following sections discuss a definition of control, a definition of controlling, and the various types of control that can be used in organizations.

Defining Control

Stated simply, **control** is making something happen the way it was planned to happen.[2] As implied in this definition, planning and control are virtually inseparable,[3] and, in fact, have been called the Siamese twins of management.[4] According to Robert L. Dewelt:

> The importance of the planning process is quite obvious. Unless we have a soundly charted course of action, we will never quite know what actions are necessary to meet our objectives. We need a map to identify the timing and scope of all intended actions. This map is provided through the planning process.
>
> But simply making a map is not enough. If we don't follow it or if we make a wrong turn along the way, chances are we will never achieve the desired results. A plan is only as good as our ability to make it happen. We must develop methods of measurement and control to signal when deviations from the plan are occurring so that corrective action can be taken.[5]

Control is making things happen as planned.

FIGURE 16.1 Newsletter emphasizing the importance of managerial control.

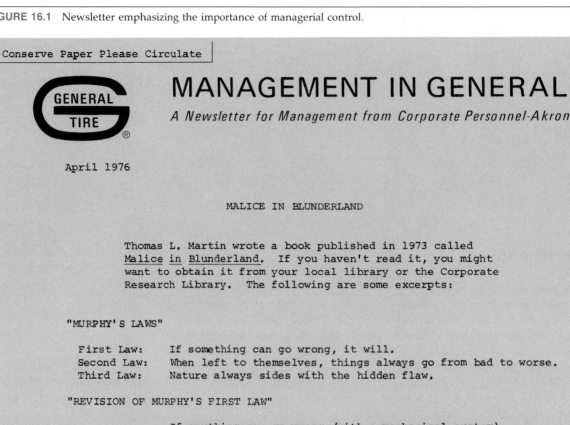

Conserve Paper Please Circulate

MANAGEMENT IN GENERAL

GENERAL TIRE

A Newsletter for Management from Corporate Personnel-Akron

April 1976

MALICE IN BLUNDERLAND

Thomas L. Martin wrote a book published in 1973 called
<u>Malice</u> in <u>Blunderland</u>. If you haven't read it, you might
want to obtain it from your local library or the Corporate
Research Library. The following are some excerpts:

"MURPHY'S LAWS"

First Law: If something can go wrong, it will.
Second Law: When left to themselves, things always go from bad to worse.
Third Law: Nature always sides with the hidden flaw.

"REVISION OF MURPHY'S FIRST LAW"

If anything can go wrong (with a mechanical system),
it will, and generally at the moment the system becomes
indispensable.

"COROLLARIES TO MURPHY'S FIRST LAW"

It is impossible to make anything foolproof because fools
are so ingenious.

Any wire or tube cut to length will be too short.

Interchangeable parts won't.

Identical units tested under identical conditions will not
perform identically in the field.

After any machine or unit has been completely assembled,
extra components will be found on the bench.

Components that must not and cannot be assembled improperly,
will be.

All constants are variables.

In any given computation, the figure that is most obviously
correct will be the source of the error.

The book goes on and on with other laws as well. The thought hit us that
you might have your own contributions. So, if you have corollaries to
"Murphy's First Law," send them to us and we will publish them in a later
issue of Management in General.

Figure 16.1 shows a newsletter sent to General Tire employees by the corporate personnel office of the General Tire Company. Although the newsletter is essentially a lighthearted discussion of Murphy's Law, it does make the serious point that managers should continually control or check to make sure that organizational activities and processes are going as planned.

Defining Controlling

Controlling is the process managers go through to control. According to Robert Mockler, controlling is:

> a systematic effort by business management to compare performance to predetermined standards, plans, or objectives to determine whether performance is in line with these standards and presumably to take any remedial action required to see that human and other corporate resources are being used in the most effective and efficient way possible in achieving corporate objectives.[6]

For example, production workers generally have production goals they must achieve per day and week. At the end of each working day, the number of units produced by each worker is recorded so that weekly production levels can be determined. If these weekly totals are significantly below the weekly goals, the supervisor must take action to ensure that actual production levels are equivalent to planned production levels. If production goals are met, the supervisor probably should allow work to continue as it has in the past.

The following sections discuss the controlling subsystem and provide more details about the control process itself.

Controlling is the process managers go through to control.

BACK TO THE CASE

Jules McDonald in the introductory case should have had a clearer understanding of control. Control within McDonald's organization would have entailed making things happen at Hospital Services, Inc. the way they were planned to happen. In essence, McDonald's control would have had to be closely related to his planning activities.

Going one step further, controlling at Hospital Services would have been the steps or process that McDonald would have had to go through to control. Ideally, this process would have included a determination of plans, standards, and objectives at Hospital Services so action could be taken to eliminate organizational characteristics that caused deviation from these factors.

The Controlling Subsystem

As with the planning, organizing, and influencing functions described previously, controlling can be viewed as a subsystem that is part of the overall management system process (Figure 16.2). The purpose of the controlling subsystem is to help managers enhance the success of the overall management system through effective controlling. Figure 16.3 shows the specific ingredients of the controlling subsystem.

Controlling is a subsystem of the overall management system.

The Controlling Process

As the process segment of Figure 16.3 implies, the three main steps of the controlling process are: (1) measuring performance; (2) comparing measured performance to standards; and (3) taking corrective action.

The controlling process has three main steps.

FIGURE 16.2   Relationship between overall management system and controlling subsystem.

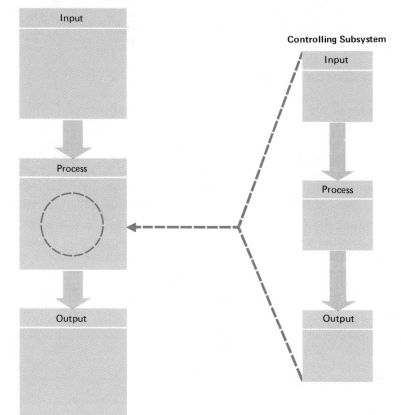

Measuring Performance

Before managers can determine what must be done to make an organization more effective and efficient, they must measure current organizational performance. And before such a measurement can be taken, some unit of measure that gauges performance must be established, and the quantity of this unit generated by the item whose performance is being measured must be observed.

For example, a manager who wants to measure the performance of five janitors first has to establish units of measure that represent janitorial performance, such as the number of floors swept, the number of windows washed, and/or the number of light bulbs changed. After designating these units of measures for janitorial performance, the manager then has to determine the number of each of these units associated with each janitor. This process of determining the units of measure and the number of units per janitor furnishes the manager with a measure of janitorial performance.

Managers also must keep in mind that a wide range of organizational activities can be measured as part of the control process. For example, the amounts and types of inventory kept on hand are commonly measured to control inventory, and the quality of goods and services being produced is commonly measured to control product quality. Performance measurements also can relate to various effects of production, such as the degree to which a particular manufacturing process pollutes the atmosphere.

FIGURE 16.3   The controlling subsystem.

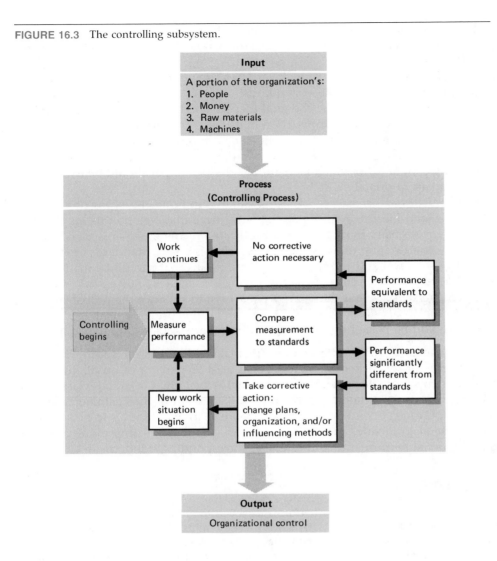

As one might suspect, the relative degree of difficulty in measuring various types of organizational performance primarily is determined by the activity being measured. For example, the relative degree of difficulty in measuring the performance of a ditchdigger would differ greatly from the relative degree of difficulty in measuring the performance of a student enrolled in a college-level management course.[7]

The difficulty of measuring performance varies greatly.

Comparing Measured Performance to Standards

Once managers have taken a measure of organizational performance, they should take the next step in controlling and compare this measure against some standard. A **standard** is the level of activity established to serve as a model for evaluating organizational performance. In essence, standards are the "yardsticks" that determine if organizational performance is adequate or inadequate.[8] General Electric set performance standards for itself in each of the following eight general areas:[9]

Standards are yardsticks of performance.

1. *Profitability standards*   In general, these standards indicate how much money General Electric would like to make as profit over a given time period—that is, return on its investment.

2. *Market position standards*   These standards indicate the share of total sales of a particular market that General Electric would like to have relative to its competitors.

3. *Productivity standards*   How much various segments of the organization should produce is the focus of these standards.

4. *Product leadership standards*   General Electric would like to assume one of the lead positions in product innovation in its field. Product leadership standards indicate what must be done to attain such a position.

5. *Personnel development standards*   Standards in this area indicate the type of training programs to which General Electric personnel should be exposed to develop appropriately.

6. *Employee attitudes standards*   These standards indicate the types of attitudes that General Electric management should strive to develop in its employees.

7. *Public responsibility standards*   General Electric recognizes its responsibility to make a contribution to the society of which it is a part. Standards in this area outline the level and types of such contributions that should be made.

8. *Standards reflecting relative balance between short- and long-range goals*   General Electric recognizes that short-range goals exist to enhance the probability that long-range goals will be attained. These standards express the relative emphasis that should be placed on attaining various short- and long-range goals.

> **Standards should be established in all important areas of organizational performance.**

Two more specific standards that American Airlines set for appropriate performance of airport ticket offices are: (1) at least 95 percent of the flight arrival times posted should be accurate in that actual arrival times do not deviate fifteen minutes from posted times; and (2) at least 85 percent of the customers coming to the airport ticket counter do not wait more than five minutes to be serviced. As a general guideline, successful managers pinpoint all important areas of organizational performance and establish corresponding standards in each area.

BACK TO THE CASE

McDonald should have viewed his controlling activities at Hospital Services Inc. as a subsystem of the organization's overall management system. For him to have achieved organizational control, his controlling subsystem would have required a portion of the people, money, raw materials, and machines available at Hospital Services.

The process portion of the controlling subsystem at Hospital Services should have involved McDonald's taking three steps: (1) measuring the performance levels of various productive units; (2) comparing these performance levels to predetermined performance standards for these units; and (3) taking any corrective action necessary to make the planned performance levels at Hospital Services consistent with actual performance levels.

Areas in which McDonald probably should have developed standards at Hospital Services include the desired profitability of various hospitals, the performance levels needed to achieve this profit level, and the training necessary to equip employees to reach the desired performance levels.

Taking Corrective Action

> **Corrective action is action to bring performance up to standard.**

Once managers have measured actual performance and compared this performance with established performance standards, they should take corrective action if necessary. **Corrective action** is managerial activity aimed at bringing organizational performance up to the level of performance standards. In other words, corrective action focuses on correcting the mistakes in the organization that are hindering organizational performance. Before taking any corrective action, however, managers should make sure that standards being used were properly established and that measurements of organizational performance are valid and reliable.

At first glance, it seems fairly simple to state that managers should take corrective action to eliminate **problems**, factors within organizations that are barriers to organizational goal attainment. In practice, however, it may be extremely difficult to pinpoint the problem causing some undesirable organizational effect. For example, a performance measurement may indicate that a certain worker is not adequately passing on critical information to fellow workers. Once the manager is satisfied that the related communication standards are appropriate and that the performance measurement information is valid and reliable, corrective action must be taken to eliminate the problem causing this substandard performance. However, what exactly is the problem causing substandard communication performance? Is the problem that the individual is not communicating because she doesn't want to communicate? Or is she not communicating adequately because the job being performed makes communication difficult? Does she have the training needed to enable her to communicate in an appropriate manner? The manager must determine whether this individual's lack of communication is a problem in itself or a **symptom**, a sign that some problem exists. For example, the individual's lack of communication could be a symptom of such possible problems as inappropriate job design or a cumbersome organizational structure.

Symptoms are signs that problems exist.

Once an organizational problem has been identified, necessary corrective action can focus on one or more of the three primary management functions of planning, organizing, and influencing. Correspondingly, corrective action can include such activities as modifying past plans to make them more suitable for future organizational endeavours, making an existing organizational structure more suitable for existing plans and objectives, or restructuring an incentive program to make sure that high producers are rewarded more than low producers. In addition, since planning, organizing, and influencing are so closely related, there is a good chance that corrective action taken in one area will necessitate some corresponding change in one or both of the other two areas.

Corrective action should focus on planning, organizing, and influencing.

In a study by Y. K. Shetty, 171 managers were surveyed from *Fortune's* list of the thirteen hundred largest U.S. industrial and non-industrial companies.[10] One purpose of the study was to investigate the types of corrective action programs managers use and the frequency with which they are used. Figure 16.4 presents the results of this study. The corrective action programs listed in the table are only a sample of such programs, not an exhaustive list.

FIGURE 16.4 Corrective action programs commonly used by managers and frequency of use.

Corrective Action Program	Frequency of Program Use
Cost reduction	2.3
Employee participation	3.1
Productivity incentives	3.3
Goal setting with productivity focus	3.5
Increased automation	3.8
Quality improvement	3.9
Increased employee training	4.7
Better labor-management relations	4.9
Increased research and development	5.3

Note: The lower the frequency, the higher the relative use of the program.

Adapted from Y. K. Shetty, "Product Quality and Competitive Strategy," *Business Horizons* (May/June 1987): 47. Copyright, 1987, by the Foundation for the School of Business at Indiana University. Reprinted by permission.

BACK TO THE CASE

If McDonald had determined that corrective action was necessary at Hospital Services, Inc., he would have had to be certain that the action was aimed at organizational problems rather than at symptoms of problems. Once Hospital Service's problems had been solved through corrective action, related symptoms eventually would have disappeared.

McDonald's corrective action at Hospital Services inevitably would have had to focus on past planning, organizing, or influencing efforts. In addition, as McDonald made changes in one of these areas, he probably would have found that some corresponding changes in another area were needed.

Types of Control

There are three types of management control: (1) precontrol; (2) concurrent control; and (3) feedback control. Each type primarily is determined by the time period in which the control is emphasized in relation to the work being performed.

Precontrol

Precontrol—controlling before people work.

Control that takes place before work is performed is called **precontrol** or feedforward control.[11] In this regard, management creates policies, procedures, and rules aimed at eliminating behaviour that will cause future undesirable work results. For example, the manager of a small record shop may find that a major factor in developing return customers is salespeople discussing various records with customers. This manager might use precontrol by establishing a rule that salespeople cannot talk to each other while a customer is in the store. This rule would be precontrol because it is aimed at eliminating anticipated problems with salespeople before those salespeople actually are faced with a customer. Precontrol focuses on eliminating predicted problems.

Concurrent Control

Concurrent control—controlling while people work.

Control that takes place as work is being performed is called **concurrent control.** Concurrent control relates not only to human performance but also to such areas as equipment performance or department appearance. For example, most grocery stores have rigid rules about the amount of stock that should be placed on the selling floor. In general, these stores desire generous amounts of all products on the shelves, with no "stock holes" or empty spaces. A concurrent control aimed at ensuring that shelves are stocked as planned could be a stock manager making periodic visual checks throughout a work period to evaluate the status of the sales shelves and, correspondingly, the performance of the stock crew.

Feedback Control

Feedback control—controlling after people work.

Control that concentrates on past organizational performance is called **feedback control**. When exercising this type of control, managers are attempting to take corrective action within the organization by looking at organizational history over a specified time period. This history may concentrate on only one factor, such as inventory levels, or on the relationships among many factors, such as net income before taxes, sales volume, and marketing costs.

Figure 16.5 is an example of a report, developed for an oil company, that can serve as the basis for feedback control. This particular report contains graphs

FIGURE 16.5 Example of report that can serve as basis for feedback control.

Trends (Years 2–7) / Months (Annualized) (Year 8 vs. Year 7)

Charts: Net Income (Thousands, $1 500–200); Total Sales Volume / S.S. Sales (Millions, 80–15); Other P.P. Sales (50–15); Gross Margin (Cents Per Gallon, 6–3); Marketing Costs (6–3). Horizontal axis: Year 2 3 4 5 6 7 8; Months J F M A M J JI A S O N D.

Annotations: "Prices depressed" · "Note trend" · "Reverse favorable volume trend of last 5 years" · "Decline in gross margin due primarily to volume; secondarily to prices"

Division "A"
Marketing — Manufacturing — Natural Gasoline Plants
Combined Net Income before Taxes: Bulk Plant and Service Station Business

Year	Net Income before Taxes ($000)	Return on Net Investment	Sales Volume (000 Gals)	S/S Volume (000 Gals)	Other Bulk Plant Sales (000 Gals)	Gross Margin Per Gal.	Marketing Costs Per Gal.	Net Income Per Gal.
1								
2								
3	348		49 451	22 416	27 035	.0497	.0427	.0070
4	413		52 715	25 551	27 164	.0494	.0425	.0069
5	478		55 833	28 243	27 410	.0507	.0421	.0086
6	435		57 896	30 719	27 177	.0522	.0447	.0075
7	768	10.8	60 481	34 544	25 937	.0552	.0425	.0127
8								
Jan	69		4 762	2 799	1 963	.0571	.0426	.0145
Feb	42		4 222	2 545	1 677	.0600	.0500	.0100
March	57		4 733	2 769	1 964	.0570	.0451	.0119
	168	8.9	13 717	8 113	5 604	.0580	.0458	.0122
April	3		4 816	2 810	2 006	.0481	.0474	.0007
May	26		4 790	2 856	1 934	.0523	.0469	.0054
June	38		5 517	3 339	2 178	.0499	.0431	.0068
	67	4.1	15 123	9 005	6 118	.0501	.0457	.0044
July	75		5 383	3 197	2 186	.0500	.0360	.0140
Aug	37		4 973	3 056	1 917	.0525	.0451	.0074
Sept	68		4 785	2 928	1 857	.0585	.0444	.0141
	180	9.4	15 141	9 181	5 960	.0535	.0416	.0119
Oct								
Nov								
Dec								
Yr. to Date	415	7.5	43 981	26 299	17 682	.0537	.0443	.0094

Annotations: "Note low return on investment; also down from last year" · "Net income per gallon lower than .0101 in jobber channel" · "Decline in net income per gallon due primarily to rising unit costs"

Variance from Last Year

	Net Income before Taxes	Return on Net Investment	Sales Volume	S/S Volume	Other Bulk Plant Sales	Gross Margin	Marketing Costs	Net Income
1st Qtr.	60	2.3	218	490	(272)	.0047	.0005	.0042
2nd Qtr.	(99)	(5.4)	(632)	117	(749)	(.0032)	.0030	(.0062)
3rd Qtr.	(133)	(7.6)	(1 493)	(471)	(1 022)	(.0046)	.0023	(.0069)
4th Qtr.								
Yr. to Date	(172)	(3.5)	(1 907)	136	(2 043)	(.0013)	.0021	(.0034)
% Change	(29.3)		(4.2)	0.5	(10.4)	(2.4)	5.0	(26.6)

Annotations: "this is one of few divisions showing decline in net income" · "Continues downtrend of last three years"

Variance from Forecast

	Net Income before Taxes
1st Qtr.	(506)
2nd Qtr.	(1 410)
3rd Qtr.	(2 285)
4th Qtr.	
Yr. to Date	(4 201)
% Change	(8.7)

Annotation: "Unit costs up because volume well below forecast"

Analysis of Change in Net Income: 9 Months

Causes of Variation	($000)	Per Gal.
Gross Margin Inc. — (Dec.) from change in:		
Volume	(128)	
Price	(23)	
Mdse. Cost	(11)	
Net Change–Gross Margin	(162)	(.0013)
Marketing Costs Inc. — (Dec.) from change in:		
Over. & Oper. Expense	7	.0020
Taxes	—	.0001
Depreciation	19	.0006
Misc. Income	—	(.0001)
T.B.A. Commissions	4	—
Subtotal	30	.0026
Loss (Gain) on Assets	(20)	(.0005)
Net Change–Mktg. Costs	10	.0021
Net Income Inc. — (Dec.)	(172)	(.0034)

Monthly Averages

	Number of Service Stations	Total Gasoline Gallons Per S.S.	Total Motor Oil Per S.S.	Ratio of Total Motor Oil to Gasoline
Year 8	239	11 990	176	1.47
Year 7	232	12 247	216	1.76
Change	7	(257)	(40)	(0.29)
% Change	3.0	(2.1)	(18.5)	

Monthly Averages – Bulk Plant Sales (Excluding Service Station Sales)

	Number Bulk Plants	Total Gasoline Per B.P.	Total Other Light Oil Per B.P.	Total Lube Oils Per B.P.
Year 8	99	17 083	2 017	722
Year 7	104	18 352	1 906	739
Change	(5)	(1 269)	111	(17)
% Change	(4.8)	(6.9)	5.8	(2.3)

Annotation: "Note declines in gasoline and motor oil sales per service station and in gasoline sales per bulk plant" that show various trends over a number of years as well as handwritten notes that highlight major trends. Management would use this report to compare actual organizational performance with planned organizational performance and then to take whatever corrective action is necessary to make actual and planned performance more equivalent. Of course, the structure of such reports varies from organization to organization, depending on the various types and forms of information needed to present an overview of specific organizational activities.

BACK TO THE CASE

In controlling Hospital Services, Inc., McDonald probably would have found good use for some combination of precontrol, concurrent control, and feedback control. Precontrol would have emphasized the elimination of the factors at Hospital Services that could cause poor productivity before the work itself actually began. Through concurrent control, McDonald would have been able to assess work performance at Hospital Services while the work was being performed. Lastly, McDonald's feedback control would have improved future performance by analyzing the history of Hospital Services. Some use of each of these types of control would have increased the probability of eliminating production problems before those problems caused too much damage. Perhaps McDonald's main mistake was that he emphasized feedback control to the exclusion of concurrent control and precontrol.

THE CONTROLLER AND CONTROL

Organization charts developed for medium- and large-sized companies typically contain a position called controller. The sections that follow explain more about controllers and their relationship to the control function by discussing the job of the controller and how much control is needed within an organization.

The Job of the Controller

The controller is usually a staff person who gathers information that helps managers to control.

From the preceding discussion, it is clear that managers have the responsibility to compare planned and actual performance and to take corrective action when necessary. In smaller organizations, managers may be completely responsible for gathering information about various aspects of the organization and developing necessary reports based on this information. In medium- or large-sized companies, however, an individual called the **controller** (also sometimes called the comptroller) usually exists. The controller's basic responsibility is assisting line managers with the controlling function by gathering appropriate information and generating necessary reports that reflect this information.[12] The information with which the controller usually works generally reflects the following various financial dimensions of the organization: (1) profits; (2) revenues; (3) costs; (4) investments; and (5) discretionary expenses.[13]

The sample job description of a controller in Figure 16.6 shows that the controller is responsible for generating appropriate information on which a manager can base the exercising of control. Since the controller generally is not directly responsible for taking corrective action within the organization and typically advises a manager of what corrective action should be taken, the controller position is primarily a staff position.

FIGURE 16.6   Sample job description for a controller in a large company.

Objectives

The Controller (or Comptroller) is responsible for all accounting activities within the organization.

Functions

1. *General accounting* Maintain the company's accounting books, accounting records, and forms. This includes:
   a. Preparing balance sheets, income statements, and other statements and reports.
   b. Giving the president interim reports on operations for the recent quarter and fiscal year to date.
   c. Supervising the preparation and filing of reports to the SEC.
2. *Budgeting* Prepare a budget outlining the company's future operations and cash requirements.
3. *Cost accounting* Determine the cost to manufacture a product and prepare internal reports to management of the processing divisions. This includes:
   a. Developing standard costs.
   b. Accumulating actual cost data.
   c. Preparing reports that compare standard costs to actual costs and highlight unfavorable differences.
4. *Performance reporting* Identify individuals in the organization who control activities and prepare reports to show how well or how poorly they perform.
5. *Data processing* Assist in the analysis and design of a computer-based information system. Frequently, the data processing department is under the controller, and the controller is involved in management of that department as well as other communications equipment.
6. *Other duties* Other duties may be assigned to the controller by the president or by corporate bylaws. Some of these include:
   a. Tax planning and reporting.
   b. Service departments such as mailing, telephone, janitors, and filing.
   c. Forecasting.
   d. Corporate social relations and obligations.

Relationships

The Controller reports to the Vice–president for Finance.

Reprinted by permission from p. 13 of *Cost Accounting: A Managerial Approach*, 2e, by Cherrington, Hubbard, and Luthy. Copyright © 1988 by West Publishing Company. All rights reserved.

How Much Control is Needed?

As with all organizational endeavours, control activities should be pursued if expected benefits of performing such activities are greater than the costs of performing them.[14] The process of comparing the cost of any organizational activity with the expected benefit of performing the activity is called **cost-benefit analysis**. In general, managers and controllers should collaborate to determine exactly how much controlling activity is justified within a given situation.

Figure 16.7 shows controlling activity over an extended period of time. According to this figure, controlling costs increase steadily as more and more controlling activities are performed. In addition, since the controlling function begins with the incurrence of related "start-up" costs, controlling costs at first usually are greater than increased income generated from increased controlling. As controlling starts to correct major organizational errors, however, increased income from increased controlling eventually equals controlling costs (point X_1 on the graph) and ultimately surpasses them by a large margin.

Managers should perform a cost-benefit analysis to determine how much controlling activity is justified.

FIGURE 16.7 Value of additional controlling.

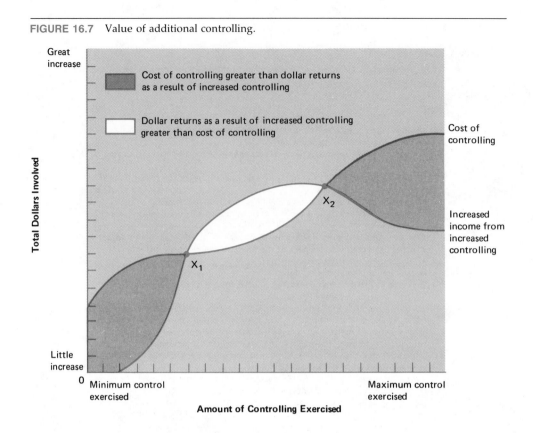

As more and more controlling activity is added beyond X_1 however, controlling costs and increased income from increased controlling eventually are equal again (point X_2 on graph). As more controlling activity is added beyond X_2, controlling costs again surpass increased income from increased controlling. The main reason why this last development takes place is that major organizational problems probably have been detected much earlier, and corrective measures taken now primarily are aimed at smaller and more insignificant problems.

The following information about Franklin M. Jarman, a past chief executive of Genesco, Inc., makes the point very emphatically that a manager can exercise too much control.[15] In 1973, Jarman fought his father, W. Maxey, for control of Genesco, a $1 billion retailing and apparel conglomerate. Jarman won. One of his first moves was to initiate a system of financial controls. These controls saved the company from ruin in 1973, when it lost $52 million. However, they ultimately may have been responsible for Jarman's downfall four years later.

According to people within Genesco, Jarman became obsessed with controls. Red tape and paperwork caused many delays and paralyzed operations. Management was centralized to the point of frustrating company executives. In its 1975 annual report, Genesco announced that in 1976 it would spend $8 million to open 63 stores and renovate 124 others. According to insiders, Jarman required so much analysis for these projects that decisions were postponed. Six months into fiscal year 1976, little of the projected work had been completed.

Because most of Genesco's business is in the fast-moving areas of apparel and retailing, delays and indecision can be very damaging. As a result, in January 1977 two dozen Genesco executives participated in a "palace revolt" that relieved Jarman of his responsibilities.

BACK TO THE CASE

The introductory case ends with the statement that McDonald's controller "failed to warn him of imminent bankruptcy." The basic job of the controller at Hospital Services, Inc. was to gather information for reports that McDonald could use to take corrective action. The controller was not to take any corrective action at Hospital Services but simply should have advised McDonald as to what corrective action should be taken. The root of the problem, however, was with McDonald. He failed to control the controller.

To have operated properly, McDonald should have determined, with or without the advice of his controller, exactly how much control was necessary at Hospital Services. In general, McDonald should have continued to increase controlling as long as the benefits from the control activities exceeded their cost. McDonald also should have kept in mind that, as in the case of Genesco, too much control could cause too much paperwork at Hospital Services and could bring decision making to a halt.

POWER AND CONTROL

To control successfully, managers must understand not only the control process itself but also how organization members relate to the control process. Up to this point, this chapter has emphasized non-human variables of controlling. This section, however, focuses on power, perhaps the most important human-related variable in the control process. The following sections discuss power by: (1) presenting a definition of power; (2) elaborating on the total power of managers; and (3) listing steps managers can take to increase their power over other organization members.

The human-related aspect of controlling is power.

A Definition of Power

Perhaps the two most often confused terms in management are *power* and *authority*. Authority was defined in Chapter 9 as the right to command or give orders. The extent to which an individual is able to influence others so that they respond to orders is called **power**. The greater this ability to influence others, the more power an individual is said to have.

Power is the ability to influence others.

Obviously, power and control are closely related. To illustrate, after a manager compares actual performance with planned performance and determines that corrective action is necessary, orders usually are given to implement this action. Although these orders are issued according to the manager's allotted organizational authority, they may or may not be followed precisely, depending on how much power the manager has over those individuals to whom the orders are issued.

Total Power of a Manager

The **total power** a manager possesses is made up of two different kinds of power: position power and personal power.[16] **Position power** is power derived from the organizational position a manager holds. In general, moves from lower-level management to upper-level management accrue more position power for a manager. **Personal power** is power derived from a manager's human relationships with others.

Total power = position power + personal power.

This Management in Action feature discusses some of the changes instituted by W. Vickery Stoughton at Toronto General Hospital to increase control and efficiency in operations, and outlines some of the factors and information that must be considered in controlling a major hospital. Stoughton's success is clearly attributable to his understanding of the control process and to the support he received to initiate changes to the hospital's operations—support that arose from his power relations with "relevant others" in the hospital.

W. VICKERY STOUGHTON: CONTROL AT TORONTO GENERAL HOSPITAL

When W. Vickery Stoughton became president of Toronto General Hospital in 1981, he took charge of something known as The Big House, or The Flagship Hospital—one of the largest hospitals in North America. A massive and bewildering complex, it is virtually a town within a city. It has 1 000 beds, 4 000 employees, its own police force, its own purified air, and its own germs. Its 1985 budget was $169 million, increased to approximately $183 million in 1986.

Toronto General is a modern teaching hospital: It is a business, a corporation, a hotel, a school, a restaurant, a charity, a supermarket of balms and medications, in short, a self-contained community that functions seven days a week, twenty-four hours a day. The hospital's threefold duties are to cure, to teach, and to conduct research. Daily, nightly, it houses birth and death, joy and sadness, fear and hope. There are some doctors and nurses whom patients regard as candidates for canonization and others whom they see as misanthropes who might want to remove their gallbladders just for the heck of it. The hospital must meet and maintain standards of excellence despite the budget limitations and restraints imposed within a highly regulated health profession, and despite public scrutiny, criticism, and the everyday crises of life and death. There are power plays involving all levels of government, labour unions, as well as physicians and surgeons.

Stoughton's office, located in the Bell Wing of Toronto General, reflects some of the day-to-day responsibility involved in running a hospital. The coffee table, for instance, is littered with sheets of statistics, part of the hospital's latest financial report that lists the number of admissions, patient days, average occupancy, and dozens of other statistical references. The figures show that the average length of stay at Toronto General for 1986 was 9.7 days, with an average occupancy rate of 86.42 percent. Stoughton studies the statistics like a baseball fan poring over the Saturday morning batting averages.

According to Stoughton, once average occupancy rates reach 93 percent or 95 percent, problems start. "We need those extra vacant beds for flexibility, for emergencies. Occupancy is highest in the middle of the week, lowest on the weekends. Saturday is the big discharge day, Sunday the big admission day. When the average

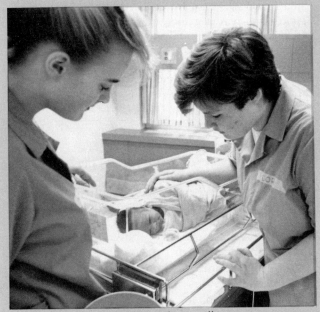

"every day . . . nine babies are born . . ."

occupancy slips over 90 percent, we start postponing elective surgery, things like gallbladders, cysts, hemorrhoids, and simple hernias. If the average occupancy is 90 percent every day, we have problems getting patients in and out, which results in beds having to be set up in corridors and spare rooms and broom closets. The optimum average occupancy rate is 85 percent. We don't like to postpone elective surgery, because it's hard on the people who have taken time off work because they've been told they would have an operation on a given date. But we've got to have the flexibility for emergencies. We don't close emergency under *any* circumstances."

More statistics: every day, 87 patients are admitted; 108 walk or are carried into emergency; 100 surgical operations are performed; 420 Xrays are taken; 4 282 meals are served; 6 122 kg of laundry are washed; three patients die; nine babies are born; ten abortions are performed. Yearly operating expenses amount to $169.3 million and include salaries and wages; medical and surgical supplies; gases; drugs; dietary provisions; housekeeping supplies; plant operation; security; employee benefits; telephone; stationery; depreciation; bad debts—in total nearly half a million dollars a day. Facing such costs, anyone who runs a hospital has to be able to look at big dollar signs without twitching. Requests keep coming in from the

452

various departments for new machines because a sprocket has worn out or because there is a now a better machine to do the same job.

It is, however, easier to be a big hospital than a little hospital when it comes to bottom lines or financial survival, or "zero-based budgeting" as hospital administrators prefer to call it. Savings tend to be "redirected," another way of saying to outside snoops to whom one may be accountable, "Try to find it if you can." Larger hospitals such as Toronto General simply have more money to throw around, to hold back, to tuck away, to invest, to roll over.

In the time leading up to the opening of Toronto General's Max Bell Research Centre in 1985, Stoughton had made a few wrong moves in his job. After five years at the hospital, he had won over the doctors, the nurses, administrators, and managers. He had done it mainly by playing tough and fair, staying outside and above the frays, and never appearing to take sides, but also by always taking the initiative, finding how things could be done—and why they couldn't.

He began by delegating authority, decentralizing power, and improving communications. The best example was nursing. In every hospital, nurses are regarded as having great potential as forces of hospital reform, particularly in patient care, but they're always kept in check—fragmented, impotent. Soon after Stoughton arrived at Toronto General, he made his head nurses "nursing managers," giving them control of money, a say in running the hospital, and effective countervailing leverage against the well entrenched power of the doctors. This helped to even things up at the hospital. Though not everyone was happy with the change, no one complained too loudly or dared to suggest that Stoughton was wrong. So well did he work behind the scenes that most people did not even notice his fingerprints.

Stoughton also encouraged group practices among the doctors within the hospital, another move that streamlined the organization and improved communication. A few specialties had formed group practices before Stoughton had arrived, but most doctors still operated as individuals, as private entrepreneurs in a clumsy and outdated system that has been described as "an army of pushcart vendors in an age of supermarkets." In a group practice, doctors' incomes are pooled and a minimum is agreed upon, perhaps $90 000 or $100 000 a year. Anything left over usually goes to research or an academic enrichment fund. When a patient is referred to orthopedics, for instance, he or she is usually referred to a specific doctor. But in orthopedics there are specialties within the specialty, so what the group will do is redirect the patient to the most qualified person, the orthopedist who does hip replacements, or the one who treats sports injuries, for example. Because it is a group practice, with all income pooled, there is no economic incentive for individual doctors to get as many patients as they can. This system has obvious benefits for patients—they get treated by the proper doctors—and it makes things easier for the president of the hospital because it is more efficient. "If you've got 600 doctors in the hospital practising as individuals, you've got no organizational structure whatsoever," says Stoughton. "Every time you want to make a decision, make a change, you've got to convince every doctor who's impacted by it. Group practices create all sorts of good things—sharing research, sharing patient referrals, building management structures within the groups."

These days, more and more big, modern hospitals are being run by non-medical administrators, specially trained management artists who know more about balancing sheets than operating room procedures. The best of them, like Stoughton, have studied and apprenticed in hospital management, a new profession as demanding and difficult as any medical specialty. Day by day, Stoughton tries to keep in touch with all departments. He wanders the hallways, drops by emergency, and visits public relations. Every Friday, shortly after dawn, he goes on a walking tour with the nurses to inspect the front lines.

In all of his work, Stoughton exudes unquenchable enthusiasm. He enjoys the company of doctors—and the doctors respect him—though he knows working with doctors can be tricky, even perilous. He is the chief executive officer and he can be tough, but his authority over the doctors is limited. "The politics are such that the only way I could fire a doctor is if he were medically incompetent. If he creates a disaster because he can't get along with anybody . . . I can put a real squeeze on him, but I'd have a tough time firing him. I've had some shouting matches, sure, but I keep them private, unless I'm attacked personally. What's nice about them (the doctors) is they are a group of people of above-average intelligence. They like good information and usually they will sit down and listen. But the politics can be *horrendous*. You don't get into ego battles with them because you'll lose. You've got to *tease* them. Watch me in a situation. It's instinctive."

Based on "Wheeling and healing," by Martin O'Malley in *Canadian Business*, November 1986. Used with permission.

Steps for Increasing Total Power

Managers can increase their total power by increasing their position power and/or their personal power. Position power generally can be increased by achieving a higher organizational position, but managers usually have little personal control over moving upward in an organization. On the other hand, managers generally have substantial control over the amount of personal power they hold over other organization members. The following statement by John P. Kotter stresses the importance of developing personal power:

> To be able to plan, organize, budget, staff, control, and evaluate, managers need some control over the many people on whom they are dependent. Trying to control others solely by directing them and on the basis of the power associated with one's position simply will not work—first, because managers are always dependent on some people over whom they have no formal authority, and second, because virtually no one in modern organizations will passively accept and completely obey a constant stream of orders from someone just because he or she is the "boss."[17]

To increase personal power, a manager can attempt to develop.[18]

Managers can develop their personal power by:

1. Making people feel obligated.

1. *A sense of obligation in other organization members that is directed toward the manager*   If a manager is successful in developing this sense of obligation, other organization members feel that they should rightly allow the manager to influence them within certain limits. The basic strategy generally suggested to create this sense of obligation is to do personal favours for people.

2. Being seen as an expert in their area.

2. *A belief in other organization members that the manager possesses a high level of expertise within the organization*   In general, a manager's personal power increases as organization members' perception of his or her level of expertise increases. To increase this perceived level of expertise, the manager must quietly make significant achievement visible to others and rely heavily on a successful track record and respected professional reputation.

3. Having others identify with them.

3. *A sense of identification that other organization members have with the manager*   The manager can strive to develop this identification by behaving in ways that other organization members respect and by espousing goals, values, and ideals commonly held by other organization members. The following description clearly illustrates how a certain sales manager took steps to increase the degree to which his subordinates identified with him:

> One vice-president of sales in a moderate-sized manufacturing company was reputed to be so much in control of his sales force that he could get them to respond to new and different marketing programs in a third of the time taken by the company's best competitors. His power over his employees was based primarily on their strong identification with him and what he stood for. Emigrating to the United States at age seventeen, this person worked his way up "from nothing." When made a sales manager in 1965, he began recruiting other young immigrants and sons of immigrants from his former country. When made vice-president of sales in 1970, he continued to do so. In 1975, 85 percent of his sales force was made up of people whom he hired directly or who were hired by others he brought in.[19]

4. Holding the "purse strings."

4. *The perception in other organization members that they are dependent upon the manager*   Perhaps the main strategy the manager should adopt in this regard is clear demonstration of the amount of authority he or she possesses over organizational resources. Action taken in this regard should emphasize not

only influence over resources necessary for organization members to do their jobs but also influence over resources organization members personally receive in such forms as salaries and bonuses. This strategy is aptly reflected in the following managerial version of the Golden Rule: "He who has the gold makes the rules."

BACK TO THE CASE

For McDonald to have been successful in controlling at Hospital Services, Inc., he would have had to have been aware of not only the intricacies of the control process itself but also of how to deal with people as they relate to the control process. With regard to people and control, McDonald would certainly have had to consider the amount of power he held over organization members—that is, his ability to encourage them to follow orders. Most of these orders would have related to implementing corrective action that McDonald had deemed advisable for Hospital Services.

The total amount of power that McDonald possessed came from the position he held and from his personal relationships with other organization members. Since McDonald was head of Hospital Services, he already possessed more position power than anyone else in the organization. Therefore, to increase his total power, McDonald would have had to develop his personal power. He could have attempted to do this by developing: (1) a sense of obligation in other organization members toward himself; (2) the belief in other organization members that he had a high level of task-related expertise; (3) a sense of identification that other organization members had with him; and (4) the perception in organization members that they were dependent on him as a manager.

PERFORMING THE CONTROL FUNCTION

Controlling can be an extremely detailed and intricate process, especially as the size of the organization increases. The two sections that follow furnish valuable guidelines for successfully executing this potentially complicated controlling function. These sections discuss potential barriers to successful controlling and making controlling successful.

Potential Barriers to Successful Controlling

Managers should take steps to avoid the following potential barriers to successful controlling:[20]

Guidelines for controlling include:

1. *Control activities can create an undesirable overemphasis on short-term production as opposed to long-term production*   As an example, in striving to meet planned weekly production quotas, a manager might "push" machines in a particular area and not allow these machines to stop running to be serviced properly. This kind of management behaviour would ensure that planned performance and actual performance are equivalent in the short term but may deteriorate the machines to the point that long-term production quotas are impossible to meet.

1. Don't overemphasize the short term.

2. *Control activities can increase employee frustration with their jobs and thereby reduce morale*   This reaction tends to occur primarily when management has a tendency to exert too much control. Employees get frustrated because they perceive management as being too rigid in its thinking and not allowing the freedom necessary to do a good job.[21] Another feeling that employees may

2. Don't frustrate through controlling.

have from overcontrol is that control activities are merely a tactic to pressure workers to higher production.

3. Don't disregard extenuating circumstances.

3. *Control activities can encourage the falsification of reports*   The following excerpt clearly makes this point:

> Not long ago, the Boy Scouts of America revealed that the membership figures coming from the field had been falsified. In response to the pressures of a national membership drive, people within the organization had vastly overstated the number of new Boy Scouts. To their chagrin, the leaders found something that other managers have also discovered: organizational control systems often produce unintended consequences. The drive to increase membership had motivated people to increase the number of new members reported, but it had not motivated them to increase the number of Boy Scouts actually enrolled.[22]

Employees may perceive management as basing corrective action solely on department records with no regard to extenuating circumstances. (The cartoon implies that people would sometimes prefer to have management consider extenuating circumstances when controlling.) If this is the case, employees may feel pressured to falsify reports so corrective action regarding their organizational unit will not be too drastic. For example, actual production may be overstated so it will look good to management or it may be understated to create the impression that planned production is too high, thereby tricking management into thinking that a lighter work load is justified.

4. Keep control activities in the proper perspective.

4. *Control activities can cause the perspective of organization members to be too narrow for the good of the organization*   Although controls can be designed to focus on relatively narrow aspects of an organization, managers must keep in mind that any corrective action should be considered not only in relation to the specific activity being controlled but also in relation to all other organizational units.

For example, a manager may determine that actual and planned production are not equivalent in a specific organizational unit because of various

"I guess no man's a hero to his controller—right, Higgins?"

New Yorker, *January 19, 1987, p. 36. Drawing by D. Reilly;*
© *1987 The New Yorker Magazine, Inc.*

periods when a low inventory of needed parts causes some production workers to pursue other work activities instead of producing a product. Although the corrective action to be taken in this situation would seem to be simply raising the level of parts inventory kept on hand, this probably would be a very narrow perspective of the problem. The manager should seek to answer questions such as the following before any corrective action is taken: Is there enough money on hand to raise current inventory levels? Are there sufficient personnel presently in the purchasing department to effect a necessary increase? Who will do the work the production workers presently are doing when they run out of parts?

5. *Control activities can be perceived as the goals of the control process rather than the means by which corrective action is taken*   Managers must keep in mind that information should be gathered and reports should be designed to facilitate the taking of corrective action within the organization. In fact, these activities only can be justified within the organization if they yield some organizational benefit that extends beyond the cost of performing them.

> 5. Remember that controlling is a means, not an end.

Making Controlling Successful

In addition to avoiding the potential barriers to successful controlling mentioned in the previous section, managers can perform certain activities to make the control process more effective. In this regard, managers should make sure that:

> To make the control process more effective, managers should:

1. *Various facets of the control process are appropriate for the specific organizational activity being focused on*[23]   As an example, standards and measurements concerning a line worker's productivity are much different than standards and measurements concerning a company vice-president's productivity. Controlling ingredients related to the productivity of these individuals, therefore, must be different if the control process is to be applied successfully.

> 1. Verify that controlling suits the situation.

2. *Control activities are used to achieve many different kinds of goals*   According to Jerome, control can be used for such purposes as standardizing performance, protecting organizational assets from theft and waste, and standardizing product quality.[24] Managers should keep in mind that the control process can be applied to many different facets of organizational life and that, for the organization to receive maximum benefit from controlling, each of these facets should be emphasized.

> 2. Use control to achieve many ends.

3. *Information used as the basis for taking corrective action is timely*[25]   Some time necessarily elapses as managers gather control-related information, develop necessary reports based on this information, decide what corrective action should be taken, and actually take the corrective action. However, information should be gathered and acted on as promptly as possible to ensure that the situation, as depicted by this information, has not changed and that the organizational advantage of corrective action will, in fact, materialize.

> 3. Act upon information quickly.

4. *The mechanics of the control process are understandable to all individuals who are in any way involved with implementing the process*[26]   Managers should take steps to ensure that people know exactly what information is necessary for a particular control process, how that information is to be gathered and used to compile various reports, what the purposes of various reports actually are, and what corrective actions are appropriate given various possible types of reports. The lesson here is simple: For control to be successful, all individuals involved in controlling must have a working knowledge of how the control process operates.

> 4. Make controlling understood.

BACK TO THE CASE

In addition to understanding the intricacies of control and how people fit into the control process, McDonald should have been aware of the potential barriers to successful controlling and the action he could have taken to increase the probability that his controlling activities would be successful.

To overcome the potential control-related barriers at Hospital Services, Inc., McDonald should have balanced his emphasis on short-term versus long-term objectives, minimized the negative influence controlling might have had on the morale of Hospital Services organization members, eliminated forces that might have led to the falsification of control-related reports, implemented a control perspective that would have

appropriately combined narrow and broad organizational focuses, and stressed controlling as a means rather than an end.

With regard to the action that could have been taken to increase the probability of effective controlling activities, McDonald should have made sure that various facets of his controlling subsystem were appropriate for Hospital Services activities, that components of the controlling subsystem were flexible and suited to many purposes, that corrective action was based on timely information, and that the controlling subsystem was understood by all organization members involved in its operation.

Action Summary

Reread the learning objectives that follow. Each objective is followed by questions. Answering these questions accurately will help you to retain the most important concepts discussed in this chapter. After answering each question, check your answer with the answer key at the end of this chapter. (*Hint*: If you have doubt regarding the correct response, consult the page that follows the answer.)

Circle:

From studying this chapter, I will attempt to acquire:

1. **A definition of *control*.**

   a. Managers must develop methods of measurement to signal when deviations from standards are occurring so that: (a) the plan may be abandoned; (b) quality control personnel may be notified; (c) the measurement standards may be checked; (d) corrective action can be taken; (e) none of the above.

   a, b, c, d, e

   T, F

   b. Control is making something happen the way it was planned to happen.

2. **A thorough understanding of the controlling subsystem.**

   a. The main steps of the controlling process include all of the following except: (a) taking corrective action; (b) establishing planned activities; (c) comparing performance to standards; (d) measuring performance; (e) all of the above are steps in controlling.

   a, b, c, d, e

   T, F

   b. Standards should be established in all important areas of organizational performance.

3. **An appreciation for various kinds of control and how each kind can be used advantageously by managers.**

   a. Which of the following is *not* one of the basic types of management control: (a) feedback control; (b) precontrol; (c) concurrent control; (d) exception control; (e) all are basic types of control.

   a, b, c, d, e

   b. An example of precontrol established by management would be (a) rules; (b) procedures; (c) policies; (d) budgets; (e) all of the above are examples.

   a, b, c, d, e

4. **Insights on the relationship between power and control.**
   a. According to Kotter, controlling others solely on the basis of position power will not work.   T, F
   b. The extent to which an individual is able to influence others to respond to orders is: (a) power; (b) sensitivity; (c) authority; (d) communication skills; (e) experience.   a, b, c, d, e

5. **Knowledge of the various potential barriers that must be overcome for successful control.**
   a. Potential barriers to successful communication can result in: (a) an overemphasis on short-term production as opposed to long-term production; (b) employees' frustration with their jobs and thereby reduced morale; (c) the falsification of reports; (d) the perception of organization members becoming too narrow for the good of the organization; (e) all of the above.   a, b, c, d, e
   b. Control activities should be seen as the means by which corrective action is taken.   T, F

6. **An understanding of steps that can be taken to increase the quality of a controlling subsystem.**
   a. All of the following are suggestions for making controlling successful *except*: (a) managers should make sure that the mechanics of the control process are understood by organization members involved with controlling; (b) managers should use control activities to achieve many different kinds of goals; (c) managers should ensure that control activities are supported by most organization members; (d) managers should make sure that information used as the basis for taking corrective action is timely; (e) all of the above are suggestions.   a, b, c, d, e
   b. Standards and measurements concerning a line worker's productivity are much the same as the standards and measurements concerning a company vice-president's productivity.   T, F

INTRODUCTORY CASE WRAP-UP

"Hospital Services, Inc." (p. 438) and its related back-to-the-case sections were written to help you better understand the management concepts contained in this chapter. Answer the following discussion questions about this introductory case to further enrich your understanding of the chapter content:

1. At the end of the introductory case, McDonald asked, "What control system should I have had?"

What do you think McDonald meant by *control system*?
2. Do you think McDonald could have controlled Hospital Services by himself? Explain.
3. List several areas of Hospital Services that McDonald's controlling activities should have emphasized.

Issues for Review and Discussion

1. What is control?
2. Explain the relationship between planning and control.
3. What is controlling?
4. What is the relationship between the controlling subsystem and the overall management system?

5. Draw and explain the controlling subsystem.
6. List and discuss the three main steps of the controlling process.
7. Define the term *standards*.
8. What is the difference between a symptom and a problem? Why is it important to differentiate between a symptom and a problem when controlling?
9. What types of corrective action can managers take?
10. List and define the three basic types of control that can be used in organizations.
11. What is the relationship between controlling and the controller?

12. What basis do managers use to determine how much control is needed in an organization?
13. What is the difference between power and authority? Describe the role of power within the control process.
14. What determines how much power a manager possesses?
15. How can a manager's personal power be increased?
16. Describe several potential barriers to successful controlling.
17. What steps can managers take to ensure that control activities are successful?

Sources of Additional Information

Bartolomé, Fernando, and André Laurent. "The Manager: Master and Servant of Power." *Harvard Business Review* (November/December 1986): 77–81.

Bruns, William J., Jr., and F. Warren McFarlan. "Information Technology Puts Power in Control Systems." *Harvard Business Review* (September/October 1987): 89–94.

Drake, Rodman L., and Lee M. Caudill. "Management of the Large Multinational: Trends and Future Challenges." *Business Horizons* 24 (May/June 1981): 83–91.

Hecht, Maurice R. *What Happens in Management: Principles and Practices.* New York: Amacom, 1980.

Hogan, Peter. "Using the Behavioural Sciences to Measure Management Performance." *Personnel Management* 13 (February 1981): 36–39.

"How TRW Tracks Multiple Programs." *Management Review* (March 1983): 44–45.

Hutchins, David. *Quality Circles Handbook.* New York: Nichols Publishing, 1985.

Kotter, John P. *Power and Influence.* New York: Free Press, 1985.

Lawler, Edward E., III, and John Grant Rhode. *Information and Control in Organizations.* Santa Monica, Calif.: Goodyear, 1976.

Ludwig, Richard. "A Team Approach to Cost Cutting." *Management World* 15 (July/August 1986): 18–19.

McTague, Michael. "Signposts on the Road to Excellence." *Business* 36 (April/May/June 1986): 3–12.

Moravec, Milan. "Performance Appraisal: A Human Resource Management System with Productivity Payoffs." *Management Review* 70 (June 1981): 51–54.

Rhodes, David, and Mike Wright. "Management Control for Effective Corporate Planning." *Long-Range Planning* 17 (August 1984): 115–21.

Rubin, Leonard R. "Planning Trees: A CEO's Guide through the Corporate Planning Maze." *Business Horizons* 27 (September/October 1984): 66–70.

Shanklin, William L. "Strategic Business Planning: Yesterday, Today, and Tomorrow." *Business Horizons* 22 (October 1979): 7–14.

Tannenbaum, A. *Control in Organizations.* New York: McGraw-Hill, 1968.

Notes

1. L.R. Bittle and J.E. Ramsey (eds.), *Handbook for Professional Managers* (New York: McGraw-Hill, 1985).
2. K.A. Merchant, "The Control Function of Management," *Sloan Management Review* 23 (Summer 1982): 43–55.
3. For an example of how a control system can be used with a formal planning model, see A.M. Jaeger and B. R. Baliga, "Control Systems and Strategic Adaptations: Lessons from the Japanese Experience," *Strategic Management Journal* 6 (April/June 1985): 115–34.
4. Donald C. Mosley and Paul H. Pietri, *Management: The Art of Working with and through People* (Encino, Calif.: Dickenson, 1975), 29–43.
5. Robert L. Dewelt, "Control: Key to Making Financial Strategy Work," *Management Review* (March 1977): 18.
6. Robert J. Mockler, ed., *Readings in Management Control* (New York: Appleton-Century-Crofts, 1970), 14.
7. Insights concerning how such measurements can influence employee performance can be found in Mark K. Hirst, "Accounting Information and the Evaluation

of Subordinate Performance: A Situational Approach," *Accounting Review* 56 (October 1981): 771–84.

8. For a discussion of how standards are set, see James B. Dilworth, *Production and Operations Management: Manufacturing and Nonmanufacturing* (New York: Random House, 1986), 637–50.

9. Robert W. Lewis, "Measuring, Reporting, and Appraising Results of Operations with References to Goals, Plans, and Budgets," in *Planning, Managing, and Measuring the Business: A Case Study of Management Planning and Control at General Electric Company* (New York: Controllership Foundation, 1955).

10. Y.K. Shetty, "Product Quality and Competitive Strategy," *Business Horizons* (May/June 1987): 46–52.

11. Harold Koontz, Cyril O'Donnell, and Heinz Weihrich, *Essentials of Management* (New York: McGraw-Hill, 1986), 454–59.

12. Vijay Sathe, *Controller Involvement in Management* (Englewood Cliffs, N.J.: Prentice-Hall, 1982).

13. James D. Wilson, *Controllership: The Work of the Managerial Accountant* (New York: Wiley, 1981).

14. For other ways in which cost-benefit analysis can be used by managers, see G.S. Smith and M.S. Tseng, "Benefit-Cost Analysis as a Performance Indicator," *Management Accounting* (June 1986): 44–49; "The IS (Information System) Payoff," *Infosystems* (April 1987): 18–20.

15. Adapted from "What Undid Jarman: Paperwork Paralysis," *Business Week*, January 24, 1977, 67.

16. Amitai Etzioni, *A Comparative Analysis of Complex Organizations* (New York: Free Press, 1961), 4–6.

17. John P. Kotter, "Power, Dependence, and Effective Management," *Harvard Business Review* (July/August 1977): 128.

18. Kotter, "Power, Dependence, and Effective Management," 135–36.

19. Kotter, "Power, Dependence and Effective Management," 131.

20. For further discussion of overcoming the potential negative effects of control, see Ramon J. Aldag and Timothy M. Stearns, *Management* (Cincinnati, Ohio: South-Western Publishing, 1987), 653–54.

21. Arnold F. Emch, "Control Means Action," *Harvard Business Review* (July/August 1954): 92–98. See also K. Hall and L.K. Savery, "Tight Rein, More Stress," *Harvard Business Review* (January/February 1986): 160–64.

22. Cortlandt Cammann and David A. Nadler, "Fit Control Systems to Your Managerial Style," *Harvard Business Review* (January/February 1976): 65.

23. Peter F. Drucker, *Management: Tasks, Responsibilities, Practices* (New York: Harper & Row, 1974).

24. W. Jerome III, *Executive Control: The Catalyst* (New York: Wiley, 1961), 31–34.

25. William Bruns, Jr., and E. Warren McFarlan, "Information Technology Puts Power in Control Systems," *Harvard Business Review* (September/October 1987): 89–94.

26. C. Jackson Grayson, Jr., "Management Science and Business Practice," *Harvard Business Review* (July/August 1973): 41–48.

Action Summary Answer Key

1. a. d, p. 439
   b. T. p. 439
2. a. b, p. 441
   b. T, pp. 443–444

3. a. d, p. 446
   b. e, p. 446
4. a. T, p. 454
   b. a, p. 451

5. a. e, pp. 455–457
   b. T, p. 457
6. a. c, p. 457
   b. F, p. 457

INTERNATIONAL PRODUCTS INC.: THE MISSING LINKS

International Products Inc. (IPI), one of the world's leading consumer products firms, is a good employer. The work at its southern Ontario plant—the company's largest in Canada—is clean and not physically demanding, and the company's wages are in the top 25 percent of those at comparable industries in the area. With regular pay, profit sharing, and a few hours of overtime each week, senior production operators can make $35 000 a year. Not surprisingly, turnover among the 900 production employees at the plant is low. Nevertheless, absenteeism is running at 4.5 percent—up from 4.1 percent five years earlier—and is costing an estimated $1.8 million a year. Michael Parker, the new human resources manager, wants to find out why.

Parker, 34, has worked at the plant for twelve years, formerly as a first-line supervisor. His interest in absenteeism was sparked by a magazine article about its causes and the cost to business. Although he knows that a 4.5 percent absenteeism rate isn't out of line with industry standards and is better than last year's 5.2 percent, the article has convinced Parker that the plant, which produces 70 percent of IPI's Canadian sales volume, can't afford to accept it: IPI faces intense competition, often accompanied by highly discounted prices, so it needs to keep quality high and costs low. In addition, few of its products are protected by patents.

The factory has a three-shift, twenty-four-hour operation and four major production departments: food products, beverages, pet foods, and toiletries. As well, it has a large shipping and storage department. Although most of the major plants in the area are unionized, IPI isn't; the company's managers pride themselves on doing their jobs well enough to make unions unattractive. Instead, an elected employee committee represents non-management staff on such issues as safety, wages, and benefits.

These good labour relations exist despite the fact that the plant, which has been in operation since 1921, operates under much less progressive management techniques than the three other IPI factories in Canada. At the newer plants, time clocks have been abolished and all employees are on salary and receive the same benefits.

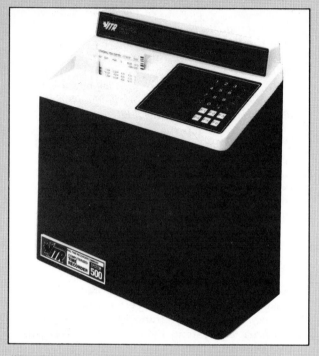

"The Ontario location . . . still has time clocks, hourly wages . . ."

The Ontario location, on the other hand, still has time clocks, hourly wages, different benefits for salaried and hourly staff, and closer employee supervision. Senior management has made a commitment to convert the Ontario plant to the more modern management style within five years.

In a report he put together to outline his concerns about absenteeism, Parker made the following observations:

- The 4.5 percent rate was probably understated because some kinds of absences, such as maternity and bereavement leaves, weren't reported.
- Variations in absenteeism among departments might be caused by different reporting methods rather than the actual differences in attendance.
- If absenteeism could be reduced to the levels of five years ago, about a quarter of the estimated $1.8 million cost would be recovered.
- Hourly paid females appeared to have about twice the absentee rate of hourly paid males.

- If absenteeism continued at the current rate or increased, the proposed changes in plant-management practices, benefits, and pay systems might prove expensive.
- The current practice of paying employees for five hours for each of the first ten days of absence in a year might be contributing to absenteeism. Nobody knew.

On the basis of this report, Parker was asked by management to develop a plan to reduce absenteeism. To get some guidance, Parker attended a one-day seminar on the subject conducted by two business school professors, which confirmed his uneasiness about the data he was getting. It was clear that annual or semi-annual summaries of the time lost were no help in diagnosing the reasons for absence or encouraging department managers to reduce it. Parker needed data on absence severity and frequency, which meant introducing a comprehensive information system.

He then decided to meet with all managers and supervisors, as well as with the executive of the employee committee. He wanted to persuade them that absenteeism was costly and that, if they measured it properly, they would be able to design programs to combat it. They agreed. In the meeting, the plant manager stressed that there could be no overnight cures to a situation that had taken years to develop.

Next, a five-day study conducted by the two business school professors confirmed that a computer program they had created could be modified for use at the plant. A task force chaired by Robert Matthews, one of Parker's employee-relations officers, was set up to do the job, which took from March to July of the following year. During this period, the members of the task force decided that data should be collected on any absences of a half-day or more and devised a data-collection system to be controlled by department secretaries. They began collecting new information from July onward, but also decided to recapture data from time cards for the January-to-July period. They felt that revised figures for the first six months of the year would be useful for comparison purposes, even though they would not be as accurate as the new information.

The first report was a shock. It showed the absenteeism rate for the month of July at 7.1 percent and for the preceding six months at an average of 6 percent. It was clear that the new system and the standardized reporting procedures were catching many absences that had previously gone unreported. But the variation between departments that the old information had shown was still there. The lowest of the departments recorded a 3.6 percent absenteeism rate, while the highest had 9.5 percent. The data also showed that the departments with the highest severity of absence weren't necessarily those with the highest frequency. For example, the paper department had a severity of 3.6 percent and a frequency of 3.2 percent, while shipping had an 8.5 percent severity and only a 2.8 percent frequency.

As the year continued, company-wide absenteeism severity decreased to 6.9 percent, 6.5 percent, and 6.1 percent in August, September, and October, respectively, with a corresponding decrease in frequency. Managers and supervisors agreed that simply being more concerned about absenteeism and letting employees know it was helping. To cut the rate still further, they wanted to develop specific goals for the next year; each department would analyze its own absenteeism and identify the training needs of its managers. They then planned to develop an absenteeism-management program.

Some managers were concerned that newly announced changes in benefits would actually increase absenteeism; all employees were to begin receiving full pay for sick days rather than the 62.5 percent they had been getting. Parker believed the risk had to be taken if the plant was to be switched to the management system in place at the other plants. Reviewing his efforts after fifteen months, Parker was pleased. He thought the problem had been tackled systematically and carefully. The new reports were more detailed and actionable. The ball was now in the court of the department managers and supervisors.

DISCUSSION ISSUES
1. What might be done to more accurately assess the significance of the absenteeism problem from a control point of view? Explain.
2. Why is the current plan of action instituted by Parker an example of effective control? Back up your answer.
3. Are there any flaws in the approach the company is taking to address the problem? What might be done to further reduce absenteeism?

From "The missing links," by Daniel Stoffman in *Canadian Business*, June 1986. Reprinted by permission of the author.

C H A P T E R

17

PRODUCTION MANAGEMENT AND CONTROL

STUDENT LEARNING OBJECTIVES

From studying this chapter, I will attempt to acquire:

1. Definitions of both *production* and *production control*.
2. An understanding of how productivity and layout patterns relate to the production process.
3. An appreciation for the significance of operations management.
4. Insights on how management by exception and break-even analysis can be used to control production.
5. An understanding of how quality control and materials requirements planning and control can contribute to production control.
6. Knowledge of how budgets and ratio analysis can be used to achieve overall or broader organizational control.

CHAPTER OUTLINE

PRODUCTION SNAGS AT COMMODORE

When Commodore International Limited, a home computer maker, began selling its Commodore 64 to mass merchandisers, only 5 to 7 percent of the machines were returned because of defects. Only a few months later, however, the rate had risen sharply. The president of CSI Distributors, Inc. said that when CSI began selling the Commodore 64, the defect rate started off at 30 percent and then went down to 15 percent. A year later, the defect rate was back up again.

Many of Commodore's problems centred around the Commodore 64 disk drive, the part of the computer that uses a floppy disk. To begin with, Commodore had opted to have the disk drives made in the Far East because of a potential savings of about $15 million annually. This decision proved troublesome for several reasons. First, the Far East manufacturer shipped the disk drives by sea, which significantly slowed deliveries. Then, an entire shipment of 170 000 Commodore disk drives was discovered to be defective. The situation apparently worsened shortly thereafter, when Commodore's disk drive maker abruptly halted production temporarily. The resulting shortage left many distributors without disk drive shipments for an average of about three months.

In an attempt to make disk drives available to its distributors, Commodore sent a rush order to its manufacturer for more than 100 000 of the drives to be sent air freight. Industry officials said, however, that Commodore's disk drive maker had a production capacity of only 50 000 units per month—far below the 8 000 to 10 000 a day capacity at Commodore's assembly plants.

In addition to the disk drive shortages and defects, Commodore had still other production problems. For example, one shipment of video screen monitors didn't fit the Commodore 64 properly. Another of Commodore's production problems involved its highest priced letter quality printer. The printer was pulled off the market because it "froze" on the print command.

Commodore's top executives, while refusing to provide any details, generally dismissed the reports of production problems as overblown. They set the defect rate of the Commodore 64 at 7 percent. Don Richard, acting vice-president at Commodore's U.S. unit, said: "Our manufacturing problems are our internal affairs. We just don't want to discuss some of this."

Based on "Commodore Hits Production Snags in Its Hot Selling Home Computer," by Dennis Kneale in *The Wall Street Journal*, October 28, 1983.

What's Ahead

The introductory case describes the reported high defect rates of various goods produced at Commodore International Limited. This chapter is designed to help managers, such as those at Commodore, who are confronted with high defect rates, as well as other production-related problems.

This chapter emphasizes the fundamentals of **production control**, which is ensuring that an organization produces goods and services as planned. The three primary discussion areas in this chapter are: (1) production; (2) operations management; and (3) production and control.

⊞ PRODUCTION

To reach organizational goals, all managers must plan, organize, influence, and control to produce some type of goods or services. Naturally, these goods and services vary significantly from organization to organization.

This production of goods and services can be explored in more detail by defining production and discussing productivity and the production facility.

Defining Production

Production is simply defined as the transformation of organizational resources into products.[1] Within this definition, *organizational resources* are all assets available to a manager to generate products, *transformation* is the set of steps necessary to change organizational resources into products, and *products* are various goods

> Production is the transformation of organizational resources into products.

467

FIGURE 17.1   Inputs, transformation processes, and outputs for three different organizations.

	Inputs	Transformation Processes	Outputs
Bus Line	Buses Gas, oil, and other supplies Terminals Drivers Ticket sellers Managers Tickets Schedules Funds Varied data	The operations system consists of selling tickets to passengers at terminals, loading buses with passengers, driving passengers to linking terminals according to schedule, and dispatching passengers at desired locations.	Transportation services to passengers
Manufacturing Firm	Trucks Plants Oil, rags, tools, and other supplies Raw materials Purchased parts Production workers Supervisors Engineers Storekeepers Bills of material Inventory records Production schedules Time records Funds Varied data	The production system consists of preparing production orders for needed or ordered products; designing products, if necessary; obtaining raw materials and parts specified by bills of material; producing and assembling products according to production schedules; recording use of materials, labor, and overhead; inspecting and packaging products, if necessary; and warehousing and shipping products to sales locations or directly to customers.	Products for use by customers

Hospital	Ambulances
	Hospital rooms
	Beds, wheelchairs,
	  X rays
	Receptionists
	Administrators
	Nurses
	Doctors
	Medicines, drugs,
	  splints, bandages,
	  food, and other
	  supplies
	Medical charts
	Funds
	Varied data
		The operations system consists
		of driving patients to hospital,
		if necessary; transporting
		patients to assigned rooms
		after being admitted; attending
		to patients' needs, including
		the administering of medication
		and drugs, taking X rays, bandaging,
		nursing, feeding, maintaining
		progress of patients on medical
		charts, and discharging patients
		upon doctor's approval.
			Health–care
			service
			to patients

From *Accounting and Information Systems* by Joseph W. Wilkinson. Copyright © 1982 John Wiley & Sons, Inc. Reprinted by permission of John Wiley & Sons Inc.

or services aimed at meeting human needs. Figure 17.1 contains examples of organizational resources (inputs), transformation processes, and goods and services produced (outputs) for each of three different types of organizations.

Productivity

Productivity is an important consideration in designing, evaluating, and improving modern production systems. The two sections that follow define productivity and discuss robotics, a means of increasing productivity.

Defining Productivity

Productivity is the relationship between the total amount of goods or services being produced (output) and the organizational resources needed (input) to produce the goods or services. This relationship is usually expressed by the following equation:[2]

$$\text{Productivity} = \frac{\text{Outputs}}{\text{Inputs}}$$

Productivity is the ratio of outputs to inputs.

The higher the value of the ratio of outputs to inputs, the higher the productivity within the production process.

Although managers should continually strive to make their production processes as productive as possible, it is no secret that over the last twenty years productivity growth related to production management and innovation in manufacturing within North America has lagged significantly behind that of countries such as Japan, West Germany, and France.[3] Some of the more traditional strategies for increasing productivity include: (1) improving the effectiveness of the organizational work force through training; (2) improving the production process through automation; (3) improving product design to make products easier to assemble; (4) improving the production facility by purchasing more modern equipment; and (5) improving the quality of workers being hired to fill open positions.

Five traditional strategies can increase productivity

The Management in Action feature for this chapter describes the increasing trend towards automation as an alternative for improving the efficiency of the production process in the traditionally low-tech retail industry. Specifically, it focuses on the developments initiated by International Retail Systems Inc. in the areas of automated point-of-sale and data collection systems targeted at the smaller end of the retail industry.

CHECKOUTS GO HIGH TECH

Twenty years ago, the self-serve gas station—with one staffer in a booth who did nothing but collect money from customers—was the ultimate in automation. But the next, inevitable step is drawing closer. With systems developed by a new Vancouver-based software firm, International Retail Systems Inc. (IRSI), motorists will pay a computer for the right to pump their own gas at an unmanned station. Adding insult to injury, the computer will charge interest on the transaction immediately, eliminating the thirty-day free float that credit card customers have long enjoyed. It's all part of the brave new world of automated point-of-sale (POS) systems, an electronic assault on a traditionally low-tech end of the retailing industry.

IRSI's edge, says president Salvatore Ruberto, lies in its unique approach to integrating systems. A filling station, for instance, has three or four operations, such as pump control, cash register, and a credit card authorization terminal. IRSI's software pulls the system together. And at some point, when debit cards replace credit cards, the system will bill the customer simultaneously.

Initially, there was little to excite investors about IRSI. In its first full fiscal year, ended October 31, 1987, it posted sales of just $1 million and managed a loss of $1.5 million. But things have since changed for the company. In March, 1988, IRSI announced the completion of two contracts that could vault the company into the big leagues: K Mart Canada Ltd. had ordered $2 million worth of hand-held data collection systems for price and inventory-checking in its 120 stores, and Fina Oil and Chemical Co. in Dallas was buying $2.2 million worth of POS software to automate 450 of its 4 000 gas stations. As a result, the company was able to report earnings of $288 823 in the quarter ending January 1988, on sales of $2.07 million.

IRSI, which projected sales of $6.3 million in 1988, works most closely as a software supplier to NCR, the world's largest point-of-sale terminal manufacturer. In most cases, IRSI writes programs in concert with NCR's 2157 POS terminal, a state-of-the-art electronic payment system that is to the traditional cash register what a computer is to a typewriter. The key to survival lies in attention to detail, says Ruberto. That means hooking up, in the case of a service station, "remote pump control devices, a card authorization terminal and data catcher, cash register, underground tank reader and electronic sign changers. Separately installed, that would run anywhere from $12 000 to $20 000." IRSI can integrate all of this with an NCR 2157 for $7 000 to $8 000, with the capability of providing similar packages to any other retail environment.

High economic payoff is the main reason why giants like NCR and IBM agree to have as a partner—or, at least, to avoid competition with—a small, creative organization such as IRSI. According to Assa Manhas, a systems consultant based in Vancouver who owns shares in IRSI, the giants tend to be preoccupied with major retail buyers, while 90 percent of all retailers are small operations that require a high degree of creativity. That's difficult for a huge organization to respond to." Deborah Hackworth, Fina's point-of-sale project manager, says that smaller units such as convenience stores and filling station outlets are generally staffed by junior personnel who require many duties to be done for them, thus increasing the need for creativity in software development.

The importance of creativity is reflected in IRSI'S staff: The company employs forty people, twenty-eight of them in systems and application development. IRSI also has a full complement of "beancounters": Apart from Ruberto and company co-founders Dwight and Nancy Romanica, "everybody on the board is an accountant."

IRSI's financial strategy for the near future will be to pump money into four areas: marketing, setting up a U.S. company, acquisitions (to enhance IRSI's marketing strengths), and continued R&D (research and development) buildup. With an earnings base established in both the U.S. and Canada, IRSI may well have an important edge over competitors already—both Fina and K Mart have many more U.S. outlets that could be automated. Overall, IRSI's customer list includes convenience-store chains in the U.S. and Canada, specialty retailers, grocery chains, and other oil companies.

Based on "Checkouts go high tech," by William Annett in *Financial Times of Canada*, March 14, 1988. Used with permission.

FIGURE 17.2   Three common applications of robots during production.

Robot Operations	Description of Operations
Assembly operations	Activities involved in constructing products. Various types of welding, parts insertion, wiring, and soldering are stressed. The automobile industry and the electronics industry commonly use robots for assembly operations.
Materials handling operations	Activities that involve moving materials from one point to another during the manufacturing process — including point-to-point transfers, machine loading, and loading and unloading palletized goods. Materials handling is one area where growth in robotics is anticipated for smaller manufacturing firms.
Spraying operations	Activities that involve applying necessary liquids during various stages of the production process. The application of paint, stain, lacquer, sealants, and rustproofing is common. Automobile and major appliance manufacturers are among the largest users of robots for spraying operations.

Based on Roger H. Mitchell and Vincent A. Mabert, "Robotics for Smaller Manufacturers: Myths and Realities," *Business Horizons* (July/August 1986): 9–16.

Robotics: A Means of Increasing Productivity

The preceding section presented a number of more traditional means for increasing productivity within organizations. Robotics, however, shows promising signs of increasing productivity in a more revolutionary way.

The use of robots is a growing trend.

Robotics is the area of study dealing with the development and use of robots. A **robot** is a machine in the form of a human being that performs the mechanical functions of a human being but lacks sensitivity. Three of today's most commonly used applications of robots during production processes are presented in Figure 17.2. The role of the robot of the future, however, will become far more complex in industrial applications as robot manufacturers master higher levels of robot design. The use of the robot as a stand-alone piece of manufacturing equipment will diminish in importance. Linking robots to many forms of production in order to achieve full factory automation will be stressed.[4]

Naturally, there are potential advantages and disadvantages to using robots to perform work functions. One disadvantage is that, since workers are generally threatened by loss of jobs, the use of robots can strain relations between management and labour.[5] An advantage, of course, is that robots can take over boring factory jobs and allow people to perform more interesting and more motivating jobs.

Robotics has its advantages and disadvantages.

The Production Facility: Layout Patterns

In addition to understanding the production process and how productivity relates to it, managers should also be aware of various layout patterns that can be used within a production facility. A **layout pattern** is the overall arrangement of machines, equipment, materials handling, aisles, service areas, storage areas, and

A layout pattern is an arrangement of a number of variables to maximize productivity.

work stations within a production facility. The primary objective of layout is to optimize the arrangement of these variables so that their total contribution to the production process is maximized.[6]

There are three basic layout patterns:

1. **Process layout** is a layout pattern based primarily on grouping similar types of equipment. Hospitals, automobile repair shops, and department stores would use process layout.
2. **Product layout** is a layout pattern based on the progressive steps by which a product is made. The automobile assembly line and furniture manufacturing are areas where product layout could be used.
3. **Fixed position layout** is a layout pattern that, because of the weight or bulk of the product being manufactured, has workers, tools, and materials rotating around a stationary product. Ships and airplanes usually are manufactured with the fixed position layout.

Figure 17.3 illustrates each of the three basic layout patterns.

FIGURE 17.3   Three basic layout patterns.

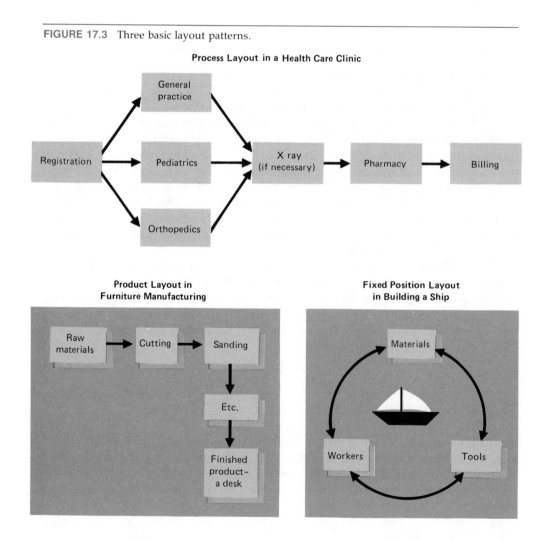

FIGURE 17.4   Criteria for effective and efficient plant layout.

Effective and efficient plant layout has:

1. Straight aisles to minimize worker and materials movement.
2. Minimum handling of materials between manufacturing or assembly operations.
3. Short distances over which materials must be moved.
4. Beginning production steps occurring as close as possible to place where resources are received from suppliers.
5. Ending production steps occurring as close as possible to place where finished goods are shipped to customers.
6. Adequate storage for tools and equipment.
7. The ability to be changed easily as circumstances change.
8. Maximum use of all production facilities.
9. Desirable levels of control for production nuisances, such as noise, dust, and heat.
10. An effective and efficient system for scrap removal.

From *Plant Layout and Materials Handling* by James M. Apple. Copyright © 1977 John Wiley & Sons, Inc., New York. Reprinted by permission of John Wiley & Sons, Inc.

In practice, what constitutes the most appropriate or "best" layout pattern differs from organization to organization. There are, however, several criteria for judging the effectiveness and efficiency of a layout pattern, regardless of the organization in which it exists. Several of these characteristics are listed in Figure 17.4.[7]

OPERATIONS MANAGEMENT

Operations management deals with managing production in organizations. The sections that follow define *operations management* and the steps involved in its use.

Defining Operations Management

According to Chase and Aquilano, **operations management** is the performance of the managerial activities entailed in selecting, designing, operating, controlling, and updating production systems.[8] Figure 17.5 describes each of these activities and categorizes them as being either periodic or continual. The distinction between periodic and continual activities is based upon the relative frequency of their performance: Periodic activities are performed from time to time, while continual activities are performed essentially without interruption.

Operations management is managing production systems.

FIGURE 17.5   Major activities performed to manage production.

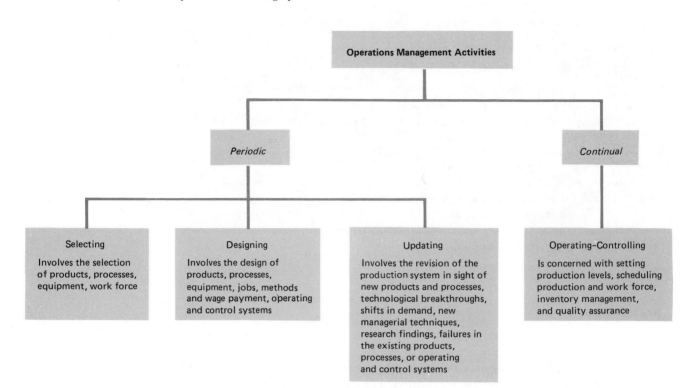

Steps in Operations Management

Successful operations management requires that managers determine:

1. The type and amount of resources needed.

There are four major steps to managing production successfully. Normally, these steps should be performed in the following order:

Step 1: Production planning   **Production planning** is determining the type and amount of resources needed to produce specified goods or services. Production planning is the foundation step in operations management in that it determines the effectiveness of the operations management steps that follow. Other general issues involved in production planning include: (1) How much should be produced? (2) At what level should inventory be kept? and (3) What materials should be ordered and from which suppliers?

2. The sequencing of work.

Step 2: Routing   **Routing** is determining the sequence in which work must be completed to produce specified goods or services. In essence, routing determines the path through a plant that materials acquired during production planning must take to become finished products. For example, wood acquired to produce furniture must be cut, sanded, glued, painted, and so on.

Step 3: Scheduling   **Scheduling** is the process of: (1) formulating detailed listings of activities that must be performed to accomplish a task; (2) allocating resources necessary to complete the task; and (3) setting up and following timetables for completing the task. Gantt charts and PERT networks are two useful scheduling tools.[9]

3. How to get the work done.

Step 4: Dispatching   **Dispatching** is simply issuing orders to those individuals actually involved in producing goods or services. Dispatching takes the results of production planning, routing, and scheduling, and puts them into actual operation within the organization.

4. How to put the other steps into operation.

BACK TO THE CASE

The high defect rate of manufactured goods at Commodore International Limited, as presented in the introductory case, may be a result of the way in which resources like people, equipment, and materials at Commodore are transformed into products—for example, the Commodore 64 and video-screen monitors.

Although the level of productivity at Commodore is not specifically mentioned in the case, managers within the company must strive to increase it to obtain the maximum number of products manufactured for the level of resources invested in the production process. In striving to increase productivity at Commodore, managers can take such actions as implementing more effective training programs for employees and being more selective in hiring people. In addition, Commodore managers should also evaluate the possibility of using robots to produce products. Besides potentially increasing productivity, the robots probably would make fewer production errors than humans.

Product layout probably would be the most advisable layout pattern for Commodore. Most high-tech manufacturers have found that efficient and effective production of their products requires using progressive steps, a type of assembly-line situation. Indeed, rotating workers, materials, and tools around a single Commodore 64 (fixed position layout) probably would be very inefficient. Commodore might also want to consider, however, if there would be any advantages to using process layout instead of product layout.

As the introductory case implies, managers at Commodore must spend much time managing production, or performing operations management activities. In essence, these managers are involved in selecting, designing, operating, controlling, and updating the Commodore production process. To carry out their operations management responsibilities, Commodore managers perform the sequential steps of production planning, routing, scheduling, and dispatching.

PRODUCTION AND CONTROL

A **control tool** is a specific procedure or technique that presents pertinent organizational information in such a way that managers are aided in developing and implementing appropriate control strategy. Control tools help managers pinpoint the organizational strengths and weaknesses on which useful control strategy must focus. This section discusses specific control tools for production as well as for broader organizational control.

Control tools provide information for implementing control strategy.

Control Tools for Production

Some of the best-known and most commonly used control tools are: (1) management by exception; (2) break-even analysis; (3) materials requirements planning and control; and (4) quality control. The specific purpose of these tools is to control the production of organizational goods and services.

Management by Exception

Management by exception is a control technique that allows only significant deviations between planned and actual performance to be brought to a manager's attention.[10] Actually, management by exception is based on the exception principle, a management principle that appears very early in management literature.[11] The exception principle recommends that subordinates handle all routine organizational matters, while managers handle only non-routine or exceptional organizational issues.

Although these exceptional issues might be uncovered when managers themselves detect significant deviation between standards and actual performance, some managers establish special rules aimed at allowing exceptional issues to surface as a matter of normal operating procedure. Two examples of such rules are:[12]

1. A department manager must immediately inform the plant manager if actual weekly labour costs exceed estimated weekly labour costs by more than 15 percent.
2. A department manager must immediately inform the plant manager if actual dollars spent plus estimated dollars to be spent on a special project exceed the funds approved for the project by more than 10 percent.

These rules focus on production-related expenditures. However, such rules can be established in virtually any organizational area.

If appropriately administered, management by exception yields the added advantage of ensuring the best use of a manager's time. Since management by exception brings only significant issues to the manager's attention, the possibility that the manager will spend valuable time working on relatively insignificant issues is automatically eliminated.

Of course, the significant issues brought to a manager's attention could be organizational strengths as well as organizational weaknesses. The manager should try to eliminate the weaknesses and reinforce the strengths.

Break-Even Analysis

Another production-related control tool commonly used by managers is break-even analysis. **Break-even analysis** is the process of generating information that summarizes various levels of profit or loss associated with various levels of production. The following sections discuss: (1) the basic ingredients of break-even analysis; (2) types of break-even analysis available to managers; and (3) the relationship between break-even analysis and controlling.

Basic Ingredients of Break-Even Analysis

Break-even analysis typically includes reflection, discussion, reasoning, and decision making relative to the following seven major ingredients:

1. *Fixed Costs*   **Fixed costs** are expenses incurred by the organization regardless of the number of products produced. Examples of these costs would be real estate taxes, upkeep to the exterior of a business building, and interest expenses on money borrowed to finance the purchase of equipment.
2. *Variable costs*   Expenses that fluctuate with the number of products produced are called **variable costs**. Examples of variable costs include costs of packaging a product, costs of materials needed to make the product, and costs associated with packing products to prepare them for shipping.

3. *Total costs*   **Total costs** are simply the sum of fixed costs and variable costs associated with production.

4. *Total revenue*   **Total revenue** is all sales dollars accumulated from selling manufactured products. Naturally, total revenue increases as more products are sold.

5. *Profits*   **Profits** are defined as that amount of total revenue that exceeds the total costs of producing the products sold.

6. *Loss*   **Loss** is that amount of the total costs of producing a product that exceeds the total revenue gained from selling the product.

7. *Break-even point*   A **break-even point** is the situation wherein the total revenue of an organization equals its total costs; the organization is generating only enough revenue to cover its costs. The company is neither gaining a profit nor incurring a loss.

Types of Break-Even Analysis

There are two somewhat different procedures for determining the same break-even point for an organization: algebraic break-even analysis and graphic break-even analysis.[13]

Algebraic Break-Even Analysis   The following simple formula is commonly used to determine that level of production at which an organization breaks even:

$$BE = \frac{FC}{P - VC}$$

where—

BE = that level of production where the firm breaks even
FC = total fixed costs of production
 P = price at which each individual unit is sold to customers
VC = variable costs associated with each unit manufactured and sold

Two sequential steps must be followed to use this formula to calculate a break-even point. First, the variable costs associated with producing each unit must be subtracted from the price at which each unit will sell. The purpose of this calculation is to determine how much of the selling price of each unit sold can go toward covering total fixed costs incurred from producing all units. The second step is to divide the remainder calculated in step one into total fixed costs. The purpose of this calculation is to determine how many units must be produced and sold to cover fixed costs. This number of units is the break-even point for the organization.

For example, a textbook publisher could face the fixed costs and variable costs per textbook presented in Figure 17.6. If the publisher wants to sell each textbook for twelve dollars, the break-even point could be calculated as follows:

$$BE = \frac{\$88\ 800}{\$12 - \$6}$$

$$BE = \frac{\$88\ 800}{\$6}$$

$$BE = 14\ 800\ \text{copies}$$

This calculation indicates that, if expenses and selling price remain stable, the textbook publisher will incur a loss if book sales are fewer than 14 800 copies,

FIGURE 17.6   Fixed costs and variable costs for textbook publisher.

Fixed Costs (Yearly Basis)		Variable Costs per Textbook Sold	
1. Real estate taxes on property	$ 1 000	1. Printing	$2.00
2. Interest on loan to purchase equipment	5 000	2. Artwork	1.00
3. Building maintenance	2 000	3. Sales commission	.50
4. Insurance	800	4. Author royalties	1.50
5. Salaried labour	80 000	5. Binding	1.00
Total fixed costs	$88 800	Total variable costs per textbook	$6.00

break even if book sales equal 14 800 copies, and make a profit if book sales exceed 14 800 copies.

Graphic Break-Even Analysis   Graphic break-even analysis entails the construction of a graph that shows all critical elements within a break-even analysis. Figure 17.7 is a break-even graph for the textbook publisher mentioned in the previous section.

Using the Algebraic and Graphic Break-Even Methods   Both the algebraic and graphic methods of break-even analysis for the textbook publisher result in the same break-even point of 14 800 books produced and sold. However, the processes used to arrive at this break-even point are quite different.

The algebraic method is quick,

The situation managers face usually determines which break-even method they should use. For example, if managers simply desire a quick yet accurate

FIGURE 17.7   Break-even analysis for textbook publisher.

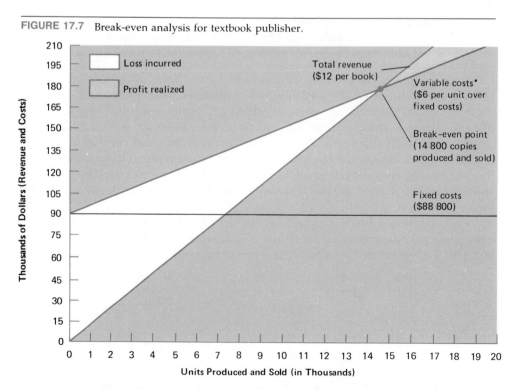

*Note that by drawing the variable costs line on top of the fixed costs line, variable costs have been added to fixed costs. Therefore, the variable costs line also represents total costs.

determination of a break-even point, the algebraic method generally suffices. On the other hand, if managers desire a more complete picture of the cumulative relationships between a break-even point, fixed costs, and escalating variable costs, the graphic break-even method probably is more useful. The textbook publisher could quickly and easily see from Figure 17.7 the cumulative relationships between fixed costs, escalating variable costs, and potential profit and loss associated with various levels of production.

but the graphic method gives a more complete picture.

Control and Break-Even Analysis

Break-even analysis is a useful control tool because it helps managers understand the relationships between fixed costs, variable costs, total costs, and profit and loss within an organization. Once these relationships are understood, managers can take steps to modify one or more of these variables to reduce significant deviation between planned profit levels and actual profit levels.[14] Increasing costs and/or decreasing selling prices have the overall effect of increasing the number of units an organization must produce and sell to break even. Conversely, managerial strategy for decreasing the number of units an organization must produce and sell to break even entails lowering or stabilizing fixed and variable costs, and/or increasing the selling price of each unit. The exact break-even control strategy a particular manager should develop and implement is dictated primarily by the manager's unique organizational situation.

Break-even analysis helps managers control profit levels.

BACK TO THE CASE

There are useful production control tools that Commodore management could use to ensure that the Commodore 64 and other products are produced as planned. Management by exception is one of these tools. The implementation of management by exception would allow Commodore workers to handle all routine production and bring only exceptional matters to management's attention. The successful use of management by exception at Commodore probably would be characterized by a number of carefully designed rules. One such rule might be that when 10 percent or more of materials purchased to be used in the production of the Commodore 64 are defective, a production worker must bring this fact to the attention of the production supervisor and the purchasing manager. The production supervisor could then inspect products more carefully to ensure that a significant number are not manufactured with defective parts, and the purchasing manager could contact the supplier for an upgrading of future delivered materials and an allowance for defective materials already delivered.

In addition to management by exception, Commodore management also could use break-even analysis as a control tool. Break-even analysis would furnish Commodore management with information regarding various levels of profit or loss associated with various levels of production. To use break-even analysis, Commodore management would have to determine total

fixed costs necessary to operate a production facility, the price at which each unit is to be offered, and the variable costs associated with producing each of those units.

For example, if Commodore management wanted to determine how many Commodore 64s had to be sold before the company would break even on that product alone, management could arrive at this break-even point algebraically by following three steps. First, management would have to total all fixed costs attributable to the Commodore 64. Examples would be lighting expenses and real estate taxes. Second, Commodore management would have to total all variable costs associated with selling each Commodore 64 and subtract this total from the price at which each unit is to be sold. Variable costs would include such expenses as the costs of materials and labour needed to produce the Commodore 64. Finally, Commodore management would have to divide the answer calculated in step 2 into the answer derived in step 1. This figure would tell management how many 64s had to be sold to break even.

Commodore management also could arrive at this break-even point by constructing a graph that showed fixed costs, variable costs, and selling price. The graph probably would provide Commodore management with a more useful picture for formulating profit-oriented production plans.

Materials require-
ments planning plots
the flow of materials.

Materials Requirements Planning and Control

Materials requirements planning is the third control tool that can increase the effectiveness and efficiency of the production process. **Materials requirements planning** is the process of creating schedules that identify specific parts and materials required to produce an item, the exact quantities of each needed to enhance the organizational production process, and the dates when orders for these quantities should be released to suppliers and be received for best timing within the production cycle.[15]

Figure 17.8 shows the main elements of a materials requirements planning system. As can be seen from this figure, the computer can be an important part of the materials requirements planning process. Input data for the computer comes from three main sources: (1) a master production schedule based on orders from consumers, sales forecasts or product demand, and plant capacity; (2) a bill of material file that considers product design changes in determining the types and quantities of materials needed within the production process; and (3) an inventory file that contains types and quantities of materials presently on hand. The computer then generates output reports that indicate what materials should be ordered or cancelled as well as what materials should be expedited or de-expedited.

A Japanese management technique sometimes considered a component of materials requirements planning is just-in-time (JIT) inventory control. The discussion of that technique, which appears in Chapter 20, will provide a richer

FIGURE 17.8   Basic elements of a materials requirements planning system.

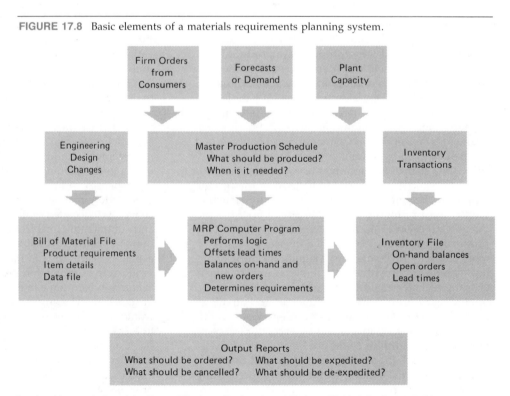

Reprinted by permission of the *Harvard Business Review*. An exhibit from "Behind the Growth in Material Requirements Planning" by Jeffrey G. Miller and Linda G. Sprague (September/October 1975): 84. Copyright © 1975 by the President and Fellows of Harvard College; all rights reserved.

understanding of the potential value of materials requirements planning to the organization.

Naturally, materials requirements planning is closely related to materials requirements control. **Materials requirements control** is simply the process of making things happen the way they were planned to happen in materials requirements planning.

Quality Control

Quality control is the process of making the quality of finished goods and services what it was planned to be. Managers compare product quality to organizational quality standards and take steps to increase, decrease, or maintain the level of product quality as dictated by the situation.[16] Products too high in quality can be too expensive to produce, while products too low in quality can alienate customers.

Product inspection may be limited to finished products or be extended to such areas as materials purchased for inventory, materials available from various suppliers, and progress inspections at different stages of production. As the cartoon illustrates, customers today are becoming intolerant of low-quality and defective merchandise.

Managers must not only determine what products or product components to inspect, but also how many products or components to inspect. One method of addressing this question is called statistical quality control.[17] **Statistical quality control** is a process used to determine how many products from a larger number should be inspected to calculate a probability that the total number of products meets organizational quality standards. Although managers limit inspection expenses by not examining all products, they must be very careful to ensure that the number of products being inspected gives an accurate measurement of the quality of a significant number of the products being produced.

Quality control measures planned versus actual product quality.

Statistical quality control determines how many units to inspect.

"Unless I'm misinterpreting the signs, gentlemen, we are approaching the end of the golden age of shoddy merchandise."

New Yorker, *December 19, 1983, p. 45. Drawing by Weber;*
© 1983 *The New Yorker Magazine, Inc.*

BACK TO THE CASE

Two additional production control tools that probably would be useful to Commodore management are materials requirements planning and control, and quality control. Materials requirements planning for the Commodore 64 would involve creating work schedules that identify specific parts and materials necessary to produce the units, determining the quantities of each needed to get maximum use of the Commodore production system, and pinpointing dates when orders for these items should be released and materials actually received from suppliers. Commodore management undoubtedly would find that the Commodore 64 itself would be invaluable in administering the complexity of the materials requirements planning process.

Materials requirements control at Commodore would involve Commodore management following up to make sure that events occur as planned during the process of materials requirements planning. If shipments of materials are not arriving as planned, for example, Commodore management must contact suppliers to expedite deliveries.

Since the most serious issue at Commodore, as depicted in the introductory case, is that of poor quality products, quality control should be an important concern of Commodore management. Commodore management must plan for some desirable level of Commodore 64 quality—neither too high nor too low—and then take steps to ensure that planned levels of quality are indeed present in the finished computers. A very important part of this quality control process would involve inspection. Commodore management first must determine *what* should be inspected—materials purchased for inventory, materials available from various suppliers, different stages of Commodore 64 production, and/or finished Commodore 64s. Then management must decide *how many* should be inspected—every Commodore 64 unit in production, all materials purchased from all suppliers, or only some proportion of each. Statistical quality control is one tool Commodore management can use to minimize inspection expenses without sacrificing accuracy of measurements of product quality.

As implied in the introductory case, Commodore in the past has somewhat limited its alternatives concerning when to inspect by subcontracting the manufacturing of certain product components. Commodore inspected subcontracted components only after they were completed, and that was too late, since the components were already defective on delivery.

Tools for Broader Organizational Control

Organizational control requires an understanding of production.

The control tools discussed in the preceding sections are commonly applied directly to the production process. The following sections discuss control tools that do not relate as directly to the production process: budgets and ratio analysis. Since the production process has impact on virtually all phases of organizational existence, however, a thorough understanding of the production process is a prerequisite for the successful use of even these control tools.

Budgets

A budget is a planning tool and a control tool.

As described in Chapter 7, a budget is a single-use financial plan that covers a specified length of time. The **budget** of an organization is its financial plan outlining how funds in a given period will be spent, as well as how they will be obtained.

In addition to being a financial plan, however, a budget is also a control tool.[18] As managers gather information on actual receipts and expenditures within an operating period, significant deviation from budgeted amounts may be uncovered. In such a case, managers can develop and implement a control strategy aimed at making actual performance more consistent with planned performance. This, of course, assumes that the plan contained in the budget is appropriate for the organization.

An illustration of how a budget can be used as an organizational plan as well as an organizational control tool is the following fictitious situation concerning a Father Walter James, rector and manager of St. Matthew's church. In response to organizational objectives, Father James developed a simple budget for St. Matthew's church (see Figure 17.9). The budget is actually Father James's financial plan of how money will be spent to achieve organizational objectives.

In addition, however, Father James can use this budget as a control tool. For example, as actual office supplies and expenses approach their maximum budgeted allowance of $2 250 during an operating period, Father James conceivably can take steps to minimize further expenditures in this area. On the other hand, after analyzing the entire situation carefully, Father James may decide to increase the budgeted amount for office supplies and expenses. Since the total amount of resources for this church or any other organization probably is fixed, an increase of the budgeted amount for one expense typically requires an equal decrease in the budgeted amount for another expense. For example, increasing the budgeted

FIGURE 17.9 Operating budget for St. Matthew's church, 1983.

Disbursements		
Diocesan assessment	$17 220.00	
Clergy salary	16 368.00	
Secretary salary	7 200.00	
Sexton	6 463.00	
Organist/St. Matthew's choirmaster salary	4 576.00	
Social security	2 000.00	
Housing allowance	3 000.00	
Auto lease	3 072.00	
Auto gas allowance	1 100.00	
Pastoral care	350.00	
Pension premium	3 500.00	
Utilities	7 920.00	
Housekeeping	2 400.00	
Repairs to property (bldg. fund)	5 000.00	
Telephone	1 760.00	
Office supplies & expenses	2 250.00	
Postage	700.00	
Bulletins & printing	1 500.00	
Kitchen supplies & expense	3 000.00	
Organ maintenance	200.00	
T. H. Greater Fed. of Churches	100.00	
Church school	2 500.00	
Worship commission		
Planning commission		
Social concerns commission		
Youth commission		
Rector's funds (music, adult education, special programs)	4 500.00	
Other expenses	3 200.00	
Convention delegate expense	800.00	
Insurance	5 500.00	
Sexton's insurance	500.00	
Clergy assistance	1 000.00	
Altar supplies	2 000.00	
Garden maintenance	500.00	
Total Disbursements	$110 179.00	
Receipts		
For general purposes:		
Plate offerings	$ 501.47	
Pledge payments	74 761.11	
Parish organizations:		
Treasure House	1 320.00	
St. Thomas's Guild	2 019.32	
From diocese	325.00	
Other miscellaneous sources	828.59	
Investment income	16 645.00	$96 400.49
For special parish use:		
Communion alms	1 240.19	
Building fund (steeple repair)	1 050.00	
Designated gifts and memorials	1 239.25	
Miscellaneous sources	485.00	$ 4 014.44
For work outside parish		$ 152.55
Nonincome receipts:		
From endowment trust transfers		$13 552.75
Day school		16 918.28
Total Receipts		$131 038.51

allowance for office supplies and expenses from $2 250 to $3 250 typically would require a $1 000 reduction in the budgeted amounts for other organizational expenses.

The following sections discuss potential pitfalls of budgets and people considerations in using budgets.

Potential Pitfalls of Budgets

To maximize the benefits of using budgets, managers must be able to avoid several potential pitfalls. These pitfalls include:

1. *Placing too much emphasis on relatively insignificant organizational expenses* As a general guideline for preparing and implementing a budget, managers should allocate more time for dealing with significant organizational expenses than for relatively insignificant organizational expenses. For example, the amount of time managers spend on developing and implementing a budget for labour costs typically should be much more than the amount of time managers spend on developing and implementing a budget for office supplies.

2. *Increasing budgeted expenses year after year without adequate information* It does not necessarily follow that items contained in last year's budget should be increased this year. Perhaps the best-known method developed to overcome this potential pitfall is zero-base budgeting.[19] **Zero-base budgeting** is a planning and budgeting process that requires managers to justify their entire budget request in detail rather than simply to refer to budget amounts established in previous years.[20]

The U.S. Department of Agriculture's Office of Budget and Finance used the following instructions to implement its zero-base budgeting program:

> A new concept has been adopted for [this year's] agency estimates; namely, that of zero-base budgeting. This means that all programs will be reviewed from the ground up and not merely in terms of changes proposed for the budget year . . . The total work program of each agency must be subjected to an intensive review and evaluation. . . . Consideration must be given to the basic need for the work contemplated, the level at which the work should be carried out, the benefits to be received, and the costs to be incurred.
>
> The fact that certain activities have been carried out for a number of years will not, per se, adequately justify their continuation. Nor will the fact that programs are prescribed by statutory law necessarily be a controlling consideration. Program goals based on statutes enacted to meet problems or needs that are today of lesser priority must be reevaluated in terms of present conditions.
>
> It is implied in the zero-base budget approach that the need for programs and their recommended magnitude in [this] fiscal year . . . be clearly and specifically demonstrated . . . The justification should be prepared on the assumption that all information needed for making budget decisions should be included.[21]

3. *Ignoring the fact that budgets must be changed periodically* Managers should recognize that such factors as costs of materials, newly developed technology, and product demand are constantly changing and that budgets should be reviewed and modified periodically in response to these changes. A special type of budget called a variable budget is sometimes used to determine automatically such needed changes in budgets. **Variable budgets** outline various levels of resources to be allocated for each organizational activity, depending on the level of production within the organization. It follows, then, that a variable budget automatically indicates increases or decreases in the amount of resources allocated for various organizational activities, depending on

whether production levels increase or decrease. Variable budgets also have been called flexible budgets.

People Considerations in Using Budgets

Many managers feel that, although budgets are valuable planning and control tools, they can result in major human relations problems in an organization. For example, in a classic article by Chris Argyris, budgets are shown to build pressures that unite workers against management, cause harmful conflict between management and factory workers, and create tensions that result in worker inefficiency and worker aggression against management.[22] Depending on the severity of such problems, budgets may result in more harm to the organization than good.

Several strategies have been suggested to minimize the human relations problems caused by budgets. The most often recommended of these strategies is the design and implementation of appropriate human relations training programs for finance personnel, accounting personnel, production supervisors, and all other key people involved in the formulation and use of budgets. These training programs should be designed to emphasize both the advantages and disadvantages of applying pressure on people through budgets and the possible results of using budgets to imply organizational member success or failure.[23]

Budgets can cause people problems.

Training can help minimize these problems.

BACK TO THE CASE

Budgets and ratio analysis are control tools available to Commodore management for broader organizational control. The prerequisite for gaining maximum benefit from the use of these tools, however, is a thorough understanding of Commodore's production process.

A budget would be Commodore's financial plan indicating how much money should be spent on such items as salaries, materials, and equipment. The budget, once prepared, would be a source of information to Commodore management regarding what steps for control, if any, should be taken. For example, if 60 percent of the annual allowance for production workers is already used up with 70 percent of the year still remaining, Commodore management must assess the situation carefully to determine what, if anything, must

be done. Management could decide to cut wages, lay off certain workers, or increase the salary allowance in the budget and decrease the monetary commitment to some other budget item such as advertising.

To use budgets successfully, Commodore management must focus on significant expenses rather than minor ones, attempt to rejustify budgeted expenses at Commodore each time a budget is revised, and change the amounts allocated to various budgeted expenses as conditions change. Commodore management also must keep in mind that budgets can cause human relations problems and that training that focuses on how to minimize such problems should be provided for all people involved in formulating and using Commodore budgets.

Ratio Analysis

In addition to budgets, the second tool for broader organizational control is ratio analysis.[24] A *ratio* is a relationship between two numbers that is calculated by dividing one number into the other. **Ratio analysis** is the process of generating information that summarizes the financial position of an organization by calculating ratios based on various financial measures that appear on the organization's balance sheet and income statement.[25] The ratios available to managers for controlling organizations typically are divided into four categories: (1) liquidity ratios; (2) leverage ratios; (3) activity ratios; and (4) profitability ratios.

Ratios are relationships.

Liquidity Ratios

Liquidity ratios indi-
cate ability to meet
financial obligations:

Ratios that indicate an organization's ability to meet upcoming financial obligations are called **liquidity ratios**. The more an organization is able to meet these obligations, the more liquid it is said to be. As a general rule, organizations should be liquid enough to meet these obligations, yet not so liquid that too many financial resources are sitting idle in anticipation of meeting upcoming debts. The two main types of liquidity ratios are the current ratio and the quick ratio.

1. Can the organiza-
tion meet current
debts?

The **current ratio** is calculated by dividing the dollar value of the organization's current assets by the dollar value of its current liabilities:

$$\text{Current ratio} = \frac{\text{Current assets}}{\text{Current liabilities}}$$

Current assets typically include cash, accounts receivable, and inventory, while current liabilities generally include accounts payable, short-term notes payable, and any other accrued expenses. The current ratio indicates to managers the organization's ability to meet its financial obligations in the short term.

2. Can the organiza-
tion meet current
debts without
inventory?

The **quick ratio**, sometimes called the acid-test ratio, is computed by subtracting inventory from current assets and then dividing the difference by current liabilities.

$$\text{Quick ratio} = \frac{\text{Current assets} - \text{Inventory}}{\text{Current liabilities}}$$

The quick ratio is the same as the current ratio except that it does not include inventory in current assets. Since inventory can be difficult to convert into money or securities, the quick ratio gives managers information on the organization's ability to meet its financial obligations with no reliance on inventory.

Leverage Ratios

Leverage ratios deal
with using borrowed
funds:

Leverage ratios indicate the relationships between organizational funds supplied by the owners of an organization and organizational funds supplied by various creditors. The more organizational funds furnished by creditors, the more leverage an organization is said to be employing. As a general guideline, an organization should use leverage to the extent that borrowed funds can be used to generate additional profit without a significant amount of organizational ownership being established by creditors. Perhaps the two most commonly used leverage ratios are the debt ratio and the times interest earned ratio.

1. Who provides organi-
zational funding?

The **debt ratio** is calculated by dividing total organizational debt by total organizational assets:

$$\text{Debt ratio} = \frac{\text{Total debts}}{\text{Total assets}}$$

In essence, this ratio gives the percentage of all organizational assets provided by organizational creditors. Whereas some managers strongly caution against using too much debt to finance an organization, Barclay Morely, the chairman and chief executive of Stauffer's, supports the theory that experiencing some debt is a critical ingredient of building a successful organization.[26]

2. Can the organiza-
tion pay interest
expenses?

The **times interest earned ratio** is calculated by dividing gross income, or earnings before interest and taxes, by the total amount of organizational interest charges incurred from borrowing needed resources:

$$\text{Times interest earned ratio} = \frac{\text{Gross income}}{\text{Interest charges}}$$

This ratio indicates the organization's ability to pay interest expenses directly from gross income.

Activity Ratios

Activity ratios indicate how well an organization is selling its products in relation to its available resources. Obviously, management's goal is to maximize the amount of sales per dollar invested in organizational resources. Three main activity ratios are: (1) inventory turnover; (2) fixed assets turnover; and (3) total assets turnover.

Activity ratios evaluate organizational performance:

Inventory turnover is calculated by dividing organizational sales by the inventory:

1. Is too much invested in inventory?

$$\text{Inventory turnover} = \frac{\text{Sales}}{\text{Inventory}}$$

This ratio indicates whether an organization is maintaining an appropriate level of inventory in relation to its sales volume. In general, as sales volume increases or decreases, an organization's inventory level should fluctuate correspondingly.

Fixed assets turnover is calculated by dividing fixed assets, or plant and equipment, into total sales:

2. Is too much invested in fixed assets?

$$\text{Fixed assets turnover} = \frac{\text{Sales}}{\text{Fixed assets}}$$

This ratio indicates the appropriateness of the amount of funds invested in plant and equipment relative to the level of sales.

Total assets turnover is calculated by dividing sales by total assets:

3. Is too much invested in total assets?

$$\text{Total assets turnover} = \frac{\text{Sales}}{\text{Total assets}}$$

The focus of this ratio is on the appropriateness of the level of funds the organization has tied up in all assets relative to its rate of sales.

Profitability Ratios

Profitability ratios focus on assessing overall organizational profitability and improving it wherever possible. Major profitability ratios include the profit to sales ratio and the profit to total assets ratio.

Profitability ratios focus on making a profit:

The **profit to sales ratio** is calculated by dividing the net profit of an organization by its total sales:

1. Is the organization making enough profit per sales dollar?

$$\text{Profit to sales ratio} = \frac{\text{Net profit}}{\text{Sales}}$$

This ratio indicates whether or not the organization is making an adequate net profit in relation to the total dollars coming into the organization.

The **profit to total assets ratio** is calculated by dividing the net profit of an organization by its total assets:

2. Is the organization making enough profit per dollar invested in total assets?

$$\text{Profit to total assets ratio} = \frac{\text{Net profit}}{\text{Total assets}}$$

This ratio indicates whether or not the organization is realizing enough net profit in relation to the total dollars invested in assets.

Using Ratios to Control Organizations

Managers should review all ratios at once,

Managers can use ratio analysis in three ways to control an organization.[27] First, managers should evaluate all ratios simultaneously. This strategy ensures that managers develop and implement a control strategy appropriate for the organization as a whole rather than one that best suits only one phase or segment of the organization.

compare organizational values to industry averages,

Second, managers should compare computed values for ratios in a specific organization with the values of industry averages for those same ratios. Managers can increase the probability of formulating and implementing appropriate control strategy by comparing their financial situation to those of competitors.

and use ratios to determine financial trends.

Third, managers' use of ratios to control an organization also should involve trend analysis. Managers must remember that any set of ratio values is actually only a determination of relationships that exist in a specified time period, perhaps a year. To use ratio analysis to its maximum advantage, values for ratios should be accumulated for a number of successive time periods to uncover specific organizational trends. Once these trends are uncovered, managers can formulate and implement appropriate strategy for dealing with them.

BACK TO THE CASE

Ratio analysis is another tool available to Commodore managers for broader organizational control. Ratio analysis would indicate the financial position of Commodore by determining relationships between various financial factors on Commodore's income statement and balance sheet. More specifically, Commodore management could use liquidity ratios to indicate Commodore's ability to pay its debts, leverage ratios to indicate appropriateness of the amount of debt used to run Commodore, activity ratios to indicate the level of activity at Commodore relative to its resources, and

profitability ratios to indicate the appropriateness of Commodore's profit level.

As with all control tools, Commodore management must use these ratios as a basis for a more subjective development and implementation of appropriate control strategy. Commodore management should evaluate all ratio information simultaneously, compare Commodore ratio values to values of industry averages for those same ratios, and analyze ratio values for several successive time periods to identify and control any financial trends that might exist at Commodore.

Action Summary

Reread the learning objectives that follow. Each objective is followed by questions. Answering these questions accurately will help you to retain the most important concepts discussed in this chapter. After answering each question, check your answer with the answer key at the end of this chapter. (*Hint*: If you have doubt regarding the correct response, consult the page that follows the answer.)

Circle:

From studying this chapter, I will attempt to acquire:

1. Definitions of both *production* and *production control*.

a, b, c, d, e

  a. *Production* is defined simply as the transformation of organizational resources into: (a) profits; (b) plans; (c) forecasts; (d) processes; (e) products.

T, F

  b. *Production control* is ensuring that an organization produces goods and services as planned.

2. An understanding of how productivity and layout patterns relate to the production process.

a, b, c, d, e

  a. The ratio that defines productivity is: (a) inputs/outputs; (b) outputs/profit; (c) outputs/inputs; (d) profits/inputs; (e) none of the above.

b. Which of the following layout patterns is usually used to manufacture airplanes: (a) process layout; (b) product layout; (c) fixed position layout; (d) customer layout; (e) assembly-line layout. a, b, c, d, e

3. **An appreciation for the significance of operations management.**
   a. Which of the following is *not* one of the operations management activities: (a) selecting; (b) designing; (c) updating; (d) operating-controlling; (e) all of the above are operations management activities. a, b, c, d, e
   b. Scheduling is the first step to be taken in operations management. T, F

4. **Insights concerning how management by exception and break-even analysis can be used to control production.**
   a. Management by exception is a control technique that allows only significant deviations between planned and actual performance to be brought to the manager's attention. T, F
   b. The overall effect of increasing costs and/or decreasing selling prices on the break-even point is that: (a) the number of products an organization must sell to break even increases; (b) the amount of profit a firm will receive at a fixed number of units sold increases; (c) the number of products an organization must sell to break even decreases; (d) a and b; (e) there is no effect on the break-even point. a, b, c, d, e

5. **An understanding of how quality control and materials requirements planning and control can contribute to production control.**
   a. A process used to determine how many products from a larger number should be inspected to calculate a probability that the total number of products meets organizational quality standards is: (a) quality control; (b) materials requirements planning; (c) materials requirements control; (d) statistical quality control; (e) all of the above. a, b, c, d, e
   b. Input data for the computer in a materials requirements planning system comes from all of the following sources except: (a) an accounts receivable file; (b) a master production schedule: (c) a bill of material file; (d) an inventory file; (e) all of the above are sources. a, b, c, d, e

6. **Knowledge of how budgets and ratio analysis can be used to achieve overall or broader organizational control.**
   a. Potential pitfalls of using budgets as control tools include: (a) too much emphasis placed on relatively insignificant organizational expenses; (b) changing budgets periodically; (c) increasing budgeted expenses year after year without adequate information; (d) a and c; (e) a and b. a, b, c, d, e
   b. Which of the following is an activity ratio: (a) inventory turnover ratio; (b) current ratio; (c) debt ratio; (d) quick ratio; (e) times interest earned ratio. a, b, c, d, e

INTRODUCTORY CASE WRAP-UP

"Production Snags at Commodore" (p. 466) and its related back-to-the-case sections were written to help you better understand the management concepts contained in this chapter. Answer the following discussion questions about this introductory case to further enrich your understanding of the chapter content:

1. What problems could be causing a high defect rate at Commodore? List as many problems as possible.
2. What would you do to solve the problems identified in question 1?
3. Does a high defect rate of products represent a serious situation for Commodore? Explain.

Issues for Review and Discussion

1. Define both *production* and *production control*.
2. Thoroughly explain the equation used to define productivity.
3. Discuss several traditional strategies that managers can use to increase organizational productivity.
4. Discuss the importance of robots in building productive organizations in the future.
5. What is a layout pattern, and what is its relationship to productivity?
6. Name the three basic types of layout patterns and give an example of each.
7. List five criteria for efficient and effective plant layout and explain how each can contribute to increasing productivity.
8. Explain the term *operations management* as well as the major managerial activities involved in operations management.
9. What steps usually are recommended to manage production successfully? Be sure to discuss each step as well as the relationships among the steps.
10. What is a control tool?
11. Define *management by exception* and describe how it can help managers to control production.
12. List and define seven major ingredients of break-even analysis.
13. How can managers use break-even analysis as an aid in controlling production?
14. What is materials requirements planning, and how can it aid in production control?
15. Define *statistical quality control* and describe its role in production control.
16. Define *budget*. How can managers use a budget to control an organization?
17. List three potential pitfalls of budgets.
18. What is ratio analysis?
19. List and define the four basic types of ratios.
20. What can the profit to sales ratio and the profit to total assets ratio tell managers about organizational profitability?
21. What guidelines would you recommend to managers using ratio analysis to control an organization?

Sources of Additional Information

Ackoff, Russell L., Jamshid Gharajedaghi, and Elsa Vergara Finnel. *A Guide to Controlling Your Corporation's Future.* New York: Wiley, 1984.

Frankson, Fred M. "A Simplified Approach to Financial Planning," *Journal of Small Business Management* (January 1981): 7–15.

Hayes, Robert H., and Kim B. Clark. "Why Some Factories Are More Productive than Others." *Harvard Business Review* (September/October 1986): 66–73.

Haywood-Farmer, John, Anthony Alleyne, Balteano Duffus, and Mark Downing. "Controlling Service Quality." *Business Quarterly* 50 (Winter 1985–86): 62.

Higgins, James M. *Human Relations: Behavior at Work*, 2d ed., New York: Random House, 1988.

Kauffman, Mort. "An Administrator's Guide to Expense Account Management." *Administrative Management* 42 (July 1981): 30–32, 39.

Mace, Edward E., and Russell Valentine. "Profit Improvement: Hope Springs Internal." *Management Focus* 31 (January/February 1984): 26–29.

McDonald, Alonzo L. "Of Floating Factories and Mating Dinosaurs." *Harvard Business Review* (November/December 1986): 82–86.

McNamee, Patrick B. "The V-Matrix–A New Tool for Plotting Earnings." *Long-Range Planning* 17 (February 1984): 19, 22.

Mockler, R. J. *The Management Control Process.* New York: Appleton-Century-Crofts, 1972.

Quelch, John A., Paul W. Farris, and James M. Olver. "The Product Management Audit." *Harvard Business Review* (March/April 1987): 30–37.

Radhakrishnan, K. S., and L. A. Soenen. "Why Computerized Financial Reporting and Consolidation Systems?" *Managerial Planning* 33 (July/August 1984): 32–36.

Raiborn, Mitchell H., and William C. Scurry, Jr. "Equity to Debt Conversion–Promoting Investments in Small Business Firms." *Financial Executive* (September 1980): 42–46, 48, 50.

Richman, Eugene, and Denis Coleman. "Monte Carlo Simulation for Management." *California Management Review* 23 (Spring 1981): 92–96.

Sadhwani, Arjan T., and Mostafa H. Sarhan. "Putting JIT Manufacturing Systems to Work." *Business* (April/May/June 1987): 30.

Schwan, Edward S. "Understanding Financial Statements," *Business* 34 (April/May/June 1984): 37–40.

Thornton, Billy M., and Paul Preston. *Introduction to Management Science: Quantitative Approaches to Managerial Decisions.* Columbus, Ohio: Charles E. Merrill, 1977.

Williamson, Nicholas C. "Japanese Productivity: Advances in Production and Marketing." *Business* 34 (April/May/June 1984): 16–22.

Wilson, Richard M. S. *Cost Control Handbook.* New York: Wiley, 1975.

Notes

1. James B. Dilworth, *Production and Operations Management: Manufacturing and Non-Manufacturing* (New York: Random House, 1986), 3.
2. John W. Kendrick, *Understanding Productivity: An Introduction to the Dynamics of Productivity Change* (Baltimore: Johns Hopkins University Press, 1977), 14.
3. Lester C. Thurow, "Other Countries Are as Smart as We Are," *New York Times*, April 5, 1981.
4. *U.S. Industrial Outlook, 1987*, p. 21–6.
5. Joann S. Lubin, "As Robot Age Arrives, Labor Seeks Protection against Work Loss," *Wall Street Journal*, October 26, 1981.
6. Jack R. Meredith, *The Management of Operations* (New York: Wiley, 1987), 243–44.
7. For more information on plant layout, see Joseph G. Monks, *Operations Management: Theory and Problems* (New York: McGraw-Hill, 1987), 122–35.
8. Richard B. Chase and Nicholas J. Aquilano, *Production and Operations Management: A Life Cycle Approach* (Homewood, Ill.: Richard D. Irwin, 1981), 4.
9. At this point, it probably would be worthwhile to review the general topic of scheduling and the more specific topics of the Gantt chart and PERT networks (pp. 178–181).
10. Lester R. Bittle, *Management by Exception* (New York: McGraw-Hill, 1964).
11. Frederick W. Taylor, *Shop Management* (New York: Harper & Bros., 1911), 126–27.
12. These two rules are adapted from *Boardroom Reports* 5 (May 15, 1976): 4.
13. For a clear discussion of more of the intricacies of break-even analysis, see Lee J. Krajewski and Larry P. Ritzman, *Operations Management: Strategy and Analysis* (Reading, Mass.: Addison-Wesley, 1987), 41–43.
14. Robert J. Lambrix and Surendra S. Singhvi, "How to Set Volume-Sensitive ROI Targets," *Harvard Business Review* (March/April 1981): 174.
15. Chase and Aquilano, *Production and Operations Management*, 516.
16. Elwood S. Buffa, *Modern Production/Operations Management* (New York: Wiley, 1983), 501.
17. Roger G. Schroeder, *Operations Management: Decision Making in the Operations Function* (New York: McGraw-Hill, 1985), 597–98.
18. Robert L. Dewelt, "Control: Key to Making Financial Strategy Work," *Management Review* (March 1977): 20.
19. George S. Minmier, "Zero-Base Budgeting: A New Budgeting Technique for Discretionary Costs," *Mid-South Quarterly Business Review* 14 (October 1976): 2–8.
20. Peter A. Phyrr, "Zero-Base Budgeting," *Harvard Business Review* (November/December 1970): 111–21. See also E.A. Kurbis, "The Case for Zero-Base Budgeting," *CA Magazine* (April 1986): 104–105.
21. Aaron Wildausky and Arthur Hammann, "Comprehensive versus Incremental Budgeting in the Department of Agriculture," in *Planning Programming Budgeting: A Systems Approach to Management*, ed. Fremont J. Lyden and Ernest G. Miller (Chicago: Markham Publishing, 1968), 143–44.
22. Chris Argyris, "Human Problems with Budgets," *Harvard Business Review* (January/February 1953): 108.
23. Argyris, "Human Problems with Budgets," 109.
24. This section is based primarily on J. Fred Weston and Eugene F. Brigham, *Essentials of Managerial Finance* 7th ed. (Hinsdale, Ill.: Dryden Press, 1985).
25. F.L. Patrone and Donald duBois, "Financial Ratio Analysis for the Small Business," *Journal of Small Business Management* (January 1981): 35.
26. "How Stauffer Outperforms the Industry," *Business Week*, November 22, 1976, 129–30.
27. For an excellent discussion of ratio analysis in a small business, see Patrone and duBois, "Financial Ratio Analysis," 35–40.

Action Summary Answer Key

1. a. e, p. 467
   b. T, p. 467
2. a. c, p. 469
   b. c, p. 472
3. a. e, p. 473
   b. F, pp. 474–475
4. a. T, p. 476
   b. a, p. 479
5. a. d, p. 481
   b. a, p. 480
6. a. d, p. 484
   b. a, p. 487

CHART INDUSTRIES: FULL SPEED AHEAD

When Gerry Horan teamed up with four other investors in November, 1981, to buy a small Pickering, Ontario, manufacturer of collision repair equipment, he thought it was barely breaking even and could readily be whipped into better financial shape. What he didn't find out until after he became president was just how troubled the company really was. Guy Chart Systems Ltd. (now Chart Industries Ltd.) was carrying a staggering $4 million debt on sales of $4.2 million. "The accounting system was a chaotic mess," he recalls. "My partners and I had based our decision to purchase the company on a lot of misinformation." He suddenly realized that the sloppy bookkeeping combined with a slow-moving, overvalued inventory would likely bankrupt Chart within two months.

Today, with nearly $10 million in sales—70 percent of them exports—and a respectable $1 million profit in 1986, Chart heads the collision repair equipment field in Canada. The company's amazing rebound is largely attributable to Chart's golden-tongued and tough-minded leader.

From the very start, Horan began finding evidence that the financial statements he had originally seen hadn't told the entire story. Among the stacks of paper, he found unpaid suppliers' bills, some more than a year old. Sometimes he'd receive a letter or a phone call demanding payment on a bill he didn't know about. "For two months I had this nagging feeling that things might be worse than I thought they were," he says. "I kept telling myself that Chart had a big inventory and that after I got the sales going again, everything would be fine. When I discovered exactly how badly off we were, I got a shock that lasted for weeks."

Horan: "The accounting system was a chaotic mess."

Horan began his fight to save Chart by persuading several bankers, suppliers, and other creditors to pull in their claws. "I simply told them that it would be better to ride along with us than to try and get cash out of a dead company," he says.

He then took a long, analytical look at what he believed was $1 million worth of inventory. When he asked distributors why they weren't moving his products faster, the answer was devastating: at least half of Chart's inventory was obsolete. The firm had implemented few equipment change since the 1960s and a growing market for front-wheel drives and other new body types had created a hunger for products (such as unibody holding fixtures to immobilize vehicles during repairs) that the company wasn't making. Before he could retool machinery to produce the new items, Horan had to clear factory space. He peddled sixty truckloads of dusty equipment he'd thought was worth about $500 000 to a scrap dealer for less than $10 000.

Next there were the foreign operations. In the mid-1970s, when Chart was turning a decent profit on sales in the $3-million-to-$4 million range and its export sales stood at 30 percent, the previous owner had taken a bold expansion leap, buying one warehouse in New York state and leasing another in Germany. Horan plowed through the paperwork, talked to clients, and realized that the warehouses were losing about $250 000 apiece every year. He sold the New York building, wound down the German operation, and began shipping merchandise directly to distributors. "The old owner was a nice guy, but he was out of his depth," says Horan. "If he had had a business background, he would never have opened the warehouses. They were completely unnecessary."

As it turned out, so were many head-office jobs. After asking the administrative staff to describe their duties, Horan discovered that some people were doing little more than reading other employees' reports, attaching memos, and passing them on to their superiors. Other office and shop staffers weren't pulling their weight or responded negatively to his demands that they change their work habits. Early in 1982, Horan swung a sharp axe, cutting the employee roster from one hundred to sixty-five; twenty administrative staff were among the casualties.

In another cost-cutting measure, Horan froze the wages of all shop workers for one year and the salaries of surviving and incoming executives for two years. The fat-trimming moves helped Chart save almost $1 million in 1982. But it wasn't until two years later that the firm finally showed a profit: a healthy $800 000 on sales of $7 million.

The successful introduction of new products spurred that recovery. The equipment the company had been making was designed primarily for vehicles built with a frame structure. However, most newer-model cars are constructed with a frameless shell and more sophisticated gear is required to handle them. Distributors had told Horan that they wanted equipment to simplify and reduce the time involved in bodyshop repairs so they could increase their earnings. With very little outside help, Chart workers retooled and adapted laser-light technology to create such new products as a $15 000 laser-repair bench that can scan a car's three dimensions simultaneously.

The new lines so impressed Bill Payne, president of Toronto distribution company Automotive Finishes and Supply Inc., that he started doing business with Chart again in 1984 after a four-year hiatus. "The old gang there was going in the wrong direction and they wouldn't listen to anything you said," Payne says. "Horan knows exactly what he's doing. I'm very happy with Chart these days."

The equipment changeover wasn't entirely trouble free, however. In its eagerness to meet customers' demands, Chart acted prematurely in putting a $10 000 measuring system on the market in 1983. One hundred units were sold — and every one of them came back within a year to have structural flaws corrected. Now virtually faultless, the item was Chart's biggest seller in 1986.

Horan obviously lacked the funds to reward his shop stewards financially during Chart's spirited climb, but he did try to convey the impression that their contribution was important. One year before he lifted the executives' wage freeze, he removed the restriction from his workers' salaries. And in 1987, Horan started up a gain-sharing plan to put extra dollars in the pockets of Chart's seventy-five employees and reward them for their loyalty.

Now that the darker days are over — Chart has paid off all its creditors — Horan envisions annual sales of $15 million by 1990. "There is only so far that Chart can go in the automotive trade because collision equipment has a limited clientele," he says. "So we're thinking of expanding into some other business. Perhaps in the automotive line but not necessarily so." Would he buy another money-losing company? "You bet," he says with a grin. "But only if I've seen every piece of paper that has ever gone through its accounting office."

DISCUSSION ISSUES

1. According to material covered in the chapter, what were the major problems faced by Chart Industries when Horan took over the business? Discuss.
2. How could Horan have improved his decision-making process before taking on Chart Industries?
3. What were the changes instituted by Horan in an effort to improve operations and gain control of the company? How do these changes tie in with the material covered in this chapter? Explain.

Based on "Full Speed Ahead," by Ted Ferguson in *Canadian Business*, May 1987. Used with permission.

C H A P T E R

18

INFORMATION

STUDENT LEARNING OBJECTIVES

From studying this chapter, I will attempt to acquire:

1. An understanding of the relationship between data and information.
2. Insights on the main factors that influence the value of information.
3. Knowledge of some potential steps for evaluating information.
4. An appreciation for the role of computers in handling information.
5. An understanding of the importance of a management information system (MIS) to an organization.
6. A feasible strategy for establishing an MIS.
7. Information about what a management decision support system is and how it operates.

CHAPTER OUTLINE

```
┌──────────┐
├──────────┤   INTRODUCTORY
├──────────┤   CASE 18
└──────────┘
```

A QUESTION OF MEASUREMENT

"Out of control? That's nonsense. Our organization has one of the most thorough control systems in the industry. I simply can't accept that statement." As Jack Wilkenson, president of Mega-Systems, Inc., made these comments, several members of the executive committee nodded in agreement. A smaller number showed no expression, while Natalie Greenberg, a new member of the executive committee, appeared unconvinced. Greenberg, a recently hired division manager, had drawn the heated remarks from the president by pointing out cost overruns on several recent projects. She had suggested that these overruns pointed to a lack of effective controls in key parts of the organization.

"We're all aware of the overruns, Natalie," said Warren Turner, the controller, "But I don't think we should blame our reporting system. It's probably the most thorough series of checks and measurements we could devise at the present time. For example, our production supervisors alone receive at least fourteen monthly measures of their department's productivity. Everything from output per hour to equipment utilization reports is made available to them. Have you seen the stack of computer printouts they receive every month? They've got everything they need to control their operations if they will only study those reports carefully."

"And we enlarged and improved our overall reporting system two years ago," added Ed Simpson, director of information systems. "We brought in a management consulting group that worked with our system design staff to create a thorough and sophisticated management information system. Then we conducted a massive campaign to 'sell' the control tools to the managers who would be using them. We've literally left no stone unturned to develop a first-class control system. I'm very satisfied with its thoroughness."

"Without trying to appear cynical," said Greenberg, "I wonder if the system is too thorough."

"Natalie, I think you'd better explain your comment," said the president, looking quizzically at the new division manager.

From *The Management of Organizations*, p. 516, by Herbert G. Hicks and C. Ray Gullett. Copyright © 1976 by McGraw-Hill, Inc. Used with permission of McGraw-Hill Book Company.

What's Ahead

The introductory case concludes with Natalie Greenberg, a recently hired division manager, implying that Mega-Systems, Inc. is not being controlled effectively due to the inadequacy of the control-related information that managers are presently receiving. This chapter presents material that Jack Wilkenson, president of Mega-Systems, should use in assessing the validity of Greenberg's implications as well as in evaluating the overall status of information within his organization.

Controlling is the process of making things happen as planned. Of course, managers cannot make things happen as planned if they lack information on the manner in which various events occur within both the organization and the organizational environment. This chapter discusses the fundamental principles of handling information within an organization by first presenting essentials of information and then examining both the management information system (MIS) and the management decision support system (MDSS).

ESSENTIALS OF INFORMATION

The process of developing information begins with the gathering of some type of facts or statistics, called **data**. Once gathered, data typically are analyzed in some manner. Generally speaking, **information** can be defined as conclusions derived from data analysis. In management terms, information can be defined as conclusions derived from the analysis of data that relate to the operation of an organization.

Data are facts; information is derived from data analysis.

The information managers receive heavily influences managerial decision making, which in turn determines what activities will be performed within the organization, which in turn dictates the eventual success or failure of the organization.[1] Some management writers consider information to be of such fundamental importance to the management process that they define *management* as the process of converting information into action through decision making.[2] The following sections discuss: (1) factors that influence the value of information; (2) how to evaluate information; and (3) computer assistance in using information.

Factors Influencing the Value of Information

Some information managers receive is more valuable than other information.[3] The value of information is defined in terms of how much benefit can accrue to the organization through the use of the information. The greater this benefit, the more valuable the information.

The benefit derived from using information defines the information's value.

497

Four primary factors determine the value of information: (1) information appropriateness; (2) information quality; (3) information timeliness; and (4) information quantity.

In general, management should encourage the generation, distribution, and use of organizational information that is appropriate, of high quality, timely, and of sufficient quantity. Following this guideline will not necessarily guarantee sound decisions, but it will ensure that important resources necessary to make such decisions are available.[4] Each of the four factors that determine information value is discussed in more detail in the paragraphs that follow.

Information Appropriateness

Appropriate information is information relevant to the decision.

Information appropriateness is defined in terms of how relevant the information is to the decision-making situation that faces the manager. If information is quite relevant to the decision-making situation, then it is said to be appropriate. As a general rule, as the appropriateness of information increases, the value of that information increases.

Figure 18.1 shows the characteristics of information appropriate for the following three common decision-making situations: (1) operational control decisions; (2) management control decisions; and (3) strategic planning decisions.[5]

Operational control decisions relate to assuring that specific organizational tasks are carried out effectively and efficiently. Management control decisions relate to obtaining and effectively and efficiently using the organizational resources necessary to reach organizational objectives. Strategic planning decisions relate to determining organizational objectives and designating the corresponding action necessary to reach those objectives.

As Figure 18.1 shows, the characteristics of appropriate information change as managers shift from making operational control decisions to management control decisions to strategic planning decisions. Strategic planning decision mak-

FIGURE 18.1   Characteristics of information appropriate for decisions related to operational control, management control, and strategic planning.

Characteristics of Information	Operational Control	Management Control	Strategic Planning
Source	Largely internal	→	External
Scope	Well defined, narrow	→	Very wide
Level of aggregation	Detailed	→	Aggregate
Time horizon	Historical	→	Future
Currency	Highly current	→	Quite old
Required accuracy	High	→	Low
Frequency of use	Very frequent	→	Infrequent

Reprinted by permission from G. Anthony Gorry and Michael S. Scott Morton, "A Framework for Management Information Systems," *Sloan Management Review*, vol. 13, no. 1 (Fall 1971): 59.

ers need information that focuses on the relationship of the organization to its external environment, emphasizes the future, is very wide in scope, and presents a broad view. Appropriate information for this type of decision is usually quite old and not completely accurate.

Information appropriate for making operational control decisions has dramatically different characteristics than information appropriate for making strategic planning decisions. Operational control decision makers need information that focuses for the most part on the internal organizational environment, emphasizes the performance history of the organization, and is well defined, narrow in scope, and quite detailed. In addition, appropriate information for this type of decision is both highly current and highly accurate.

Information appropriate for making management control decisions generally has characteristics that fall somewhere between the extreme characteristics of appropriate operational control information and appropriate strategic planning information.

Information Quality

The second primary factor that determines the value of information is **information quality**, which is the degree to which information represents reality. The more closely information represents reality, the higher the quality and the greater the value of the information. In general, the higher the quality of information available to managers, the better equipped managers are to make appropriate decisions and the greater the probability that the organization will be successful over the long term.

> High-quality information is information that represents reality.

Information Timeliness

Information timeliness is the third primary factor that determines the value of information. The timeliness of information refers to the extent to which the receipt of information allows decisions to be made and resulting action to be taken so that the organization can gain some benefit from possessing the information. Information received by managers at a point when it can be used to the advantage of the organization is said to be timely.

> Timely information is information received in time to benefit the organization.

For example, a product may be selling poorly primarily because its established market price is significantly higher than that of competitive products. If this information is received by management after the product has been discontinued, the information would be untimely. If, however, this information is received by management soon enough to adjust the selling price of the product and thereby significantly increase sales, the information would be timely.

Information Quantity

The fourth and final determinant of the value of information is called **information quantity**. Information quantity refers to the amount of decision-related information managers possess. Before making a decision, managers should assess the quantity of information they possess that relates to the decision being made. If this quantity is judged to be insufficient, more information should be gathered before the decision is made. If the amount of information is judged to be as complete as necessary, managers can feel justified in making the decision.

> Sufficient information quantity is necessary for making justifiable decisions.

BACK TO THE CASE

Information at Mega-Systems, Inc. in the introductory case is the conclusions derived from the analysis of data relating to the way in which Mega-Systems operates. Natalie Greenberg has implied that managers currently are unable to make sound control decisions at Mega-Systems primarily because of the type of decision-related information they are receiving.

If Jack Wilkenson, the president of Mega-Systems, finds that the control-related information Mega-Systems managers currently are receiving is relatively valueless, he cannot fault his managers for making poor control decisions. Instead, he should strive to provide them with more valuable control-related information. Wilkenson might be able to increase the value of the information his managers presently are receiving by forcing it to more closely represent activities as they actually occur at Mega-Systems, by making sure that the information is received by managers in sufficient quantity and in time to make controlling decisions, and by ensuring that the information is relevant to the control decisions of the managers receiving the information.

FIGURE 18.2   Flowchart of main activities in evaluating information.

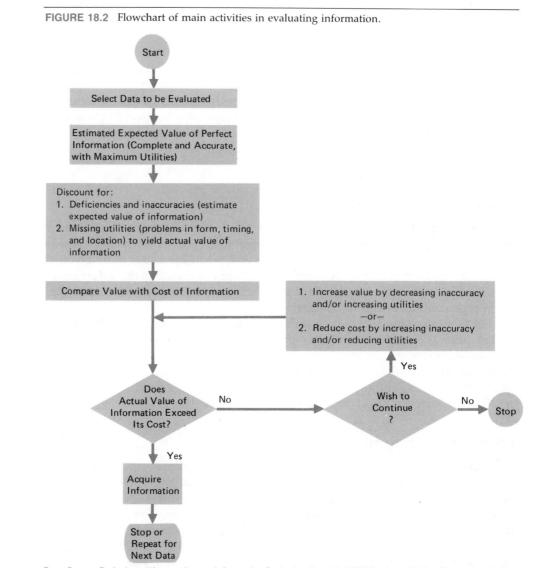

From Roman R. Andrus, "Approaches to Information Evaluation," p. 44, *MSU Business Topics* (Summer 1971). Reprinted by permission of the publisher, Division of Research, Graduate School of Business Administration, Michigan State University.

Evaluating Information

Evaluation of information is the process of determining whether or not the acquisition of specified information is justified. As with all evaluations of this type, the primary concern of management is to weigh the dollar value of benefit gained from using some quantity of information against the cost of generating that information.

According to the flowchart in Figure 18.2, the first major step in evaluating organizational information is determining the value of that information by pinpointing the data to be analyzed and then determining the expected value or return to be received from obtaining perfect information based on this data. Next, this expected value should be reduced by the amount of benefit that will not be realized because of deficiencies and inaccuracies expected to appear in the information.

Then the expected value of organizational information should be compared with the expected cost of obtaining that information. If the expected cost does not exceed the expected value, the information should be gathered. If, however, the expected cost does exceed the expected value, managers either must increase the information's expected value or decrease its expected cost before the information gathering can be justified. If neither of these objectives is possible, management cannot justify gathering the information.

One generally accepted strategy for increasing the expected value of information is to eliminate those characteristics of the information that tend to limit its usefulness. Figure 18.3 shows characteristics of information that tend to limit its usefulness and possible action that management can take to eliminate these characteristics.

Evaluation of information involves determining

whether the expected value of the information

exceeds the expected cost.

FIGURE 18.3 Characteristics that tend to limit the usefulness of information and how to eliminate them.

Characteristics That Tend to Limit the Usefulness of Information	Possible Actions to Eliminate These Characteristics*
Language and/or format not understood	Translate, revise, or change format
Volume excessive: Time required to examine information exceeds the intuitive estimate of the value of the contents	Condense
Received before need perceived	Store for possible future need
Received after needed	Insure against future occurrence
Inaccessible	Create access
Time or cost of access excessive	Relocate data, change access
No right of use, or closed communication channels due to conflicting subunit goals, authority relationships, and so forth	Relocate information; alter or open transmission channels; change relationships

*The organization will incur some additional cost by taking one or more of these actions.

From Roman R. Andrus, "Approaches to Information Evaluation," p. 44, *MSU Business Topics* (Summer 1971). Reprinted by permission of the publisher, Division of Research, Graduate School of Business Administration, Michigan State University.

BACK TO THE CASE

Jack Wilkenson's analysis of the status of organizational information at Mega-Systems should include a determination of whether all of the information furnished to Mega-Systems managers can be justified. To make this determination, Wilkenson should compare the value of the information with its cost. If its value is greater than its cost, the information received by managers can be justified. If its cost is greater than its value, however, the process of furnishing information should be modified—and Greenberg's inference that managers are receiving too much control related information would be valid. Wilkenson also should consider the possibility of increasing the value of organizational information by increasing its usefulness.

Computer Assistance in Using Information

Computers are extremely helpful in generating information from raw data.

Managers have an overwhelming amount of data to gather, analyze, and transform into information before making numerous decisions. Materials distributed by the Xerox corporation indicate that American businesses currently have more than 324 billion documents to generate annually, and this number is increasing by 72 billion each year.[6] A computer is a tool managers can use to assist in the complicated and time-consuming task of generating this information. A **computer** can be defined as an electronic tool capable of accepting data, interpreting data, performing ordered operations on data, and reporting on the outcome of these operations.

In general terms, Joseph D. Wessekamper, a director of the Haskins and Sells computer services department, indicates that computers give managers the ability to store vast amounts of financial, inventory, and other data so that it is readily accessible for making day-to-day decisions.[7] Figure 18.4 complements Wessekamper's more general statement by listing several more specific computer operations for handling information.

Of course, the mere possession of a computer does not guarantee that management will receive a desirable level of data-processing support. Managers must strive to acquire appropriate computers for their organization and take steps to ensure that the computers are performing the necessary data-processing functions.

The following Management in Action feature highlights the importance of appropriate and efficient ways of generating and analyzing data into informational profiles in enabling doctors to better serve their patients and control their practices. The use of a specialized software program provides a comprehensive information system that renders information easily accessible to doctors.

FIGURE 18.4   Computer operations that assist management in handling information.

Operation	How a Computer Can Aid Managers
Billing	Control of buying, inventory, selling; rapid paying cycle; improved cash position; data about customers, products, items, costs, prices, sales representatives, sales statistics
Accounts receivable	Shorten average collections of accounts receivables; highlight past due statements, improve cash flow, invoice summary
Sales analysis	Review sales volume on the basis of profit contributions as well as gross profit contribution; compute sales representatives' commission plans; pinpoint sales improvement for customers and sales representatives
Inventory	Provide control of inventory, generation of distribution–by–value report; i.e., quantity sold annual sales are accumulated and printed as percentage of total number of items and total annual sales; pinpoint marginal items; segment inventory; establish order quantities and order points; cycle reviewing of vendor lines
Payroll	Construct payroll accounting system; produce reports to management, employees, government agencies; reduce peak work loads, strengthen managerial control over human resources
Materials planning	Determine components requirements; plan inventory per item by time period; determine how change in order quantity or delivery will affect production schedule; consolidate requirements of multiple–use items; reduce materials planning costs
Purchasing	Provide performance figures by item, supplier, and buyer in terms of cost, quality, and delivery; achieve tangible savings by meeting discount dates through faster processing of invoices; simplify analysis of historical data; expedite purchase orders based on production shortages and late deliveries
Dispatching and shop-floor control	Reduce expediting costs because job status records are current; give early notification of exceptions requiring corrective action plus daily revisions of order priority by machine group
Capacity planning and operation scheduling	Make available labour requirements by time period in time to take corrective action; immediate information about effect of changes on work orders, simplified planning on availability of tools, realistic order release dates

Reprinted by permission from Alice M. Greene, "Computers Big Pay-off for Small Companies," *Iron Age*, March 30, 1972, pp. 63–64.

CAREFILE: EFFICIENCY IN INFORMATION GENERATION

"In some ways medicine is really in the stone age," says Tom Astle, referring to the medical community's often archaic methods of record keeping. In his late twenties, Astle is president and co-founder of Carefile Medical Systems Inc. "If a company was to keep its records the way a doctor manages his, it'd be out of business in no time," he remarks. While most office employees call up and enter data on personal computers, send facsimile messages around the globe, and dial the phone with the push of a single button, many physicians still fight through hand-scribbled charts and wrestle with outmoded filing and billing systems to keep a finger on the health of their patients—and of their practice. So Astle has collaborated with Dr. Doug Ackman, senior urologist at the Montreal General Hospital, to develop a software system that handles doctors' medical data, statistical records, and billing procedures at the tap of a computer key. Billing is done by modum (over telephone lines) direct to the provincial Medicare office.

Since its founding three years ago, Carefile has been developing and refining its strategy and products. Its systems are installed at the Royal Victoria Hospital and the Montreal General, as well as about sixty other hospitals and medical clinics across the country. Sales totalled $250 000 in 1987, a figure that will be at least doubled in 1988. Carefile's software, essentially a spread sheet tailored specially to the needs of the medical profession, is priced at about $5 000.

According to Astle, the system is especially efficient because it has been developed in close consultation with medical specialists. The Carefile system evolved from an idea Ackman had mulled over for fifteen years. Because specialists repeatedly see the same type of patient, they look for the same blocks of information over and over again. For instance, 90 percent of urology patients fit into ten categories of diseases or problems. Consequently, the program for each specialty, of which nine are complete, is based on an extensive computer profile of common ailments such patients encounter.

One aspect of the system includes a checklist for the doctor to follow to help ensure that he or she doesn't overlook any elements of an examination—a feature which may prove to be a big draw in the U.S., where malpractice suits are commonplace and doctors are paying about $100 000 in liability insurance. About a third of these malpractice suits are settled due to improper documentation. "If we could prove that our system reduces the incidence of malpractice suits by 5 percent, that per-

"The Carefile system evolved from an idea Ackman had mulled over for fifteen years."

centage of $100 000 pays for a system pretty quick," says Astle.

The Carefile system consists of four main components: a "CareFiler," used to enter all patient data and general referral letters and chart notes; a "CareAnalyzer," used to analyze historical patient data; a "CareEditor," used to organize data and reports; and a "CareBook," a scheduling and appointment system. These systems may be linked to a hospital's mainframe computer system; a password required to open any file helps maintain and ensure confidentiality. Medicare numbers are also verified upon entry, thus eliminating physicians' headaches over not getting paid when they accept invalid insurance numbers.

Astle estimates that although about twenty software programs for billing exist, Carefile has a jump of about eighteen months on U.S. competitors in terms of offering a more comprehensive, overall software package for doctors and hospitals. "We're going as fast as we can into a full-blown marketing plan," he says. Some Carefile systems already have been installed as far away as California and New Orleans. Regional sales offices were scheduled to open in late 1988 in Boston, Atlanta, San Francisco, and Los Angeles. A Toronto sales office will open in the summer of 1989 and the Carefile system is being translated into French.

Proud of the company's innovations, Astle likes to recount the reaction to Carefile of several software specialists encountered at recent trade shows: "We were asked if we were from California." As anyone who has heard of the "Silicone Valley" knows, California is the traditional trendsetter in the world of computer technology.

Based on "Carefile develops software system to take medicine out of stone age," by Nancy McHarg in *This Week In Business*, March 26, 1988. Used with permission.

Main Functions of a Computer

A computer function is a computer activity that must be performed to generate organizational information. Computers perform five main functions: (1) the input function; (2) the storage function; (3) the control function; (4) the processing function; and (5) the output function. The relationships among these functions are shown in Figure 18.5.

The **input function** consists of computer activities through which the computer enters the data to be analyzed and the instructions to be followed to analyze that data appropriately. As Figure 18.5 implies, the purpose of the input function is to provide data and instructions to be used in the performance of the storage, processing, control, and output functions.

The **storage function** consists of computer activities involved with retaining the material entered into the computer during the performance of the input function. The storage unit, or memory, of a computer is similar to the human memory in that various facts can be stored until they are needed for processing. In addition, facts can be stored, used in processing, and then restored as many times as necessary. As Figure 18.5 implies, the storage, processing, and control activities are dependent on one another and ultimately yield computer output.

The **processing function** consists of the computer activities involved with performing both logic and calculation steps necessary to analyze data appropriately. Calculation activities include virtually any numerical analysis. Logic activities include such analysis as comparing one number to another to determine which is larger. Data, as well as directions for processing the data, are furnished by input and storage activities.

The five functions of a computer involve:

1. Getting material into the computer.

2. Retaining material that has been input.

3. Analyzing data.

FIGURE 18.5   Relationships among the five main functions of a computer.

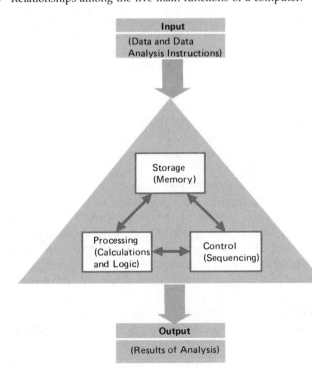

4. Ordering computer activities.

Computer activities that dictate the order in which other computer functions are performed comprise the **control function**. Control activities indicate: (1) when data should be retrieved after it has been stored; (2) when and how this data should be analyzed; (3) if and when the data should be restored after analysis; (4) if and when additional data should be retrieved; and (5) when output activities, (described in the next paragraph), should begin and end.

5. Communicating computer analysis results.

The **output function** is comprised of those activities that take the results of the input, storage, processing, and control functions and transmit them outside of the computer. These results can appear in such diversified forms as data on punched computer cards or words typed on paper tapes. Obviously, the form in which output should appear primarily is determined by how the output is to be used. Output that appears on punched computer cards, for example, can be used as input for another computer analysis but is of little value for analysis by human beings.

Possible Pitfalls in Using a Computer

Managers should keep in mind that:

The computer is a sophisticated management tool with the potential of making a significant contribution to organizational success. For this potential to materialize, however, the following possible pitfalls should be avoided:

1. Computers are not self-directed.

1. *Thinking that a computer is capable of independently performing creative activities* A computer is only capable of following precise and detailed instructions provided by the computer user. The individual using the computer must tell the computer exactly what to do, how to do it, and when to do it. One computer expert describes his working with a computer as follows:

> It's like talking to a moron. You have to tell it every little detail . . . When I was working my way through college, I used to work in a laundry. One of the boys . . . there had very low intelligence. I could say, "Jimmy, go over to the bench and pick up that empty bucket and bring it to me." Jimmy would do it. But, if he found that the bucket was full of water instead of empty, he would become very confused. So I would have to tell him to take it to the sink and pour the water out. The trouble was that I had left out a step in his instructions, and he didn't have the ability to think what to do. It's the same with machines.[8]

[handwritten margin note: to not be a moron you have to stop wanting to go to someone for instructions, all the time, an d make some decisions on your own.]

This section makes the point that computers are simply pieces of equipment that must be directed very precisely by computer users in order to perform some function. The cartoon makes much the same point by implying that people and computers are equals.

2. Using computers is expensive.

2. *Spending too much money on computer assistance*[9]   In general, computers can be of great assistance to managers. The initial cost of purchasing a computer as well as updating it when necessary, however, can be very high.[10] Managers need to continually compare the benefit obtained from computer assistance with the cost of obtaining this assistance. A.R. Zipf makes the point that this comparison can help managers to eliminate the seeming desire of many organization members to purchase computer time simply to "play with a new toy."[11]

3. People determine the worth of computer output.

3. *Overestimating the value of computer output*   Some managers fall into the trap of assuming that they have "the answer" once they have received information generated by computer analysis. Managers must recognize that computer output is only as good as the quality of data and directions for analyzing that

Reprinted by permission of the cartoonist, Douglas Blackwell.

data that human beings have put into the computer. Inaccurate data or inappropriate computer instructions yield useless computer output. A commonly used phrase to describe such an occurrence is "garbage in, garbage out."

 BACK TO THE CASE

Part of Wilkenson's investigation of the status of information at Mega-Systems, Inc. should include an analysis of the company's present computer assistance in handling information. Not only should the computer be storing and processing data related to performing the control function at Mega-Systems, but it also should be handling additional operations related to such areas as payroll, sales analysis, billing, and pur-

chasing. To encourage wise use of Mega-Systems' computer, Wilkenson should tell organization members using the computer to keep in mind that a computer is not capable of performing creatively, that the benefits of using a computer should be greater than the costs of using it, and that computer output should be scrutinized carefully and not used as "the answer."

THE MANAGEMENT INFORMATION SYSTEM (MIS)

In simple terms, a **management information system (MIS)** is a network established within an organization to provide managers with information that will assist them in decision making. The following more complete definition of an MIS was developed by the Management Information System Committee of the Financial Executives Institute:

An MIS gets information to where it is needed.

> An MIS is a system designed to provide selected decision-oriented information needed by management to plan, control, and evaluate the activities of the corporation. It is designed within a framework that emphasizes profit planning,

performance planning, and control at all levels. It contemplates the ultimate integration of required business information subsystems, both financial and nonfinancial, within the company.[12]

The title of the specific organization member responsible for developing and maintaining an MIS varies from organization to organization. In smaller organizations, a president or vice-president may possess this responsibility. In larger organizations, an individual with a title such as "Director of Information Systems" may be solely responsible for appropriately managing an entire MIS department. The term *MIS manager* is used in the sections that follow to indicate that person within the organization who has the primary responsibility for managing the MIS. The term *MIS personnel* is used to designate those non-management individuals within the organization who possess the primary responsibility of actually operating the MIS. Examples of these non-management individuals are computer operators and computer programmers.

The sections that follow describe an MIS more fully and outline the steps managers take to establish an MIS.

Describing the MIS

The MIS is perhaps best described by summarizing the steps necessary to properly operate an MIS and by discussing the different kinds of information various managers need to make job-related decisions.

Operating the MIS

The six-step process of operating an MIS involves:
1. Determining what information is needed.

MIS personnel generally perform six sequential and distinct steps to properly operate an MIS.[13] The first of these steps is to determine what information is needed within the organization, when it will be needed, and in what form it will be needed. Since the basic purpose of the MIS is to assist management in making decisions, one way to begin determining management information needs is to analyze: (1) decision areas in which management makes decisions; (2) specific decisions within these decision areas that management actually must make; and (3) alternatives that must be evaluated in order to make these specific decisions. Figure 18.6 presents such an analysis for the manager making decisions related to production and operations management.

2. Gathering data to fill information needs.

The second major step in operating the MIS is pinpointing and collecting data that will yield needed organizational information. This step is just as important as determining the information needs of the organization. If data collected do not relate properly to information needs, it will be impossible to generate needed information.

3. Summarizing the data.
4. Analyzing the data.

After the information needs of the organization have been determined and appropriate data have been pinpointed and gathered, summarizing the data and analyzing the data are, respectively, the third and fourth steps MIS personnel generally should take to properly operate an MIS. It is in the performance of these steps that MIS personnel find computer assistance of great benefit.

5. Transmitting the information.
6. Using the information.

The fifth and sixth steps are transmitting the information generated by data analysis to appropriate managers and having managers actually use the information. The performance of these last two steps results in managerial decision making.

Although each of these six steps is necessary if an MIS is to run properly, the time spent on performing each step naturally will vary from organization

FIGURE 18.6 Decision areas, decisions, and alternatives related to production and operations management.

Decision Areas	Decisions	Alternatives
Plant and equipment	Span of process	Make or buy
	Plant size	One big plant or several smaller ones
	Plant location	Locate near markets or locate near materials
	Investment decisions	Invest mainly in buildings or equipment or inventories or research
	Choice of equipment	General-purpose or special-purpose equipment
	Kind of tooling	Temporary, minimum tooling or "production tooling"
Production planning and control	Frequency of inventory taking	Few or many breaks in production for buffer stocks
	Inventory size	High inventory or a lower inventory
	Degree of inventory control	Control in great detail or in lesser detail
	What to control	Controls designed to minimize machine downtime or labor cost or time in process, or to maximize output of particular products or material usage
	Quality control	High reliability and quality or low costs
	Use of standards	Formal or informal or none at all
Labor and staffing	Job specialization	Highly specialized or not highly specialized
	Supervision	Technically trained first-line supervisors or nontechnically trained supervisors
	Wage system	Many job grades or few job grades; incentive wages or hourly wages
	Supervision	Close supervision or loose supervision
	Industrial engineers	Many or few such men
Product design/engineering	Size of product line	Many customer specials or few specials or none at all
	Design stability	Frozen design or many engineering change orders
	Technological risk	Use of new processes unproved by competitors or follow-the-leader policy
	Engineering	Complete packaged design or design-as-you-go approach
	Use of manufacturing engineering	Few or many manufacturing engineers
Organization and management	Kind of organization	Functional or product focus or geographical or other
	Executive use of time	High involvement in investment or production planning or cost control or quality control or other activities
	Degree of risk assumed	Decisions based on much or little information
	Use of staff	Large or small staff group
	Executive style	Much or little involvement in detail; authoritarian or nondirective style; much or little contact with organization

FIGURE 18.7   Six steps necessary to operate an MIS properly and the sequential order of their performance.

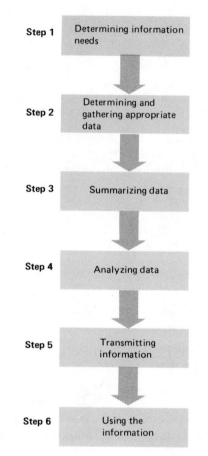

to organization. Figure 18.7 summarizes the steps discussed and indicates the sequential order in which they generally are performed.

Different Managers Need Different Kinds of Information

MIS information should be appropriate for the manager receiving it.

For maximum benefit, an MIS must collect relevant data, transform that data into appropriate information, and transmit that information to appropriate managers. Appropriate information for one manager within an organization, however, may not be appropriate information for another. Robert G. Murdick suggests that the degree of appropriateness of MIS information for a manager depends on the activities for which the manager will use the information, the organizational objectives assigned to the manager, and the level of management at which the manager functions.[14] All of these factors, of course, are closely related.

Murdick's thoughts on this matter are best summarized in Figure 18.8. As can be seen from this figure, since the overall job situations of top managers, middle managers, and first-line managers are significantly different, the types of information these managers need to satisfactorily perform their jobs also are significantly different.

FIGURE 18.8   Appropriate MIS information under various sets of organizational circumstances.

Organizational Level	Type of Management	Manager's Organizational Objectives	Appropriate Information from MIS	How MIS Information Is Used
1. Top management	CEO, president, vice-president	Survival of the firm, profit growth, accumulation and efficient use of resources	Environmental data and trends, summary reports of operations, "exception reports" of problems, forecasts	Corporate objectives, policies, constraints, decisions on strategic plans, decisions on control of the total company
2. Middle management	Middle managers such as marketing, production, and financial	Allocation of resources to assigned tasks, establishment of plans to meet operating objectives, control of operations	Summaries and exception reports of operating results, corporate objectives, policies, constraints, decisions on strategic plans, relevant actions and decisions of other middle managers	Operating plans and policies, exception reports, operating summaries, control procedures, decisions on resource allocations, actions and decisions related to other middle managers
3. First-line management	First-line managers whose work is closely related	Production of goods to meet marketing needs, supplying budgets, estimates of resource requirements, movement and storage of materials	Summary reports of transactions, detailed reports of problems, operating plans and policies, control procedures, actions and decisions of related first-line managers	Exception reports, progress reports, resource requests, dispatch orders, cross-functional reports

Adapted from Robert G. Murdick, "MIS for MBO," *Journal of Systems Management* (March 1977): 34–40. Used with permission of *Journal of Systems Management*, 24587 Bagley Road, Cleveland, Ohio 44138.

BACK TO THE CASE

Wilkenson's analysis of the status of information at Mega-Systems, Inc. should include an assessment of the MIS within the organization. The MIS at Mega-Systems is the organizational network established to provide managers with information that helps them make job-related decisions. In assessing the MIS, Wilkenson should check to see that activities performed by MIS personnel include determining information needs at Mega-Systems, determining and collecting appropriate Mega-Systems data, summarizing and analyzing these data, transmitting analyzed data to appropriate Mega-Systems managers, and having managers actually use received MIS information. Wilkenson also should check to see if information sent to managers through the MIS is appropriate for their respective levels within the organization.

Establishing an MIS

The process of establishing an MIS can be broken down into four stages: (1) planning for the MIS; (2) designing the MIS; (3) implementing the MIS; and (4) improving the MIS.

Planning for the MIS

The planning stage is perhaps the most important stage of establishing an MIS. Commonly cited factors that make planning for the establishment of an MIS an absolute necessity are the typically long periods of time needed to acquire MIS-related data-processing equipment and to integrate it within the operation of the organization, the difficulty of hiring competent personnel to operate the equipment, and the major amounts of financial and managerial resources typically needed to operate an MIS.[15]

The specific form that plans for an MIS take varies from organization to organization. However, a checklist of topics that should be addressed in all such plans is presented in Figure 18.9. In general, the more of the topics on this checklist that an MIS plan thoroughly addresses, the greater the probability the plan will be successful.

A sample plan for the establishment of an MIS at General Electric is shown in Figure 18.10. This particular plan, of course, is abbreviated. Much more detailed

---

FIGURE 18.9 Checklist for the contents of an MIS plan.

1. *Introduction*
   a. Summary of major goals, a statement of their consistency with corporate goals, and current state of planning vis-à-vis these goals
   b. Summary of aggregate cost and savings projections
   c. Summary of human resources requirements
   d. Major challenges and problems
   e. Criteria for assigning project priorities
2. *Project Identification*
   a. Maintenance projects, all projects proposed, and development projects
   b. Estimated completion times
   c. Human resources requirements, by time period and job category
   d. Computer capacity needed for system testing and implementation
   e. Economic justification by project — development costs, implementation costs, running costs, out-of-pocket savings, intangible savings
   f. Project control tools
   g. Tie-ins with other systems and master plans
3. *Hardware Projections (Derived from Projects)*
   a. Current applications — work loads and compilation and testing requirements
   b. New applications — work loads and reruns
   c. Survey of new hardware, with emphasis on design flexibility which will allow the company to take full advantage of new developments in hardware and in software
   d. Acquisition strategy, with timing contingencies
   e. Facilities requirements and growth, in hardware, tape storage, offices, and supplies
4. *Human Resources Projections (Derived from Projects)*
   a. Human resources needed by month for each category
      1. General — management, administrative, training, and planning personnel
      2. Developmental — application analysts, systems designers, methods and procedures personnel, operating system programmers, and other programmers
      3. Operational — machine operators, key punchers/verifiers, and input/output control clerks
   b. Salary levels, training needs, and estimated turnover
5. *Financial Projections by Time Period*
   a. Hardware rental, depreciation, maintenance, floor space, air conditioning, and electricity
   b. Human resources — training and fringe benefits
   c. Miscellaneous — building rental, outside service, telecommunications, and the like

FIGURE 18.10   Plan for establishing an MIS at General Electric.

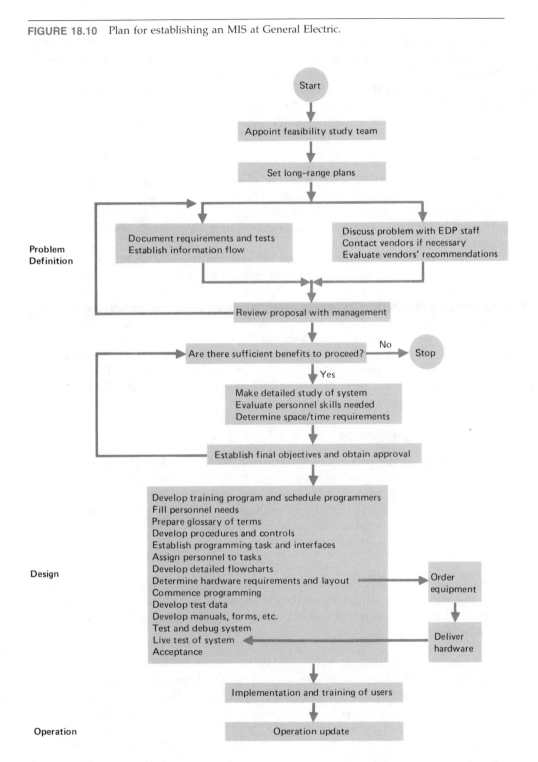

Reprinted by permission from R. E. Breen et al, *Management Information Systems: A Subcommittee Report on Definitions* (Schenectady, N.Y.: General Electric Co., 1969), p. 21.

outlines of each of the areas in this plan would be needed before it could be implemented. It is interesting to note that this plan includes a point (about a third of the way down the figure) at which management must decide if there is enough potential benefit to be gained from the existence of the MIS to continue the process of establishing it. This particular plan specifies that if management decides that there is not sufficient potential benefit to be gained by establishing the MIS, given its total costs, the project should be terminated.

Designing the MIS

Although data-processing equipment is normally an important ingredient of management information systems, the designing of an MIS should not begin with a comparative analysis of the types of such equipment available. Many MIS managers mistakenly think that data-processing equipment and an MIS are synonymous.

The design of an MIS should stress decision making.

Stoller and Van Horn indicate that, since the purpose of an MIS is to provide information that will assist managers in making better decisions, the designing of an MIS should begin with an analysis of the types of decisions managers actually make in a particular organization.[16] These authors suggest that designing an MIS should consist of four steps: (1) defining various decisions that must be made to run an organization; (2) determining the types of existing management policies that may influence the ways in which these decisions should be made; (3) pinpointing the types of data needed to make these decisions; and (4) establishing a mechanism for gathering and appropriately processing this data to obtain needed information.[17]

Implementing the MIS

Implementation is putting the MIS into action.

The third stage in the process of establishing an MIS within an organization is implementation; that is, putting the planned for and designed MIS into operation. In this stage, the equipment is acquired and integrated into the organization. Designated data is gathered, analyzed as planned, and distributed to appropriate managers within the organization, and line managers make decisions based on the information they receive from the MIS.

Improving the MIS

Once the MIS is operating, MIS managers should continually strive to maximize its value. The two sections that follow provide insights on how MIS improvements might be made.

Symptoms of an Inadequate MIS

Managers must evaluate the symptoms of an inadequate MIS to determine MIS weaknesses.

To improve an MIS, MIS managers must first find symptoms or signs that the existing MIS is inadequate. A list of such symptoms, developed by Bertram A. Colbert, a principal of Price Waterhouse & Company, is presented in Figure 18.11.[18]

Colbert divides these symptoms into three types: (1) operational symptoms; (2) psychological symptoms; and (3) report content symptoms. Operational symptoms and psychological symptoms relate, respectively, to the operation of the organization and the functioning of organization members. Report content symptoms relate to the actual make-up of the information generated by the MIS.

Although symptoms in Figure 18.11 are clues that an MIS is inadequate, the symptoms themselves may not actually pinpoint MIS weaknesses. Therefore, after

FIGURE 18.11 Symptoms of an inadequate MIS.

Operational	Psychological	Report Content
Large physical inventory adjustments	Surprise at financial results	Excessive use of tabulations of figures
Capital expenditure overruns	Poor attitude of executives about usefulness of information	Multiple preparation and distribution of identical data
Inability of executives to explain changes from year to year in operating results	Lack of understanding of financial information on part of nonfinancial executives	Disagreeing information from different sources
Uncertain direction of company growth	Lack of concern for environmental changes	Lack of periodic comparative information and trends
Cost variances unexplainable	Executive homework reviewing reports considered excessive	Lateness of information
No order backlog awareness		Too little or excess detail
No internal discussion of reported data		Inaccurate information
Insufficient knowledge about competition		Lack of standards for comparison
Purchasing parts from outside vendors when internal capability and capacity to make is available		Failure to identify variances by cause and responsibility
Record of some "sour" investments in facilities, or in programs such as R&D and advertising		Inadequate externally generated information

Reprinted by permission of the Institute of Management Services from Bertram A. Colbert, "The Management Information System," *Management Services* 4, no. 5 (September/October 1967): 18.

such symptoms are detected, MIS managers usually must gather additional information to determine what MIS weaknesses exist. Answering questions such as the following would be of some help to MIS managers in determining these weaknesses:[19]

1. Where and how do managers get information?
2. Can managers make better use of their contacts to get information?
3. In what areas is managers' knowledge weakest, and how can managers be given information to minimize these weaknesses?
4. Do managers tend to act before receiving information?
5. Do managers wait so long for information that opportunities pass them by and the organization becomes bottlenecked?

Typical Improvements to an MIS

MIS inadequacies vary from situation to situation, depending on such factors as the quality of an MIS plan, the appropriateness of an MIS design, and the type of individuals operating an MIS. However, several activities have the potential of improving the MIS of most organizations. These activities include:

1. *Building cooperation among MIS personnel and line managers*[20] Cooperation of this sort encourages line managers to give MIS personnel honest opinions of

To improve an MIS, managers should:

1. Build cooperation.

the quality of information being received. Through this type of interaction, MIS designers and operators should be able to improve the effectiveness of an MIS.

2. Stress decision making.

2. *Constantly stressing that MIS personnel should strive to accomplish the purpose of the MIS: providing managers with decision-related information*   In this regard, it probably would be of great benefit to hold line managers responsible for continually educating MIS personnel on the types of decisions organization managers make and the corresponding steps taken to make these decisions. The better MIS personnel understand the decision situations that face operating managers, the higher the probability that MIS information will be appropriate for decisions these managers must make.

3. Use cost-benefit analysis.

3. *Holding, wherever possible, both line managers and MIS personnel accountable for MIS activities on a cost-benefit basis*[21]   This accountability reminds line managers and MIS personnel that the benefits the organization receives from MIS functions must exceed the costs. In effect, this accountability emphasis helps to increase the cost conscientiousness of both line managers and MIS personnel.

4. Consider people.

4. *Operating an MIS in a "people-conscious" manner*   An MIS, like the formal pyramidal organization, is based on the assumption that organizational affairs can and should be handled in a completely logical manner.[22] Logic, of course, is extremely important to the design and implementation of an MIS. In addition, however, MIS activities should also include people considerations.[23] After all, even if MIS activities are well thought out and completely logical, an MIS can be ineffective simply because people do not use it as intended.

According to Dickson and Simmons, several factors can cause people to resist using an MIS.[24] A summary of these factors according to working groups is presented in Figure 18.12. This study implies that for managers to improve MIS effectiveness, they may have to take steps to reduce such factors as threats to power and status that might be discouraging MIS use.

FIGURE 18.12   Causes for four different working groups' resistance to an MIS.

	Operating (Nonclerical)	Operating (Clerical)	Operating Management	Top Management
Threats to Economic Security		X	X*	
Threats to Status or Power		X	X*	
Increased Job Complexity	X		X	X
Uncertainty or Unfamiliarity	X	X	X	X
Changed Interpersonal Relations or Work Patterns		X*	X	
Changed Superior–Subordinate Relationships		X*	X	
Increased Rigidity or Time Pressure	X	X	X	
Role Ambiguity		X	X*	X
Feelings of Insecurity		X	X*	X*

X = The reason is possibly the cause of resistance to MIS development.
X* = The reason has a strong possibility of being the cause of resistance.

From Dickson/Simmons, "The Behavioral Side of MIS," *Business Horizons* (August 1970): 68. Copyright, 1970, by the Foundation for the School of Business at Indiana University. Reprinted by permission.

BACK TO THE CASE

Mega-Systems presently has an MIS. Wilkenson, however, may be able to gain valuable insights on the status of information at Mega-Systems by evaluating the way in which the existing MIS was established. For example, Wilkenson should ask the following questions about the planning stage of Mega-Systems' MIS: Was appropriate data-processing equipment acquired and integrated? Have appropriate personnel been acquired to operate the equipment?

About the design and implementation stages of Mega-Systems' MIS, Wilkenson should seek answers to such questions as: Did the design of the present MIS begin with an analysis of managerial decision making? Does the present MIS exist as designed and implemented?

Wilkenson also should try to determine whether MIS managers, other MIS personnel, and line managers are continually trying to improve the MIS. All such organization members should be aware of the symptoms of an inadequate MIS and should be attempting to pinpoint and eliminate corresponding MIS weaknesses.

Finally, Wilkenson should consider the possibilities of improving his MIS by: (1) building additional cooperation between MIS managers, MIS personnel, and line managers; (2) stressing that the purpose of the MIS is to provide managers with decision-related information; (3) using cost-benefit analysis to evaluate MIS activities; and (4) ensuring that the MIS operates in a people-conscious manner.

THE MANAGEMENT DECISION SUPPORT SYSTEM (MDSS)

Traditionally, the MIS that uses electronic assistance in gathering data and providing related information to managers has been invaluable. This MIS assistance has been especially useful in areas where programmed decisions (see Chapter 5) are necessary, since the computer continually generates the information that helps managers make these decisions. An example is using the computer to track cumulative labour costs by department. The computer can be used to automatically gather and update the cumulative labour costs per department, compare the costs to corresponding annual budgets, and calculate the percentage of the budget that each department has reached to date. Such information would normally be useful in controlling departmental labour costs.

Electronic assistance is invaluable to an MIS.

Closely related to the MIS is the **management decision support system (MDSS)**—an interdependent set of decision aids that help managers make nonprogrammed decisions (see Chapter 5).[25] Figure 18.13 illustrates possible components of the MDSS and describes what they do. The MDSS is typically characterized by the following:[26]

Management decision support systems are characterized by:

1. *One or more corporate databases*   A **database** is a reservoir of corporate facts consistently organized to fit the information needs of a variety of organization members. These databases (also termed corporate databases) tend to contain facts about all important facets of company operations, including financial as well as non-financial information. These facts are used to explore issues important to the corporation. For example, a manager might find it helpful to use facts from the corporate database to forecast profits for each of the next three years.

1. Corporate databases.

2. *One or more user databases*   In addition to the corporate databases, an MDSS tends to contain several additional user databases. A **user database** is a database developed by an individual manager or other user. These databases may be

2. User databases.

FIGURE 18.13 Possible components of a management decision support system (MDSS) and what they do.

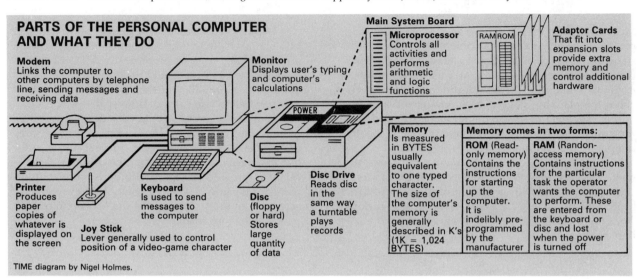

PARTS OF THE PERSONAL COMPUTER AND WHAT THEY DO

Main System Board

Microprocessor Controls all activities and performs arithmetic and logic functions

RAM ROM

Adaptor Cards That fit into expansion slots provide extra memory and control additional hardware

Modem Links the computer to other computers by telephone line, sending messages and receiving data

Monitor Displays user's typing and computer's calculations

POWER

Printer Produces paper copies of whatever is displayed on the screen

Joy Stick Lever generally used to control position of a video-game character

Keyboard Is used to send messages to the computer

Disc (floppy or hard) Stores large quantity of data

Disc Drive Reads disc in the same way a turntable plays records

Memory Is measured in BYTES usually equivalent to one typed character. The size of the computer's memory is generally described in K's (1K = 1,024 BYTES)

Memory comes in two forms:

| **ROM** (Read-only memory) Contains the instructions for starting up the computer. It is indelibly pre-programmed by the manufacturer | **RAM** (Random-access memory) Contains instructions for the particular task the operator wants the computer to perform. These are entered from the keyboard or disc and lost when the power is turned off |

TIME diagram by Nigel Holmes.

derived from but are not necessarily limited to the corporate database. They tend to address specific issues peculiar to the individual users. For example, a production manager might be interested in exploring the specific issue of lowering production costs. To do so, the manager might build a simple user database that includes departmental facts about reject rates of materials purchased from various suppliers. The manager might be able to lower production costs by eliminating the materials from the suppliers with the highest reject rates.

3. Model databases.

3. *A set of quantitative tools stored in a model base* A **model base** is a collection of quantitative computer programs that can assist MDSS users in analyzing data in databases. For example, the production manager discussed in item 2 might use a correlation analysis program stored in a model base to accurately determine any relationships that might exist between reject rates and the materials from various suppliers.

One desirable feature of a model base is its ability to allow the user to perform **"what if" analysis**—the simulation of a business situation over and over again using somewhat different data for selected decision areas. For example, a manager might first determine the profitability of a company under present conditions. The manager might then ask *what* would happen *if* materials costs increased by 5 percent. Or *if* products were sold at a different price. Popular programs such as Lotus 1-2-3 and the Interactive Financial Planning System (IFPS)[27] allow managers to ask as many "what if's" as they want and to save their answers without changing their original data.

4. Dialogue capability.

4. *A dialogue capability* The ability of an MDSS user to interact with an MDSS is **dialogue capability**. Such interaction typically involves extracting data from a database, calling various models stored in the model base, and storing analysis results in a file. How this dialogue capability interacts with other MDSS ingredients is depicted in Figure 18.14.

FIGURE 18.14   How dialogue capability interacts with other MDSS ingredients.

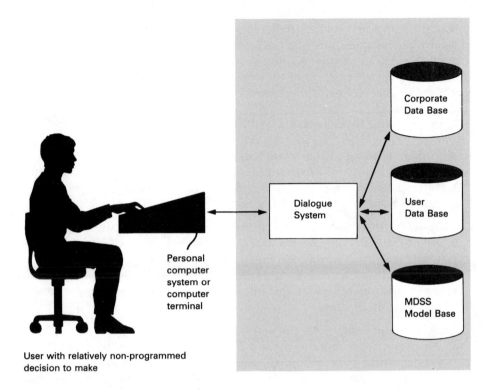

User with relatively non-programmed
decision to make

The continued technological developments related to microcomputers have made the use of the MDSS concept feasible and its application available to virtually all managers. In addition, the continued development of extensive software to support information analysis related to more subjective decision making is contributing to the popularity of MDSS.

BACK TO THE CASE

The information about MDSS should be particularly interesting to Wilkenson in evaluating Greenberg's comments. Perhaps information is not being appropriately used at Mega-Systems simply because managers are not familiar with the use of the MDSS. Wilkenson should make sure that managers are balancing MIS reports for programmed decisions with MDSS reports for non-programmed decisions.

In exploring this issue, Wilkenson must answer several questions: Do managers have adequate equipment to operate an MDSS? Do they have adequate access to a corporate database? Are managers properly employing user databases? Is there an appropriate model base available to managers? Is there adequate dialogue capability within the existing MDSS? If the answers to these and other related questions are yes, then the probability is high that the Mega-Systems MDSS is being properly used. If the answers are no, then Wilkenson would probably be able to improve operations within his company by encouraging his managers to appropriately use an MDSS.

Action Summary

Reread the learning objectives that follow. Each objective is followed by questions. Answering these questions accurately will help you to retain the most important concepts discussed in this chapter. After answering each question, check your answer with the answer key at the end of this chapter. (*Hint*: If you have doubt regarding the correct response, consult the page that follows the answer.)

Circle:

From studying this chapter, I will attempt to acquire:

1. An understanding of the relationship between data and information.

a, b, c, d, e

    a. Data can be: (a) information; (b) opinion; (c) premises; (d) facts; (e) gossip.

a, b, c, d, e

    b. Information can be defined as conclusions derived from: (a) data analysis; (b) opinion; (c) premises; (d) gossip; (e) none of the above.

2. Insights on the main factors that influence the value of information.

a, b, c, d, e

    a. All of the following are primary factors determining the value of information except: (a) appropriateness; (b) expense; (c) quality; (d) timeliness; (e) quantity.

T, F

    b. The appropriateness of the information increases as the volume of the information increases.

3. Knowledge of some potential steps for evaluating information.

a, b, c, d, e

    a. All of the following are main activities in evaluating information except: (a) acquiring information; (b) comparing value with cost of information; (c) selecting data to be evaluated; (d) using information in decision making: (e) discounting expected value for deficiencies and inaccuracies.

T, F

    b. The primary concern of management in evaluating information is the dollar value of the benefits gained compared to the cost of generating that information.

4. An appreciation for the role of computers in handling information.

a, b, c, d, e

    a. All of the following are main computer functions except: (a) input; (b) storage; (c) control; (d) heuristic; (e) output.

a, b, c, d, e

    b. All of the following are possible pitfalls in using the computer except: (a) thinking that a computer is independently capable of creative activities; (b) failing to realize that a computer is capable only of following precise and detailed instructions; (c) training and retraining all computer operating personnel; (d) spending too much money on computer assistance; (e) over-estimating the value of computer output.

5. An understanding of the importance of a management information system (MIS) to an organization.

T, F

    a. A management information system is a network established within an organization to provide managers with information that will assist them in decision making.

a, b, c, d, e

    b. "Determining information needs" is which of the steps necessary to operate an MIS: (a) first; (b) second; (c) third: (d) fourth; (e) none of the above.

6. A feasible strategy for establishing an MIS.

a, b, c, d, e

    a. All of the following are stages in the process of establishing an MIS except: (a) planning; (b) designing; (c) improving; (d) implementing; (e) all of the above are stages.

b. Which of the following activities has the potential of improving an MIS: (a) stressing that MIS personnel should strive to accomplish the purpose of an MIS; (b) operating an MIS in a "people-conscious" manner; (c) encouraging line managers to continually request additional information through the MIS; (d) a and b; (e) all of the above.   a, b, c, d, e

7. **Information about what a management decision support system is and how it operates.**
    a. A management decision support system is a set of decision aids aimed at helping managers make non-programmed decisions.   T, F
    b. There is basically no difference between a corporate database and a user database.   T, F
    c. Dialogue capability allows the MDSS user to interact with an MIS.   T, F

INTRODUCTORY CASE WRAP-UP

"A Question of Measurement" (p. 496) and its related back-to-the-case sections were written to help you better understand the management concepts contained in this chapter. Answer the following discussion questions about this introductory case to further enrich your understanding of the chapter content:

1. How does the series of "checks and measurements" mentioned by Turner fit into the control process of Mega-Systems, Inc.?
2. What do you think Greenberg meant by, "I wonder if the system is too thorough"?
3. How do managers determine if too many checks and measurements are being taken during the controlling process?

Issues for Review and Discussion

1. What is the difference between data and information?
2. List and define four major factors that influence the value of information.
3. What are operational control decisions and strategic planning decisions? What characterizes information appropriate for making each of these decisions?
4. Discuss the major activities involved in evaluating information.
5. What factors tend to limit the usefulness of information, and how can these factors be overcome?
6. Is a computer a flexible management tool? Explain.
7. How do the main functions of a computer relate to one another?
8. Summarize the major pitfalls managers must avoid when using a computer.
9. Define *MIS*, and discuss its importance to management.
10. What steps must be performed to operate an MIS properly?
11. What major steps are involved in establishing an MIS?
12. Why is planning for an MIS such an important part of establishing an MIS?
13. Why does the designing of an MIS begin with analyzing managerial decision making?
14. How should managers use the symptoms of an inadequate MIS as listed in Figure 18.11?
15. How could "building cooperation among MIS personnel and line managers" typically improve an MIS?
16. How can management use cost-benefit analysis to improve an MIS?
17. Describe five possible causes of resistance to using an MIS. What can managers do to ensure that these causes do not affect their organization's MIS?
18. How does an MDSS differ from an MIS? Define *"what if" analysis* and give an illustration of how a manager might use it.

Sources of Additional Information

Ahituv, Niv, and Seev Neumann. *Principles of Information Systems for Management*. Dubuque, Iowa: Wm. C. Brown, 1982.

Attaran, Mohsen, and Hossein Bidgoli. "Developing an Effective Manufacturing Decision Support System." *Business* 36 (October/November/December 1986): 9–16.

Berg, Norman A. *General Management: An Analytical Approach*. Homewood, Ill.: Richard D. Irwin, 1984.

Brabb, George J. *Computers and Information Systems in Business*. Boston: Houghton Mifflin, 1980.

Chen, Dr. Richard. "Hospital Information System Design." *Journal of Systems Management* (May 1984): 24–28.

Ehrlemark, Ulla. "Design Your Own Management Information Systems." *Long-Range Planning* 17 (April 1984): 85–95.

Gillenson, Mark L., and Robert Goldberg. *Strategic Planning, Systems Analysis, and Database Design*. New York: Wiley, 1984.

Henderson, Marjorie, Marti J. Rhea, and Joe L. Welch. "How to Manage the Information Resource—The Xerox Case." *Business* 37 (April/May/June 1987): 3–10.

Middaugh, J. Kendall, III. "Data Transmission: Guarding the System." *Business* 35 (January/February/March 1985): 3–10.

Murray, John P. "How an Information Center Improved Productivity." *Management Accounting* (March 1984): 38–44.

Orlicky, Joseph A. *The Successful Computer System*. New York: McGraw-Hill, 1969.

Panko, Raymond R. "A Different Perspective on Office Systems." *Administrative Management* 42 (August 1981): 30–32ff.

"The Spreading Danger of Computer Crime." *Business Week*, April 20, 1981, 86–92.

Wagner, G. R. "Decision Support Systems: Computerized Mind Support for Executive Problems." *Managerial Planning* 30 (September/October 1981): 3–8, 16.

Notes

1. Henry Mintzberg, "The Myths of MIS," *California Management Review* (Fall 1972): 92–97.
2. Jay W. Forrester, "Managerial Decision Making," in *Management and the Computer of the Future*, ed. Martin Greenberger (Cambridge, Mass., and New York: MIT Press and Wiley, 1962), 37.
3. The following discussion is based largely on Robert H. Gregory and Richard L. Van Horn, "Value and Cost of Information," in *Systems Analysis Techniques*, ed. J. Daniel Conger and Robert W. Knapp (New York: Wiley, 1974), 473–89.
4. John T. Small and William B. Lee, "In Search of MIS," *MSU Business Topics* (Autumn 1975): 47–55.
5. G. Anthony Gorry and Michael S. Scott Morton, "A Framework for Management Information Systems," *Sloan Management Review* 13 (Fall 1971): 55–70.
6. "A Wealth of Information Can Be Worthless," *Newsweek*, August 7, 1978, 28.
7. *H & S Reports: For the People of Haskins and Sells* 14 (Autumn 1977): 28.
8. Robert Sanford, "Some Loose Talk about and with Computers," *Beehive* (United Aircraft Corporation), Fall 1960.
9. John Dearden and Richard L. Nolan, "How to Control the Computer Resource," *Harvard Business Review*. (November/December 1973): 68–78.
10. Martin D. J. Buss, "Penny-wise Approach to Data Processing," *Harvard Business Review* (July/August 1981): 111.
11. A.R. Zipf, "Retaining Mastery of the Computer," *Harvard Business Review* (September/October 1968): 70.
12. Robert W. Holmes, "Twelve Areas to Investigate for Better MIS," *Financial Executive* (July 1970): 24.
13. This section is based on Richard A. Johnson, R. Joseph Monsen, Henry P. Knowles, and Borge O. Saxberg, *Management, Systems, and Society: An Introduction* (Santa Monica, Calif.: Goodyear, 1976), 113–20.
14. Robert G. Murdick, "MIS for MBO," *Journal of Systems Management* (March 1977): 34–40.
15. F. Warren McFarlan, "Problems in Planning the Information System," *Harvard Business Review* (March/April 1971): 75.
16. David S. Stoller and Richard L. Van Horn, *Design of a Management Information System* (Santa Monica, Calif.: Rand Corporation, 1958).
17. More detail on the design of an MIS can be found in Robert G. Murdick, "MIS Development Procedures," *Journal of Systems Management* 21 (December 1970): 22–26.
18. Bertram A. Colbert, "The Management Information System," *Management Services* 4 (September/October 1967): 15–24.

19. Adapted from Henry Mintzberg, "The Manager's Job: Folklore and Fact," *Harvard Business Review* (July/August 1975): 58.

20. William R. King and David I. Cleland, "Manager-Analysts Teamwork in MIS," *Business Horizons* 14 (April 1971): 59–68.

21. Regina Herzlinger, "Why Data Systems in Non-profit Organizations Fail," *Harvard Business Review* (January/February 1977): 81–86.

22. Chris Argyris, "Management Information Systems: The Challenge of Rationality and Emotionality," *Management Science* (February 1971): 275–92.

23. Robert W. Holmes, "Developing Better Management Information Systems," *Financial Executive* 38 (July 1970): 24–31.

24. G. W. Dickson and John K. Simmons, "The Behavioral Side of MIS," *Business Horizons* (August 1970): 59, 71.

25. Steven L. Mandell, *Computers and Data Processing: Concepts and Applications with BASIC* (St. Paul, Minn.: West Publishing, 1982, 370–91.

26. Mark G. Simkin, *Computer Information Systems for Business* (Dubuque, Iowa: Wm. C. Brown, 1987), 299–301.

27. For additional information on these software packages, see *Lotus 1-2-3 Reference Manual* (Cambridge, Mass.: Lotus Development Corporation, 1985); *IFPS User's Manual* (Austin, Tex.: Execucom Systems Corporation, 1984).

Action Summary Answer Key

1. a. d, p. 497
   b. a, p. 497
2. a. b, pp. 497–498
   b. F, p. 498

3. a. d, p. 501
   b. T, p. 501
4. a. d, p. 505
   b. c, pp. 506–507

5. a. T, p. 507
   b. a, pp. 508–510
6. a. e, p. 511
   b. d, p. 515–516

7. a. T, p. 517
   b. F, pp. 517–518
   c. F, p. 518

MANAGING INFORMATION TECHNOLOGY IN THE '90s

According to Andrew Grindlay, a professor of business administration at the University of Western Ontario, during the next decade it is Canadians' skill in managing that will distinguish us from competing nations in a way nothing else can and only our management skills will keep us at the forefront in the world economic arena. This means that Canadians will have to take whatever steps are necessary to ensure that their management practices are as good as, if not better than, those of any other country in the world. In the final decade of the twentieth century, Canadians will find themselves searching constantly for new ways of enhancing the performance of their managers, either by enabling them to reduce costs or improving their decision making, or both.

THE ROLE OF THE COMPUTER

Despite the ready availability of the necessary hardware, software, and projection equipment, few companies meet to set strategy by viewing numbers and graphs in brilliant colour on a large screen on the wall. Most of the early predictions about how important computers would be for senior executives have turned out to be rather naive. The reason for this is quite apparent if one observes managers at work. According to McGill University professor Henry Mintzberg in his book, *The Nature of Managerial Work*:

> Managers strongly favor the verbal media—namely telephone calls and meetings. They seem to cherish soft information—especially gossip, hearsay and speculation. Today's gossip may be tomorrow's fact. Managers do not write down much of what they hear. The strategic data bank of the organization is not in the memory of its computers but in the minds of its managers.

After studying dozens of companies and trying to identify what differentiated the excellent firms from the others, Tom Peters and Robert Waterman wrote in their book, *In Search of Excellence*: "While it is true that good companies have superb analytical skills, we believe their major decisions are shaped more by their values than by their dexterity with numbers."

Despite such findings, the computer is still a useful management tool according to Grindlay. As he points out, management is much more than just talking to people and having a sense of values. There is usually a substantial amount of analytical work which must precede important decisions and there is a critical need for control to ensure that plans are implemented and results achieved. All of this is a part of management, and the

"managers . . . are finding the computer an ever more useful analytical and control tool."

last two activities, analysis and control, are precisely where the computer is making its greatest contribution. If one thinks of the typical organization as having a classic pyramid shape, it is probable that one will find the strategic decision making being done by a few people at the very top and the analysis and control being performed at the middle and lower levels.

This, however, is not true in all cases. Harold Geneen, the controversial former CEO of International Telephone and Telegraph Company, was a fanatic for control. During his seventeen years at the helm of IT and T, he increased the annual operating profit from $14 million to $562 million. Having a strong vision of what he wanted IT and T to be, Geneen was constantly looking for inefficiencies because he believed that all large organizations were inefficient. According to him:

> . . . anyone in business, if he sets up the proper kinds of controls—controls that tell him when any segment of his company is not doing what he expected, and tell him promptly enough and in enough detail so that he can go back behind the numbers and analyze precisely where it is that he has to take action— . . . could run a progressive, profitable and growth-oriented company. That's what a good set of numbers will do for you.

THE IMPACT ON MANAGEMENT

Emerging from the many advances made in technology and information systems is the fact that managers everywhere at all levels are finding the computer an ever more useful analytical and control tool. The possibility for waste and error in this environment of strong technological growth is, however, high, to say the least. Almost every day there is a story in the papers about some company or government department that, because of a computer, has got itself into trouble. Generally, the computer is blamed but it is widely known that these machines do absolutely nothing except what they have been told to do by humans. Keeping track of the vast quantities of information in a large organization and making it available to people when they need it is an enormous task and one which only a properly managed computer system can perform. Somebody has to plan, organize, and control the introduction and use of information technology if it is to be done effectively. This "somebody" includes senior executives, the information systems (IS) people, and the users.

Organizations large and small, public and private are rethinking the role of these groups. Information technology has become so important to the survival of some enterprises that it demands the time and attention of the most senior executives. Many companies are finding that without a well-managed IS department, they would suffer a distinct competitive disadvantage and eventually be ineffective in the marketplace.

TRENDS IN INFORMATION TECHNOLOGY

Four major interrelated trends in information technology that have had a substantial impact on management in both the private and public sectors are:

1. The increasing desire and ability of users to do some or all of their own computing.
2. A vast improvement in the capabilities and cost of office workstations.
3. A dramatic increase in power and simplicity of the new programming languages.
4. Increasing availability and capability of networks that connect workstations to each other and to a mainframe.

These four trends, all occurring together and pushing in the same direction, are having a significant effect on the way organizations use and manage their computing resources. The first trend has appeared partly because of a better informed user-base and partly because of the tremendous improvements in the information technology as reflected in the other three trends. According to Scott G. Abbey, vice-president of Morgan Stanley, a large U.S. investment house that has pioneered user development applications, "In the future, we expect MIS to become primarily a data administration and operations organization. End users will develop 90 percent of their own applications."

A particular concern to some organizations is the hidden cost of personal computers. The capital cost of $5 000 or so is only the beginning. The Gillette Company in the U.S. estimates that over its three-year life, a personal computer—with its furniture, training, technical support, communications items, extra memory, and maintenance—costs between $25 000 and $30 000.

Emerging from all these advances is a significant change in the role of the users and the users' managers who, more and more, are taking responsibility for application systems planning, system design, project management and data entry, as well as for the security and use of their workstations. This responsibility is giving them freedom to explore new and important ways of improving the efficiency and effectiveness of their organizational units.

The impact on the IS department and its manager is equally dramatic. The IS manager who will provide the technological leadership necessary for the coming decade will have a solid understanding of information technology, will have a deep appreciation of the organization and what is important to it, and will have demonstrated strong management skills. Most important, that person will have a vision, a vision of where and how the organization should be using information technology to help it achieve its strategic goals. It will be an informed vision, based on such an appreciation of the mission of the enterprise, its competitors, and its clients that the perspective the IS manager holds will coincide closely with that of the other senior executives. The person will also need to be able to implement his or her ideas.

As well, this manager will need to overcome the inertia that every organization possesses, and move the enterprise steadily in the envisioned direction. Although one tends to think of the users as the ones who resist change, they are not alone. According to Scott Abbey, "Despite their roles as agents of change for the rest of the organization, technical people often turn out to be very conservative in their approach to their own work." One way of facilitating the change is through the training of the employees. The skills of the IS professional become obsolete after about three years and unless constantly upgraded will become practically useless. The person then becomes defensive and can actually inhibit the change that is necessary.

DISCUSSION ISSUES

1. According to the article, how might computers aid managers in improving their performance of the various managerial functions? Explain.
2. What are some of the potential pitfalls associated with implementing computerized information systems?
3. Given advances in computer technology, how will the MIS department contribute to future organizational performance? What are some of the considerations associated with making an MIS more effective? Discuss.

Based on "Managing Information Technology: The Challenge of the '90s," by Andrew Grindlay in *Business Quarterly*, Spring 1986. Copyright 1986, *Business Quarterly*, School of Business Administration, The University of Western Ontario, London, Canada. Used with permission.

TOPICS FOR SPECIAL EMPHASIS

Sections 1 to 5 of this text introduced the subject of management and presented detailed discussions of the four management functions: planning, organizing, influencing, and controlling. This last section emphasizes carefully selected topics that represent special challenges for modern managers. These topics are social responsibility, international management, and management skills for the future.

Chapter 19

Chapter 19, "Social Responsibility: An Emphasis on Ethics," focuses on the responsibilities that managers have to society. Social responsibility is defined as the managerial obligation to take action that protects and improves the welfare of society as a whole along with organizational interests. Although there are arguments both for and against businesses meeting social responsibilities, it is hypothesized that modern managers must spend a significant amount of time dealing with social issues. This chapter recommends that modern managers strive to make organizations socially responsive by being both effective and efficient in pursuing social responsibilities. The chapter also discusses the idea that modern managers should plan, organize, influence, and control for social responsibility activities and that society should take positive steps to help businesses meet their social responsibilities. The chapter concludes with a discussion of ethics and their relationship to social responsibility.

Chapter 20

Chapter 20, "International Management," focuses on the international arena in which modern managers operate. International management is defined as performing management activities across national borders and is designated as a critical and growing challenge of modern managers. A multinational corporation is defined as a company that has significant operations in more than one country. The complexity and risk associated with managing multinational corporations also are discussed. Planning, organizing, influencing, and controlling within multinational corporations is emphasized, as is the topic of comparative management. Comparative management is the study of management processes within different countries to examine their potential under different environmental conditions. In this text, a primary focus of comparative management is the study of Japanese management techniques.

Chapter 21

Chapter 21, "Management Skills for the Future," discusses the skills that managers will need to be successful in the future. The hypothesis is made that, for individuals of the future to be successful as managers, they must possess the skills to apply both systems theory and functional theory to unique organizational situations. This chapter also predicts that the organizational situations of the future will be somewhat different in that the management systems will tend to be larger and more complicated and the work force will tend to be older and more deeply interested in such issues as quality of life, and will contain more women managers. Energy, as known today, will be in short supply. The chapter concludes with a recommendation that training programs aimed at preparing managers for the future should stress that managers become future-oriented, approach the study of management as a profession, and bear in mind that the job of a manager is continually changing.

SOCIAL RESPONSIBILITY: AN EMPHASIS ON ETHICS

STUDENT LEARNING OBJECTIVES

From studying this chapter, I will attempt to acquire:

1. An understanding of the term *social responsibility*.
2. An appreciation for the arguments both for and against business assuming social responsibilities.
3. Useful strategies for increasing the social responsiveness of an organization.
4. Insights on the planning, organizing, influencing, and controlling of social responsibility activities.
5. An understanding of the relationship between social responsibility and ethics.

CHAPTER OUTLINE

ASSISTING THE DISABLED

Tony Fortunato is president of Bonaventure Coiffures, a chain of thirty-six beauty shops spread out over Ottawa, Montreal, Halifax, and Toronto. Fortunato presently resides in Montreal where company headquarters are located. By almost any criteria, Bonaventure Coiffures shops have been extremely successful over the past several years. In fact, Fortunato has just recently completed plans for opening seven new Bonaventure Coiffures shops in Winnipeg in about six months.

It was Tuesday morning, and Fortunato had just arrived at his office. His secretary handed him a special delivery envelope that had been delivered only twenty minutes earlier. Fortunato opened the envelope and began to read the following letter from a woman in Halifax:

Mr. Tony Fortunato, President
Bonaventure Coiffures
3045 rue St. Catherine
Montreal, Quebec H3R 2G7

Dear Mr. Fortunato:

I have a special problem that I hope you can help me solve. I live in the Halifax area and hear nothing but fantastic comments about the beauticians you have in your shops in our city. I also hear very good things about how clean and well kept the shops themselves actually are.

My problem is that I am disabled and am confined to a wheelchair. I can arrange transportation to and from any of your shops but cannot climb the several steps in front of each of them. From what I hear, it also would be difficult for me to have my hair washed in one of your basins, even if I could get into one of your shops. Friends also tell me that your shops are somewhat cramped and that there may be some areas where I would find it difficult to manoeuvre.

To solve my problem, I thought you might be able to install a ramp on the outside of your shops so that wheelchair customers like myself could enter your place of business. I also wonder if you could alter your equipment and facilities somewhat so that individuals like myself could get hair washed and manoeuvre wheelchairs once within one of your establishments.

Thank you for your attention to this matter, and I hope you can make it easier for the disabled to be your customers.

Sincerely yours,

Tiffany McGill

Tiffany McGill

When Fortunato had finished the letter, he was quite perplexed. All of Tiffany McGill's information about his beauty salons was accurate. He wondered, however, if he could or really should do anything about Tiffany McGill's problem.

What's Ahead

The introductory case ends with Tony Fortunato, the president of Bonaventure Coiffures, reflecting on a customer request to modify his beauty shops so that they are more easily accessible to the disabled. This chapter presents material that a manager like Fortunato should understand to assess his social responsibility in this situation. Specifically, this chapter discusses: (1) fundamentals of social responsibility; (2) social responsiveness; (3) social responsibility activities and management functions; (4) how society can help business meet social obligations; and (5) ethics and social responsibility.

FUNDAMENTALS OF SOCIAL RESPONSIBILITY

The term *social responsibility* means different things to different people.[1] For purposes of this chapter, however, **social responsibility** is defined as the managerial obligation to take action that protects and improves the welfare of society as a whole and also of organizational interests.[2] The manager in the cartoon is not being socially responsible, because he is stressing societal goals and de-emphasizing organizational goals. According to the concept of social responsibility, a manager must strive to achieve both organizational and societal goals.

Social responsibility is the managerial obligation to protect the interests of society and the organization.

"You know what I think, folks? Improving technology isn't important. Increased profits aren't important. What's important is to be warm, decent human beings."

New Yorker, *June 1, 1987, p. 39. Drawing by Handelsman; © 1987 The New Yorker Magazine, Inc.*

The amount of attention given to the area of social responsibility by both management and society has increased in recent years and probably will continue to increase in the future.[3] The following sections present the fundamentals of social responsibility by discussing: (1) the Davis model of social responsibility; (2) areas of social responsibility activity; and (3) varying opinions on social responsibility. Since the main thrust of recent social responsibility issues has focused primarily on business, this chapter focuses primarily on the social responsibility of business systems.

The Davis Model of Social Responsibility

Davis has proposed the following:

A generally accepted model of social responsibility was developed by Keith Davis.[4] Stated simply, Davis's model is a list of five propositions that describe why and how business should adhere to the obligation to take action that protects and improves the welfare of society and the organization. These propositions and corresponding explanations are:

1. Social responsibility comes from social power.

Proposition 1: Social responsibility arises from social power   This proposition is built on the premise that business has a significant amount of influence or power over such critical social issues as minority employment and environmental pollution. In essence, the collective action of all business in the country mainly determines the proportion of minorities employed and the prevailing condition of the environment in which all citizens must live.

Building on this premise, Davis reasons that, since business has this power over society, society can and must hold business responsible for social conditions that result from exercising this power.[5] Davis explains that society's legal system does not expect more of business than it does of each individual citizen exercising his or her own personal power.

2. Society and business must be partners.

Proposition 2: Business shall operate as a two-way open system with open receipt of inputs from society and open disclosure of its operation to the public   According to this proposition, business must be willing to listen to societal representatives on what must be done to sustain or improve societal welfare. In turn, society must be willing to listen to the reports of business on what it is doing to meet its social responsibilities. Davis suggests that continuing, honest, and open communications between business and societal representatives must exist if the overall welfare of society is to be maintained or improved.

3. Business must consider how proposed activities will affect society.

Proposition 3: Both social costs and benefits of an activity, product, or service shall be thoroughly calculated and considered to decide whether or not to proceed with it   This proposition stresses that technical feasibility and economic profitability are not the only factors that should influence business decision making. Business should also consider both the long- and short-term societal consequences of all business activities before such activities are undertaken.

4. Society must ultimately pay for business's social costs.

Proposition 4: Social costs related to each activity, product, or service shall be passed on to the consumer   This proposition states that business cannot be expected to finance completely activities that may be economically disadvantageous but socially advantageous. The cost of maintaining socially desirable activities within business should be passed on to consumers through higher prices for the goods or services related to those socially desirable activities.

Proposition 5: Business institutions, as citizens, have the responsibility to become involved in certain social problems that are outside of their normal areas of operation   This last proposition makes the point that, if a business possesses the expertise to solve a social problem with which it may not be directly associated, it should be held responsible for helping society to solve that problem. Davis reasons that, since business eventually will share increased profit from a generally improved society, business should share in the responsibility of all citizenry to generally improve that society.

5. Business must be willing to help others help society.

BACK TO THE CASE

Social responsibility is the obligation of a business manager to take action that protects and improves the welfare of society along with the interests of the organization. Tony Fortunato, the president of Bonaventure Coiffures beauty shops in the introductory case, presently is considering his social responsibility to the disabled.

Following the logic of Davis's social responsibility model, Fortunato should attempt to service Tiffany McGill because such an activity generally would help to improve society and thereby profit Fortunato as well as others. By making Bonaventure Coiffures wheelchair-accessible, Fortunato would be addressing not only McGill's problem, but also that of many other disabled people who might like to visit his salon. Furthermore, Fortunato's actions might encourage other businesses to respond to the needs of the disabled.

The information presented thus far in this chapter also implies that Fortunato should decide what to do about McGill's situation by considering not only the technical feasibility and economic profitability of various actions, but also the possible effects of those actions on society as a whole. Of course, depending on what Fortunato actually does about this situation, the costs he would incur as a result of taking action would be passed on to his patrons. Obviously, he should not do so much that his prices are no longer competitive.

As a result of handling McGill's problem, Fortunato could acquire some expertise in the general area of assisting the disabled. This expertise could benefit society if Fortunato shared it with businesspeople in other areas. For example, Fortunato might be able to help the president of another company make barbershops more accessible to disabled customers.

Areas of Social Responsibility Activity

The areas in which business can become involved to protect and improve the welfare of society are numerous and diversified (see Figure 19.1). Perhaps the most publicized of these areas are urban affairs, consumer affairs, and environmental affairs.[6]

The following Management in Action feature deals with a specific example of corporate philanthropy—corporate volunteerism. The imperatives and advantages pushing for increased corporate volunteerism are explored and specific examples of actions undertaken by numerous organizations are outlined. A discussion of the organizational conditions necessary for successfully undertaking these activities is also included.

FIGURE 19.1   Major social responsibility areas in which business can become involved.

Categories of Social Responsibility Issues

Product Line

Internal standards for product
- Quality, e.g., does it last?
- Safety, e.g., can it harm users or children finding it?
- Disposal, e.g., is it biodegradable?
- Design, e.g., will its use or even "easy" misuse cause pain, injury, or death?

Average product life comparisons versus
- Competition
- Substitute products
- Internal standards or state-of-the-art regular built-in obsolescence

Product performance
- Efficacy, e.g., does it do what it is supposed to do?
- Guarantees/warranties, e.g., are guarantees sufficient, reasonable?
- Service policy
- Service availability
- Service pricing
- Utility

Packaging
- Environmental impact (degree of disposability; recycleability)
- Comparisons with competition (type and extent of packaging)

Marketing Practices

Sales practices
- Legal standards
- "Undue" pressure (a qualitative judgment)

Credit practices against legal standards

Accuracy of advertising claims—specific government complaints

Consumer complaints about marketing practices
- Clear explanation of credit terms
- Clear explanation of purchase price
- Complaint answering policy
  - Answered at all
  - Investigated carefully
  - Grievances redressed (and cost)
  - Remedial action to prevent future occurrences

Adequate consumer information on
- Product use, e.g., dosage, duration of use, etc.
- Product misuse

Fair pricing
- Between countries
- Between states
- Between locations

Packaging

Employee Education and Training

Policy on leaves of absence for
- Full-time schooling
- Courses given during working hours

Dollars spent on training
- Formal vocational training
- Training for disadvantaged worker
- OJT (very difficult to isolate)
- Tuition (job-related versus nonjob-related)
- Special upgrading and career development programs
- Compare versus competition

Special training program results (systematic evaluations)
- Number trained in each program per year
- Cost per trainee (less subsidy)
- Number or percent workers still with company

Plans for future programs

Career training and counseling

Failure rates

Extend personnel understanding
- Jobs
- Skills required later
- Incentive system now available
- Specific actions for promotion

Corporate Philanthropy

Contribution performance
- By category, for example:
  - Art
  - Education
  - Poverty
  - Health
  - Community development
  - Public service advertising
- Dollars (plus materials and work hours, if available)
  - As a percent of pretax earnings
  - Compared to competition

Selection criteria for contributions

Procedures for performance tracking of recipient institutions or groups

Programs for permitting and

encouraging employee involvement in social projects
- On company time
- After hours only
- Use of company facilities and equipment
- Reimbursement of operating units for replaceable "lost" time
- Human resources support
  - Number of people
  - Work hours

Extent of employee involvement in philanthropy decision making

Environmental Control

Measurable pollution resulting from
- Acquisition of raw materials
- Production processes
- Products
- Transportation of intermediate and finished products

Violations of government (federal, state, and local) standards

Cost estimates to correct current deficiencies

Extent to which various plants exceed current legal standards, e.g., particulate matter discharged

Resources devoted to pollution control
- Capital expenditures (absolute and percent)
- R & D investments
- Personnel involved full time; part time
- Organizational "strength" of personnel involved

Competitive company performance, e.g., capital expenditures

Effort to monitor new standards as proposed

Programs to keep employees alert to spills and other pollution-related accidents

Procedures for evaluating environmental impact of new packages or products

External Relations

Community Development

Support of minority and community enterprises through
- Purchasing
- Subcontracting

FIGURE 19.1   (continued)

External Relations (continued)
Investment practices
- Ensuring equal opportunity before locating new facilities
- Identifying opportunities to serve community needs through business expansion (e.g., housing rehabilitation or teaching machines)
- Funds in minority banks

Government Relations

Specific input to public policy through research and analysis

Participation and development of business/government programs

Political contributions

Disclosure of Information/ Communications

Extent of public disclosure of performance by activity category

Measure of employee understanding of programs such as:
- Pay and benefits
- Equal opportunity policies and programs
- Position on major economic or political issues (as appropriate)

Relations/communications with constituencies such as stockholders, fund managers, major customers, and so on

International

Comparisons of policy and performance between countries and versus local standards

Employee Relations, Benefits, and Satisfaction with Work

Comparisons with competition (and/or national averages)
- Salary and wage levels
- Retirement plans
- Turnover and retention by level
- Profit sharing
- Day care and maternity
- Transportation
- Insurance, health programs, and other fringes
- Participation in ownership of business through stock purchases

Comparisons of operating units on promotions, terminations, hires against breakdowns of
- Age
- Sex
- Race
- Education level

Performance review system and procedures for communication with

employees whose performance is below average

Promotion policy—equitable and understood

Transfer policy

Termination policy (i.e., how early is "notice" given)

General working environment and conditions
- Physical surroundings
  - Heat
  - Ventilation
  - Space/person
  - Lighting
  - Air conditioning
  - Noise
- Leisure, recreation, cultural opportunities

Fringe benefits as a percent of salary for various salary levels

Evaluation of employee benefit preferences (questions can be posed as choices)

Evaluation of employee understanding of current fringe benefits

Union/industrial relations
- Grievances
- Strikes

Confidentiality and security of personnel data

Minority and Women Employment and Advancement

Current hiring policies in relation to the requirements of all affirmative action programs

Specific program of accountability for performance

Company versus local, industry, and national performance
- Number and percent minority and women employees hired by various job classifications over last five years
- Number and percent of new minority and women employees in last two to three years by job classification
- Minority and women and nonminority turnover
- Indictments for discriminatory hiring practices

Percent minority and women employment in major facilities relative to minority labour force available locally

Number of minority group and women members in positions of high responsibility

Promotion performance of minority groups and women

Specific hiring and job upgrading goals established for minority groups and women
- Basic personnel strategy
- Nature and cost of special recruiting efforts
- Risks taken in hiring minority groups and women

Programs to ease integration of minority groups and women into company operations, e.g., awareness efforts

Specialized minority and women career counseling

Special recruiting efforts for minority groups and women

Opportunities for the physically handicapped
- Specific programs
- Numbers employed

Employee Safety and Health

Work environment measures
- Government requirements
- Other measures of working conditions

Safety performance
- Accident severity—work hours lost per million worked
- Accident frequency (number of lost time accidents per million hours)
- Disabling injuries
- Fatalities

Services provided (and cost of programs and human resources) for:
- Addictive treatment (alcohol, narcotics)
- Mental health

Spending for safety equipment
- Required by law/regulation
- Not required

Special safety programs (including safety instruction)

Comparisons of health and safety performance with competition and industry in general

Developments/innovations in health and safety

Employee health measures, e.g., sick days, examinations

Food facilities
- Cost/serving to employee; to company
- Nutritional evaluation

MANAGEMENT IN ACTION

ON SOCIAL RESPONSIBILITY AND CORPORATE VOLUNTEERISM

Although generally a corporation's principal objectives are profitability and return on investment, most people expect that this will not be at the expense of the quality of life in today's society. Many feel that a corporation must put something back into society—that it must make a positive social contribution as it goes about its business. As recent statistics on corporate giving compiled by the Institute of Donations and Public Affairs Research show, there have, in fact, been increases in corporate contributions and intentions.

Although few hard data on corporate involvement and effectiveness in encouraging employee volunteerism and community involvement exist, finding ways of accommodating the needs of the workplace and the needs of employees who perform volunteer work in the community is becoming an important corporate issue. Two trends in Canadian society have increased the importance of corporate responses. First, there is a declining population of "professional" volunteers, those for whom volunteer work is a vocation. Second, there is an increasing market for volunteer services. Canadian firms have had to respond to this situation in creative ways.

Volunteers will usually come forward when there is a combination of interest, motivation, and belief in community need. These elements frequently come together in the workplace, which can provide useful opportunities to identify and enrol volunteers. The corporation, too, has become well known as a supporter of community, cultural, and educational projects through corporate contribution activities. Nearly 70 percent of more than 900 respondents to a recent Conference Board of Canada survey reported adopting a supportive approach to employees engaged in volunteer work. Among volunteer activities in which Canadian employers especially encourage participation, the United Way ranks first. Other voluntary activities near the top of the ranking include participation in professional associations, business and trade associations, and Chambers of Commerce.

"the workplace ... can provide useful opportunities to identify and enrol volunteers."

Often, corporate and community interests can be matched and needs met through contributions of cash and services. There are many examples of corporations combining financial resources, goods and services, and employee volunteerism to the benefit of the community. Some examples:

- Xerox Canada, as an official supplier to Expo 86, was entitled to its own "day" at Expo. The company decided to be host to senior citizens in the Vancouver area who might otherwise have found it difficult to get to and from the Expo site. By combining company cash and resources with employee time, several thousand senior citizens were helped to get to and from Expo and were given tours of the site, refreshments, and souvenirs of the occasion.
- Warner-Lambert Canada Inc. and its employees "adopted" a camp near Toronto that offers special facilities for children who have cancer. Support is provided through corporate funds, through corporate gifts in kind, and through the voluntary efforts of current and retired Warner-Lambert employees.
- Several companies, among them Shell Canada Ltd. and Xerox Canada Inc., provide financial contributions to organizations in which employees play an active volunteer role. As a result, significant benefits have accrued to organizations in areas as diverse as daycare centres, lifeboat stations, and programs for children with learning disabilities.

- Many companies will undertake the organization of a volunteer fair, on company premises, for which community organizations are invited to provide exhibits portraying their objectives, activities, and associated volunteer opportunities. This allows employees to "shop" for volunteer interests and may expose them to volunteer organizations that they otherwise might have overlooked.
- Some companies present awards to employees who have demonstrated particular dedication to community work. The Toronto-Dominion Bank uses awards to recognize and encourage employee dedication to community projects.
- A few companies have offered limited leaves of absence to employees who wish to become involved in community activities. Xerox Corporation (U.S.) has had such a program for several years. Under this program, employees leave the company for periods of up to a year to undertake work in education, community service, counselling, or agency management.

For such programs to work well, a particular environment must exist. Management must indicate that voluntary involvement by employees in community projects is a commendable and desirable activity. Such encouragement should include a reasonable amount of visible involvement by management personnel. Simultaneously, there must be flexibility by management in recognizing that some volunteer activities will occasionally encroach on the nine-to-five working day.

Few employers, however, have formal policy statements on employee volunteerism. Among those that do, the policies fall into three categories. *Encouraging policy statements* are used to set an organizational tone for policies that are given substance in the business units, or to preface more explicit corporate policies. *Enabling policies* set boundaries and establish procedures to assist employees in resolving any competing demands made by the job and the voluntary activity. *Promoting policy statements* establish rewards for employee achievement in the voluntary, civic, artistic, or athletic fields.

For those employers who encourage employee volunteerism, there are obvious benefits for the community and the organizations involved, just as there are benefits for the employers and employees. Among the benefits to employers are:

- A better community environment where the corporation conducts business and where employees live and work.
- Opportunities for a team-building environment among management, employees, and the community at large.
- Genuine and effective "image-building" opportunities for the corporation.

The benefits to employees include:

- Improvements in their quality of life through personal involvement.
- Opportunities for education and personal growth through the contacts and voluntary work experience.
- Faster acceptance into the community and its lifestyle for employees new to a community.

There are some negative aspects to encouraging employee involvement in volunteer work however. For instance the amount of personal and corporate time to be committed must be thought through carefully. In a work environment where overtime, irregular work hours, and heavy travel are part of the corporate culture, adding an expectation of commitment to community service might harm the entire notion of the voluntary ethic. Any perception by employees that volunteerism is really involuntary would be totally counterproductive.

CONCLUSION

By and large, the corporation has a role to play in maintaining and cultivating interest in voluntary activities by its employees. Although employer involvement in stimulating employee interest in volunteerism can be a promising source of new volunteers, such a program must be developed carefully and with attention to employee concerns and community conditions. A more externally-oriented form of social responsibility, corporate volunteerism is an obvious area of socially responsible behaviour where standards and ethical supremacy (and, hence, advantages) are clear-cut, thus rendering such behaviour easier to undertake on the part of organizations. Less clear-cut and harder to undertake are more internally-oriented areas such as product standards and safety, which may have important (and possibly negative) implications for an organization's bottom line and/or survival.

Based on "Emerging Patterns of Volunteerism," by Kenneth D. Hart, and "Corporate Volunteerism: Putting Something Back," by Peter M. Brophey, in *Canadian Business Review*, Spring 1987 (Ottawa: The Conference Board of Canada). Used with permission of *Canadian Business Review* and the authors.

Varying Opinions on Social Responsibility

Although numerous businesses are, and will continue to be, involved in social responsibility activities, much controversy persists about whether such involvement is necessary or appropriate. The two sections that follow present some of the arguments against and for businesses performing social responsibility activities.[7]

Arguments AGAINST Business Performing Social Responsibility Activities

Friedman argues that business exists mainly to make profits

The best-known argument against business performing social responsibility activities is advanced by Milton Friedman, one of North America's most distinguished economists. Friedman argues that to make business managers simultaneously responsible to business owners for reaching profit objectives and to society for enhancing societal welfare represents a conflict of interest that has the potential to cause the demise of business as it is known today.[8] According to Friedman, this demise almost certainly will occur if business is continually forced to perform socially responsible behaviour that is in direct conflict with private organizational objectives.[9]

and that social responsibility may be unethical.

Friedman also argues that to require business managers to pursue socially responsible objectives may in fact be unethical since it requires managers to spend money that really belongs to other individuals:

> In a free enterprise, private property system, a corporate executive is an employee of the owners of the business. He has direct responsibility to his employers. That responsibility is to conduct the business in accordance with their desires, which generally will be to make as much money as possible while conforming to the basic rules of society, both those embodied in law and those embodied in ethical custom. . . . Insofar as his actions reduce returns to stockholders, he is spending their money. Insofar as his actions raise the price to customers, he is spending the customers' money.[10]

Arguments FOR Business Performing Social Responsibility Activities

Proponents of social responsibility argue that all members of society must maintain society.

The best-known argument supporting the performance of social responsibility activities by business was alluded to earlier in this chapter. This argument begins with the premise that business as a whole is a subset of society as a whole and exerts a significant impact on the way in which society exists. The argument continues that, since business is such an influential member of society, it has the responsibility to help maintain and improve the overall welfare of society. After all, the argument goes, since society asks no more or less of any of its members, why should business be exempt from such responsibility?

In addition, some make the argument that business should perform social responsibility activities because profitability and growth go hand in hand with responsible treatment of employees, customers, and the community. In essence, this argument implies that performing social responsibility activities is a means of earning greater organizational profit.[11]

Many more arguments for and against business performing social responsibility activities are presented in Figure 19.2.

FIGURE 19.2 Major arguments for and against business performing social responsibility activities.

Major Arguments for Social Responsibility

1. It is in the best interest of the business to promote and improve the communities where it does business.
2. Social actions can be profitable.
3. It is the ethical thing to do.
4. It improves the public image of the firm.
5. It increases the viability of the business system. Business exists because it gives society benefits. Society can amend or take away its charter. This is the "iron law of responsibility."
6. It is necessary to avoid government regulation.
7. Sociocultural norms require it.
8. Laws cannot be passed for all circumstances. Thus, business must assume responsibility to maintain an orderly legal society.
9. It is in the stockholders' best interest. It will improve the price of stock in the long run because the stock market will view the company as less risky and open to public attack and therefore award it a higher price–earnings ratio.
10. Society should give business a chance to solve social problems that government has failed to solve.
11. Business, by some groups, is considered to be the institution with the financial and human resources to solve social problems.
12. Prevention of problems is better than cures—so let business solve problems before they become too great.

Major Arguments against Social Responsibility

1. It might be illegal.
2. Business plus government equals monolith.
3. Social actions cannot be measured.
4. It violates profit maximization.
5. Cost of social responsibility is too great and would increase prices too much.
6. Business lacks social skills to solve societal problems.
7. It would dilute business's primary purposes.
8. It would weaken the balance of payments because price of goods will have to go up to pay for social programs.
9. Business already has too much power. Such involvement would make business too powerful.
10. Business lacks accountability to the public. Thus, the public would have no control over its social involvement.
11. Such business involvement lacks broad public support.

From R. Joseph Mansen, Jr., "The Social Attitudes of Management," in Joseph W. McGuire, *Contemporary Management*, © 1974, p. 616. Reprinted by permission of Prentice-Hall, Inc., Englewood Cliffs, New Jersey.

BACK TO THE CASE

Figure 19.1 indicates that there probably are many other social responsibility areas in which Bonaventure Coiffures could become involved, in addition to McGill's situation. McGill's situation, however, could be categorized under the heading of marketing practices, since McGill is suggesting that Bonaventure Coiffures's present method of marketing its services makes it extremely difficult for the disabled to be consumers of those services.

Whatever Fortunato would do to ease McGill's problem probably would cost him money and, as a result, raise the cost of his services to his customers. While this action would cost him profits and perhaps seem unbusinesslike, performing such social responsibility activities could improve the public image of Bonaventure Coiffures and therefore seem very businesslike. Fortunato must decide to what degree, if at all, he will try to solve McGill's problem.

Conclusions about Business Performing Social Responsibility Activities

The preceding two sections presented several major arguments against and for businesses performing social responsibility activities. Regardless of which argument or combination of arguments particular managers might support, they generally should make a concentrated effort to: (1) perform all legally required social responsibility activities; (2) consider the possibility of voluntarily performing social responsibility activities beyond those legally required; and (3) inform all relevant individuals of the extent to which their organization will become involved in performing social responsibility activities. The following sections further discuss each of these topics.

Performing Required Social Responsibility Activities

Both federal and provincial legislation and agencies require businesses to perform certain social responsibility activities. At the federal level the Canadian Human Rights Commission is responsible for this activity, while at the provincial level these rights are ensured as well. As an example, the Quebec *Charte des Droits et Libertés de la Personne* (Charter of Human Rights Act) not only deals with issues of discrimination and due process but focuses a large amount of attention upon language rights. The effect on corporations operating in Quebec has been felt, including the francization of documents and personnel policies favouring francophones. The Ontario Human Rights Commission and Code attempts to enforce human rights legislation but does not become overly involved with language issues.

There are few aspects of the environment of Canada which are not covered by at least one government department and quite comprehensive legislation. At the federal level, environmental protection is spread among four major departments: Ministry of the Environment (1972); Ministry of Fisheries; Ministry of Health and Welfare; and Ministry of Agriculture. Since 1970, the Ministry of the Environment and the Ministry of Fisheries have been responsible for twenty-nine different acts affecting water, wildlife, clean air, fisheries, inspection, forestry, freshwater fish, migratory birds, ocean dumping, whales, pacific fur seals, international rivers, and more. In addition to those specific assignments, other environmental protection mandates are spread among other government departments. Agriculture regulates animal health and parasites; Labour regulates industrial hygiene and safety; Energy, Mines, and Resources controls mineral extraction processes and chemical uses; and External Affairs deals with international air and water pollution. The federal structures are largely paralleled by similar operations within the provinces.[12]

The Department of Consumer and Corporate Affairs is the main government agency concerned with consumer complaints and products (each provincial government has a comparable department). It has three main divisions: Consumer Affairs, Corporate Affairs, and Combines Investigation. The Consumer Affairs section administers four major acts:

1. *Hazardous Product Act*   The act gives the government the right to ban outright or to regulate sales, distribution, labelling, and advertising of potentially dangerous products.
2. *Consumer Packaging and Labelling Act*   The law defines the labels, ingredients, weight, and so forth, of consumer products.

Laws require certain social responsibility activities.

3. *Food and Drug Act*   The main purpose of this act is to protect the consumer from injuries, fraud, and other deceptive practices relating to food and drugs.
4. *Weight and Measures Act*   The law regulates weighing and measuring devices, as well as the use of the metric system.

The Combines Investigation Act prohibits price fixing, price discrimination, resale price maintenance, and mergers and monopolies. Deceptive advertising, fictitious sales, and provision of misleading information to consumers are criminal offences under this act. Section 36(l)(h) of the act says that no person shall make a statement to the public that is not based on an adequate and proper test thereof, proof of which lies on the person making the representation.[13]

The Canadian Labour Code at the federal level and the commissions on working conditions at provincial levels handle occupational safety and health issues affecting employees. Transport Canada, another agency at the federal level is responsible for highway codes, interprovincial transportation, and so forth. The Ministry of Energy, Mines & Resources is responsible for safety conditions for mine workers and the enforcement of mine safety and equipment standards as one of its social issues. The Environmental Protection Agency has the authority to enforce the law requiring businesses to adhere to certain socially responsible environmental standards.

Voluntarily Performing Social Responsibility Activities

Adherence to legislated social responsibilities represents the minimum standards of social responsibility performance that business managers must achieve. Managers must ask themselves, however, how far beyond these minimum standards, if at all, they should attempt to go.

Managers must determine how much social responsibility is enough.

The process of determining how far to go is simple to describe, yet difficult and complicated to implement. The process simply entails managers assessing both positive and negative outcomes of performing social responsibility activities over both the short and long terms, and then performing only those social responsibility activities that maximize management system success while making some desirable contribution to maintaining or improving the welfare of society.

Sandra L. Holmes asked top executives in 560 of the major firms in such areas as commercial banking, life insurance, transportation, and utilities to indicate the possible negative and positive outcomes their firms could expect to experience from performing social responsibility activities.[14] Figure 19.3 lists these positive and negative outcomes and indicates the percentage of executives questioned who expected to experience the outcomes. Although the information in this figure furnishes managers with several general insights on how involved their organization should become in social responsibility activities, it does not and cannot furnish them with a clear-cut answer to this question. Managers can determine the appropriate level of social responsibility involvement for a specific organization only by examining and reacting to specific factors related to that organization.

Communicating the Degree of Social Responsibility Involvement

Determining the extent to which a business should perform social responsibility activities beyond legal requirements is an extremely subjective process. Despite this subjectivity, however, managers should have a well-defined opinion in this vital management area, should establish a personal code of ethics that relates to this position, and should inform all organization members of this position.[15]

An organization's position on social responsibility should be known.

FIGURE 19.3   Outcomes of social responsibility involvement expected by executives and the percent who expected them.

Positive Outcomes	Percent Expecting
Enhanced corporate reputation and goodwill	97.4
Strengthening of the social system in which the corporation functions	89.0
Strengthening of the economic system in which the corporation functions	74.3
Greater job satisfaction among all employees	72.3
Avoidance of government regulation	63.7
Greater job satisfaction among executives	62.8
Increased chances for survival of the firm	60.7
Ability to attract better managerial talent	55.5
Increased long-run profitability	52.9
Strengthening of the pluralistic nature of... society	40.3
Maintaining or gaining customers	38.2
Investors prefer socially responsible firms	36.6
Increased short-run profitability	15.2
Negative Outcomes	
Decreased short-run profitability	59.7
Conflict of economic or financial and social goals	53.9
Increased prices for consumers	41.4
Conflict in criteria for assessing managerial performance	27.2
Disaffection of shareholders	24.1
Decreased productivity	18.8
Decreased long-run profitability	13.1
Increased government regulation	11.0
Weakening of the economic system in which the corporation functions	7.9
Weakening of the social system in which the corporation functions	3.7

From Sandra L. Holmes, "Executive Perceptions of Social Responsibility," *Business Horizons* (June 1976). Copyright, 1976, by the Foundation for the School of Business at Indiana University. Reprinted by permission.

Taking these steps will ensure that managers and organization members behave consistently to support this position, and that societal expectations of what a particular organization will achieve in this area will be realistic.

BACK TO THE CASE

Some social responsibility activities are legislated and therefore must be performed by business. Most of these legislated activities, however, are aimed at larger companies. There probably is no existing legislation that would require Fortunato to make Bonaventure Coiffures beauty shops more accessible to the disabled.

Since Fortunato probably is not required by law to modify his shops for the benefit of the disabled, whatever modifications he might decide to make would be strictly voluntary. In making this decision, Fortunato should assess both positive and negative outcomes of modifying his shops over both the long and short terms, and then make those modifications, if any, that would maximize the success of Bonaventure Coiffures as well as make some desirable contribution to the welfare of the disabled. Fortunato should let all organization members, as well as Tiffany McGill, know what he decides and, perhaps, his reasons for that decision.

⊞ SOCIAL RESPONSIVENESS

The previous section discussed social responsibility as the business obligation to take action that protects and improves the welfare of society along with business's own interests. This section defines and discusses **social responsiveness** as the degree of effectiveness and efficiency an organization displays in pursuing its social responsibilities.[16] The greater the degree of effectiveness and efficiency an organization displays while pursuing its social responsibilities, the more socially responsive the organization is said to be.[17] The two sections that follow discuss: (1) social responsiveness and decision making; and (2) approaches to meeting social responsibilities.

Social responsiveness is the degree of effectiveness and efficiency in pursuing social responsibilities

Social Responsiveness and Decision Making

The socially responsive organization that is both effective and efficient meets its social responsibilities and does not waste organizational resources in the process. Deciding exactly which social responsibilities an organization should pursue and then how to accomplish activities necessary to meet those responsibilities are perhaps the two most critical decision-making aspects of maintaining a high level of social responsiveness within an organization.

Figure 19.4 is a flowchart that managers can use as a general guideline for making social responsibility decisions that enhance the social responsiveness of an organization. This figure implies that, for managers to achieve and maintain a high level of social responsiveness within an organization, they must pursue only those social responsibilities that their organization actually possesses and has a right to undertake. Furthermore, once managers decide to meet a specific social responsibility, they must decide the best way in which activities related to meeting this obligation should be undertaken; that is, managers must decide if their organization should undertake the activities on its own or acquire the help of outside individuals with more expertise in the area.

Socially responsive organizations must decide which social responsibilities to pursue and how best to pursue them.

Approaches to Meeting Social Responsibilities

In addition to decision making, various managerial approaches to meeting social obligations are another determinant of an organization's level of social responsiveness.

According to Harry Lipson, a desirable and highly socially responsive approach to meeting social obligations: (1) incorporates social goals into the annual planning process; (2) seeks comparative industry norms for social programs; (3) presents reports to organization members, the board of directors, and shareholders on social responsibility progress; (4) experiments with different approaches for measuring social performance; and (5) attempts to measure the costs of social programs as well as the return on social program investments.[18]

S. Prakash Sethi presents three management approaches to meeting social obligations: (1) the social obligation approach; (2) the social responsibility approach; and (3) the social responsiveness approach.[19] Each of these approaches and the types of behaviour typical of them on several different dimensions are presented in Figure 19.5.

FIGURE 19.4   Flowchart of social responsibility decision making that will generally enhance the social responsiveness of an organization.

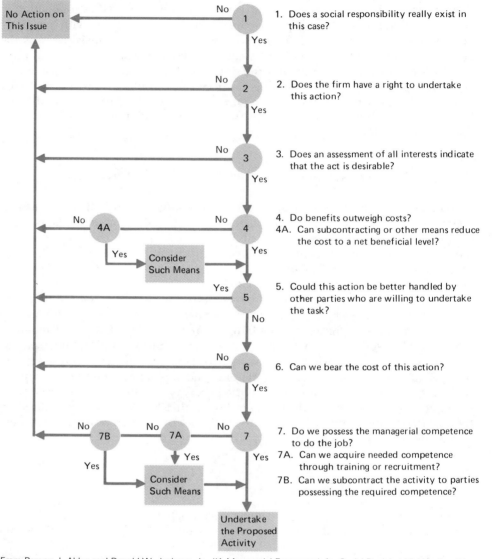

1. Does a social responsibility really exist in this case?
2. Does the firm have a right to undertake this action?
3. Does an assessment of all interests indicate that the act is desirable?
4. Do benefits outweigh costs?
4A. Can subcontracting or other means reduce the cost to a net beneficial level?
5. Could this action be better handled by other parties who are willing to undertake the task?
6. Can we bear the cost of this action?
7. Do we possess the managerial competence to do the job?
7A. Can we acquire needed competence through training or recruitment?
7B. Can we subcontract the activity to parties possessing the required competence?

From Ramon J. Aldag and Donald W. Jackson, Jr., "A Managerial Framework for Social Decision Making," p. 34, *MSU Business Topics* (Winter 1975). Reprinted by permission of the publisher, Division of Research, Graduate School of Business Administration, Michigan State University.

Sethi's approaches reflect three different business dispositions toward social responsibility.

As Figure 19.5 indicates, each of Sethi's three approaches contains behaviour that reflects a somewhat different attitude with regard to business performing social responsibility activities. The **social obligation approach**, for example, reflects an attitude that considers business as having primarily economic purposes and confines social responsibility activity mainly to conformance to existing legislation. The **social responsibility approach** is characterized by an attitude that sees business as having both economic and societal goals. The third approach, the **social responsiveness approach**, reflects an attitude that considers business as having both societal and economic goals as well as the obligation to anticipate upcoming social problems and to work actively toward preventing their appearance.

FIGURE 19.5 Three approaches to social responsibility and types of behaviour associated with each.

Dimensions of Behaviour	Approach One: Social Obligations Prescriptive	Approach Two: Social Responsibility Prescriptive	Approach Three: Social Responsiveness Anticipatory and Preventive
Search for legitimacy	Confines legitimacy to legal and economic criteria only; does not violate laws; equates profitable operations with fulfilling social expectations	Accepts the reality of limited relevance of legal and market criteria of legitimacy in actual practice; willing to consider and accept broader extralegal and extramarket criteria for measuring corporate performance and social role	Accepts its role as defined by the social system and therefore subject to change; recognizes importance of profitable operations but includes other criteria
Ethical norms	Considers business value-neutral; managers expected to behave according to their own ethical standards	Defines norms in community-related terms, i.e., good corporate citizen; avoids taking moral stand on issues which may harm its economic interests or go against prevailing social norms (majority views)	Takes definite stand on issues of public concern; advocates institutional ethical norms even though they may be detrimental to its immediate economic interest or prevailing social norms
Social accountability for corporate actions	Construes narrowly as limited to shareholders; jealously guards its prerogatives against outsiders	Construes narrowly for legal purposes, but broadened to include groups affected by its actions; management more outward looking	Willing to account for its actions to other groups, even those not directly affected by its actions
Operating strategy	Exploitative and defensive adaptation; maximum externalization of costs	Reactive adaptation; where identifiable, internalizes previously external costs; maintains current standards of physical and social environment; compensates victims of pollution and other corporate related activities even in the absence of clearly established legal grounds; develops industry-wide standards	Proactive adaptation; takes lead in developing and adapting new technology for environmental protectors; evaluates side effects of corporate actions and eliminates them prior to the action's being taken; anticipates future social changes and develops internal structures to cope with them
Response to social pressures	Maintains low public profile, but if attacked, uses PR methods to upgrade its public image; denies any deficiencies; blames public dissatisfaction on ignorance or failure to understand corporate functions; discloses information only where legally required	Accepts responsibility for solving current problems; will admit deficiencies in former practices and attempt to persuade public that its current practices meet social norms; attitude toward critics conciliatory; freer information disclosures than approach one	Willingly discusses activities with outside groups; makes information freely available to public; accepts formal and informal inputs from outside groups in decision making; is willing to be publicly evaluated for its various activities
Activities pertaining to governmental actions	Strongly resists any regulation of its activities except when it needs help to protect its market position; avoids contact; resists any demands for information beyond that legally required	Preserves management discretion in corporate decisions, but cooperates with government in research to improve industry-wide standards; participates in political processes and encourages employees to do likewise	Openly communicates with government; assists in enforcing existing laws and developing evaluations of business practices; objects publicly to governmental activities that it feels are detrimental to the public's good
Legislative and political activities	Seeks to maintain status quo; actively opposes laws that would internalize any previously externalized costs; seeks to keep lobbying activities secret	Willing to work with outside groups for good environmental laws; concedes need for change in some status quo laws; less secrecy in lobbying than approach one	Avoid meddling in politics and does not pursue special-interest laws; assists legislative bodies in developing better laws where relevant; promotes honesty and openness in government and in its own lobbying activities
Philanthropy	Contributes only when direct benefit to it clearly shown; otherwise, views contributions as responsibility of individual employees	Contributes to noncontroversial and established causes; matches employee contributions	Activities of approach two, *plus* support and contributions to new, controversial groups whose needs it sees as unfulfilled and increasingly important

Organizations characterized by attitudes and behaviours consistent with the social responsiveness approach generally are more socially responsive than organizations characterized by attitudes and behaviours consistent with either the social responsibility approach or the social obligation approach. Also, organizations characterized by the social responsibility approach generally achieve higher levels of social responsiveness than organizations characterized by the social obligation approach.

BACK TO THE CASE

Fortunato should strive to maintain a relatively high level of social responsiveness when pursuing issues such as those brought up by Tiffany McGill. To do this, he should make decisions appropriate to his social responsibility area and also approach the meeting of those social responsibilities in an appropriate way.

In terms of decision making and the Tiffany McGill situation, Fortunato must first decide if Bonaventure Coiffures has a social responsibility to service customers such as McGill. Assuming that Fortunato decides that Bonaventure Coiffures has such a responsibility, he must then determine exactly how to accomplish the activities necessary to meet those responsibilities. For example, can the people presently employed by Bonaventure Coiffures install ramps in front of the beauty shops, or should Fortunato hire independent contractors to make the installations? Making appropriate decisions will help Bonaventure Coiffures meet social obligations both effectively and efficiently.

In terms of an approach to meeting social responsibilities that probably will increase Bonaventure Coiffures's social responsiveness, Fortunato should try to view his organization as having both societal and economic goals. In addition, he should attempt to anticipate the arrival of social problems, such as the one depicted by McGill's situation, and actively work to prevent their appearance.

SOCIAL RESPONSIBILITY ACTIVITIES AND MANAGEMENT FUNCTIONS

This section discusses a social responsibility as a major organizational activity. As such, it should be subjected to the same management techniques used to perform other major organizational activities, such as production, personnel, finance, and marketing. Managers have known for some time that desirable results in these areas are not achieved if managers are not effective in planning, organizing, influencing, and controlling. Achieving social responsibility results is not any different.[20] The following sections discuss planning, organizing, influencing, and controlling social responsibility activities.

Planning Social Responsibility Activities

Planning is defined in Chapter 4 as the process of determining how the organization will achieve its objectives or get where it wants to go. Planning social responsibility activities, therefore, involves determining how the organization will achieve its social responsibility objectives or get where it wants to go in the area of social responsibility. The following sections discuss how the planning of social responsibility activities is related to the overall planning process of the organization and how to convert the social responsibility policy of the organization into action.

The Overall Planning Process

The model shown in Figure 19.6 depicts how social responsibility activities can be handled as part of the overall planning process of the organization. According to this figure, social trends should be forecast within the organizational environment along with the more typically performed economic, political, and technological trends forecasts. Examples of such social trends would be prevailing and future societal attitudes toward water pollution or safe working conditions. In turn, each of these forecasts would influence the development of the strategic and tactical plans of the organization as well as the corresponding activities undertaken.

Social responsibility activities can be integrated into the overall planning effort.

FIGURE 19.6 Integration of social responsibility activities and planning activities.

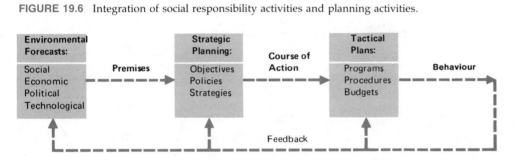

From Kenneth E. Newgren, "Social Forecasting: An Overview of Current Business Practices," in Archie B. Carroll, ed., *Managing Corporate Social Responsibility*. Copyright © 1977 by Little, Brown and Company (Inc.). Reprinted by permission of the author.

Converting Organizational Policies on Social Responsibility into Action

A *policy* is a standing plan that furnishes broad guidelines for channeling management thinking in specific directions. Managers should establish organizational policies in the social responsibility area just as they do in some of the more generally accepted areas, such as hirings, promotions, and absenteeism.

To be effective, however, such social responsibility policies must be converted into appropriate action. According to Figure 19.7, conversion of social responsibility policy into action involves three distinct and generally sequential phases.

Phase 1 consists of top management recognizing that its organization possesses some social obligation. Top management then must formulate and communicate some policy to all organization members about its acceptance of this obligation.

Phase 2 involves staff personnel as well as top management. In this phase, top management gathers information related to actually meeting the social ob-

Conversion of social responsibilities into action requires efforts by:
1. Top management.

2. Staff personnel.

FIGURE 19.7   Conversion of social responsibility policy into action.

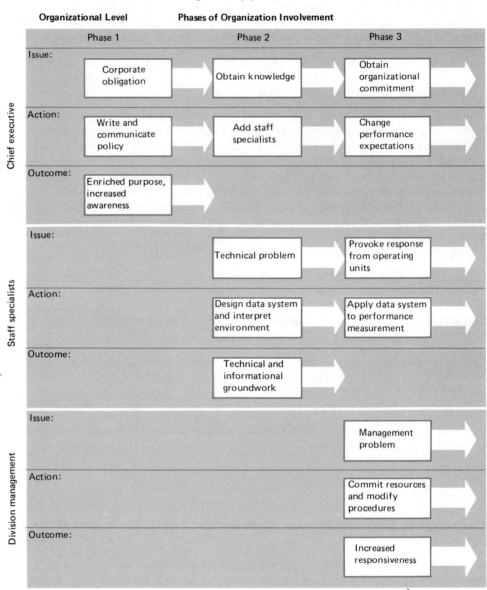

ligation accepted in phase 1. Staff personnel generally are involved at this point to give advice on technical matters related to meeting the accepted social obligation.

3. Division management.

Phase 3 involves division management in addition to organization personnel already involved from the first two phases. During this phase, top management strives to obtain the commitment of organization members to live up to the accepted social obligation and attempts to create realistic expectations about the effects of such a commitment on organizational productivity. Staff specialists encourage those responses within the organization that are necessary to properly meet the accepted social obligation, properly. Finally, division management commits resources and modifies existing procedures so that appropriate socially-oriented behaviour can and will be performed within the organization.

BACK TO THE CASE

Fortunato should know that pursuing social responsibility objectives probably will be a major management activity at Bonaventure Coiffures. As such, Fortunato should plan, organize, influence, and control Bonaventure Coiffures's social responsibility activities if the company is to be successful in reaching social responsibility objectives.

In terms of planning social responsibility activities, Fortunato should determine how Bonaventure Coiffures will achieve its social responsibility objectives. He can do this by incorporating social responsibility planning into his overall planning process at Bonaventure Coiffures. That is, Fortunato can make social trends forecasts along with his economic, political, and technological trends forecasts. In turn, these forecasts would influence the development of strategic plans, tactical plans, and ultimately, the action taken by Bonaventure Coiffures in the area of social responsibility.

Fortunato also must be able to turn Bonaventure Coiffures's social responsibility policy into action. For example, Fortunato may want to make Bonaventure Coiffures beauty shops more accessible to disabled customers. To convert this policy into action, he should first communicate such a policy to all organization members. Next, he should obtain additional knowledge of exactly how to make his shops more accessible and retain staff personnel who can help him with technical problems in this area. Lastly, Fortunato should make sure that all people at Bonaventure Coiffures are committed to meeting this social responsibility objective and that lower-level managers are allocating funds and establishing appropriate opportunities for organization members to fulfill this commitment.

Organizing Social Responsibility Activities

Organizing is defined in Chapter 8 as the process of establishing orderly uses for all resources within the organization. These uses, of course, emphasize the attainment of management system objectives and flow naturally from management system plans. Correspondingly, organizing for social responsibility activities entails establishing for all organizational resources logical uses that emphasize the attainment of the organization's social objectives and also are consistent with the organization's social responsibility plans.

Figure 19.8 shows how Standard Oil Company decided to organize for the performance of its social responsibility activities. The vice-president for Law and Public Affairs hold the primary responsibility in the area of societal affairs within this company and is responsible for overseeing the related activities of numerous individuals who report directly to this person. This figure, of course, is intended only as an illustration of how a company might include its social responsibility area on its organization chart. The specifics of how any single company organizes in this area always should be tailored to the unique needs of that company.

Organizational resources should be organized to attain the organization's social responsibility objectives.

FIGURE 19.8 How Standard Oil Company of Indiana includes the social responsibility area on its organization chart.

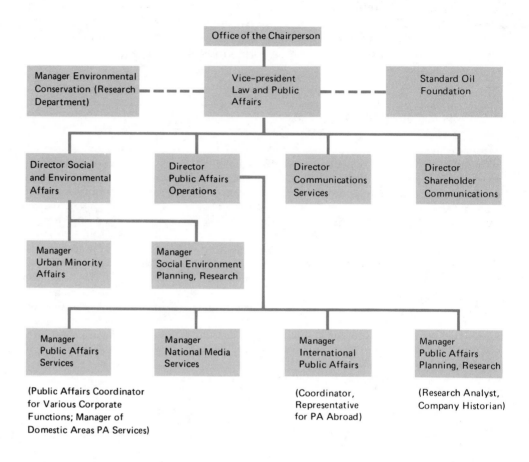

Influencing Individuals Performing Social Responsibility Activities

Activities of organization members should be guided toward reaching social responsibility objectives.

Influencing is defined in Chapter 12 as the management process of guiding the activities of organization members in directions that enhance the attainment of organizational objectives. As applied to the social responsibility area, influencing is simply the process of guiding the activities of organization members in directions that will enhance the attainment of the organization's social responsibility objectives. More specifically, to influence appropriately in this area, managers must lead, communicate, motivate, and work with groups in ways that result in the attainment of existing social responsibility objectives.

Controlling Social Responsibility Activities

Controlling, as defined in Chapter 16, is making things happen as they were planned to happen. To control, managers assess or measure what is occurring in the organization and, if necessary, change these occurrences in some way to make them conform to plans. Controlling in the area of social responsibility entails these same two major tasks. The following sections discuss various areas in which social responsibility measurement takes place, and the social audit, a tool for determining and reporting progress in the attainment of social responsibility objectives.

Controlling involves determining whether social responsibility activity is going as planned.

Areas of Measurement

To be consistent, measurements to gauge organizational progress in reaching its social responsibility objectives could be taken in any of the areas listed in Figure 19.1. The specific areas in which individual companies actually take such measurements vary, of course, depending on the specific social responsibility objectives of those companies. All companies, however, probably should take such social responsibility measurements in at least the following four major areas.[21]

Social responsibility measurements should be taken in at least four areas.

1. *The economic function area*   A measurement should be made of whether or not the organization is performing such activities as producing goods and services that people need, creating jobs for society, paying fair wages, and ensuring worker safety. This measurement gives some indication of the economic contribution the organization is making to society.
2. *The quality of life area*   In this area, the measurement should focus on determining if the organization is improving or degrading the general quality of life in society. Producing high-quality goods, dealing fairly with employees and customers, and making an effort to preserve the natural environment all could be indicators that the organization is upholding or improving the general quality of life within society. As an example of not upholding the quality of life, cigarette companies, because they produce goods that actually can harm the health of society overall, are viewed by some as socially irresponsible.[22]
3. *The social investment area*   This area deals with the degree to which the organization is investing both money and human resources to solve community social problems. Here, the organization could be involved in assisting community organizations related to education, charities, and the arts.
4. *The problem-solving area*   Measurement in this area should focus on the degree to which the organization deals with social problems, as opposed to dealing with just the symptoms of these problems. Such activities as participating in long-range community planning and conducting studies to pinpoint social problems generally could be considered dealing with social problems.

The Social Audit: A Progress Report

A **social audit** is the process of actually taking social responsibility measurements such as those discussed in the preceding section to assess organizational performance in the social responsibility area. The basic steps taken to conduct a social audit are monitoring, measuring, and appraising all aspects of an organization's social responsibility performance. The audit itself can be performed by organization personnel or by an outside consultant.[23]

A social audit monitors, measures, and appraises social responsibility performance.

Figure 19.9 is an example of a social audit that would be prepared by a bank. It should be noted that this figure does not illustrate any type of standard format used for writing up the results of a social audit. In fact, probably no two organizations conduct and present the results of a social audit in exactly the same way.[24]

FIGURE 19.9   Portion of sample social audit report made by a practising manager.

MNB Social Performance Report
Part 1—Mainstream Issues

Priority—Consumer Issues

Issue—Discrimination in Credit—Women

Potential   Growing public awareness of issue. Consumer Finance Commission Report should stimulate legislation within two years. Class actions a possibility.

Progress   New guidelines instituted for credit cards and small loans (under $5 000). Women's full income and employment now considered. No restrictions on married women obtaining credit in own name.

Problems   No change in real estate or larger personal loans because of Michigan's community property laws.

Position   Well ahead of competition. Better advertising of this fact would generate considerable new business.

Issue—Complaints and Errors

Potential   Errors prime reason for customers leaving bank. Five percent reduction in closed accounts would be equal to raising profits by $280 000. Quick handling of complaints could increase this to $400 000.

Progress   Instituted double-check system. Check-processing errors down 27 percent. Cost: $110 000. Instituted 800 line to handle complaints and questions. Good results. Cost for line, officer, and advertising: $90 000.

Problems   No progress in credit card billing errors.

Position   Reputation for personalized service improved. Closed accounts down 4.3 percent.

Priority—Employee Development

Issue—Affirmative Action

Potential   Close monitoring by government and others assured. Recent class actions indicate severe penalties for nonaction. Potential liability $1 million to 10 million. Upgrading large pool of underutilized talent in bank (especially women) could significantly increase productivity. Growing number of qualified minorities in Detroit.

Progress   Strong minority program instituted during year with goals, timetables, and enforcement mechanism. The record is good: *1968*, 18.3 percent of employees minority; *1970*, 20.5 percent; *1972*, 24.1 percent; *1975* goal is population parity (31.7 percent). Similar program for women (now 62 percent of labor force) will be ready in mid-1973.

Problems   Minorities and women still concentrated in lower rank:

Percent Bank Officers Who Are:	1968	1970	1972	1975 Goal
Minority	5.6%	6.1%	7.3%	12.0%
Women	18.2%	20.8%	23.3%	30.0%

To reach 1975 goals, we must develop a better system of isolating promotables, training and placing them. Difficulty of attracting top minorities to banking. Some resentment from white males expected.

Position   This effort largely required. Other Detroit banks at essentially the same position. No competitive advantage or disadvantage.

▤ BACK TO THE CASE

In addition to planning social responsibility activities at Bonaventure Coiffures, Fortunato also must organize, influence, and control them. To organize social responsibility activities, Fortunato must establish orderly use of all resources at Bonaventure Coiffures to carry out the company's social responsibility plans. Despite the relatively small size of his company, developing an organization chart that shows the social responsibility area at Bonaventure Coiffures along with corresponding job descriptions, responsibilities, and specifications for the positions on this chart might be an appropriate step for Fortunato to take.

To influence social responsibility activities, Fortunato must guide the activities of organization members in directions that will enhance the attainment of Bon-

aventure Coiffures's social responsibility objectives. He must lead, communicate, motivate, and work with groups in ways appropriate for meeting these objectives.

To control, Fortunato must make sure that social responsibility activities at Bonaventure Coiffures are happening as planned. If they are not, he should make changes to ensure that they will in the near future. One tool Fortunato can use to check Bonaventure Coiffures's progress in meeting social responsibilities is the social audit. With the audit, he can check and assess management system performance in such areas as economic function, quality of life, social investment, and problem solving.

▦ ETHICS AND SOCIAL RESPONSIBILITY

The study of ethics can be approached from many different viewpoints. Perhaps the most practical approach is to view ethics as a catalyst, causing managers to take socially responsible actions. According to Dr. Albert Schweitzer, a famous humanitarian, **ethics** is "our concern for good behavior. We feel an obligation to consider not only our own personal well-being, but also that of other human beings." Overall, ethics is similar to following the golden rule: Do unto others as you would have them do unto you. In general, the more ethical its manager, the more socially responsible the organization.

> Ethics is a catalyst for socially responsible actions.

General Dynamics, McDonnell Douglas, Chemical Bank, and American Can Company are examples of corporations that conduct training programs aimed at encouraging ethical practices within their organizations.[25] Such programs do not attempt to teach managers what is moral or ethical but rather give managers criteria they can use to help determine how ethical a certain action might be. Managers can feel confident that a potential action will be considered ethical by the general public if it is consistent with one or more of the following standards:[26]

> Some important criteria for determining if actions are ethical:

1. *The golden rule*   Act in a way you would expect others to act toward you.
2. *The utilitarian principle*   Act in a way that results in the greatest good for the greatest number.
3. *Kant's categorical imperative*   Act in such a way that the action taken under the circumstances could be a universal law, or rule, of behaviour.
4. *The professional ethic*   Take actions that would be viewed as proper by a disinterested panel of professional peers.
5. *The TV test*   Managers should always ask, "Would I feel comfortable explaining to a national TV audience why I took this action?"

> 1. Golden rule.
> 2. Utilitarian principle.
> 3. Kant's categorical imperative.
> 4. Professional ethic.
> 5. TV test.

Top management in many organizations commonly strives to encourage ethical practices not only to be morally correct, but also to gain whatever business advantage there may be in having potential consumers as well as employees view their companies as being ethical. In addition to preserving their corporate image, such companies are concerned about future ethical dilemmas that could

> Encouraging ethical practices is good business.

FIGURE 19.10   Martin Marietta's corporate ethics office.

To ensure continuing attention to matters of ethics and standards on the part of all Martin Marietta employees, the Corporation has established the Corporate Ethics Office. The Director of Corporate Ethics is charged with responsibility for monitoring performance under this Code of Ethics and for resolving concerns presented to the Ethics Office.

Martin Marietta calls on every employee to report any violation or apparent violation of the Code. The Corporation strongly encourages employees to work with their supervisors in making such reports and, in addition, provides to employees the right to report violations directly to the Corporate Ethics Office. Prompt reporting of violations is considered to be in the best interest of all.

Employee reports will be handled in absolute confidence. No employee will suffer indignity or retaliation because of a report he or she makes to the Ethics Office. . . .

The Chairman of the Corporate Ethics Committee will be the President of the Corporation. The Committee will consist of five other employees of the Corporation including representatives of the Corporation's operating elements, each of whom will be appointed by the Chairman of the Committee subject to the approval of the Audit and Ethics Committee of the Corporation's Board of Directors.

The Chairman of the Corporate Ethics Committee reports to the Audit and Ethics Committee of the Martin Marietta Corporation Board of Directors.

Reprinted by permission from "Code of Ethics and Standards of Conduct" (Orlando, Fla.: Martin Marietta, n.d.), p. 3.

FIGURE 19.11   The Johnson & Johnson code of ethics.

We believe our first responsibility is to the doctors, nurses and patients, to mothers and all others who use our products and services.
In meeting their needs everything we do must be of high quality.
We must constantly strive to reduce our costs in order to maintain reasonable prices.
Customers' orders must be serviced promptly and accurately.
Our suppliers and distributors must have an opportunity to make a fair profit.

We are responsible to our employees, the men and women who work with us throughout the world.
Everyone must be considered as an individual.
We must respect their dignity and recognize their merit.
They must have a sense of security in their jobs.
Compensation must be fair and adequate, and working conditions clean, orderly and safe.
Employees must feel free to make suggestions and complaints.
There must be equal opportunity for employment, development and advancement for those qualified.
We must provide competent management, and their actions must be just and ethical.

We are responsible to the communities in which we live and work and to the world community as well.
We must be good citizens—support good works and charities and bear our fair share of taxes.
We must encourage civic improvements and better health and education.
We must maintain in good order the property we are privileged to use, protecting the environment and natural resources.

Our final responsibility is to our stockholders.
Business must make a sound profit.
We must experiment with new ideas.
Research must be carried on, innovative programs developed and mistakes paid for.
New equipment must be purchased, new facilities provided and new products launched.
Reserves must be created to provide for adverse times.
When we operate according to these principles, the stockholders should realize a fair return.

Reprinted by permission of Johnson & Johnson.

prove costly. Unethical practices commonly result in expensive consequences, such as fines, loss of company reputation, and legal fees.

Instances of companies pursuing ethical issues are plentiful. For example, Martin Marietta, a major supplier of missile systems and aircraft components, has established a corporate ethics office; Figure 19.10 explains what this office is and how it functions. Johnson & Johnson, a leading manufacturer of health care products, included in its annual report the code of ethics it developed to guide company practices (see Figure 19.11).

BACK TO THE CASE

As indicated earlier, there probably is no legislation that would require Fortunato to modify his beauty shops to make them more accessible to disabled customers. If such legislation were being developed, however, there are certain steps legislators could take to help Fortunato meet social responsibilities in this area. For example, laws should be clear, consistent, and technically feasible. This would ensure that Fortunato would know what action was expected of him and that technology existed to help him take this action.

Laws should also be economically feasible, emphasize the future, and allow flexibility. Fortunato should be able to follow them without going bankrupt and should not be penalized for what has happened in the past. Fortunato also should be given the flexibility to follow these laws to the best advantage of Bonaventure Coiffures. In other words, he should not be told to conform to the laws by following specific steps.

Assuming that Fortunato is an ethical manager, he would be inclined to consider the well-being of other people. As a result, he would be likely to seriously consider reasonable action to aid disabled customers such as Tiffany McGill. If Fortunato assisted disabled customers to an extent that significantly limited the success of his company, however, he could probably be accused of being unethical in regard to his employees or anyone else who had a genuine interest in organizational success.

Action Summary

Reread the learning objectives that follow. Each objective is followed by questions. Answering these questions accurately will help you to retain the most important concepts discussed in this chapter. After answering each question, check your answer with the answer key at the end of this chaper. (*Hint*: If you have doubt regarding the correct response, consult the page that follows the answer.)

From studying this chapter, I will attempt to acquire:	Circle:

1. An understanding of the term *social responsibility*.

a. According to Davis, since business has certain power over society, society can and must hold business responsible for social conditions that result from exercising this power.   T, F

b. Major social responsibility areas in which business can become involved include the following except: (a) urban affairs; (b) consumer affairs; (c) pollution control; (d) natural resource conservation; (e) all of the above are areas of potential involvement.   a, b, c, d, e

2. An appreciation for the arguments both for and against business assuming social responsibilities.

a. Some argue that performing social responsibility activities is a means for a business to gain greater profit.   T, F

b. Milton Friedman argues that business cannot be held responsible for performing social responsibility activities. He does *not* argue that: (a) doing so has the potential to cause the demise of American business as we know it today; (b) doing so is in direct conflict with the organizational objectives of business firms; (c) doing so would cause the nation to creep toward socialism, which is inconsistent with American business philosophy; (d) doing so is unethical because it requires business managers to spend money that rightfully belongs to the firm's investors; (e) doing so ultimately would either reduce returns to the firm's investors or raise prices charged to consumers.

a, b, c, d, e

3. **Useful strategies for increasing the social responsivenesss of an organization.**
   a. When using the flowchart approach in social responsibility decision making, which of the following questions is out of appropriate sequential order: (a) can we afford this action? (b) does a social responsibility actually exist? (c) does the firm have a right to undertake this action? (d) does an assessment of all interests indicate that the act is desirable? (e) do benefits outweigh costs?

a, b, c, d, e

T, F

   b. The social obligation approach to performing social responsibility activities is concerned primarily with complying with existing legislation on the topic.

4. **Insights on the planning, organizing, influencing, and controlling of social responsibility activities.**
   a. Organizational policies should be established for social responsibility matters in the same manner as, for example, for personnel relations problems.

T, F

   b. Companies should take social responsibility measurements in all of the following areas except: (a) economic utility area; (b) economic function area; (c) quality of life area; (d) social investment area; (e) problem-solving area.

a, b, c, d, e

5. **An understanding of the relationship between social responsibility and ethics.**
   a. The utilitarian principle suggests that managers should act in such a way that the action taken under the circumstances could be a universal law, or rule, of behaviour.

T, F

   b. Management might strive to encourage ethical behaviour in organizations in order to: (a) be morally correct; (b) gain a business advantage by having employees perceive their company as ethical; (c) gain a business advantage by having customers perceive the company as ethical; (d) avoid possible costly legal fees; (e) all of the above.

a, b, c, d, e

INTRODUCTORY CASE WRAP-UP

"Assisting the Disabled" (p. 530) and its related back-to-the-case sections were written to help you better understand the management concepts contained in this chapter. Answer the following discussion questions about this introductory case to further enrich your understanding of the chapter content:

1. Do you think Fortunato has a responsibility to make it possible for customers such as McGill to enter his beauty salons? Explain.

2. Assuming that Fortunato has such a responsibility, when would it be relatively easy for him to be committed to living up to it?

3. Assuming that Fortunato has such a responsibility, when would it be relatively difficult for him to be committed to living up to it?

Issues For Review and Discussion

1. Define *social responsibility*.
2. Explain three of the major propositions in the Davis model of social responsibility.
3. Summarize Milton Friedman's arguments against business pursuing social responsibility objectives.
4. Summarize three arguments that support business pursuing social responsibility objectives.
5. What is meant by the phrase *performing required social responsibility activities*?
6. What is meant by the phrase *voluntarily performing social responsibility activities*?
7. List five positive and five negative outcomes a business could experience as a result of performing social responsibility activities.
8. What is the difference between social responsibility and social responsiveness?
9. Discuss the decision-making process that can help managers increase the social responsiveness of a business?
10. In your own words, explain the main differences among Sethi's three approaches to meeting social responsibilities.
11. Which of Sethi's approaches has the most potential for increasing the social responsiveness of a management system? Explain.
12. What is the overall relationship between the four main management functions and performing social responsibility activities?
13. What suggestions does this chapter make about planning social responsibility activities?
14. Describe the process of turning social responsibility policy into action.
15. How do organizing and influencing social responsibility activities relate to planning social responsibility activities?
16. List and define four main areas in which any management system can take measurements to control for social responsibility activities.
17. What is a social audit? How should the results of a social audit be used by management?
18. How can society help business meet its social responsibilities?
19. What is the relationship between ethics and social responsibility?
20. Explain how managers can try to judge if a particular action is ethical.

Sources of Additional Information

Anshen, Melvin, ed. *Managing the Socially Responsible Corporation*. New York: Macmillan, 1974.

Christopher, William F. *Management for the 1980s*. New York: Amacom, 1980.

Cowan, William M. "Office Accidents: Painful, Profitless—and Preventable." *Administrative Management* 42 (September 1981): 68–70, 78.

Cressey, Donald R., and Charles A. Moore. "Managerial Values and Corporate Codes of Ethics." *California Management Review* 25 (Summer 1983): 53–77.

Davis, Keith, and Robert L. Blomstrom. *Business and Society: Environment and Responsibility*, 3d. ed. New York: McGraw-Hill, 1975.

Diebold, John. *The Role of Business in Society*. New York: Amacom, 1982.

Donaldson, Thomas. *Corporations and Morality*. Englewood Cliffs, N.J.: Prentice-Hall, 1982.

Harding, Charles F. "Why Administrative Offices Are Moving to Smaller Cities." *Administrative Management* 42 (September 1981): 40–42, 66.

Hay, Robert D., and Edmund R. Gray. *Business and Society: Cases and Text*. Cincinnati, Ohio: South-Western, 1981.

Hosmer, LaRue Tone. *The Ethics of Management*. Homewood, Ill.: Richard D. Irwin, 1987.

"Johnson & Johnson Suspends Shipments of Some Tylenol." *Wall Street Journal*, September 1983, 21.

Kapp, K. William. *The Social Costs of Private Enterprise*. New York: Schocken, 1971.

Kinicki, Angelo, Jeffrey Bracker, Robert Kreitner, Chris Lockwood, and David Lemak. "Socially Responsible Plant Closings." *Personnel Administrator* 32 (June 1987): 116–36.

McGuire, Joseph F. *Business and Society*. New York: McGraw-Hill, 1963.

Rose, Robert L. "Ethics Policies Gain Favor but Leave Major Questions." *Wall Street Journal*, November 24, 1986, 35.

Ruth, Stephen R., and Linda Samuels. "Perspectives on Computer Ethics and Crime." *Business* 36 (January/February/March 1986): 30–36.

Scott, William G., and Terrence R. Mitchell. "The Moral Failure of Management Education." *Chronicle of Higher Education*, December 11, 1985, 35.

Soothill, Keith. "The Extent of Risk in Employing Ex-Prisoners." *Personnel Management 13 (April 1981): 35–37, 43.

Steiner, George A., and John F. Steiner. *Business, Government, and Society: A Managerial Perspective*, 5th ed. New York: Random House, 1988.

Stone, Christopher D. *Where the Law Ends: The Social Control of Corporate Behavior*. New York: Harper & Row, 1975.

Sutton, Robert I., and Anat Rafaeli, "Characteristics of Work Stations as Potential Occupational Stressors." *Academy of Management Journal 30 (June 1987): 260–76.

Thomas, Dr. Edward (C.A.M.). "Conserving Energy— What's Being Done." *Management World 10 (March 1981): 14–17.

Walton, Clarence C. *Corporate Social Responsibilities*. Belmont, Calif.: Wadsworth, 1967.

Watson, John H., III. *20 Company-Sponsored Foundations: Programs and Policies*. New York: Conference Board, 1970.

Weidenbaum, Murray L. "The True Obligation of the Business Firm to Society." *Management Review 70 (September 1981): 21–22.

Notes

1. D. Votaw and S.P. Sethi, *The Corporate Dilemma: Traditional Values Versus Contemporary Problems* (Englewood Cliffs, N.J. Prentice-Hall, 1973), 9–46, 167–91.
2. Keith Davis and Robert L. Blomstrom, *Business and Society: Environment and Responsibility*, 3d. ed. (New York: McGraw-Hill, 1975), 6.
3. Peter L. Berger, "New Attack on the Legitimacy of Business," *Harvard Business Review* (September/October 1981): 82–89.
4. Keith Davis, "Five Propositions for Social Responsibility," *Business Horizons* (June 1975): 19–24.
5. Stahrl W. Edmunds, "Unifying Concepts in Social Responsibility," *Academy of Management Review* (January 1977): 38–45.
6. For a worthwhile study on these social responsibility areas, see Vernon M. Buehler and Y.K. Shetty, "Managerial Response to Social Responsibility Challenge," *Academy of Management Journal* (March 1976): 66–78.
7. For a more detailed summary of the arguments for and against business pursuing social responsibility activities, see Keith Davis, "The Case For and Against Business Assumptions of Social Responsibilities," *Academy of Management Journal* (June 1973): 312–22.
8. Milton Friedman, "The Social Responsibility of Business Is to Increase Profits," *The New York Times Magazine*, 13 September 1970, 33, 122–26.
9. Neil M. Brown and Paul F. Haas, "Social Responsibility: The Uncertain Hypothesis," *MSU Business Topics* (Summer 1974): 48.
10. Milton Friedman, "Does Business Have Social Responsibility?" *Bank Administration* (April 1971): 13–14.
11. Elizabeth Gatewood and Archie B. Carroll, "The Anatomy of Corporate Social Response: The Rely, Firestone 500, and Pinto Cases," *Business Horizons 24 (September/October 1981): 9–16.
12. Harold A. Gram and Ronald L. Crawford, *Canadian Management, Responses to Social Issues*. (New York: McGraw-Hill, 1981), 103.
13. Ibid., 117.
14. Sandra L. Holmes, "Executive Perceptions of Corporate Social Responsibility," *Business Horizons* (June 1976): 34–40.
15. William C. Gergold, "Corporate Responsibility and the Industrial Professional," *Industrial Managment* (November/December 1976): 5–8.
16. Frederick D. Sturdivant, *Business and Society: A Managerial Approach* (Homewood, Ill.: Richard D. Irwin, 1977), 109–25.
17. For an interesting discussion of the comparative social responsiveness of Ford, Firestone, and Proctor & Gamble, see Gatewood and Carroll, "The Anatomy of Corporate Social Response," 9–16.
18. Harry A Lipson, "Do Corporate Executives Plan for Social Responsibility?" *Business and Society Review* (Winter 1974—75): 80–81.
19. S. Prakash Sethi, "Dimensions of Corporate Social Performance: An Analytical Framework," *California Management Review* (Spring 1975): 58–64.
20. Donald S. McNaughton, "Managing Social Responsiveness," *Business Horizons* (December 1976): 19–24.
21. Frank H. Cassell, "The Social Cost of Doing Business," *MSU Business Topics* (Autumn 1974): 19–26.

22. Donald W. Garner, "The Cigarette Industry's Escape from Liability," *Business and Society Review*, no. 33 (Spring 1980): 22.

23. Archie B. Carroll and George W. Beiler, "Landmarks in the Evolution of the Social Audit," *Academy of Management Journal* (September 1975): 589–99.

24. Raymond A. Bauer and Dan H . Fenn, Jr., "What Is a Corporate Social Audit?" *Harvard Business Review* (January/February 1973): 37–48.

25. Alan L. Otten, "Ethics on the Job: Companies Alert Employees to Potential Dilemmas," *Wall Street Journal*, July 14, 1986, 25.

26. Gene R. Laczniak, "Framework for Analysing Marketing Ethics," *Journal of Macromarketing* (Spring 1983): 7–18.

Action Summary Answer Key

1. a. T, p. 532
   b. e, pp. 533–535
2. a. T, p. 538
   b. c, p. 538

3. a. a, pp. 543–544
   b. T, pp. 543–545
4. a. T, p. 546
   b. a, p. 551

5. a. F, p. 553
   b. e, pp. 553–555

THE CRIMINALIZATION OF TOBACCO?

Jacques LaRivière, vice-president of public affairs for the Canadian Tobacco Manufacturers' Council, has been leading the cigarette makers' year-long rearguard battle against a federal bill that would phase out all tobacco advertising by 1993. LaRivière, a former Radio-Canada reporter, says he has helped to write hundreds of protest letters and has coordinated dozens of meetings with cabinet ministers, MPs, and senators in recent months to preserve what he terms "the freedom of commercial speech."

At contention is Bill C-51, introduced in April 1987 by Health Minister Jake Epp. The bill is still bottled up in the House of Commons after protracted committee hearings that generated nineteen amendments, the most important of which would water down provisions against tobacco industry sponsorship of sports and cultural events. The legislation, long advocated by non-smokers' and public health groups, received approval in principle towards the end of 1987, but no date has been set for resumption of the Commons debate over the amendments. After the vote on third reading, the bill must be ratified by the Senate to become law.

Tobacco companies and their supporters in the business, sports, and arts communities fear that the bill will be passed unless opposition to it strengthens. Claude Garcia, president of Montreal's Chamber of Commerce, says that the legislation sets "a dangerous precedent, and violates Canada's Charter of Rights and Freedoms."

The tobacco lobby contends that the ban on cigarette advertising will threaten the future of an industry that employs 50 000 Canadians directly and indirectly, including a large proportion in Quebec. The industry, dominated by just three companies, subsidizes and promotes numerous community orchestras and sports events across Canada—among them the Player's International and Player's Challenge tournaments for the world's top male

LaRivière, fighting "to preserve what he terms 'the freedom of commercial speech.'"

and female tennis professionals—to the tune of $10 million annually.

Governments should not be in the business of regulating sponsors, say officials of both the Rothmans Porche Challenge and the Benson & Hedges International Fireworks Competition in Toronto. Without tobacco's help, orchestras that present duMaurier concerts have predicted they would surely fold. To mollify these groups, Epp has accepted amendments to his bill that would allow them to continue using cigarette brand names in their promotion campaigns and in the names of their special events.

Many representations, however, continue to pour in from anti-smoking groups that are campaigning for the elimination of smoking in public places and of tobacco promotion, especially when it is aimed at young people. But as LaRivière argues, "If the government is absolutely convinced that tobacco is dangerous, then it strikes me that its only consistent position is to ban it, outright."

LaRivière is quick to point out that federal taxes on a pack of cigarettes total 95 cents. In Quebec, provincial taxes amount to $1.13 per pack, meaning that taxes eat up two thirds of the cost of a pack, which retails between $3.25 and $3.50. Tobacco taxes in Canada total more than $4 billion a year, an amount federal and provincial governments split almost evenly. "It is quick money for which neither need do much work," LaRivière says. "The feds will be pretty hard-pressed to find another consumer product, sold at the same price and in the same volume, which they can tax right off the top at nearly two thirds of its selling price."

The tobacco industry has always maintained that its advertising has not reached out for new smokers, but instead to those who, like Jacques LaRivière, already smoke. "Besides," he says, "what can the federal government do about all that tobacco advertising in all those foreign magazines that absolutely dominate our stands?" Sixty percent of publications sold in Canada come from foreign countries, and they cannot be legislated.

Imperial Tobacco, which has more than half of the Canadian cigarette market, has its head office in Montreal. Its two competitors, Rothmans Benson & Hedges and RJR-MacDonald have Montreal sales offices but are based in Toronto. All three are adamant that if Bill C-51 is intended to reduce cigarette consumption, it is unnecessary. Government publicity campaigns have worked so well, they say, that the number of cigarettes sold in Canada has declined by more than 20 percent since 1982. It is predicted to drop by another 5 percent by the time the bill is expected to become law.

ORGANIZATIONS URGE CANADIANS TO BUTT OUT

Bill Pratt, who has been agitating for a smoke-free Canada since he stopped smoking a pack of cigarettes a day thirty years ago, vows to fight the tobacco companies "every inch of the way." Pratt, president of the Ottawa-Hull branch of Non-Smokers for Clean Air, declares: "The tobacco industry is selling a lethal product and any advertising they are allowed to do—however meek—will never negate the shocking dangers of what they are selling to an unsuspecting public."

Nearly twenty organizations like Pratt's group have sprung up across the country in recent years to lobby Health and Welfare Canada for a ban on cigarette advertising and promotion. These associations fervently disbelieve cigarette manufacturers' claims that their advertising does not reach out for new smokers, but merely encourages people who already smoke to switch brands. According to the Toronto-based Physicians for a Smoke-Free Canada, 35 000 people die from the effects of smoking every year in this country, and many thousands more are hospitalized. "Tobacco firms will always have the need to replace these prime customers. That's exactly what their ads will amount to," says Pratt.

Gabriel Durocher, head of the Montreal branch of the Non-Smokers' Rights Association, warns that most new smokers are teenagers and children; he cites studies indicating that people who started smoking as adults account for only 1 percent of cigarette sales. Durocher and his colleagues will continue to press the federal government to stop all advertising, even that "cloaked in sponsorship of sports and artistic events." Support for these worthy events, anti-smoking groups agree, must come from someone else—and doubtless will. Comments Bill Pratt, "Wait and see just how many other corporations will be prepared to help tennis tournaments and symphony concerts when tobacco money is finally out of the way."

DISCUSSION ISSUES

1. Under which social responsibility categories would the current debate surrounding the tobacco industry fall? Explain.
2. What are the arguments both for and against the tobacco industry's position and Bill C-51? Refer to both the chapter content and the case.
3. How might the government respond to the tobacco industry's arguments? How should it respond? What's the difference, if any? Discuss.

Based on "Tobacco lobby fights ban on advertising," by Adrian Waller in *This Week In Business*, March 19, 1988. Used with permission.

C H A P T E R

20

INTERNATIONAL MANAGEMENT

STUDENT LEARNING OBJECTIVES

From studying this chapter, I will attempt to acquire:

1. An understanding of international management and its importance to modern managers.
2. An understanding of what constitutes a multinational corporation.
3. Insights concerning the risk involved in investing in international operations.
4. Knowledge about planning and organizing in multinational corporations.
5. Knowledge about influencing and controlling in multinational corporations.
6. Insights about what comparative management is and how it might help managers to do their jobs better.
7. Ideas on how to be a better manager through the study of Japanese management techniques.

CHAPTER OUTLINE

NABISCO BRANDS IN THE INTERNATIONAL ARENA

In 1985, Nabisco merged with R.J. Reynolds to form a new company called RJR Nabisco. Nabisco Brands, a subsidiary of RJR Nabisco, is a leading North American producer of cookies and crackers. The Nabisco Brands product line includes such recognizable brands as Oreos, Chips Ahoy!, Fig Newtons, Ritz, and Saltines. Nabisco Brands also produces nuts and snack products, candy products, dog food products, margarine products, and cereal products for North American markets. Popular product names in these areas include Planters, Life Savers, Milk Bone, Blue Bonnet, and Shredded Wheat.

Although many North Americans are very familiar with the Nabisco Brands products mentioned in the previous paragraph, they probably are less familiar with Nabisco Brands product penetration in other parts of the world. In some years, product sales to "other parts of the world" have contributed over 40 percent of total company annual sales at Nabisco Brands. The following excerpts from the 1987 Nabisco Brands annual report indicate how involved this company is in the international arena:

> In the United Kingdom, International Nabisco's largest single market, good volume growth came from Walkers and Smiths crisps and snacks, as well as Nabisco cereals. Successful product introductions included Smiths Jackets crisps, a chip made using unpeeled potatoes, and Team Flakes cereal.
>
> In France, volume and market share increases for the Belin line of cookies extended the company's position as one of the country's top biscuit producers. The acquisition of ULA Bahlsen, a French frozen pastry business, made Nabisco the leading marketer of this popular French dessert.

Other major European markets also showed good progress. In Italy, Nabisco continued to register market share gains for the Saiwa line of cookies. In Spain, the company's biscuit business achieved sharply higher volume and market share improvements. To enhance its distribution channels there, the company entered into a partnership with Tabacalera, S.A., Spain's government-owned tobacco and foods company.

International Nabisco expanded its operations in a number of other countries as well. Britannia Industries, Nabisco's 38 percent-owned business in India, began operating a new soya processing plant and maintained its leadership position in the biscuit category. In New Zealand, the company added to its number one position in biscuit products by acquiring the country's leading snack producer, Abels Industries, Ltd.

Nabisco Brands' joint venture in the People's Republic of China completed construction and began start-up of a new bakery in late 1987. The Beijing bakery will begin producing crackers for sale in China and other Far East countries during 1988. In addition, a joint-venture business in Thailand began operating a new bakery during 1987.

Nabisco Brands does business in several countries in addition to those just mentioned. Although there is great potential reward for such an international focus, the task of managing an organization such as Nabisco Brands is generally much more involved than that of managing most organizations of similar size that focus on doing business in only one country.

Excerpts reprinted by permission of RJR Nabisco, Inc., from the 1987 Nabisco Brands Annual Report.

What's Ahead

The introductory case gives examples of Nabisco Brands operations in the United Kingdom, France, Italy, Spain, New Zealand, and China. The material in this chapter provides insights on how to manage in diverse multinational circumstances like those at Nabisco Brands. Major topics covered are fundamentals of international management, the multinational corporation, management functions and multinational corporations, and comparative management.

⊞ FUNDAMENTALS OF INTERNATIONAL MANAGEMENT

International management is simply defined as performing management activities across national borders. In essence, international management entails reaching organizational objectives by extending management activities to include an emphasis on organizations in foreign countries.

International management is management activities that cross national borders.

In practice, this emphasis may take any of several different forms and can vary from simply analyzing and fighting foreign competition to establishing a formal partnership with a foreign company. An example of the former is the Canadian beer industry.

Canada's ability to compete in the U.S. beer market is exemplified by Molson—one of Canada's biggest brewers and the oldest one in North America. Molson, which sells four of its over twenty brands in the U.S., is the number two imported beer, behind Heineken. U.S. marketing efforts are conducted through a wholly owned subsidiary, Martlet Importing Company Incorporated of Great Neck, New York. Molson's primary target market is young, affluent males and college students. Molson's competitive strategy includes pricing their brands between the domestic U.S. brands and the European imports. The firm concentrates its advertising in radio and print media rather than television. Product quality is stressed. The emphasis is on providing a product with a wider, more flavourful taste than that of domestic brands. Molson's phenomenal rise in the U.S. attests to the Canadian firm's ability in international business activity.[1]

Outstanding progress in areas like transportation, communication, and technology makes access to foreign countries more feasible and attractive as time passes. As a result, many modern managers face numerous international issues that can have a direct and significant impact on organizational success. For example, the following situation is facing managers at Xerox:

Business with foreign countries is growing.

> Xerox corporation is racing to meet deadlines at once. It must slim its copier business fast enough to beat the Japanese. Japanese competition in small copiers, a nagging worry since the mid-1970s, has shrunk Xerox's market share in North America to roughly half of total copier revenue. In Europe, its other big market, Xerox has only a quarter of the revenues. Xerox has had to accept slimmer profit margins to stop the rot.[2]

FIGURE 20.1   Canada's exports by country (thousands of dollars).

Country	Year	Live Animals	Food, Feed, Beverages and Tobacco	Crude Materials, Inedible	Fabricated Materials, Inedible	End Products, Inedible	Special Trans-actions, Trade	Total Domestic Exports	Re-Exports	Total Exports
Western Europe	1987	9 617	1 159 213	2 369 611	4 465 691	2 256 593	9 544	10 270 268	518 207	10 788 476
Eastern Europe	1987	1 729	783 270	67 153	50 634	102 938	45	1 005 769	7 352	1 013 121
Middle East	1987	8 172	544 373	58 442	225 304	398 506	1 711	1 236 508	38 201	1 274 708
Other Africa	1987	402	211 652	334 812	130 439	151 111	10 298	838 713	13 369	852 082
Japan	1987	1 642	1 200 716	2 817 797	2 672 894	343 074	125	7 036 248	37 666	7 073 914
Other Asia (incl. Japan)	1987	8 823	2 355 917	3 892 598	4 953 941	1 085 304	7 206	12 303 789	102 903	12 406 692
Oceania	1987	81	72 000	107 791	395 025	259 369	3 085	837 351	18 417	855 768
South America	1987	14 673	377 206	256 334	488 030	454 588	4 822	1 595 652	123 223	1 718 875
Central America and Antilles	1987	3 529	474 244	180 462	450 388	465 613	8 798	1 583 033	50 068	1 633 102
United States	1987	318 819	4 260 067	9 532 991	30 642 164	46 719 719	282 644	91 756 404	2 749 279	94 505 683
Total North America (incl. U.S.)	1987	319 022	4 265 169	9 533 717	30 661 453	46 728 944	282 953	91 791 258	2 752 619	94 543 877
All Countries	1987	366 049	10 243 041	16 800 920	41 820 903	51 902 965	328 463	121 462 342	3 624 359	125 086 701

From Statistics Canada, Exports—Merchandise Trade 1987 Catalogue 65–202.

FIGURE 20.2   Canada's imports by country and section—January to December (thousands of dollars).

Country	Year	Live Animals	Food, Feed, Beverages and Tobacco	Crude Materials, Inedible	Fabricated Materials, Inedible	End Products, Inedible	Special Trans-actions, Trade	All Sections	Year-to Year Percentage Change
Western Europe	1987	4 537	1 136 828	2 071 115	3 826 915	8 547 230	206 472	15 793 098	6.4
Eastern Europe	1987	—	28 253	10 032	131 435	211 718	5 376	386 814	15.2
Middle East	1987	—	42 611	449 729	109 880	94 854	7 535	704 609	7.5
Other Africa	1987	—	129 339	461 044	119 632	36 068	14 060	760 143	− 24.8
Japan	1987	34	74 474	22 827	635 515	6 760 400	57 459	7 550 709	− 1.1
Other Asia (incl. Japan)	1987	1 057	454 865	230 885	1 684 958	12 064 839	134 963	14 571 568	5.1
Oceania	1987	160	413 085	251 707	36 699	73 587	8 989	784 227	14.2
South America	1987	127	567 995	428 558	780 645	359 165	6 234	2 142 724	12.6
Central America and Antilles	1987	463	419 849	280 206	339 323	948 461	18 362	2 006 664	− 3.6
United States	1987	155 713	3 434 838	3 221 125	13 826 588	56 844 289	1 586 765	79 069 318	2.5
Total North America (incl. U.S.)	1987	155 769	3 436 145	3 221 145	13 826 767	56 858 857	1 590 084	79 088 767	2.5
All Countries	1987	162 114	6 628 970	7 404 422	20 856 255	79 194 780	1 992 074	116 238 614	3.3

From Statistics Canada, International Trade Division—Imports by Country Jan.-Dec. 1987, Catalogue 65–006 Vol. 44, No. 4.

FIGURE 20.3   Top ten countries for exports and imports.

Country	Top 10 for Exports 1987 Estimate ($ million)	5-Year Change	Country	Top 10 in Imports 1987 Estimate ($ million)	5-Year Change
U.S.	91 756	+64%	U.S.	79 069	+65%
Japan	7 036	+54%	Japan	7 551	+114%
Britain	2 850	+7%	Britain	4 339	+128%
W. Germany	1 515	+23%	W. Germany	3 534	+155%
China	1 432	+17%	Taiwan	2 023	+206%
S. Korea	1 167	+130%	S. Korea	1 844	+215%
Belgium-Luxemburg	1 137	+47%	Italy	1 703	+135%
France	1 037	+47%	France	1 489	+70%
Netherlands	1 021	−2%	Mexico	1 170	+17%
Italy	843	+27%	Hong Kong	1 138	+70%

From Statistics Canada, International Trade Division Catalogues 65–006 and 65–202.

FIGURE 20.4   Five largest export markets for Canada in 1987.

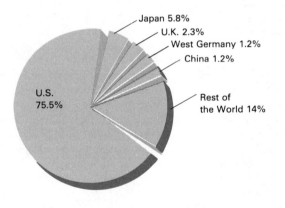

The notable trend that already exists in North America and other countries toward developing business relationships in and with foreign countries is expected to accelerate even more in the future.[3] Figures 20.1, 20.2, and 20.3 indicate the amount of investment by other countries in Canada, Canada's leading trading partners, and the top ten countries for exports and imports. Figure 20.4 graphically illuminates Canada's largest export markets. Information of this nature has caused many management educators, as well as practising managers, to voice the opinion that an understanding of international management is necessary in order to have a thorough and contemporary understanding of the fundamentals of management.[4]

The Management in Action feature for this chapter details the increasing importance of overseas experience as a precondition for success in an environment where global markets are the norm, rather than the exception. Some issues related to international management, such as an ability to understand and adapt to cultural differences, are highlighted.

and therefore so must an understanding of international management.

FOREIGN POSTINGS:
THE WAY TO THE TOP

Robert Maich was just twenty-six years old when the telephone call came from Colgate-Palmolive's president in New York. Maich was in marketing with the company in Toronto, and the news was surprising, exciting, and flattering. Maich had a promotion; he was to be the president—the youngest president ever—of a Colgate-Palmolive subsidiary. His mind jumped ahead of the conversation: Would he be going to London? To Paris? "We'd like you to run the subsidiary in East Africa," said the president. "The head office is in Nairobi."

Today, some twenty years later, Maich is back in Toronto, and president of Silcorp Ltd., a management holding company with sales of $551 million in 1985. He looks back upon his overseas posting as a truly invaluable business experience. It gave him an entirely different outlook, he says, a new attitude based on the realization that what works very well in one instance may be absolutely wrong in another.

Doug Caldwell, the president of Caldwell Partners International, Canada's largest executive search company, says overseas experience may be the most valuable asset one can have in the tough struggle up the corporate ladder. Companies are beginning to realize that executives who perform well in these foreign operations are presidential contenders. "These foreign postings are a great opportunity for individuals to demonstrate how good they are," says Caldwell. Clarke Jackson, a Caldwell partner in Vancouver, adds, "You have to be truly excellent to succeed in a new country without the familiar support systems such as friends, family, and one's own cultural traditions. Executives who have passed the international test with flying colors will surpass limitations of doing business in Canada. They are aware of the world outside; they are independent; and they will be the leaders in reaching beyond Canada's borders to develop world markets."

This is especially true in a time when world markets are becoming increasingly important, where business is conducted in a "global village." As competition intensifies for top spots in corporations, many young executives are driven to search for foreign postings. "It's a tougher and more competitive world," says Anne Fawcett, a Caldwell partner. "Anything you can do to differentiate yourself from the rest of the pack, you want to do."

Roger Garland spent four years in Zurich for Citibank, managing its corporate banking activities in Switzerland. Now based in Toronto, he is executive vice-president of Four Seasons Hotels. He recalls that his European experience was a true eye-opener. "What you tend to forget when you are in North America," he says, "is that you *don't* have all the answers. You get very smug over here. For example, you tend to think of Italy as all screwed up, when the fact is that its economy has a very solid base."

According to Garland, one of the most important benefits of having an international posting is the way it switches an executive's thinking onto an international track. "You learn to think in terms of international trade. You look at the currency as international. You look at international exchange rates. You begin following what is going on politically and economically in other countries." Besides the invaluable business experience, Garland is quick to point out the personal development that takes place, partly due to the adjustments that overseas executives have to make.

Another equally important learning experience is understanding and adapting to cultural differences. An early starter, Garland initially ran into some trouble in Zurich. The custom in Switzerland is for junior people to get to the office first. So when Garland bagan showing up at 8:30 a.m., the junior people began arriving at 8:15. Then, trying to get in early enough to take advantage of an empty office, Garland began starting at 8:00 a.m.; soon his juniors were showing up at 7:45 a.m. "I think I finally gave up at around 7 o'clock—and went back to 8 a.m."

When he first arrived at the Zurich job, Garland produced an awkward situation by walking through the office, past an assistant's desk without saying, "Good morning." This violated Swiss custom; the assistant thought something was wrong, and he was ready to quit, until somebody explained things to Garland. Misunderstandings of this sort are one reason why some companies such as the Royal Bank—an old hand at international operations—provide a special service for executives headed overseas. For half a day or as much as three days, they meet with national representatives of the country to which they've been posted. They discuss the culture and customs of the country, so they can head off social boo-boos—or worse.

Clay Coveyduck is the Royal's vice-president for corporate personnel services, and he notes that, while overseas service undoubtedly strengthens a person's self-reliance, the person selected for an overseas posting must possess certain strengths in the first place. "They have to have emotional stability," he says. "If a man and his wife are going, they have to have a solid relationship. And you have to make sure that they have the technical competence. They have to know how to do business, and they have to understand the risks."

Another big Canadian company with extensive overseas operations is Canadian Pacific. Robert Ballantyne, vice-president in charge of its international consulting services, says there is certainly no doubt that overseas service is a career plus. "Essentially," he says, "these people have wound up better than okay. When you're overseas, you have to live by your wits. You've got to be adaptable. You've got to be flexible. It usually makes people a hell of a lot more self-reliant."

There's another type of foreign service experience which is just as valuable. Stephen Wilgar, president of the Canadian operations of Warner Lambert, the large international health care company, was posted to the company's head office in the U.S. He moved from the Canadian presidency to a job in Morris Plains, New Jersey, just outside New York City, where he supervised both the Canadian and South American operations. "I learned a whole bunch of things," he says. "From a business standpoint, I learned how people think in head office and why it is so easy for there to be differences in opinion between the head office and the field. People in head office only have the time and the resources to get a certain amount of the story, whereas the people in the field are dealing with the whole piece of cloth. And sometimes a one-page report on results really doesn't give people the whole story. It's easy for misunderstandings to develop. So I learned to appreciate the other guy's point of view by working the system myself."

But often, says Doug Caldwell, the greatest impact can be made in some far-off outpost of business where the challenge can be immense—like selling Pepsi-Cola in Jakarta. He says today's ambitious young executives should leap at the opportunity. "You get a chance," says Caldwell, "to show management how good you are."

Based on "Out of the country and up to the top," by Judy Weaver in *Goodlife*, October 1986. Used with permission.

BACK TO THE CASE

As the introductory case shows, Nabisco Brands is an example of an organization involved in international management. Managers within Nabisco Brands perform management activities across national borders of countries like Italy and France. Given the international trend toward greater foreign investment, Nabisco Brands is likely to continue to emphasize worldwide expansion in the future. In addition, this trend will likely be characterized by foreign companies attempting to compete with Nabisco Brands in North America.

THE MULTINATIONAL CORPORATION

This section presents more specifics about managing organizations in the international arena by defining *multinational corporation* and discussing the complexities of and risks involved in managing the multinational corporation.

Defining the Multinational Corporation

A multinational corporation has significant operations in more than one country.

The term *multinational corporation*, having first appeared in the dictionary sometime in the 1970s, has been defined in several different ways in conversation and textbooks alike.[5] For the purposes of this text, a **multinational corporation** is a company that has significant operations in more than one country. In essence, a multinational corporation is an organization that is involved in doing business at the international level. The multinational corporation carries out its activities on an international scale that disregards national boundaries and on the basis of a common strategy from a corporation centre.[6]

A list of multinational corporations in this country would include companies like Ford, General Motors, Shell Oil, Firestone Tire, Varity Corporation (formerly Massey-Ferguson Limited), Noranda, Consolidated Bathurst and McMillan Bloedel. A former Massey-Ferguson executive described Massey-Ferguson's international involvement as combining French-made transmissions, British-made engines, Mexican-made axles, and United States-made sheet metal parts to produce in Detroit a tractor for sale in Canada.[7] Xerox Canada, Incorporated (100 percent owned by Xerox Corporation of Stamford, Connecticut) produces document sorters that are sold in tandem with the American-made copying machine. The Canadian product must suit the world market, but although production is in the subsidiary's hands, the parent has the marketing function because the two are sold together.

Those Canadian subsidiaries that have the world market function as well as the manufacturing include Black and Decker Canada, Incorporated (100 percent owned by Black and Decker, Incorporated of Townson, Maryland) and Westinghouse Canada, Incorporated (95 percent owned by Westinghouse Electric Corporation of Pittsburgh, Pennsylvania). For the latter, the sophisticated nature of the product, huge turbines, necessitates its own sales force.

FIGURE 20.5 Six stages of multinationalization.

Stage I	Stage II	Stage III	Stage IV	Stage V	Stage VI
Exports its products to foreign countries	Establishes sales organizations abroad	Licenses use of its patents and know-how to foreign firms that make and sell its products	Establishes foreign manufacturing facilities	Multinationalizes management from top to bottom	Multinationalizes ownership of corporate stock

IBM Canada Limited (100 percent owned by IBM World Trade of New York) is often cited as a hope-inspiring example of global product-mandating used as a means of enhancing and developing a sophisticated Canadian manufacturing sector. But while IBM Canada produces for the world, it does not market for it, thus lacking what many consider to be a true indication that a company is operating as an independent unit.[8]

Neil H. Jacoby implies that there are six stages a company goes through to reach the highest degree of multinationalization (see Figure 20.5.)[9] As Figure 20.5 indicates, multinationalization can range from a slightly multinationalized organization that simply exports products to a foreign country to a highly multinationalized organization that has some of its owners in other countries.

There are six stages of multinationalization.

In general, the larger the organization, the greater the likelihood that it participates in international operations of some sort. Companies like General Electric, Lockheed, and DuPont, which have annually accumulated over $1 billion from export sales, support this generalization. Exceptions to this generalization in the form of smaller firms, however, also exist. In the future, an increasing number of smaller organizations almost certainly will become involved in international operations.

In the future, even smaller companies will become more involved in international operations.

Complexities of Managing the Multinational Corporation

The definition of *international management* and the discussion of what constitutes a multinational corporation clearly indicate that international management and domestic management are quite different. International management differs from domestic management because it involves operating:[10]

1. Within different national sovereignties.
2. Under widely disparate economic conditions.
3. With peoples living within different value systems and institutions.
4. In places experiencing the industrial revolution at different times.
5. Often over greater geographical distance.
6. In national markets varying greatly in population and area.

Six variables in the international management situation

Figure 20.6 shows some of the more important management implications generated by the preceding six variables and some of the relationships among them. For example, according to the "Different national sovereignties" variable

complicate the multinational corporation's operations.

FIGURE 20.6   Management implications based on six variables in international systems and relationships among them.

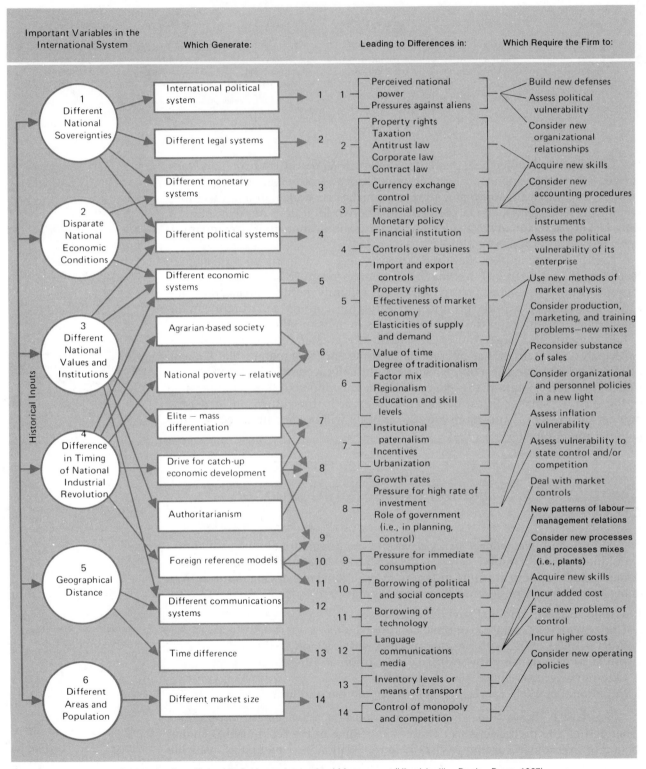

Reprinted by permission of the author from Richard D. Robinson, *International Management* (Hinsdale, Ill.: Dryden Press, 1967).

"Problems with your conference call—Los Angeles is out to breakfast, New York's out to lunch and London's out to dinner."

Wall Street Journal, *February 24, 1987. From the Wall Street Journal—permission, Cartoon Features Syndicate.*

in the figure, different national sovereignties generate different legal, monetary, and political systems. In turn, each legal system implies a unique set of relevant rights and obligations in relation to property, taxation, antitrust (control of monopoly) law, corporate law, and contract law. These, in turn, require the firm to acquire new skills to assess these international legal considerations. The skills are new in the sense of being different from those required in a purely domestic setting. The cartoon emphasizes the point that the management process generally becomes more complicated when an organization functions in the international business arena.

Risk and the Multinational Corporation

Naturally, developing a multinational corporation requires a substantial investment in foreign operations. Normally, managers who make foreign investments feel that such investments: (1) reduce or eliminate high transportation costs; (2) allow participation in the rapid expansion of a market abroad; (3) provide foreign technical, design, and marketing skills; and (4) earn higher profits.[11]

The benefits of foreign investments

FIGURE 20.7   Political risk in investing in a foreign country.

Sources of Political Risk	Groups Through Which Political Risk Can Be Generated	Political Risk Effects: Types of Influence on International Business Operations
Competing political philosophies (nationalism, socialism, communism)	Government in power and its operating agencies	Confiscation: Loss of assets without compensation
Social unrest and disorder	Nonparliamentary opposition groups (e.g., anarchist or guerrilla movement working from within or outside of country)	Expropriation with compensation: Loss of freedom to operate
Vested interests of local business groups		Operational restrictions: Market shares, product characteristics, employment policies, locally shared ownership, and so forth
Recent and impending political independence	Nonorganized common interest groups: students, workers, peasants, minorities, and so forth	
Armed conflicts and internal rebellions for political power		Loss of transfer freedom: Financial (for example, dividends, interest payments), goods, personnel, or ownership rights
New international alliances	Foreign governments or intergovernmental agencies	
	Foreign governments willing to enter into armed conflict or to support internal rebellion	Breaches or unilateral revisions in contracts and agreements
		Discrimination such as taxes, compulsory subcontracting
		Damage to property or personnel from riots, insurrections, revolutions, and wars

From Stefan H. Robock and Kenneth Simmonds, *International Business and Multinational Enterprise*, 3d ed. Copyright © 1983 Richard D. Irwin, Inc. Reprinted by permission.

cannot be claimed without some risk taking.

There is, however, some risk associated with the decision to invest in foreign operations. For example, political complications between the **parent company**, the company investing in international operations, and various factions within the **host country**, the country in which the investment is made, could prohibit the outcomes in the preceding paragraph from materializing. Figure 20.7 presents various possible sources of political risk, several groups within the host country that might generate the risk, and possible effects of the risk on the investing organization.

The likelihood of desirable outcomes related to foreign investments probably will always be somewhat uncertain and will vary from country to country. Nevertheless, managers faced with the decision of a foreign investment must assess this likelihood as accurately as possible. Obviously, a poor decision to invest in another country can cause serious financial problems for the organization. Figure 20.8 describes how some managers subscribe to services that weigh political, economic, and social factors to assess various risk levels associated with investing in different foreign countries.

FIGURE 20.8   How some managers assess the risk of doing business abroad.

Can a Computer Tell the Ratio of Risk?

To help them cope with the uncertainties of doing business abroad, many companies subscribe to services that publish country risk indexes, somewhat like Moody's bond or Value Line stock ratings. Though there is some debate about the usefulness of numerically rating countries for risk, the client lists of the three organizations read like the Fortune 500.

A company considering expanding into Indonesia, for example, might well consult all three of that country's ratings. It could look at the BERI (for Business Environment Risk Index) rating, which ranks countries on a scale of 1 to 100. Indonesia scores a 45.5, a low enough rating to be marked a "high risk." A similar index put out by Business International (BI), an advisory service for multinationals, gives Indonesia a slightly more respectable 58. Finally, the World Political Risk Forecasts (WPRF) service of Frost & Sullivan, a business research organization, expresses its own rather dim view of Indonesia in its January, 1980 forecast: a company doing business there stands a 31 percent chance of a major business loss owing to political developments in the next eighteen months and a 45 percent chance of loss within five years. A better bet for investment would be nearby Singapore — BERI score 74.9, BI rating 79, and WPRF loss probability of only 19 percent in the next five years.

Executives appreciate these rating services because they are relatively cheap ($500 a year for BERI, $1 500 for WPRF), and they boil down the complex forecast to simple numbers. Says Frederick Haner, the University of Delaware business professor who compiles the BERI rating, "Executives treat these numbers as though they came from God directly." In fact, they are derived from weighting and averaging the evaluations of economic, political, and social factors in foreign countries made by panels of "experts." BI's information comes from its employees around the world; WPRF and BERI don't identify their panelists beyond describing them as experts from business, government, and academia.

The most frequent criticism of this indexing is that, although it is based on largely subjective evaluations, the figures imply a mathematical precision that really isn't there. One risk analyst for a major U.S. corporation calls indexing "a substitute for thought." But the purveyors of risk ratings—and many of their clients—claim indexing is a useful tool, though obviously not the only one, for assessing risk. In any case, the troubled world of international business has made risk rating a growth industry.

From Grant F. Winthrop, "Can a Computer Tell the Ratio of Risk?" *Fortune*, March 24, 1980, p. 95. © 1980 Time Inc. All rights reserved.

BACK TO THE CASE

It is apparent from the introductory case that Nabisco Brands is a multinational corporation, an organization with significant operations in more than one country. In addition, Nabisco Brands can be classified as being in the sixth stage of multinationalization; that is, multinational ownership of corporate stock.

Managing at Nabisco Brands under such international circumstances is an extremely complex matter. This complexity is mostly caused by Nabisco Brands managers managing within different foreign countries that are separated by significant distances and that are characterized by different economic conditions, people, levels of technology, and market sizes. Comparison of Nabisco Brands Chinese and United Kingdom markets on each of these variables for example, illustrates how complex management at Nabisco Brands can be.

Naturally, Nabisco Brands management has attempted to minimize risk in making foreign investments. In the past few years, political situations in France, Italy, and the United Kingdom have seemed mostly stable. Of course, political situations can change quickly and should be constantly monitored by multinational corporations. On additional dimensions like economy and social factors, Nabisco Brands management obviously has decided that investments in these countries represent a tolerable amount of risk when weighed against the prospect of increased return from foreign operations.

⊞ MANAGEMENT FUNCTIONS AND MULTINATIONAL CORPORATIONS

The sections that follow discuss performing the four major management functions—planning, organizing, influencing, and controlling—as they occur at multinational corporations.

Planning for Multinational Corporations

Planning was defined in Chapter 4 as determining how the management system will achieve its objectives. This definition is applicable to the management of either domestic or multinational organizations. In general, such management tools as policies, procedures, rules, budgets, forecasting, Gantt charts, and the program evaluation and review technique (PERT) are equally valuable in planning for either domestic or multinational organizations.

> Multinational corporations must have an international strategy.

Perhaps the primary difference between planning in multinational versus domestic organizations involves strategic planning. Organizational strategy for the multinational organization must include provisions that focus on the international arena, while such strategy for the domestic organization does not. Increased environmental uncertainties along with a growing sense of international competition are causing more and more managers to evaluate internationalization as an organizational strategy.

> International strategies usually involve

To develop appropriate international strategies, managers explore issues such as: (1) establishing a new sales force in a foreign country; (2) developing new manufacturing plants in other countries through purchase or construction; (3) financing international expansion; and (4) determining which countries represent the most suitable candidates for international expansion. Although organizations' international strategies vary, most include some emphasis in one or more of the following areas: imports/exports, licence agreements, direct investing, and joint ventures.

Imports/Exports

> importing or exporting goods or services to another country,

Strategy in imports/exports emphasizes attempting to more successfully reach organizational objectives by **importing**—buying goods or services from another country—or **exporting**—selling goods or services to another country.

Organizations of all sizes are importing and exporting. There are very small organizations, and there are extremely large and complex organizations such as Eastman Kodak, which exports photographic products to a number of foreign countries.[12]

Licence Agreements

> buying or selling licence agreements,

A **licence agreement** is a right granted by one company to another to use its brand name, technology, product specifications, and so on, in the manufacture or sale of goods and services. Naturally, the company to whom the licence is extended pays some fee for the privilege. International strategy in this area involves more successfully reaching organizational objectives through either the purchase or sale of licences at the international level.

Direct Investing

Direct investing is using the assets of one company to purchase the operating assets (for example, factories) of another company. International strategy in this area emphasizes reaching organizational objectives through the purchase of operating assets of a company in another country.

purchasing operating assets in another country,

For example, Robinson Nugent, Incorporated, of New Albany, Indiana, manufactures sophisticated electronic parts that are first purchased and then used as parts of other products assembled by high-tech manufacturers throughout the world. The company recently opened a manufacturing facility in Delemont, Switzerland, in an effort to maintain its share of the European market. Overall, the company feels that this Swiss plant has had a good effect on European sales and has even increased demand for exports from the United States to Europe by 40 percent.[13]

Joint Ventures

A **joint venture** is a partnership formed by a company in one country with a company in another country for the purpose of pursuing some mutually desirable business undertaking. International strategy that includes joint ventures emphasizes the attainment of organizational objectives through partnerships with foreign companies.

or forming partnerships with foreign companies.

Joint ventures between car manufacturers in Europe are becoming more and more common as companies strive for greater economies of scale and higher standards in product quality and delivery. Renault, for example, formulated a network of deals for diesel engines from Fiat, gasoline engines from Volvo, forgings and castings from Peugeot, and gearboxes from Volkswagen.[14]

Organizing Multinational Corporations

Organizing was defined in Chapter 8 as the process of establishing orderly uses for all resources within the organization. This definition is equally applicable to the management of either domestic or multinational organizations. Two organizing topics regarding multinational corporations, however, bear further discussion. These topics are organization structure and the selection of managers.

Organization Structure

Organization structure was defined in Chapter 8 as established relationships among resources within the management system, and the *organization chart* is the graphic illustration of organization structure. Chapter 8 also notes that departments as

FIGURE 20.9 Partial multinational organization charts based upon function, product, territory, customers, and manufacturing process.

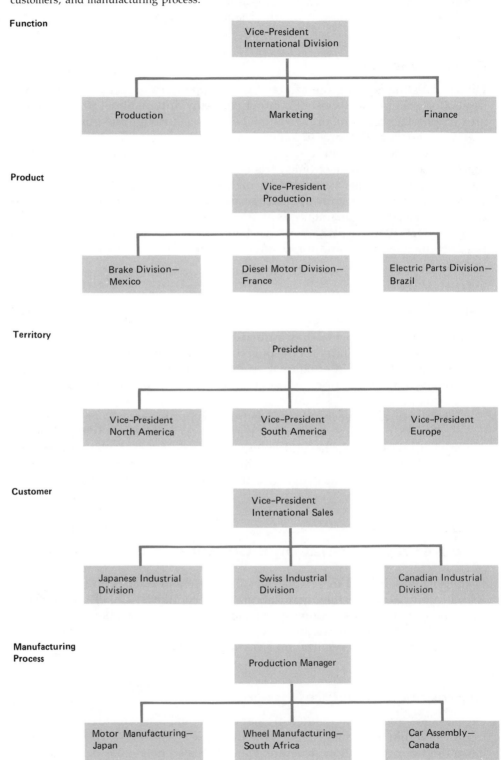

shown on organization charts are most commonly established according to function, product, territory, customers, or manufacturing process. Internationally oriented organizations also normally establish structure based upon these five areas (see Figure 20.9).

Five factors usually determine the organization structure of multinational corporations.

As with domestic organizations, there is no one best way to organize all multinational corporations. Instead, managers of these organizations must analyze the multinational circumstances that confront them and develop an organization structure that best suits those circumstances.

Selection of Managers

Naturally, for multinational organizations to thrive, they must have competent managers. One important characteristic that is believed to be a primary determinant of how competently managers can guide multinational organizations is their attitude toward how such organizations should operate.

Managerial attitudes toward the operations of a multinational corporation can range from

Over the years, management theorists have identified three basic managerial attitudes toward the operations of a multinational corporation: ethnocentric, polycentric, and geocentric.[15] The **ethnocentric attitude** reflects a feeling that multinational corporations should regard home country management practices as superior to foreign country management practices. The **polycentric attitude** reflects a feeling that, since foreign managers are closer to foreign organizational units, they probably understand them better, and, therefore, foreign management practices should generally be viewed as more insightful than home country management practices. Managers with a **geocentric attitude** believe that the overall quality of management recommendations, rather than the location of managers, should determine the acceptability of management practices used to guide multinational corporations.

ethnocentric

to polycentric

to geocentric.

Understanding the potential worth of these three attitudes within multinational corporations is extremely important. The ethnocentric attitude, although perhaps having the advantage of keeping the organization simple, generally causes organizational problems since feedback from foreign operations is eliminated. In some cases, the ethnocentric attitude even causes resentment toward the home country within the foreign society. The polycentric attitude can create the advantage of tailoring the foreign organizational segment to its culture, but can lead to the sizeable disadvantage of creating numerous individually run, relatively unique, and therefore difficult to control foreign organizational segments.

The geocentric attitude is generally thought to be the most appropriate for managers in multinational corporations. This attitude promotes collaboration between foreign and home country management and encourages the development of managerial skill regardless of the organizational segment or country in which managers operate. An organization characterized by the geocentric attitude generally incurs high travel and training expenses, and many decisions are made by consensus. Although risks like wide distribution of power in such an organization are real, payoffs like better-quality products, worldwide utilization of the best human resources, increased managerial commitment to worldwide organizational objectives, and increased profit generally outweigh the potential harm of such risks. Overall, managers with a geocentric attitude generally tend to create organizations that contribute more to the long-term success of the multinational

The geocentric attitude generally is considered most appropriate for long-term organizational success.

FIGURE 20.10   Different organizational characteristics typical of ethnocentric, polycentric, and geocentric attitudes.

Organization Design	Ethnocentric	Polycentric	Geocentric
Complexity of organization	Complex in home country: simple in subsidiaries	Varied and independent	Increasingly complex and interdependent
Authority; decision making	High in headquarters	Relatively low in headquarters	Aim for a collaborative approach between headquarters and subsidiaries
Evaluation and control	Home standards applied for persons and performance	Determined locally	Find standards that are universal and local
Rewards and punishments; incentives	High in headquarters; low in subsidiaries	Wide variation; can be high or low rewards for subsidiary performance	International and local executives rewarded for reaching local and worldwide objectives
Communication; information flow	High volume to subsidiaries; orders, commands, advice	Little to and from headquarters; little between subsidiaries	Both ways and between subsidiaries: heads of subsidiaries part of management team
Identification	Nationality of owner	Nationality of host country	Truly international company but identifying with national interests
Perpetuation (recruiting, staffing, development)	Recruit and develop people of home country for key positions everywhere in the world	Develop people of local nationality for key positions in their own country	Develop best people everywhere in the world for key positions everywhere in the world

Reprinted with permission from Howard V. Perlmutter, "The Tortuous Evolution of the Multinational Corporation," *Columbia Journal of World Business* 4 (January/February 1969): 12.

corporation. Figure 20.10 compares in more detail the types of organizations generally created by managers who possess ethnocentric, polycentric, and geocentric attitudes.

BACK TO THE CASE

The preceding information gives hints on how to carry out the management functions within a multinational corporation like Nabisco Brands. Regarding planning, planning tools like policies and procedures are equally valuable at Nabisco in managing either domestic or foreign operations. Being a multinational corporation, Nabisco has strategies that focus on the international sector, whereas a totally domestic organization would not. Such strategies could include Nabisco Brands buying products (importing) from foreign companies or selling products (exporting) to foreign companies, selling the rights (licence agreements) to a foreign company to manufacture and sell a product like Oreos, purchasing facilities (direct investing) in foreign countries, or entering a partnership (joint venture) with a foreign company to pursue some mutually desirable opportunity.

Regarding organizing a multinational corporation

such as Nabisco, organization structure, as with totally domestic organizations, generally should be based upon one or more of the important variables of function, product, territory, customers, or manufacturing process. Nabisco managers must consider all of the variables within the situations that confront them and then design an organization structure that is most appropriate for those situations.

Over the long term, management at Nabisco should try to select for multinational positions those managers who possess geocentric attitudes, as opposed to polycentric or ethnocentric attitudes. Such Nabisco managers would tend to build operating units in countries such as France and the United Kingdom that would use the best human resources available and be highly committed to the attainment of organizational objectives.

Influencing People in Multinational Corporations

Influencing was defined in Chapter 12 as guiding the activities of organization members in appropriate directions through such activities as communicating, leading, motivating, and managing groups. Influencing people within a multinational corporation, however, is more complex and challenging than within a domestic organization.

Influencing within multinational corporations is more complex because of culture.

The one factor that probably most contributes to this increased complexity and challenge is culture. **Culture** is the total characteristics of a given group of people and their environment. Factors generally designated as important components of a culture include customs, beliefs, attitudes, habits, skills, state of technology, level of education, and religion. As a manager moves from a domestic corporation involving basically one culture to a multinational corporation involving several cultures, the task of influencing usually becomes progressively more difficult.

To successfully influence people, managers in multinational corporations should:

Multinational managers are more successful at influencing if they:

1. *Acquire a working knowledge of the languages used in countries that house foreign operations*   Multinational managers attempting to operate without such knowledge are prone to making costly mistakes. For example, one North American company was shaken when it discovered that the Spanish brand name of the well-known cooking oil it had just introduced in Latin America translated as "jackass oil."[16] Naturally, such a mistake could have been avoided if the management of this organization had had a working knowledge of the Spanish language.

1. Understand the languages.

2. *Understand the attitudes of people in countries that house foreign operations*   An understanding of these attitudes can help managers to design business practices that are most suitable for unique foreign situations. For example, Americans generally accept competition as a tool to encourage people to work harder. As a result, U.S. business practices that include some competitive aspects seldom create significant disruption within organizations. Such practices, however, could cause disruption if introduced in either Japan or the typical European country. Figure 20.11 compares the American, European, and Japanese attitudes toward competition in more detail.

2. Understand the attitudes.

3. *Understand the needs that motivate people in countries housing foreign operations*   For managers in multinational corporations to be successful in motivating people in different countries, they must present these individuals with the opportunity to satisfy personal needs while being productive within the organization. In designing motivation strategies, multinational managers must understand that people in different countries often have different personal needs. For example, people in countries like Switzerland, Austria, Japan, and Argentina tend to have high security needs, while people in countries like Denmark, Sweden and Norway tend to have high social needs. People in countries like Great Britain, Canada, the United States, New Zealand, and Australia tend to have high self-actualization needs.[17] Thus, to be successful at influencing, multinational managers must understand their employees' need priorities and mold such organizational components as incentive systems, job design, and leadership style to correspond to these priorities.

3. Understand the personal needs.

FIGURE 20.11   Comparison of American, European, and Japanese viewpoints on competition.

Nature and Effect of Competition	Typical American Viewpoints	Typical European Viewpoints	Typical Japanese Viewpoints
Nature of competition	Competition is a strong moral force: it contributes to character building.	Competition is neither good nor bad.	There is conflict inherent in nature. To overcome conflicts, individuals must compete, but our final goal is harmony with nature and other human beings.
Business competition compared	Business competition is like a big sport game.	Business competition affects the livelihood of people and quickly develops into warfare.	The company is like a family. Competition has no place in a family. Aggressive action against competitors in the marketplace is in order for the survival and growth of the company.
Motivation	One cannot rely on an employee's motivation unless extra monetary inducements for hard work are offered in addition to a base salary or wage.	A key employee is motivated by the fact that he or she has been hired by the company.	Same as the European viewpoint.
Reward system	Money talks. A person is evaluated on the basis of his or her image (contribution) to the company. High tipping in best hotels, restaurants, etc., is expected.	An adequate salary, fringe benefits, opportunities for promotion, but no extra incentives–except in sales. Very little tipping (service charge is included in added-value tax).	Same as the European viewpoint.
Excessive competition	Competition must be tough for the sake of the general welfare of society. No upper limit on the intensity and amount of competition is desirable.	Too much competition is destructive and is in conflict with brotherly love and the Christian ethic.	Excessive competition is destructive and can create hatred. Only restrained competition leads to harmony and benefits society.
Hiring policy	Aggressive individuals who enjoy competition are ideal employees. Individuals who avoid competition are unfit for life and company work.	Diversity of opinion. How competitiveness or aggressive behaviour of an individual is viewed varies with national ideology and the type of work. In England, it is not a recommendation to describe a job applicant as being aggressive.	Individuals are hired usually not for specific jobs but on the basis of their personality traits and their ability to become an honorable company member. Team play and group consensus are stressed.

From Hugh E. Kramer, "Concepts of Competition in America, Europe, and Japan," in *Business and Society* (Fall 1977). © 1977 Business and Society. Reprinted by permission.

Controlling Multinational Corporations

Controlling was defined in Chapter 16 as making something happen the way it was planned to happen. As with domestic corporations, control in multinational corporations requires that standards be set, performance be measured and compared to standards, and corrective action be taken if necessary. In addition, control in such areas as labour costs, product quality, and inventory is very important to organizational success regardless of whether the organization is domestic or international.

Control of a multinational corporation, however, has additional complexities. First, there is the problem of different currencies. Management must decide how to compare profit generated by organizational units located in different countries and therefore expressed in terms of different currencies.

Another complication is that organizational units within multinational corporations are generally more geographically separated. This increased distance normally makes it more difficult for multinational managers to keep a close watch on operations in foreign countries. For example, this physical distance certainly contributed to adverse publicity PepsiCo received when an employee in Pepsi's overseas bottling branch blew the whistle on an elaborate scam that had puffed up unit profits for several previous years. Using stacks of false documents, finance staffers in the Philippines and Mexico had overstated assets and profits and deferred expenses. As a result, PepsiCo's financial position was overstated by $224 million.[18]

Controlling in multinational corporations is complicated by different currencies

and greater distances.

BACK TO THE CASE

Influencing people in a multinational corporation like Nabisco Brands is a complicated process. Cultures of people in Italy, France, the United Kingdom, and China, as well as Canada and the United States, must be thoroughly understood. Nabisco managers of foreign operations must have a working knowledge of languages spoken in these countries and also an understanding of the attitudes and personal needs that motivate individuals within the foreign work forces. At Nabisco, for example, if motivation strategy is to be successful for the company as a whole, rewards used to motivate Chinese workers may need to be very different from rewards used to motivate United Kingdom workers.

The control process at Nabisco should involve standards, measurements, and needed corrective action just as it should within a domestic company. The different currencies used in France, Italy, Canada, the United States, the United Kingdom, and China, however, tend to make control more complicated at Nabisco than within a domestic organization. Significant distance between all of these countries also tends to complicate control at Nabisco.

COMPARATIVE MANAGEMENT: AN EMPHASIS ON JAPANESE MANAGEMENT

Perhaps the most popular international management topic today is comparative management. The sections that follow define *comparative management* and provide insights on Japanese management practices that can be of value to North American managers.

Defining Comparative Management

Comparative management is the study of the management process in different countries to examine the potential of management action under different environmental conditions. Whereas international management focuses on management activities across national borders,[19] comparative management analyzes management practices in one country for their possible application in another country.[20]

The sections that follow discuss motivation, management practice, and manufacturing insights that were formulated by analyzing Japanese management

Comparative management is studying management in other countries.

methods. These insights currently are being applied by many North American managers.

Insights from Japanese Motivation Strategies

Japanese managers motivate by:

The one country that probably is being studied the most from a comparative management viewpoint is Japan, and knowledge of the overall success of today's Japanese managers is widespread.[21] Perhaps the most analyzed area of this success deals with how Japanese managers effectively motivate organization members. So successful are the Japanese in this area that Americans are traveling to Japan to try to gain insights on Japanese motivation strategies.[22]

Japanese managers seem to be able to motivate their organization members by:

1. Hiring for life.

1. *Hiring an employee for life rather than some shorter period of time*   A close relationship between worker and organization is built through this lifetime employment. Since workers know that they have a guaranteed job and that their future is therefore heavily influenced by the future of the organization, they are very willing to be flexible and cooperative.[23]

2. Treating everyone equally.

2. *Elevating employees to a level of organizatonal status equal to that of management*   In Japanese factories, employees at all levels wear the same work clothes, eat in the same cafeteria, and use the same restrooms.[24]

3. Making employees feel valued and secure.

3. *Making them feel that they are highly valued by management and that the organization will provide for their material needs*[25]   For example, new workers and their relatives attend a ceremony at which the company president welcomes them to the firm. The newcomers often live in company-built housing for several years until they can afford to buy their own housing. Also, much employee life outside of work is spent in company social clubs, with weddings and wedding receptions often held in company facilities. Some Japanese companies even help pay for wedding expenses.

Imitating Japanese management in other countries could backfire.

Japanese managers obviously go to great lengths to build positive working relationships with their employees. In addition, there is some evidence that similar actions have been applied successfully by Japanese managers in motivating American employees at the Japanese Sony plant in San Diego.[26] Since the general Japanese culture has been shown to be a significant factor influencing the success of Japanese management,[27] however, managers of other countries should imitate Japanese actions with extreme caution.[28] After all, what Japanese workers feel are desirable or need-satisfying actions by management may not be the same as what workers from other countries feel are desirable or need-satisfying.[29]

Insights from Japanese Management Practices: Theory Z

Given the recent success of organizations like Nissan and Sanyo, many U.S. management writers have been carefully analyzing Japanese organizations and comparing them to American organizations. The purpose of this analysis and comparison is to make recommendations regarding how Japanese management practices can be used to improve the operation of American organizations.

One such recommendation, called Theory Z, was introduced by William Ouchi in 1981.[30] **Theory Z** suggests integration of significant management practices in the United States and Japan into one, middle-ground, improved framework. Basically, Ouchi studied the following management practices in American and Japanese organizations: (1) the length of time workers were employed; (2) the way in which decisions were made; (3) where responsibility existed within the organization; (4) the rate at which employees were evaluated and promoted; (5) the type of control tools used; (6) the degree to which employees had specialized career paths; and (7) the type of concern organizations showed for employees. Figure 20.12 summarizes Ouchi's findings regarding how these management practices differ in American and Japanese organizations.

In addition, Figure 20.12 contains Ouchi's suggestions for how to integrate American and Japanese management practices to develop a new, more successful American organization, called a Type Z organization. According to Ouchi, the Type Z organization is characterized by the "individual responsibility" of American organizations, as well as the "collective decision making, slow evaluation and promotion, and holistic concern for employees" of Japanese organizations. The length of employment, control, and career path characteristics of the Type

Ouchi proposed Theory Z, which integrates U.S. and Japanese management practices.

FIGURE 20.12   Combining significant American and Japanese management practices to form the Type Z organization.

Organization Type A
(American)

1. Short-term employment
2. Individual decision making
3. Individual responsibility
4. Rapid evaluation and promotion
5. Explicit control mechanisms
6. Specialized career path
7. Segmented concern for employee as an employee

Organization Type J
(Japanese)

1. Lifetime employment
2. Collective decision making
3. Collective responsibility
4. Slow evaluation and promotion
5. Implicit control mechanisms
6. Nonspecialized career path
7. Holistic concern for employee as a person

1. Long-term employment
2. Collective decision making
3. Individual responsibility
4. Slow evaluation and promotion
5. Implicit, informal control with explicit, formalized measures
6. Moderately specialized career paths
7. Holistic concern, including family

Organization Type Z
(Modified American)

Z organization are essentially compromises between American and Japanese organizations.

Theory Z is popular, but Ouchi's research methods are being questioned.

In a very short time, Ouchi's Theory Z concept has gained much popularity not only among management theoreticians but also among practising managers. Anecdotes abound about how the application of Theory Z principles has aided managers in such organizations as Chrysler and Mead Merchants.[31] However, since some question has arisen regarding the quality of Ouchi's research methods,[32] the validity of his Theory Z conclusions has become somewhat questionable. Much more investigation is needed before Ouchi's Theory Z can be conclusively evaluated.

Insights from Japanese Manufacturing: Just-in-Time Inventory Control

JIT reduces inventory to a minimum.

The previous two sections focused on improving U.S. companies through the use of Japanese motivation strategies and manangement practices. This section focuses on improving U.S. companies through the use of **just-in-time (JIT) inventory control**, the inventory control technique that reduces inventories to a minimum by arranging for them to be delivered to the production facility "just in time" to be used. The concept, developed primarily by the Toyota Motor Company of Japan,[33] is also called "zero inventory" and "kanban"—the latter a Japanese term referring to purchasing raw materials by using a special card ordering form.

JIT is based on the management philosophy that products should be manufactured when customers need them and in the quantities customers need them in order to minimize levels of raw materials and finished goods inventories kept on hand.[34] It is sometimes considered a component of materials requirements planning (MRP). The discussion of MRP, which appears in Chapter 17, will provide a more complete understanding of JIT and its potential role in organizations. Overall, JIT emphasizes maintaining operations within a company by using only the resources that are absolutely necessary to meet customer demand.

JIT is most suitable for companies with standardized products and consistent demand for them.

JIT works best in companies that manufacture relatively standardized products and that have consistent product demand. Such companies can comfortably order materials from suppliers and assemble products in several small, continuous batches. The result is a smooth, consistent flow of purchased materials and assembled products and little inventory buildup. Companies that manufacture non-standardized products that have sporadic or seasonal demand generally must face more irregular purchases of raw materials from suppliers, more uneven production cycles, and greater accumulations of inventory.

JIT can enhance organizational performance.

If implemented successfully, JIT can enhance organizational performance in several important ways. First, it can reduce unnecessary labour expenses generated by products manufactured but not sold. Second, it can minimize the tying up of monetary resources needed to purchase production-related materials that do not result in sales on a timely basis.[35] Third, it can help management minimize expenses normally associated with maintaining an inventory—for example, storage and handling costs. Better inventory management and improved control of labour costs are two of the most commonly cited benefits of JIT.[36]

Many U.S. businesses are adopting JIT as a means of improving organizational performance.[37] General Motors has used JIT since 1980 and has slashed its annual inventory related costs from $8 billion to $2 billion. One American Motors plant has cut its inventories to less than one day's supply, compared to the more usual six-day reserve. Recent reports indicate that the use of JIT is spreading from the automotive industry to other industries—for example, the small appliances industry. General Electric and RCA are two small appliance firms seriously experimenting with JIT.[38]

Experience indicates that successful JIT programs tend to have certain common characteristics:[39]

1. *Closeness of suppliers*   Manufacturers using JIT find it beneficial to have suppliers of raw materials within short distances of them. As companies begin to order smaller quantities of raw materials, suppliers sometimes must be asked to make one or more deliveries per day. Short distances make multiple deliveries per day feasible.

2. *High Quality of materials purchased from suppliers*   Manufacturers using JIT find it difficult to overcome problems caused by defective materials purchased from suppliers. Since the materials inventory is kept small, defective materials may mean that the manufacturer must wait until the next delivery from the supplier before the production process can continue. Such production slowdowns can be disadvantageous, causing late delivery to customers or lost sales because finished products are unavailable.

3. *Well-organized receiving and handling of materials purchased from suppliers*   Companies using JIT must be able to receive and handle raw materials effectively and efficiently. Such materials must be available for the production process where and when they are needed. Naturally, if the materials are not available, extra costs are built into the production process.

4. *Strong management commitment*   Management must be strongly committed to the concept of JIT. The system takes time and effort to plan, install and improve—and is therefore expensive to implement. Management must be willing to commit funds to initiate the JIT system and to support it once it is functioning.

> Four common characteristics of JIT programs are:
> 1. Short distances.
> 2. Avoidance of defective materials.
> 3. Well-organized receiving and handling of materials.
> 4. Management commitment.

BACK TO THE CASE

Managers at Nabisco Brands undoubtedly are involved with comparative management. In this regard, they study the management practices in foreign operations for the purpose of applying them to improve operations at Nabisco. Company managers probably take a number of trips annually to see firsthand how foreign operations are run.

One comparative management insight that Nabisco managers might want to consider applying within their company involves Japanese motivation strategies. Japanese managers seem to be very successful in motivating their workers by implementing such strategies as elevating the workers to the same status as managers and making workers believe that the organization will provide for their material needs. Since the Japanese culture is much different from the French, Italian, United Kingdom, Chinese, Canadian, and U.S. cultures with which Nabisco deals, however, Nabisco managers should be careful in applying Japanese methods to workers in other countries.

Another comparative management insight that

could be valuable to Nabisco managers is Theory Z, which suggests a blend of American and Japanese management practices. With Theory Z, Nabisco managers could make their company more successful by implementing such strategies as hiring employees for the long term and having only moderately specialized career paths for workers. If Theory Z is to be implemented in a non-Japanese company, however, the worth and impact of the concept should be carefully monitored. More research is needed to test Theory Z's true worth.

JIT, another Japanese concept, could prove to be a valuable inventory control method for Nabisco. Keeping inventory to a minimum by ordering materials from suppliers only as they are needed for production could significantly enhance organizational performance. Minimizing storage and handling costs related to inventories and engaging only the organizational resources needed to meet customer needs are advantages that Nabisco could gain by using JIT.

Action Summary

Reread the learning objectives that follow. Each objective is followed by questions. Answering these questions accurately will help you to retain the most important concepts discussed in this chapter. After answering each question, check your answer with the answer key at the end of this chapter. (*Hint*: If you have doubt regarding the correct response, consult the page that follows the answer.)

Circle:

From studying this chapter, I will attempt to acquire:

1. **An understanding of international management and its importance to modern managers.**
   T, F
   a. To reach organizational objectives, management may extend its activities to include an emphasis on organizations in foreign countries.
   b. Canada's ability to rise in international business activity is attested to by: (a) the amount of investment by other countries in Canada; (b) its trading partners; (c) its business relationships with foreign countries; (d) all of the above; (e) none of the above.
   a, b, c, d, e

2. **An understanding of what constitutes a multinational corporation.**
   a. According to Jacoby, which of the following is the first stage in multinationalization: (a) multinationalizes ownership of corporate stock; (b) multinationalizes management from top to bottom; (c) establishes foreign manufacturing facilities; (d) establishes sales organizations abroad; (e) exports its products.
   a, b, c, d, e
   b. In general, the smaller the organization, the greater the likelihood that it participates in international operations of some sort.
   T, F

3. **Insights concerning the risk involved in investing in international operations.**
   a. Which of the following factors affects the risk of an organization doing business in a foreign country; (a) economic factors; (b) political factors; (c) social factors; (d) a and b; (e) a, b, and c.
   a, b, c, d, e
   b. Before a company does business in a foreign country, some managers think that it should check the country's BER1 rating, its B1 rating, and its WPRF rating.
   T, F

4. **Knowledge about planning and organizing in multinational corporations.**
   a. The primary difference between planning in multinational versus domestic organizations probably involves operational planning.
   T, F
   b. The feeling that multinational corporations should regard home country management practices as superior to foreign country practices is known as which of the following attitudes: (a) egocentric attitude; (b) ethnocentric attitude; (c) polycentric attitude; (d) geocentric attitude; (e) isocentric attitude.
   a, b, c, d, e

5. **Knowledge about influencing and controlling in multinational corporations.**
   a. The one factor that probably most contributes to the increased complexity and challenge of influencing in multinational organizations is: (a) language; (b) attitudes; (c) personal needs; (d) culture; (e) none of the above.
   a, b, c, d, e
   b. Different currencies and distance are the two major contributors to the difficulty of controlling in multinational corporations.
   T, F

6. **Insights about what comparative management is and how it might help managers to do their jobs better.**
   a. Comparative management emphasizes analyzing management practices in one country to determine how to best counteract the effectiveness of a foreign competitor.   T, F
   b. A group of Canadian business executives learning the virtues of self-discipline and group decision making through the vehicle of a business game developed by a Japanese firm is an example of: (a) industrial sabotage; (b) comparative management; (c) kibutshi; (d) foreign intervention; (e) none of the above.   a, b, c, d, e

7. **Ideas on how to be a better manager through the study of Japanese management techniques.**
   a. Since the Japanese have been so successful and there is little relationship between their culture and their success, American management would be wise to immediately implement the Japanese techniques.   T, F
   b. Which of the following is *not* one of the significant management practices that Ouchi studied in American and Japanese organizations: (a) the length of time workers were employed; (b) the way in which decisions were made; (c) the type of incentive plan used; (d) where responsibility existed within the organization; (e) the rate at which employees were evaluated and promoted.   a, b, c, d, e
   c. JIT emphasizes the improvement of organizational performance primarily through more accurate sales forecasts.   T, F

INTRODUCTORY CASE WRAP-UP

"Nabisco Brands in the International Arena" (p. 564) and its related back-to-the case sections were written to help you better understand the management concepts contained in this chapter. Answer the following discussion questions about this introductory case to further enrich your understanding of the chapter content:

1. Do you think that at some point in your career you will become involved in international management? Explain.

2. Assuming that you become involved in international management, what challenges do you think will be the most difficult for you to meet? Why?
3. Evaluate the following statement: We can learn to manage our organizations better by studying how successful managers in other countries run their organizations.

Issues for Review and Discussion

1. Define *international management*.
2. How significant is the topic of international management to the modern manager? Explain fully.
3. What is meant by the term *multinational corporation*?
4. List and explain four factors that contribute to the complexity of managing multinational corporations.

5. Should managers be careful in making investments in foreign operations? Explain.
6. List and define four areas in which managers can develop internationally oriented strategies.
7. What is the difference between direct investing and joint ventures at the international level?
8. Draw segments of organization charts that organize a multinational corporation on the basis of product, function, and customers.

9. Is there one best way to organize all multinational corporations? Explain fully.
10. What are the differences between ethnocentric, polycentric, and geocentric attitudes? Describe advantages and disadvantanges of each.
11. How does culture affect the international management process?
12. Discuss three suggestions that would be helpful to a manager attempting to influence organization members in different countries.
13. How does geographic distance relate to controlling multinational corporations?
14. How can comparative management help managers of today?
15. What insights can be learned from Japanese managers about ways to motivate people? Should caution be exercised by a Canadian manager in applying these insights? Explain.
16. Discuss what is meant by Theory Z. How much value should a manager place on the Theory Z concept? Explain.
17. What is JIT, and how can it improve organizational performance?

Sources of Additional Information

Berenbeim, Ronald. *Managing the International Company: Build a Global Perspective.* New York: Conference Board, 1982.

Bylinsky, Gene. "America's Best-Managed Factories." *Fortune,* May 1984, 16–24.

Frame, J. Davidson. *International Business and Global Technology.* Lexington, Mass.: D.C. Heath, 1983.

Garvin, David A. "Quality Problems, Policies, and Attitudes in the United States and Japan: An Exploratory Study." *Academy of Management Journal* 29 (December 1986): 653–73.

Goehle, Donna A. *Decision Making in Multinational Corporations.* Ann Arbor: University of Michigan Research Press, 1980.

Gregory, Gene. "The Japanese Enterprise: Sources of Competitive Strength." *Business and Society* 24 (Spring 1985): 13–21.

Herbert, Theodore T. "Strategy and Multinational Organization Structure: An Interorganizational Perspective." *Academy of Management Review* 9, no. 2 (1984): 259–71.

Keys, J. Bernard, and Thomas R. Miller. "The Japanese Management Theory Jungle." *Academy of Management Review* 9, no. 2 (1984): 342–53.

Marr, Norman E. "Impact of Customer Service in International Markets." *International Journal of Physical Distribution and Materials Management* 14, no. 1 (1984): 33–40.

Negandhi, Anant R. *International Management.* Boston: Allyn and Bacon, 1987.

Scott, Bruce R. "National Strategies for Stronger U.S. Competitiveness." *Harvard Business Review* (March/April 1984): 77–91.

Sloan, Michael P. "Strategic Planning by Multiple Political Futures Techniques." *Management International Review* 24, no 1 (1984): 4–17.

Tung, Rosalie L. "Selection and Training Procedures of U.S., European, and Japanese Multinationals." *California Management Review* 25 (Fall 1982): 57–71.

Tyson, Laura, and John Zysman. *American Industry and International Competition: Government Policies and Corporate Strategies.* Ithaca, N.Y.: Cornell University Press, 1983.

Vlachoutsicos, Charalambos A. "Where the Ruble Stops in Soviet Trade." *Harvard Business Review* (September/October 1986): 82–86.

Notes

1. S.H. Appelbaum, M.D. Beckman, L.E. Boone, and D.L. Kurtz. *Contemporary Canadian Business* (Toronto: Holt, Rinehart and Winston of Canada, 1984), 516.
2. "Trying to Copy Past Success." *The Economist,* 6 February 1982, 70.
3. Ben J. Wattenberg, "Their Deepest Concerns," *Business Month* (January 1988): 27–33.
4. American Assembly of Collegiate Schools of Business, *Accreditation Council Policies, Procedures, and Standards,* 1980–1981. St. Louis, Mo.; Sylvia Nasar, "America's Competitive Revival," *Fortune,* January 4, 1988, 44–52.
5. J. Behrman, *Some Patterns in the Rise of the Multinational Enterprise* (Chapel Hill, N.C., University of North Carolina Press, 1969).
6. U.S. Department of Commerce, *The Multinational Corporation: Studies on U.S. Foreign Investment* vol. 1 (Washington, D.C.: U.S. Government Printing Office.)

7. Robert W. Stevens, "Scanning the Multinational Firm," *Business Horizons* 14 (June 1971): 53.

8. Patricia Best, "Just Because of the Children," *Financial Post 500,* Summer 1984, 24.

9. Neil H. Jacoby, "The Multinational Corporation," *The Center Magazine* 3 (May 1970): 37–55.

10. This section is based primarily on Richard D. Robinson, *International Management* (New York: Holt, Rinehart & Winston, 1967) 3–5.

11. 1971 Survey of National Foreign Trade Council, cited in Frederick D. Sturdivant, Business and Society: A Managerial Approach (Homewood, Ill.: Richard D. Irwin, 1977), 425.

12. Karen Paul, "Fading Images at Eastman Kodak," *Business and Society Review* 48 (Winter 1984): 56.

13. Joan Servaas Marie, "Robinson Nugent, Inc.: Working Smarter, Not Harder," *Indiana Business* (June 1983): 4–7.

14. Peter J. Mullins, "Survival through Joint Ventures," *Automotive Industries* (May 1983): 17–18.

15. Howard V. Perlmutter, "The Tortuous Evolution of the Multinational Corporation," *Columbia Journal of World Business* (January/February 1969): 9–18.

16. John S. Hill and Richard R. Still, "Adapting Products to LDC Tastes," *Harvard Business Review* (March/April 1984): 92.

17. Geert Hofstede, "Motivation, Leadership and Organization: Do American Theories Apply Abroad?" *Organizational Dynamics* 9 (Summer 1980): 42–63.

18. Anne B. Fisher, "Peering Past Pepsico's Bad News," *Fortune,* November 14, 1983, 124.

19. R.N. Farmer, "International Management," in *Contemporary Management Issues and Viewpoints,* ed. J.W. McGuire (Englewood Cliffs, N.J.: Prentice-Hall, 1974), 302.

20. Frank Ching, "China's Managers Get U.S. Lessons," *Wall Street Journal,* January 23, 1981, 27.

21. Peter F. Drucker, "Behind Japan's Success," *Harvard Business Review* (January/February 1981): 83–90.

22. "How Japan Does It," *Time,* March 30, 1981, 55.

23. Charles McMillan, "Is Japanese Management Really So Different?" *Business Quarterly* (Autumn 1980): 26–31.

24. Masaru Ibuka, "Management Opinion," *Administrative Management* May 5, 1980, 86.

25. "How Japan Does It".

26. "Consensus in San Diego," *Time,* March 30, 1981, 58.

27. Lane Kelly and Reginald Worthley, "The Role of Culture in Comparative Management," *Academy of Management Journal* 24, no. 1 (1981): 164–73.

28. Linda S. Dillon. "Adopting Japanese Management: Some Cultural Stumbling Blocks," *Personnel* (July/August 1983): 73–77.

29. Isaac Shapiro, "Second Thoughts about Japan," *Wall Street Journal,* June 5, 1981.

30. William Ouchi, *Theory Z* (Reading, Mass.: Addison-Wesley, 1981)

31. Charles W. Joiner, " One Manager's Story of How He Made the Theory Z Concept Work," *Management Review* (May 1983): 48–53.

32. William Bowen, "Lessons from behind the Kimono," *Fortune,* June 15, 1981, 247–50.

33. Lee J. Krajewski and Larry P. Ritzman, *Operations Management: Strategy and Analysis* (Reading, Mass.: Addison-Wesley, 1987), 573.

34. Krajewski and Ritzman, *Operations Management,* 572–84.

35. A. Ansari and Modarress Batoul, "Just-in-Time Purchasing: Problems and Solutions," *Journal of Purchasing and Materials Management* (August 1986): 11–15.

36. Albert F. Celley, William H. Clegg, Arthur W. Smith, and Mark A. Vonderembse, "Implementation of JIT in the United States," *Journal of Purchasing and Materials Management* (Winter 1987): 9–15.

37. Jack R. Meredith, *The Management of Operations,* 3d ed. (New York: Wiley, 1987), 391–92.

38. Information about companies that have adopted JIT methods appears in Sumer C. Aggarwal, "MRP, JIT, OPT, FMS?" *Harvard Business Review* (September/October 1985): 8–16.

39. John D. Baxter, "Kanban Works Wonders, but Will it Work in U.S. Industry?" *Iron Age,* June 7, 1982, 44–48.

Action Summary Answer Key

1. a. T, p. 565
   b. d, p. 567
2. a. e, p. 571
   b. F, p. 571

3. a. e, p. 574
   b. T, pp. 574–575
4. a. F, p. 576
   b. b, p. 579

5. a. d, p. 581
   b. T, p. 583
6. a. F, p. 583
   b. b, pp. 583–584

7. a. F, p. 584
   b. c, p. 585
   c. F, p. 586

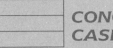
THE JAPANESE INDUSTRIAL MIRACLE IS NO MIRACLE

In the early 1950s, cheap Japanese Christmas tree lights, running shoes, and T-shirts were a source of considerable amusement to North American business people. Today, the Japanese produce three-quarters of the world's video cassette recorders, single lens cameras, and motorcycles, half the world's ships, two-fifths of its televisions, and a third of its semi-conductors and cars. For the future, the Japanese have taken dead aim at telecommunications, robotics, bioengineering, modern materials, lasers, fashions, and, perhaps most startling of all, financial services. No one is laughing at the Japanese anymore.

Why the Japanese have been so successful has been the subject of numerous scholarly and popular articles and books. Investigating the Japanese industrial miracle has become something of a cottage industry in itself. Though the high quality of commentaries on Japan Incorporated abound, it often does not appear as if North American executives and policy makers have taken note. More often than not, these executives and policy makers have attributed the success of the Japanese to "cheating."

According to John S. McCallum, a professor with the Faculty of Administrative Studies at the University of Manitoba, such rationalizations tend to absolve us of responsibility without explaining the extent or the long time frame of Japanese industrial dominance. While it is a huge mistake to attribute Japan's industrial success to cheating, there is no question that they have engaged in a number of highly questionable industrial practices. This does not, however, explain why the Japanese share of world markets in established products continues to increase at the same time that they are taking dominant positions in products just hitting the world's consumer and industrial marketplaces.

CULTURE

That the Japanese are culturally different is clearly evident. That their devotion to family and the work ethic have contributed mightily to their success is also clear. But while some of Japan's industrial success can obviously be explained by their culture, ascribing Canada's industrial difficulties and failures largely to cultural differences is to go much too far. Moreover, if Japan's culture is so crucial to their success, why have other countries with more or less similar cultural lineages, such as China, not achieved the same pre-eminence? Even those remarkable four dragons—Hong Kong, Taiwan, Singapore, and Korea—would not mind some protectionist help against Japan. Since their own success is so great, so diverse, and

so dynamic, other factors must be explored. The bulk of Japan's success may, in fact, be explained by basics like reliance on competitive markets, industrial priorities, flexibility, and rates of saving—precisely the things that once put North America at the top of the world economy.

COMPETITION

An important reason for Japan's industrial success is its reliance on a ruthlessly competitive marketplace to discipline those who are systematically unable to provide quality goods and services at prices people want to pay. Uncompetitive industrial hulks that survive, year after year, courtesy of either direct government aid or some complicated set of market regulations and interventions, just do not exist in Japan.

James Abegglen and George Stalk's book, *Kaisha: The Japanese Corporation*, documents the importance of Japan's reliance on competitive markets in its industrial success. They describe an industrial system that works in the following manner: government identification of key markets, heavy government subsidization of basic industrial research and information accumulation, a period of time over which the domestic market is heavily protected, and a no-holds-barred battle for market supremacy among domestic competitors, where the spoils do belong to the victor and the vanquished really do not live to fight another day.

PRIORITIES

Accumulated evidence suggests that Japanese corporate priorities are quite different from those of North Americans. Where the North American corporation is obsessed with return on equity, dividend maintenance, stock price increases, this year's earnings, and shareholder satisfaction, Japanese corporations relentlessly pursue lifetime jobs for their employees and evergrowing world market shares. Japanese unemployment has averaged about 3 percent of the workforce over the last decade, whereas North America and Western Europe are close to, or in, double digits. In return for modest dividends, Japanese shareholders are expected to keep quiet and let professional managers run the operation. Japan currently boasts a U.S. $50 billion trade surplus.

Focusing on lifetime jobs and market shares results in an important difference between North American and Japanese business practices. For one thing, it enables the Japanese to take a much longer-term view of investment. Instead of looking to quick financial paybacks, the Japanese are able to concentrate on long-term product development, product quality, basic industrial research into new manufacturing technologies, applications, and processes, worker training and education, and world market penetration and development through aggressive promotion and cutthroat—bordering on predatory—pricing.

Because of such investments, the Japanese are now more productive than North Americans in many industries, countering a long-held view that the only reason the Japanese have been so successful is because they work like Trojans for subsistence wages. For example, it is estimated that Japanese car stamping and assembly plants are twice as productive as those in North America, while engine, transmission, and machinery plants are about 50 percent better. Across all manufacturing, Japan is estimated to have about a 30 percent cost advantage over North America.

The Japanese are also obsessed with product quality, recognizing that it is a "must" for worldwide market success. Not much annoys a consumer faster, and more, than something that does not work as implied or promised. The way the Japanese achieve product quality involves emphasizing simplicity in manufacturing processes and products, worker incentive programs that reward quality, and quality control circles. The Japanese preoccupation with cleanliness in the workplace also contributes to their capacity to consistently deliver quality products.

FLEXIBILITY

Another important difference between Japan and North America is the Japanese emphasis on a flexible economy. Japanese preoccupation with problem-recognition times and the speed of industrial adjustment must be rated an important factor in their industrial success, given a rapidly changing or highly technological business world. Examples of Japanese flexibility abound. For instance, they do not cushion their economy against ups and downs in the prices of important industrial commodities. When oil prices rocketed in 1973, rather than using subsidies to cushion industry and consumers, the Japanese immediately went to the world price throughout their economy, forcing everyone to abruptly adjust. For a country that imports all its oil, a 1,000 percent increase in the price of this most crucial of industrial inputs was no small matter, but by moving right away to the world price, the Japanese were quicker than most to rethink their economy along energy efficient lines. The result: world leadership in energy efficient products, technologies, and manufacturing processes.

The Japanese wage and salary system is also very flexible. That Japanese workers from the executive suite to the shop floor earn much less than their counterparts in Canada has already been noted as a contributing factor to their industrial success. But how the Japanese compensate is also relevant. A significant part of a Japanese worker's pay is flexible, dependent on how the employing organization prospers. This not only provides a strong incentive, but also gives the organization financial breath-

ing room when things turn down—as they did in 1973, after the OPEC shock, and again during the worldwide recession of 1981-1982. Those heated North American battles between labour and management over "give-backs" (voluntary wage cuts), did not occur in Japan. Why? Because Japanese pay is at least partly tied to what is available, and is not governed by a series of obligations contracted under possibly entirely different economic and financial circumstances.

The Japanese factory is a model of flexibility too. Quite different from a North American factory, it has a minimum of fixed facilities in order to accommodate fast redeployment and adjustment should it be necessary. The Japanese do not put much time or energy into the physical housing of their workplaces, because they are forever changing. The "factory" in the conceptual sense is a constantly evolving thing in Japan. It is continually being remade by small innovations, additions of new machinery, and adaptations. The inside changes every five to seven years, allowing the factory to be constantly at the edge of whatever technology is available. With the introduction of robotics and automation, factories will soon be able to change within hours. The Japanese factory and assembly line—where products are actually made—is the focus of Japanese business, whereas here it is the office and executive suite that are emphasized.

The Japanese categorically see the worker as the most important element in the production process and great emphasis is put on the worker's flexibility and adaptability. To them, the key to turning out a high-quality, world-competitive product is a worker who can think for him or herself and do several different tasks. By focusing on the factory and making the worker the most important element in the production process, Japanese manufacturers get production help through suggestions, etc., that manufacturers here can only dream of getting from those on the assembly lines. Recognizing that the key to worker flexibility is worker capability, Japanese firms invest staggering sums each year in training.

The Japanese are also flexible because of what they do not do. They are far less involved in such flexibility-dissipating schemes as high minimum wages, excessive rent controls, price subsidies, and marketing boards—elements that have become a staple for North American politicians seeking a quick hit at the next ballot box.

SAVINGS

A final difference that has helped their economy enormously is the Japanese tendency to save, particularly in long-term plans. As a consequence, much more capital is available at much lower interest rates. Japanese interest rates of about one-third to one-half of ours enable them to invest two to three times as much with the same interest payment. As well, the lower interest rates imply a lower cost of capital, which makes long-term infrastructure-type investments much more likely to satisfy conventional net-present-value investment decision criteria.

DISCUSSION ISSUES

1. According to the case, what are the real reasons behind Japan's industrial success? Elaborate.
2. How do such findings support what we know about comparative management? Explain.
3. What are some of the practices that may be transferable to North American workplaces? What considerations must be taken into account in transferring these Japanese practices? Discuss.

Based on "The Japanese Industrial Miracle: It is not Hard to Explain," by John S. McCallum in *Business Quarterly*, Summer 1986. Copyright 1986, *Business Quarterly*, School of Business Administration, The University of Western Ontario, London, Canada. Reprinted with permission.

C H A P T E R

MANAGEMENT SKILLS FOR THE FUTURE

STUDENT LEARNING OBJECTIVES

From studying this chapter, I will attempt to acquire:

1. An understanding of how systems skill relates to management in the future.

2. Insights about how functional skill relates to management in the future.

3. An understanding of how situational analysis skill relates to management in the future.

4. A better understanding of the labour force of the future.

5. An appreciation for the impact of such factors as system size, energy, and technology on management in the future.

6. A practical strategy for training managers for the future.

CHAPTER OUTLINE

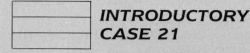

WHAT ABOUT TOMORROW?

Max Barton was feeling a real sense of accomplishment. He had worked at the Pleasant Ridge Candy Company managing the molded chocolate candy department for twelve months and was just receiving a well-deserved compliment from his supervisor, Judy Shull.

Shull was telling Barton that his people had been very productive as a unit, having increased their output of molded candy by 12 percent over the past six months. She also mentioned that the department's efficiency was above average and that Barton's people seemed to identify with the company's goal of becoming the largest producer of chocolate candy on the West Coast during the next five years. Barton could only surmise from Shull's statements that, overall, he was doing an excellent job as department manager.

Shull's concluding statements, however, left Barton somewhat perplexed. Shull indicated that Barton cer-

tainly would have a good future with the Pleasant Ridge Candy Company if he decided to remain. This, of course, pleased Barton. What puzzled him was that, as Shull left, she turned around and advised him to prepare himself carefully for managing in the future.

Barton had never really thought about consciously and systematically trying to prepare himself for a management position later on. He was managing well today, but what about tomorrow? How would the company's growth affect his department? How could technological advances change the production of molded candy? Would he be able to continue the efficiency and productivity of his department in the face of rising costs and greater company demands? After giving some thought to these issues, Barton concluded that Shull was right. He did need to plan carefully for the future as manager of the molded chocolate candy department. The question was: How?

What's Ahead

The introductory case ends with Max Barton, a relatively new department manager at the Pleasant Ridge Candy Company, thinking about conscientiously and systematically preparing himself to be a good manager in the future. This chapter gives managers like Barton some insights on what such preparation involves. More specifically, this chapter discusses various skills that managers of the future should possess and how a management system can train its present managers for the challenges they inevitably will face in the future.

⊞ ESSENTIAL SKILLS FOR FUTURE MANAGERS

Up to this point, this text has recommended that, to manage successfully, managers should apply both knowledge of systems theory and the four basic management functions to the unique management situations they face. However, will this recommendation change sometime in the future? The sections that follow attempt to answer this question by discussing: (1) systems skill in the future; (2) functional skill in the future; and (3) situational analysis skill in the future.

Systems Skill in the Future

Systems skill is the ability to view and manage a business or some other concern as a number of components that work together and function as a whole to achieve some objective. In essence, the systems approach to management is a way of analyzing and solving managerial problems.[1] Managers analyze problems and implement corresponding solutions only after examining those system parts related to the problem and evaluating the effect of a problem solution on the functioning of all other system parts.[2]

Frank T. Curtin, vice-president of machine tools at Cincinnati Milacron, has seen the value of applying the systems approach to management problems in the past and indicates that the systems approach will be an extremely valuable tool for managers of the future.[3] According to Curtin, only after managers understand the "big picture," or see all parts of a company as a whole, will they be able to solve managerial problems appropriately. For the systems approach to management to become more useful to businesses in the future, however, Curtin suggests that more individuals be formally educated in the value of this approach and shown the steps that can be taken to implement it.

Systems skill involves seeing parts as a whole.

599

FIGURE 21.1 Relationships among the four major functional subsystems and the overall management system.

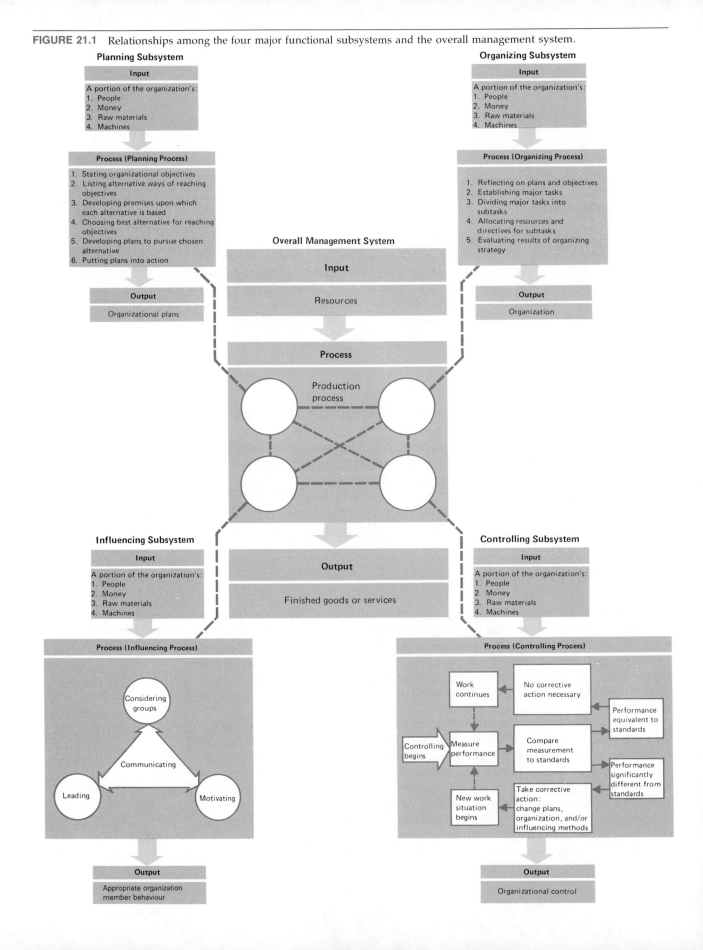

Functional Skill in the Future

Functional skill is the ability to apply appropriately the concepts of planning, organizing, influencing, and controlling to the operation of a management system. The application of these four basic functions is of such vital concern to management that this text presents them as subsystems of the process of the overall management system (Figure 21.1).

Functional skill involves applying managerial functions to the operation of the management system.

The application of these four functions to managerial problems, of course, has long been suggested as sound management practice. In fact, the evolution of theory related to each of these functions has evolved over many decades as a result of insights contributed and accumulated by both management practitioners and management researchers. The probability is quite high, therefore, that functional skill will continue to be extremely valuable to managers of the future.

BACK TO THE CASE

Max Barton, in the introductory case, probably has achieved his present level of managerial success primarily by applying systems skill and functional skill to the fundamental aspects of his job at Pleasant Ridge. Systems skill enables Barton to see and manage all parts of his department as a group of components that function as a whole with other departments to help his company achieve its objectives. For example, Barton is able to understand how his department's increased productivity will affect the chocolate making and the packaging departments and how changes in these other departments will affect the company as a whole.

Functional skill enables Barton to successfully plan, organize, influence, and control the various compo-

nents in his department. He is able to plan to produce more chocolate candy, and he can then implement his plan by organizing his work force, encouraging his people to produce, and controlling each part of his department to ensure that the department as a whole will be coordinated with other departments to obtain the company's goal of increased production.

Because these skills are so entrenched in management theory, a sound strategy for Barton in preparing himself for a future management position would be to continue developing his systems and functional skills.

Situational Analysis Skill in the Future

Situational analysis skill is the ability to apply both systems theory and functional theory to the particular situations managers face. This skill emphasizes that managers must thoroughly understand their own unique management situations before they can use systems and functional skills to their best advantage. Obviously, the importance of situational analysis skill is supported by the thoughts and ideas of the contingency approach to management.

Situational analysis skill involves managers understanding their unique management situations.

Situational analysis skill probably will be extremely important to managers of the future. However, managers of the future almost certainly will face much different situational factors than either past or present managers,[4] such as: (1) the size of future management systems; (2) the characteristics of future management system members; (3) the amount of energy available to future management systems; and (4) the technology available to future management systems. The following sections discuss each of these future situational factors in more detail and offer possible strategies for dealing with them.

Situational factors of the future will be different.

Size of Management Systems of the Future

Generally speaking, a tendency exists in North American society for successful businesses and other types of concerns to grow larger over time. As this trend continues into the future, managers of the future, as a group, probably will be faced with managing larger systems than has any other generation of managers.[5] Also, since as management systems grow they tend to become more difficult to manage, managers of the future, as a group, probably also will be challenged by the most difficult-to-manage set of management systems that has ever existed. Specific characteristics of large management systems that tend to make the systems more difficult to manage include:

1. *A diminishing ability of individuals within the system to comprehend the overall system*   As a system increases in size, fewer and fewer individuals within that system are able to understand all system parts and the complicated relationships between those parts. Generating and disseminating information that adequately defines system parts and their corresponding relationships becomes both a formidable and important task for managers of large management systems. One of the trends emerging to counter the problems created by size is stated by John Naisbitt in *Megatrends*: "We will restructure our businesses into smaller and smaller units, more entrepreneurial units, more participatory units."[6]

2. *A diminishing level of participation in decision making*   Overall, as management systems grow larger, managers tend to believe that large-group involvement in decision making becomes less and less feasible, and thus some system members are excluded from decision making. As a general guideline, even as management systems grow larger, managers should continue to try to raise the quality of their decisions by allowing other system members to participate in the making of those decisions.[7]

3. *A declining access of organization members to top decision makers within the system*   As the number of system members increases, the proportion of those members who can communicate directly with upper management becomes smaller and smaller. If not overcome in some way—perhaps through special meetings of various kinds with system members—this characteristic of a large management system can put top management completely out of touch with its people.

4. *A growing involvement of experts in decision making within the system*   As systems grow, they necessarily become more and more complex. As problem complexity related to those systems increases, managers tend to ask various kinds of experts for help in solving these problems. These experts only can be of help, however, if they can discuss specialized information in a way that managers can understand and apply. This can be, and often is, very challenging for experts. Managers, however, must do everything possible to ensure that experts meet this challenge.

5. *Increasing costs of coordination and control*   As management systems grow larger, more and more authority must be delegated to various system levels and segments. To maintain coordination and control, however, managers must establish adequate communication between the various levels and segments, and establish effective plans to guide them. The cost of coordinating and controlling system segments never should exceed the contribution those segments can make to the system as a whole.

6. *Increasing system rigidity*   As systems grow in size, rules and regulations must be established so that new system segments operate in a predetermined and predictable fashion. Managers must recognize, however, that too many of such rules and regulations creates a rigid and inflexible system. Large systems should have enough regulations to ensure order but not so many that flexibility and creativity in solving unique management system problems become non-existent.

6. The system becomes less flexible.

7. *A gowing deterioration of the overall system*   The point was made earlier that, as management systems grow larger, fewer and fewer system members are able to understand them fully. As a result of this lack of understanding, the deterioration of various segments of large management systems likely will go unnoticed and, therefore, remain uncorrected. Managers of growing management systems must take steps to ensure that such deterioration is noticed and eliminated as soon as possible.

7. The system's weaknesses go undetected.

BACK TO THE CASE

Since Max Barton is presently successful, he probably possesses situational analysis skill in addition to the systems and functional skills discussed earlier. In other words, Barton is able to look at and analyze the unique issues in his own department before he uses his systems and functional skills to solve problems.

Barton should consider that his department will grow and be more difficult to manage as the Pleasant Ridge Candy Company becomes more successful. Barton will need to analyze his department's growth and instill in its members, as well as in himself, an understanding of the department's components and how they relate to one another and to the rest of the company. He must also recognize that it is important to continue to involve department members in decision making, despite the fact that group involvement will become more difficult as the department gets larger.

Other issues, such as Barton's accessibility to his subordinates and the amount of control he exerts over them, will also come into play as the molded candy department grows. Currently, Barton is available to listen to employee suggestions and complaints. He spends time walking through the production line, talking to and encouraging his workers. He is also relaxed about his employees' hours and vacation time. As Pleasant Ridge grows, however, Barton will probably have less time for his employees and will also have to establish new rules to keep his growing department under control. If he uses his situational analysis skill effectively, he will find ways to make himself accessible to his workers and provide some flexibility in the new regulations, despite the department's increased size.

It seems, then, that Barton's situational analysis skill is very valuable to him as manager of the molded chocolate candy department. He should continue to develop this skill as he prepares for management in the future.

Characteristics of Future Management System Members

The characteristics of future management system members is another significant situational factor that will face managers of the future. In this regard, the sections that follow discuss union membership of professional workers in the future and characteristics of the work force of the future.

Union Membership of Professional Workers in the Future

A significant number of management theorists predict that in the future an increasing number of professional workers, such as engineers, professors, and doctors, will join unions and that the traditional image of the union member as a factory employee fighting for better wages will change. This probably will be especially true for professionals employed by government agencies.[8] It appears

Future professional workers will turn to unions.

that the needs of professionals who work within management systems simply are not being met by management.[9] Unless this trend is reversed, managers of the future probably can look forward to dealing with professional workers primarily through union representatives.

Characteristics of the Work Force of the Future

Characteristics of the future human resources of management systems can be obtained by studying the general make-up of the work force from which those resources will come. The next sections discuss the following characteristics of this work force of the future: (1) average age of the work force; (2) size of the work force; (3) number of professional workers in the work force; (4) jobs performed by the work force; (5) employment of the work force according to industries; (6) interest of the work force in the quality of work life; and (7) number of women in management.

The work force of the future will consist of older workers.

Average Age of Work Force   Overall, the work force of the future will have a much higher average age than the work force of today. In addition, these older workers will not be forced to retire because of age and generally will be sought by managers much more intensely than their counterparts today.[10] As a result, managers of the future probably will have to deal with generally older workers who may have been employed within the management system for much longer periods of time.[11]

There will be fewer workers than once expected,

Size of Work Force   Work forces of the future probably will be smaller than was at one time anticipated. As a result, managers of the future probably will have to face higher labour costs and more intense competition in hiring good employees than predicted earlier. The decreasing national population rate generally is cited as the basis for this prediction of a smaller work force in the future.

and more professionals.

Number of Professional Workers in Work Force   Another characteristic of the work force of the future probably will be that the number of white-collar or professionally and technically trained workers will increase relative to the number of blue-collar or non-professional workers. This growth of professional and technical workers implies that managers of the future probably will have to modify their strategies to suit generally more sophisticated workers.[12] In addition, the competition for managerial positions will become more intense. Naisbitt's *Megatrends* suggests that between 1982 and 1990, the number of workers competing for such positions will have doubled.[13]

The work force of the future will work less in production areas and more in maintenance and professional areas.

Jobs Performed by Work Force   A fourth characteristic of the work force of the future is that the future work force as a whole will be performing somewhat different jobs than the work force of today. In addition, the work force of the future will want to be responsible and efficient if it perceives its work as serving some meaningful purpose.[14] There probably will be primarily three types of jobs that human resources of the future will perform in management systems:

> There will be a few "workers"—probably a smaller part of the total labour force than today—who will be part of the in-line production, primarily doing tasks requiring relatively flexible eye-brain-hand coordination.
>
> There will be a substantial number of people whose task is to keep the system operating by preventative and remedial maintenance. Machines will

play an increasing role, of course, in maintenance functions, but machine power will not likely develop as rapidly in this area as in-line activities. Moreover, the total amount of maintenance work—to be shared by people and machines—will increase. In the near future at least, this group can be expected to make up an increasing fraction of the total work force.

There will be a substantial number of people at professional levels responsible for the design of product, for the design of the productive process, and for general management.[15]

If these three types of jobs materialize as predicted, managers of the future will be faced with a number of challenging problems. For example, if fewer employees work in production areas, differences in the perceived level of importance of production work groups within the management system relative to the perceived level of importance of other work groups within the management system could develop. Other work groups within the management system might believe that, since they are larger than the production work group, they are more important. Naturally, this type of situation easily could result in jealousy and a lack of cooperation between production and other work groups.

Another problem managers of the future will have to face will be to determine how to use their blue-collar employees as blue-collar jobs begin to disappear.[16]

Employment of Work Force According to Industries   A greater percentage of the work force of the future will be employed within the service industry, such as retailing, banking, insurance, and education. The service industry does not directly produce goods as do the manufacturing, farming, and construction industries. Figure 21.2 suggests the service sector will continue to increase faster than other areas and more than four times faster than manufacturing.

In the future, more people will work for service industries.

Since service jobs probably will become more prevalent as society continues to grow, managers' ability to apply management concepts to this particular job situation will become increasingly important. However, it must be noted that managers of the future must understand that government involvement will be a fact of life.

FIGURE 21.2   Actual growth in the number of jobs 1971–1987.

	1971	1987	% Change 1971–87	Annual % Change 1971–87
Agriculture	514	475	− 7.6	−0.5
Manufacturing	1766	2044	+15.7	0.9
Construction	489	680	+39.0	2.1
TCOU	707	906	+28.1	1.6
Trade	1335	2116	+58.5	2.9
FIRE	399	695	+74.2	3.5
Services	2128	3934	+84.9	3.9
Pub. Admin.	545	814	+49.4	2.5

From Employment Canada—Catalogue 71–201.

The work force of the future will be interested in making decisions about work situations.

Interest of Work Force in Quality of Work Life   Generally, the work force of the future probably will be more seriously interested in the overall quality of work life than any other work force that has preceded it. **Quality of work life** can be defined as the opportunity of workers to make decisions that influence their work situation. The greater the opportunity of workers to make such decisions within a management system, the higher the quality of work life within that system is said to be. Overall, the work force of the future probably will strive to make decisions that tend to create:[17]

1. Jobs that are interesting, challenging, and responsible.
2. Worker rewards through fair wages and recognition for their contribution.
3. Workplaces that are clean, safe, quiet, and bright.
4. Minimal but available supervision.
5. Secure jobs that promote the development of friendly relationships with other system members.
6. Organizations that provide for personal welfare and medical attention.

Managers of the future, as managers of both the present and the past, will have to emphasize the attainment of management system objectives. Unlike managers of the past, however, future managers may find that providing workers with a high quality of work life is an extremely important prerequisite for attaining these objectives.[18]

Women will fill more managerial positions in the future.

Women in Management   As in the recent past, the future should contain a number of legal, educational, and social developments that will move a greater percentage of women into the mainstream of corporate management.[19] As an indication of this trend, not only is the percentage of women attending four-year colleges increasing faster than that of men, but a significant number of business schools are now offering courses aimed specifically at preparing women for management positions.[20] As Figure 21.3 indicates, women account for over three fifths of the growth in the labour force over the last decade. Naisbitt's *Megatrends* indicates

FIGURE 21.3   Women as percentage of labour force growth.

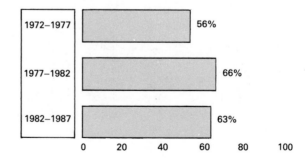

From *Women in the labour force,* 1986–87 Edition, Labour Canada.

FIGURE 21.4   Factors that seem to make it difficult for men and women to work together productively.

Organizational Problems and Inequities	Characteristics of Men and Women	Men's Perception of Women	Women's Perception of Men
Many women feel they are left out of the informal communication network. Women are seen by men as making advances because of government regulations and not ability. Customers may have difficulty dealing with women. Women feel they are discriminated against for promotions. Women are seen as having more problems than men in relocating in another community. Men are seen by other men as having more long-term career goals than women.	Men seem to have difficulty understanding the subtle ways in which they discriminate or treat women. Women compete and discriminate more against each other than do men. Women appear to give their marriages and family roles greater importance relative to their jobs than men. Women behave with more emotion than men. Women are required to be more competent than men in comparable positions.	Women are obsessed with terminology (a "he" rather than a "he/she" etc.). Women use the idea of discrimination as a "crutch." Women don't make a real commitment. Women misconstrue being courteous as being patronizing. Women overreact.	Men treat women differently than men. Men exhibit niceties, not acceptance. Men don't help women grow. Men don't relate to problems women have. Men either lack confidence in women's abilities or are afraid women are capable.

that "by 1990, the number of women earning business B.A.s will be eight times that of the 1960s."[21]

Although at first glance, "more women in management" may seem to be a simple variable with which managers of the future must deal, in reality it is extremely complex. For example, Baron and Witte determined that several factors seem to increase the difficulty involved in men and women being able to work together productively.[22] Figure 21.4 shows these factors divided into four categories: (1) organizational problems and inequities; (2) personal characteristics of men and women; (3) men's perception of women; and (4) women's perception of men.

Naturally, managers of the future must strive to minimize the effects of these factors if organizations are to maximize gains through men and women working together. Perhaps through special training programs, managers can help men and women to better understand one another and, as a result, work more productively as a team.

The following Management in Action feature deals with the increasing presence of women in the traditionally male-dominated business community. As women have moved into management positions, their presence in the top echelons of power has not increased in a corresponding manner. Access 51 is an attempt to respond to these discrepancies by highlighting and generating a data bank of women eminently qualified for top management and governmental positions, thereby providing an essential networking function for women.

MANAGEMENT IN ACTION

ACCESS 51: HELPING WOMEN MOVE UP

At a glittering dinner one year ago, a computerized program was officially launched to help women executives break into the so-called "network of influence" at the top level of Quebec's business community. The data bank, dubbed Access 51, then contained a mere sixty names. Word of its existence spread afar, and the list compiled by the Montral Chamber of Commerce has since grown to more than 425 names.

All names belong to women who are eminently qualified to sit on boards of directors, economic advisory committees, or task forces, and to be referred as guest speakers on major issues. "We don't compete with head hunters or do any placing of personnel," says Paule Dore, the Chamber's general manager. "We simply believe that women have been under-represented and need to be promoted." At the centre of Access's beliefs is the feeling that a growing number of organizations and government agencies actually want to appoint women to senior positions, but don't know where or how to find them.

There is a special significance to Access 51's name. In Quebec, women make up 51 percent of the population, yet they hold only 2 percent of the directors' positions with provincial companies. "We have come to realize," says Dore, "that only between twenty and twenty-five women have penetrated Quebec's so-called inner circle of power, and nearly all of them sit together on several boards. The same names return to the same directorships over and over again."

As more names trickled in, businesses began to draw from the list for some of their appointments of directors and advisers. Now, as then, most women are recommended for the program by executives who already hold senior posts. Each woman's name, and the full range of her qualifications and experience, comprise a confidential computer file. Organizations, companies, or governments use the Access 51 data bank by telling the Chamber, as precisely as they can, the kind of woman they seek, and for what post.

The rest is up to the program's coordinator, Dominique Groleau. She sets the computer to work, telling it to match the backgrounds of those women listed in the bank with the kind of canditate being sought. No sooner has the computer done its job by naming the most suitable women for the post—usually three or four—than they are contacted so meetings can be arranged between themselves and the requesting firm or organization. The final choice depends entirely on human evaluation.

An assessment of the program's effectiveness is being made to establish just how accurately the computer makes

Groleau: "Access 51 has really begun to address an issue that has gone on for far too long."

its choices. "The computer has proved to be very accurate," Groleau says cheerfully. "But as the years roll on and we refine our data base by including more variables and possibilities, the program will become even more sophisticated."

Groleau and her part-time secretary have received more than 150 inquiries about the data bank, of which 115 have been serious attempts to recruit women. These have come from seventy different enterprises, six of them large corporations, but most of them small and medium-sized businesses and non-profit organizations. So far sixty-four women have been considered for posts and thirty-five of them have been appointed, a dozen or so to boards of directors and the remainder to task forces and various government advisory committees. Comments Groleau, "Access 51 has really begun to address an issue that has gone on for far too long."

Former Employment Minister Barbara McDougall, who was also formerly responsible for the status of women in the federal cabinet, supports this view. "Competence alone is not enough," she says. "One of the biggest problems facing many qualified women is their lack of visibility, and a program like Access 51 is helping to change all that."

Based on "Access 51 helps women executives to move into circle of influence," by Adrian Waller in *This Week In Business*, April 23, 1988. Used with permission.

BACK TO THE CASE

One reason the management situation Barton will face in the future will probably be different is that the nature of the work force in his department and in the company as a whole will be different. Barton will probably find that the professionals in his department will be represented by unions, making it necessary for him to abide by union rules regarding wages, hours, and working conditions.

Barton will also have to consider that the number of blue-collar workers and the types of jobs they perform will probably decrease. This will result in fewer assembly-line workers making the chocolate candy and more employees at the professional level planning and designing the candy-making process.

In addition, Barton may find that the average age of his employees is rising and that more of his fellow

managers are women, making it necessary for him to adapt his working conditions and relationships. Overall, Barton will need to recognize that his employees (and all the other employees at Pleasant Ridge Company) will be more concerned with the quality of their work life, making it necessary for him to provide more challenging positions, a clean, comfortable workplace, and appropriate compensation for jobs well done.

Of course, Barton should not view any of these people-oriented issues as unmanageable. Instead, he should strive to apply systems and functional theory to help him plan for managing in the future. He can begin by considering such issues as how to accommodate more professionals in his department, how to alter regulations to abide by union rules, and how to make assembly-line jobs more interesting.

Energy in the Future

The previous two sections discussed management system size and characteristics of system members as two major situational variables for managers of the future. Energy is a third such variable.

In the past, managers seem to have operated under the assumption that an unlimited supply of energy could be obtained for such worthwile and important purposes as powering equipment and providing adequate working light. Energy sources as known in the past, however, probably will become more and more scarce in the future. Although this scarcity is not expected to be crippling, the cost of energy available to management systems of the future probably will be very high. This prediction is based primarily on the premise that the world's oil supply is expected to begin vanishing in about 1990.[23]

In the future, there will be less energy at higher cost.

As new ways of using coal, solar, and nuclear energy are discovered in years to come, energy may again become readily available. Managers of the more immediate future, however, probably will need to become involved in such activities as investing in reserve supplies of energy, finding or developing alternative sources of energy, and quickly cutting back production activities due to unexpected depletion of energy supplies.

Future energy shortages probably will force managers of the future to modify somewhat the way in which they operate their management systems. The most significant of these modifications typically will be forced on future managers who are directly responsible for management systems that exist primarily to supply energy products to consumers.

Technology in the Future

Technology is the fourth major situational factor that will face managers of the future. The future undoubtedly will contain numerous possible technological improvements that managers of the future must evaluate for use within the management system.[24] This evaluation, of course, necessarily must weigh the cost of using such technological improvements against the contribution they can make toward the attainment of management system objectives. In essence, managers

Future technological improvements will have to be evaluated on a cost-benefit basis.

of the future will be faced with the hard fact that sophisticated equipment is expensive to use and therefore must make a substantial contribution to the attainment of management system objectives.

Specific technological improvements available to managers of the future undoubtedly will be many and varied. The further sophistication of computers and calculators for use in the area of information handling is likely. Indeed, Naisbitt's book *Megatrends* identifies the "new information economy" as the "most important megatrend." Naisbitt devotes his first chapter to the proposition that "we have shifted from an industrial society to one based on the creation and distribution of information."[25] New and different means of distributing products to customers, as well as faster and safer means of human transportation, are expected. In addition, further developments in the area of communication will make it easier for people to share information more effectively and efficiently.[26]

BACK TO THE CASE

In the future, Barton may find that the energy supply to his company is diminished, making it necessary for him to consider such conservation measures as cutting down the hours of the night shift, utilizing fewer machines for production, and purchasing more energy-efficient equipment. However, Barton will not need to be as concerned about energy shortages as will managers who supply energy products to consumers.

Barton could also be greatly affected by improved technology. Faster, more efficient machines could lead to an increase in the amount of molded candy Barton's department can produce but could also result in a decrease in the need for assembly-line workers. Of course, Barton will have to evaluate technological improvements to decide if the increase in production will be more valuable than the cost of the improved machinery.

TRAINING MANAGERS FOR THE FUTURE

Organizations can prepare their managers for the future.

Managers of tomorrow, if they are competent, certainly will be in high demand and of critical importance to the success of a management system. One strategy a company can adopt to ensure an adequate supply of future managers is to train its managers of today so that they are ready to cope with tomorrow's challenges. The sections that follow discuss three main issues related to this training of managers for the future: (1) objectives in training managers for the future; (2) developing future-oriented managers; and (3) emphasizing professionalism and change.

Objectives in Training Managers for the Future

Objectives for training managers for the future should consider skills, decisions, and practices.

To develop and maintain an effective and efficient program for training managers for the future, an appropriate set of objectives for such a program must be developed and pursued. These objectives should consider skills that managers will need in the future, decisions future managers will have to make, and practices that managers of the future will follow.

An earlier section of this chapter already discussed three skills that inevitably will be helpful to managers of the future: systems skill, functional skill, and situational analysis skill. In addition Figure 21.5 indicates that managers of the future probably will need somewhat different skills than their predecessors. Thus, objectives for training managers for the future should focus on developing man-

FIGURE 21.5   Useful skills of managers of the past and future.

Skills Useful to Past Managers	Skills Useful to Future Managers
Familiar problem solver	Novel problem solver
Intuitive problem solver	Analytic problem solver
Conservative risk taker	Entrepreneurial risk taker
Convergent diagnostician	Divergent diagnostician
Lag controller	Lead controller

Adapted from H. Igor Ansoff, "Management in Transition," in Edward C. Bursk, ed., *Challenge to Leadership: Managing in a Changing World* (New York: The Free Press, 1973), p. 41. Copyright 1973 by the Conference Board, Inc. Used with permission.

agers who are novel problem solvers, analytical problem solvers, risk takers, divergent diagnosticians, and lead controllers.

Objectives for training managers for the future also should take into consideration the decisions that managers of the future will have to make. Figure 21.6 compares the content of decisions, the decision process, and decision information as used in the company of today versus the company of the future. Since these two decison-making situations are dramatically different, objectives for training managers for the future should reflect these differences. For example,

FIGURE 21.6   Decision making in the firm of today and the firm of the future.

Firm of Today	Firm of the Future
Content of Decisions	
Operating issues, corporate policies	Strategy formulation, design of systems for strategy implementation
Exploitation of firm's current position	Innovation in patterns of firm's products, markets, and technology
Economic, technological, national, intraindustry perspective	Economic, sociopolitical, technological, multinational, multiindustry perspective
Decision Process	
Emphasis on historical experience, judgment, past programs for solving similar problems	Emphasis on anticipation, rational analysis, pervasive use of specialist experts, techniques for coping with novel decision situations
Personnel-intensive process	Technology-intensive process
Information for Decisions	
Formal information systems for internal performance history	Formal systems for anticipatory, external-environment information
One–way, top down, flow of information	Interactive, two–way communication channels linking managers and other professionals with knowledge workers
Computer systems emphasizing volume and fast response information for general management	Computer systems emphasizing richness, flexibility, and accessibility of information for general management
Emphasis on periodic operations plans, capital, and operating expenditure budgets	Emphasis on continuous planning, covering operations, projects, systems resource development; control based on cost–benefits forecasts

© 1969 by the Regents of the University of California. Reprinted from H. Ansoff and R. Brandenburg, "The General Manager of the Future," *California Management Review*, Vol. 11, No. 3, p. 69, by permission of the Regents.

FIGURE 21.7   Past and future management practices.

Past	Future
Assumption that a business manager's sole responsibility is to optimize shareholder wealth	Profit still dominant but modified by the assumption that a business manager has other social responsibilities
Business performance measured only by economic standards	Application of both an economic and a social measure of performance
Emphasis on quantity of production	Emphasis on quantity and quality
Authoritarian management	Permissive/democratic management
Short-term intuitive planning	Long-range comprehensive structured planning
Entrepreneur	Renaissance manager
Control	Creativity
People subordinate	People dominant
Financial accounting	Human resources accounting
Caveat emptor ("let the buyer beware")	Ombudsman
Centralized decision making	Decentralized and small-group decision making
Concentration on internal functioning	Concentration on external ingredients for company success
Dominance of economic forecasts in decision making	Major use of social, technical, and political forecasts as well as economic forecasts
Business viewed as a single system	Business viewed as a system within a larger social system
Business ideology calls for aloofness from government	Business-government cooperation and convergence of planning
Business has little concern for social costs of production	Increasing concern for internalizing social costs of production

From Presidential Address by Dr. George Steiner to American Academy of Management, Minneapolis, August 15, 1972. Courtesy of Dr. Steiner.

objectives for training managers for the future should emphasize the relationship between managerial decision making and such factors as strategy formulation, the use of expert specialists, and the use of computer systems to increase management system flexibility. Figure 21.6 indicates that objectives for training managers of today that relate to these same areas typically emphasize the relationship between managerial decision making and existing corporate policies, the use of personal judgment and operating history, and the use of computer systems to analyze large amounts of information quickly.

Objectives for training managers for the future also should consider the management practices that future managers will be following. Naturally, such objectives should be aimed at training managers to carry out these future practices both effectively and efficiently. Figure 21.7 compares past and future management practices. According to this figure, training objectives for developing managers for the future should emphasize such factors as carrying out long-range comprehensive planning as opposed to short-term intuitive planning, meeting social responsibilities as opposed to meeting only profit responsibilities, and establishing a decentralized decision process within the management system as opposed to a primarily centralized decision process.

Developing Future-Oriented Managers

In addition to developing and pursuing appropriate objectives, the process of training managers for the future should involve encouraging today's managers to be future oriented.[27] According to Burt Nanus, **future-oriented managers** attempt to create their own future, whenever possible, and adapt to this future, when necessary, through a continuous process of research about the future, long-range planning, and the setting of objectives. Such managers make no important decisions without a systematic and thorough analysis of the future consequences of such decisions. Future-oriented managers see the future not as an *uncontrollable* development but as a factor that can be influenced significantly by present managerial behaviour. Here, Nanus is suggesting that managers are best prepared for the future when they are shown how to participate in creating that future to the best advantage of the management system.

Future-oriented managers participate in creating their own future.

Emphasizing Professionalism and Change

Besides an appropriate set of objectives and a future orientation, the process of training managers for the future should emphasize both professionalism and change. The extremely complex nature of the future manager's job indicates that this job can best be learned by approaching its study as the learning of a profession. A **profession** is a vocation whose practice is based on an understanding of both a specific body of knowledge and the corresponding abilities necessary to apply this understanding to vital human problems. Additionally, professionalism stresses that knowledge related to a profession should be seen as constantly evolving and being modified as a result of insights derived from individuals actually practicing the profession.[28]

Management is a profession

   Professionalism necessarily involves changes. Managers trained for the future, therefore, should be warned of the inevitable changes that will occur over time. This warning should help managers of the future to overcome "future shock," or an inability to adapt to changes.[29] Although some management theorists argue that such changes probably will be insignificant,[30] others believe strongly that these changes will be both extensive and significant.[31]

and, as such is constantly changing.

BACK TO THE CASE

Even though the discussion has focused primarily on the process a company can implement to prepare its managers for future challenges, there are many things Max Barton can do as an individual to prepare himself for his own management position. For example, Barton should realize that, in addition to using his excellent systems, functional, and situational analysis skills, he will need to be an imaginative problem solver and risk taker. In other words, he must look at new and innovative ways to accomplish his department's objectives rather than simply relying on what has worked well in the past.

   In addition, Barton must recognize that the decision-making process in the future will be quite different from the way it is now. As he prepares himself for the future, Barton should consider how he can use computers and expert specialists to aid him in future decision-making situations.

Barton must also become future-oriented and learn to anticipate the inevitable changes that will occur as the company grows. As he makes decisions such as increasing the number of employees in his department or purchasing improved machinery, he should look ahead and analyze how such changes will lead to other developments. In other words, Barton must see his present managerial decisions as factors that will help shape the developments to come.

   Overall, Barton must recognize that his role as manager is a professional one, requiring him not only to understand the workings of his department but to modify his understanding as the department evolves. By developing his professionalism, learning to be future-oriented, and improving his decision-making and other managerial skills, Max Barton should be well prepared for his future management position at Pleasant Ridge Candy Company.

Action Summary

Reread the learning objectives that follow. Each objective is followed by questions. Answering these questions accurately will help you to retain the most important concepts discussed in this chapter. After answering each question, check your answer with the answer key at the end of this chapter. (*Hint*: If you have doubt regarding the correct response, consult the page that follows the answer.)

Circle:

From studying this chapter, I will attempt to acquire:

1. An understanding of how systems skill relates to management in the future.

T, F

    a. In solving organizational problems, managers of the future must understand the "big picture," or see all parts of a company as a whole.

T, F

    b. Systems skill is intuitive to most managers, and, according to Curtin, successful managers don't require any type of formal education to develop systems skill.

2. Insights about how functional skill relates to management in the future.

a, b, c, d, e

    a. The functional skill of a manager requires the application of activities associated with: (a) the influencing subsystem; (b) the implementing subsystem; (c) the organizing subsystem; (d) a and b; (e) a and c.

T, F

    b. To manage successfully, a manager need only apply knowledge of the four basic management functions to the unique management situation faced.

3. An understanding of how situational analysis skill relates to management in the future.

a, b, c, d, e

    a. Which of the following is *not* a major situational factor that managers of the future will face: (a) the characteristics of future management system members; (b) the technology available for future management systems; (c) the amount of energy available for future management systems; (d) the size of future management systems; (e) all of the above are major factors.

a, b, c, d, e

    b. All of the following are characteristics of a large management system that tend to make this system harder to manage except: (a) a decrease in the overall number of component units that comprise the total system; (b) increasing costs of coordinating and controlling the system; (c) a diminishing level of participation in decision making; (d) a declining access of organization members to top decision makers in the system; (e) an increase in system rigidity.

4. A better understanding of the labour force of the future.

T, F

    a. Projections for future employment opportunities indicate that there will be more blue-collar than white-collar workers in the labour force by 1990.

a, b, c, d, e

    b. Which of the following is *not* an organizational problem that causes inequities between men and women workers: (a) women tend to overreact; (b) customers may have difficulty in dealing with women employees; (c) women tend to feel they are omitted from the organization's informal communication network; (d) men are perceived by other men as having more long-term career goals than women; (e) women are perceived as having more difficulty than men in relocating to another community.

5. An appreciation for the impact of such factors as system size, energy, and technology on management in the future.

    a. Technological improvement in equipment can be expected in the future in all of the following areas except: (a) communication; (b) legislation; (c) information processing; (d) product distribution; (e) human transportation.   a, b, c, d, e

   b. In the future, managers will need to recognize that sophisticated equipment will have to contribute significantly to meeting organizational objectives to be justified.   T, F

6. A practical strategy for training managers for the future.

   a. All of the following are useful characteristics for managers in the future to possess except being: (a) a lag controller; (b) a divergent diagnostician; (c) an analytical problem solver; (d) an entrepreneurial risk taker; (e) a solver of novel problems.   a, b, c, d, e

   b. The process of training future-oriented managers should stress a need for professionalism and change.   T, F

▤ INTRODUCTORY CASE WRAP-UP

''What about Tomorrow?'' (p. 598) and its related back-to-the-case sections were written to help you better understand the management concepts contained in this chapter. Answer the following discussion questions about this introductory case to further enrich your understanding of the chapter content:

1. What skills does Barton probably possess now that should still be valuable to him five or ten years from now?

2. Do you agree that Barton should be preparing himself for managing in the future? Why?

3. If you were Barton, what would you do to prepare yourself for managing in the future at the Pleasant Ridge Candy Company?

Issues for Review and Discussion

1. Define *systems skill* and describe its probable value to managers of the future.
2. What is functional skill? How valuable will this skill probably be to managers of the future?
3. What is the relationship between situational analysis skill, systems skill, and functional skill?
4. List and discuss four factors that can make large management systems difficult to manage.
5. If the predicted trend of more professional workers of the future joining unions actually materializes, how do you think it will affect management practices in the future?
6. State three probable characteristics of the work force of the future. Explain how each of these characteristics could affect the practice of management in the future.
7. What is meant by the phrase *quality of work life?*
8. Describe the types of decisions that employees of the future will attempt to make to increase the quality of their work life.

9. How will the predicted energy shortage, if it materializes, probably affect the practice of management in the future?
10. What is the major criterion that managers of the future should use to decide if a particular technological improvement will be employed within their management system?
11. Describe a strategy that a company can adopt to ensure that its managers will be able to face management challenges of the future.
12. Considering the decision-making situation future managers will face, how should managers be trained for the future?
13. What is a ''future-oriented'' manager?
14. Fully explain the implications of the following statement: Management is a profession.

Sources of Additional Information

Amara, Roy, and Andrew J. Lipinski. *Business Planning for an Uncertain Future: Scenarios and Strategies.* New York: Pergamon, 1983.

Bowonder, B. "The Energy Manager and His Corporate Role." *Long-Range Planning* 17 (Autust 1984): 74–78.

Flamholtz, Eric G., Yvonne Randle, and Sonja Sackmann. "Personnel Management: The Tone of Tomorrow." *Personnel Journal* 66 (July 1987): 42–65.

Guth, William D. *Handbook of Business Strategy 1986/1987 Yearbook.* New York: Warren, Gorham & Lamont, 1986.

Harris, Philip R. *New World, New Ways, New Management.* New York: Amacom, 1983.

Hickok, Richard S. "Looking to the Future: A Key to Success." *Journal of Accountancy* (March 1984): 77-82.

"High Technology—Wave of the Future or a Market Flash in the Pan?" *Business Week,* November 10, 1980, 86–98.

Leavitt, Harold J. *Corporate Pathfinders: Building Vision and Value into Organizations.* Homewood, Ill.:Richard D. Irwin, 1986.

Lehrer, Robert N. *Participative Productivity and Quality of Work Life.* Englewood Cliffs, N.J.: Prentice-Hall, 1982.

Mills, D. Quinn. *The New Competitors: A Report on American Managers from D. Quinn Mills of the Harvard Business School.* New York: Wiley, 1985.

Naisbitt, John. *Megatrends.* New York: Warner Books, 1984.

Nykodym, Nick, Jack L. Simonetti, Joseph C. Christen, and Judith A. Kasper. "Stress and the Working Woman." *Business* 37 (January/February/March 1987): 8–12.

Pascarella, Perry. "Futurists Sound a More Positive Note." *Industry Week* (August 1982): 76–86.

Quinn, James Brian, and Christopher E. Gagnon. "Will Services Follow Manufacturing into Decline?" *Harvard Business Review* (November/December 1986): 95–105.

Sample, Robert L. "Coping with the 'Work-at-Home' Trend." *Administrative Management 42 (August 1981): 24–27.*

Suojanen, Waino W., Tricia Working, Jane S. Goldner, Kelley Ort, and Sherrie Cribbs. "The Emergence of the Type E Woman." *Business* 37 (January/February/March 1987): 3–7.

Talpaert, Roger. "Looking into the Future: Management in the Twenty-first Century." *Management Review* (March 1981): 21–25.

"What's Ahead for In-House Training." *Administrative Management* 42 (July 1981): 41–47.

Whitsett, David A., and Lyle Yorks. "Looking Back at Topeka: General Foods and the Quality-of-Work-Life Experiment." *California Management Review* 25 (Summer 1983): 93–109.

Zoffer, H.J. "Restructuring Management Education." *Management Review* 70 (April 1981): 37–41.

Notes

1. J. Buckley, "Goal-Process-System Interaction in Management: Correcting an Imbalance," *Business Horizons* 14 (December 1971): 81–92.

2. Paul Adler, Jr., "Toward a System of General Management Theory" *Southern Journal of Business,* July 1969.

3. "Stressing the System Approach," *Manufacturing Engineering* (August 1969): 75.

4. Richard Allen Stull, "A View of Management to 1980," *Business Horizons* (June 1974): 5–12.

5. Duane S. Elgin and Robert A. Bushnell, "The Limits to Complexity: Are Bureaucracies Becoming Unmanageable?" *The Futurist* (December 1977): 493–49.

6. John Naisbitt, *Megatrends* (New York: Warner, 1984), 229.

7. Kenneth A. Kovach, Ben F. Sands, Jr., and William W. Brooks, "Management by Whom?—Trends in Participative Management," *S.A.M. Advanced Management Journal* (Winter 1981): 4–14.

8. Thomas A. DeScissciolo, "Labor Relations—Friends and Future," Third National Capitol Conference, International Personnel Management Association, Washington, D.C., May 28, 1975.

9. Dennis Chamot, "Professional Employees Turn to Unions," *Harvard Business Review* (May/June 1976): 119–28.

10. Patricia Skalka, "Farewell to the Youth Culture," *Ambassador* (April 1978): 43–48.

11. Susan R. Rhodes, Michael Schuster, and Mildred Doering, "The Implications of an Aging Work force," *Personnel Administrator* (October 1981): 19–22.

12. Peter F. Drucker, "Management's New Role," *Harvard Business Review* (November/December 1969): 49–54.

13. Naisbitt, *Megatrends,* 223.

14. Frederick Herzberg, "Herzberg on Motivation for the '80s," *Industry Week* (October 1979): 58–61.

15. Herbert A. Simon, "The Corporation: Will It Be Managed by Machines?" in *Management and Corporations—*

1985, eds. Anshen and Bach (New York: McGraw-Hill, 1960), 17–55.

16. Robert Schrank, "Horse-collar, Blue-collar Blues," *Harvard Business Review* (May/June 1981): 133.

17. Tom Lupton, "Efficiency and the Quality of Work Life," *Organizational Dynamics* (Autumn 1975): 68

18. John F. Mee, "The Manager of the Future," *Business Horizons* (June 1973): 5–14.

19. Linda Keller Brown, "Women and Business Management," *Signs: Journal of Women in Culture and Society* 5, no. 2 (1979): 266–88.

20. Rose K. Reha, "Preparing Women for Management Roles," *Business Horizons* (April 1979): 68–71.

21. Naisbitt, *Megatrends,* 264.

22. Alma S. Baron and Robert L. Witte, "The New Work Dynamic: Men and Women in the Work Force." *Business Horizons* (August 1980) 56–60.

23. "The Future Revised: No Crippling Shortage of Energy Expected, But Cost Will Be High," *Wall Street Journal,* March 29, 1976, 1.

24. Henry B. Schacht, "The Impact of Changes in the Seventies," *Business Horizons* (August 1970): 29–34.

25. Naisbitt, *Megatrends,* xxii.

26. Douglas P. Brush, "Internal Communications and the New Technology," *Public Relations Journal* (February 1981): 10–13.

27. Burt Nanus, "The Future-Oriented Corporation," *Business Horizons* (February 1975) 5–12.

28. For more information on professionalism, see Kenneth R. Andrews, "Toward Professionalism in Business Management," *Harvard Business Review* (March/April 1969): 49–60.

29. Alvin Toffler, *Future Shock* (New York: Random House, 1970), 4.

30. Charles Perrow, "Is Business Really Changing?" *Organization Dynamics* 3 (Summer 1974): 30–62.

31. Gordon H. Coperthwaite, "Management: Its Changing Patterns," *Management Controls* (December 1972): 281–86

Action Summary Answer Key

1. a. T, p. 599
   b. F, p. 599
2. a. e, p. 601
   b. F, p. 601

3. a. e, p. 601
   b. a, pp. 602–603
4. a. F, p. 604
   b. a, p. 607

5. a. b, p. 610
   b. T, pp. 609–610
6. a. a, p. 611
   b. T, p. 613

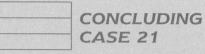
IN SEARCH OF THE FUTURE MANAGER

Between July 1985 and April 1986, the Banff Centre School of Management conducted a national survey of sixty-two chairpersons, CEOs, presidents, and senior executives. In personal interviews, they were asked to identify the most crucial executive and management development needs facing Canadians in the foreseeable future. The following summary represents the top ten executive and management development priorities expressed by the senior executives.

1. COMMUNICATION SYSTEMS AND SKILLS

The most acutely-felt need in both the private and public sectors lies in the functional area of communication systems and skills. In the area of communication, executives see a need for improvement in their various forecasting, monitoring, and reporting systems, including financial reporting systems and client contact reports. Most are calling for more effective performance planning, management and evaluation systems to be in place over the short to medium terms.

Meanwhile, an overwhelming number of executives see an important need for the following skills in the future:

- Basic oral and written communication skills, including the interpersonal or behavioural skills required to motivate employees and build teams.
- Negotiation skills, to deal with labour relations situations, conflict resolution, and the myriad of daily situations requiring varying levels of influence.
- Customer service skills, including communications to the general public.
- The skills required to deal effectively with the media.
- Presentational skills, covering in-house activity, sales, and public speaking.

These skill sets are seen to be required at all levels of management, but most particularly by middle managers.

2. CREATIVE, TRANSFORMATIONAL, OR INSPIRATIONAL LEADERSHIP

Many of the chief executives who were interviewed are at the helm of downsized, "lean and mean" organizations. While they generally seem pleased with their organizations' collective abilities to be as productive or more productive with fewer staff, they are also concerned about the morale of their middle managers. Faced in many cases

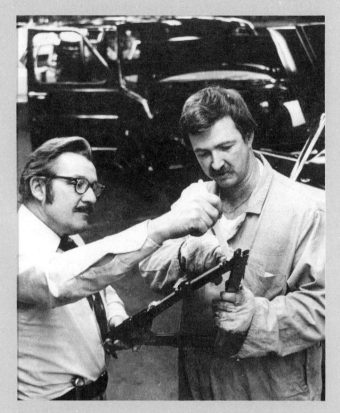

"executives see an important need for . . . the interpersonal or behavioural skills required to motivate employees and build teams."

with the phenomenon of the baby boomers' plateaued careers, and with the lack of adequate rewards, chief executives are looking for the leadership and insight needed to inspire or transform their managers' motivations over the next few years. They also make a positive connection between an innovative, marketing-oriented management group and the organization's ability to compete.

Nurturing creative leadership skills within ranks of senior and middle managers in both the public and private sectors must deal with:

- Cultivating New Visions.
- Clarifying and confirming the human values which underlie corporate excellence, and helping people make emotional and intellectual links to the corporate vision.
- Understanding managerial leadership as a high art and an intensely creative process.
- Developing this creative capacity and then managing creativity effectively.
- Developing flexibility in thinking.

618

- Developing the inner strength of people called upon to make tough decisions.
- Persevering in the face of adversity.

3. MANAGEMENT DEVELOPMENT

Third on the list is the on-going need for management development, a general management program for middle-level managers in the private sector. While management development has different meanings for different people, chief executives seem to look to such programs to develop their people's abilities in:

- Determining what's important, what contributes to achieving major skills, and how to keep on track.
- Developing a sense of accountability, initiative, risk-taking, entrepreneurship, and the freedom to act.
- Understanding the importance of taking time to see, get to know, and help employees.
- Auditing one's own operations.
- Maintaining and developing outside contacts.

The actual components seen as desirable in a management development program include:

- Business policy, planning, and environmental scanning.
- Financial management.
- Marketing.
- Motivation, interpersonal skills, and communications.
- Contracts and industrial relations.
- Government relations.
- Administration and office automation.

4. THE MANAGEMENT OF CHANGE

The next most frequently mentioned aspect of management requiring an on-going concentration is the management of change. Seen as a western, private sector need by a four-to-one margin, chief executives want their middle and senior managers to be able to recognize opportunities quickly and to keep their operations competitive in rapidly changing conditions. Here again, such qualities as innovation, flexibility, creativity, and imagination continue to surface as integral to the ability to manage change in diverse situations. The objective of a program of this nature would be:

- To develop the thinking ability to cope with and manage change in an environment characterized by a great amount of rapid change.
- To handle a multitude of expectations, technologies, and regulations, and the competition.

The program would include components designed to develop functional, interpersonal, motivational, and resource allocation skills.

5. STRATEGIC PLANNING AND MANAGEMENT

Very closely related to the question of managing change is the need for strategic planning and management. Effective executive and management development programs designed to increase strategic abilities in order to compete in a global environment will integrate skills in:

- Establishing corporate mission and corporate development philosophies.
- Analyzing the external environment and developing individual indicators to monitor and interpret it.
- Understanding the competition and developing competitive strategies, particularly for mature markets.
- The management of strategic business units.
- Communications.

6. BUSINESS-GOVERNMENT RELATIONS

The main recurring executive and management program need of an issue-oriented nature is that of business-government relations. The provision of "a forum of equals" in which senior managers from the private and public sectors can improve communications is much needed in the west, according to private sector chief executives. Nineteen of those executives see a need, where only two public sector executives made mention of the usefulness of a new, on-going program that would deal with such politically sensitive issues as freer trade, deregulation, management of the environment, safety, the transportation of hazardous goods, and the like. The overall objectives of a short, intensive program of this nature would be:

- To foster development and to improve the economy.
- To understand changes in the labour market.
- To underline the importance of profits and jobs.
- To understand the political system, how to get things done through government, and how to influence change.
- To redefine the blurring roles of legislators, administrators, and bureaucrats for more effective government.

The private sector sees these forums as part of a consultative process necessary both provincially and federally, yet would prefer to refine this process in separate forums. A few executives also see the need for such programs at the middle management level, and suggest including on-site visits in that particular curriculum.

7. MANAGING TECHNOLOGY

Included in the general management challenge of the management of change will be the specific need of managing technology. Chief executives from both private and public sectors in Western and central Canada aim to have their middle managers "understand the microchip." Professional development programs in this field will centre around effective and efficient corporate management information systems, as well as keep managers updated on trends in computer-assisted decision making, in new personal-computer applications, and in automated customer service and automated offices.

8. MARKETING STRATEGY

Refining the marketing strategy of both private and public sector organizations is the goal of a significant number of chief executives, particularly in Western Canada. Their specific needs are:

- Increasing market reponsiveness.
- Developing a consumer orientation, including public participation programs and improved communications.
- Improving product information and client analysis systems and skills.
- Sales, including the marketing of self.

9. ORGANIZATIONAL EFFECTIVENESS

This was cited often as a set of attitudes, systems, and skills required by middle managers from both private and public sectors right across the country. Such an externally delivered program (i.e., delivered by persons outside the firm) would be comprised of:

- Organizational theory and design.
- Restructuring for more effectiveness and efficiency.
- Succession planning and manpower planning.
- Understanding the legal implications of actions, such as labour and safety laws, and the impact of equal employment opportunities programs.
- Program evaluation.

10. THE BASICS

Finally, this commonly expressed need of a general nature is aimed at middle managers in the private sector. It is a need perceived to be inadequately met either on an in-house basis or on the open market at the present time. It surfaced frequently as a gap in management training. The basics is defined as developing managerial competence in:

- Planning, organizing, staffing, directing, and controlling.

- Setting priorities, integrating operations and measuring effectiveness.
- Problem solving and decision making.
- Interpersonal skills, such as influencing and negotiating.

THE CHALLENGE

Canada can boast of a healthy executive and management development industry. Business and government, to say nothing of the not-for-profit sector, annually invest staggering amounts of time and money in both open-market and in-house programs. The Canadian institutions and organizations offering these programs can and do call upon world-class teachers, and employ relevant learning materials and effective methodologies. Indeed, the number of international participants attracted each year to Canadian programs, as well as the overseas demand for Canadian teachers and their made-in-Canada programs, all attest to a high-quality national product.

Yet it is clear that much remains to be done if Canada is to sharpen its competitive abilities. The findings here provide a challenge to the executive and management development industry, to business and government organizations, and to individual executives and managers. Canadian CEOs have some very specific and common concerns about getting their people to deal with the future.

DISCUSSION ISSUES

1. It is obvious from the case that systems, functional, and situational analysis skills will be important considerations for future managers. Why? Elaborate.
2. It appears that managers of the future will have to pay considerable attention to people. Comment on the theme that managing human resources is a key to competitive success.
3. What will be the characteristics of future managers that the senior executives interviewed are trying to emphasize and anticipate with regard to survival?

Based on "Future Executive and Management Training Needs in Canada—A National Survey," by G. Peter Greene in *Business Quarterly*, March 1984. Copyright 1984, *Business Quarterly*, School of Business Administration, The University of Western Ontario, London, Canada. Reprinted with permission.

APPENDIX
Video Cases

This is a unique appendix designed to give you another means of applying the management theory you are learning. Three video-assisted cases appear on the following pages:

Fired: A Focus on Management Careers
Battle of the Blimps: A Focus on Strategic Planning
The Colonel Comes to Japan: A Focus on International Management

Your instructor will inform you when to use this material.

Note: Video synopses are reprinted by permission of Coronet/MTI. Videos are available from Marlin Motion Pictures Ltd., 211 Watline Avenue, Mississauga, Ontario L4Z 1P3, 416-890-1500.

VIDEO CASE 1

FIRED: A FOCUS ON MANAGEMENT CAREERS

(An extension of materials in Chapter 1—Introducing Management and Management Careers)

SYNOPSIS: Tens of thousands of executives lose their jobs each year. "Fired" is the true story of one of those executives, 44-year-old Douglas "Biff" Wilson.

Before he was dismissed, Biff Wilson was Vice-President of Marketing for Universal Foods (fictional name), a multi-divisional packaged-goods firm. After 15 years, Wilson's career at Universal was terminated by a man who had reached the presidency after vying with Biff for the position. The new president wanted to aim toward a new era for Universal, and Biff was part of the old era. Clearly, the new president and Biff had contrasting personalities and styles, so Biff was out. One Monday morning, in less than an hour, Biff Wilson had gone from a vice-president of a large company to unemployment.

Douglas Wilson was shaken. For $10 000, Universal hired an executive outplacement firm to help Biff find a job elsewhere. Eric Barton, Biff's counselor and a former sales representative, met his client at Universal minutes after the firing. His challenge: to help piece together Biff Wilson's shattered professional life.

The first step was a visit to the outplacement center, which, like a hospital, has its patients. Only these patients are some 100 fired executives seeking a new job in mid-life. As in a hospital, counselors prescribed a pro-

tocol for each patient, or client. Wilson's protocol included self-exploration exercises, fitness training, new clothing, new hairstyle, and most importantly, a new confidence in this exciting new product—himself.

After mock interviewing and evaluation, Biff's counselors determined that he was out of his league in attempting another career with a large packaged-goods firm. They felt he should set his sights lower; Wilson did not agree. He answered newspaper advertisements, called on friends, and contacted executive search firms. From his search, one job possibility emerged. After interviewing, Biff did not get the job; he claimed age was the deciding factor.

Finally, Wilson lowered his expectations and followed Eric Barton's advice: "Use people like never before and don't be ashamed to do it." After talking with several people in the food industry, Wilson homed in on a medium-sized organization, run by its owner, Ray Morris. Before seeing Morris, Biff chatted with suppliers, buyers and employees, and eventually landed the all-important interview with Ray Morris. Biff Wilson was lucky, he was offered the job with Morris—replacing a man that Ray Morris was about to fire.

INTRODUCTION: Now that you have had the opportunity to read and reflect on the Chapter 1 materials and concepts pertaining to management and management careers, you are ready to view the video case entitled "Fired." This case vividly portrays the true story

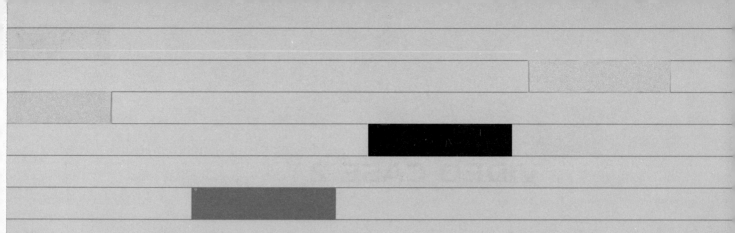

of forty-four-year-old Douglas "Biff" Wilson, one of the tens of thousands of managers who lose their jobs each year. The major difference in the video case situation and the background reading you have done in Chapter 1 is that this type of career change is not within the control of the individual . . . or is it? After you view the case and discuss its implications, your perspective on managment careers will be broadened. Management is one of the most challenging and rewarding of all careers. It is also one of the most demanding and, in some instances, one of the least secure career choices.

PART 1: In preparation for viewing the video, familiarize yourself with the following questions. When the video is shown, make notes on the case issues that appear especially relevant:

a. Is there anything in the text that provides a hint that Biff Wilson's career could be approaching a period of transition?
b. Which management skills did Wilson appear to be lacking to cause the new president to view him as he did? Jot down specific examples and statements from the video to support your contentions. Was there any evidence at the end of the video that Wilson had made adjustments and upgraded his skills? Explain.
c. When Wilson finally realized that he was going to have to lower his sights and get serious about the search process if he was to find a job, how did he approach the job search process? Would the steps he

took be helpful for anyone else looking for a job? Explain.
d. One of the recommendations made to Wilson by outplacement executive Eric Barton was to "use people" to make the contacts necessary to get the job he wanted. Is this type of behaviour appropriate job search behaviour? If it is, should college students begin developing links to individuals in business organizations who can assist them in making career moves? If so, how?
e. What specific strategy did Wilson follow to land the job at Morris Corporation? Would it be beneficial to you to tuck away this strategy for your own future reference? Explain.
f. Was Wilson in a position to do anything about being fired after the decision was made? Could he have taken action earlier to keep this from occurring? Explain.

PART 2: After you view the case and document the issues you find especially pertinent, meet with three or four of your classmates to discuss and develop a group reaction to each question. Groups may be asked to share their views (or case analysis) with the rest of the class. The presenting group's comments will provide the basis for a class discussion of the issue at hand.

PART 3: Now that you have viewed the video case and have answered and discussed the questions, what specific points do you want to remember to assist you in your management career? ∎

VIDEO CASE 2

BATTLE OF THE BLIMPS: A FOCUS ON STRATEGIC PLANNING

(An extension of materials in Chapter 6—Types of Planning: Strategic and Tactical)

SYNOPSIS: Founded in 1979 by Roger Munk, the small British company Airship Industries has built eight airships with seven more in the works. Using Porsche engines and sporting $4 million price tags, Airship Industries' products are presently the best in the field, making Airship the undisputed leader in modern airship technology. Yet being a technological leader is of little advantage when the market for your product is practically nonexistent. In late 1984, $14 million in debt, Airship Industries was sold to Australian tycoon Alan Bond.

The only other major producer of blimps, Goodyear Aerospace (a wholly-owned subsidiary of Goodyear Tire and Rubber), did not even compete for Airship Industries' few customers. Goodyear's heyday for blimps lasted from World War I until the early 1960s, when it built almost 300 airships for the U.S. Navy. Now Goodyear has only four blimps, which it uses for its own promotional purposes.

Unlike balloons, blimps or airships have a propulsion system and a steering mechanism. Although the first successful airship was built in 1852, the age of commercial use really began in 1900 when Count Ferdinand von Zeppelin of Germany designed a "rigid airship." Dubbed "Zeppelins," these aircraft had aluminum frames and gas-filled cells inside.

Zeppelins were used for military purposes during World Wars I and II, and for long-distance passenger travel until 1937, when the hydrogen-filled *Hindenberg* exploded in Lakehurst, New Jersey. Today's blimps are far smaller than the zeppelins of the 1930s; they do not have internal frames, and are filled with helium, a stable gas that will not explode.

The market for airships reawakened in the early 1980s when the U.S. Coast Guard announced its intention to use blimps in surveillance and search-and-rescue operations. Both Goodyear and Airship Industries showed early interest in participating in the Coast Guard's six-month feasilibility trials.

Airship Industries spent the summer of 1985 pursuing a contract for the Coast Guard trials, a move they hoped would put $4 million into their cash-poor coffers. Goodyear, realizing that extensive modifications to its 30-year-old blimp designs would be necessary just to participate in the trials, decided to withdraw from the competition. In the end, this conservative action turned out to be the right course: as of September, 1985, the Coast Guard indefinitely postponed its airship program. Airship Industries' summer of negotiations had gained them nothing.

In the meantime, the U.S. Navy decided to re-enter the airship market. For the first time since 1963, the Navy was making plans to use airships for surveillance. Airships are large enough to carry the 100-foot radar antennae necessary to track small, faster targets. The Navy contract would be worth an estimated $3 to $5 billion. To date, three groups have submitted proposals for the Navy contract:

- Airship Industries, teamed with the American company Westinghouse
- Goodyear, in conjunction with Sperry and Litton
- A consortium led by aircraft manufacturer Boeing

All three groups have been lobbying intensively for the contract, particulary at the Navy League's annual Sea and Air Exposition. Each competitor's position is unique:

- *Airship Industries* represents the latest in airship tech-

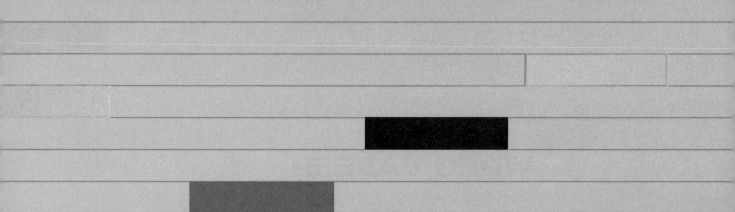

nology, with its vectored-thrust propellers and greater lifting capacity. The company's small size and lack of a history in the market, however, could be detrimental.

- *Goodyear's* airships are of an older design, but it has a longstanding relationship with the Navy and a name that has been closely associated with blimps.
- *Boeing*, the dark horse in the competition, has drawn on its experience in aircraft technology to create a design radically different from either Airship Industries' or Goodyear's. Boeing's airship has a rigid internal structure, like the zeppelins of the 1930s, for greater stability and safety.

At the time this program was filmed, the Navy's final decision was not known. The company that wins the Navy contract could become the dominant force in a market few people even know exists. Whether there is room for competitors in that market remains to be seen.

INTRODUCTION: Now that you have read and reflected on the Chapter 6 materials and concepts pertaining to strategic and tactical planning, you are ready to analyze the decisions and actions of a small British company called Airship Industries. This video case, entitled "Battle of the Blimps," provides a unique behind-the-scenes opportunity to evaluate the strategy and tactics of the organizations involved in an apparent revival of the lighter-than-air airship industry.

PART 1   Part of this video case analysis will be carried out in work teams. Your instructor will assign specific questions to various teams. It will be the responsibility of each team to extract the requested information from the video as the case is played out. If more than one team is assigned the same question, teams may be asked to pool their findings in preparation for presenting them to the rest of the class.

a. An organization can be successful only if it is appropriately matched to its environment. With information provided in the video, your group is to perform an environmental analysis of the situation facing Airship Industries. Use Figure 6.3 in the text as the framework for your analysis.

b. An organization's strategy can be systematically developed through the use of one of a number of specially formulated techniques. The responsibility of your group is to conduct a SWOT analysis of Airship Industries' situation, using the points appearing in Figure 6.7, in an attempt to judge the appropriateness of the company's existing strategy.

c. What is Airship Industries' organizational strategy? Would you categorize it as a growth, stability, retrenchment, or divestiture strategy? Explain.

d. What specific tactics were implemented to support the established strategy?

e. One of the companies competing for the Navy's contract has resurrected technology that may make its design the most competitive of all. What is this design feature and what is its special advantage?

f. Which company do you think will secure the Navy's contract? Why? Justify your answer with the information that your group assimilated in the team assignment in either a or b above.

PART 2:   After fulfilling your team's assignment, answer questions c through f. Be prepared to present your views to your classmates if called upon to do so.

PART 3:   Now that you have viewed the video case and have answered and discussed the questions, what specific points do you want to note so you will be able to effectively handle strategic and tactical planning in a similar situation?   ■

VIDEO CASE 3

THE COLONEL COMES TO JAPAN: A FOCUS ON INTERNATIONAL MANAGEMENT

(An extension of materials in Chapter 20—International Management)

SYNOPSIS: Japan is the restaurant capital of the world. The country has one eating establishment for every 81 people. Compeitition, understandably, is fierce.

One outfit that has been able to penetrate the market is Kentucky Fried Chicken. KFC was actually asked by the enormous Japanese conglomerate Mitsubishi to participate in a joint fast-food venture. The gesture was not simply hands-across-the water generosity. Mitsubishi just happens to be the largest chicken grower in Japan. KFC would have had trouble finding enough chicken to fry elsewhere in the country, and imported birds develop skin disease. The partnership has turned out to be mutually rewarding, with Mitsubishi leading the Colonel through the maze of the Japanese bureaucracy, and KFC netting a solid profit.

The progam follows the opening of one restaurant in a relatively traditional Tokyo neighborhood. While the product itself is the same as in the United States, just about everything else is not. KFC is positioned differently in the market, appealing to a higher-paying customer. The familiar restaurant design is altered to fit a limited space. Outside, the restaurant displays little plastic models of the food available inside, as is customary in Japan. In one scene, the Japanese store manager and workers go door-to-door to drum up new business.

KFC seems to be catching on. The Japanese have obviously developed a fondness for the Colonel and his chicken. And the total operation is bringing in $200 million a year.

INTRODUCTION: Now that you have become thoroughly familiar with the Chapter 20 materials and concepts pertaining to international management, you are ready to view the video case entitled "The Colonel Comes to Japan." This case should provide you with a great deal of insight into what is required to successfully set up and run a business in a foreign country.

PART 1: In preparation for viewing the video, familiarize yourself with the following questions.[1] When the video is shown, make notes on the case issues that appear especially pertinent.

a. What examples of planning, organizing, influencing, and controlling did you see in the video case? Does there appear to be any difference in the way these management functions are carried out in an international setting?

b. At what stage of multinationalization is Kentucky Fried Chicken? Explain.

c. Think of some American-made goods that, following the example of Kentucky Fried Chicken, might be successfully exported to Japan. What cultural, linguistic, or technological barriers would have to be overcome before the enterprises would flourish?

d. If you were an American entrepreneur trying to start up a chain of Kentucky Fried Chicken restaurants in Tokyo, what typical Japanese policies should you implement toward your employees?

e. What characteristics should a manager possess if the manager is to be transferred to a foreign location?

PART 2: After you view the case and document the issues you find especially pertinent, meet with three or four of your classmates to discuss and develop a group reaction to each question. Groups may be asked to share their views (or case analysis) with the rest of the class. The comments of the presenting group will provide the basis for a class discussion of the issues.

PART 3: Now that you have viewed the video case and have answered and discussed the questions, what generalizations can you make about managing in a foreign setting? ■

1. Some of the questions are adapted from *A Guide to Enterprise: The Colonel Comes to Japan*, Learning Corporation of America, distributed by Coronet/MTI Film & Video, 108 Wilmot Road, Deerfield, IL 60015.

GLOSSARY

This glossary contains important management terms and their definitions as used in this text. Since it is sometimes difficult to understand a term fully simply by reading its definition, page numbers after each definition indicate where a more complete discussion of the term can be found.

Accountability Management philosophy that individuals are held liable, or accountable, for how well they use their authority and live up to their responsibility of performing predetermined activities. (page 233)

Activities In the PERT network, specified sets of behaviour within a project. (page 179)

Activity ratios In ratio analysis, ratios that indicate how well an organization is selling its products in relation to its available resources. (page 487)

Affirmative action programs In the area of equal employment opportunity, programs whose basic purpose is to eliminate barriers against and increase opportunities for under-utilized or disadvantaged individuals. (page 261)

Appropriate human resources The individuals in the organization who make a valuable contribution to management system goal attainment (page 249)

Assessment centres Programs in which participants engage in and are evaluated on a number of individual and group exercises constructed to simulate important activities at the organizational levels to which these participants aspire. (page 265)

Authority The right to perform or command. (page 226)

Behavioural approach to management Management approach that emphasizes increasing organizational success by focusing on human variables within the organization. (page 40)

Behaviour modification Program that focuses on managing human activity by controlling the consequences of performing that activity. (page 392)

Break-even analysis Control tool based on the process of generating information that summarizes various levels of profit or loss associated with various levels of production. (page 476)

Break-even point The situation wherein the total revenue of an organization equals its total costs. (page 477)

Budget Control tool that outlines how funds in a given period will be spent, as well as how they will be obtained. (pages 167, 482)

Bureaucracy Management system with detailed procedures and rules, a clearly outlined organizational hierarchy, and, mainly, impersonal relationships among organization members (page 197)

Business portfolio analysis The development of business-related strategy that is based primarily on the market share of businesses and the growth of markets in which businesses exist. (page 144)

Career An individual's perceived sequence of attitudes and behaviours associated with the performance of work-related experiences and activities over the span of the person's working life. (page 19)

Centralization The situation in which a minimal number of job activities and a minimal amount of authority are delegated to subordinates. (page 238)

Change agent Anyone inside or outside the organization who tries to modify an existing organizational situation. (page 288)

Changing The second of Kurt Lewin's three related conditions, or states, that result in behavioural change—the state in which individuals begin to experiment with performing new behaviours. (page 301)

Changing an organization The process of modifying an existing organization to increase organizational effectiveness. (page 285)

Classical approach to management Management approach that emphasizes organizational efficiency to increase organizational success. (page 33)

Classical organizing theory The cumulative insights of early management writers on how organizational resources can best be used to enhance goal attainment. (page 197)

Closed system System that is not influenced by and does not interact with its environment. (page 46)

Command groups Formal groups that are outlined in the chain of command on an organization chart. (page 406)

Commitment principle Management guideline that advises managers to commit funds for planning only if they can anticipate, in the foreseeable future, a return on planning expenses as a result of the long-range planning analysis. (page 133)

Committee   Task group that is charged with performing some type of specific activity. (page 407)

Communication   The process of sharing information with other individuals. (page 322)

Communication effectiveness index   Intended message reactions divided by the total number of transmitted messages. (page 328)

Communication macrobarriers   The factors that hinder successful communication and that relate primarily to the communication environment and the larger world in which communication takes place. (page 325)

Communication microbarriers   The factors that hinder successful communication and that relate primarily to such variables as the communication message, the source, and the destination. (page 325)

Comparative management   The study of the management process in different countries to examine the potential of management action under different environmental conditions. (page 583)

Complete certainty condition   The decision-making situation in which the decision maker knows exactly what the results of an implemented alternative will be. (page 120)

Complete uncertainty condition   The decision-making situation in which the decision maker has absolutely no idea what the results of an implemented alternative will be. (page 120)

Computer   Electronic tool capable of accepting data, interpreting data, performing ordered operations on data, and reporting on the outcome of these operations. (page 502)

Conceptual skills   Skills that involve the ability to see the organization as a whole. (page 18)

Concurrent control   Control that takes place as some unit of work is being performed. (page 446)

Consensus   Agreement on a decision by all individuals involved in making the decision. (page 111)

Consideration behaviour   Leadership behaviour that reflects friendship, mutual trust, respect, and warmth in the relationship between the leader and the followers. (page 361)

Contingency approach to management   Management approach that emphasizes that what managers do in practice depends on a given set of circumstances—a situation. (page 46)

Contingency theory of leadership   Leadership concept that hypothesizes that, in any given leadership situation, success is determined primarily by: (1) the degree to which the task being performed by the followers is structured; (2) the degree of position power possessed by the leader; and (3) the type of relationship that exists between the leader and the followers. (page 365)

Control   Making something happen the way it was planned to happen. (page 439)

Control function   Computer activities that dictate the order in which other computer functions are performed. (page 506)

Controller   Staff individual whose basic responsibility is assisting line managers with the controlling function by gathering appropriate information and generating necessary reports that reflect this information. (page 448)

Controlling   The process the manager goes through to control. (page 441)

Control tool   Specific procedure or technique that presents pertinent organizational information in such a way that a manager is aided in developing and implementing appropriate control strategy. (page 475)

Coordination   The orderly arrangement of group effort to provide unity of action in the pursuit of a common purpose. (page 205)

Corporate database   See Database.

Corrective action   Managerial activity aimed at bringing organizational performance up to the level of performance standards. (page 444)

Cost-benefit analysis   The process of comparing the cost of some activity to the benefit or revenue that results from the activity to determine the total worth of the activity to the organization. (page 449)

Critical path   The sequence of events and activities within a program evaluation and review technique (PERT) network that requires the longest period of time to complete. (page 180)

Critical question analysis   Strategy development tool composed mainly of four questions: What are the purposes and objectives of the organization? Where is the organization presently going? In what kind of environment does the organization presently exist? What can be done to better achieve organizational objectives in the future? (page 144)

Culture   The total characteristics of a given group of people and their environment. (page 581)

Current ratio   The liquidity ratio that indicates the organization's ability to meet its financial obligations in the short term. (page 486)

$$\text{Current ratio} = \frac{\text{Current assets}}{\text{Current liabilities}}$$

Data   Facts or statistics. (page 497)

Database   A reservoir of corporate facts consistently organized to fit the information needs of a variety of organization members. Also termed corporate database. (page 517)

Debt ratio   The leverage ratio that indicates the percentage of all organizational assets provided by organizational creditors. (page 486)

$$\text{Debt ratio} = \frac{\text{Total debts}}{\text{Total assets}}$$

Decentralization The situation in which a significant number of job activities and a maximum amount of authority are delegated to subordinates. (page 238)

Decision Choice made between two or more available alternatives. (page 109)

Decision-making process The steps a decision maker takes to make a decision. (page 117)

Decision tree Graphic decision-making tool typically used to evaluate decisions containing a series of steps. (page 123)

Decline stage The fourth and last stage in career evolution, which occurs near retirement and during which individuals about sixty-five years of age or older show declining productivity. (page 21)

Decoder/destination The person or people in the interpersonal communication situation with whom the source/encoder attempts to share information. (page 323)

Delegation The process of assigning job activities and related authority to specific individuals in the organization. (page 233)

Demographics The statistical characteristics of a population. (page 138)

Department Unique group of resources established by management to perform some organizational task. (page 199)

Departmentalization The process of establishing departments in the management system. (page 199)

Dialogue capability The ability of a management decision support system (MDSS) user to interact with a management decision support system. (page 518)

Direct investing Using the assets of one company to purchase the operating assets of another company. (page 577)

Dispatching Issuing orders to the individuals involved in producing goods or services. (page 475)

Divestiture Strategy generally adopted to eliminate a strategic business unit that is not generating a satisfactory amount of business and has little hope of doing so in the future. (page 148)

Division of labour The assignment of various portions of a particular task among a number of organization members. (page 205)

Downward organizational communication Communication that flows from any point on an organization chart downward to another point on the organization chart. (page 332)

Economics Science that focuses on understanding how people of a particular community or nation produce, distribute, and use various goods and services. (page 136)

Environmental analysis Study of the organizational environment to pinpoint environmental factors that can significantly influence organizational operations. (page 136)

Establishment stage The second stage in career evolution, during which individuals of about twenty-five to forty-five years of age typically start to become more productive or higher performers. (page 20)

Esteem needs Maslow's fourth set of human needs—including the desire for self-respect and respect from others (page 384)

Ethics Our concern for good behaviour; our obligation to consider not only our own personal well-being but also that of other human beings. (page 553)

Ethnocentric attitude Attitude that reflects a belief that multinational corporations should regard home country management practices as superior to foreign country management practices. (page 579)

Events In the PERT network, the completions of major product tasks. (page 179)

Expected value Measurement of the anticipated value of some event; determined by multiplying the income an event would produce by its probability of making that income. (page 122)

Exploration stage The first stage in career evolution, which occurs at the beginning of a career and is characterized by self-analysis and the exploration of different types of available jobs by individuals of about fifteen to twenty-five years of age. (page 20)

Exporting Selling goods or services to another country. (page 576)

Extrinsic rewards Rewards that are extraneous to the task accomplished. (page 380)

Feedback In the interpersonal communication situation, the decoder/destination's reaction to a message. (page 327)

Feedback control Control that takes place after some unit of work has been performed. (page 446)

Financial objectives Organizational targets relating to monetary issues. (page 66)

Fixed assets turnover The activity ratio that indicates the appropriateness of the amount of funds invested in plant and equipment relative to the level of sales. (page 487)

$$\text{Fixed asset turnover} = \frac{\text{Sales}}{\text{Fixed assets}}$$

Fixed costs Expenses incurred by an organization regardless of the number of products produced. (page 476)

Fixed position layout Layout pattern that, because of the weight or bulk of the product being manufactured, has workers, tools, and materials rotating around a stationary product. (page 472)

Flat organization chart Organization chart that is characterized by few levels and relatively large spans of management. (page 209)

Flextime Program that allows workers to complete their jobs within a workweek of a normal number of hours that they schedule themselves. (page 390)

Forecasting Planning tool used to predict future environmental happenings that will influence the operation of the organization. (page 173)

Formal group Group that exists in an organization by virtue of management decree to perform tasks that enhance the attainment of organizational objectives. (page 406)

Formal organizational communication Organizational communication that follows the lines of the organization chart. (page 332)

Formal structure Relationships among organizational resources as outlined by management. (page 198)

Friendship groups Informal groups that form in organizations because of the personal affiliation members have with one another. (page 416)

Functional authority The right to give orders within a segment of the management system in which the right is normally non-existent. (page 231)

Functional objectives Targets relating to key organizational functions. (page 67)

Functional similarity method Method for dividing job activities in the organization. (page 222)

Functional skill Skill involving the ability to apply appropriately the concepts of planning, organizing, influencing, and controlling to the operation of a management system. (page 601)

Future-oriented managers Managers who attempt to create their own future, whenever possible, and adapt to this future, when necessary, through a continuous process of research about the future, long-term planning, and setting objectives. (page 612)

Gangplank Communication channel extending from one organizational division to another but not shown in the lines of communication outlined on an organization chart. (page 211)

Gantt chart Scheduling tool composed essentially of a bar chart with time on the horizontal axis and the resource to be scheduled on the vertical axis. (page 178)

General environment The level of an organization's external environment that contains components normally having broad long-term implications for managing the organization. (page 136)

Geocentric attitude Attitude that reflects a belief that the overall quality of management recommendations, rather than the location of managers, should

determine the acceptability of management practices used to guide multinational corporations. (page 579)

Geographic contiguity The degree to which subordinates are physically separated. (page 207)

Goal integration Compatibility between individual and organizational objectives. (page 63)

Graicunas's formula Formula that makes the span of management point that as the number of a manager's subordinates increases arithmetically, the number of possible relationships between the manager and the subordinates increases geometrically. (page 208)

Grapevine Network for informal organizational communication. (page 336)

Grid organization development (grid OD) Commonly used organization development technique based on a theoretical model called the managerial grid. (page 298)

Group Any number of people who: (1) interact with one another; (2) are psychologically aware of one another; and (3) perceive themselves to be a group. (page 405)

Group cohesiveness The attraction group members feel for one another in terms of the desire to remain a member of the group and to resist leaving it. (page 422)

Group norms Appropriate or standard behaviour that is required of informal group members. (page 423)

Groupthink The mode of thinking that people engage in when seeking agreement becomes so dominant in a group that it tends to override the realistic appraisal of alternate problem solutions. (page 411)

Growth Strategy adopted by management to increase the amount of business that a strategic business unit is currently generating. (page 147)

Hierarchy of objectives The overall organizational objective(s) and the subobjectives assigned to the various people or units of the organization. (page 68)

Host country The country in which an investment is made by a foreign company. (page 574)

Human resource inventory Accumulation of information concerning the characteristics of organization members; this information focuses on the past performance of organization members as well as on how they might be trained and best used in the future. (page 254)

Human resource planning Input planning that involves obtaining the human resources necessary for the organization to achieve its objectives. (page 170)

Human resources *See* Appropriate human resources.

Human skills Skills involving the ability to build cooperation within the team being led. (page 17)

Hygiene, or maintenance, factors   Items that influence the degree of job dissatisfaction. (page 389)

Importing   Buying goods or services from another country. (page 576)

Individual objectives   Personal goals that each organization member would like to reach as a result of personal activity in the organization. (page 62)

Influencing   The process of guiding the activities of organization members in appropriate directions, involving the performance of four primary management activities: (1) leading; (2) motivating; (3) considering groups; and (4) communicating. (page 319)

Informal groups   Groups that develop naturally in organizations as people interact. (page 415)

Informal organizational communication   Organizational communication that does not follow the lines of the organization chart. (page 336)

Informal structure   Patterns of relationships that develop because of the informal activities of organization members. (page 198)

Information   Conclusions derived from data analysis. (page 497)

Information appropriateness   The degree to which information is relevant to the decision-making situation that faces the manager. (page 498)

Information quality   The degree to which information represents reality. (page 499)

Information quantity   The amount of decision-related information a manager possesses. (page 499)

Information timeliness   The extent to which the receipt of information allows decisions to be made and action to be taken so the organization can gain some benefit from possessing the information. (page 499)

Input function   Computer activities through which the computer enters the data to be analyzed and the instructions to be followed to analyze the data appropriately. (page 505)

Input planning   Development of proposed action that will furnish sufficient and appropriate organizational resources for reaching established organizational objectives. (page 168)

Interest groups   Informal groups that gain and maintain membership primarily because of a special concern each member possesses about a specific issue. (page 416)

Intermediate-term objectives   Targets to be achieved within one to five years. (page 65)

Internal environment   The level of an organization's environment that exists inside the organization and normally has immediate and specific implications for managing the organization. (page 142)

International management   Performing management activities across national borders. (page 565)

Intrinsic rewards   Rewards that come directly from performing a task. (page 380)

Inventory turnover   The activity ratio that indicates whether an organization is maintaining an appropriate level of inventory in relation to its sales volume. (page 487)

$$\text{Inventory turnover} = \frac{\text{Sales}}{\text{Inventory}}$$

Job analysis   Technique commonly used to gain an understanding of what a task entails and the type of individual who should be hired to perform the task. (page 250)

Job description   Specific activities that must be performed to accomplish some task or job. (pages 221, 250)

Job enlargement   The process of increasing the number of operations an individual performs in a job. (page 389)

Job enrichment   The process of incorporating motivators into a job situation. (page 390)

Job rotation   The process of moving individuals from one job to another and not requiring individuals to perform only one job over the long term. (page 389)

Job specifications   Characteristics of the individual who should be hired to perform a specific task or job. (page 250)

Joint venture   Partnership formed by a company in one country with a company in another country for the purpose of pursuing some mutually desirable business undertaking. (page 577)

Jury of executive opinion method   Method of predicting future sales levels primarily by asking appropriate managers to give their opinions on what will happen to sales in the future. (page 174)

Just-in-time (JIT) inventory control   An inventory control technique that reduces inventories to a minimum by arranging for them to be delivered to the production facility just in time to be used. (page 586)

Lateral organizational communication   Communication that flows from any point on an organization chart horizontally to another point on the organization chart. (page 332)

Layout patterns   The overall arrangement of machines, equipment, materials handling, aisles, service areas, storage areas, and work stations within a production facility. (page 471)

Leader flexibility   The ability of leaders to change their leadership styles. (page 365)

Leadership   The process of directing the behaviour of others toward the accomplishment of objectives. (page 349)

Leadership style   Behavioural pattern a leader establishes while guiding organization members in appropriate directions. (page 361)

Lecture   Primarily one-way communication situation in which an instructor trains by orally presenting information to an individual or group. (page 268)

Level dimension (of plans)   The level of the organization at which plans are aimed. (page 162)

Leverage ratios   In ratio analysis, the ratios that indicate the relationship between organizational funds supplied by the owners of an organization and organizational funds supplied by creditors. (page 486)

Licence agreement   Right granted by one company to another to use its brand name, technology, product specifications, and so on in the manufacture or sale of goods and services. (page 576)

Life cycle theory of leadership   Leadership concept that hypothesizes that leadership styles should reflect primarily the maturity level of the followers. (page 362)

Line authority   The right to make decisions and to give orders concerning the production, sales, or finance-related behaviour of subordinates. (page 227)

Liquidity ratios   In ratio analysis, the ratios that indicate an organization's ability to meet upcoming financial obligations (page 486)

Long-term objectives   Targets to be achieved within five to seven years. (page 65)

Loss   The amount of the total costs of producing a product that exceeds the total revenue gained from selling the product. (page 477)

Maintenance stage   The third stage in career evolution, during which individuals of about forty-five to sixty-five years of age become more productive, stabilize, or become less productive. (page 21)

Management   The process of reaching organizational goals by working with and through people and other organizational resources. (page 9)

Management by exception   Control tool that allows only significant deviations between planned and actual performance to be brought to the manager's attention. (page 476)

Management by objectives (MBO)   Management approach that uses organizational objectives as the primary means by which to manage organizations. (page 73)

Management decision support system (MDSS)   An interdependent set of computer-oriented decision aids that help managers make non-programmed decisions. (page 517)

Management functions   Activities that make up the management process, including planning, organizing, influencing, and controlling. (page 10)

Management information system (MIS)   Network established in an organization to provide managers with information that will assist them in decision making. (page 507)

Management inventory card   Form used in compiling a human resource inventory—containing an organizational history of an individual and an explanation of how the individual might be used in the future. (page 254)

Management manpower replacement chart   Form used in compiling a human resource inventory—people-oriented and presenting a total composite view of the individuals whom management considers significant to human resource planning. (page 255)

Management responsibility guide   Tool that can be used to clarify the responsibilities of various managers in the organization. (page 223)

Management science approach   Management approach that emphasizes the use of the scientific method and quantitative techniques to increase organizational success. (page 44)

Management system   Open system whose major parts are organizational input, organizational process, and organizational output. (page 47)

Managerial effectiveness   The degree to which management attains organizational objectives. (page 13)

Managerial efficiency   The degree to which organizational resources contribute to productivity. (page 13)

Managerial grid   Theoretical model based on the premise that concern for people and concern for production are the two primary attitudes that influence management style. (page 298)

Materials requirements control   The process of making things happen the way they were planned to happen in materials requirements planning. (page 481)

Materials requirements planning (MRP)   Creating schedules that identify the specific parts and materials required to produce an item, the exact quantities of each needed to enhance the production process, and the dates when orders for these quantities should be released to suppliers and be received for best timing in the production cycle. (page 480)

Matrix organization   Traditional organizational structure that is modified primarily for the purpose of completing some type of special project. (page 294)

Maturity   As used in the life cycle theory of leadership, an individual's ability to independently perform the job, to assume additional responsibility, and to desire success. (page 362)

Means-ends analysis   The process of outlining the means by which various objectives, or ends, in the organization can be achieved. (page 71)

Message   Encoded information that the source/encoder intends to share with others. (page 323)

Message interference   Stimuli that compete with the communication message for the attention of the decoder/destination. (page 325)

Model base   A collection of quantitative computer programs that can assist management decision support system (MDSS) users in analyzing data within databases. (page 518)

Motion study   Finding the one best way to accomplish a task by analyzing the movements necessary to perform the task. (page 35)

Motivating factors   Items that influence the degree of job satisfaction. (page 389)

Motivation   The inner state that causes an individual to behave in a way that ensures the accomplishment of some goal. (page 377)

Motivation strength   Individual's degree of desire to perform a behaviour. (page 378)

Multinational corporation (MNC)   Company that has significant operations in more than one country. (page 570)

Need for achievement (n Ach)   The desire to do something better or more efficiently than it has ever been done before. (page 385)

Needs-goal model   Motivation model that hypothesizes that felt needs cause human behaviour. (page 378)

Negative norms   Informal group standards that limit organizational productivity. (page 423)

Negative reinforcement   Reward that is the elimination of an undesirable consequence of behaviour. (page 393)

Non-programmed decisions   Decisions that typically are one-shot occurrences and usually are less structured than programmed decisions. (page 110)

Non-verbal communication   The sharing of ideas without the use of words. (page 330)

On-the-job training   Training technique that blends job-related knowledge with experience in using that knowledge in the job. (page 270)

Open system   System that is influenced by and is constantly interacting with its environment. (page 47)

Operating environment   Level of the organization's external environment that contains components normally having relatively specific and immediate implications for managing the organization. (page 141)

Operational objectives   Objectives that are stated in observable or measurable terms. (page 69)

Operations management   The process of managing production in organizations. (page 473)

Organizational communication   Interpersonal communication in organizations. (page 331)

Organizational objectives   Targets toward which the open management system is directed. (page 59)

Organizational purpose   What the organization exists to do, given a particular group of customers and customer needs. (page 60)

Organizational resources   Assets available for activation during normal operations, among which are human resources, monetary resources, raw materials resources, and capital resources. (page 13)

Organization chart   Graphic representation of organizational structure. (page 197)

Organization development   Process that emphasizes changing an organization by changing organization members and that bases these changes on an overview of structure, technology, and all other organizational ingredients. (page 297)

Organizing   The process of establishing orderly uses for all resources in the organization. (page 193)

Output function   Computer activities that take the results of input, storage, processing, and control functions and transmit them outside the computer. (page 506)

Overlapping responsibility   Situation in which more than one individual is responsible for the same activity. (page 222)

Parent company   The company investing in international operations. (page 574)

People change   Changing certain aspects of organization members to increase organizational effectiveness. (page 297)

People factors   Attitudes, leadership skills, communication skills, and all other characteristics of the organization's employees. (page 289)

Perception   Interpretation of a message as observed by an individual. (page 326)

Performance appraisal   The process of reviewing past productive activity to evaluate the contribution individuals have made toward attaining management system objectives. (page 271)

Personal power   Power derived from the relationship that one person has with another. (page 451)

PERT   *See* Program evaluation and review technique (PERT). (page 179)

Physiological needs   Maslow's first set of human needs—for the normal functioning of the body—including the desire for water, food, rest, sex, and air. (page 383)

Plan   Specific action proposed to help the organization achieve its objectives. (page 161)

Plan for planning   Listing of all steps that must be taken to plan for an organization. (page 94)

Planning   The process of determining how the management system will achieve its objectives. (page 85)

Planning tools   Techniques managers can use to help develop plans. (page 173)

Plant facilities planning   Input planning that involves developing the type of work facility an organization will need to reach its objectives. (page 168)

Policy   Standing plan that furnishes broad guidelines for channeling management thinking in specified directions. (page 163)

Polycentric attitude   Attitude that reflects a belief that since foreign managers are closer to foreign organizational units, they probably understand them better—and therefore that foreign management practices generally should be viewed as more insightful than home country management practices. (page 579)

Porter-Lawler model   Motivation model that hypothesizes that felt needs cause human behaviour and that motivation strength is determined primarily by the perceived value of the result of performing the behaviour and the perceived probability that the behaviour performed will cause the result to materialize. (page 379)

Position power   Power derived from the organizational position that one holds. (page 451)

Position replacement form   Form used in compiling a human resources inventory—summarizing information about organization members who could fill a position should it open. (page 254)

Positive norms   Informal group standards that contribute to organizational productivity. (page 423)

Positive reinforcement   Reward that is a desirable consequence of behaviour. (page 393)

Power   The extent to which an individual is able to influence others so they respond to orders. (page 451)

Precontrol   Control that takes place before some unit of work is actually performed. (page 446)

Premises   Assumptions on which alternate ways of accomplishing objectives are based. (page 88)

Principle of supportive relationships   Management guideline that indicates that all human interaction within an organization should build and maintain the sense of personal worth and the importance of those involved in the interaction. (page 395)

Principle of the objective   Management guideline that recommends that before managers initiate any action, organizational objectives should be clearly determined, understood, and stated. (page 65)

Probability theory   Decision-making tool used in risk situations—situations in which the decision maker is not completely sure of the outcome of an implemented alternative. (page 122)

Problems   Factors within organizations that are barriers to organizational goal attainment. (page 445)

Procedure   Standing plan that outlines a series of related actions that must be taken to accomplish a particular task. (page 165)

Processing function   Computer activities involved with performing the logic and calculation steps necessary to analyze data appropriately. (page 505)

Process layout   Layout pattern based primarily on grouping together similar types of equipment. (page 472)

Production   The transformation of organizational resources into products. (page 467)

Production control   Ensuring that an organization produces goods and services as planned. (page 467)

Production planning   Determining the type and amount of resources needed to produce specified goods or services. (page 474)

Productivity   The relationship between the total amount of goods or services being produced (output) and the organizational resources needed (input) to produce the goods or services. (page 469)

Product layout   Layout pattern based mostly on the progressive steps by which the product is made. (page 472)

Product life cycle   Five stages through which most new products and services pass—introduction, growth, maturity, saturation, and decline. (page 176)

Product-market mix objectives   Objectives that outline which products and the relative number or mix of these products the organization will attempt to sell. (page 67)

Profession   Vocation whose practice is based on an understanding of a specific body of knowledge and the corresponding abilities necessary to apply this understanding to vital human problems. (page 613)

Profitability ratios   In ratio analysis, the ratios that indicate the ability of an organization to generate profits. (page 487)

Profits   The amount of total revenue that exceeds total costs. (page 477)

Profit to sales ratio   The profitability ratio that indicates whether the organization is making an adequate net profit in relation to the total dollars coming into the organization. (page 487)

$$\text{Profit to sales ratio} = \frac{\text{Net profit}}{\text{Sales}}$$

Profit to total assets ratio   The profitability ratio that indicates whether the organization is realizing enough net profit in relation to the total dollars invested in assets. (page 487)

$$\text{Profit to total assets ratio} = \frac{\text{Net profit}}{\text{Total assets}}$$

Program Single-use plan designed to carry out a special project in an organization. (page 167)

Program evaluation and review technique (PERT) Scheduling tool that is essentially a network of project activities showing estimates of time necessary to complete each activity and the sequential relationship of activities that must be followed to complete the project. (page 179)

Programmed decisions Decisions that are routine and repetitive and that typically require specific handling methods. (page 110)

Programmed learning Technique for instructing without the presence of a human instructor—small pieces of information requiring responses are presented to individual trainees. (page 268)

Punishment The presentation of an undesirable behavioural consequence or the removal of a desirable one that decreases the likelihood of the behaviour continuing. (page 393)

Quality circles Small groups of workers that meet regularly with management to discuss quality-related problems. (page 416)

Quality control The process of making the quality of finished goods and services what it was planned to be. (page 481)

Quality of work life Opportunity of workers to make decisions that influence their work situation. (page 606)

Quick ratio The liquidity ratio that indicates an organization's ability to meet its financial obligations with no reliance on inventory. (page 486)

$$\frac{\text{Quick}}{\text{ratio}} = \frac{\text{Current assets} - \text{Inventory}}{\text{Current liabilities}}$$

Ratio analysis Control tool based on the process of generating information that summarizes the financial position of an organization by calculating ratios based on various financial measures appearing on balance sheets and income statements. (page 485)

Recruitment The initial screening of the total supply of prospective human resources available to fill a position. (page 250)

Refreezing The third of Kurt Lewin's three related conditions, or states, that result in behavioural change—the state in which an individual's experimentally performed behaviours become part of the person. (page 302)

Relevant alternatives Alternatives that are considered feasible for implementation and for solving an existing problem. (page 116)

Repetitiveness dimension (of plans) The extent to which plans are used again and again. (page 161)

Responsibility The obligation to perform assigned activities. (page 221)

Responsibility gap Situation in which certain organizational tasks are not included in the responsibility area of any individual organization member. (page 222)

Retrenchment Strategy adopted by management to strengthen or protect the amount of business a strategic business unit is currently generating. (page 147)

Risk condition The decision-making situation in which the decision maker has only enough information to estimate how probable the outcome of implemented alternatives will be. (page 121)

Robot Machine in the form of a human being that performs the mechanical functions of a human being but lacks sensitivity. (page 471)

Robotics The area of study dealing with the development and use of robots. (page 471)

Routing Determining the sequence in which work must be completed to produce specified goods or services. (page 474)

Rule Standing plan that designates specific required action. (page 165)

Sales force estimation method Method of predicting future sales levels primarily by asking appropriate salespeople for their opinions of what will happen to sales in the future. (page 175)

Scalar relationships The chain of command positioning of individuals on an organization chart. (page 210)

Scheduling The process of formulating detailed listings of activities that must be performed to accomplish a task, allocating resources necessary to complete the task, and setting up and following timetables for completing the task. (pages 178, 475)

Scientific management Management approach that emphasizes the one best way to perform a task. (page 34)

Scientific method Problem-solving method that entails the following sequential steps: (1) observing a system; (2) constructing a framework that is consistent with the observations and from which the consequences of changing the system can be predicted; (3) predicting how various changes would influence the system; and (4) testing to see if these changes influence the system as intended. (page 44)

Scope dimension (of plans) The portion of the total management system at which the plans are aimed. (page 162)

Scope of the decision The proportion of the total management system that a particular decision will affect. (page 111)

Security, or safety needs Maslow's second set of human needs—reflecting the human desire to keep free from physical harm. (page 383)

Selection Choosing an individual to hire from all of those who have been recruited. (page 262)

Self-actualization needs Maslow's fifth set of human needs—reflecting the human desire to maximize potential. (page 384)

Serial transmission The passing of information from one individual through a series of individuals. (page 335)

Short-term objectives Targets to be achieved in one year or less. (page 65)

Signal A message that has been transmitted from one person to another. (page 323)

Single-use plans Plans that are used only once or several times because they focus on organizational situations that do not occur repeatedly. (page 163)

Site selection Determining where a plant facility should be located. (page 168)

Situational analysis skill Skill involving the ability to apply both systems theory and functional theory to the unique conditions of a particular organizational situation. (page 601)

Situational approach to leadership Relatively modern view of leadership that suggests that successful leadership requires a unique combination of leaders, followers, and leadership situations. (page 351)

Social audit The process of measuring the social responsibility activities of an organization. (page 551)

Social needs Maslow's third set of human needs—reflecting the human desire to belong, including the desire for friendship, companionship, and love. (page 384)

Social obligation approach Approach to meeting social obligations that reflects an attitude that considers business to have primarily economic purposes and confines social responsibility activity mainly to conformance to existing legislation. (page 544)

Social responsibility The managerial obligation to take action that protects and improves the welfare of society as a whole and organizational interests as well. (page 531)

Social responsibility approach Approach to meeting social obligations that is characterized by an attitude that considers business as having both societal and economic goals. (page 544)

Social responsiveness The degree of effectiveness and efficiency an organization displays in pursuing its social responsibilities. (page 543)

Social responsiveness approach Approach to meeting social obligations that reflects an attitude that considers business to have societal and economic goals as well as the obligation to anticipate upcoming social problems and to work actively toward preventing their appearance. (page 544)

Social values The relative degrees of worth society places on the manner in which it exists and functions. (page 138)

Sociogram Sociometric diagram that summarizes the personal feelings of organization members about the people in the organization with whom they would like to spend free time. (page 417)

Sociometry Analytical tool that can be used to determine what informal groups exist in an organization and who the members of those groups are. (page 417)

Source/encoder The person in the interpersonal communication situation who originates and encodes information that the person wants to share with others. (page 323)

Span of management The number of individuals a manager supervises. (page 206)

Stability Strategy adopted by management to maintain or slightly improve the amount of business a strategic business unit is generating. (page 147)

Staff authority The right to advise or assist those who possess line authority. (page 227)

Standard The level of activity established to serve as a model for evaluating organizational performance. (page 443)

Standing plans Plans that are used over and over because they focus on organizational situations that occur repeatedly. (page 163)

Statistical quality control Process used to determine how many products from a larger number should be inspected to calculate a probability that the total number of products meets organizational quality standards. (page 481)

Status The positioning of importance of a group member in relation to other group members. (page 425)

Storage function Computer activities involved with retaining the material entered into the computer during the performance of the input function. (page 505)

Strategic business unit (SBU) In business portfolio analysis, a significant organizational segment that is analyzed to develop organizational strategy aimed at generating future business or revenue. (page 145)

Strategic planning Long-term planning that focuses on the organization as a whole. (page 133)

Strategy Broad and general plan developed to reach long-term organizational objectives. (page 133)

Strategy management The process of ensuring that an organization possesses and benefits from the use of an appropriate organization strategy. (page 134)

Stress   The bodily strain that an individual experiences as a result of coping with some environmental factor. (page 304)

Stressor   Environmental demand that causes people to feel stress. (page 306)

Structural change   Type of organizational change that emphasizes modifying an existing organizational structure. (page 294)

Structural factors   Organizational controls, such as policies and procedures. (page 289)

Structure   Designated relationships among resources of the management system. (page 197)

Structure behaviour   Leadership activity that: (1) delineates the relationship between the leader and the leader's followers; or (2) establishes well-defined procedures that the followers should adhere to in performing their jobs. (page 360)

Suboptimization   Condition wherein organizational subobjectives are conflicting or not directly aimed at accomplishing overall organizational objectives. (page 68)

Subsystem   System created as part of the process of the overall management system. (page 90)

Successful communication   Interpersonal communication situation in which the information the source/encoder intends to share with the decoder/destination and the meaning the decoder/destination derives from the transmitted message are the same. (page 324)

Suppliers   Individuals or agencies that provide organizations with resources needed to produce organizational goods or services. (page 141)

SWOT analysis   Strategy development tool that matches internal organizational strengths and weaknesses with external opportunities and threats. (page 144)

Symptom   Sign that a problem exists. (page 445)

System   Number of interdependent parts functioning as a whole for some purpose. (page 46)

System approach to management   Management approach based on general system theory—the theory that to understand fully the operation of an entity, the entity must be viewed as a system. (page 46)

Systems skill   The ability to view and manage a business or some other concern as a number of components that work together and function as a whole to achieve some objective. (page 599)

Tactical planning   Short-range planning that emphasizes current operations of various parts of the organization. (page 149)

Tall organization chart   Organization chart that is characterized by many levels and relatively small spans of management. (page 209)

Task groups   Formal groups of organization members who interact with one another to accomplish mostly non-routine organizational tasks (members of any one task group can and often do come from various levels and segments of an organization). (page 406)

Technical skills   The ability to apply specialized knowledge and expertise to work-related techniques and procedures. (page 17)

Technological change   Type of organizational change that emphasizes modifying the level of technology in the management system. (page 294)

Technological factors   Any types of equipment or processes that assist organization members in the performance of their jobs. (page 289)

Testing   Examining human resources for qualities relevant to performing available jobs. (page 264)

Theory X   Set of essentially negative assumptions about the nature of people. (page 387)

Theory Y   Set of essentially positive assumptions about the nature of people. (page 387)

Theory Z   Effectiveness dimension that implies that managers who use either Theory X or Theory Y assumptions when dealing with people can be successful, depending on their situation. (pages 388, 585)

Time dimension (of plans)   The length of time plans cover. (page 162)

Time series analysis method   Method of predicting future sales levels by analyzing the historical relationship in an organization between sales and time. (page 175)

Times interest earned ratio   The leverage ratio that indicates an organization's ability to pay interest expenses directly from gross income. (page 486)

$$\frac{\text{Times interest}}{\text{earned ratio}} = \frac{\text{Gross income}}{\text{Interest charges}}$$

Total assets turnover   The activity ratio that indicates the appropriateness of the level of funds an organization has tied up in all assets relative to its rate of sales. (page 487)

$$\frac{\text{Total assets}}{\text{turnover}} = \frac{\text{Sales}}{\text{Total assets}}$$

Total costs   The sum of fixed costs and variable costs associated with production. (page 477)

Total power   The entire amount of power an individual in an organization possesses, mainly the amount of position power and the amount of personal power possessed by the individual. (page 451)

Total revenue   All sales dollars accumulated from selling goods or services that are produced. (page 477)

Training   The process of developing qualities in human resources that ultimately will enable them to be more productive and thus to contribute more to organizational goal attainment. (page 266)

Training need Information or skill area of an individual or group that requires further development to increase the organizational productivity of the individual or group. (page 266)

Trait approach to leadership Outdated view of leadership that sees the personal characteristics of an individual as the main determinants of how successful the individual could be as a leader. (page 351)

Triangular management Management approach that emphasizes using information from the classical, behavioural, and management science schools of thought to manage the open management system. (page 48)

Unfreezing The first of Kurt Lewin's three related conditions, or states, that result in behavioural change — the state in which individuals experience a need to learn new behaviours. (page 301)

Unity of command Management principle that recommends that an individual have only one boss. (page 210)

Universality of management skills The idea that the principles of management are universal, or applicable to all types of organizations and organizational levels. (page 18)

Unsuccessful communication Interpersonal communication situation in which the information the source/encoder intends to share with the decoder/destination and the meaning the decoder/destination derives from the transmitted message are different. (page 324)

Upward organizational communication Communication that flows from any point on an organization chart upward to another point on the organization chart. (page 332)

User database Database developed by an individual manager or other user. (page 517)

Variable budgets Budgets that outline various levels of resources to be allocated for each organizational activity, depending on the level of production within the organization. Also called flexible budgets. (page 484)

Variable costs Organizational expenses that fluctuate with the number of products produced. (page 476)

Verbal communication The sharing of ideas through words. (page 330)

Vroom expectancy model Motivation model that hypothesizes that felt needs cause human behaviour and that motivation strength depends on an individual's degree of desire to perform a behaviour. (page 378)

"What if" analysis The simulation of a business situation over and over again using somewhat different data for selected decision areas. (page 518)

Work team Task group used in organizations to achieve greater organizational flexibility or to cope with rapid growth. (page 412)

Zero-base budgeting The planning and budgeting process that requires managers to justify their entire budget request in detail rather than simply to refer to budget amounts established in previous years. (page 484)

NAME INDEX

SUBJECT INDEX

PHOTO CREDITS

1. Official organization - report etc.

2. Unofficial
   politics, favorites, etc. —